FOUNDATIONS OF DEMOCRATIC EDUCATION

Foundations of Democratic Education

MARY JOHN O'HAIR
University of Oklahoma

H. JAMES MCLAUGHLIN
University of Georgia

ULRICH C. REITZUG
University of North Carolina at Greensboro

Harcourt College Publishers

Fort Worth Philadelphia San Diego New York Orlando Austin San Antonio
Toronto Montreal London Sydney Tokyo

Publisher	Earl McPeek
Executive Editor	Carol Wada
Developmental Editor	Tracy Napper
Project Editor	Elaine Richards
Art Director	Carol Kincaid
Production Manager	Linda McMillan

ISBN: 0-03-017348-5
Library of Congress Catalog Card Number: 99-67768

Literary and photo permissions appear on pages 476 and 477, which constitute a continuation of the copyright page.

Address for Domestic Orders
Harcourt College Publishers, 6277 Sea Harbor Drive, Orlando, FL 32887-6777
800-782-4479

Address for International Orders
International Customer Service
Harcourt, Inc., 6277 Sea Harbor Drive, Orlando, FL 32887-6777
407-345-3800
(fax) 407-345-4060
(e-mail) hbintl@harcourtbrace.com

Address for Editorial Correspondence
Harcourt College Publishers, 301 Commerce Street, Suite 3700, Fort Worth, TX 76102

Web Site Address
http://www.harcourtcollege.com

Harcourt College Publishers will provide complimentary supplements or supplement packages to those adopters qualified under our adoption policy. Please contact your sales representative to learn how you qualify. If as an adopter or potential user you receive supplements you do not need, please return them to your sales representative or send them to: Attn: Returns Department, Troy Warehouse, 465 South Lincoln Drive, Troy, MO 63379.

Printed in the United States of America

9 0 1 2 3 4 5 6 7 8 048 9 8 7 6 5 4 3 2 1

Harcourt College Publishers

This book is dedicated to everyONE who makes a positive difference in the lives of children.

PREFACE

Although some may argue otherwise, there is no such thing as an objective textbook. Textbooks, like all books, are shaped by the beliefs, values, and ideals of their authors. This book is no different. Thus, before you read this book, we believe it is important for you to understand a bit about our beliefs as authors and educators. We want you to see how our beliefs are reflected in this book and assess the extent to which you agree or disagree with these beliefs. We want to emphasize from the outset that you do not need to agree with us. Indeed, as you read this book, we encourage you to question and challenge. We want you to encourage your students to develop their own beliefs about schools and education—rather than simply accepting ours. It is, however, important to be able to support whatever beliefs one holds. Thus, we hope this book begins a journey for your students that results in their developing a strong foundation for their practice as a teacher, educator, and socially responsible citizen.

So, what do we believe? We believe schools should be about more than high test scores, job preparation, and perpetuating existing cultural norms. We believe schools should be about developing young people who not only achieve, who not only become qualified for well-paying jobs, but who also are and will continue to be as concerned with the good of society as they are with their personal well-being. We believe schools should be about individual growth and development but, more importantly, we believe schools should be about providing students with a purpose for growing and developing, and an end toward which to channel their growth and development. That purpose and end is working toward a society that is just, caring, and democratic—a society which reflects "liberty and justice *for all.*" In essence, we believe the purpose of schools is to prepare students for morally-involved citizenship in a democratic society. Further, we believe that in order to accomplish this, schools themselves must function as democracies.

Schooling *for democracy* and *as democracy* does not, however, reflect conventional practice in American education. Witness the following examples.

- Many states have implemented high-stakes testing programs in which teachers and schools are financially rewarded or punished depending on the scores their students receive on standardized tests.
- Across the country thousands of schools participate in school-to-work initiatives, with students often spending a portion of the school day in the workplace, potentially losing sight of the intrinsic value of education.
- Hundreds of schools nationwide have adopted a Core Knowledge curriculum which enculturates students in the knowledge and norms of the Western world while essentially excluding cultural perspectives of non-White races and ethnic groups.

As a result of these and similar programs and policies, many schools have become places which train students for high test achievement; places which prepare students for the world of work; and places which legitimate the cultural norms of one group to the exclusion of others.

We believe these are insufficient purposes for education. As we write this, fresh on our minds is the worst school shooting in U.S. history, perpetrated by two academically high achieving students who shot and killed 12 of their classmates, a teacher, and themselves. On our minds also are the millions of adults in this country with well-paying jobs—but unfulfilling lives. And, on our minds are the cultural norms that perpetuate the tracking of a disproportionate percentage of white students into gifted and talented programs and ethnic students into special education. It is because of factors like these that we believe that education which focuses only on high test scores, job preparation, and the perpetuation of existing social and cultural norms is insufficient. It is for reasons like these that we believe that other foundations of education books are inadequate and that future teachers are better served by being prepared for schools that work toward and mirror a just, caring, and democratic society. And, it is because of factors like these that we wrote this book, *The Foundations of Democratic Education.*

We hope this book can help serve as a road map for your students' personal and professional journey toward democratic practice. Road maps are designed to provide travelers with assistance, direction, choices, and security of mind when traveling. Our road map is no different. It is designed to help your students chart a course for becoming a teacher in a democratic society and at the same time giving them the tools to "survive" their first few years of teaching. We want to help readers discover, connect with, and model democratic education. As a result of this journey, we hope that readers will construct their own beliefs about schooling in a democracy rather than maintaining a neutral, seemingly objective stance—or merely adopting our viewpoint.

In *Foundations of Democratic Education,* we examine issues from both a classroom perspective and a whole-school focus. We believe that a whole-school focus is as important for us to examine as the classroom perspective. Neither you nor your students live in isolation. We all interact daily with other teachers, other students, and with individuals outside the school. Democratic schools require that teachers work collaboratively; that they develop and pursue a clear, shared purpose; and that they take collective responsibility for all students—whether or not those students are in their classroom.

Many textbooks attempt to provide the reader with an overview of a variety of topics often with few connections from chapter to chapter. In this textbook we attempt to be different. We explore connections and relationships rather than merely asking readers to memorize disconnected pieces of information. As authors, we emphasize the importance of making connections—connections within the classroom; connections with the school, community, and society; connections that help link historical, philosophical, social, and political understandings to daily practice as a teacher; and connections that help readers become successful with all students and families.

The book does not attempt to provide comprehensive coverage of every topic. Rather, the discussion and your work revolves around the most salient aspects of the topic being discussed and how these aspects relate to a set of concepts which we call the IDEALS of democratic education. These IDEALS include *I*nquiry, *D*iscourse, *E*quity, *A*uthenticity, *L*eadership, and *S*ervice. The central issue for us is not how many isolated facts, statistics, and "hot" new topics we can present in this book, but rather how information and knowledge connect to democratic IDEALS, our expanding knowledge of what works well in schools and classrooms, and with our daily practice as teachers. The IDEALS of democratic education provide a consistent and coherent focus for inquiry throughout the book while ensuring that there is conceptual integration across the different topical areas that make up the foundations of education.

In order to ensure that the IDEALS are fully integrated in each chapter and to help them come alive for you, each chapter contains *IDEALS Challenges.* IDEALS Challenges are exercises that challenge the reader to think about and apply the foundations of democratic education to real-world situations. Frequently they are based on real world situations we have either experienced or read about, conversations we have been part of, or interviews we have conducted.

There are six different types of IDEALS Challenges. *Initiating Inquiry* Challenges typically ask the readers to gather additional information or collect data about an issue or situation that will help them more fully understand the dilemma and ways of addressing it. *Deepening Discourse* Challenges pose reflective questions or engage thinking in other ways with the intent to deepen the discourse that occurs in class. *Examining Equity* Challenges describe practices or dilemmas and ask readers to examine the situations and to discover and discuss the equity issues involved. *Achieving Authenticity* Challenges describe practices that reflect aspects of authentic pedagogy or authentic relationships with the reader's task being to assess how and why the practices reflect authenticity. *Learning Leadership* Challenges present scenarios in which teacher leadership is exhibited or could potentially be exhibited. Finally, *Supporting Service* Challenges present examples of students, teachers, and schools engaged in activities that serve others. Please note that not all of these types of boxes will appear in each chapter but only where they are most salient.

In addition to IDEALS Challenges, the book provides several other types of learning opportunities. Most chapters contain *Technology Challenges* which either present issues involved in the use of technology, give examples of the use of technology in democratic schools, or ask the reader to use technology in some fashion. Most chapters also include *Global Challenges* which provide descriptions and insight into education practices in other countries. Each chapter contains a *Doing Democracy* exercise which asks the reader to engage in the practice of democracy in some fashion. Finally, we have included "Click on It!" boxes that list Web site addresses for students to explore for further information.

The book is divided into six units. Unit 1 describes a framework for democratic education. The unit introduces the IDEALS of democratic education in the first chapter, describes practices in schools that are consistent with the IDEALS in the second chapter, discusses how schools might embark on the journey from conventional schooling to democratic schooling in the third chapter, and connects democratic IDEALS and practices to their historical and philosophical foundations in the fourth chapter.

Units 2 through 5 examine in more detail how democratic IDEALS get played out in schools. Although all the IDEALS are woven throughout every chapter, each chapter focuses on a specific IDEAL. For example, chapter 5, the first chapter in Unit 2, is entitled, "The Nature of Teacher Inquiry," and describes how teachers can engage in inquiry about their practice and the practice of their school. The chapter also discusses the role *discourse* plays in inquiry, how examining *equity* aspects of issues is key in inquiry, how *authenticity* can be enhanced via inquiry, the way in which inquiry can be a form of teacher *leadership,* and the relationship between inquiry and *service.* Chapter 6, the other chapter in Unit 2, discusses the role discourse plays in democratic schools and how schools can engage in productive discourse.

Unit 3 focuses on equity. Chapter 7 focuses on issues of equity that pervade schools, particularly in terms of race, class, gender, and sexuality. The chapter also describes ways that schools can and have responded to issues of equity. Chapters 8 and 9 explore how law serves to protect equity, especially in terms of protecting the access of all groups to education and ensuring the personal liberty of each individual. Chapter 10, the last chapter in Unit 3, discusses issues of equity involved in school governance and finance.

Unit 4 is focused on authenticity. Chapter 11 examines teaching and learning, with a particular focus on authentic pedagogy and the characteristics of authentic democratic classrooms. Chapter 12 moves from teaching and learning to curriculum, exploring the nature of curriculum in democratic schools and influences on the construction of the curriculum.

Unit 5 deals with leadership and service. Chapter 13 focuses primarily on the nature of leadership in democratic schools and on the implications for leadership from teachers. Chapter 14 examines the necessity for democratic classrooms and schools to connect with the world beyond their walls via serving others.

The concluding Unit 6, chapter 15 of the book, ties together what it means to be a democratic educator and how teachers can engage in the practice of "doing democracy."

Throughout the book we attempt to integrate historical events and philosophical thought which serve as foundations for the contemporary democratic practices that are the focus of our discussion. We do this through the use of "Present to Past" sections. Typically these sections immediately follow the discussion of the contemporary beliefs or practices they ground. Our belief is that reading about present practices before reading about their historical roots will serve to make the historical discussion more meaningful to you. In essence, our objective is to "connect" history to the present, rather than having it stand alone as something that happened a long time ago with seemingly little relevance to what we do now.

What are the qualifications we bring to writing a book about democratic education? While we could cite the usual degrees and publication records that textbook authors tend to have, we believe these are less important than other qualifications. Perhaps what qualifies us most is that we are teachers, professors, students, parents, administrators, authors, and citizens. As teachers, we struggle to teach democratically as well as to teach about democratic education. As professors/students, we struggle to learn with and from schools through our active involvement with schools and school renewal networks. As parents, we struggle to raise our children democratically and to promote democratic practices in our children's schools. As administrators, we struggle within our own colleges and universities as we work toward more democratic practices. As citizens we struggle to find the time and means to provide service in our communities to help make them better, more equitable, and more just places for all those who live in them. As authors we struggle to connect our teaching, learning, parenting, and service to what we write about democratic schooling. Perhaps what qualifies us most to write this book are the multiple perspectives which our experiences and struggles in these roles provide us as we continue in our personal journeys toward "doing democracy." Perhaps this, more than anything, qualifies us to write this book.

Finally, we wish to acknowledge a few of the many individuals who influenced us in our personal and continuing journeys toward democratic education. We thank Ally Audas, Judi Barber, Martha Dauway, Michale Gentry, Dean Ketchum, Kim Nickerson, Isaac Sithole, and the teachers, administrators, students, and parents who are part of the Oklahoma Networks for Excellence in Education member schools; Bob McCarthy, Ted Sizer, and Nancy Walwood from the Coalition of Essential Schools; Lew Allen, Carl Glickman, and Francis Hensley from the League of Professional Schools; graduate assistants Ruth Ference and Mary Greco; Colleen Capper, David Clark, Jeffrey Cornett, Beverly Cross, Elaine Jarchow, John McIntyre, Ray McNulty; and our international friends, Abla A. AL-Essa, Ahmad AL-Bustan, Eero Ropo, and Johannes Slabbert. Thanks to Julie Mead for contributing chapters 8 and 9. Finally, we thank Linda Darling Hammond, Ann Lieberman, Paul Schwarz, and George Wood, whose insights about schools have helped us see much to which we might otherwise have been blind. We thank also the reviewers of earlier drafts of this book: Paul Burden, Kansas State University; Jeff Cornett, University of Central Florida; Larry Daniel, University of Southern Mississippi; Bryan Deever, Georgia Southern University; Dorothy Engan-Barker, Mankato State University; Erwin Epstein, Ohio State University; Don Kauchak, University of Utah; Jean Luckowski, York College; Averil McClelland, Kent State University; John McLure, University of Iowa; Robert Morris, West Georgia College; George Noblitt, University of North Carolina-Chapel Hill; Evelyn Powers, formerly of East Carolina University; Alan Quick, Central Michigan University; Vance Randall, Brigham Young University; Clement Seldin, University of Massachusetts-Amherst; Robert Sherman, University of Florida; Angela Spaulding, West Texas A & M University; Phil Tate, Boston University; Atilano Valencia, California State University-Fresno; Caroline Wactler, Arizona State University; Paul Wagner, University of Houston-Clear Lake; and John Zelazek, Central Missouri State University. Tracy Napper, Carol Wada, Jo-Anne Weaver, Elaine Richards, Linda McMillan, Lili Weiner, Carol Kincaid, and all the others on the Harcourt staff supported us, stimulated our thinking, and worked with us in various capacities on this book. Last, but certainly not least, we thank our families—Dan, Maggie, Mary, Erica, Jonathan, Carrie, Meghan, Ben, and Rebecca—for their unwavering understanding, support, and sacrifice. To all of you and to all those whom we have not mentioned but who are a part of us: Thanks for being our road map.

Connect to the IDEALS framework and read real-life examples of teachers and students practicing democratic education when you study the IDEALS Challenge boxes found in every chapter. There are six kinds of boxes: Initiating Inquiry; Deepening Discourse; Examining Equity; Achieving Authenticity; Learning Leadership; and Supporting Service, although each chapter may not have examples of all six boxes.

IDEALS CHALLENGE: *Learning Leadership*

(Adapted from Brodhagen, 1995, pp. 96–97.)

I was nervous. "Will this really work?" I wondered. "Will these kids really conduct their own parent-teacher conferences? Had there been enough preparation? Will parents want to listen to their child?"

My first conference was with Holly, a bright young adolescent who does consistently good work, but doesn't seem to want to participate in large- or small-group discussions. Holly walked into the room first. Trailing behind was her mother, who was carrying a younger sibling. Holly began.

She introduced her mother, her sister, and me and then plunged into discussion of her work. "This is my best work." She took papers out and gave a brief explanation of each. Her mom asked questions and made comments such as "I remember when you were working on this" and "This turned out pretty good." Holly explained that the "best work" papers would be kept at school in a folder that would be sent home at year's end, with all the other best work.

Holly then read her written self-evaluation to her mom. When she had finished, she and her mom started to talk about why Holly didn't want to talk in front of her peers. Her mom admitted that as a teenager she didn't want to talk in class either. They talked about what was easy and challenging for Holly. They laughed about Holly's admission that doing her homework in front of the television wasn't such a good idea. And they discussed her goals for the next quarter, with mom saying Holly was too hard on herself.

I just sat there, amazed. Holly had said all I would have said, and much more that I never could or should. I simply validated a lot of what they had said. When it was over, the three of us stood, smiling at one another, exchanging looks that seemed to say, "This felt good, let's do it again."

- Which IDEALS of democratic education are represented in the scenario?
- What is the connection between the teacher's parent-teacher conference practices and leadership?
- How do you think the teacher prepared students for conducting conferences with their parents?
- Why do you think that Holly said much more than the teacher ever "could or should" say?
- In what other areas of the school, might students expand their leadership roles?

Spark interesting discussion of the contrasts between educational practices in the United States and other countries by studying the Global Challenge boxes. A complete listing follows, along with an example:

GLOBAL CHALLENGE ***The Maori***

(Excerpted from Barrington, 1991, pp. 318–319, 321–322.)

Maori children remain disadvantaged in terms of overall educational achievement compared with Europeans. . . . In the 1960s and 1970s, explanations of underachievement were closely modeled upon American or English theories: the problem was seen as being located in the personality and home experience of Maori children—that is, outside schools. . . .

In more recent years, there has been a shift away from this "blaming the victim" approach to a much closer look at what is happening in schools and classrooms. Factors identified here as likely to impede the progress of Maori children include inadequate provision of the Maori language in schools . . . use of unsuitable tests and assessment methods . . . low expectations by teachers . . . curriculum content and organization which is inadequate or inappropriate . . . school climate and teaching styles . . . and monocultural European teachers.

Global Challenge

Consider the issues involved in the use of technology in democratic schools or complete an exercise using technology when you read the Technology Challenge boxes. Below is a listing of the boxes, including an example:

TECHNOLOGY CHALLENGE

Access to Technology

(From The Parents' Guide to the Information Superhighway *(2nd ed.), by the National Center for Education Statistics, 1998, Washington, DC: The Children's Partnership.)*

HAVES	HAVE NOTS
88% of schools with students from high-income families have access to the Internet	63% of schools with a large proportion of students from poor families have access to the Internet
39% of households with annual incomes of $20,000–$39,999 own computers	19% of households with annual incomes less than $20,000 own computers
58% of households with annual incomes of $40,000–59,999 own computers	
68% of households with annual incomes of over $60,000 own computers	

- What is the relationship of the democratic IDEALS of equity to these statistics?
- What are some possible solutions to the access problem for poor schools and children?

Technology Challenge

Integrate historical events and philosophical thought with their contemporary democratic education practices by reading the Present to Past sections. These sections follow the contemporary beliefs or practices they ground, to allow the reader to see how the historical roots are connected to today's practices.

PRESENT TO PAST

Examining Historical Bases for Teaching Practices

THE 19TH CENTURY: MAINTAINING CONTROL

During the 19th century the growth of cities led to a tremendous increase in the number of urban schools. Urban schools were much larger than rural schools and urban classrooms often contained 40–48 desks per room, accommodating as many as 60 students. The growth of these schools and classroom populations combined with the effects of industrialization led to a push for greater efficiency and student control. Schools began using subtle but powerful means of control. For example, instead of working at communal tables or benches, students sat at desks bolted to the floor, in rows, facing forward. Schools became graded by age groups, and ability grouping within classes was expanded. Specific textbooks were mandated and curriculum guidelines became formalized. Blackboards replaced the individual slates of students in country schools, and individual report cards replaced student performances and exhibits as a means of showing learning or achievement.

Present to Past

Explore the Internet for further information of relevance and interest by following the links provided in the "Click on It!" boxes found in the margins of every chapter.

CLICK ON IT

Visit the Web site of the Center for Living Democracy at

www.livingdemocracy.org

and the Web site of the Hubert H. Humphrey Center for Democracy and Citizenship at

www.hhh.umn.edu/centers/cdc/

and

wwwou.edu/org/one/network.html

for examples of individuals and groups "doing democracy."

About the Authors

MARY JOHN O'HAIR is a professor at the University of Oklahoma and the Director of the Center for School Renewal and Democratic Citizenship. She is also the founder and Executive Director of the Oklahoma Networks for Excellence in Education (O.N.E.), a school-university-community partnership that has international links with South Africa, Kuwait, Nicaragua, Peru, Finland, and the Netherlands. Her teaching and scholarly work forms an intersecting collage that incorporates themes dealing with the democratic restructuring of schools, enhancing the quality of student learning, and viewing children as our highest priority. She is the author of seven books and dozens of articles and other professional publications. She views education from the multiple perspectives of professional educator, citizen, and parent of two school-aged children.

ULRICH C. REITZUG is a professor at the University of North Carolina at Greensboro and chair of the Department of Educational Leadership and Cultural Foundations. His teaching and scholarly interests are concerned with issues of democratic education, school renewal, inquiry, and educational leadership. He has written and published extensively, received the William J. Davis Award for one of his scholarly publications, and recently became the editor of the Journal of School Leadership. He has worked with schools striving to become more democratic in Florida, North Carolina, Indiana, Ohio, and Wisconsin and internationally in South Africa. For the past four years he has served as the external critical friend for the Oklahoma Networks for Excellence in Education, a democratic school renewal network. He views education from the multiple perspectives of professional educator, citizen, and parent of two school-aged children.

H. JAMES MCLAUGHLIN is an associate professor at the University of Georgia in the Middle School Education Program. Dr. McLaughlin is a former elementary and middle school teacher, and he has maintained strong ties with classroom practitioners by planning with teachers to develop an innovative field-based teacher education program. He is a former editor of Action in Teacher Education and has a number of publications related to teacher reflection, teacher action research, and the benefits of multiage grouping of students. Dr. McLaughlin's current scholarly and community work is directed toward involving educators in international experiences and community action projects in order to increase our understanding of how to teach children from different language and national backgrounds. He views education from the multiple perspectives of teacher educator, after-school tutor, community activist, and parent of two school-aged children.

CONTENTS IN BRIEF

CONTENTS

CONTENTS

CONTENTS

CONTENTS

Foundations of Democratic Education

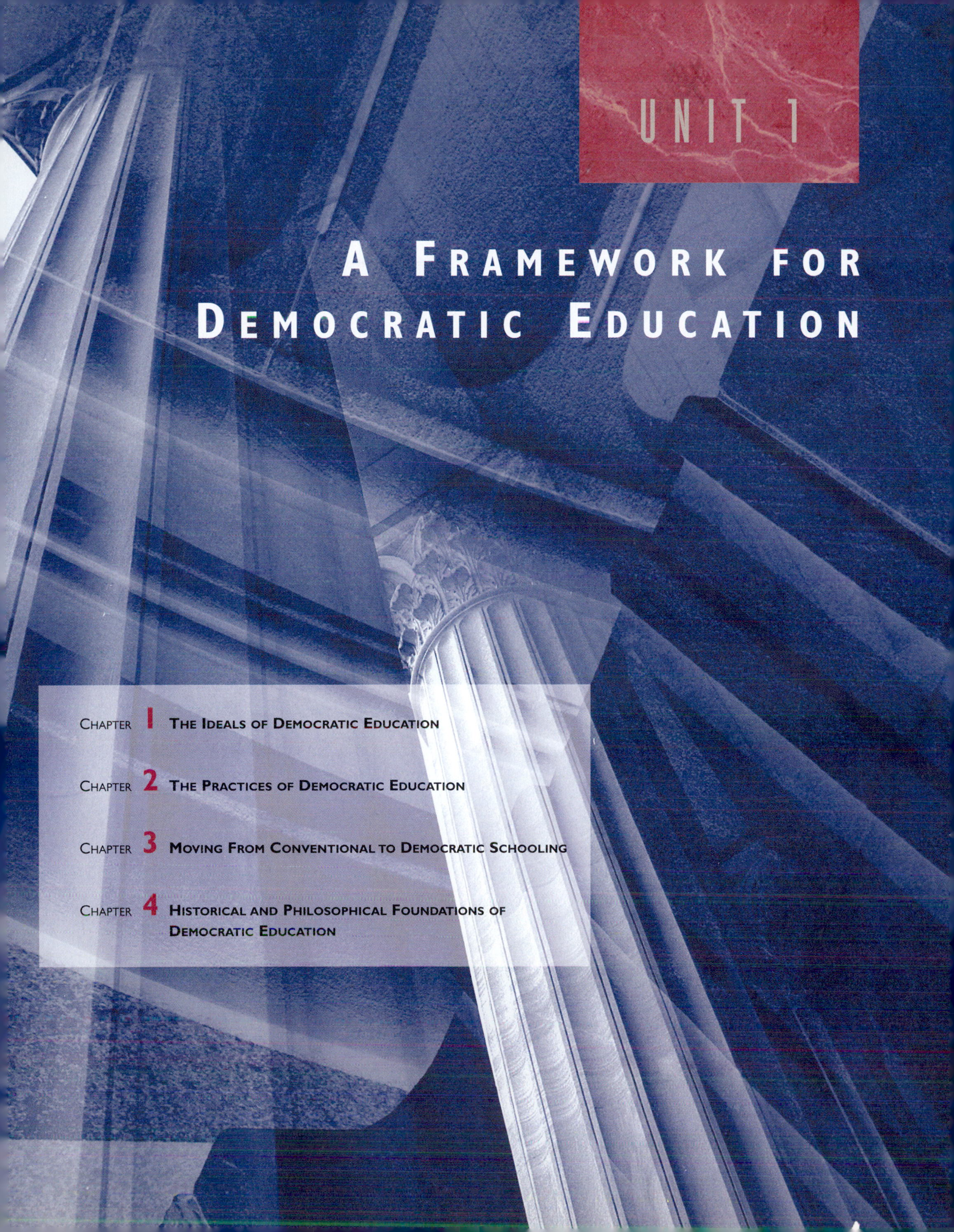

UNIT 1

A Framework for Democratic Education

What materials did the workers use to build the foundation for this school?

What role does the foundation of the building serve?

What role do you think the foundations of education will play in your teaching practice?

What types of "materials" do you think will serve as the foundation for your teaching practice?

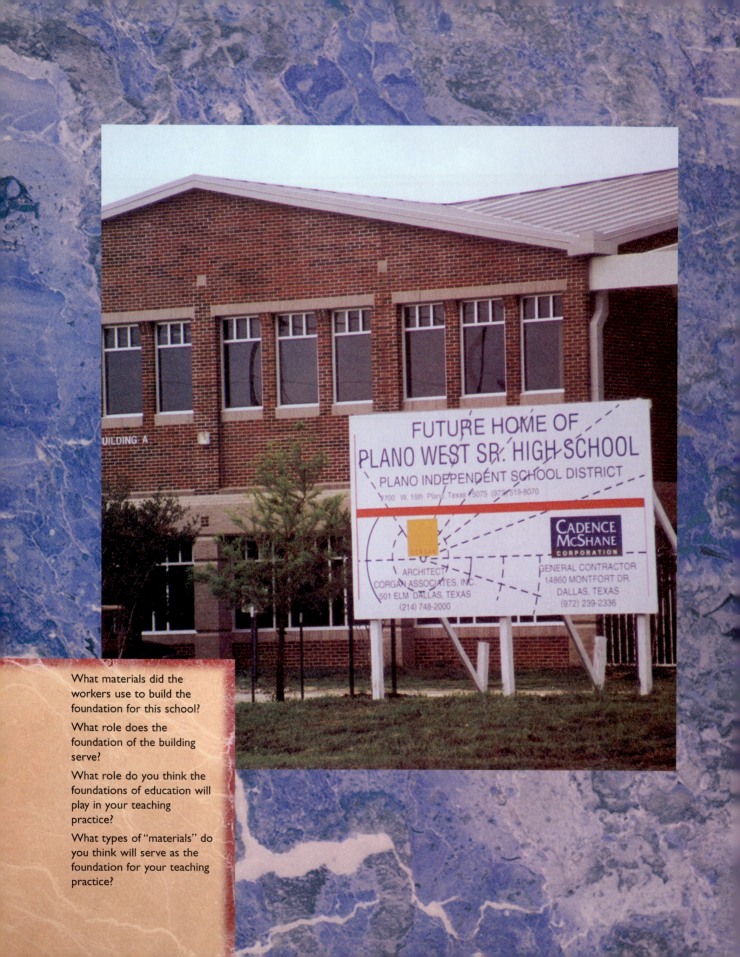

CHAPTER 1

The Ideals of Democratic Education

IDEALS CHALLENGE: *Deepening Discourse*

Complete the following statement:
A truly educated person is someone who ____________________.

INTRODUCTION

Belvidere, IL: Looking out a classroom window at the dumpster below, a student asks the teacher, "Where does that garbage go?" Since she is just as curious, the teacher arranges for a class field trip to an area landfill. Concerned about the size and contents of the landfill, the students undertake a campaign for conservation and recycling in their school. Over several months, their efforts begin to take hold. Though they are just first graders, they have made a difference in their school. (Apple & Beane, 1995, p. 2)

Madison, WI: On a warm September day, a group of nearly 60 middle school students and their teachers are working together to create their curriculum out of questions and concerns they have about themselves and their world. Eventually they cluster their questions into themes like "Living in the Future," "Problems in the Environment," "Isms," and "Conflict." After selecting their first theme and planning relevant activities, they will spend the year trying to answer those questions—their questions. (Apple & Beane, 1995, p. 2)

Purcell, OK: In the wake of the bombing of the Murrah Building on April 19 [1995], our elementary students were trying to deal with their anger and distress. Several of the students asked if they could donate money to help the children.

We set up a clear Lucite cube in a central location in the school and began to collect "Change for the Children." Many of our schoolchildren brought all they had in their piggy banks. A first grader donated her birthday money. By the end of a week, students had collected over $1,200 for the littlest victims of the tragic bombing. (Davis, 1996)

The teachers and students in these scenarios demonstrate what valuable and beneficial education should look like. As unpublicized as these stories and others like them are, we know that all took place in public schools involving young people, educators, and communities no different on the surface than many other communities across the country. In these schools, teachers help students relate classroom learning to the world outside of school. They move beyond the study of isolated facts to identifying, analyzing, and solving problems facing their schools and local communities.

While these stories are refreshing and worthwhile, we sometimes forget the original idea that links these stories. This idea was intended to guide the philosophy and practices of our public schools. The idea is democracy.

The only social institution charged with teaching children for democracy is our public schools. Often, however, public schools lose focus on democracy as their primary purpose. Unless we as teachers develop strong democratic foundations and guiding beliefs, we leave ourselves open to being influenced and overwhelmed by educational fads and trends, regardless of their merit and congruence with our needs and context. In this book our goal is to reexamine the original purposes of education; reduce fragmentation and emphasis on trendy, quick-fix programs to improve schools; and challenge future teachers to develop strong democratic foundations of education that withstand external pressures and that promote high quality intellectual growth for all students.

Specifically in this chapter, we examine:

- Why is building an educational foundation important?
- What are the purposes of education?
- What is the meaning of democracy and democratic education?
- What IDEALS guide democratic school communities?

WHY IS BUILDING AN EDUCATIONAL FOUNDATION IMPORTANT?

Our purpose in writing this book is not to overload you with disconnected pieces of information about teaching and schools, but rather to assist you in examining and connecting new information to your practice as a teacher and to your beliefs and values about American education. As these connections become clear, you begin to create your own educational foundations, your own understanding of how to relate philosophy and practice. These connections not only help provide meaning for your educational foundations class, but they also help you make sense of your entire preservice education program. Connections continue to grow and develop as you experience your first classroom and well beyond your first year of teaching. These connections, rather than a course, a textbook, or a teacher education program, become your educational foundation—the beliefs and values that help guide your actions, inform your sense of inquiry and, in general, create the teacher you become. Thoreau perhaps describes this process best:

> If one advances confidently in the direction of his [sic] dreams and endeavors to live the life which he has imagined, he will meet with a success unexpected in common hours. He will put some things behind, and will pass an invisible boundary; new, universal, more liberal laws will begin to establish themselves around and within him. . . . If you have built castles in the air, your work need not be lost; this is where they should be. Now put the foundations under them. . . .

Note the word "foundations" in the Thoreau quote. The metaphor "foundations" is the heart of this book. Perhaps the "foundations of education" should be perceived as the support and infrastructure for our "castles in the air"—our ideals and visions of what education should be. Without the foundational understanding of education as a historical, sociocultural, political, and moral enterprise, the walls of our castles will not hold up. They will crumble as soon as the first-year teacher hears experienced teachers talk in the teachers' lounge about "how kids really are." Or perhaps, the walls of the castle will crumble when the first-year teacher has a veteran tell him or her what won't work and what "real life" is like in schools. Castle walls and towering turrets without a firm foundation cannot hold. Likewise, a foundation that has no visionary castle constructed over it is empty, devoid of meaning and direction.

The central aim of this book is to help you see clearly the purposes, philosophies, and practices of public education and your role as a teacher in a democratic society. We examine our successes and our failures in educating all students. We discuss why schools have not been successful in the past in educating all students and what democratic teachers and schools must accomplish in the future to get us back on track and be true to the most vital purposes of American education.

WHAT ARE THE PURPOSES OF EDUCATION?

There have been many, often conflicting, purposes of American education. For example, many people believe that schools' primary purpose is to prepare students to get a job. Some other common purposes of schooling include:

- political purposes primarily concerned with "educating citizens . . . and socializing individuals for political systems" (Spring, 1994, p. 7)

- social purposes intended to promote "social control, improving social conditions, and reducing social tensions caused by economic inequalities" (Spring, 1994, p. 12)
- economic purposes, such as increasing national wealth, advancing technological development, and maintaining the global economic position of the United States (Spring, 1994).

Purposes for public education such as these are not always clearly understood by the public and educators. Often, purposes may conflict or even work at cross-purposes. As one frustrated teacher describes:

> I've been teaching for 20 years now, and I can't remember all the reforms I've been through. I'm not sure that I can take another one! It seems that every three years someone—whether it's a new hotshot superintendent, the state department, the governor, or a university professor—comes up with a great new idea of how American education can be saved. What happens is that I and my colleagues become the punching bag recipients of someone else's plan. . . . To be blunt, I've seen these ideas come and go. . . . Each new idea that comes down from on high doesn't improve my teaching—it often takes away from my teaching. (Glickman, 1990, p. 434)

Another teacher discusses the priority placed on the economic purpose of schools and the indifference to a democratic focus.

> My goal is to help my kids become active, involved members of the community. I try to reach this by having them become active, involved members of our classroom, school, and neighborhood. But what I'm told now is that what we are really to do is just get kids ready to take tests so we can make better cars than the Japanese. So I'm told to drill, and sort, and measure; and whether or not my kids can think, cooperate, and be creative, or work for a common goal is irrelevant. (Blase & Blase, 1997)

Students themselves feel that learning without connections to the real world is meaningless:

> In your classes you learn, but you forget. You run from class to class and it is always something different and not connected. You might carry seven or eight books home every day, but I didn't read them, I just looked for the answer. (Wood, 1992, p. 201)

As reflected in these teachers' and students' voices, power structures that use a top-down hierarchical approach to change and mandate reforms without teacher, student, or parent input have often worked at cross-purposes and have been ineffective in improving education.

Our Beliefs

While many purposes of American education exist, we believe they should be *to promote individual growth and participation in a democratic society*. Our beliefs are aligned with Thomas Jefferson, who wrote that the purpose of education in a democratic state is "to furnish all citizens with the knowledge and training that will enable them to pursue happiness as private persons [and] to prepare all citizens to exercise their rights to self-government

. . ." (Heslep, 1969, p. 50). Also, we believe in democracy *as* education and that an educated citizenry and a democracy are one and the same—the lack of one endangers the other (Glickman, 1998).

In order to better understand the purpose of American education and the connections between schools and democracy, we must first examine the meaning of democracy and democratic education.

WHAT IS THE MEANING OF DEMOCRACY AND DEMOCRATIC EDUCATION?

Democracy is the word we use to describe "how we govern ourselves, the concept by which we measure the wisdom and worth of social policies and shifts, the ethical anchor we seek when our political ship seems to drift" (Beane & Apple, 1995, p. 4–5). We hear it used daily, for example to justify almost any action: "Hey, this is a free country, right? Don't we live in a democracy?" But what does democracy really mean? Should it be used to justify our every action?

We believe that democracy is more than a form of governance—*democracy is a way of life*. It is "not what we have, but what we do" (Center for Living Democracy, 1998). Democracy is integrally linked to education and schooling. It is essential that you as a beginning teacher develop a personal understanding of the linkages between democracy and education. While frequently associated with the governance of countries and practices such as voting in elections, we believe these are merely tokens of democracy. Democracy is a *process* rather than a *product* and extends far beyond merely decision making and governance structures. Perhaps John Dewey (1966) states it best when he describes democracy as occurring not just in voting and in formal governance structures, but rather in all areas of life. He notes that democracy includes a whole range of "associated living" and occurs in the various realms of social life (p. 87). What might this "way of life" or "associated living" look like? We believe the following conditions undergird a democratic way of life.

- The open flow of ideas, regardless of their popularity, that enables people to be as fully informed as possible.
- Faith in the individual and collective capacity of people to create possibilities for resolving problems.
- The use of critical reflection and analysis to evaluate ideas, problems, and policies.
- Concern for the welfare of others and "the common good."
- Concern for the dignity and rights of individuals and minorities.
- The organization of social institutions to promote and extend the democratic way of life. (Beane & Apple, 1995)

Additionally, democracy is not a state that you achieve but rather "an 'idealized' set of values that we must live and that must guide our life as a people" (Beane & Apple, p. 7). We believe the examples provided at the

In addition to voting, what else does "*living* democracy" require?

CLICK ON IT

Visit the Web site of the Center for Living Democracy at

www.livingdemocracy.org

and the Web site of the Hubert H. Humphrey Center for Democracy and Citizenship at

www.hhh.umn.edu/centers/cdc/

and

wwwou.edu/org/one/network.html

for examples of individuals and groups "doing democracy."

IDEALS CHALLENGE: *Deepening Discourse*

- A truly educated person *in a democracy* is someone who ____________________.
- Assess the three examples in this chapter's opening in terms of the conditions of democracy outlined in the list on page 7. Which conditions does each example illustrate?
- Divide into small groups of four to six members each. Choose three of the conditions of democracy and give examples of each. Include at least one school example.
- What are some common obstacles or barriers to the conditions of democracy? How would a truly educated person in a democracy respond to these obstacles? Discuss examples with your small group.

beginning of this chapter are illustrations of students and schools involved in the process of "doing democracy."[1]

In this book we define democracy as *a way of living that requires the open flow and critique of ideas with an authentic concern for the interest of the individual as well as the common good.* Perhaps what is most important to remember for you as a beginning teacher is that if people are to strive for and maintain a democratic way of life, they must have opportunities to learn what that way of life means and how it might be led (Dewey, 1916). Schools provide such an opportunity to practice and model democracy. In the next section, we explore connections of democracy and education.

What Is Democratic Education?

Two core concepts best describe democratic education: schooling *for* democracy and schools *as* democracies. In combination, these concepts facilitate the development of democratic school communities.

Schooling for Democracy

The focus on schooling for democracy has emphasized reconnecting schools to their original purpose, that is, to prepare students for life in a democracy. Many argue that the number one goal of our schools is to prepare students to engage productively in a democracy by understanding and practicing their rights and responsibilities as citizens in a democracy. Schooling for democracy requires schools to practice authentic teaching and learning designed to connect students with the real issues of their communities and their lives. If this were the case, then:

> Rarely would we hear students describing school as "a hassle you put up with during the day until you can return to the real world." If the primary goal of schools were to prepare students to engage productively in a democracy, then students and teachers would be working on the concerns of students' immediate and future lives and on the concerns of their immediate and local communities. Students would learn to speak and listen, read and write, and understand mathematics, science, art, and music in order to gain the power to make a better life for themselves and their communities. (Glickman, 1993, pp. 9–10)

Schooling for democracy focuses on authenticity, relevance, and making connections. In a later section, we describe these concepts through the democratic ideals of authenticity and service.

Schools as Democracies

The focus on schools *as* democracies has been on creating schools that are organized, governed, and practiced as democracies. The discourse has frequently concentrated on the governance of schools and specifically on increasing the participation of various stakeholders in school decision making through initiatives such as site-based management.

Unfortunately, a focus exclusively on democratic governance overlooks significant aspects of schools as democracies that are played out in various aspects of school policy as well as in issues of daily practice. As described earlier, democracy includes a whole manner of "associated living" and occurs in "multiple realms of social life" (Dewey, 1916). Democracy requires that (1) all stakeholders are represented in governance and the other realms of social life, (2) there is widespread inclusion and sharing of perspectives, and (3) the objective is the reconstruction of perspective and practice (Dewey, 1916). Additionally, in a democracy discourse must be equitable, with no individual or group dominating due to power differentials, and inquiry (rather than power) should determine the strongest argument (Strike, 1993). However, democratic practices do not always serve democratic ends. Specifically "local populist politics" may result in practices such as "racial segregation and denial of access to all but the wealthy" (Beane & Apple, 1995, pp. 9–10). Thus, democracy requires not only equity in discourse, but also equity in practice. In a later section, we describe these concepts through the democratic ideals of inquiry, discourse, equity, and shared leadership.

Democratic education involves schooling *for* democracy as well as schools *as* democracies. When we combine both concepts we end up with schools that serve their students, families, teachers, staff members, and communities well. These schools are best described as democratic school communities.

Democratic School Communities Linked to High Student Achievement

OK, you might ask, "What's the bottom line? Do students learn more in democratic school communities than in conventional schools?" Empirical evidence and moral arguments suggest that student success in schools that function as democratic school communities is substantially higher than in traditional schools. After studying over 1,500 schools, researchers found that students learn more when teachers:

- pursue a clear, shared purpose for all students' learning;
- engage in collaborative activities to achieve that purpose;
- take collective responsibility for student learning. (Newmann & Wehlage, 1995; Newmann & Associates, 1996)

Further, schools as democratic communities require strong, collaborative leadership from the principal; undivided support from the district administrators; broad-based support from teachers and parents; and engagement of and support from citizens who live in the larger community. At the systems level, collaborative leadership is required of superintendents and other administrators, as well as from school board members and other policy makers who represent local and state government (Newmann & Wehlage, 1995). Researchers believe the findings are due to the contrast between schools that are organized bureaucratically and those that are organized democratically. Researchers from the University of Michigan describe teachers who work in democratic schools as:

> Teachers working collaboratively, often in teams that are formed across subjects. Instead of being governed by top-down directives, teachers have more input into decisions affecting their work. And instead of slotting students into different educational paths, [the school] would group students of diverse talents and interests together for instruction. . . . Schools with this form have more meaning for their members. (p. 2)

These findings support the hypotheses about the effects of democratic school communities on student success. Not only were students' achievements in the first two years significantly higher in democratic school communities but those gains also were distributed more equitably. That is, the achievement gap between students of lower socioeconomic status, or SES, and students of higher SES was narrower in democratic school communities (Lee & Smith, 1994).

WHAT IDEALS GUIDE DEMOCRATIC SCHOOL COMMUNITIES?

Democratic education has at its core ideals of inquiry, discourse, equity, authenticity, shared leadership, and service. We must remember that democracy and democratic education are not conditions that have been achieved, but ideals that we must strive for together. That is, democracy and democratic education are not a destination, but rather a journey or a pilgrimage. Even if we work in the most democratic of schools it is better to think of "becoming" a democratic school rather than of "being" a democratic school. Democracy and democratic schooling are an ongoing struggle toward putting into practice a set of democratic IDEALS, which stem from the purposes of public education and include:

I — Inquiry

D — Discourse

E — Equity

A — Authenticity

L — Leadership

S — Service

These IDEALS represent our interpretation of democratic education. Their framework is not intended to include everything involving democracy and education, but rather to assist as you begin to develop your own educational foundations as a teacher.

Each of these IDEALS is rich in meaning and in implications for practice, and are discussed throughout this book. We also will ask you to work with the IDEALS via periodic IDEALS Challenges scattered throughout each chapter. Table 1.1 gives an initial explanation and overview of each IDEAL.

Inquiry

Inquiry refers to the ongoing study, reflection, and analysis of one's own practice as a teacher and the collective practice of the school. Inquiry allows educators to examine their practice and the school's programs and policies and to make decisions based on careful study rather than on educational trends or fads. Before making decisions, inquiring teachers and administrators continually ask, "How can we improve our practices? Is this the best decision for our students? On what data or information are we basing this decision?"

Table 1.1 The IDEALS of Democratic Education

Inquiry	The study of individual and school practice.
Discourse	Conversation and debate about teaching, learning, and schooling.
Equity	Concern for achieving fair and just practices in school and society.
Authenticity	Teaching and learning that engages and has value beyond the classroom.
Leadership	Initiation of experiences that result in inquiry, discourse, and critique.
Service	Experiences that develop and exhibit social responsibility.

Although inquiry will be discussed in greater detail in chapter 5, it requires two minimum conditions that we will discuss here: access and collaboration. First, individuals and schools engaged in inquiry must have access to a wide range of information and ideas. Access, which involves the open flow of ideas regardless of their popularity, enables people to be as fully informed as possible. Access to information and ideas for teachers and others involved in school decision making is limited if, for example, communication from superintendents, school boards, state governing bodies, and professional organizations is shared only with principals. Access to information and ideas for students is limited if textbooks and supplementary reading materials are censored because of complaints from a particular interest group, if teachers utilize solely a textbook-centered curriculum, or if certain valuable subjects (such as the arts) are largely left out of the curriculum.

Second, teachers and other members of the school community must collaborate to accept collective responsibility for what occurs in the school. For example, if a teacher cannot determine how to meet a student's needs, teachers should work together to study the student's situation and develop strategies for his or her education. Collaborative inquiry fosters an atmosphere of collegiality in which teachers give up a degree of personal autonomy in order to gain collective school autonomy. They spend time discussing, studying, and debating issues of curriculum, teaching, and learning. Collaboration among teachers and administrators ensures that the success or failure of classroom events and of the school does not rest with the strengths or weaknesses of one person, such as the classroom teacher or the principal. Rather, faculty and staff collectively share the responsibility for student and school success.

True collaboration requires mutual respect and open communication. Mutual respect is not limited to tolerance, although tolerating others' viewpoints is a beginning. Mutual respect involves a shared effort to listen to and attempt to understand what others think. Without mutual respect, we may take turns talking, but we do not really listen to one another and attempt to understand and communicate in the face of conflicting views.

Teachers and other staff in schools cannot make students have mutual respect for one another. Adults, however, can strive for open communication in their interactions with students, parents, and the community, as well as among themselves. Communication combines written, oral, and nonverbal skills with one's personal commitment to and conscious actions when listening and understanding. The aim of communicating in classrooms is to provide the opportunity to speak and to be heard as part of the inquiry

IDEALS CHALLENGE: *Initiating Inquiry*

(Adapted from Reitzug & Reeves, 1992. The narrator is a teacher in the school.)

One time the other third-grade teachers and I went to see Mr. Sage (the principal) to talk with him about our reading and language instruction. We told him that we wanted to change our current way of teaching reading and language arts. We had been mostly using basal readers for reading and were using a lot of skill worksheets with the students. The students were doing very little reading out of trade books and little expository writing. One of the district language arts resource teachers, Miss Lincoln, had visited us and enthusiastically told us about whole language and how wonderful it was to use children's literature and trade books instead of basal readers, and to have the kids expressing themselves through elaborated written and oral communication. It sounded pretty neat, so we thought we'd ask Mr. Sage if it was OK if we switched to this type of an approach. We told him that Miss Lincoln was in favor of a whole language approach. We also happened to know that Mr. Sage personally favored this way of teaching language arts.

To our amazement Mr. Sage said he didn't want us to use this type of an approach. When we asked him why, he said, "You haven't convinced me that you know why you want to do this, how you will do it, or why you think it will be good for the kids in your classrooms. Miss Lincoln doesn't teach here—you do." We went back to our classrooms dumbfounded and a little angry. After we calmed down and talked about it we realized Mr. Sage was right. We were just trying to jump on another educational bandwagon without having thought about, studied, and discussed whether this was an approach that was supported by research. More importantly, we hadn't thought about, studied, and discussed whether it was a good approach for us and our students.

Fortunately, we didn't stop there. We started reading all the articles about whole language and process approaches to writing that we could get our hands on. We started documenting how our students responded during our reading and language arts classes. We asked them what they were learning and how they liked reading and language arts. We asked Miss Lincoln to refer us to some teachers who were already using whole language methods in their classrooms. We observed in those teachers' classrooms and talked with them about their experiences with whole language. We talked with each other, sharing what we were learning and discussing how we felt it fit with our teaching styles and how it would impact our students. We became more and more convinced that this was the way we wanted to teach and wondered why we hadn't started teaching this way years ago. We concluded that we had been seduced by the ease of using prepackaged reading and language arts series. We didn't have to do much thinking or planning when we used them—we just had to do what the book told us to do. It was easy, but not very satisfying, and it didn't seem real good for kids either.

We went back to see Mr. Sage, determined to teach using whole language methods even if he denied us permission. When we started talking with him we couldn't stop. I think we overwhelmed him with what we knew and with our enthusiasm. The names rolled off our tongues—Allington, Pearson, Graves, Calkins. We told him about what we and our students didn't like about our current practices. We told him about how we intended to do things differently. When we finally finished, all he said was, "Initially I didn't want you to use a whole language approach because I wasn't sure that you knew what you were doing. If I didn't think that you were able to handle a whole language approach I couldn't justify letting you use it. Now you've convinced me. Go for it!"

- How is the scenario an example of inquiry/critical study?
- In what ways did the teachers inquire about their practice? What sources of data and knowledge did they use?

Using discourse to gain a deeper understanding of others' perspectives is a characteristic of democratic schools.

process. It provides a means to give voice to those unwilling or unable to speak. Open communication during inquiry means that we are willing to entertain opposing points of view. It does not mean that we capitulate in order to gain a quick consensus.

Discourse

In the simplest sense, discourse refers to conversations, discussions, and debates. In democratic schools, **discourse** refers to conversations, discussions, and debates that result in the development of a clear, shared purpose for schooling and for student learning. Additionally, discourse in democratic schools explores how classroom and school practices and policies are consistent with and promote the school's shared purpose.

Discourse is closely related to inquiry and equity, two other democratic IDEALS. Discourse should be informed by the inquiry process. That is, discourse should not involve exchanging uninformed opinions. Rather, discourse should identify information, data, and knowledge that needs to be collected in order to have informed discussions. Subsequent to collecting this information, it should play a central part in the discourse surrounding a question, issue, or decision.

Equity in discourse is essential and refers to ensuring that the voices of all are heard—not simply those who are powerful, aggressive, or favored. Thus, it is important that in schools the voices of teachers who typically act more like "lambs" than "lions," not speaking or deferring to those with louder or more aggressive voices, are proactively solicited in school discourse (Glickman, 1993, p. 63). Similarly, the voices of others who are typically not asked or heard must be solicited—custodians, secretaries, and

IDEALS CHALLENGE: *Deepening Discourse*

(Narrator is Dana Hemphill, a teacher at Norman (OK) High School, as she questions the equitable discourse practices in her classroom.)

I wonder what unintentional messages I may send my students. If I compliment a girl's haircut, have I sent the message that I only think of her as a person who needs to look pretty? When I respond to students' comments in class, do I use critical thinking questions for the girls as well as for the boys? Do I call on disruptive boys as a method of classroom management? Does this leave the quiet, well-behaved girl out in the cold? Do I send the message that as long as you are well-behaved, you don't have to be responsible for learning? By focusing on what boys think and say, do I ignore the possibility that the quiet girl in the corner has valuable insights to share?

- How would you respond to Dana's questions? Discuss your responses with your classmates.

other school support staff; parents, especially those who are less affluent or are minority group members; students; and community members. A comprehensive discussion of discourse is found in chapter 6.

Equity

Equity refers to seeking fair and just practices both within the school and outside of the school. There are many dimensions to equity. Equity in discourse and in having a voice in school decision making already has been discussed. Other dimensions include equity in terms of access to schools, access to school programs and educational opportunities, and achieving a balance between the rights of the individual and the welfare of others—in other words, the common good.

On one level equity simply involves the opportunity to attend school. Not so long ago in our country, students were segregated into different schools on the basis of race, disability, religion, national origin, or gender. In some cases the segregation was tacitly agreed upon by those involved. In other cases, certain groups of people (such as minorities and girls) were denied access to quality schooling and sometimes to schooling at all. In any case, segregation that denies access to educational institutions for certain groups is unacceptable in a democratic society. Indeed, equity in access to quality schools still does not exist in our society. For example, research has documented that a tremendous disparity exists between school facilities and programs in economically impoverished urban areas versus those in suburban areas (Kozol, 1991). Even within a school district, great disparities exist between one public school and another, or between public schools and parochial or elite private schools. Thus, some proponents of school choice ground their arguments in equity, arguing that students (especially those in impoverished urban areas) should be allowed to choose the school they wish to attend rather than to be assigned to a school that may be inferior to others in the area.

On another level, equity is ensuring that all students have an equal opportunity to learn once they are in school. For example, can students with disabilities have access to equal educational opportunity when they are

IDEALS CHALLENGE: *Examining Equity*

(A conversation between Jonathan Kozol and Mrs. Washington, a New York City, South Bronx, resident. Excerpted from Kozol (1995), pp. 243–244.)

"Do you think that America likes children?" Mrs. Washington asks me the next evening in her kitchen after we have dinner. It is the last time I will see her for a long while.

"What do you think?" I say, turning back her question, as I probably do too often.

"I don't think so," she replies, and hands me a clipping she has saved. The story, which is from *Newsday*, is about an abandoned steel plant that is going to be used this fall as a school building. The factory, which is next to a cemetery and beside a pipeline that carries "combustible fuel," is in an area, according to a Board of Education engineer, that "appears to be a dumping ground" for "tires, rugs, and parts of bodies." Because of unexpected overcrowding, some 500 children will be forced to go there.

In the margin, next to a sentence that says the site of the building is "a haven" for rats, Mrs. Washington has written, "This is the rock-bottom. So what else is new?"*

- Would we as a society tolerate the deplorable conditions under which some black, Hispanic, and other minority children experience schooling if those children were white?

*Are the deplorable conditions under which some black, Hispanic, and other children experience life due to our inability to eradicate poverty, or are they better explained by a societal lack of will in providing adequate living conditions for "other people's children" (Delpit, 1995; Kozol, 1991, 1995).

Democratic schools focus on equity for all children.

separated from nondisabled students throughout the day? Under current federal and state laws, students with disabilities have a right to the best education possible. Some argue, however, that the inclusion of students with disabilities in the regular classroom may make a teacher's job more difficult and may be detrimental to the education of nondisabled students. This is an issue of equitable access, because it is concerned with every student's opportunity to learn.

Another issue of equitable access is the argument posed by some that many school practices intentionally or unintentionally favor white, middle-

and upper-class students and discriminate against students from economically poor families or students from racial or ethnic minority groups. Tracking, that is, the separation of students into different academic tracks primarily on the basis of standardized test scores, is one commonly cited inequitable practice. Tracking is *believed* to provide vastly superior educational experiences for students in the upper tracks. However, when advantages to students in the high-ability tracks do accrue, and even this result is not always found, "they do not seem to be primarily related to the fact that these tracks are homogeneously grouped. Controlled studies of students taking similar subjects in heterogeneous and homogeneous groups show that high-ability students (like other students) rarely benefit from these tracked settings" (Oakes & Guiton, 1995; Slavin, 1996). An additional inequitable factor is that in racially diverse schools, African American and Hispanic students are typically disproportionally represented in the lower tracks while white students overly populate the upper tracks.

Other potentially inequitable school practices range from discipline policies that are developed based on white, middle-class norms of communication and interaction (Reitzug, 1994) to frequently revered practices such as whole language instruction (Delpit, 1995). Access to programs or experiences can also be inhibited by inequitable public funding or a lack of community resources. A poor rural school with a much lower tax base than a suburban school, or an inner-city school with little chance for financial support from local businesses, both offer reduced access to a quality education. Finally, the expulsion, suspension, or lengthy isolation of students who have misbehaved also denies them access to education.

A democratic school must be continually concerned with seeking fair and just practices both within the school and outside the school. In Unit 3, these practices are examined in-depth.

What do the students appear to be doing? How does it reflect authentic instruction?

Authenticity

Authenticity as a democratic IDEAL refers to something that is genuine and connected, rather than something that is fake and fragmented. Teachers who practice authenticity help students view learning as valuable and that they are judged not by a test but by the quality of their lives. Authentic teaching actively engages students in understanding new knowledge in more meaningful ways. Authentic teaching and learning has some value beyond the classroom and school for students and teachers.

Unfortunately, we often find that in our fragmented academic world what students fail to gain is a more coherent view of knowledge and a more integrated, authentic view of life (Boyer, 1993). In many schools, education is based on seat time rather than on meaningful learning. The schoolwork students experience in order to earn credit, grades, and high test scores is considered trivial, contrived, and meaningless by both students and adults. In the absence of meaning, students lose their excitement for learning and schools. When the most frequently asked question by students is "Will this be on the test?" then we know that something is amiss.

Meaningless schoolwork is a consequence of a number of factors. Perhaps the most significant factor involves a curriculum that emphasizes the concept "more is better." Students spend their time attending 50-minute classes without any real understanding about how subjects connect with each other or with the real world. As a result, students receive a superficial exposure to hundreds of pieces of isolated information. Knowledge is perceived by students as for test purposes only rather than as worthwhile, significant, and meaningful. In addition to a fragmented curriculum, other factors that make authenticity difficult involve heavy teaching loads, rigid school schedules, and lack of planning time for teachers.

IDEALS CHALLENGE: *Achieving Authenticity*

(The late Ernest Boyer, president of the Carnegie Foundation, believed that to see things as authentic and connected is what being an educated person is all about. The following is excerpted from a speech he once delivered on this topic; Boyer, 1993.)

School is a place where values are examined rather than answers dictated.

School provides a climate that makes honorable the quest. I am also convinced that the search for meaning is not taught so much in the curriculum but that it seems to be taught most effectively by great teachers who model values in their own lives. . . . What makes a great teacher? Four characteristics are found in great teachers. They are knowledgeable and well-informed; relate what they know to the readiness of students; create active not passive learning in the classroom; and the most important characteristic is that influential teachers are those that are authentic, honest, and open human beings. They teach not only their subjects, but they teach themselves. They are willing to be vulnerable. They laugh. They cry. They say, "I don't know!" And as I observe them I am observing not just the content to be covered, but I observe the quality of their lives. Values are taught, in my opinion, most especially by the integrity, honesty, openness, and *authenticity* of the teacher.

- Describe a great teacher from your own school experiences. What made this teacher great? Why did the teacher stand out among all of the others? How did this teacher make you feel?

Restructuring schools for authentic teaching and learning is explored in-depth in Unit 4.

Leadership

Leadership as a democratic IDEAL refers to facilitating strong collaborative leadership and shared decision making. While traditionally leadership is thought of as being the responsibility of someone in a particular position (for example, the principal), leadership in democratic schools is viewed as being embodied in acts that may come from anyone in the school community. Leadership in a democratic school may come from teachers, support staff, students, parents, community members, principals, and superintendents. Rather than leadership being described as influencing or directing others to pursue the goals and direction identified by one individual or group of individuals, leadership in democratic schools involves facilitating processes that cause individuals or groups to examine, study, and challenge goals, directions, and practices. The intent of leadership in democratic schools is the development of shared understandings that lead to a common direction and improve the school experience for all members of the democratic school community (Lambert, 1995). Democratic leadership is grounded in assumptions that hold that all individuals in the school community have knowledge and insight that can contribute to and enhance the work of the school. In chapter 13, we explore in-depth the sharing of leadership and responsibilities in classrooms and schools.

IDEALS CHALLENGE: *Learning Leadership*

(Adapted from Brodhagen, 1995, pp. 96–97.)

I was nervous. "Will this really work?" I wondered. "Will these kids really conduct their own parent-teacher conferences? Had there been enough preparation? Will parents want to listen to their child?"

My first conference was with Holly, a bright young adolescent who does consistently good work, but doesn't seem to want to participate in large- or small-group discussions. Holly walked into the room first. Trailing behind was her mother, who was carrying a younger sibling. Holly began.

She introduced her mother, her sister, and me and then plunged into discussion of her work. "This is my best work." She took papers out and gave a brief explanation of each. Her mom asked questions and made comments such as "I remember when you were working on this" and "This turned out pretty good." Holly explained that the "best work" papers would be kept at school in a folder that would be sent home at year's end, with all the other best work.

Holly then read her written self-evaluation to her mom. When she had finished, she and her mom started to talk about why Holly didn't want to talk in front of her peers. Her mom admitted that as a teenager she didn't want to talk in class either. They talked about what was easy and challenging for Holly. They laughed about Holly's admission that doing her homework in front of the television wasn't such a good idea. And they discussed her goals for the next quarter, with mom saying Holly was too hard on herself.

I just sat there, amazed. Holly had said all I would have said, and much more that I never could or should. I simply validated a lot of what they had said. When it was over, the three of us stood, smiling at one another, exchanging looks that seemed to say, "This felt good, let's do it again."

- Which IDEALS of democratic education are represented in the scenario?
- What is the connection between the teacher's parent-teacher conference practices and leadership?
- How do you think the teacher prepared students for conducting conferences with their parents?
- Why do you think that Holly said much more than the teacher ever "could or should" say?
- In what other areas of the school, might students expand their leadership roles?

Service

Simply engaging in inquiry and discourse and being concerned with equity, authenticity, and shared leadership is insufficient in a democratic school. Democratic schools must connect principles and beliefs to practice within and outside the school. This involves moving beyond inquiry and study to action and service. Dewey (1966) argued that democratic discourse should lead to a "continuous reconstruction or reorganizing of experience" (p. 322). In other words, as a result of the exchange, debate, and exploration of different perspectives, the viewpoints and practices of individuals and groups should be modified or changed. Changes in thinking should also be accompanied by changes in practice. At the end of each chapter, a Doing Democracy section is included. These exercises ask you to serve, take action, and do something. Doing Democracy exercises are designed to help you to see the value beyond this book.

Service as a democratic IDEAL refers to the belief that making a difference in the lives of children and families requires serving the needs of the community as well as the school. One of the primary responsibilities of public education is to enable students to develop a strong sense of individual and social responsibility.

IDEALS CHALLENGE: *Supporting Service*

Elementary school children are often given greater responsibility than are students in middle schools or even high schools. For example, taking care of animals in the classroom, cleaning up after themselves, protecting student-made projects that have been left in the room, serving on safety patrols—in many ways, elementary students are held accountable for their environment and their actions. By contrast, older students are generally only held responsible for their homework and for sitting quietly and not causing trouble.

- Why do you think that younger children are given more responsibilities than older children in schools?
- How might we increase responsibilities for older children?
- How might all children learn to serve their classrooms, schools, and local communities?

How might this picture reflect the democratic ideal of serving others?

Responsibility is essential to learning. Students without a well-developed sense of responsibility may come to depend on other students to do their work in school, or they may not take responsibility for doing their work outside of school. Likewise, students who will not or cannot participate socially may reject group work and thus fail to realize the possibilities of collaborative learning. Self-reliance and responsibility does not entail isolation or self-centeredness, just as social participation does not mean simply giving in to the group sentiment. We must strive toward both autonomy and community. This can result from a sense of how to take individual and social responsibility and how to serve. In chapter 14, we will examine how democratic schools might work to serve others.

Connecting Democratic IDEALS to Classroom Practices

Democratic educators in schools continually seek to provide access to equal educational opportunity for all students, to require individual and social responsibility of themselves and their students, and to foster collaboration among people. We need as much as is possible to connect philosophy (our ideals and beliefs) and practice (our classroom actions). The story of Christy, a teacher intern, demonstrates how this connection might be made.

Christy was participating in a four-week practicum as part of an education course on Middle School Curriculum. She was placed in a seventh-grade social studies classroom during Black History Month, and she and her mentor teacher decided that Christy would teach about the antebellum South. Here is Christy's portrayal of an occurrence in class, and our conversation in a conference afterward, that exemplifies the six IDEALS of democratic education.

Christy's Story

It was about halfway through class, and I was trying to describe for students the social and economic structure of the South at that time. To do that I had drawn a pyramid on the board. At the top of the pyramid I had written "planters." A third of the way down I had written "middle class," further down "poor whites," and on the bottom level "free blacks and slaves." While asking questions of students about this hierarchy, I commented that people could sometimes move up and down on these levels (except for the free blacks and slaves, whose social mobility was fixed). Right at that point, a girl sitting in the middle row asked, in an abrupt but not hostile manner, "How in the world can poor people move up?" I was intent on getting to the next point in the lesson, and I'm not sure I really thought about her reason for asking the question. I replied, "Well, in our society, if you work hard you have a chance to do better in life. That's different than in those days, when black people couldn't really advance themselves."

We went on, and I didn't think more about it until the conference with my university and teacher mentors after class. The university mentor asked my thoughts about that incident, and then said, "Christy, how would you show the student that you were really listening to what she said?" We agreed that I could have said, "Yes, you're right. It is difficult for many poor people to rise in life." That would validate the worth of her question, and also show that I understood her position (she was from a low-income family). I might even have said, "How do you think people can achieve a better job or have a better life if they're poor?" It's the listening and the validation of the student's thinking that I needed to consider and that I have to keep in mind as I learn how to teach.

Christy's experience during and after the lesson can help us understand the manner in which democratic IDEALS are reflected in practice.

The student's question reflected a comfort level with *inquiry*, that is, being comfortable responding to the curriculum by asking perplexing questions which may have multiple answers. For Christy, the conference situation gave her a chance to inquire about what happened in class, why it happened, and in what other ways she might have acted, which also is a means of taking responsibility for what we do and how we think.

Christy's interaction with her university supervisor involved *discourse*, that is, discussion about how the situation had been handled and alternative ways in which she could have responded. Unfortunately, the opportu-

IDEALS CHALLENGE: *Deepening Discourse*

- "A truly educated person *who is also a teacher* is someone who ______________."
- How did Christy enact the democratic IDEALS of inquiry, discourse, equity, authenticity, leadership, and service in her lesson?
- How else might she have enacted the democratic IDEALS?

nity for this type of inquiry and discourse is not readily available for many teachers once they move beyond their student teaching. Christy could have initiated discourse among her students by not only listening to the student, but by validating the student's question, asking for elaboration (which also would place responsibility on the student to think about what she said), and by then having the class respond to the student's question. The students, with Christy's facilitation, could have discussed whether it is possible for poor people to advance economically. The students could have identified and discussed the barriers they see in their lives and the lives of others that make it difficult for the poor to advance economically.

Christy's entire lesson was, in a sense, about *equity* and its absence in that time period in the South. However, Christy missed an opportunity to connect the past to the present by not viewing the student's question as an opportunity to link historical inequities with an exploration of economic inequities that exist today.

By asking students, "How do you think people can achieve a better job or have a better life if they're poor?" Christy immediately would have sparked *authenticity* in her lesson. The lesson would have come alive and seemed real, relevant, and connected to her students' lives, rather than merely being a discussion of something that happened over a hundred years ago with little relevance today. Also, by addressing an individual student's question directly, Christy would have demonstrated an authentic, caring relationship for that student.

Following a discussion of continuing inequities in society, Christy could have engaged the class in a discussion about the nature and extent of responsibility that we all have for each other in our society. The philosophical discussion could have been followed by the development of a *service*-oriented plan of action for what students could do to address economic inequities in their community.

Christy's teaching practice in engaging the class in discourse and action planning would have been an example of *leadership*. However, Christy should have shared leadership for the actual student action-oriented service project with her students. In other words, Christy should not have been the one to do all the planning and implementation. Christy could have allowed students to take the lead, perhaps by simply asking of the class, "What do we need to do to make this happen?" and allowing leadership to emerge from the students.

Enacting Democratic IDEALS Is Not Easy

As schools are confronted with increasing societal problems and political pressures, the challenge to act on democratic IDEALS may seem difficult or impossible at times. Working in schools and society in democratic ways is not simple. It is much easier to make quick and popular decisions, follow trendy educational reforms, and simply just do as you are instructed. To carefully study one's own practice, adopt changes based on data and not fads, participate in schoolwide decision making, and accept responsibility for successes and for failures is challenging.

Despite the difficulties of moving beyond the "talk" of democratic education, John Dewey (1916) remained committed to the concept that the cure for the problems of democracy is not less democracy but more democracy. Educators in democratic schools act on democratic IDEALS by committing to and demonstrating the "walk" of democratic education. These schools are goal-oriented and guided by a shared and collaboratively developed vision of education. They encourage all students, teachers, administrators, and parents to participate in developing common principles or beliefs about learning that help guide curriculum, instruction, and daily practices in schools.

Educators in democratic schools constantly examine school practices through a critical study process. They make decisions based on data and on notions of what is best for students. Some decisions may be unpopular ones, but these schools demonstrate a willingness to take risks for students regardless of popular trends or powerful special interest groups.

You may ask: "Are educators willing to tackle the hard work of democratic education? Can all schools be successful? Can we challenge the norms of bureaucratic schools and strengthen the emphasis on democratic education?" We believe the answer is yes; all schools can become more democratic and can continually struggle to model democratic IDEALS for their students and community.

Robert Silver, principal of Cloward Middle School, describes the democratic struggle to educate:

> If a problem surfaces in our building, teachers have ownership of it—"OK, this is a problem. What are we going to do about it?" That's the attitude that exists, instead of the attitude, "Oh, my goodness, they've done this or they've done that, and all these terrible things are happening. What's wrong with these people? Don't they know what's going on?" Instead of complaining about a problem, our teachers have accepted ownership for it, and they know they can solve it if we all work together. (Blase et al., 1995, p. 105)

SUMMARY

Democratic education involves believing in ourselves, our students and their parents, and the original purposes of public education. We believe that democratic education is not simply a matter of determining political processes and establishing shared governance in schools, though that is part of it. It is also defined by the collaborative way in which students, teachers, principals, staff members, parents, and community members interact with each other on a daily basis. It is defined by the extent to which inquiry, discourse, equity, authenticity, leadership, and service guide our work. It is defined by the content of the academic curriculum, by the social curriculum that is modeled and maintained in classrooms, by grouping and inclusion practices, by the uses and misuses of testing, and by the nature and content of staff development. In short, democratic education is fostered within a range of relationships among members of the school community, the content of the curriculum, and the processes of instruction.

Now with a clearer description of purposes of public education and with an understanding of democratic education and the IDEALS it entails, you may wonder: How do I fit into the larger purpose of public education? What can one person do? We invite you to come along with us on our journey as we travel through this book, reading, thinking about, and doing democracy. We begin in chapter 2 by exploring the practices of democratic schools. Bon voyage!

DOING DEMOCRACY

When thinking about or attempting to enact democratic IDEALS, often teachers are confronted by a number of dilemmas. Discuss the following questions with a practicing teacher. Share insights gained from your discussion with your professor and fellow students.

- How do you act on your own beliefs about teaching and learning when these conflict with the direction of your school?
- How do you honor students' and other teachers' beliefs when your own beliefs convince you that their beliefs are wrong or misguided?
- How do you ensure that individual student rights are protected while simultaneously acting in the best interests of the common good? (For example, the inclusion of students with disabilities in "regular" classrooms.)
- How do you reconcile conflicts between individual and social responsibility? That is, given limited time, how do you reconcile the conflict between spending time on your job, family, and immediate surroundings with spending time participating in civic affairs and working toward the improvement of community and global conditions?

END NOTE

[1]The term "doing democracy" comes from the literature and work of the Center for Living Democracy in Brattleboro, Vermont. We are indebted to them.

REFERENCES

Apple, M. W., & Beane, J. A. (1995). *Democratic schools.* Alexandria, VA: Association for Supervision and Curriculum Development.

Beane, J. A., & Apple, M. W. (1995). The case for democratic schools. In M. W. Apple & J. A. Beane (Eds.). *Democratic schools* (pp. 1–25). Alexandria, VA: Association for Supervision and Curriculum Development.

Blase, J., & Blase, J. (1997). *The fire is back.* Thousand Oaks, CA: Corwin.

Blase, J., Blase, J., Anderson, G. L., Dungan, S. (1995). *Democratic principals in action: Eight pioneers.* Thousand Oaks, CA: Corwin.

Boyer, E. (1993, March). *What is an educated person?* Keynote address at the annual meeting of the Association for Supervision and Curriculum Development, Washington D.C.

Brodhagen, B. L. (1995). The situation made us special. In M. W. Apple & J. A. Beane (Eds.). *Democratic schools.* Alexandria, VA: ASCD.

Center for Living Democracy (1998). *What is living democracy?* Brattleboro, VT: Author.

Davis, S. (1996, April). *Principal discusses aftermath of the Oklahoma City bombing.* Paper presented at the annual meeting of the American Educational Research Association, New York City.

Delpit, L. (1995). *Other people's children: Cultural conflict in the classroom.* New York: The New Press.

Dewey, J. (1916). *Democracy and education.* New York: Macmillan.

Dewey, J. (1966). *Democracy and education.* New York: Free Press.

Glickman, C. D. (1990). *Supervision for instruction: A developmental approach* (2nd ed.). Needham Heights, MA: Allyn & Bacon.

Glickman, C. D. (1993). *Renewing America's schools: A guide for school based action.* San Francisco: Jossey-Bass.

Glickman, C. D. (1998). *Revolutionizing America's schools.* San Francisco: Jossey-Bass.

Heslep, R. (1969). *Thomas Jefferson and education.* New York: Random House.

Kozol, J. (1991). *Savage inequalities.* New York: Crown.

Kozol, J. (1995). *Amazing grace: The lives of children and the conscience of a nation.* New York: Harper Perennial.

Lambert, L. (1995). Toward a theory of constructivist leadership. In L. Lambert, D. Walker, D. P. Zimmerman, J. E. Cooper, M. D. Lambert, M. E. Gardner, & P. J. Slack (Eds.), *The constructivist leader.* New York: Teacher College Press.

Lee, V. E., & Smith, J. B. (1994). High school restructuring and student achievement: A new study finds strong links. In *Issues in Restructuring Schools.* University of Wisconsin: Center on Organization and Restructuring of Schools.

Newmann, F. M. (1996). *Authentic achievement: Restructuring schools for intellectual quality.* San Francisco: Jossey-Bass.

Newmann, F. M., & Wehlage, G. G. (1995). *Successful school restructuring.* Alexandria, VA: Association for Supervision and Curriculum Development.

Oakes, J., & Guiton, G. (1995). Matchmaking: The dynamics of high school tracking decisions. *American Educational Research Journal, 32*(1), 3–33.

Reitzug, U. C. (1994). A case study of empowering principal behavior. *American Educational Research Journal, 31*(2), 283–307.

Reitzug, U. C., & Reeves, J. E. (1992). "Miss Lincoln doesn't teach here": A descriptive narrative and conceptual analysis of a principal's symbolic leadership behavior. *Educational Administration Quarterly, 28*(2), 185–219.

Slavin, R. E. (1996). *Education for all.* Exton, PA: Swets & Zeitlinger.

Spring, J. (1994). *American education* (6th ed.). New York: McGraw-Hill.

Strike, K. A. (1993). Professionalism, democracy, and discursive communities. *American Educational Research Journal, 30*(2), 255–275.

Wood, G. (1992). *Schools that work.* New York: Dutton.

What is connecting the atoms in the double helix?

What are the connections in democratic education?

What types of practices connect schools to the concept of democracy?

CHAPTER 2

The Practices of Democratic Education

IDEALS CHALLENGE: *Deepening Discourse*

The following statements are adapted from Darling-Hammond (1997):

A quality education for all children is necessary in order to maintain a democratic society.
Schools should prepare students for democratic citizenship.
Schools rarely practice democratic ideals.
Schools are more often authoritarian than participative.
Schools are more frequently segregative by social class, race, and culture than integrative.

- Discuss each of the statements above. With which ones do you agree? Disagree? Why?
- Is there an incongruency between the first two statements and the last three? If so, what is the nature of the incongruency, and why do you think it exists?

INTRODUCTION

In this chapter we will explore the *practices* of schools that are democratic learning communities. We begin the chapter by briefly discussing why we form organizations (including schools) and the characteristics of the dominant form of organizing: the bureaucracy. We then contrast the principles of bureaucratic ways of organizing, which serve as the foundation for many current school practices, with democratic ways of organizing. Subsequently, we explore in general terms the practices of schools grounded in bureaucratic thought with the practices of schools that are more democratic. We then spend the remainder of the chapter describing in greater detail the practices of democratic schools.

COMPARING BUREAUCRATIC SCHOOLS AND DEMOCRATIC SCHOOLS

Organizations are formed to bring together a group of individuals for purposes of accomplishing a goal or goals that none of the individuals would be able to accomplish by themselves. A school is an organization that is formed for purposes of educating students.

Principles of a Bureaucratic Way of Organizing

The dominant form of organization is grounded in bureaucratic thought. While the term "bureaucracy" is frequently used pejoratively to complain about unbending adherence to rules or excessive paperwork requirements, the bureaucratic organizational model was actually formed to counteract abuses in organizations. Specifically, prior to the development of the bureaucratic organizational model, organizations were often characterized by inefficiency, capriciousness, and unfair treatment of employees. Bureaucracy was intended to counteract organizational inefficiency and injustice.

Several principles characterize a bureaucratic way of organizing. Specifically, in a bureaucracy:

1. positions are organized into a *hierarchical authority structure* that designates reporting relationships, superiors, and subordinates (e.g., in schools, teachers report to their superior, the principal; principals to their superior, the superintendent, etc.);
2. a clear cut *division of labor* exists, typically exemplified by job descriptions that delineate specific responsibilities for every position in the organization (e.g., school districts have formal job descriptions for teachers, principals, counselors, etc.);
3. there is an extensive and written system of *rules, regulations, and procedures* (e.g., school districts have policy manuals and extensive teacher contracts, and schools have teacher and student handbooks);
4. relationships are characterized by *impersonality* in order to help ensure *objective application of rules and regulations*, as well as objective distribution of rewards based on technical competence.

Although organizational scholars have debated whether schools are truly bureaucracies or whether they more nearly resemble other organizational forms (see, e.g., Weick, 1978), it is clear that bureaucratic thinking significantly influences the structure and practices of schools.

Disadvantages of a Bureaucratic Way of Organizing Schools

Although bureaucracy was a well-intended organizational model, changing social and cultural conditions and excessive adherence to bureaucratic principles have often caused bureaucratic ways of organizing to be counterproductive. Organizing schools along bureaucratic lines can have drawbacks.

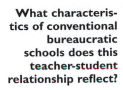

What characteristics of conventional bureaucratic schools does this teacher-student relationship reflect?

Excessive adherence to the bureaucratic principles of hierarchical authority structure, division of labor, extensive rules and regulations, and impersonality in relationships can result in the following:

1. A hierarchical authority structure may result in the knowledge and perspectives of those in positions of greater authority being considered superior to the knowledge and perspectives of those with less authority. In schools, this means the knowledge and perspectives of principals might be considered more valuable than the knowledge and perspectives of teachers, and the knowledge and perspectives of superintendents more valuable than that of principals. As a result, decisions are handed down from superintendents to schools, or principals to teachers, without calling on the expertise of those who are on the front line—the teachers. Interestingly, in bureaucratic schools the further an individual is removed from the core work of schools—teaching and learning—the more valued is that individual's knowledge and perspective.
2. A clear-cut division of labor can result in individuals striving for minimums, that is, doing what their job description stipulates and nothing more. This frequently occurs, for example, when prescriptive teacher contracts are approved. One result in schools is teachers isolating themselves in their classrooms with little connection to other teachers, between what occurs in their classroom and other classrooms, and between the school and the community. Another result is that teachers

leave at the end of the school day the minute their contract specifies that they may, whether or not they are well-prepared for the following day.

3. An extensive and written system of rules, regulations, and procedures can result in unthinking action and blind application of rules, regulations, and procedures even when these make little sense due to the contextually specific nature of a situation. For example, in one recent incident, a first grader was expelled from school for bringing a small, squirt water toy shaped like a dinosaur to school. The reason for the expulsion was because, in some school officials' eyes, the toy too nearly resembled a weapon and the school had a zero-tolerance policy on weapons. In a second incident, a first-grade boy was expelled for kissing a first-grade girl because school officials decided the first grader's actions violated their sexual harassment policy.

4. Relationships characterized by impersonality may lead to alienation—antithetical to the needs of many students (and adults) in today's schools and contrary to recent findings on successful schools (see, e.g., Kruse, Louis, & Bryk, 1995). For example, high schools are frequently set up to maximize efficiency and thus have students switching classes every hour. The result is that a teacher may see 150 different students each day, making it difficult to know students' names and virtually impossible to develop genuine relationships with students.

IDEALS CHALLENGE: *Examining Equity*

(Paraphrased from a keynote address by George Wood, principal of Federal Hocking High School in rural southern Ohio, at the Oklahoma Networks for Excellence in Education 1997 Summer Institute in Norman, Oklahoma.)

We do our best work in communities, not in institutions. Yet our public schools too often resemble institutions. Public schools are where our young people develop habits of the heart and mind. We must insure that our public schools are democratic communities and not impersonal institutions.

I believe there are three steps in nurturing a democratic community. First, we must make sure we build a deep, lasting relationship with every child. Anonymity is the biggest enemy of democracy. Most of our schools are fairly anonymous in terms of students. We need to structure schools in terms of size, time, and place so that they are personal rather than anonymous. In terms of size, it is crucial that our schools have 500 or fewer students. School buildings that house more than 500 students must be restructured internally into smaller schools of 500 or less. In terms of time, teachers at the high school level see five to six classes of 25 to 30 students each. There is no way anyone can reach the hearts and minds of 140 to 180 students per day. We must recreate our schedules so that teachers see a reasonable number of students per day. In terms of place, all students must have a place in the school where they can go, where they can interact with an adult who knows them personally. That's why every adult in our building serves as an adviser. Our ratio is about 15 students to 1 adult. Even the secretaries and custodians serve as advisers. We all know that the most important thing in our school is developing deep, lasting relationships with our young people.

The second essential in nurturing a democratic community is to make sure that the curriculum makes sense to the kids. It should be about who we are and what we are. The curriculum should be localized. Kids should see how what goes on in the rest of the world happens to people in our area. The curriculum should be integrated. We don't do subjects separately in life. Finally, there should be no tracking. If it's valuable for some kids, it's valuable for all kids.

The third essential is to give kids the keys. School is typically about control rather than about responsibility. Why? School is a wonderful place to give kids opportunities to fail at things. Why not let them fail when we are there to help them? In our school we have flex time. During flex time students do not have classes, but have access to all school facilities. The facilities are staffed during that time. Not only does flex time equalize access for those kids who don't have resources such as computers at home, it also results in many meaningful conversations between adults and students that are different from conversations that occur during classes. Another way in which we give kids the keys to our school is by allowing them to serve internships in the community where they are not under our direct supervision, nor under anyone's supervision as they are traveling to and from their internship. Finally, we give kids the keys to the school through student government, which is involved in many significant activities and decisions, including the hiring of teachers for the school.

- What other steps can you identify that might build a democratic community in schools?
- In what other ways might schools create deep, lasting relationships with students; make the curriculum meaningful to students; and give students the keys to the school?
- How do the steps articulated by George Wood promote equity in the school?

Principles of a Democratic Way of Organizing

In many respects, bureaucratic and democratic ways of organizing exist in opposition to each other. Although there is no one-to-one relationship between bureaucratic principles and democratic ideals and principles there is a rough juxtaposition between them. As you read the principles of democratic schools in the list below, relate them to George Wood's description of the democratic community in his school (see IDEALS Challenge: Examining Equity).

- In contrast to the bureaucratic principle of a hierarchical authority structure, which results in an individual or a few select individuals making decisions and "being in charge," a democratic way of organizing strives for access and equal opportunity for all. Teachers, parents, and students all should be involved in the decision making and governance of a school (the democratic ideals of equity and shared leadership). Additionally, in democratic schools the hierarchical divisions separating school staff from students, resulting in an emphasis on control rather than on responsibility, are weakened.
- In contrast to a bureaucratic division of labor resulting in the isolation of teachers from each other and a separation between teachers and administrators, a democratic way of organizing strives for collaboration of teachers across classroom lines and between teachers and administrators

(the democratic ideals of discourse, inquiry, and shared leadership). Additionally, in democratic schools both teachers and students should view themselves as learners and facilitators of learning for others.

- In contrast to the rule-boundedness of a bureaucracy, a democratic way of organizing strives for individual and social responsibility (the democratic ideal of service). For teachers and students, behaviors and practices are directed less by rules, contracts, and policies, and more by a concern for the rights of others and for the common good.
- In contrast to the impersonal relationships that characterize a bureaucratic organization, a democratic way of thinking about organizations strives for deep, personal relationships, by active involvement in the school community, and by a concern for social justice (the democratic ideals of equity, authenticity, and service).

Comparing Bureaucratic With Democratic Schools

Many of the practices of schools are grounded in the principles of bureaucracy. For example, in schools important decisions are often made hierarchically by superintendents, school boards, and principals. Decisions are handed down to teachers in the form of rules, policies, programs, and curriculum packages. In many schools, little emphasis is placed on teacher knowledge and expertise. For purposes of efficiency, teachers teach primarily in isolation. In most cases they are the lone adult educator within the classroom. They rarely have the opportunity to engage in serious and extended professional talk with their colleagues, observe each others' teaching, or work collaboratively on curricular or instructional matters. Bureaucratic efficiency is also served by teachers being responsible for large numbers of students. While the typical American family has one to three children, the typical elementary school teacher is responsible for 25 to 30 students and the typical high school teacher may teach as many as 180 students per day. The result can be that students move from classroom to classroom with little personal attention from their teachers. School can become a cold and impersonal place for both students and teachers. Due to the large number of students for whom teachers are responsible, the focus of teachers' work often becomes more on the control of student behavior than on the development of intellectual and social growth (Darling-Hammond, 1997).

In addition to controlling student behavior, bureaucratically grounded schools also attempt to control what students learn. That is, rather than building on and connecting to what students already know, such schools are driven by uniform state or local curriculum documents. Typically these documents have been correlated with standardized tests and there is a strong emphasis on how students do on the test. In some cases teachers' salaries and principals' job security are linked to student standardized test scores. The result is that rather than *teaching students,* much of a teacher's efforts are put into "teaching the test." That is, teachers and principals spend their time planning and monitoring curriculum and instructional practices to ensure that they match the types of information and questioning formats found on state- or district-mandated standardized tests. Unfortunately, standardized tests typically measure low-level cognitive skills rather than assessing intellectual growth and high-level cognitive functioning.

Due to the prescriptive and controlling aspects of bureaucratically driven schools, many teachers in such schools believe that they are locked into a nonfunctional system. They believe they have been victimized by politically oriented superintendents and school boards, unknowledgeable principals, uncaring parents, and apathetic and deviant students. They often are uncertain about how to change the system and feel powerless in making their teaching and students' learning exciting, meaningful, and valued beyond school.

While not all schools share these characteristics, many do. As we contrast bureaucratically grounded schools with democratic ones, we realize that many schools fall somewhere in between. Unfortunately, we believe most American schools bear a closer resemblance to bureaucratically grounded schools than to democratic schools. Thus, we will refer throughout this book to schools as "conventional" whose practices are more consistent with bureaucratic principles than with democratic ideals.

In contrast to bureaucratically grounded "conventional" schools, democratic school communities are more personal, collaborative, and participatory. Democratic schools are characterized by a respect for teacher and student knowledge and a collective sense of responsibility for student and teacher learning. They embrace shared values and collaboratively developed learning principles that guide curriculum, instruction, and the daily operation of the school. In democratic schools, shared leadership exists among teachers, administrators, parents, and students. School and classroom decisions are based on critical study rather than on self-interest (Glickman, 1993). Teachers learn from and with each other via discussion and critique of teaching and school practices, and by working collaboratively on initiatives related to curriculum and instruction. Finally, in democratic schools there is a concern for connecting curriculum with the world beyond the school (Newmann & Wehlage, 1995) and especially in terms of exploring and addressing social conditions such as racism, sexism, poverty, and other forms of injustice and oppression (Beane & Apple, 1995).

THE PRACTICES OF DEMOCRATIC SCHOOLS

In a sense, to talk about the practices of democratic schools can be misleading. It makes it sound as if there is a well-defined set of practices that make a school democratic—as if democratic schooling is a static state a school attains. In reality, a school never becomes a democratic school. Democratic schooling is more of a process than a state that one attains. It is a continuing journey of working to become more democratic, of striving toward a set of ideals. A democratic school is not one that has "made it" or has "arrived," but rather a school that continually assesses its practices in terms of the democratic IDEALS described in this book. The practices we describe in this chapter reflect these ideals, and all have one thing in common—they result in the school being a place that respects all members of its community, a place where *all* children *and* adults learn and grow. (See Table 2.1.) These practices include:

- shared value systems (Kruse, Louis, & Bryk, 1995; Glickman, 1993; Sergiovanni, 1994);

- authentic pedagogy (Darling-Hammond, 1997; Newmann & Associates, 1996; Sizer, 1992; Wood, 1992);
- critical study (Glickman, 1993; Kruse, Louis, & Bryk, 1995; Meier, 1995);
- shared decision making (Glickman, 1993; Meier, 1995; King, Louis, Marks, & Peterson, 1996);
- internal and external support (Newmann & Wehlage, 1995);
- a moral and professional community (Beane & Apple, 1995; Darling-Hammond, 1997; Kruse, Louis, & Bryk, 1995; Sergiovanni, 1994).

Shared Value Systems

Democratic school communities have a collective identity. That is, the teachers, administrators, parents, students, and others who are actively involved in the school community are in agreement about what is important in the school. They know what the school stands for, what it sees as its purpose, and what it is trying to accomplish. This is in contrast to conventional schools where there often is little that binds teachers and other staff members together because the school is structured and operates so that individuals work largely in isolation.

The **shared value systems** in authentic school communities consist of two components. First, there is a set of shared values about students, the purposes of education, and human and professional interaction. For example, a democratic school may value student choice (see chapter 11), see its purpose as preparing students for democratic citizenship, and believe human and professional interaction should be characterized by intrinsic worth and unconditional respect (see Purpel, 1989).

Second, there is a collaboratively developed set of core learning principles that guide curriculum, instruction, and instructionally related operations of the school (Glickman, 1993). For example, a democratic school might embrace learning principles which hold that students learn best when

Table 2.1 The Practices of Democratic Schools

Shared Values About	Core Learning Principles	Authentic Pedagogy	Shared Decision Making	Critical Study	Internal Support	External Support	Moral & Professional Community
Purposes of education	Curriculum	Construction of knowledge	Teachers	Data	Supportive principal leadership	School autonomy	Caring
Students	Instruction	Disciplined inquiry	Parents	Knowledge	Connective communication structures	Access to external expertise	Collective responsibility for students
Personal & professional interaction		Value beyond school	Students	Perspectives	Time to meet & talk		Collaboration
			Community	Reflective dialogue	Leadership by teachers & others		Connection to home & community
							Concern for equity

What are the shared values that connect this teacher and student? What types of shared values might connect members of a democratic school community?

they (1) are required to personally construct knowledge about the topics being addressed, (2) engage in disciplined inquiry to gather more information and data about the topic, and (3) work on tasks that have some value beyond the lesson and the assignment (Newmann & Associates, 1996).

The outcomes of shared value systems are synergistic effects that result when individuals work collectively toward something. Shared values serve as a basis for decision making (i.e., "How does that decision fit with what we believe in?") and give individuals an enhanced sense of purpose. They make individuals part of a bigger cause—of a cause beyond one's self (Glickman, 1993).

IDEALS CHALLENGE: *Learning Leadership*

(Learning principles adapted from "Foxfire Core Practices," 1991.)

1. All the work teachers and students do together must flow from student desires and student concerns.
2. The role of the teacher must be that of collaborator and team leader and guide, rather than boss.
3. The work is characterized by student action, rather than by passive receipt of processed information.
4. A constant feature of the process is its emphasis on peer teaching, small-group work, and teamwork.
5. Connections between the classroom work, surrounding communities, and the real world outside the classroom are clear.

6. There must be an audience beyond the teacher for student work.
7. As teachers, we must acknowledge the worth of aesthetic experience [and provide students] the chance to use their imaginations.
8. Reflection—some conscious, thoughtful time to stand apart from the work itself—is an essential activity that must take place at key points throughout the work.
9. The work must include unstintingly honest, ongoing evaluation for skills and content, and changes in student attitude.

- Are these learning principles primarily from a conventional or a democratic school? Provide support for your answer.
- Develop a set of learning principles for the type of school not reflected in the set of learning principles above (i.e., conventional or democratic).
- If you were currently teaching, how would you proceed in helping your school identify or develop a set of learning principles?
- Return to this IDEALS Challenge and repeat this exercise after you have read more about democratic schools in this chapter.

Authentic Pedagogy

Rather than teaching in a didactic manner that focuses primarily on the memorization of factual information, **authentic pedagogy** requires that teachers design and facilitate learning experiences that:

- engage students in the personal construction of new knowledge;
- result in their conducting disciplined inquiry about the topic at hand;
- have some value beyond the school (Newmann & Wehlage, 1995).

Researchers found that when teachers taught authentically, their students consistently outperformed those taught in more conventional ways (Newmann & Associates, 1996). That is, when teaching focused on the development of understanding and meaning and on connecting lessons to students' interests and experiences, rather than on memorization, students did better both on assessments of advanced skills as well as on standardized tests. These findings suggest that students who think carefully about subjects, study them in-depth, and connect them to their personal experiences also are more likely to remember the facts and definitions called for on standardized tests.

Authentic pedagogy is democratic because it treats students as individuals rather than as a generic mass. In a sense, authentic pedagogy gives "voice" to student individuality. That is, it is grounded in assumptions about student differences, recognizing that they bring various experiences to the classroom and that they construct knowledge in different ways. In contrast to conventional teaching, which is grounded in assumptions that students who are not "average" have deficits that need to be rectified, authentic pedagogy views student differences as intrinsic and natural.

Authentic pedagogy will be discussed in greater detail in chapter 11. Here we will simply provide you with an example from practice that contrasts conventional teaching with authentic pedagogy.

CLICK ON IT

Visit the Web site of the Center for the Organization and Restructuring of Schools at

www.wcer.wisc.edu/completed/cors

for more information about authentic pedagogy and the research supporting it.

Authentic learning has a value beyond school, like these students who are learning about marine biology and the world's food supply.

IDEALS CHALLENGE: *Achieving Authenticity*

(As you read the two excerpts that follow, think about how each does or does not reflect authentic pedagogy. Adapted from Newmann & Wehlage, 1995, p. 24.)

"OK class, get out your books. We will read aloud Chapter 3 and then you will work independently to answer the following questions":

1. What did Prince Henry encourage?
2. What was an important instrument for sea captains?
3. What happened after Columbus returned from his visit to America?
4. Who destroyed the Aztec and Inca civilizations?
5. What did Cortés use to help conquer the Aztecs?
6. After Columbus, when Europeans came to America, in what did they live?
7. Europeans who came to the New World included *missionaries*. (True or False?)
8. Several explorers searched for a *southwest passage*. (True or False?)

(*From the* Greensboro News and Record, *October 14, 1997, p. B1.*)

CLASS EXAMINES SCIENCE FROM A BIRD'S-EYE VIEW

RALEIGH, NC—A middle school class has turned what many people consider a nuisance—thousands of birds in their chimneys—into an epic science project.

Teachers realized that nature had provided that project one day in September when all the students in science class at Ligon Middle School flocked to the window. What looked like smoke billowing from the chimney was a dense cloud of birds.

Since that day, the chimney swifts roosting in Ligon's massive smokestack have taken over Virginia Owens' class. The migrating birds are considered a nuisance in most Wake County schools, but Owens has used the swifts' visit as a lesson in scientific method and environmental education.

She transformed her classroom into the "Ligon Roost Stop of the Chimney Swift Flyway." Her pupils are junior researchers who clock the birds' schedules, habits, and characteristics.

"They're kind of getting the idea that an inquiry starts with an observation," said Owens. "They're investigating their world."

Owens' class is mobilized with scientific fervor. They have contacted a Cornell University ornithologist by e-mail. They log meteorological data to detect any connection between the weather and their bird counts.

Owens intends to turn the project into an annual event to coincide with the birds' fall roosting.

- Based on what you currently know, how do the excerpts reflect authentic pedagogy? Conventional pedagogy?
- How does each lesson promote or not promote:

  the construction of knowledge?

  disciplined inquiry?

  value beyond school?
- Based on the excerpts, speculate on other possible characteristics of conventional teaching and authentic pedagogy.
- If you were teaching the lessons described in the excerpts, what would you do differently to make one or both of them more authentic?

Shared Decision Making

Shared decision making, which involves teachers, administrators, parents, and students is at the heart of becoming a *democratic* school. In conventional schools, decisions are made by one individual or by the individual in consultation with a few select others. This results in one individual having the authority to determine the direction of the school and to influence or control others to pursue that direction. Such hierarchical decision-making practices are antithetical to democracy.

Decision making that promotes one individual's perspective honors that singular perspective while essentially discounting and dishonoring the perspectives of all others in the school community. It makes one individual the "expert" who knows the way, with teachers and others in the school community being merely "technicians" who carry out his or her wishes. This is especially problematic since the decision maker is usually the principal or the superintendent who currently are primarily white, middle class males.

Democratic schools find and create times for people to meet and talk including times for conversations between teachers, students, and parents.

This is likely to silence the voices of women, racial and ethnic minorities, and the poor. Thus, schooling is more likely to continue to be grounded in values of efficiency, rationality, and control—values typically associated with white males—rather than values of caring, community, and empowerment—values more typically associated with women and other cultures (see, e.g., Noddings, 1984; Irvine, 1991).

In essence, what hierarchical decision-making practices do is close down the conversation about what the school stands for, the school's purpose, and the multiple ways in which the school's purposes can be accomplished. Given the lack of consensus on school purpose and best educational practices (indeed, conflicting research exists on most educational practices), it is critical that the varying perspectives of school community members be publicly articulated. Shared decision making permits the articulation and exploration, via discourse and critical study, of the diverse perspectives of the school community's stakeholders. It permits members of the school community to collectively decide which decisions are consistent with the school's purpose, core values, and learning principles, and how to best promote these purposes, values, and principles.

Critical Study

Critical study (Glickman, 1993), also known as inquiry, drives shared decision making and other practices in democratic schools. Without engaging in critical study we have no basis for determining whether what we are doing works and how it fits with the things we believe in. Formal and informal critical study should inform schoolwide and classroom decision making. It should inform instructional practices as well as the development of school policies, curriculum, and programs.

In democratic schools, learning and growing is important not only for students, but also for teachers and other members of the school community. **Critical study**—the process that can facilitate this growth—is the study of practice by considering relevant perspectives, data, and knowledge. It involves asking questions such as:

- On what basis are we doing what we are doing? What evidence or support do we have to justify our practice? How do we know whether what we are doing is effective?
- What information, data, knowledge, and perspectives can we gather to assist us in studying our practice?
- How does what we are doing fit with our values and beliefs as a school?
- How does what we are doing serve the needs of the diverse individuals and groups who make up our community? Whose interests do our practices serve? Whose interests do they not serve?

The primary purpose of critical study is the improvement of teaching, learning, and school practice in the classrooms and schools that engaged in it. Rather than trying to identify what works in all classrooms and schools, critical study gives insight into what works in a particular classroom or school (Cochran-Smith & Lytle, 1993). Chapter 5 will discuss critical study and inquiry in greater detail.

Our understanding of successful schools supports the importance of critical study. Studies suggest that successful schools are, in essence, democratic communities of inquiry (critical study). In such communities, the practice of all individuals, as well as institutionwide practices, are the subject of continuous study and discussion (see, e.g., Kruse, Louis, & Bryk, 1995).

Internal Support

Research and our personal work with schools indicates that **internal support** conditions can alter a school's progress in becoming democratic (see, e.g., Kruse, Louis, & Bryk, 1995; Reitzug & O'Hair, 1998). Facilitative in-school conditions include supportive principal leadership, connective communication structures, time for the school staff to meet and talk, and leadership that is shared by teachers and others.

CLICK ON IT

Visit the Web site of Northwest Regional Education Lab at

www.nwrel.org/scpd/natspec/catalog/leagueprofsch.htm

for more information about the League of Professional Schools and its use of critical study, core learning principles, and decision-making charters.

IDEALS CHALLENGE: ***Initiating Inquiry***

Identify a common educational practice or program (e.g., cooperative learning, whole language instruction, Reading Recovery, shared decision making, homogeneous grouping/tracking, outcomes-based education, school-to-work) and develop a plan for how you might critically study the efficacy of this practice. Be sure to consider the questions listed in the discussion of critical study as you develop your inquiry plan. Conduct your critical study to the extent possible.

Supportive Principal Leadership

In our work with schools attempting to become more democratic, we found that the nature of principal support varied. Principal involvement in a school's efforts to become more democratic can range from being actively resistant to actively supportive of democratic efforts. Active principal resistance involves placing obstacles in the way of teachers attempting to become more democratic (e.g., withholding financial or material resources) or simply refusing to engage in certain practices (e.g., sharing decisions). Passive forms of principal support consist of "letting democratic efforts happen" in their school. That is, principals exhibiting passive support neither block the efforts of teachers engaged in the work of becoming more democratic, nor do they proactively support or become personally involved in such efforts. Active principal support includes regularly publicly and privately communicating support for democratic efforts, personally participating in such efforts, *and* providing time for *discussing* the school's movement toward democratic schooling (Reitzug & O'Hair, 1998).

Connective Communication Structures

A second internal factor that affects the progress of schools toward becoming democratic communities are the structures and processes developed for individuals to carry out the schools' work. These structures and processes can potentially serve as vehicles to enhance communication across classrooms, grades, and departments, thus connecting individuals with each other. This serves to help teachers and others move beyond the isolation of their individual classrooms and to continuously define and redefine the collective work of the school as a by-product of their completing more routine tasks. For example, one school in which we worked developed a process for awarding a nominal amount of mini-grant funding the school had at its disposal. The process involved a committee of teachers discussing each mini-grant application in the context of the school's democratic initiatives. As a result, the teachers on the committee had to clarify for themselves what it meant to be a democratic school. The school also formed a number of subcommittees that were structured around the school's various democratic initiatives. All teachers worked on at least one subcommittee. Structures and processes such as these serve to connect all teachers to the democratic work of the school (Reitzug & O'Hair, 1998).

Time to Meet and Talk

A third internal factor that affects the progress of schools toward becoming democratic communities is the availability of time for teachers and school staff to meet and talk about the work of the school. As early as 1982, Judith Warren Little found that "high success" schools were characterized by "norms of collegiality" which involved a great deal of shared discussion and shared work among staff members. Little (1982) found that in high success schools, teachers engaged in frequent talk that helped them develop a "shared language adequate to the complexity of teaching" (p. 331). Kruse and Louis (1995) similarly found that successful schools were characterized by a prevalence of "teacher talk . . . in a variety of contexts" and "sustain[ed] conversation centered around curriculum and instruction" (p. 190).

Our experience with schools is that teachers and others in *conventional* schools complain that there is *no time* to talk collectively about classroom and school practice. Teachers and others in *democratic* school communities also bemoan the lack of *sufficient* time to talk about their practice, but individuals in these schools find or create times in which to meet, reflect, talk, and study about it. Chapter 6 discusses in greater detail the ways schools find time to meet and talk.

Shared Leadership

A fourth internal factor that affects the progress of schools toward becoming democratic communities is the extent to which leadership is shared by teachers and others. Leadership in democratic schools is the responsibility of everyone in the school community. Shared leadership occurs not merely by the representation and participation of teachers and others in school decision making (see chapter 10 for discussion of shared decision making), but perhaps more importantly, from "constructivist" forms of leadership (Lambert, 1995).

Constructivist leadership is based on the belief that adults learn just like children do—through reflection and the construction of knowledge. The function of such leadership is to engage people in processes that cause them to inquire into and discuss issues and dilemmas of classroom and school practice. Linda Lambert describes leadership acts consistent with this approach as, "the next essential question is asked, ideas and traditions are challenged, people volunteer to lead, groups form, curiosity is aroused, verbal and nonverbal interactions change" (p. 50). Constructivist leadership acts can come from anyone, at anytime, anywhere in the school community. A constructivist leadership act is any act that engages people in examining "the way we do things around here." Constructivist leadership helps democratic communities increase their capacity for learning how to be more democratic. Chapter 13 will discuss shared leadership in greater detail.

IDEALS CHALLENGE: *Learning Leadership*

(*From the* Greensboro News and Record, *October 4, 1997,* p. B1, B2.)

SCHOOL GETS PLAN TO RAISE TEST SCORES

By John Temple (Staff Writer)

HIGH POINT—Union Hill Elementary School students, teachers, and parents need to better coordinate efforts to boost test scores.

That's the initial conclusion of a team of educators spending the year in search of solutions at Union Hill, which scored among the state's 15 worst-performing schools on end-of-year tests.

Specifically, said the team, teachers at different grade levels should consult each other more often to make sure the knowledge their students are taking in prepares them for next year's curriculum. Teachers must also make sure that their own books, classroom teaching, and tests are focused on the same material.

The report also said more attention needs to be focused on grades three through five, whose students are the ones being tested. Before this year, the school's literacy programs mostly have pinpointed the youngest students.

The report recommended ways to get parents involved. In particular, parents and students might help set up parent-teacher conferences. Also, they could draw up a contract, outlining what is expected of each person: the teacher, the parent, the student.

- What do you think of the committee's recommendations?
- Do you believe the committee's recommendations are focused on conventional or democratic schooling? Support your answer.
- If you were a teacher in Union Hill Elementary School, what would you do? How might you practice constructivist leadership?

External Support

Schools that function as democratic school communities have typically managed to benefit from favorable external support conditions. These include a reasonable level of school autonomy and access to external expertise.

School Autonomy

Reasonable school autonomy refers to schools being free to pursue their work without excessive external constraints. For example, teachers often feel pressured by state accountability measures, superintendents, or principals to focus their instruction on the low-level cognitive skills measured by standardized tests. This detracts from their teaching in more authentic ways that promote higher level cognitive functioning. Schools also often feel constrained by contractual agreements that assign teachers and principals to their school when there is a position open, rather than permitting the school community to select an individual who shares the school's value system. Such constraints do not prevent a school from becoming a democratic school community—they simply make the school's work more difficult.

Access to External Expertise

Thus far we have discussed dimensions such as critical study, shared decision making, and supportive internal conditions that contribute to schools becoming more like democratic communities and that also have been linked to successful schooling. Each of these dimensions promotes individuals in the school community turning inward to themselves and to their colleagues for growth in teaching and school practice. None of these roles requires individuals or the school to go outside their immediate environment for ideas or growth. However, as Andrew Hargreaves (1992) observes,

> Teachers do not develop entirely by themselves. . . .They also learn a great deal from contact with many other people who are knowledgeable about and have experience of teaching and learning. They learn from "experts" by taking courses, studying for higher degrees,

or undergoing programs of staff training in new techniques and approaches. (p. 216)

Teachers and other members of democratic school communities cannot presume that all worthwhile knowledge can be developed within the school. Michael Fullan (1993) notes that the isolation of a teacher within a classroom is limiting because it restricts learning to the experiences of that individual. Similarly, he notes, the isolation of a school from the wider environment is limiting because it creates "a ceiling effect" if the school "does not connect to . . . networks of others involved in similar and different pursuits" (p. 87).

In democratic schools teachers and others are regularly exposed to ideas and knowledge from sources external to the school. Our experience is that teachers and other staff members in successful schools are constantly participating in individual or collective staff development efforts. In these schools, ideas and knowledge brought in from external sources are not simply "adopted" and put into practice, but rather are discussed, debated, and subjected to critical study.

The primary way in which schools have traditionally accessed ideas and knowledge is through formal staff development efforts such as workshops, in-services, and conferences. A second way of accessing new ideas and knowledge is through participation in school renewal networks, which help schools learn from each other's efforts.

School renewal networks consist of educators from a number of schools who are connected by a shared vision and a typically loose organizational structure that facilitates their interaction across schools. Networks are based on the beliefs that you cannot improve student learning without improving teacher learning (Fullan, 1995; 1996) and that teachers learn best by working collaboratively, supervising and guiding one another, planning courses together, and reducing the isolation encountered in most schools. The intent of cross-school networks is to accelerate the change process in schools. The glue that connects network schools with each other is regular meetings of school coordinators, professional development institutes, cross-school visitation, attendance at professional development opportunities consistent with the network and participating schools' visions, and a network resource staff that works to facilitate sharing between network schools.

In conclusion, teachers in democratic schools are provided with many staff development opportunities and search out even more. Additionally, their schools often belong to national school renewal networks, such as the Coalition of Essential Schools, or smaller, more personal networks, such as the Oklahoma Networks for Excellence in Education.

Moral and Professional Community

Democratic schools are pervaded by a sense of professional and moral community, which are most noticeably characterized by connection and relationship. Connections and relationships are both within the school and beyond the school.

Caring and Collective Responsibility for Students

Within the school one form of connection and relationship is a sense of caring and collective responsibility for all students. Unlike conventional schools where teachers feel responsible for their students while they are in their classrooms, in democratic schools teachers believe they are responsible for all students in the school all the time. As one teacher noted in talking about her school where collective responsibility is the norm, "Everyone has all the students here—it isn't my kid versus your kid." Another teacher observed, "One person doesn't just own a child. You may be able to work well with a child in one area of their life and somebody else needs to give you some ideas to work with [in another area]. . ." (Burrello & Reitzug, 1993, p. 672).

In schools where collective responsibility for students does not exist, students often feel disconnected from teachers and uncared for. In Linda Darling-Hammond's book, *The Right to Learn*, two dropouts from a well-regarded New York City comprehensive high school explain:

> At one time school was important to me. I liked getting good grades and making my parents proud of me. [But in high school] I never felt part of the school. It didn't make a difference if I was there or not. . . . The teachers just threw me aside. . . . I felt like I was being ignored, like I wasn't important. (Carrajat, 1995)

The second dropout from the same school continues,

> I had passing grades when I decided to drop out, but nobody tried to stop me. Nobody cared. . . . None of the counselors paid any attention to me. The individual classes were too big for students to learn. Students should have longer exposure to individual teachers. If students could have the same subject teachers throughout their high school careers, this would allow teachers to get to know them better. (Carrajat, 1995)

Collaboration

In order for teachers to live out their sense of collective responsibility, there should be collaboration among teachers and between teachers and other members of the school staff (a second form of connection and relationship within the school). Teachers realize that students' lives will be touched by many teachers in the school and that, therefore, what happens across the school is as important as what happens within their classroom. Teachers and other staff members should work collaboratively as they talk about curriculum and instruction, engage in critical study, observe and discuss each others' teaching, plan courses and programs together, and teach each other new practices via leading in-school workshops and in-services.

Connection to Home and Community

Outside the classroom, democratic schools are connected to their parents and community. Neither children nor schools exist as islands. They are part of a global society that is made up of many communities, including the family, and local and global communities. These communities impact who and what the child and school are and can be.

In order to be democratic, a school must connect itself with families and communities in various ways. On one level it should involve families and communities in the work of the school, that is, educating students for

How does this picture illustrate a connection between school and community?

democratic citizenship (see chapter 14 for further discussion). On a second level it should involve itself in the work of the family and community. This is particularly true in terms of working for improved living conditions for all people and being concerned with issues of equity and justice. Educators in democratic school communities care deeply about young people. They understand that caring requires them to stand firm both within and outside the school against undemocratic practices such as racism, injustice, centralized power, poverty, and other gross inequities in schools and society (Beane & Apple, 1995).

IDEALS CHALLENGE: *Supporting Service*

(*Adapted from Wood,* 1992, p. 217.)

One morning a week every student at Central Park East Secondary School (CPESS) can be found somewhere other than inside the school. You might find students in an elementary school, hospital, nursing home, museum, community newspaper, just about anywhere in Harlem. They may be working with a small group of children, sharing stories with an elder, moving hospital equipment or transferring patients, writing a story, answering the phone, conducting tours, or sorting the mail. They are carrying out one of the central parts of their educational experience at CPESS—the community/school service requirement.

Every CPESS student spends two and a half to three hours a week at community service. The purpose of the program is clearly stated in school materials: "CPESS believes that all of its students are capable of contributing service/work on a more adult level. Our students need to realize that they are able to contribute to the community now, not at some far-off time in the future. . . ."

- Do you think the community/school service requirement detracts from students' academic learning?
- How would you respond to a parent who was critical of the community/school service requirement?

Concern for Equity

Schools that have a sense of professional and moral community concern themselves with issues of equity and justice not only in the local and global communities, but also within the school. These schools realize that undemocratic practices inside the school are reflective of the larger conditions on the outside. For example, in democratic schools students are heterogeneously grouped, partially for reasons of academic and social achievement, but more because of the democratic ideals of justice and equitable access for all students (Oakes, 1985).

Other types of equity issues that a school might examine include:

- Why is there a disparity between races in achievement in our school?
- How can we provide less affluent students with equitable access to technology?
- Do our instructional practices legitimate the background and culture of some students at the expense of others?
- How do we group students and how does this affect different groups of students?
- How do our classroom (and school) discipline policies and practices affect students from nondominant cultural groups?
- Do our classroom interactions and language subtly and subconsciously promote socially constructed gender roles and expectations to students?
- Do our shared decision making procedures ensure that the voices of *all* teachers, parents, and students get heard?

In democratic schools staff members search out potential issues of equity in all decisions, practices, and policies.

CLICK ON IT

Visit the Web site of Central Park East Secondary School at

www.csd4.k12.ny.us/cpess/index.html

for more information about the school and their democratic practices.

SUMMARY

This chapter compared bureaucratic organizations and schools with democratic organizations and schools and then described the practices of democratic schools. These practices have been linked in theoretical and research literature to school effectiveness. The schools in which you work may not mirror all (or even any) of these dimensions. Even successful schools are not always strong on every one of these dimensions. Democratic schooling is a continual process. No matter what our schools are like, our responsibility as democratic educators is to help them become more democratic.

As we noted earlier in this chapter, being a democratic school is not a static state a school attains. Rather, democratic schooling is a set of ideals toward which a school strives and which are reflected in practices like the ones described in this chapter. In essence, we are continually on a journey to become more democratic. We will discuss more of this journey in chapter 3.

DOING DEMOCRACY

(Adapted from Darling-Hammond, 1997, p. 149.)

School X

Upon entering the school the office is the first thing one sees, the quietest and best-outfitted part of the school, a forbidding place with its long, high counter separating the office staff from others who enter. The next sight is a glass-enclosed trophy case and a bulletin board of announcements about meetings, sports events, and rules to be followed. Long, clear corridors of egg-crate classrooms are broken by banks of lockers and an occasional tidy bulletin board. Classrooms look alike, teachers' desks at the front of each room commanding the rows of smaller desks for students. The teachers themselves work independently, their time and efforts managed by periodic bells that structure classes and duties and by the announcements boomed by the loudspeaker. Occasional faculty meetings ensure that further announcements are shared. Otherwise teachers make their way through the day largely isolated from colleagues.

School Y

The office is often difficult to find, stashed away in a corner, full of desks and curriculum materials that mark working spaces for both teachers and administrators. Students and parents enter the office comfortably with questions and announcements of their own: the place belongs to them too. Symbolically, office, hallway, and classroom walls are plastered with student work: writing, designs, models, and artwork are everywhere along with the notices of conferences, workshops, and other learning events. Classrooms usually have clusters of desks or tables; the teacher's desk often sits at the back. Handmade models of planets or skeletons hang from the ceilings. Graphs and charts, explanations, questions, and classroom constitutions written by students adorn walls. Wooden cubbies provide a home for students' things. Teachers frequently work in teams and visit one another's classrooms. Teacher workrooms host planning meetings throughout the day. Classes and hallways are busy but more relaxed than in traditional schools, because class periods are longer, classes change infrequently, and announcements over the public address system are rare. Most communication occurs during faculty teams' and committees' regular meetings and through the collectively compiled school newsletter.

- Identify the elements of each school that you would consider to be conventional. Identify the elements that you would consider to be democratic. Provide support for your responses.
- After discussing School X and School Y, discuss the practices of your university classroom and of the university in general. How are they democratic? How could they be more democratic? What actions can be taken to make them more so?
- Visit a local school and look for evidence that supports it being a conventional or a democratic school. Ask for feedback from a teacher, parent, or student about your initial impressions.

REFERENCES

Beane, J. A. & Apple, M. W. (1995). The case for democratic schools. In M. W. Apple & J.W. Beane (eds.), *Democratic schools* (pp. 1–25). Alexandria, VA: Association for Supervision and Curriculum Development.

Burrello, L. C. & Reitzug, U. C. (1993). Transforming context and developing culture in schools. *Journal of Counseling and Development, 71*, 669–677.

Carrajat, M. A. (1995). *Why do academically able Puerto Rican males drop out of high school.* Unpublished dissertation. New York: Teachers College, Columbia University.

Cochran-Smith, M. & Lytle, S. L. (1993). *Inside/Outside: Teacher research and knowledge.* New York: Teachers College Press.

Darling-Hammond, L. (1997). *The right to learn: A blueprint for creating schools that work.* San Francisco: Jossey-Bass.

Foxfire Core Practices. (1991). *Hands On, 40*, 4–5.

Fullan, M. (1993). *Change forces: Probing the depths of educational reform.* Bristol, PA: The Falmer Press.

Fullan, M. (1995). Contexts: Overview and framework. In M. J. O'Hair & S. J. Odell (Eds.), *Educating teachers for leadership and change: Teacher education yearbook III* (pp. 1–10). Thousand Oaks, CA: Corwin Press.

Fullan, M. (1996). Turning systemic thinking on its head. *Phi Delta Kappan, 77*, 420–423.

Glickman, C. D. (1993). *Renewing America's schools.* San Francisco: Jossey-Bass.

Hargreaves, A. (1992). Cultures of teaching: A focus for change. In A. Hargreaves & M. G. Fullan (Eds.), *Understanding teacher development* (pp. 216–240). New York: Teachers College Press.

Irvine, J. J. (1991). *Black students and school failure*. New York: Praeger.

King, B. M., Louis, K. S., Marks, H. M., & Peterson, K. D. (1996). Participatory decision making. In F. M. Newmann & Associates, *Authentic achievement: Restructuring schools for intellectual quality* (pp. 245–263). San Francisco: Jossey-Bass.

Kruse, S. D. & Louis, K. S. (1995). Developing professional community in new and restructuring urban schools. In K. S. Louis & S. D. Kruse (Eds.), *Professionalism and community: Perspectives on reforming urban schools* (pp. 187–207). Thousand Oaks, CA: Corwin Press.

Kruse, S. D., Louis, K. S., & Bryk, A. S. (1995). An emerging framework for analyzing school-based professional community. In K. S. Louis & S. D. Kruse (Eds.), *Professionalism and community: Perspectives on reforming urban schools* (pp. 3–22). Thousand Oaks, CA: Corwin Press.

Lambert, L. (1995). Toward a theory of constructivist leadership. In L. Lambert, D. Walker, D. P. Zimmerman, J. E. Cooper, M. D. Lambert, M. E. Gardner, & P. J. Ford Slack (Eds.), *The constructivist leader* (pp. 28–51). New York: Teachers College Press.

Little, J. W. (1982). Norms of collegiality and experimentation: Workplace conditions of school success. *American Educational Research Journal, 19*, 325–340.

Meier, D. (1995). *The power of their ideas: Lessons for America from a small school in Harlem.* Boston: Beacon Press.

Newmann, F. M. & Wehlage, G. G. (1995). *Successful school restructuring.* Alexandria, VA: Association for Supervision and Curriculum Development.

Newmann, F. M. & Associates (1996). *Authentic achievement: Restructuring schools for intellectual quality.* San Francisco: Jossey-Bass.

Noddings, N. (1984). *Caring: A feminine approach to ethics and moral education*. Berkeley: University of California Press.

Oakes, J. (1985). *Keeping track: How schools structure inequality*. New Haven, CT: Yale University Press.

Purpel, D. E. (1989). *The moral and spiritual crisis in education*. New York: Bergin & Garvey.

Reitzug, U. C. & O'Hair, M. J. (1998, April). *Educational Reform Networks: Charting the Path from Conventional School to Democratic School Community.* Paper presented at the annual meeting of the American Educational Research Association; San Diego, California.

Sergiovanni, T. J. (1994). *Building community in schools*. San Francisco: Jossey-Bass.

Sizer, T. R. (1992). *Horace's school: Redesigning the American high school.* New York: Houghton Mifflin.

Temple, J. (1997, October 4). School gets plan to raise test scores. *Greensboro (NC) News and Record,* p. B1, B2.

Weick, K. A. (1978). Educational organizations as loosely-coupled systems. *Administrative Science Quarterly, 21,* 1–19.

Wood, G. (1992). *Schools that work: America's most innovative public education programs.* New York: Penguin Books.

How is the journey of these high school cross country runners similar to the journey of democratic education?

How is it different?

CHAPTER 3

Moving From Conventional to Democratic Schooling

IDEALS CHALLENGE: *Deepening Discourse*

As a teacher who would like to see the school in which you work become more democratic, a first step that you could initiate is to ______________.

She was thirty-four. She wore a white skirt and yellow sweater and a thin gold necklace, which she held in her fingers, as if holding her own reins, while waiting for her children to answer. At about ten of eight in the morning, before the children arrived, she stood at the chalkboard, coffee cup in her right hand, a piece of chalk in her left. The chalk rattled, never squeaked, as she wrote down the word of the day in penmanship under the lists of children who owed her work (Kidder, 1989, p. 27–28).

You have spent the first two chapters reading about and discussing democratic IDEALS and some ways these translate into practices for teachers in democratic schools. In this chapter we examine how a school moves from being a conventional school to becoming a more democratic school. We do this by discussing what we have learned from our work with teachers and schools as they move through various stages of conventional to democratic practices (Reitzug & O'Hair, 1998). As we examine each stage, we periodically will return to the voice of Tracy Kidder (1989), the author of the best-selling book *Among Schoolchildren,* from which the opening vignette was taken. *Among Schoolchildren* describes the experiences of one teacher, Chris Zajac, whom Kidder spent a year observing. Chris teaches in an elementary school and was carefully selected by Kidder as representative of a typical teacher in a typical American school. The descriptions of Chris provide brief glimpses of what teaching in a conventional school is like.

STAGES IN THE MOVE FROM CONVENTIONAL TO DEMOCRATIC

In discussing the stages of conventional and democratic schooling, it is important to remember that not all schools and teachers will experience the journey toward democratic schooling in the same way. Some will move more rapidly than others from conventional practices, such as teaching in isolation and competing with each other, to more authentic practices, such as working together based on trust and cooperation. Some schools will move further toward democratic practices than others. Some will progress to critically studying struggles and practices, developing authentic teaching, truly sharing power, and acting on issues of equity, while others may never get beyond sharing best practices. Finally, some teachers and schools may move through an entirely different set of stages. The stages described here are not presented as the only way to progress toward democratic schooling, but rather representative of the stages we have observed.

The stages schools and teachers experience as they move from conventional toward democratic schooling are:

- teaching in isolation
- sharing best practices
- establishing trust and cooperation
- sharing leadership and noncritical decisions
- critiquing struggles and practices through critical study
- developing authentic and democratic practices
- sharing/"seizing" power, authority, and critical decisions
- moving from individual classroom concerns to collective school identity
- examining and acting on equity issues
- serving other learning communities

The first stage is characteristic of conventional schools, the middle stages of schools that have achieved a sense of professional community (Louis & Kruse, 1995), and the latter stages of schools that are democratic communities. (See Figure 3.1.)

As teachers and schools progress to a subsequent stage, they do not necessarily leave behind the practices of a previous stage. Schools may exhibit practices from a number of stages during the same period of time. Indeed, schools seldom completely abandon the practices of the first stage. That is, a great deal of teaching and working in isolation continues to occur in most schools, no matter how democratic they have become. However, the work of teachers and other educators becomes less isolated as a school becomes more democratic.

Teaching in Isolation

Educational analysts suggest that one of the most powerful reasons why attempts to reform educational practices have been largely unsuccessful is the isolation in which teachers operate (see, e.g., Fullan, 1996; Wasley, 1991). Tracy Kidder's account reflects the sense of the isolation that teachers in conventional schools feel.

Figure 3.1 **Continuum of Practices in Moving From Conventional Schooling to a Democratic Community**

CONVENTIONAL SCHOOLING	PROFESSIONAL COMMUNITY				DEMOCRATIC COMMUNITY				
Teaching in isolation and other conventional practices	Sharing best practices	Establishing trust and cooperation	Sharing leadership and some decisions	Critiquing struggles and practices	Developing authentic and democratic practices	Sharing power, authority, and critical decisions	Moving from individual classroom concerns to collective school identity	Examining and acting on issues of equity	Serving others

IDEALS CHALLENGE: *Initiating Inquiry*

(Adapted from Kidder, 1989.)

Eleven-thirty was lunchtime. She ate in the Teachers' Room, a small, grubby sanctuary with three tables and a couple of orange vinyl sofas and a coffee machine. She usually sat with her best school friend, Mary Ann, and they talked about wakes and weddings, sales and husbands, and only rarely about students and lessons (p. 31).

The principal mostly visited the classrooms of new teachers who needed help in keeping order. This year he'd observed only one lesson taught by each of his veteran teachers. After watching Chris in action, he'd say little more than that she was doing a good job. Chris appreciated his restraint, but she thought she'd like more advice.

She didn't get much advice of any sort from her students' parents. . . . These days, Chris always had a hard time persuading some of her students' parents to visit her, even for the scheduled biannual conferences. This year she would receive just one note from a parent that contained a request about her teaching. The note came from the upper-class Highlands, from Alice's mother. It read: "Alice seems to be having trouble with her math homework. Would you please go over her work with her in class." Chris felt grateful for the message. "I'd like to have one year of parents pushing me," she said. "Just one year."

She had always pushed herself. Over the years she had volunteered for almost all of the extra training that the school system occasionally offered. She had a reputation, not to all minds flattering, for signing up to serve on committees—the School Improvement Council and the Language Arts Curriculum Committee were her current ones. In the past, Chris had gotten some push from other teachers, swapping ideas and tips about instruction. Once in a while, she had taught classes jointly with other teachers. The opportunities for that kind of collegiality always arose by accident, when like-minded teachers were placed in the same grade as she and had similar schedules. The arrangements were always informal. They seemed precious because they resembled acts of free will, and because in her experience they were relatively rare.

Some evenings that fall Chris called up teacher friends—Candy or Mary Ann or Debbie—to discuss ways of handling Clarence. In between lessons during the day, she often conferred with Debbie about strategies for teaching reading. But the faculty did not routinely discuss academic matters when groups of them on the same schedules met over coffee and lunch in the Teachers' Room. In there, banter and complaints were more common than shoptalk (p. 48–49).

- Spend several hours or a day observing a teacher. Keep track of the following:

  How often does he or she interact with teachers or other adult educators?

  What are the interactions about?
- Develop categories and subcategories, such as professional, personal, complaints, exchanges, discussions, to categorize the interactions.
- What have you learned about "teaching in isolation" from your inquiry exercise?

Several factors contribute to the isolation of teachers. First, time is a major obstacle. In conventional schools, teacher "engaged time" with students is controlled and inflexible. Teachers are with students for almost their entire day. They have little time to go to the bathroom, make a phone call, or get a drink of water, let alone engage in deep conversation about professional practices with colleagues. During the few minutes without students that teachers do have, they often simply want to relax because of the intensity of their work when they are engaged with students. Therefore they talk about weddings, funerals, spouses, their children, shopping, and sports, rather than reading, writing, and arithmetic or authentic pedagogy, learning principles, and democratic schooling.

Not only is time important in helping reduce isolation and facilitating collaboration, but the mental attitude of educators regarding collaborative work is also crucial. Chris was different from many of her colleagues in her belief that the best way to meet students' needs is by working and learning together. Chris and her colleagues could have benefited greatly from more frequent discussions about teaching and learning, about how to meet the needs of individual students, about how parents and school could work more collaboratively in educating children, and about what they as a school stood for.

You might think you would prefer that no one see you teach until you became a polished teacher. Actually, teaching in collaboration is both stimulating and fun. One teacher observed,

> It's not only team teaching, but it's collaborative consultation. I can't begin to tell you how many ideas are generated by us teaching a subject [together]. Neither of us could accomplish as much as we are doing because we are both communicating our perspectives and ideas" (Burrello & Reitzug, 1993, p. 672)

Other teachers working in teams describe collaborative work environments as being ". . . so much better and more interesting . . . the team keeps me more on task, it helps me to look at students as whole individuals who take more than just [my class]." Another teacher said, "Teaming helps me to know what is going [on] in other teachers' classes. I can plan lessons to work with what other teachers are doing and help kids understand the concepts better" (Kruse & Louis, 1997, p. 262).

The isolation of teachers hinders the progression of schools toward democratic schooling. Teacher isolation makes it impossible to collaboratively develop core learning beliefs that guide the individual and collective practice of a school. Teachers working in isolation are unable to plan, share,

How are these teachers working to reduce the isolation that characterizes many conventional schools?

and discuss successes and struggles with anyone. They are unaware of what occurs in other classrooms and may unknowingly actually be working at cross-purposes with colleagues. Perhaps the most devastating result of teacher isolation is that schools fail to model for students the belief that you can make a difference in society if you work together and practice public problem solving.

The first step toward developing a collaborative caring environment and away from teaching in isolation is to begin sharing best practices with colleagues.

Sharing Best Practices

Teachers are hungry for opportunities for professional growth that are meaningful and that show respect for them and their knowledge. When asked from whom they would prefer learning, teachers usually say from other teachers in similar situations; for example a ninth-grade English teacher would like to share information with other ninth-grade English teachers. But teaching schedules in conventional schools rarely allow for this sharing to occur. Consequently, teachers are unaccustomed to discussing and sharing their best practices publicly or even sharing with the teacher next door or down the hall.

When opportunities to share do occur, however, teachers usually are willing and enthusiastic about sharing what they do well. First, they are willing to tell other teachers, either individually or in a group setting such as a faculty meeting, about what they did in a particular lesson or unit that engaged students, or to share a classroom management technique that accomplished the objectives they had for it. Second, they are willing to let other teachers observe them using their best practices. Third, they are willing to bring in knowledge and expertise from outside the school, either through sharing what they have learned in traditional forms of staff development or by networking with other schools.

The power of sharing best practices and observing different practices enhances teachers' willingness to try new practices in their classrooms. It begins to change the professional culture of the school. Teachers talk more among themselves about school concerns, rather than personal or trivial matters, which in turn stimulates professional growth. More importantly, sharing best practices moves teachers beyond the counterproductive and often dysfunctional mode of "complaining and blaming" students, parents, principals, and other teachers for any difficulties they have. Sharing is a first step in learning how to talk with each other professionally.

While teachers are eager to adopt the best practices of others in their classrooms, they are unlikely to challenge and critique how well those practices fit in—with their personal values and beliefs, their school's values and beliefs, and their classroom context. As described in the next sections, the critique of practice is likely to occur only when teachers have developed a sense of trust and community with each other.

Establishing Trust and Cooperation

Before challenge and critique can occur, trust must be built through communication among colleagues, parents, and students. As in most relationships, this trust is earned and grows over time. But as teachers move out of isolation and share best practices, trust develops more quickly because several things occur. First, at a very basic level, they begin to get to know their colleagues; the adage "You can't trust someone if you don't know them" was never more true. Second, they begin to build relationships that go beyond the superficial "Hi, how are you?" "I'm fine. How are you?" exchanges that occur in schools. Third, they develop confidence in their own professional knowledge and skills; in a sense, they begin to trust themselves professionally. This personal trust and confidence is necessary before they can build a relationship of trust with others. Finally, the well-intentioned nature of most teachers is affirmed; that is, that teachers are not out to "get" each other but want to work cooperatively and collaboratively.

Building trust is one of the most important factors affecting the decision to self-disclose the problems and struggles all teachers face. Trust must be established firmly before teachers can begin to provide meaningful feedback to each other. Such feedback and critique helps to accelerate the movement of conventional schools towards democratic school communities.

Sharing Leadership and Noncritical Decisions

In schools where a degree of trust and cooperation has developed and in which teachers have moved beyond teaching in isolation to sharing best practices, the pool of teachers who assume leadership tasks or roles broadens. Teacher leadership in these schools often involves not merely the *representation* of teachers in school decision making, but the *participation* of all teachers in some way in these decisions. This may be via membership on committees such as the curriculum committee, budget committee, community-building committee, or similar standing committees, or it may be via membership on ad hoc committees formed on a short-term basis to address specific school issues. Other times shared leadership is evident in teachers taking responsibility for initiating, organizing, or coordinating activities. It is essential, however, that shared leadership also involves more constructivist forms of leadership (see discussion in chapters 2 and 13), such as teachers initiating conversations about practices, conducting and sharing research, and raising critical questions focused on enhancing mutual understanding of practices (e.g., "Oh, I never thought about that. Why are you saying that?"). Constructivist leadership practices result in teachers and others in the school community continually constructing and reconstructing knowledge about their teaching practices.

In schools where teachers are beginning to share leadership, principals also typically begin to do the same. They become willing to let teachers make decisions that they, as principals, had previously made. For example, they may let teachers organize the school's staff development activities for the year or help select the textbook series that will be adopted the following year. However, principals appear unwilling to let go of critical decisions at this point. As one principal argued, "There are some decisions we as principals just need to make. After all, if the wrong decisions are made in those areas, we will be the ones who lose our jobs."

Critiquing Struggles and Practices Through Critical Study

While sharing best practices and leadership can begin to break down the isolation in which teachers work, it may simply result in a less conventional form of conventional schooling. Progressing toward democratic schooling requires raising a number of issues with respect to a best practice focus. What makes something a best practice? Is a best practice merely something that teachers or students like doing and that results in outcomes desired by some individuals (e.g., keeping students under control, making teachers' lives easier)? Simply because a best practice works in one school or classroom, does it mean it will work in all schools and classrooms?

Democratic schooling suggests that simply applying best practices across classroom and school settings is insufficient. Rather, exposure to best practices must be followed by critique and critical study that results in teachers personally "constructing knowledge" about the "best" practice and assessing the practice's fit with their classroom and school.

IDEALS CHALLENGE: *Learning Leadership*

- What do you think of the statement made by the principal that there are some decisions in schools that principals need to make and in which teachers should not be involved? Do you agree? Disagree? Why?
- If you believe there are some decisions that principals need to make and in which teachers should not be involved, which decisions are they? Provide reasons why teachers should not be involved in helping to make those decisions.

Teachers sharing their best practices with each other is an early step on the journey toward democratic schooling. Electronic mail is one way to share these practices quickly and efficiently with many people, especially those who teach in different schools.

As noted previously, teachers are frequently willing to share best practices but are often less willing to critique others' practice. Similarly, they are even less likely to voluntarily submit their own *daily* practice to critique. It is a lot safer to tell someone about what you do best as a teacher or to have them observe your best practices than it is to let them see your everyday routine. Educators typically tend to be congenial with each other rather than critical. Congeniality and acceptance in terms of each others' practices is often the result of a fear that if we criticize (or critique) what other teachers do, they may do the same to us. Some educators may lack confidence in their work and have fragile egos that are easily bruised. Therefore they avoid critique. As a result, conventional schools tend to be characterized not only by norms of isolation, but also by norms of congeniality.

Democratic schools operate from collegial norms of practice that encourage critique and critical study of all school practices. They examine needs of their students and families, plan and implement actions, and assess results. In effect, democratic schools gather information from within the school as well as from outside its current knowledge bases to make informed decisions affecting students and the community. For example, one high school teacher in Kentucky who as part of a critical study exercise followed ten students through an entire school day, commented on the

This teacher is trying to more thoroughly understand the school's practices by shadowing a student for a day.

student's day afterward by saying, "It was boring" (Kerchner, 1993). A second teacher who participated in the exercise said, "You know, this isn't a very humane place to be" (p. 39). A third teacher reported that no adult had spoken to the child she was following the entire day. As a result of critiquing their practices through critical study, these teachers subsequently helped make major changes in their school that resulted in students feeling more valued and appreciated.

Developing Authentic Practices and Relationships

If critique occurs with authentic teaching practice in mind, then it can lead to the initial stirring of such practices; that is, those that involve disciplined inquiry and the construction of knowledge, and that have value beyond school (Newmann & Associates, 1996). Teachers, however, often struggle with adopting authentic practice for such reasons as that it takes more time. Teachers teach for five or more hours per day. They correct papers and assess student work. They serve on various committees, complete miscellaneous paperwork, and participate in periodic schoolwide assessments. As one teacher noted, "You start looking at all the time this takes and you get to the point where there are just too many demands" (Prestine & McGreal, 1997, p. 383). Another teacher observed, "Authentic assessment became more something you could mess around with when you had time—and, of course, there never was time" (Prestine & McGreal, 1997, p. 383).

A second reason teachers struggle with moving toward authentic practice is the tension they feel between teaching, which prepares students for high-stakes standardized tests, versus teaching students in authentic ways.

One Oklahoma teacher noted that she felt she was doing a "disservice to kids" when her teaching practices were not authentic, yet she felt great pressure from school and district administrators to ensure that her students did well on standardized tests. She was afraid that teaching in authentic ways that focused on higher-level cognitive functioning would be detrimental to student performance on standardized tests that measure primarily low-level skills. As previously noted, however, research has found the opposite to be true (Newmann & Wehlage, 1995; Newmann & Associates, 1996; see discussion in chapter 2). Students who are taught in authentic ways actually perform better on standardized tests than students who have been taught in more conventional ways.

A third reason that inhibits progress toward authentic practice is that even though teachers may want to teach more authentically, they are only moderately successful in doing so due to the difficulty of permanently reconstructing long-ingrained didactic teaching practices to more authentic practices. One teacher noted that when other problems emerge (e.g., new students who are unruly), "Teachers get on edge. They retrench and go back to old ways that they know well and are comfortable with" (Prestine & McGreal, 1997, p. 385).

Even given all these potential obstacles to authentic practice, the desire to engage in authentic pedagogy stimulates a degree of reflection, discussion, study, and change in teachers. Reflection, discussion, and study provide insight both into what authentic pedagogy is, how it might be practiced, and the relationship between authentic teaching and student achievement. Collaborative study often has the side effect of further enhancing trust and the formation of "authentic" relationships in which teachers respond to each other both as caring individuals and as growth-oriented professionals. Authentic relationships link teachers with each other so that authentic practices have an opportunity to become schoolwide and not just restricted to individual classrooms.

IDEALS CHALLENGE: *Achieving Authenticity*

(Adapted from Kidder, 1989.)

Chris had three different reading groups composed of children from various fifth-grade classrooms. Two of her groups were lodged in the third-grade-level and one in the fourth-grade-level "basal" readers. The school had brand-new basals. They were more than reading books. They were mountains of equipment: big charts for teaching what were called "skill lessons," big metal frames to hold those charts erect, workbooks for the children to practice those skills, readers full of articles and stories that did not fairly represent the best of children's literature, and, for each grade level, a fat teacher's manual that went so far as to print out in boldface type the very words that Chris, or any other teacher anywhere, should say to make the children learn to read. Chris didn't teach reading by the numbers, right out of the manual. She made up her own lessons from the basal's offerings.

She spoke with each of her groups for twenty-five minutes every day about skills and stories. Most of the time her reading students enjoyed these conversations, and many enjoyed the twenty-five minutes each group spent in reading whatever they liked to themselves—she let them lie on the floor if they wanted during that time but almost every child hated the twenty-five minutes spent in the basal's workbooks. Junior, a most proficient reader who went to another room for reading, said, "I love to read, but I hate reading-reading." Chris couldn't quit the basal altogether, but she knew she ought to make the children see that there is more to reading than workbooks (p. 29–30).

Chris wished she could vary the morning's timetable now and then so that she could linger over certain lessons. . . . She left science for last. For several other subjects she used textbooks, but only as outlines. She taught science right out of the book; this was one of those texts that takes pains with the obvious and gives the complex short shrift. Chris didn't know much science and didn't usually enjoy teaching it. Sometimes she let creative writing encroach on science's time. About one day in ten she canceled science altogether and announced—to cheers, Felipe's the loudest—an informal art lesson. She often felt guilty about science.

- In what ways is Chris's teaching authentic?
- In what ways is her teaching conventional?
- Which of the obstacles to authentic pedagogy seem to be real for Chris?

Sharing or Seizing Power and Critical Decisions

In our discussion of a previous stage we noted that principals begin to share leadership by letting teachers participate in making noncritical decisions. We also noted, however, that some principals are unwilling to let go of all decisions because "if the wrong decisions are made . . . we will be the ones who lose our jobs" (Oklahoma principal, personal interview). Essentially, at this earlier stage principals are willing to let teachers participate in or make decisions that are not crucial to the performance or reputation of the school, or to the principal's career or well-being. In essence, they are willing to let teachers share leadership and decision making without letting them truly share power and authority.

The unwillingness on the part of some principals to share power and authority at this earlier stage is understandable. Typically teachers in conventional schools have not been legitimately involved in school decision making. Principals may be skeptical of their decision-making abilities. Just as teachers need to develop trust in each other before they are willing to critique each others' practice, so also may principals need to develop trust in teachers' decision-making capabilities before they are willing to share true power and authority. Sharing leadership and decision making on less significant decisions and participating with teachers in critical study of those decisions is likely to help principals develop sufficient trust in teachers' decision-making capabilities so that they are willing to share true power and authority. In order for a school to be authentic and democratic, principals *do not* need to share all decisions with teachers. They do, however, need to share all *critical* decisions. Decisions that are critical include: Who do we hire? What should we teach? How should we teach? How do we spend our money? Which decision do we make when there is disagreement in our community?

Principals sharing power and authority with teachers by letting them participate in critical decisions is one factor that distinguishes democratic school communities from those that are merely professional communities. There are different ways in which schools can get to this stage. In some schools the good intentions and cooperation of principals and teacher may evolve into a shared power relationship. In other schools teachers become aware of their own ability to make things happen and begin regularly acting on that belief (in a sense, they "seize power," although not necessarily in a confrontational way). That is, teachers begin to generate ideas, develop plans, and initiate activities, with or without the principal's approval. This does not mean that principals no longer have a voice, or that teachers develop an adversarial relationship with the principal. Rather it means that while being a democratic school community requires hearing the voices and perspectives of all members of the community, the opposition of some (e.g., principals or some teachers) should not be used as an excuse for failing to initiate and pursue actions that move the school toward becoming more democratic.

In democratic schools everyone realizes that no one has a monopoly on wisdom and knowledge. Further, in democratic schools all teachers and administrators have the best interests of children in mind when they make decisions. Differences of opinion may exist, however, regarding how the best interests of children should be met. Democratic schooling requires that all perspectives of how this might be accomplished are heard and discussed. Finally, although the discussion in this section has been about teachers, democratic schools must ensure that students and parents also are participants in sharing power and authority.

Moving From Individual Classroom Concerns to Collective School Identity

In addition to sharing power and authority, a second factor that distinguishes democratic school communities from schools that are merely professional communities is teachers moving from concerns for only their classroom to a concern for the collective identity of the school. As teachers talk about their work, they frequently talk about it in terms of their own classroom. For example, one teacher, in talking about democratic schools, forcefully observed:

> I don't care about charters. I don't care about democratic. What's in it for me? I'm in the classroom. I've got kids. How's it gonna help me? If you start saying to teachers, 'Let's write a [decision-making] charter. Let's do this thing democratic, etc.', you lose them because their hearts are in their classroom with their kids. (Oklahoma teacher, personal interview)

As teachers share practices, leadership, and power, they often move out of the narrowness of the "my classroom is my kingdom" focus and look beyond it to broader concerns. Teachers begin to see their work as going beyond their individual classroom responsibilities. They begin to see part of their role as helping to develop a collective vision of schooling with their colleagues.

In truly democratic school communities, teachers' roles extend beyond responsibility for *only* their students and their classroom. While their students and classroom remain their primary responsibility, their role also includes being concerned about the school as a whole. Students' school lives are not restricted to interactions in only one classroom with only one teacher. Thus, teachers must be concerned with what happens in the school beyond their classroom. This includes helping develop and pursue a clear, shared purpose for the school; engaging in collaborative activity with teachers, principals, parents, and students to achieve the purpose; and taking collective responsibility for student learning (Newmann & Associates, 1996).

Examining and Acting on Issues of Equity

A third factor that distinguishes democratic school communities from schools that are merely professional communities is the concern of the school for examining and acting on equity issues. In democratic school communities, there must be an explicit and proactive concern for equitable practice. A proactive concern is exemplified by inquiry and critical study into the nature of equity in the school; for example, by looking at issues such as tracking, Eurocentric curriculum, differential achievement levels between white students and minority students or between males and females in math and science, access to technology (see Technology Challenge that follows), and by acting to rectify inequities both within the school and in the community.

Being proactively concerned with issues of equity is a difficult stage for many schools to attain. This is because most middle-class white educators (who make up a large majority of all educators) have typically not been subjected to the significant inequities during their lives to which African Americans, Hispanics, and some other racial and cultural minorities

TECHNOLOGY CHALLENGE

Access to Technology

(*From* The Parents' Guide to the Information Superhighway *(2nd ed.), by the National Center for Education Statistics, 1998, Washington, DC: The Children's Partnership.*)

HAVES	HAVE NOTS
88% of schools with students from high-income families have access to the Internet	63% of schools with a large proportion of students from poor families have access to the Internet
39% of households with annual incomes of \$20,000–\$39,999 own computers	19% of households with annual incomes less than \$20,000 own computers
58% of households with annual incomes of \$40,000–59,999 own computers	
68% of households with annual incomes of over \$60,000 own computers	

- What is the relationship of the democratic IDEALS of equity to these statistics?
- What are some possible solutions to the access problem for poor schools and children?

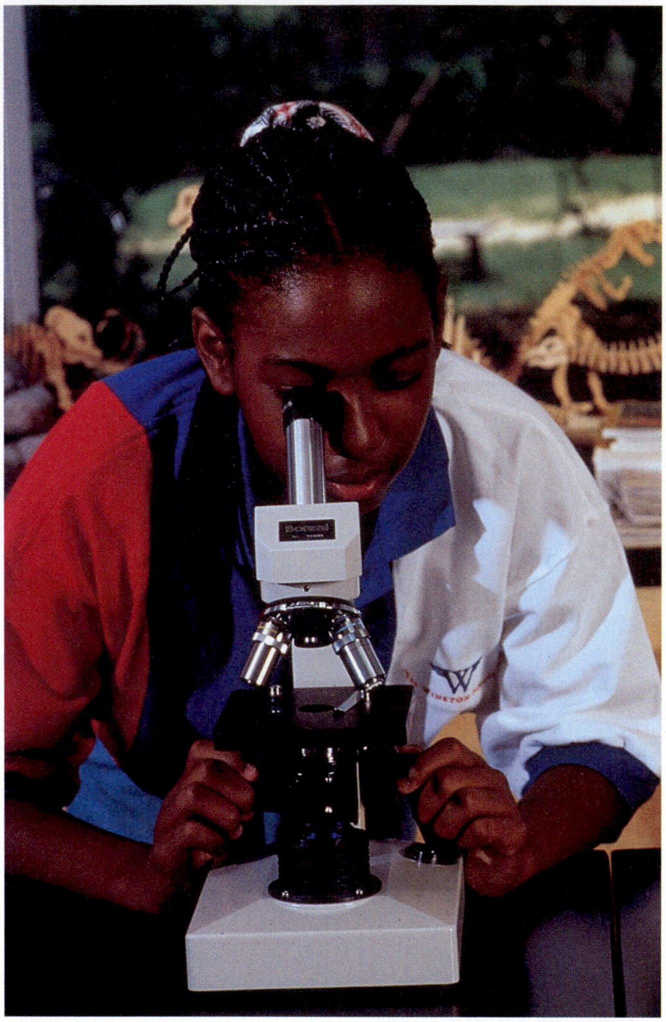

Authentic learning often involves inquiring in the same way as a professional does; for example, this girl uses a microscope just as a "real" biologist would.

have been subjected. Additionally, in some cases educators who *have* been subjected to inequities have been socialized to believe that they are responsible for the inequitable conditions they face or that there is a legitimate and rational reason for differential conditions. For example, female students are often subtly (and frequently unintentionally) socialized to believe that they are not good at math (see, e.g., American Association of University Women Educational Foundation, 1992). Similarly, the passive and subdued oral communication style common among European Americans is typically considered most appropriate, while the active, emotionally engaged, and vocal style that is more characteristic of African Americans is considered inappropriate (see Kochman, 1981). These factors often make it difficult for us to see inequities in school practice. Our tendency is to talk about *all* children, but to mean white, middle-class children. Thus, schools often do not think in terms of the differential and perhaps inequitable effects of programs, policies, and practices and may overlook differential levels of achievement based on race, class, or gender.

IDEALS CHALLENGE: *Examining Equity*

(Adapted from Kidder, 1989.)

At 8 o'clock, a high-pitched beep from the intercom announced math, which lasted an hour. Some children left Chris's room for math, replaced by other children from the room next door. For math and reading, children were "levelized," which means the opposite of "leveled"—they were grouped by abilities. Her lower math group began the year with a review of the times tables and her top group with decimals. She would take each group as far as she could, but every child had to improve in problem solving, every member of the low group had to at least master long division, and all of the top group should progress to the brink of geometry (p. 28).

- Is the type of grouping described in this scenario equitable? Why or why not?

For a school to be truly democratic it must progress to the stage of examining and acting on issues of equity. One way of moving toward this stage is by proactively thinking in terms of equity implications of each decision that is made and every practice or policy in which the school engages. The types of questions discussed in the Moral and Professional Community section of chapter 2 are examples of those that schools might ask as they move toward this stage.

Serving Other Communities

The fourth factor that moves schools from professional communities to democratic school communities is a concern in the school for serving other communities, which means those outside of the immediate classroom or school. This might be serving another classroom, another school, the neighborhood surrounding the school, the local community, a particular racial or cultural community, or the global community.

A school cannot be considered democratic if it exists in a vacuum. It must see itself as connected to the world beyond its school. This involves a concern on at least two levels. One level is a concern for issues of equity and justice not just within the school, but also in the larger context of the local and global community. The second level is a concern for the learning of other learning communities. That is, democratic schools must share what they have learned not only among school staff members, but also with other schools who are on journeys to become democratic learning communities.

Frequently schools have difficulty reaching the stage where they focus on serving other communities. Conventional schools are too concerned with what is going on inside their school. They believe that they do not have time to be concerned about the outside world. They believe they must cover the material in their textbooks and once they have done that, then they can participate in extra projects that involve communities outside the school. Unfortunately, that time never arrives. There is always more "material" to cover.

If you work in a conventional school where textbook and content coverage is the prime focus, you should consider engaging your colleagues in a discussion of the significance of textbooks and the outside world. In order to function as a democratic school, there must be an understanding that *communities* are the *locus of learning*. Textbooks are significant only to the extent that they inform our understanding of those communities and our work in helping them be more equitable, humane, and just places. Educators in democratic schools should always keep in mind what one principal writes in a note to her teachers at the beginning of every school year.

> Dear Teacher:
>
> I am a survivor of a concentration camp. My eyes saw what no man [sic] should witness:
>
> Gas chambers built by *learned* engineers.
>
> Children poisoned by *educated* physicians.
>
> Infants killed by *trained* nurses.
>
> Women and babies shot and burned by *high school* and *college* graduates.
>
> So I am suspicious of education.
>
> My request is: Help your students become human. Your efforts must never produce learned monsters, psychopaths, educated Eichmanns. Reading, writing, and arithmetic are important only if they serve to make our children more humane. (Shapiro, 1996, p. 227)

Becoming more democratic as a school requires a transformation that goes beyond merely transforming school facilities.

IDEALS CHALLENGE: *Supporting Service*

(From: Beane & Apple, 1995, p. 1.)

A group of third graders has spent several weeks studying problems in their school, homes, neighborhoods, and community. Besides looking at problems they know of, they also have gathered examples from parents, teachers, and community officials. After a month of research and discussion, they collect their recommendations for solving these problems in a booklet that will be distributed throughout the community.

(From Ladson-Billings, 1994, p. 72; narrated by Pauline Dupree, fourth-grade teacher.)

From the day that they walk into my room they know they have to select a buddy. This is their learning partner for the year. A lot of times when a student is having a hard time, I'll call the buddy to my desk and really give him or her an earful. "Why are you letting your buddy struggle like this? What kind of partner are you? You're supposed to be the helper." Within a couple of months I begin to see them looking out for one another. One student will hesitate before he turns in his paper and will go check to make sure the buddy is doing OK. Eventually, they begin to check very carefully and they may discover some errors that they themselves have made. Having the buddy is just really another level of learning. Those that are helping are really helping themselves.

- How do the two examples reflect the democratic IDEALS of inquiry, discourse, equity, authenticity, shared leadership, and, especially, service?

SUMMARY

We have discussed a continuum of stages that schools progress through as they move from conventional schooling to democratic schooling. The continuum may be useful to you as a new teacher in several ways. At one level, it can help you understand the schools in which you conduct your field experiences. At another level, once you have attained your first teaching position it may help you address the question, "Where do I start in my school?" That is, although the continuum is not a recipe for practice, it can help you understand how you might proceed in facilitating your school's progress from conventional schooling to democratic schooling. For example, if the school in which you teach is characterized by teachers working in isolation, you might consider initiating activities or conversations that result in teachers sharing best practices. The journey toward becoming more democratic starts with a single step. Taking the first step of sharing best practices may lead to the second step, the development of trust, which may in turn lead to further steps.

Keep in mind that the continuum also is not a shortcut for transforming conventional schools into democratic schools. Schools are complex places. Frameworks such as the continuum, while enhancing our

CLICK ON IT

For more information on how you might get started as a teacher in working toward democratic school improvement, visit the Web site of the Center for Applied Research and Educational Improvement at

http.//carei.coled.umn.edu/General/Otheresources

Click on the "Links to Other Resources" icon that is part of this site for access to a vast array of resources dealing with school improvement.

understanding of schools, also risk oversimplifying reality. Remember, you will always know the school you work in much better than we do. You are the individual who can critically study your school and reflect on what you find. You are the individual who can discuss with your colleagues what it means to be a democratic school, whether you want to be part of one, and, if so, how your school might move toward democratic schooling. Chapter 4 will help you learn about the philosophical and historical background of today's schools.

IDEALS CHALLENGE: *Deepening Discourse*

At the beginning of the chapter you responded to the following probe. Now, after having read this chapter, how would you respond? Would you still respond in the same way?

As a teacher who would like to see the school in which you work become more democratic, a first step that you could initiate is to ______________.

DOING DEMOCRACY

In many respects this book is about our beliefs as educators and human beings. What are your beliefs as an educator and a human being? What values are important to you in your practice and your life? What do you believe is the purpose of schools? How do you believe students learn best? What do you believe is your role as a teacher in your classroom? As a member of the school? As a member of multiple communities? What evidence exists that you "practice what you preach"—that your actions are consistent with your beliefs? What evidence of your beliefs do you anticipate will be visible in your practices once you are a teacher? Completing a table similar to the one that follows will provide you with the beginnings of an educational platform. We recommend that after completing the table, you periodically review and update it as you proceed through this course, your teacher education program, and once you are a teacher. You also may wish to use the table to inquire or critically study the congruency between your beliefs and your practice (see chapter 5).

TOPIC	YOUR BELIEFS	EVIDENCE OF BELIEFS
Important Values	______________	______________
Purpose of schools	______________	______________
How students learn	______________	______________
Role as a teacher:		
in the classroom	______________	______________
in the school	______________	______________
as a community member	______________	______________

REFERENCES

American Association of University Women Educational Foundation. (1992). *How schools shortchange girls: The AAUW report*. Boston: Author.

Beane, J. A., & Apple, M. W. (1995). The case for democratic schools. In M. W. Apple & J. W. Beane (Eds.), *Democratic schools* (pp. 1–25). Alexandria, VA: Association for Supervision and Curriculum Development.

Burrello, L. C., & Reitzug, U. C. (1993). Transforming context and developing culture in schools. *Journal of Counseling and Development, 71*, 669–677.

Fullan, M. (1996). Turning systemic thinking on its head. *Phi Delta Kappan, 77*, 420– 423.

Kerchner, C. T. (1993). Building the airplane as it rolls down the runway. *School Administrator, 50*(10), 8–15.

Kidder, T. (1989). *Among schoolchildren*. Boston: Houghton Mifflin Co.

Kochman, T. (1981). *Black and white: Styles in conflict*. Chicago: The University of Chicago Press.

Kruse, S. D., & Louis, K. S. (1997). Teacher teaming in middle schools: Dilemmas for a schoolwide community. *Educational Administration Quarterly, 33*, 261–289.

Ladson-Billings, G. (1994). *The dreamkeepers: Successful teachers of African-American children*. San Francisco: Jossey-Bass.

Louis, K. S., & Kruse, S. D. (1995). *Professionalsim and community: Perspectives on reforming urban schools.* Thousand Oaks, CA: Corwin Press.

Newmann, F. M., & Wehlage, G. G. (1995). *Successful school restructuring*. Alexandria, VA: Association for Supervision and Curriculum Development.

Newmann, F. M., & Associates (1996). *Authentic achievement: Restructuring schools for intellectual quality.* San Francisco: Jossey-Bass.

Prestine, N., & McGreal, T. L. (1997). Fragile changes, sturdy lives: Implementing authentic assessment in schools. *Educational Administration Quarterly, 33*, 371–400.

Reitzug, U. C., & O'Hair, M. J. (1998, April). *Educational Reform Networks: Charting the Path from Conventional School to Democratic School Community.* Paper presented at the annual meeting of the American Educational Research Association, San Diego, CA.

Shapiro, H. S. (1996). Memo to the president—Clinton and education: Policies without meaning. In F. Mengert, K. Casey, D. Liston, D. Purpel, & H. S. Shapiro (Eds.), *The institution of education* (2nd ed., pp. 219–227). Needham Heights, MA: Simon & Schuster.

Wasley, P. A. (1991). Stirring the chalkdust: Changing practices in Essential Schools. *Teachers College Record, 93*(1), 28–58.

What do you think this boy is wondering about as he studies the turtle?

What do you wonder about as a future teacher?

What are the questions that you think are worth thinking about for teachers?

What thoughts have previous teachers, educators, and philosphers had about these questions?

CHAPTER 4

Historical and Philosophical Foundations of Democratic Education

IDEALS CHALLENGE: *Deepening Discourse*

Complete and then discuss the following statement.
The purpose of schools is ______________________.

Philosophy is a Greek word that combines *philo*, meaning "love of," and *sophia*, meaning "wisdom." A "love of wisdom" leads us to think deeply about important matters. Philosophical ideas do not provide *an* answer to anything, but thinking philosophically enables you to consider the possible and the ideal, and how they are related.

It is easy to think that philosophy consists of abstractions created by professors sitting in armchairs, but philosophy is a part of everyday life. Teachers develop a philosophy of education by publicly expressing their ideals and by taking action in their classrooms, schools, and communities. All of us carry ideal images of how we ought to teach or how the classroom ought to be, and our actions embody a "philosophy-in-practice." "[T]o think philosophically is to reflect upon who we are, what we are doing, why we are doing it, and how we justify all these things" (Ozman & Craver, 1986, p. x). Educational philosophies, then, are based on complex and often implicit beliefs about *purposes*, *people*, and *practices*. Here is how Steven Levy (1996), a fourth-grade teacher in Massachusetts, describes his philosophy of education. The questions that follow Levy's writing form the basis for the rest of the chapter.

IDEALS CHALLENGE: *Supporting Service*

(Excerpted from Levy, 1996, pp. 3–4, 7–8.)

Teachers often labor under the assumption that we need to meet the needs of *all* the children in our classes. We have children who are able to read Shakespeare and children who can barely read at all. We have children who can do algebra and children who cannot do simple addition. To compound these tremendous discrepancies, we are expected to teach our students in heterogeneous groups rather than separate them by ability. And if this weren't enough, with the advent of inclusion we have some children in our classes who can't see or hear and some who are confined to wheelchairs. We also have an increasing number of children who cannot speak English. I am all for inclusion, but . . . how can we meet the needs of all these children?

I found I needed to set a new goal to guide my teaching, one that I had a reasonable chance of reaching. So I asked myself a new question: how can I create an environment that allows every child to express and develop his or her true genius, the essence of who he or she really is? In doing so I had shifted my entire focus: rather than trying to meet the needs of every single child, I concentrated on shaping the learning environment to enable each child to manifest the genius that he or she brought to the classroom.

I use the word *genius* intentionally. I do not mean to suggest that every child is a genius as we understand that word today, but rather that everyone *has* a genius according to the word's essential meaning of "a particular character of essential spirit." It is the quality that makes something unique.

Jenny [a former student] had many difficulties in school. She couldn't read, and she couldn't do even the most basic math. There seemed to be nothing in school for her. I tried dancing, singing, poetry, but nothing awakened her confidence. She was good at knitting, but it brought her no real pleasure. It wasn't until the last week of school I found the activity that revealed her genius. We were creating watercolor paintings to cover books we were making. Jenny's pictures were extraordinary. Her sense of form and color was magnificent. I did not have to praise her paintings, as I had tried to do with her knitting and singing to no avail. Her accomplishment was intrinsically satisfying. The other children saw it immediately and crowded around her table, offering encouragement and praise. But it was the last week of school. Had I known earlier, I would have painted with the whole class every week!

- How are your current beliefs similar to and different from Levy's?
- What does Levy have to say about why we should educate children?
- Who does he believe should have access to the curriculum?
- What does he believe should happen in classrooms?
- Do you think Levy sees himself most as an individual who teaches, an individual who leads, or an individual who serves? Discuss the relationship between teaching, leadership, and service.

We began with the words of a practicing teacher like Steven Levy because we wanted to stress the point that every teacher expresses and lives out a philosophy. In chapters 1, 2, and 3, we examined the essential IDEALS and practices of democratic education and the journey from conventional to democratic schooling. In this chapter you will have the chance to reflect upon the IDEALS, practices, and journey of democratic education through an examination of philosophical ideas and historical patterns that have influenced our schools and how we think about children and education. We have interwoven philosophy and history around the IDEALS framework because we think historical events influence people's philosophical beliefs about education, and philosophical writings can influence educational practices and policies. We will examine how certain ideas led to others, and how different labels may really encompass similar ideas. Exploring these ideas in-depth is like conducting an archaeological dig, during which we find layer-upon-layer of educational artifacts. None of these broadly defined philosophies have disappeared—we can still find their remnants in school and classrooms today.

Our philosophical and historical "dig" will focus on the following general questions:

- What are the purposes of education?
- From where do the purposes and beliefs come?
- How did democratic purposes for education develop in the United States?
- Who had access to education for democracy?

WHAT ARE THE PURPOSES OF EDUCATION?

In chapter 1, we discussed the meaning of democracy and democratic education. Specifically, we examined two core concepts as best describing democratic education: schooling *for* democracy and schools *as* democracies. We believe that in combination, these concepts facilitate the development of democratic school communities. Now, we ask you to expand your analysis of democratic school communities by examining the cultural, political, and economic purposes of education. Also, we ask you to consider issues of access, organization, people, and practices. As you consider these purposes, make comparisons with democratic education. Which support, extend, or oppose democratic education and the IDEALS framework?

Cultural Purposes

All philosophies of education—and, certainly, all educators—would claim that education should aim to increase students' knowledge. Through the ages there have been two aspects of knowledge that are central to cultural conceptions of education: *virtue* and *enlightenment*. These terms, which sound old-fashioned, actually carry the authority of many centuries of use by philosophers and even educational practitioners. Aristotle spoke of "character and intellect," while more than 2,000 years later Horace Mann, the forceful advocate of American common schools, talked about "virtue and knowledge." They both were trying to express the ideas conveyed through *virtue* and *enlightenment*.

Education is intended to influence or even mold our attitudes and actions. It is a means of socializing young people so that they will act virtuously. Virtue involves knowing how to act, and such knowledge can derive from religious or secular teachings. Virtue is also associated with the concept of *character*. When we act virtuously it is said that we are "showing our character," which is our sense of the right thing to do. Virtue may reflect our conformity to cultural beliefs or our sense of what is right—regardless of prevailing opinion.

Enlightenment entails knowing how to think, and knowing about vital information and ideas. People have tried to attain knowledge that leads to enlightenment by traveling to other societies, meditating, studying texts, and talking with someone who is considered wise. It is only in the last two centuries that those traditional paths to enlightenment have been supplemented and in some ways supplanted for most young people by a secular, institutional form of enlightenment: formal schooling.

Educators in modern schools have promoted their own ideals of virtue and enlightenment. The two purposes are not always compatible, depending on how they are defined. In societies such as ours there is a tension between expecting that children will simply accept our cultural beliefs about what is right and wrong and encouraging children to ask questions and "think for themselves"—a call for enlightenment. The pull between *conformity* and *autonomy* is an important feature of life as an educator in our times.

Political Purposes

Leadership elites in every society have tried to maintain their political power, and have developed educational structures in order to maintain the social order. In many societies, there have also been people who want to reconstruct the existing power arrangements that are part of educational practice. For example, do teachers want to educate students to be democratic citizens who question authority and societal inequities, or do they want to educate students to work within the current political system—even though this may at times limit them to perpetuating the status quo? While this question may artificially dichotomize the choices available, teachers do have to confront issues of *stability* and *transformation* when considering the political purposes of education.

Economic Purposes

Traditionally, education served to train young people in the occupations of their elders. Apprenticeships in traditional preindustrial societies served to continue vital crafts and arts within the group. In more modern times, formal education has been linked to economic productivity and efficiency. Vocational education in early 20th-century America, for example, was initiated to train workers who would assume jobs in the manufacturing trades. Individual choice in the traditional or modern situations just described was limited. However, since the mid-18th century some educators have called for schooling that enables students to develop their talents and interests without being overly concerned with future vocation or their contribution to the country's economic productivity.

FROM WHERE DO PURPOSES AND BELIEFS COME?

What teachers believe about school purposes is linked to their beliefs about various aspects of education. Specifically, it is linked to beliefs about questions such as:

- How should the people involved in education (i.e., students, teachers, parents) be treated?
- Who should have access to formal education?
- Who should have access to different curricular experiences?
- What are the perceptions of children and adolescents?
- How are students understood in relation to their gender, ethnicity, socioeconomic status, language, place of origin, and special characteristics?

These are complex questions that teachers need not answer alone. Educational philosophers (and educational practitioners) have contemplated these questions for centuries. Different societies have developed different cultural beliefs about these questions. Similarly, different time periods have been characterized by favored beliefs about these questions. Before you fully form your beliefs, we ask you to first examine three broad philosophical "schools of thought" that are grouped according to their commonalities: *communitarian, Western classical,* and *liberal.* Exploring these "schools of thought" will help us better understand the various ways that teaching and learning, the treatment of children, schools, and schooling can be thought of. Within each "school of thought" there are different "subphilosophies" that reflect the particular beliefs of different racial or ethnic groups, or the predominant thinking of a particular historical period of time. Finally, we would caution you that any individual philosopher or educator may take a position that crosses into several philosophical groups.

The quest begins with communitarian philosophies of education, because they predate the other philosophical schools.

Communitarian Philosophy: How Do We Pass Our Culture on to Our Children?

Communitarianism, the oldest of all philosophies, represents the attempt of traditional communities to maintain their way of life. Until relatively recently, in most societies education was a process of preparing children to survive in a particular culture by inculcating the prevailing cultural values and practices.

Three purposes are emphasized in communitarian societies. The first of these is *cultural virtue*. Virtue is defined in many different ways, but every society has a cultural standard for how children are supposed to act and the sort of character they are supposed to show. In many cases, communitarian groups have been theocracies, which are societies organized around strict adherence to religious precepts. Being virtuous and maintaining the faith has been a major goal, particularly when that faith was threatened (as with Jews) or when religious groups were trying to expand (as with Christians and Muslims).

The second purpose emphasized in communitarian societies is *political stability*. Group solidarity is a central aim of communitarian philosophies. Solidarity is ensured by teaching children to be loyal to elders and to the rulers, and often by having inflexible practices for the power of adults over children and the transfer of governmental power.

The third purpose emphasized in communitarian societies is *economic continuity*. Historically, life has been difficult for most groups of people, who have had to scrape out a living by hunting, fishing, farming, and bartering for goods with other groups. The children have had to learn survival skills and the trades of their ancestors, which has given economic continuity a higher priority than young people's choice of occupation.

To give a more concrete idea of what "communitarian" means, important communitarian ideas will be explored in traditional African, Native American, and Chinese societies. Then, other communitarian societies and groups will be discussed, such as Sparta, the Greek city-state; the Jewish and Christian groups around the time of the Greek and Roman empires; and some early American communitarian groups. In many of these groups, theological traditions were the core of the community.

CLICK ON IT

For links to many sources of information about philosophy and philosophers, visit the following Web sites

www.yahoo.com/Arts/Humanities/Philosophy

www.yahoo.com/Arts/Humanities/Philosophy/Philosophers

Traditional African Society

Life in traditional African societies revolved around the largely unchanging rhythms of village life. The following description applies to communitarian life in Africa in the past, and not as much to education in the more Westernized African cities of today. Though there are still thousands of different cultural groups across the continent, and customs vary widely from area to area, there have been seven general goals of African education (Fafunwa, 1974, p. 20):

1. to develop the child's physical skills
2. to develop character
3. to inculcate respect for elders and those in position of authority
4. to develop intellectual skills

Although this African classroom resembles American classrooms in many ways, there are distinct differences between the African communitarian tradition of education and conventional schooling. What are they?

5. to acquire specific vocational training and a healthy attitude toward honest labor
6. to develop a sense of belonging and to participate actively in family and community affairs
7. to understand, appreciate, and promote the cultural heritage of the community at large

Thus, in traditional African communities, political stability and economic continuity are ensured by children's acceptance of authority and of their adult roles. Cultural agreement is assumed and not negotiated—children *will* follow in their elders' footsteps.

In terms of educational practice, traditional African societies have five major characteristics (Reagan, 1996). First, in village life, there is a *communal approach to teaching.* The overused phrase "It takes a whole village to raise a child" accurately represents African education. All adults, especially same-sex adults, are responsible for teaching children how to act.

Second, African societies have long relied on *nonformal educational experiences,* such as informal and formal apprenticeships. Girls work alongside the women, and boys imitate the men's activities. Children's participation in the economic life of the community is crucial for its survival, so they are taught the necessary skills that their ancestors learned.

Third, African educational practices emphasize *oral culture* in the form of proverbs, riddles, puzzle stories, or folk tales. Proverbs are a concise source of traditional wisdom and they are intended to strengthen the child's reasoning abilities. "Your guest is a guest for two days; after that, give him a hoe" and "The tree is bent while young" are examples of two proverbs, the first Swahili and the second Zulu, that communicate the traditional wisdom of these tribes (Reagan, 1996, pp. 22–23). Riddles and puzzles also are commonly used as a playful way to teach children how to think. A Yoruba riddle states: "We cut off the top and bottom, yet it produces wealth. What is it?" (a drum) (Reagan, 1996, p. 25). This sort of language play is part of many communitarian societies because it calls attention to important cultural wisdom and artifacts.

Fourth, traditional African societies believed in the importance of *local knowledge about the world.* Whether it is the plants used as medicines or the folklore recounted as village history, community knowledge is transmitted from one generation to the next.

Finally, *ritual and custom* play a large role in communal education in African societies. Children are grouped in "age-sets" and undergo initiation ceremonies in this group. Becoming an adult occurs after a gradual process of learning for years about the occupational, social, and religious life of the tribe.

As you can see, traditional African societies practiced a communitarian philosophy in their educational efforts at maintaining their way of life. They did this via the educational practices just outlined, which advanced their sense of cultural virtue and promoted economic and political stability.

Native Peoples of North America

As in Africa and other parts of the world, there was great diversity among groups of native peoples in North America. In many of the most well-known tribes, however, it is quite clear that spirituality was a central purpose of education. Adults focused on maintaining harmony with nature and passing along traditional religious customs. Cultural groups such as the Hopi developed intricate and compelling spiritual systems which, like other communitarian societies, formed the basis for education about the world.

Teaching the young how to survive in a sometimes harsh environment was another main purpose of education. In 1774, Benjamin Franklin reported how the Six Nations of the Iroquois Confederacy responded to an offer to send their children to the College of William and Mary; the speaker is a member of the Iroquois:

> [B]ut you, who are wise must know that different nations have different conceptions of things; and you will therefore not take it amiss, if our ideas of this kind of education happen not to be the same with yours. We have had some experience of it; several of our young people were formerly brought up at the colleges of the Northern Provinces; they were instructed in all your Sciences; but, when they came back to us, they were bad runners, ignorant of every means of living in the woods, unable to bear either cold or hunger, knew neither how to build a cabin, take a deer, or kill an enemy, spoke our language imperfectly, were therefore neither fit for hunters, warriors, nor counselors; they were totally good for nothing. We are however not the less obliged by your kind Offer, though we decline accepting it: And to show our grateful sense of it, if the gentlemen of Virginia will send us a dozen of their sons, we will take great care of their education, instruct them in all we know, and make *Men* of them. (Reyhner, 1992, p. 36)

Play activities, engaged in by children and adults alike, served to test the Native American child's mental and physical skills—and to let them have fun! In order to pass along ritual and ceremonial knowledge, children imitated and were directly instructed by same-sex adults. Respect for tribal elders was paramount, and oratory played a big part in the educational process (which is similar to Greece and Rome, as discussed later). Decisions about tribal matters often were made by councils of elders, after lengthy discussions and speeches intended to sway opinions. Children imitated this form of group interaction and assumed their place during adulthood.

Chinese Societies

China presents a slightly different picture of communitarian education. Historically, the thinking of Confucius and the numerous texts based on his teachings formed the foundation of Chinese education. Confucius (551–479 B.C.) stressed that the primary purpose of education should be to develop a good person who has the qualities of benevolence *(ren)* and an understanding of how to act in accordance with the right principles *(li)*. By being educated about the basic virtues of life and by accepting obligations based on one's relationship to others of higher and lower status, one could become a good person. This philosophy was founded on political stability and economic continuity—carrying out the wishes of political and familial leaders and carrying on the occupations of family members. The ultimate goal of formal education was to train good administrators for the government (which would be run by an elite, well-educated, male cadre)—rather than to develop all children's capacity to learn.

Confucian scholars in the centuries following his death systematized his ideas. Over the centuries, Chinese rulers developed a civil service examination, which required years of laborious study and a rigorous set of tests to determine who would fill governmental positions. Basic education, what is called "elementary," remained the responsibility of parents. Schooling began later, at the age of 7 or 8, when children studied with a tutor. There was an authoritarian and formal relationship between tutor and student. Children memorized long texts and learned how to write the essays required on the national examinations. Confucius believed that education should be widely available and based on the premise that the most able and virtuous students would assume governmental leadership. This is the notion of a *meritocracy,* a system where individual merit rather than economic or social standing is the determinant of success. Since many poor families had little time to educate their children and no money to hire a tutor, and the state did not provide monies or resources to do so, the result was at best a limited meritocracy. Educational practices in China remained the same until the 20th century upheavals of civil war and communist rule.

Greek Societies—Sparta

In the centuries leading up to the time of Christ, societies surrounding the Mediterranean Sea fought for control of trade routes and resources. The two most famous Greek societies vying for power were Sparta and Athens, which each developed as a *polis*—a governmental entity that was both a city and a state. Perhaps because Athens and Sparta represent such different views of the relationship between citizens and the state, they frequently have been analyzed and held up as archetypes of governmental and cultural systems. For our purposes, the two societies contrast the communitarian and Western classical philosophies of education.

Reaching its zenith in the 6th century B.C., Sparta was a communitarian society founded on unquestioning devotion to the state. Spartan males were constantly warring or preparing for battle, so boys had to be trained to be warriors and girls to be wives and mothers of warriors. Spartan children were cared for by nurses from a young age so that their loyalty to the state would supersede attachment to a family. Young men from age 7 to 20 engaged in rigorous military training in boarding schools. They memorized heroic epics, but physical skills and discipline were far more important than literary abilities.

Girls received training in gymnastics, javelin throwing, and the like, though this was intended to toughen them for childbirth. Greeks from the more sophisticated and fractious city-state of Athens, including Plato and Aristotle, remarked approvingly about Sparta's way of raising children. Despots and antidemocrats through the centuries seeking a "perfect, changeless society" have desired the "simplicity and public spirit of the Spartans" (Sommerville, 1990, pp. 23–24).

Jewish Communities

Jewish culture in the millennium before Christ provides a view of a theocratic society that, like the philosophers of ancient Greece and Rome, was concerned with moral behavior. A crucial event for Jews occurred in 587 B.C., when they went into exile after the Babylonians destroyed the Temple. During the Babylonian exile, maintaining the faith, preserving cultural identity, and becoming an ethical person were all vital to a religious culture struggling to survive. "Religion became a matter of thought and reflection rather than ritual behavior" (Sommerville, 1990, p. 34). This differs from Greek and Roman education because of the stress on humans' relationship with God.

In Jewish society before the exile, the family was the primary educational unit. After the exile, when the scriptures were written in the adopted language of Aramaic, all boys had to attend school so that they could memorize the proverbs and religious laws. There developed a three-tiered educational system akin to present-day elementary, secondary, and higher education schools. Those fortunate enough advanced after age 15 to pursue Talmudic studies in rabbinical schools, which demanded in-depth readings of the scriptures in order to unveil spiritual truths and pursue a search for meaning. Teachers had a revered place in the society because teaching the holy laws was the highest calling. Education came to be seen not as a matter of how much knowledge one had gained, but as a matter of one's commitment to holiness, morality, and continual learning from Biblical texts—essential elements in preserving the Jewish culture.

Christian Communities

Early Christian communities focused on survival and spreading the faith. Clement, Origen, and Augustine developed the first Christian schools, which provided a blend of classics (Greek and Roman texts) and Christian religious texts. Christian schools housed in monasteries prepared students to understand the Bible and to be active members of the church, while training for the clergy. The curriculum for those fortunate enough to attend school in a monastery consisted of the trivium (grammar, dialectic, and rhetoric) and the quadrivium (geometry, arithmetic, music, and astronomy). Church educators attempted to meld parts of Western classical philosophy (especially Plato's idealism—see subsequent discussion) with their theocratic communitarian beliefs.

For nearly 15 centuries the Christian church was the primary deliverer of education in Europe, while political rulers engaged in war after war to extend their tenuous hold on the lands of Europe. Throughout the long Medieval period, educational philosophy and practice focused on spiritual virtue and a close adherence to church and local beliefs. Not until the Renaissance was there a rethinking of educational practices and philosophy in Europe.

Early American Schools: Communitarian Groups in North America

In 1619, the first slave ship to dock in the British colonies unloaded its human cargo in Virginia. Africans would create their own unique culture and would be the centerpiece of a human drama about whether the ideals of democracy included all people. Subsequently, in 1620 a small band of 102 Puritans seeking religious freedom rowed onto the shore at Plymouth, Massachusetts. By 1640 there would be 20,000 Puritan immigrants to "New England," and the foundations of an American educational system already would be under construction. This section describes how the Puritans and other European colonists conceived of education.

The Puritans. Puritans and other theocratic communal groups in the British colonies wanted to transmit knowledge of their religious faith. The schools emphasized cultural conformity and virtue, and continuity of the community's economic and occupational patterns. The Massachusetts School Act of 1647, quoted below, expressed the theocratic nature of Puritan society that would hold true for most European colonizers of America into the 19th century.

> It being one chief project of that old deluder, Satan, to keep men from the knowledge of the Scriptures, as in former times by keeping them in an unknown tongue, so in these latter times by persuading from the use of tongues. . . . It is therefore ordered, that every township in this jurisdiction, after the Lord hath increased them to the number of fifty householders, shall then forthwith appoint one within their town to teach all such children as shall resort to him to write and read, whose wages shall be paid either by the parents or masters of such children, or by the inhabitants in general. . . . and it is further ordered, that where any town shall increase to the number of one hundred families or householders, they shall set up a grammar school, the master thereof being able to instruct youth so far as they may be fitted for the university. . . . (Pulliam & Van Patten, 1995, p. 15)

Puritans held to a strong belief in sin, a fundamental distrust of Catholic ritual and the use of Latin (which had kept the Scriptures from most people), a hope that literacy and reading the Bible would allow their children to know the Scriptures, a demand that education be open to all, and a declaration that public schooling was a community responsibility. Puritans essentially rejected governmental democracy and did not tolerate diverse (to them, false) religions. In early Colonial societies, education and religion were not separable. The limited education that existed was intended to strengthen children's belief in God and church, and to ensure the survival of the community.

Colonial children of the 17th and 18th centuries were treated as miniature adults. At age 6–8 they began wearing adult clothing, engaging in the same family activities, and attending the same church services as adults. The child-rearing practices of Puritans were quite influential—and controversial. It is true that they practiced corporal punishment, and the word "Puritan" has assumed the negative cast of one who is completely intolerant and lives by the belief that if you "spare the rod" you "spoil the child." But much of the writing about how to raise children focused on providing an upbringing that was directed by love and consistency of response, not merely punishment. Puritans in America and England were prolific authors of picture books for children, though the books emphasized humans' sinful nature and the horrors of damnation. Famous Puritan preachers such as Jonathan Edwards bellowed their grim visions of life from the pulpits, while Puritans like William Gouge would counsel tenderness. It can be argued that the Puritans were trying to balance what they saw as the chaos of permissiveness with the harshness of an overly strict discipline.

Children, especially those of the poor, were often "binded out" to live for a time with another family as servants or apprentices, or for such reasons as the death of parents or unreconcilable domestic conflict. Childhood

How do you feel about colonial beliefs that children should dress and be treated like miniature adults? What are the advantages and disadvantages of such an approach?

was seen more as a time of ignorance than of innocence. Early education at home was focused on learning the alphabet and the skills of housework and farmwork. Until ages 6–10, children of both sexes attended "dame schools." A local woman would teach "the three R's" to small groups of children in her kitchen, often while doing chores and attending to babies. Students first learned how to read, then tackled writing, and finally studied arithmetic. Girls often stopped after learning how to read. If the parents were willing, children could then attend "writing school" and "grammar school," which was open only to boys. There is evidence that teaching was primarily done through recitations, when children would come one-by-one to the teacher's desk to recite verbatim from a text. Conditions in the schools were crude, and many schoolmasters routinely flogged or publicly humiliated students for the slightest infraction of the strict rules.

Colonial communities clung to the tradition that education was primarily a parental obligation, a private concern that required some public oversight. There was little formal schooling for the Colonial children of European settlers until the late 1600s. The family was a "school," "vocational institute," "church," "house of correction," and "welfare institution" (Demos, 1970, pp. 183–184). The Massachusetts School Act was passed about 350 years ago, but the Puritans' ideas of education exerted a powerful influence for most children in America until the late 19th century. The Middle Colonies and the South, however, developed somewhat different educational patterns than the New England Puritans.

Quakers and the inner light. Quakers and other religious dissenters leaving Europe settled throughout the Colonies, although Quakers settled in large numbers in Pennsylvania. Quakers believed that parents should be compelled to educate their children. Quaker faith was predicated on seeing an "inner light" and stressed a more individual approach to religion. Education had secular as well as spiritual aims. In 1685 Pennsylvania passed a law requiring elementary education for girls and boys so that they could read the Scriptures and write by the time they were age 12, when they would be taught some useful trade or skill. It was the Quakers also who first included Native Americans and freed slaves in their schools, because all were equal in God's eyes.

Conclusion

There are notable differences between early American educational thought, Jewish and Christian education, education in Sparta, traditional Confucian education, and education in a small African town. In the end, however, such societies share a belief that conformity to community values and cultural norms should be valued over individual autonomy. This usually resulted in a unity of purpose that late 20th-century societies may find *appealing* and a willingness to submit to authority that many people would find *appalling*.

IDEALS CHALLENGE: *Deepening Discourse*

Communitarian philosophies are based on the existence, acceptance, and promotion of a cohesive community.

- What is your "community"? What do you hold in common (especially your beliefs and customs) with the people in this community?
- Communitarian societies are marked by powerful oral traditions. What oral culture exists in your community, or elsewhere in our society?
- How do adults transmit their knowledge in your community? How do schools reflect communitarian tendencies?
- How is your community different from the communitarian societies just described?
- What are the strengths of communitarian societies? The weaknesses?
- Does a relationship exist between communitarian societies and democratic school communities? If so, explain the connection.

Western Classical Philosophy: How Do We Prepare Good Citizens?

Athenian and Roman thought about the education of young people represent a *Western classical* philosophy that differs in several fundamental ways from communitarian societies.

Greek Societies—Athens

The city-state of Athens had a long and turbulent history. The height of its cultural and military powers came during the classical period, around 400

B.C. In Athens, male children under age 7 were cared for by their mothers, mainly apart from men. Schools then became important for those who were not slaves or had not apprenticed at an early age. "Schooling was not compulsory, nor were schools organized or staffed by the community (though education was encouraged and schools were regulated by law); attendance was essentially a private matter between a boy's father or guardian and the teacher, an independent entrepreneur" (Golden, 1990, p. 62). Upper-class boys were assigned a *pedagogue,* a companion who accompanied them to school and exercised control over their behavior. Pedagogues were often slaves or men considered of little use to society.

The Athenian approach to education challenged the idea that students should learn only what reflected certain religious beliefs, formal examinations, or occupational knowledge. The free-born boys were schooled in reading and writing *(grammata),* athletics *(gymnastike),* music and poetry *(mousike),* and sometimes painting or drawing. Here is an example of Athenian education.

IDEALS CHALLENGE: *Deepening Discourse*

The following text is a fourth century B.C. description of the teaching of Diogenes the Cynic, a philosopher who had been captured by pirates, sold as a slave, and purchased by a Corinthian, to whose sons he became a tutor.

"After their other studies [primary education] he taught them to ride, to shoot with the bow, to sling stones and to hurl javelins. Later, when they reached the wrestling-school, he would not permit the instructor to give them full athletic training, but only so much as would heighten their complexion and keep them in good condition. The boys used to get by heart many passages from poets, historians and the writings of Diogenes himself; and he would practice them in all the quick ways to cultivate a good memory. In the house, too, he taught them to wait upon themselves, and to be content with plain fare and with water to drink. . . . He would also take them out hunting. They, for their part, had a great regard for Diogenes, and made requests of their parents in his favor" (Golden, 1990, p. 62).

- What were the most important skills in Greek society? What are the most important skills that students should learn today?
- What were the purposes of educating these boys? Why do we require that children today attend school?
- What aspects of the boys' education might we be missing in our own formal education?

In Athens, there was a constant struggle between those who wanted to create a democratic republic (in which only free-born males would be considered citizens) and those who supported a more autocratic approach like Spartan society. Athens and later societies that reflected a Western classical philosophy emphasized *individual enlightenment,* because self-knowledge and understanding of how and why the world operates the way it does were seen as worthy purposes for education. As Thomas Jefferson and others would argue 2,000 years later, Athenians who supported a republican form of government asserted that a democratic society required an edu-

How were schools in Athens similar to and different from our schools today? With which Athenian ideas do you agree?

cated citizenry. In Athens, male citizens debated openly about the best means of education; Sparta and other communitarian societies would not have countenanced such discussions about purpose or practice. At the same time, Athenian society embraced some of the aspects of communitarian societies, such as its focus on *civic virtue, political stability, economic continuity,* and *limited individual autonomy* for most people.

In practice, Athenian social and political systems were not challenged. Access to education was not open to slaves or the "lesser born." In spite of the few calls for educating Athenian girls, they were not educated outside the home and were considered minors all their lives. They had limited social contacts, and while they might participate in community choruses, they did not compete in athletic contests or other community events as did Spartan girls.

The contributions of major Athenian philosophers. Numerous Greek philosophers wrote about education, but here we focus on four of the most important: Protagoras, Socrates, Plato, and Aristotle. Each has influenced later educators, and remnants of their ideas still can be found in our schools.

Protagoras (c. 490–420 B.C.) was a Sophist philosopher. While traditional Athenian education had revolved around the family, Protagoras and other Sophists asserted that formal education was necessary if citizens were to make wise decisions about their future. His curriculum centered on managing one's personal affairs and participating in public affairs, and he thought that all men (not women) should have the chance to be educated.

In Protagoras' view, knowledge came through the senses and through practical action. In addition to the traditional purposes of transmitting cultural heritage and inculcating moral values (becoming virtuous), Protagoras and like-minded Greek educators believed that schooling should prepare leaders by teaching students how to reason clearly and speak persuasively.

Socrates (469–399 B.C.) was one of the great teachers of Athens, and a man who challenged prevailing orthodoxies or beliefs. He thought that knowledge developed through logic and reasoning, and that education should involve a question-and-response dialectic that has since come to be called the "Socratic method." Socrates was more concerned with whether people thought deeply than with the practical matters associated with the Sophists and the societal leaders.

Socrates was a complex man. On the one hand, he supported rule by an elite and not by a truly democratic government. He never considered schooling for everyone. He also was courageous and willing to stand up for what he believed. He was eventually convicted on a charge of corrupting the youth of Athens and then sentenced to death by a jury of Athenian citizens. Rather than renounce his ways of thinking or admit to any wrong, Socrates committed suicide by taking hemlock, a deadly poison.

Plato (428–347 B.C.) was one of Socrates' students. In his writings Plato paid homage to his mentor by describing dialogues between Socrates and young Athenian students, and these writings expanded and reshaped the ideas of Socrates. Like Socrates, Plato believed that the ultimate purpose of education was to discover truth in the form of abstract ideals that underlie our everyday sensory perceptions. Because of those philosophical beliefs, Plato and people who think like him have been called "idealists."

Plato held that children should be educated by the state and raised in public nurseries—which reminds us of the Spartan model. Unlike Socrates and the prevailing male sentiment, Plato argued that girls should receive the same education as males. This included military training, which was always a part of Greek education in those violent times. Like classical Confucianism, Plato wanted a lengthy process of education to cull out the most talented potential leaders, though he had no plan for systematic testing akin to the Chinese civil service examinations. Plato's curriculum focused on subjects such as mathematics, because it required the development of abstract thought. Most of the curriculum he espoused contained the common Greek mix of literacy, athletics, and the arts (especially music and poetry). The curriculum was intended to revolve around large concepts and ideas and not get lost in the thicket of facts and information.

Aristotle (384–322 B.C.) has been called a "realist" because of his interest in empirical investigation. Aristotle was Plato's student and he operated his own school, called the Lyceum. Like communitarian approaches, Aristotle thought that education should lead to "goodness" of action and to enhanced character. In accordance with Plato, Aristotle accepted the reality of ideal forms or properties (for example, the ideal of being "human"). Aristotle, however, believed that our understanding of such universal ideas, or of any broad concept or idea, was derived by examining material objects that exist independent of human thought. He believed that by carefully studying, categorizing, and engaging in careful reasoning about material aspects of life (what could be called a "scientific" approach to education), one can arrive at a deeper knowledge of ideas.

Methods of teaching in ancient Greece, however, did not square with the philosophical writings about democracy, ideal forms, and rational investigation of phenomena described above. Harsh discipline, including beatings, was the rule (*paideuo,* meaning "to teach," also means "I correct, I discipline"; Golden, 1990, p. 64). Schools emphasized courage and self-control as the marks of character. Good behavior was more important than academic skills.

In summary, Protagoras' approach to practical action, Socrates' approach to teaching, Plato's approach to curriculum, and Aristotle's approach to learning represented a wide-ranging attempt to seek truth and learn how to live in the world. The Athenian philosophy of education is the basis for Western classicism, which has had a powerful influence on European education—and education across the world since the 19th century.

Roman Society

Many of our notions of democracy and the workings of a republic are drawn from Rome, whose educational ideas largely were based on the Greeks. One of the enduring Roman approaches to education was laid out by *Quintilian* (A.D. 35–95). Quintilian was a Spanish-born teacher who was appointed to the first professorship in rhetoric in the Roman Empire. In *The Institutes of Oratory,* written toward the end of his life, Quintilian issued an appeal for a humane education that ran counter to his society and many others since then. To Quintilian, the goal of education should be that the student become a virtuous person, with skill in speech and knowledge of social affairs. He asserted that through supervised play as an infant, the child could learn valuable lessons. It was the teacher's job to know every student's talents and to treat the student with respect. Quintilian was opposed to corporal punishment, at a time when flogging was endemic in Roman schools. He thought that students needed the social interactions schools provided, although class sizes should be small to promote such interactions. Quintilian's ideas were quite well known by later educators, and he was quoted at length by da Feltre, Erasmus, Comenius, and others during the Renaissance.

The Renaissance

The Renaissance, which literally means "rebirth," signaled a revival of interest in Greek and Roman classical culture and an accompanying emphasis on human talents and accomplishments. First in 15th-century Italy and later in other European societies, there was a powerful push for economic expansion and artistic achievement.

Families, particularly aristocratic households, were changing. With economic prosperity came the building of larger houses and, ironically, an increased emphasis on the nuclear family. But the growing individualism represented by male artists and entrepreneurs did not extend to women and children. Writers sentimentalized children and painters depicted them as cherubs floating through the heavens. In truth, however, children were important "primarily as family heirs and not as individuals" (Sommerville, 1990, pp. 87–88). Many women gave their children to peasants to be wet-nursed and children often were neglected and passed to a series of stepmothers or relatives.

Just as art represented ideals often incommensurate with actual events in society, so the writing about education did not reflect changes in schools. Schools, for the few who attended them, emphasized hard work, routine, and a striving for excellence, rather than self-expression. Teachers still were drawn from the clergy, who largely maintained a rigid adherence to Biblical text. With some exceptions, teachers relied on physical punishment to enforce order and academic drill to ensure memorization. "All the prints we have of schoolrooms then show a switch, usually a bundle of twigs, either in the master's hand or within easy reach. Often we see it in use" (Sommerville, 1990, p. 94). Most educators had no intention of challenging prevailing orthodoxies.

The early 15th-century Italian Renaissance: Vittorino da Feltre. By the 15th century there were forces at work that would forever alter education. During Medieval times, the Arabs had discovered how to make paper. The first paper mill was established in Italy in 1276, and by the 15th century paper was widely used in Europe. This new resource, coupled with Gutenberg's invention of the printing press (the first complete book, the *Latin Bible,* was printed in 1456), enabled reading materials to be produced in great quantities. More people could read what they chose to, and the influence of monastic scholars and schools waned. Scribes in cloistered, candle-lit cells no longer would be solely responsible for saving and transmitting the cultural heritage. A few educators began to think more creatively about how to educate children.

One of the most famous schoolmasters of the period was *Vittorino da Feltre* (1378–1446), an Italian. He first taught children of the nobility and later worked to educate poor children. Da Feltre believed that the goal of schooling was to create a good citizen, who might become an orator or statesman. Virtue and moral character were the marks of this citizen. The school must be a community of learners and must accentuate the development of social conscience.

Through his emphasis on cultural norms and his love of abstract classical thought, da Feltre took a bow toward Greek and Roman traditions. However, da Feltre also was concerned with the individual learning of children. Self-improvement was one of the goals of schooling, and so instruction needed in some way to be individualized. The individual should be the standard for thought and conduct.

Like Aristotle, da Feltre emphasized that students need to learn through firsthand observation of the world. Physical activity, a chance to play, and a pleasant learning environment were crucial for the development of the child. Like Quintilian, da Feltre believed that learning should be enjoyable, and close contacts between students and teacher should be encouraged.

Reformation and the late Renaissance: The life of John Amos Comenius. Ideas of the Renaissance spread from Italy in the 16th century. One central question for Renaissance thinkers interested in changing education was how one could be both a Christian (associated with a communitarian philosophy) and a Humanist (associated with a Western classical philosophy). *John Comenius* (1592–1670) was a churchman and educator whose ideas in the late Renaissance were quite influential, and who tried to bridge both of the perspectives just noted. He was a member of the Unity of Brethren, a Moravian group that sought to emulate the life of early Christians by practicing a kind of Christian democracy. They were persecuted and sometimes burned at the stake for their pacifism and nonorthodox beliefs. Comenius was critical of the harsh manner in which he had been taught, and when he became a minister he instructed the congregation's children. For decades he led an itinerant life, dodging the constant chaos of the Thirty Years War between Catholics and Protestants. He moved from what is now the Czech Republic to England, France, Sweden, Hungary, and finally the Netherlands. Always he promoted his radical ideas of education as a lifelong process that might bring people together. In 1657, at the age of 65, he collected his life's writings. Many of the manuscripts were kept by a religious order in Germany and subsequently discovered in 1935 in an orphanage library—265 years after his death!

Comenius took da Feltre's efforts to educate the poor a step further by insisting that there be universal schooling. He issued a call to the warring churches of Europe to collaborate in providing a free primary education for all children regardless of ethnicity, gender, creed, social origin, or nationality. He believed that this international organization of education might lead to a fundamental reform of society.

For Comenius, schooling should serve larger moral and religious ends. The purpose of education was not individual self-consciousness, but knowledge of and adherence to religious and social norms: "to make men as like as possible to the image of God . . . truly rational and wise" (Piaget, 1957, p. 98).

Comenius also reflected the Renaissance concern with the individual. He was interested in the physical, mental, and emotional development of children. He asserted that schooling should be organized around four developmental stages or "schools of life": the School of Infancy (birth through age 6), the School of Childhood (ages 6–11), the School of Adolescence or Boyhood *(sic)* (ages 12–18), and Youth. Instruction should be geared to the child's age and maturational level. This developmental thinking, clearly stated in his rules and principles of teaching, has quite a modern ring to it. Comenius wanted students to engage in practical activities by manipulating objects in the environment. "It is the world which is our school," he said (Sucholdsky, 1970, p. 36). Positive encouragement of student learning should replace negative sanctions such as corporal punishment, this "in an age when the cane was a teaching instrument and the only school morality was a morality of obedience" (Piaget, 1957, p. 21).

The lives of da Feltre and Comenius encompass the Renaissance, early to late, southern to northern. One could argue that the Renaissance marked a turning point in Western conceptions of knowledge. Humanists moved away from a preoccupation with copying and transmitting traditional religious knowledge. Instead, humanist thinkers sought to adapt classical knowledge, as redefined by individuals. Learning about *the nature of the individual and the ideal* became important, as it had been to the Greeks. Yet, family bindings remained tight and the rhythms of village life carried on.

IDEALS CHALLENGE: *Initiating Inquiry*

The tension between Western classical ideas about individual enlightenment and communitarian ideas of socializing young people to cultural values, beliefs, and norms continues to exist in schools today.

- Identify and describe examples of the influence of each of these philosophies in schools today.
- Which philosophy more closely matches your philosophy of education?
- What are the advantages and disadvantages of the coexistence of the two philosophies in schools?
- As part of your field experiences in schools, gather data about further examples of the influence of these philosophies. Did your data and your analysis of it cause you to change your thinking in any way about your responses to the previous two questions?

What made the humanist educators so remarkable for any age was their insistence on the education of all children and their notions of the practical. They believed that formal schooling could help to enlighten children, not for the purpose of individual advancement but in order to promote civic and religious virtue. The path to enlightenment lay through individual striving within the limitations established by custom.

Even today, there are communitarian groups that live within modernized societies, struggling to maintain their traditional ways while somehow adapting to 21st-century life. Their situation is analogous to what people experienced throughout the Renaissance and Reformation, as humanists sought to balance the sacred and the secular, the social and the individual. The Global Challenge that follows is an example of what currently faces the Maori, the original inhabitants of New Zealand.

GLOBAL CHALLENGE *The Maori*

(Excerpted from Barrington, 1991, pp. 318–319, 321–322.)

Maori children remain disadvantaged in terms of overall educational achievement compared with Europeans. . . . In the 1960s and 1970s, explanations of underachievement were closely modeled upon American or English theories: the problem was seen as being located in the personality and home experience of Maori children—that is, outside schools. . . .

In more recent years, there has been a shift away from this "blaming the victim" approach to a much closer look at what is happening in schools and classrooms. Factors identified here as likely to impede the progress of Maori children include inadequate provision of the Maori language in schools . . . use of unsuitable tests and assessment methods . . . low expectations by teachers . . . curriculum content and organization which is inadequate or inappropriate . . . school climate and teaching styles . . . and monocultural European teachers.

Greater recognition of the importance of Maori language in schools had been a feature of curriculum change and is seen by many as likely to have a positive effect on self-concept and achievement. There are now 11 official bilingual schools and over 100 primary schools with bilingual classes (New Zealand Planning Council, 1989). Experience has shown that while many initial difficulties often must be overcome in establishing such programs, the results can be extremely positive. Teachers in one of the bilingual schools report that the children have greater self-esteem, their spoken and written Maori and English and their reading in both languages have improved, they are enthusiastic about being taught in Maori, and the school now has a better spirit. . . .

One approach has been to develop *whanaus* (small "schools within schools"), which provide students with greater opportunities for close interaction and the growth of a "caring family feeling." Maori language and culture courses now are taught in all teachers' training colleges, and multicultural courses are compulsory for all primary teacher trainees. The Department of Maori Affairs also has been active with schemes to assist Maori youth, promoting the *Tu Tangata* (stand tall) program. This program is designed to encourage ethnic pride and confidence through school visits by prominent Maoris and through visits to rural *maraes* [meeting grounds] by young Maoris in urban areas to acquaint them with traditional values and practices.

- How is the struggle between a communitarian philosophy and a Western classical philosophy evidenced in this excerpt about Maori schools?
- How is the situation of Maoris similar to that of Native Americans, African Americans, and Hispanics in the United States? How is it different?
- Why is language so important to communitarian groups such as the Maori? What do you think about the proposition that schools ought to teach students in both their first and second languages?
- As an educator, how do you think we could highlight the "traditional values and practices" of different cultural groups in classrooms and schools? What difficulties do we face in doing this?

Early American Schools: The Anglican South

Unlike New England and the Middle Colonies, which had been colonized by significant numbers of religious dissenters and where carrying on religious traditions was the primary purpose of schooling, the American South was dominated politically by English aristocrats and religiously by the state-sanctioned Anglican Church. What schooling there was in the Southern colonies took many forms and constituted a blend of communitarian and Western classical approaches to educating children. Additionally, schooling reflected a rigid social hierarchy. Socioeconomic status, and thus access to education, was largely inherited.

The children of wealthy southern plantation owners received an elementary education from tutors brought to the home and a secondary education from tutors or in academies. Sons were sent to college, often in Europe, in order to learn law and politics, to become skillful at land management, or to receive religious training. Daughters attended "finishing schools" to learn refinement. The sons of ministers, merchants, small planters, and shopkeepers were able to attend secondary academies while the daughters had to be content with an elementary education. The

IDEALS CHALLENGE: *Initiating Inquiry*

Characteristics of Communitarian and Western Classical Philosophies

COMMUNITARIAN GOALS:	WESTERN CLASSICAL GOALS:
Cultural virtue	Civic virtue
Political stability	Individual enlightenment
Economic continuity	Political stability/economic continuity

TIME PERIOD	SOCIETIES	CHARACTERISTICS OF EDUCATION	MODERN ECHOES
	(Theorists)	**(Major goals, curricular emphases, and ways of teaching)**	**(How might this philosophy still influence our schools—"the echoes in the hallways"?)**
Since ancient times	Traditional societies in Africa and North America	• Mainly oral culture • Emphasis on spirituality and respect for elders • Preparing to learn the local customs, apprenticing for the same jobs as parents • Nonformal and communal approach to teaching	
Since ancient times	China (Confucius)	• Oral and written culture • Preparing elite classes for leadership • National examinations and a form of meritocracy • Tutoring and memorization	
8th century B.C. to 323 B.C.	Sparta	• Unquestioning devotion to the state • Preparing to be a warrior (males) or a wife and mother (females) • Apprenticeship and tutoring	
6th century B.C. to 323 B.C.	Athens (Protagoras, Socrates, Plato, Aristotle)	• Attempt to seek truth and live virtuously • Preparing to reason logically, argue persuasively, and participate in civic matters (for males) • Curricular focus on literacy, athletics, and the arts • Apprenticeship and tutoring	
3rd century B.C. to A.D. 476	Roman Empire (Quintilian, Cicero)	• Similar to Greeks • Curricular focus on oratory and practical application of what is learned	
Since 538 B.C. (the return from exile)	Communitarian Jews (also influenced by Western classical ideas)	• Curricular focus on maintaining the faith, preserving cultural identity, and becoming an ethical person • For some boys, preparing to be learned rabbis • Curricular focus on understanding the Scriptures	
Since 1st century A.D.	Communitarian Christians (also influenced by Western classical ideas)	• Similar focus to communitarian Jews • For some boys, preparing to be ministers • In more recent communitarian Christians (like the Puritans and the Mennonites), a focus on formal literacy for all	
14th–17th centuries	Renaissance and Reformation in Europe (da Feltre, Erasmus, Comenius)	• Strongly influenced by Western classical philosophies and by communitarian beliefs • Emphasis on individual learning and self-expression, and on a practical curriculum • Calls for universal schooling	

- This table provides an overview of the characteristics of communitarian and Western classical philosophies as played out in various cultures and societies. On a separate sheet of paper, complete the "Modern Echoes" section of the table with ways you think the philosophy of each culture or society might still influence schools today.

children of artisans and poor shopkeepers, people with a small income and no servants, received a primary education or went into apprenticeships. The few children of nonelite families who had access to education attended "old field schools" (primitive buildings erected in the midst of a fallow agricultural field), while in some areas there were charity schools run by the Anglican Church to permit poor children to learn the rudiments of reading and arithmetic.

As in some other regions of the Colonies, a large segment of the southern population was left standing outside the schoolhouse door. Farmers working small plots of land in isolated areas far from the coastal lowlands usually had no access to schools or tutors. By halfway through the 18th century, slavery had become a powerful socioeconomic institution that would shape the South's history. For example, in Virginia in 1708 there were approximately 12,000 slaves; by 1763 there were perhaps 120,000 (Heslep, 1969, p. 12). Slaves, who were widely considered inferior to Europeans, and conquered Native Americans, who were simply a hindrance to the acquisition of land, were not allowed to be publicly schooled. Numerous pauper children who were orphaned, neglected, or dirt poor, regardless of ethnicity, remained illiterate.

Liberal Philosophy: How Do We Educate Children to Reach Their Potential?

Few educators of the Colonial period had linked education with political or social change or concerned themselves with questions about universal education. It would take a revolution before new questions about the purposes of schooling would be raised.

1787–1837: The Rise of Liberal Thought in a New Republic

On September 17, 1787, the U.S. Constitution was signed by its framers after an intense summer of political and philosophical wrangling in Philadelphia. In that same year, the Northwest Ordinance was enacted, which was the precursor to a universal, free public school system governed by local authorities and supported by federal involvement. Liberal philosophies in both politics and education lay behind these significant events.

Liberal is a word that commonly is misinterpreted because it is taken out of its historical context. There are three meanings of the word that relate to education. From a Western classical point of view, Aristotle talked about the "liberal and illiberal arts." "Liberal" in this case meant subjects of study that provide a more intellectual and artistic understanding of the world, those suitable for free citizens who do not have to perform manual labor or consider practical applications. A second, related meaning arose from the Athenian definition of "liberal" as broad-minded, tolerant of other ways of thinking or acting. A third meaning is connected with political thinking and has strongly influenced education. Liberal ideas arose in the Renaissance and Reformation periods in Europe, when some people expressed opposition to aristocratic control of governmental and economic power, and many people seriously opposed control of religious power by one church. Subsequently, in the 18th and 19th centuries, a liberal philosophy entailed a belief in individual rights and of the consent of the governed.

Liberal thinkers of this era had diverse views that incorporated communitarian and Western classical ideas. They tended to support the prevailing societal ideas of virtue and character, and the classical curriculum remained dominant in the schools. At the same time, they called for political autonomy, but were uninterested in seriously reforming the economic system (especially the plantation economy based on slavery). Though there was certainly a call for societal reform (there had been, after all, a revolution to rid the American Colonies of British aristocratic rule), there was little push to reform a system that allowed some children to attend college in England while others never attended a day of formal school.

The *Enlightenment* was the movement of that era that was associated with a liberal philosophy. The Enlightenment embodied a shift toward individualism and away from the religious communalism of groups such as the Puritans. To be enlightened was not simply to know God's will, but to know how to realize one's potential as a person. The path to this personal enlightenment lay through rational thought and practical action. John Locke and Benjamin Franklin were two of the major Enlightenment figures who wrote about education.

John Locke (1632–1704) was an 18th-century philosopher whose ideas profoundly affected scientific inquiry and educational thinking. According to Locke, government is the "product of human contrivance," and its function should be to ensure citizens' "natural rights." Government is only legitimated by "the rational contractual consent of the free" who are securing their personal interests (Pulliam & Van Patten, 1995, pp. 37–38). This new "liberal" view of politics differed from the classical view that government—and education—should cultivate virtue. Unlike classical republicans, Locke believed that morality and religion are not the legitimate concern of government. Likewise, education is not a duty of government, but the duty of parents.

According to Locke's ideas of learning, the child's mind is a "tabula rasa," a blank slate. Knowledge originates in sensory perceptions, and it is human reflection and the ability to reason that create ideas. This means that human differences emerge from experience, including formal and informal educational experiences. Educators, then, should concern themselves with the impact of the environment on the individual child. Locke's ideal was a private education at home (for males only), with a parent and tutor presiding. Because he held that human nature was malleable and not fully determined by inborn traits, Locke was especially concerned with infancy and childhood.

Benjamin Franklin (1706–1790) was an Enlightenment philosopher who acted on the political, scientific, and educational stages of Colonial and post-Colonial America during a long and wondrous life. Franklin promoted the public discussion of ideas by founding the American Philosophical Society for Promoting Useful Knowledge. One of the questions that potential members of the society were asked was: "Do you love truth for truth's sake?" "Truth" for Franklin could be ascertained by reasoning and by using the methods of science. His was a worldly truth, a secular enlightenment. Following upon Locke, Franklin expressed a belief in the power of human reason to solve social problems and saw schooling as a means to teach reasoning. Unlike Locke, Franklin focused on teachers in schools and not on tutors as the purveyors of knowledge. He wanted to educate an elite of young people for public service.

Franklin was not concerned with schooling all children. He supported some combination of charity schools for the poor and scholarships for less fortunate students to attend the secondary academies. His academy was intended to educate talented young men for civic office because he felt that education can lead to a "general virtue," an improved society. To that end, he focused the curriculum on a study of practical matters. He wanted to promote "useful knowledge."

Franklin also saw education as a means of self-fulfillment, as a path to individual virtue. This thinking was an extension of the Renaissance humanists' emphases on self-improvement and the needs of individual children. Each individual has a unique temperament and set of abilities. Scientific experimentation and a strong grounding in history and philosophy can enable students to utilize these mental capacities. Franklin subscribed, as had Locke, to the notion that subjects such as mathematics can develop habits of using the mind—that they are forms of "mental exercise." Though he had little faith in most schools of his time, Franklin possessed a great faith in education and schooling as a means of learning how to reason, and thus to attain individual and civic virtue.

While Enlightenment ideas coexisted uneasily with theocratic education, Jean-Jacques Rousseau (1712–1778) and other Europeans issued a challenge to traditional religion and to rationality such as that proposed by Locke and Franklin. Rousseau espoused radical ideas, and he was uninterested in holding down a regular job, so he was constantly harassed by religious and civil authorities. He offered up a vision of "romanticism" that was to be, in terms of its general sentiments, influential for centuries after his tortured life ended.

> We are born weak, we need strength; helpless, we need aid; foolish, we need reason. All that we lack at birth, all that we need when we come to man's estate, is the gift of education. This education comes to us from nature, from men, or from things. . . . Forced to combat either nature or society, you must make your choice between the man and the citizen, you cannot train both. (Dobinson, 1970, p. 71)

Right away, we see Rousseau's emphasis on natural development, and his barely concealed distaste for the "citizen." He was distrustful of society, especially society's impact on children below the age of 12. His book *Emile* depicted how boys should grow up far from the restrictive realms of society. (Rousseau thought girls should adhere to the feminine roles and domestic jobs that were widely thought to be suited to their sex.)

> The mind should be left undisturbed 'til its faculties have developed; for while it is blind it cannot see the torch you offer it. . . . Therefore the education of the earliest years should be merely negative. It consists not in teaching virtue or truth, but in preserving the heart from vice and from the spirit of error. . . . Exercise his body, his limbs, his senses, his strength, but keep his mind idle as long as you can. (Dobinson, 1970, pp. 81–82)

With which of Rousseau's ideas do you agree? With which do you disagree? Why?

Rousseau's antisocial sentiments are overstated, but his beliefs in understanding children's (boys') development and basing education on that understanding have a modern ring. You can see the connections between Rousseau's thinking and subsequent educators' desires to provide children with interesting experiences and to refrain from pushing children too quickly into academic work.

Mary Wollstonecraft (1759–1797) was a British writer who intermingled Enlightenment and Romantic thinking about education and gender. She is most famous for penning *The Rights of Woman* in 1792. She stated that females were in a "state of degradation" due to limited education, lack of access to other societal institutions, and prevailing opinion. The popular thinking in the late 18th century was that women were not supposed to reason as men did. The belief was that women's arena was the home and their strength was a "sensibility," an affective approach toward life. Wollstonecraft's focus was on the self-education of women and the need to question these debilitating stereotypes.

Wollstonecraft challenged Rousseau's writing on romanticism by emphasizing the rationality of women and calling for rigorous coeducational schooling. While she opposed Rousseau's portrayal of women in *Emile,* she agreed with some of his educational ideas. The child should be allowed to "unfold" naturally in order to integrate reason and feeling, which is the sort of "non-interventionist" approach favored by Rousseau and later by the Swiss educator Pestalozzi.

Wollstonecraft also reflected the social order of her day. Even in the new education for womanhood, virtue would be a primary aim. For example, she held that after age 9 schools should be tracked according to probable future occupation, thus perpetuating the systems of economic privilege.

IDEALS CHALLENGE: *Learning Leadership*

Another woman who reflected Mary Wollstonecraft's combination of traditional sentiments and rational challenge to a male-dominated society was Emma Hart Willard (1787–1870). Willard was a pioneer in women's education. As a young woman she taught in female academies and then opened the Troy Female Seminary, the first college for women in the United States. Women who graduated from Troy became teachers, at a time when there was no special preparation to teach. Willard worked tirelessly to improve teacher education and teaching in the early common schools, and she authored a number of history textbooks. In the following excerpt, Willard describes teaching in a boarding school in Vermont (1997, pp. 45–46).

When I began my boarding school in Middlebury, in 1814, my leading motive was to relieve my husband from financial difficulties. I had also the further object of keeping a better school than those about me; but it was not until a year or two after, that I formed the design of effecting an important change in education, by the introduction of a grade of schools for women, higher than heretofore known.... I began to write "an address to the—Legislature, proposing a plan for improving Female Education." ...

My exertions, meanwhile, became unremitted and intense. My school grew to seventy pupils. I spent from ten to twelve hours a day in teaching.... Hence every new term some new study was introduced; and in all their studies, my pupils were very thoroughly trained.... During this first part of the process, I talked much more than the pupils were required to do, keeping their attention awake by frequent questions, requiring short answers from the whole class—for it was ever my maxim, if attention fails, the teacher fails. Then in the second stage of my teaching, I made each scholar recite, in order that she might *remember*—paying special attention to the meaning of words, and to discern whether the subject was indeed understood without mistake. Then the *third* process was to make the pupil capable of *communicating.* And doing this in a right manner, was to prepare her for examination.... At this time I personally examined all my classes.

The professors of the college attended my examinations; although I was by the President advised, that it would not be becoming in me, nor be a safe precedent, if I should attend theirs.... But I had full faith in the clear conclusions of my own mind.

- How does this school reflect a Western classical philosophy?
- How could the school, and Willard's educational ideas, be seen as a liberal approach?
- How does Willard's job as a teacher in 1814 appear to differ from teaching today?
- Which democratic IDEALS did her approach support?
- Discuss the leadership aspects of Willard's work. How was she a leader as a woman? As an educator? As a teacher in the school/classroom?

In summary, liberal thinking of this era supported *civic virtue* and *individual enlightenment, economic continuity,* certain sorts of *political change,* and *individual autonomy.* The Enlightenment emphasized creating knowledge through science. Locke and Franklin believed that reason could guide students to enlightenment about the workings of the world and about how one ought to attain virtue. Rousseau and Wollstonecraft portrayed the interplay of Enlightenment rationality and a growing Romantic sentiment. Emma Hart Willard heralded the rise of women as teachers, and reflected the 19th-century blend of Western classical and liberal thinking. Except for Rousseau, who distrusted society so much that he would delay formal schooling until adolescence, all of these people expressed support for individual liberty and a great faith in the power of formal education to effect positive changes in children. In that sense, regardless of their differences, they shared a common faith.

IDEALS CHALLENGE: *Initiating Inquiry*

The central thesis of this book is that students should be educated for democracy. In chapter 1, we discussed the IDEALS of democratic education: inquiry, discourse, equity, authenticity, shared leadership, and service. Now that you have read about communitarian, Western classical, and liberal philosophies of education, assess their fit with the IDEALS of democratic education. Specifically, which of the IDEALS are congruent with each of the philosophies? Which are incongruent? Provide support for your answers. The table below provides a framework for your task.

IDEALS	COMMUNITARIAN	WESTERN CLASSICAL	LIBERAL
Inquiry			
Discourse			
Equity			
Authenticity			
Leadership			
Service			

HOW DID DEMOCRATIC PURPOSES FOR EDUCATION DEVELOP IN THE UNITED STATES?

After the Revolutionary War and particularly the passage of the Constitution and the Bill of Rights, the purposes of education in the United States needed to be redefined. A democratic government by the people and for the people required a citizenry that was knowledgeable, questioning, and proactive. The Northwest Ordinance of 1787 stated it as follows: "Religion, morality, and knowledge, being necessary to good government and the happiness of mankind, schools and the means of education shall forever be encouraged" (Tyack, 1987, p. 20).

People believed that the absence of formal education was related to, and perhaps a cause of, social problems. Although it would be at least another five decades before the South and West experienced some of these conditions, in New England during the 1820s–1840s, citizens expressed concern about the effects of population growth, manufacturing, urbanization, and poverty. Education was seen as a means of stabilizing society by creating an educated citizenry capable of participating in public problem solving and of electing political leaders, who were adept problem-solvers and had the interests of the common good in mind.

The problem was that there was no mechanism in place in this country to establish a system of public education. As you will read in chapter 8, the U.S. Constitution does not directly address education. There were federal ordinances, though, that helped the cause of public education. For example, the Land Ordinance of 1785 stipulated that revenue from the sale of a one-mile-square lot in each township should be devoted to maintaining a public primary school. There were no provisions for funding of public schools through taxation, but the ordinance paved the way for local and state funding of public education. The subsequent Northwest Ordinance of 1787 attempted to integrate the old with new regions of the country (i.e., Michigan, Wisconsin, Illinois, Indiana, and Ohio) and provide for an orderly expansion of the nation's territory by stipulating that "lot No. 16 of every township" be reserved "for the maintenance of public schools." Since basic education was not a federal mandate in the U.S. Constitution, land policies were a way to influence state and local leaders to support public education.

Through the years, however, land policies as the sole means of funding public education were generally ineffective. School reformers wanted to divide responsibility for funding schools not only between local, county, and state governments, but also wanted parents to share funding responsibility. Public school proponents of the time faced severe problems when they tried to pass funding laws for schools, because the wealthy sent their children to private academies and most citizens opposed increased taxes to support public enterprises of any kind. To fund schools, communities relied on "rate bills," which were school charges based on the number of days the child attended school. Parents low on money opted to have their children stay home rather than pay a higher rate bill.

In order for a change in school financing and community support to occur, people had to believe that everyone had a stake in local common schools, and that there was a social responsibility to support them. Radicals in the French Revolution had already proposed compulsory universal schooling, as did Samuel Knox and others in the United States in the late 1790s. Such efforts largely failed during the first half of the 19th century. The first compulsory attendance law in the United States was passed in 1852 (in Massachusetts, the leader in many policy matters), and by 1900 many, but not all, states had such laws on the books. With public schooling becoming more universal in this country, the question remained, however, of what constitutes an education for democracy.

Key Proponents of Democratic Education

What sort of education promoted democratic citizenship? What sort of education was "necessary to good government" mentioned in the Northwest Ordinance of 1787? How do you integrate continuing communitarian impulses to promote religion and cultural virtue with democratic needs for knowledge, inquiry, questioning, and equity? Many educational leaders of the time (and of our time as well!) felt that education should be more concerned with civic virtue and loyalty to the republic than with inquiry, questioning, literacy, and other academic skills. Some called for a Spartan model of education, while others wanted to promote classical learning without importing the authoritarian overtones. John Locke had offered a "trickle-down" theory of education: the clergy and the upper classes would be transformed, which would gradually change the economic opportunities in society and lead to higher educational attainment for the masses of citizens. There were several key figures in the movement toward a mass system of public schools focused on educating students for democracy.

Thomas Jefferson (1743–1826) was a central character because he wanted to extend educational opportunity and clearly defined its purpose in the new republic. His life reflected a clash of ideals and practices, legislative victories and defeats, that even today can be informative for us.

It is essential to understand that for Jefferson, educational practice should reflect political ideas and ideals. He read widely in philosophy, history, law, and the sciences, and he held that moral education was not bound by religious tenets. Jefferson accepted Locke's philosophy of natural rights and laws. People had a right to belong to a society of their choice and to govern themselves (that is, if they were male, free, and owned property). But they would only be able to govern wisely if enough people were educated to be knowledgeable and responsible citizens. Jefferson believed that the purposes of education should be to enhance private happiness and to promote successful self-government by enabling society's most gifted citizens to lead. He wanted the poor to understand their rights and to participate in government, which can be seen as a step forward from classical republican beliefs that ignored the lower classes. He wanted less "religious indoctrination" but more "civic instruction" and "utilitarian studies" (Heslep, 1969, p. 51).

Jefferson's first political effort to influence educational practice came in 1779, when he proposed a Bill for the Diffusion of General Knowledge for the state of Virginia. The bill was eventually defeated, but is illustrative of Jefferson's beliefs about democratic education. It would have created a system of primary schools free to all white children in Virginia, in which they would take arithmetic, geography, and history. Reading, writing, and moral study would be incorporated into the three basic subjects. Secondary schools, whose curriculum would be a mix of classical and utilitarian studies, would offer scholarships to the most qualified students from poor families across the state. He did not think secondary school was appropriate for females or for many nonelite males, because not all students in a republic were entitled to the same educational opportunities. There should be a social order based on merit, not "family, wealth, military prowess, popularity, race, and religion" (Heslep, 1969, p. 120). College would be free to the best students in the state, regardless of economic background. The Virginia legislature was controlled by the planter aristocracy whose children attended elite private schools. They were adamantly opposed to public taxation for schools that most of their children would not attend and thus ensured that Jefferson's bill was defeated.

From 1781–1809, Jefferson busied himself serving in political offices, but in 1817 he again advanced a bill proposing a system of public education—38 years after his first bill! It was similar to the one in 1779, only it also created a public university, the University of Virginia. Other states such as Georgia and North Carolina had created state universities decades earlier, but Jefferson's plans were unique. He wanted to establish diverse courses in different schools within the university and permit students to choose what courses they would take. This time, the university idea was approved but Jefferson's ideas for the other two levels of education were found unacceptable. The IDEALS Challenge that follows offers you a chance to read some of Jefferson's ideas from his report to the Virginia legislature in 1818. Even though his plea for a free primary education had been rebuffed, he insisted on describing what was needed.

IDEALS CHALLENGE: *Examining Equity*

(Excerpted from Jefferson, 1982, pp. 395–396.)

The objects of this primary education determine its character and limits. These objects would be,

To give to every citizen the information he needs for the transaction of his own business;

To enable him to calculate for himself, and to express and preserve his ideas, his contracts and accounts, in writing;

To improve, by reading, his morals and faculties;

To understand his duties to his neighbors and country, and to discharge with competence the functions confided to him by either;

To know his rights; to exercise with order and justice those he retains; to choose with discretion the fiduciary of those he delegates; and to notice their conduct with diligence, with candor, and judgment;

And, in general, to observe with intelligence and faithfulness all the social relations under which he shall be placed.

To instruct the mass of our citizens in these, their rights, interests and duties, as men and citizens, being then the objects of education in the primary schools, whether private or public, in them should be taught reading, writing and numerical arithmetic, the elements of mensuration (useful to so many callings), and the outlines of geography and history.

- Who might Jefferson include in his idea of "citizen"? Who might not be included?
- What aspects of Jefferson's ideal curriculum for primary school students do we teach now? What don't we teach? Why don't we teach it?
- What is missing from Jefferson's curriculum?
- Looking back at your responses to the previous questions, in what ways would Jefferson's ideas promote or not promote equity in a society?

While Jefferson advocated for education *for* democracy in the United States, Johann Pestalozzi, a Swiss educator, was promoting many of the child-centered practices that we believe are essential in schools that are both *for* democracy and function *as* democracies.

Johann Pestalozzi (1746–1827) was perhaps the most famous educator of the time. He was a schoolmaster who late in life achieved fame for his school at Yverdon in Switzerland, where he taught from 1805–1825. Pestalozzi concurred with Rousseau that the child is innately good and that society often corrupts the child's nature. Pestalozzi used the metaphor of the child as a bud not yet opened. Our job as teachers is to help the bud to

Which of Pestalozzi's ideas are consistent with schools *as* democracies and schools *for* democracy?

unfold, to allow the natural course of development to take place. Like Rousseau, Pestalozzi spoke of the importance of nurturance for young children during the process of unfolding. He perceived the school as a family, wherein there existed mutual love between teacher and student. Pestalozzi wanted desperately to improve the lot of the poor. He believed that the practical goal of education should be to benefit all people for whatever function they had in society.

Borrowing from da Feltre, Comenius, Locke, Franklin, and Rousseau, Pestalozzi upheld the value of practical activities in school. Taking Locke one step further, he held that the mind is not passive, but is an analytical force. One should not depend on rote memorization and mental training. Pestalozzi focused on learning by discovery, and saw learning as an individual mental interaction with objects in the environment. Instruction should consist of "object teaching," that is, teaching children how to "observe, analyze, compare, and count objects."

IDEALS CHALLENGE: *Initiating Inquiry*

The central thesis of this book is that students should be educated for democracy. In chapter 2, we discussed the practices of democratic education. See if you can identify dimensions of philosophies or aspects of the thinking of the individuals about whom you have read in this chapter that may have served as "foundations" for the practices discussed in chapter 2. The following table provides a framework for your task.

Practices	Philosophies/ Individuals	Foundational Aspects/Dimensions
Shared Value Systems		
Authentic Pedagogy		
Critical Study		
Shared Decision Making		
Internal/External Support		
Moral/Professional Community		

Johann Pestalozzi and his followers had a large effect on writing and theorizing about education, but a negligible immediate effect on day-to-day life in most schools. There was little effort made to educate teachers about the "new educational gospel."

WHO HAD ACCESS TO EDUCATION FOR DEMOCRACY?

By the early 1800s formal education was seen as "an indispensable instrument of popular sovereignty, an intellectual resource against tyranny" (Welter, 1971, p. lvii). While public schooling began to be linked with the concept of a democratic citizenry and the maintenance of democratic institutions, schools and other institutions of that time had complex views of children and females, and rarely included African Americans and Native Americans. The republican revolutionaries espoused a more egalitarian society, but only Franklin and some other northerners wanted to educate African Americans, and Thomas Jefferson and John Adams were among the few founders to propose a public primary school system for all children. It was unclear for whom education for democracy would be democratic.

Women

There were conflicting conceptions of women and children in the new republic. Children were portrayed as either innocent *or* wicked; either in need of protection *or* ready at an early age for adult responsibilities. John Locke's belief in environmental effects on intelligence, like Rousseau's emphasis on "natural development," had pulled the underpinnings from many educators' conceptions of children as sinful and almost willfully ignorant. In the view of many of the republic's founders, children were seen as prospective citizens.

Women were also seen in conflicting ways. Emma Hart Willard notwithstanding, they were often thought *rationally* inferior to men, yet *morally* at least their equal. It was commonly believed that the early education of children ought to be carried out by mothers in the new republic. The "cult of motherhood" focused on women's place in raising democratically inclined citizens, but did not call for women to participate in that democracy—to be enfranchised to vote or to be given equal rights. As a result, most girls continued to work in the home or "board out" at an early age, and most women took it as their duty (and sole choice) to raise good citizens.

Native Americans

Earlier in this chapter you read about the traditional communitarian ways of Native Americans. The invading European Americans of the 18th and 19th centuries tended to value strict discipline of children, property as a private good, the accumulation of wealth, and formal schooling, all of which differed from Native Americans. These cultural clashes were accompanied by European American leaders' belief in the "manifest destiny" of the country to spread across the entire continent. Governmental relationship with Native Americans evolved from a measured coexistence in the 17th century to a sense of superiority in tune with the 18th-century European fixation on assigning physical and mental characteristics to peoples of different ethnic groups and nationalities. Native Americans might indeed be "noble," but they were still "savages."

Native Americans were either left alone or enjoined to attend missionary schools. Christian missionaries had long operated in "Indian Territory," working under the premise that the natives needed to be saved and taught how to read and write in English. The Civilization Fund Act of 1819 provided $10,000 to pay for federal contracts with missionary societies so that they could operate Indian schools. Missionary schools were intended to assimilate the Native Americans, to teach them about Western ways. Southern tribes, however, continued to live on lands coveted by settlers moving west, and so in 1830 the Indian Removal Act required all Native Americans to move west of the Mississippi River, into "Indian Territory" (modern day Texas and Oklahoma). Some peoples, such as the Cherokees, held out until being forcibly moved west in 1838. Thousands of Native Americans died during these long and brutal treks, and the route came to be called the "Trail of Tears." After this time there would be less emphasis on missionaries and more on federal government intervention, especially when the reservation system was created in the 1850s.

African Americans

It seems ironic to use the term "African *American,*" since slaves in the antebellum South had no rights of citizenship at all, and black people in areas outside the South faced routine segregation and discrimination. Some southern spokesmen even questioned whether public education and democracy were compatible and believed that certainly they were not if democracy entailed educating people of African descent. Nevertheless, until the 1830s there were freed slaves and sympathetic whites in the South who found a way to teach them, and we have a few glimpses of what they did. For example, a Frenchman named Julien Froumontaine opened a school for "Free Negroes" in Savannah, Georgia, sometime around 1818 or 1819 (Du Bois, 1992, p. 644). After the Nat Turner Rebellion occurred in 1831 in Virginia, however, laws were passed in every southern state making the education of African Americans illegal, and schools such as Froumontaine's were closed. In the IDEALS Challenge that follows, Daniel Payne (1997), a free black man from Charleston, South Carolina, who opened his own school in 1830, describes his efforts to teach in the school. Payne went on to become a bishop in the African Methodist Episcopal Church and was later the president of Wilberforce University. He was the first African American to be a college president in the United States.

IDEALS CHALLENGE: *Achieving Authenticity*

(Excerpted from Payne, 1997, pp. 59–61.)

On the first of the year 1830 I re-opened my school, which continued to increase in numbers until the room became too small, and I was constrained to procure a more commodious place. This in turn became too small, and one was built for me on Anson Street. . . . Here I continued to teach until April, 1835.

I had a geography class, but had never seen an atlas, and, what was more, I knew not how or where to get one. Fortunately for me, one day as I was sitting on the piazza endeavoring to learn some lesson, a woman entered the gate and approached me with a book in her hand. Said she: "Don't you want to buy this book?" Taking it, I opened it, and to my great joy I beheld the colored maps of an atlas—the very thing I needed. . . . Immediately I went to work with my geography and atlas, and in about six months was able to construct maps on the Mercator's and globular projection. After I had acquired this ability I introduced geography and map-drawing into my school. At the same time with geography I studied and mastered English grammar. I began with "Murray's Primary Grammar," and committed the entire book to memory, but did not understand it; so I reviewed it. . . . I then made a second review of it, and felt conscious of my power to teach it.

My researches in botany gave me a relish for zoology; but as I could never get hold of any work on this science. I had to *make* books for myself. This I did by killing such insects, toads, snakes, young alligators, fishes, and young sharks as I could catch. I then cleaned and stuffed those that I could, and hung them upon the walls of my school-room. . . . My enthusiasm was the inspiration of my pupils. I used to take my first class of boys into the woods every Saturday in search of insects, reptiles, and plants, and at the end of five years I had accumulated some fine specimens of each of these. . . . My school increased in popularity, and became the most popular of five which then existed. It numbered about sixty children from most of the leading families of Charleston.

- What do you think Payne saw as the purposes of education?
- Why does Payne spend time describing what and how he learned? In what ways is his teaching "authentic"?
- Does his way of teaching remind you of educational experiences you have had? How is it similar or different?

TECHNOLOGY CHALLENGE

Parents and Technology in the Last 100 Years

(*Adapted from* The Parents' Guide to the Information Superhighway *(2nd ed.), 1998, Washington, DC: The Children's Partnership.*)

1890s	How can I afford a telephone at home?
1900s	Why do my children know more about automobiles than I do?
1910s	Should I take my children to the moving pictures?
1920s	Why do my children know more about radio than I do?
1930s	Are radio programs too violent?
1940s	Are comic books a bad influence on my kids?
1950s	Is TV good for my child—or not?
1960s	What are my children learning from rock 'n' roll?
1970s	Are TV programs too violent?
1980s	Is my child playing too many video games?
1990s	Is being online safe and beneficial for my child?

- Discuss parents' concerns over the past century. Do you recognize any trends?
- What concerns might parents have about technology in the future?
- Do you agree or disagree with this statement: "It isn't the technology, it's the way people use the technology that makes the difference." Provide support for your belief.

SUMMARY

There are many similarities among past educators' ideas about schooling. In most societies, civic virtue, political stability, and economic continuity were paramount purposes. We can think of this as the impulse to *conform*. There were two main reasons for this conformity: people in small communities generally held strong religious beliefs about the right way to act or think, and the ruling elites wanted to maintain their powerful economic and political positions in their communities.

In societies that enacted Western classical philosophies of education, there was a strong push to conform, but alongside that grew the impulse to *inform* and to be informed. The Greek and Roman philosophers had emphasized reasoning and the ability to inform oneself, to think deeply. For an elite literate group, that came to mean reciting the classic texts and having the ability to write.

The Enlightenment spurred two major movements in the 18th and early 19th centuries, from which a liberal philosophy of education arose, a philosophy whose impulse was to *transform*. One was the democratic movement that led to the American Revolution, the creation of the Constitution, and the development of laws and policies to support education. The question asked after the revolution was: *What does it mean to be educated as a democratic citizen?* The answer to the question was quite complex. On the one hand, individual enlightenment and scientific knowledge were necessary. Many innovative educators of the time believed in the importance of first-hand observations of the world through practical activities. It was seen as essential that teachers focus on the individual development of students' abilities. There are many ideas about democratic schooling that are included in this book and other sources that grew out of the work of Comenius, da Feltre, Franklin, Jefferson, Pestalozzi, and others. (See IDEALS Challenge: Initiating Inquiry that followed the discussion of Johann Pestalozzi.)

In addition to individual enlightenment, educators influenced by liberal democratic philosophies believed that social responsibility was a primary goal of schooling. The survival of a democracy depended on a literate citizenry that participated in political life. These goals of individual enlightenment and democratic governance required personal autonomy coupled with a concern for the needs of others and for the common good.

Alongside the question about democracy, there was another question of reform that would be asked repeatedly by loud and powerful voices in the 20th century: *How can we maintain the most economical, efficient, competitive schools possible?* Economy and efficiency did not seem so important when the scale of communities was small, when most children ended up working on the farm or in a small local business. But when the Industrial Revolution (and later the information age) kicked into high gear, cities grew, and notions of scientific efficiency expanded, the fascination with efficiency would return.

In conclusion, we would note that Johann Pestalozzi's epitaph declared him to be a "man, Christian, and citizen." This epitaph reflects the confluence of currents that run through communitarianism, Western classicism, liberalism, and democratic purposes for education. As a Christian, Pestalozzi wanted to conform to the community. As a man, he wanted to reach his potential. Finally, as a democratic citizen, he needed to stay informed in order to participate in the continual transformation of education, government, and society. We hope that the selected review of historical and philosophical foundations underlying school purpose has helped you understand how the present has been influenced by the past, and why educating for democracy remains a key purpose for schools.

IDEALS CHALLENGE: *Deepening Discourse*

At the beginning of this chapter you completed the following statement. Do so again. Has your response changed since you read this chapter?

The purpose of schools is ______________________________.

DOING DEMOCRACY

- Is it possible to have a democratic society that adheres to a communitarian or Western classical philosophy of education? In what ways?
- Which educational policies that were enacted in the period of American colonization and the early republic do you believe represented your understanding of a democratic approach to education? Why?
- Of all the educators described in this chapter, whose ideas would you most like your teaching to exemplify? Why? How can you learn more about this person?
- Plan a lesson that reflects communitarian purposes. Plan a lesson that reflects Western classical purposes. Plan the same or a different lesson that reflects democratic purposes. Teach the lesson or lessons to children or to your university classmates. Chapter 5 brings us to a discussion of teacher inquiry.

REFERENCES

Barrington, J. M. (1991). The New Zealand experience: Maoris. In M. A. Gibson & J. U. Ogbu (Eds.), *Minority status and schooling: A comparative study of immigrant and involuntary minorities* (pp. 309–326). New York: Garland Publishing.

Comenius: Selections. (1957). Introduction by J. Piaget, Trans. by Iris Urwin. Geneva: United Nations.

Conger, S. M. (1994). *Mary Wollstonecraft and the language of sensibility.* Cranbury, NJ: Associated University Presses.

Demos, J. (1970). *A little commonwealth: Family life in Plymouth Colony.* New York: Oxford University Press.

Dobinson, C. H. (Ed.). (1970). *Comenius and contemporary education.* Hamburg, Germany: UNESCO Institute for Education.

Du Bois, W. E. B. (1992). *Black Reconstruction in America, 1860–1880.* New York: Atheneum.

Fafunwa, A. B. (1974). *A history of education in Nigeria.* London: Allen & Unwin.

Ford, P. L. (Ed.). (1897). *The New England Primer.* New York: Dodd, Mead & Co.

Freeman, K. J. (1907). *Schools of Hellas: An essay on the practice and theory of ancient Greek education from 600 to 300 B.C.* Port Washington, NY: Kennikat Press.

Golden, M. (1990). *Children and childhood in classical Athens.* Baltimore: Johns Hopkins Press.

Heslep, R. D. (1969). *Thomas Jefferson and education.* New York: Random House.

Jefferson, T. (1982; original from 1819). Excerpts from the report to the legislature of Virginia relative to the University of Virginia. In *Education: Ends and means* (pp. 395–404). Lanham, MD: University Press of America.

Jenkins, K. (1991). *Re-thinking history*. London: Routledge.

Kaestle, C. F. (Ed.). (1973). *Joseph Lancaster and the monitorial school movement: A documentary history.* New York: Teachers College Press.

Levy, S. (1996). *Starting from scratch: One classroom builds its own curriculum.* Portsmouth, NH: Heinemann.

Mattingly, P. (1981). *The classless profession: American schoolmen in the Nineteenth Century.* New York: New York University Press.

Monroe, W. S. (1969). *History of the Pestalozzian movement in the United States.* New York: Arno Press and the *New York Times.*

Ozman, H. A., & Craver, S. M. (1986). *Philosophical foundations of education* (3rd ed.). Columbus, OH: Merrill.

Payne, D. A. (1997). The school-master in the dark South. In R. M. Cohen & S. Scheer (Eds.), *The work of teachers in America: A social history through stories* (pp. 57–61). Mahwah, NJ: Lawrence Erlbaum.

Pulliam, J. D., & Van Patten, J. (1995). *History of education in America.* (6th ed.). Englewood Cliffs, NJ: Prentice-Hall.

Reagan, T. (1996). *Non-Western educational traditions: Alternative approaches to educational thought and practice.* Mahwah, NJ: Lawrence Erlbaum.

Reyhner, J. (Ed.). (1992). *Teaching American Indian students.* Norman, OK: University of Oklahoma Press.

Smith, L. G. (1984). *Lives in education: People and ideas in the development of teaching.* Ames, IA: Educational Studies Press.

Sommerville, C. J. (1990). *The rise and fall of childhood.* New York: Vintage Books.

Tyack, D. (1987). *". . . schools and the means of education shall forever be encouraged": A history of education in the Old Northwest.* Athens, OH: Ohio University Libraries.

Welter, R. (1971). *American writings on popular education: The Nineteenth Century.* Indianapolis: Bobbs-Merrill.

Willard, E. H. (1997). Memoirs of a woman teacher. In R. M. Cohen & S. Scheer (Eds.), *The work of teachers in America: A social history through stories* (pp. 41–46). Mahwah, NJ: Lawrence Erlbaum.

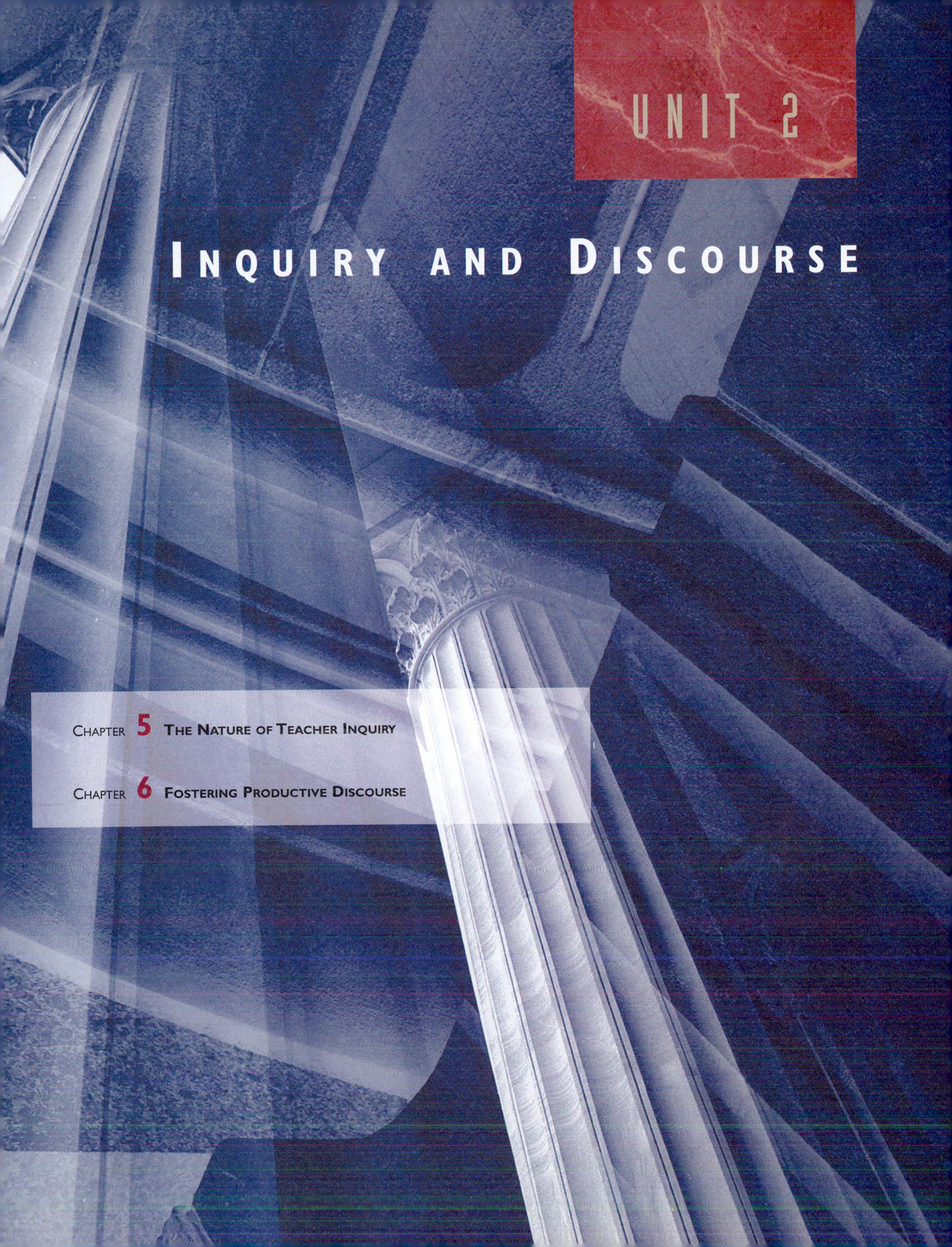

UNIT 2

INQUIRY AND DISCOURSE

What do you think the boy in the photo is wondering about as he looks at the sky?

How might he go about getting answers to his questions?

How might you go about getting answers for the things you wonder about as a teacher?

CHAPTER 5

THE NATURE OF TEACHER INQUIRY

IDEALS CHALLENGE: *Deepening Discourse*

- A recent important decision I made was ________________. The information, knowledge, data, and perspectives I considered in making my decision were ________________.
- When I make a professional decision as a teacher, the information, knowledge, data, and perspectives I anticipate using are ________________.

In democratic schools it is important not only for students to continue to learn and grow, but also for teachers and other members of the school community to learn and grow. Inquiry, also known as critical study, can facilitate the growth of all members of the school community. The term *inquiry* is used here to capture a wide range of thinking about and assessment of learning and teaching. Inquiry is the study of our practice by considering relevant perspectives, data, and knowledge. It refers not only to a formal way of researching or studying something related to education, but also to the way teachers reflect on, gather information about, and analyze the effectiveness of what they do in their classrooms and schools.

As we noted in chapter 2, without engaging in inquiry we have no basis for determining whether what we are doing works and how it fits with the things we believe in. Formal and informal inquiry should guide classroom and schoolwide decision making. It should inform instructional practices as well as the development of school policies, curriculum, and programs. Inquiry involves asking questions such as:

- On what basis are we doing what we are doing? What evidence or support do we have to justify our practice? How do we know whether what we are doing is effective?

- What information, data, knowledge, and perspectives can we gather to assist us in studying our practice?
- How does what we are doing fit with our values and beliefs as a school?
- How does what we are doing serve the needs of the diverse individuals and groups who make up our community? Whose interests do our practices serve? Whose interests do they not serve?

The primary purpose of inquiry is the improvement of teaching, learning, and school practice in the classrooms and schools of those engaged in critical study. Rather than trying to identify what works in all classrooms and schools, the purpose of personal inquiry is insight into what works in a particular classroom or school (Cochran-Smith & Lytle, 1993).

In this chapter the following questions will be addressed:

- What are the ways in which teachers can inquire about their practice?
- How do teachers go about inquiring into their practice?
- What are the issues and topics about which teachers might inquire?

IDEALS CHALLENGE: *Initiating Inquiry*

In the excerpt that follows, we read how Dottie McCaffrey (1997), a fifth/sixth-grade teacher, involved her students in helping her make decisions about the classroom environment. (From McCaffrey, 1997, pp. 123–125, 128–130.)

I resolved to work on the physical organization of our classroom in concert with my students. I introduced my plan after Christmas vacation. The first day back in January, I put all of the tables askance and wrote on the message board that the class could arrange the room as they liked and sit where they wanted. There was a buzz of excitement and a flurry of activity. The class immediately divided into two kinds of groups: those who grabbed a buddy and sat down where a table was without moving it . . . and those who had a grand plan that they tried to convince others was the best. The planners couldn't budge the sitters, so they worked among themselves to arrange, discuss and rearrange around the sitters. . . . After about twenty minutes, the class settled into seats that they kept for several weeks.

Over the next few days, I conducted class discussions in which I told the children that I wanted to hear their ideas about what a good school needs to have. During the first discussion, I asked them to brainstorm what perfect classrooms need. . . .

That night I thought about our discussion. I noted sadly that in neither discussion did any child mention the importance of being able to choose a topic or activity. I also noticed that this list reflected the children's need to be protected and taught by the adults around them. Satisfying that need while showing them how to be more independent was the task at hand.

In the next discussion I shared with them what I wanted physically to happen in the room and invited them to help decide how we could best achieve these things together.

[Based on the discussion, the students decided first on "Mary's plan" and later on "Sam's plan," an open rectangular arrangement. Neither of these satisfied the students.]

Sam's plan lasted only one week. After discussing its obvious drawbacks privately with Sam and then with the class, I proposed a slightly different room arrangement based on their ideas. Because we were beginning a unit about Greece organized around learning teams, we arranged clusters of tables where three or four children could work together. After several weeks we discussed this arrangement's merits. The consensus was that they liked this setup. They appreciated having several people to interact with and they enjoyed having more elbow room. A few who complained about being stuck at the corner of the table or having to share with a space hog discovered they could remedy the situation by simply repositioning their chairs. . . .

As the Greek unit got under way with its group decision-making component and many art projects, I was pleased to see more choice occurring. The children selected a greater variety of materials for their projects and the new central organization helped them keep the room neater as they worked. The groups were even functioning as I had hoped—not all as complete democracies, but at least with the consent of their members. . . .

As I look back on the problem I chose to work on, I wonder if our discussions about the room changed the students' involvement or if their interest in and love of the Greek unit inspired more participation in the class. I don't know. . . . Did the discussions about furniture placement and supplies cause changes that worked for them? Certainly our own classroom now better reflected the Greek ideals we were discussing. Perhaps as children thought out loud about Greek democratic ideals they were reminded of similar moments in their own room. . . . I learned again, as I do every year, that it is my job to teach children how to become more involved in their learning, whether it is through discussing our classroom space or by introducing them to the wider world of learning they otherwise might not have experienced. . . . But we cannot teach the ethics of democracy without giving them opportunities to experience real democracy in the daily operations of their lives.

- How is this an example of teacher inquiry? How is it an example of student inquiry?
- The teacher said the groups were functioning "not all as complete democracies, but at least with the consent of their members." In what ways do you think they were functioning as democracies? What else would be required for them to function as "complete democracies"?
- What do you think are the relationships between:

  room arrangement

  how well students work together

  classrooms functioning democratically
- How might you inquire further into these relationships?
- The teacher proposed a list of what the students needed to consider in arranging the room. Are there other factors that you might consider?

How to best arrange classroom furniture to facilitate meeting instructional objectives is only one of many aspects of teaching to inquire about.

WHY IS TEACHER INQUIRY IMPORTANT?

What makes classroom inquiry so vital and so difficult is the complexity of classroom life. Educational researchers have long studied students, teachers, and schools. The goal of such traditional research inquiry is to develop promising theories and examine issues that have direct or indirect application to practice. Researchers typically report their findings in journals and at conferences. In doing so, they hope that knowledge from their results will "trickle down" to teachers when they participate in in-service workshops, attend professional conferences, take graduate courses, and read on their own. However, such traditional research inquiry, while valuable, has limits in its ability to contribute to your personal growth and to inform your classroom practice. Let's look at an example.

One body of research that significantly influenced teaching practice is the research conducted on "effective teaching" in the 1970s and 1980s. This research was known as process-product or process-outcome research. Based on different theories that they were trying to confirm, researchers studied what teachers and students did in classrooms, and then tried to determine what teacher actions ("processes") were correlated with student achievement on standardized tests ("products"). As a result of this research, many teachers adopted teaching "processes" that were determined to be effective by the research. However, more recent research has shown that effective teaching is much more complex and *dependent on specific contextual circumstances* than the simple implementation of specific teaching processes. For example, one of the findings of this research was that, "[I]ndependent seatwork is probably overused and is not an adequate substitute either for active teacher instruction or for recitation and discussion opportunities" (Good & Brophy, 1994, p. 397). This could well be true in some circumstances, but does it mean that teachers should never give independent seatwork? Certainly not. In what situations is independent seatwork appropriate? In what situations is it not? Which students need more independent work and which students need more direct instruction? These are all questions teachers might examine as they inquire into their teaching practice. It is because of such complexity that *teacher* inquiry is so important.

Doyle (1986) describes five characteristics that contribute to the complexity of classrooms.

1. Classroom life is *multidimensional.* For example, while teachers keep in mind the plans they have made for today, they must also be cognizant of what they did yesterday, as well as plans for tomorrow and the days after, and the directions in which they wish to go.

2. Classroom life is *simultaneous.* For example, teachers must pass out papers, consider students' questions, deal with internal and external interruptions, and attend to multiple other aspects of classroom life, sometimes all at once.

3. Classroom life is *immediate*. For example, there is an immediacy about students needing help or wanting attention, about a knock on the classroom door that must be answered, about the attendance roll which must be taken to the office by 9 A.M., and so on.

4. Classroom life is *historical.* For example, there is a history of interpersonal expectations and patterns of behavior that has built up during the course of the school year. Perhaps a teacher's immediate response to a student is different than it was at the start of the year because the teacher has learned what to expect and how to respond.

5. Classroom life is *unpredictable.* For example, a teacher's plans and expectations for a lesson and the directions set for the day are regularly diverted by the flow of classroom events.

Philip Jackson (1968) noted that there are three other aspects of the classroom context that also contribute to the complexity of teaching—that classrooms are crowded, public, and isolated, all at once. Consider that in classrooms 25 to 30 students are *crowded* into a space much smaller than most homes (which typically house 2–6 people). Almost all the events that occur in classrooms are *public* because teachers are constantly under students' scrutiny. Simultaneously, many teachers feel *isolated* because they are almost always confined in their classrooms, away from other adults.

In order to make sense of their complex environment, inquiring teachers constantly ask questions about what is happening. Questioning is the first step in *inquiry*. Questions typically are ones teachers ask themselves based on what they experience. Inquiry involves considering and reconsidering questions such as: "What have I just done? What's happening with the students? What's the best way to do this? How do I know?"

When teachers ask such questions, they may have a number of different goals in mind. They might, for example, simply want to find a short-term solution that will enable them to get through the following day without a confrontation or a worsening problem. Or, they may be searching for a more consistent approach to solving a common problem. Teachers also question students in order to learn about their interpretations of what is occurring in the classroom. This can take place in the midst of a classroom discussion, while standing in the hallway, in the cafeteria, or in other informal settings throughout the day.

In essence, inquiry serves to identify the reasons for current practice as well as to inform future practice. As a result, the questions around which teachers and schools inquire should not be contrived but rather should spring from the uncertainties and complexities of daily practice.

Questions that teachers and school administrators ask often emerge from discrepancies between what they would like to see happen and what actually occurs. This may range from a concern about a student's progress, a classroom practice that is not working as expected, or a desire to assess how a new approach is working (Cochran-Smith & Lytle, 1993). Why can't Johnny read? Why can Susie? Should whole language or basal readers be used, or both? Which form of classroom management is most effective? Which fits what we believe in? What does it mean for discipline to be effective? What can we do to better educate our students who live in poverty? Inquiring about complex questions may not result in definitive answers and solutions to the dilemmas that confront us. Inquiring about complex questions should, however, enhance our understanding and inform our practice so that we can become more effective and compassionate educators. For example, inquiry may not answer, "Why can't Johnny read?" It may, however, help us identify some alternative strategies to use in developing Johnny's reading ability.

Our intention in this section is to explore the nature of inquiry about teaching and learning. Throughout the rest of the chapter, you will find examples of how teachers might inquire in a conscious way, so that they can increase the chances for their long-term growth and the growth of their students. The IDEALS Challenge that follows is an example of teacher inquiry. In it you hear the voice of Chelsea Caivino (1997), a student teacher in a high school journalism class. Caivino is initially overwhelmed by a curriculum that seems vague and by a cooperating teacher who has a different viewpoint on some curriculum issues.

IDEALS CHALLENGE: *Deepening Discourse*

(Excerpted from Caivino, 1997, pp. 65–66.)

Within a few weeks, I realized how difficult creating a curriculum can be with few guidelines and with little collaboration with other educators and professional journalists. It was at this point that I decided to focus my research paper on the development of a journalism curriculum from the perspectives of a first-year teacher.

In addition to recording and reflecting on my own experiences in the classroom, I read more than two dozen articles written by both journalism teachers and professional journalists. . . . Further, I set up interviews with two local first-year journalism teachers.

. . . In late September, we began a two-week unit covering both journalism ethics and communication law. Only one of the six class days, however, was devoted to ethics. . . . During the one day when ethics were discussed, the majority of the 87 minute period was spent reading the Society of Professional Journalists' Code of Ethics, a lofty piece of rhetoric that seemed to go over the students' heads. When I suggested that the class might need a real-world example in order to make these ethics more tangible, Mr. Fletcher [the cooperating teacher] said the kids could answer one of the two scenarios at the end of the chapter.

. . . Dylan [one of the students] took journalism last year and now is a member of our newspaper staff. At the beginning of the school year, Dylan approached us requesting to write the editorial pages. We decided that Dylan could write responses to the published letters to the editor. We didn't receive any letters to the editor for the first issue, and when the October deadlines came with still nary a letter, Dylan became frustrated. He persuaded a member of the class to write a letter about the tardy policy. The letter filled only half the allotted space, though, so Dylan asked the same person to write a second letter, this time signing it under a pseudonym.

. . . A week later another newspaper student came to me and said the letters were a joke, that Stan Tracy doesn't exist and Jack wrote both letters at Dylan's request.

That afternoon we sat down with Dylan and discussed the ethics and potential legal problems of what he did—soliciting letters and knowingly running them under false pretenses. I told him that the credibility of the paper had been damaged by his lack of forethought.

> He really didn't get it. Mr. Fletcher reminded Dylan that he learned this last year in journalism. Dylan was faced with a situation where he needed to apply one of the codes of ethics we just tested this year's journalism students on, and he couldn't do it. The challenge now is to come up with another way of driving those ethics home and making them very real to students. (Personal Journal [Caivino's], pp. 67–68)

In retrospect, I believe we did our students a great disservice by dedicating so little class time to ethics. Dylan (who, incidentally, earned an A in both semesters of journalism) and his ethical blunder demonstrates how ineffectual the lesson plan was. The revision includes many more real-life examples for class discussion and resolution. Moreover, I want to have the students analyze the Society's Code of Ethics, which was written in 1987, critique its strengths and weaknesses, and create a code that they feel is superior and perhaps more applicable today" (Caivino, 1997, pp. 58, 65–66).

- How did Caivino's writings help her in this situation? In addition to her observations and journal entries, what other data sources could she use to learn more about developing a meaningful journalism curriculum?
- How is Caivino's study different from what you think of as traditional research?
- How did Caivino "systematically" collect data?
- How is Caivino's inquiry different from merely thinking about your work? Is it more valuable? Do you think the outcomes of her curriculum development would have been the same without her "data collection"?

HOW DO TEACHERS INQUIRE?

Formal Versus Informal Inquiry

How do teachers go about inquiring into their (and the school's) practice? Inquiry is generally guided by questions. Questions may be recurring dilemmas or more immediate issues springing from the events of that day. The way these questions are studied can range from formal to informal. Informal inquiry may be as simple as individual reflection or discussion about teaching practice with colleagues. As a result of sharing perspectives, teachers become more aware of aspects of teaching they did not know about or had not thought about. They also may alter personal opinions and modify aspects of their practice. While additional knowledge may be acquired in informal inquiry by listening to the perspectives of others, some forms of data are typically not systematically gathered and analyzed.

Do the cultural backgrounds of students like these affect how they learn? Why or why not?

More formal inquiry, however, involves the systematic collection and analysis of data, which requires teachers to:

- formally identify specific questions that guide their study (e.g., How does a shift to whole language practices affect student attitudes toward reading?)
- formally identify specific means of data collection (e.g., discussions or interviews with students, written surveys)
- engage in data collection and analysis over an extended period of time (e.g., one week, month, or semester)

Types of Information, Data, and Knowledge

What types of information, knowledge, or data can be used in inquiry? In a democratic school community it seems clear that, at a minimum, the perspectives of various individuals and groups must be considered. This alone will broaden teachers' knowledge and perspectives in addressing an issue. For example, in attempting to assess the impact of whole language instruction, teachers might ask students whether they are enjoying reading and writing more. Their parents might be asked if they are reading more frequently at home.

While soliciting a variety of perspectives is important, a variety of other data sources also exist. These might include various types of documents, such as student work products, reports, handbooks, policy statements, program evaluations, printouts of test scores, attendance figures, dropout rates, discipline referrals, enrollment figures for various programs, and course grades. For example, in addressing the whole language question, collecting student writing samples over a period of time could help assess changes in writing ability, as may looking at their standardized test scores in reading and language arts.

In addition to addressing questions, the study of information and data coming from documents also can serve to identify questions. For example, studying documents containing program enrollment information for a school might lead to questions such as: "Why are male students represented much more heavily in advance-level mathematics classes in our school than female students?" and "Why are white students disproportionally represented in the gifted program?" Or, document evidence collected in critically studying the whole language question may show that one group of students is improving while another is not. This may lead to further questions such as: "Why does girls' writing improve with whole language instruction while boys' does not?" and "Why do the average test scores of white children improve in reading and language arts with whole language instruction, while those of black children do not?" (Delpit, 1995).

Other sources of data that can be used in inquiry include:

- surveys of students, parents, community members, and faculty
- interviews with students, teachers, community members, and faculty
- student work samples
- direct observation
- student exhibits and portfolios
- videotapes of teachers or students in the classroom
- performance assessments
- the formal research literature in an area

In addition, efforts such as keeping a reflective journal over time or using technology to get insights from teachers around the country are other ways to better understand an aspect of teaching practice. Good teachers look to others for ideas and support. One of the newest ways to do this is being part of a "listserv," a group of people from across the country or around the world who communicate about a particular subject by e-mail. The Technology Challenge that follows provides more information about listservs.

It is important to remember that the inquiry process should not be viewed as an add-on by teachers and schools, but rather as an integral part of the sense-making process about "why we do what we do."

Action Research

Action research is one form of inquiry that is typically on the formal end of the inquiry continuum but which has gained increasing usage and attention as a means of professional development.

As previously discussed, the traditional process of research requires an outsider to come into the classroom or school and formally study what is occurring. Now we look at how teachers systematically study an aspect of their own practice in order to inform their future actions. This is commonly referred to as action research or participant research.

TECHNOLOGY CHALLENGE ***Using Listservs***

- The e-mail address for ERIC, a federally funded center for educational resources, is askeric@ericir.syr.edu. Search through its menu for "Education Listservs Archives," a collection of previous postings for some major listservs.
- What other listservs can you find? Look for such sources as the *Internet Yellow Pages* and talk with K–12 teachers, your college instructors, and fellow students to put together a list. Join one of the listservs.
- If possible, set up a listserv with your own class. How might you use the listserv for educational purposes?
- As a classroom teacher, is there any way you could use a listserv to aid your teaching and your communication with families and other teachers?

The idea of teachers and other professionals conducting research on their practice began early in the 20th century, but there was not much talk about it until the 1950s. In fact, it is only in the last 20 years that teacher research has been given serious consideration. There still are many more people talking about it or attending conferences where it is discussed than there are teachers conducting formal inquiries over a period of time. Nonetheless, an increasing number of teachers are inquiring about life in their schools (Hubbard & Power, 1993; Noffke & Stevenson, 1995).

How is participant action research different from the self-reflection that teachers already do? Fundamentally, in action research teachers ask questions about their practice that *they* deem important, rather than questions an outside researcher considers important. Compared with informal reflection and inquiry about teaching, action research involves a more systematic approach to data collection and analysis and a somewhat different role as teacher and researcher. We begin with a discussion of the possible goals of action research, and then describe the phases of a practitioner study.

The Action Researcher's Goals

Among the many possible goals of inquiry into school life, are these three: First, and most commonly, is the examination of practices, values, and the congruency between beliefs and practices. What do you believe about good teaching? How do students learn best? What do you believe is your role as a teacher? What is the purpose of schooling? These are the types of beliefs that might be articulated. Subsequently, you would study your teaching to see what you do that puts these beliefs into practice. This entails being self-aware and willing to criticize your own ideas. If this is your goal, you might write an autobiography, keep a teacher journal, or videotape yourself teaching.

A second goal is to improve curriculum and the teaching skills necessary to implement the curriculum. To do this you would examine how different classroom activities influence students' interactions. For example, you might audiotape class meetings or small group work, conduct a survey to uncover students' judgments about class rules and procedures, or keep careful notes during student-led conferences to see whether the students' sense of responsibility in the classroom increases.

These first two goals of action research involve improving teaching and enhancing students' learning and development in the classroom. The third goal takes you beyond the classroom walls, into the school halls and offices, and amid the community life around the school. This goal involves examining the consequences of school policies and programs. Central to this goal is trying to understand what other teachers and school staff, parents, administrators, and community members think about the policies and programs. For example, you could analyze observational, interview, or survey information derived from conflict resolution sessions, from student support team meetings, from what occurs during in-school suspension, and from various methods of communicating with parents.

The Research Process

Although there is no single "best" way to conduct action research, there are generally five phases to an action research inquiry. Overall, it is important to remember that throughout the inquiry process the focus is on *acting* as well as on *asking*.

1. One way of beginning an inquiry is to document what is already happening. Reflecting on the documented events can lead to questions about why certain things happen the way they do.

2. From the initial questions, determine a research focus by deciding which specific questions to pursue as you study your classroom or school life.

3. After specifying the questions for inquiry, determine what data might help address the questions and help in understanding the things that perplex you. Gather this data over a period of time and analyze it as it is collected to try to makes sense of what is occurring. Analyzing the data in an on-going fashion will likely result in additional questions both about the best ways of making sense of the data and about perplexing aspects of your practice of which you were not previously aware.

4. With additional insight about perplexing questions, take action. For example, you might change a reading method or the way you assess student work.

5. Finally, if you want to share your insights with others, write a report about what you learned, do a presentation for your colleagues or at a professional conference, lead a discussion with others about your inquiry, or simply have a conversation with a close colleague about your study. Sharing, though not essential, can serve to increase your understanding even more as a result of questions and insights that others may have about your work and topic.

To get a feel for how a prospective teacher might engage in participant action research, the IDEALS Challenge that follows is a description of such a study conducted by Monica Richards (1989), a classroom teacher.

IDEALS CHALLENGE: *Initiating Inquiry*

(Adapted from Richards (1989) and based on a discussion in Anderson, Herr, & Nihlen, 1994. Bracketed material is explanatory and transitional text added to Monica Richards's verbatim description of her action research study.)

Every year I ask myself the same question, "How am I going to motivate a group of students who do not want to learn?" . . . In the past I had relied on suggestions by published researchers and educators or techniques recommended by my colleagues (p. 65). . . .

[This time I decided to study my own practice. I developed several questions I wanted to examine in terms of my practice.] What behavior must I exhibit/model to elicit an interested response at the onset of the class; how can I maintain that interest? . . . What is it that occurs in highly motivational situations? I wanted to determine what environmental factors in the classroom might influence motivation, and what types of rewards are effective (p. 66).

[I collected data about my work by keeping a daily journal, tape recording class activities, conducting student interviews, and having students complete questionnaires. I also decided to enlist their help and talked with them about my research.] They all listened attentively. Even George, who usually cannot resist laying his head down for a short snooze, remained alert. "If we agree to work together, you will have to communicate with me." They all agreed to do so.

I had no idea 8H [her class] could be so serious, so understanding. [Telling them about my study] had been the first step in working together. I knew my perceptions of them were accurate, and they knew how I really felt about them and their neglect of the learning process (p. 70).

[I began to try some different things in my classroom. One day I decided to send positive notes home to parents.] About seven people had completed their homework. . . . As I praised each one, I handed them a positive note to take home to their parents. . . . Norman was especially happy about his. Proudly he showed it to the person in front of him—comparing notes, possibly. Or was he laughing, making fun of it? This was my fear. Is Norman (and others like him in 8H) too cool, too macho to get a positive note from the teacher? I'll talk to them about this tomorrow (p. 69).

[I devised a list of things that I thought would motivate my students.] I discussed the priority of items on the checklist [with them]. I had assumed the number one item would be a bonus point system where the class earning the most bonus points in one six-week period would choose their own reward. 8H rated it number ten, and after a little discussion decided it didn't even need to be on the list. They rated teaching resources number one. How wrong I was about them! I was also wrong about the positive notes home. I shared my fear about them being "too cool" for a positive note. Norman, Scott, and Dawn all said that's not true. They said they took their notes home and showed them. Norman was serious. Dawn and Kim rated them especially high on their list—about second, with verbal praise a close third (p. 70). . . .

[I also did some reading about motivation. I realized that] if I want my students to be motivated to achieve, I must care about them as persons (p. 72). [I believe things improved in my classroom] because we had a common understanding that getting good grades was important; we were interested in the content of the lesson; we valued each others' ideas; we were working and learning together. This interchange of teaching and learning was the most valuable lesson to be learned.

I also believe that what will be remembered in the minds of the students of 8H will not be a letter grade received in a class, but rather the memories of having experienced success and praise for achieving, regardless of how small the achievements (pp. 75–76).

- What has Monica Richards learned about her teaching by conducting this action research study?
- What did she learn about motivating students?
- Is it likely that Richards would have learned the same things without doing the action research?
- How does her action research study reflect the action research process described in this chapter? How does it differ?
- Review Alfie Kohn's writing on rewards (e.g., his book *Punished by Rewards*). How does what Richards learned compare with Kohn's arguments? What is your perspective about motivation and rewards?

WHAT ARE THE ISSUES AND TOPICS TEACHERS MIGHT INQUIRE ABOUT?

Inquiring About the School and Community

Part of the challenge educators face is to learn about the school and the local community. Perhaps the first thing to do is to inquire about the community in which the school functions. Many teacher education programs provide a bus tour of the local community, or require students to do a "school profile" about the community in which they will do their student teaching. To complete the school profile, teacher education students drive around various sections of the community, summarize demographic information, and even interview community members.

It is also vital to gain a historical and sociological understanding of the school. Bullough and Gitlin (1995) argue that a school history should not simply include data gathering, a summary of the observations and interviews conducted, and a description of the school, but it should also evoke questions and identify "themes" that raise essential ideas. The IDEALS Challenge that follows includes an excerpt from a prospective teacher's school history.

CLICK ON IT

For more information about action research and links to related Web sites, visit

www.winona.msus.edu/library/acq/actres.htm

http.//elmo.scu.edu.au/schools/sawd/ari/links.html

IDEALS CHALLENGE: *Deepening Discourse*

(Excerpted from Bullough & Gitlin, 1995.)

From what I had seen and observed in the classrooms and halls, I assumed that Central Heights had no more than 10–12 percent minority students. I was surprised when I discovered the actual figure was 24 percent, and I couldn't help but ask myself just where Central Heights "was keeping" its minorities. The "mystery" was solved, however, when I began observing remedial and basic skills courses, which were literally filled with minority students. . . . When asked about race relations at Central Heights High School, students, both minority and majority, came to the same conclusions: students tend to form "cliques" or groups which exclude others who do not fit the criteria for the group. . . . Some of the teachers at Central Heights think that there is nothing wrong with "the way things are currently done," [others] feel that there is much to be done at Central Heights. When asked what approaches to teaching style, curriculum, and management need to be altered to suit the needs of all students [one teacher] agreed that there needs to be more cooperative learning approaches taken with students and that assessment needs to be more flexible and reflective of the different ways that students learn. Citing portfolios as an example [this teacher] explained that her Asian students hated this method, but her Hispanic students loved the approach and were very successful (Bullough & Gitlin, 1995, pp. 80–83).

- What are the educational issues raised by the writer of this excerpt?
- What questions would *you* want to ask the teachers about these issues?
- What are the possible problems associated with doing a school profile or history?

In addition to the perspective provided by a school history, there are many other kinds of questions that can be asked when observing in a school. What follows is part of an "orientation checklist" that one university requires prospective teachers to complete within one week after arriving in a school.

Know the Community

- Find demographic information about the student population at your school, related to ethnicity, income levels, percentage of students on free and reduced lunch, types of parental occupations, and other data you think is important.
- Take a tour of the communities your school serves, and talk with teachers in the school about community life. If possible, talk with several parents or guardians about the community and about their views of the school. Write a brief description of the different residential housing and business areas near the school, and important issues that the community faces.
- Make a list of community agencies that provide services for the students at the school. Visit at least one of those agencies to get information and to talk informally with someone about their services.

Know the Building

- Tour the school building and locate the following (where applicable): media center, teachers' workroom for your grade level, school offices, school nurse's room, cafeteria, materials and equipment storage rooms, computer lab(s).
- Write down and memorize the names of the principal, assistant principal(s), all teachers on your school wing, custodians for your wing, secretaries in the main office, special services people, the school or grade-level counselor.

Know School Procedures

- What are the fire drill and severe weather drill procedures?
- What are the rules for using the phones in school?

How can knowledge of the community in which you teach be helpful to you as a teacher?

- What are the teachers' supervisory duties (e.g., cafeteria, halls, bus)?
- What meetings or events will you be expected to attend (e.g., staff meetings, PTA, students clubs, athletic events)?
- What is the procedure to use in case of student illness or injury?
- How is daily attendance taken, recorded, and reported to the office?
- What are the regulation and procedures for taking students on out-of-school trips?
- What are the checkout procedures for audiovisual equipment, films and videotapes, and other materials? (Can a cart of books be taken from the media center for students to use in a classroom?)

Inquiring About Students

The primary inquiry task teachers have is to learn about their students and how best to teach them. This begins by gathering information about students and establishing strong relationships with them. Inquiring about students entails examining your images, beliefs, and theories about students in general and about your students in particular.

Bullough and Gitlin (1995) offer a number of suggestions for learning about school and student life. One suggestion they offer is to conduct a "shadow study" prior to becoming a teacher. A shadow study is an inquiry designed to learn how students experience and make sense of school. As part of a field experience, a prospective teacher might shadow a student for one complete day, taking observational notes, talking informally with students, and perhaps formally interviewing the shadowed student. What follows is an example of a shadow study that Veronica, a prospective teacher, cowrote with Janie, a high school student. In this piece, they each describe the last class of the day.

Janie: This class is a pretty good one. English isn't my favorite subject, but Mrs. B. usually makes it pretty interesting. We have been reading *I Heard the Owl Call My Name.* Have you read it? Yeah, it's pretty good. Looks like we're going to start with free writing today. I'm glad we're going to talk about some ideas we can write on. I can never think of anything to write. . . .

Veronica: I have to admit to some disappointment at what seemed to me to be the tedious and lackluster nature of Janie's day. . . . Janie's last class was the highlight of the day for me. . . . [I] also sincerely felt that Mrs. B. made a genuine attempt to employ various activities to help students with different learning styles to find a way to relate to the novel they were reading. She took the time to brainstorm with the class to make sure everyone had an idea requiring them to complete a ten-minute free-writing exercise. (Bullough & Gitlin, 1995, pp. 110–114)

In her shadow study paper, Veronica made a real effort to see what school was like from Janie's eyes, and to consider how the teacher responded to students' actions and interests.

Both in your student teaching and as a teacher, at the beginning of the school year your students are likely to be simply an assortment of alphabetized names on a class roster. It is a daunting challenge to *really* learn about every student. It is especially difficult to learn about students in secondary schools, where you may have five or six classes of 28 students each. What can you do to get to know your students? Two teachers from Chicago, Yolanda Simmons and Pat Bearden (1996), have developed a multicultural, start-of-the-year unit that enables them to really get to know their students each year. Simmons teaches high school and Bearden is a third-grade teacher. The IDEALS Challenge that follows contains a description of how the unit is enacted in Simmons's high school classroom over a two-week period.

IDEALS CHALLENGE: *Achieving Authenticity*

(Excerpted from Simmons & Bearden, 1996.)

DAY ONE

Students choose partners and conduct three-minute interviews with one another, taking notes on the following questions:

- Where were you born?
- Who were you named after, and what does your name mean?
- Where do your ancestors come from within the United States? Where do they come from outside the United States?
- Have you or anyone in your family researched your family history?

While the students are working, Simmons circulates around the room taking Polaroid pictures of each kid. She also makes sure she has a bit of information of her own about at least one student. Students then take a minute or two to review and select from their notes, in preparation for oral presentations.

Next, each student introduces his or her partner "culturally." Simmons provides a model by doing the first introduction, giving some of the information briefly: "This is John. He was born here in Chicago on the South Side, and he was named after his great uncle. His family comes from Macon, Georgia, where he used to visit every summer when he was small. He loved his grandmother's cooking, but hated the farm work he had to do. He doesn't know anything about where his family came from before that, but he wishes he did. Meeeeeet John Coleman!"

Day Two

The students complete and edit one-page written versions of their interviews, with space left on each page for a photograph. These are pasted on, and someone with artistic talent is drafted to make a cover. Overnight, Simmons photocopies the interviews to produce a class book, and everyone receives a copy the next day. The kids immediately check their own photographs and moan that they don't do the owner justice. But they save and browse through this information about their peers for weeks.

Day Three

The students come in to class to find newsprint sheets taped to the walls with the headings "English," "Language Arts," "Math," "Social Studies," "Science," "Phys. Ed.," plus a few blank sheets. Students are told to gather next to the sheets according to their strongest interests, with the option of also using the blank sheets to create their own categories—often "Dance," "Music," and "Home Economics/Foods." Their task is now to brainstorm and list questions for researching information about some of the locations on the "Origins" chart for their chosen subject area. The students especially warm up to this work, no doubt because it offers a rare opportunity to share in control of the curriculum. Simmons remarks that no subject area seems to go without a few devotees in each class. Some typical questions the kids put on their charts are:

- English: Who were some famous authors from this place, and what did they write?
- Social Studies: What is the student drop-out rate in this city?
- Science: What are some of the diseases that occur especially in this area, and what are their causes?
- Math: What are the population statistics, comparisons among them, and trends for various ethnic groups in this area?

Days Four and Five

These are spent in the library. Each group chooses one of the research questions listed on their chart . . . and looks for answers to that question for each place of family origin in the United States for their particular group.

Day Six

The students bring in their research reports and each group compiles an information book on their subject area.

Days Seven and Eight

Each group gives an oral report to the class, sharing some of the knowledge they've gained on their particular aspect of the locations of family origins.

DAY NINE

At the end—and also at various points all along—the students "debrief" their research work in short discussion sessions. Among the important questions Simmons poses are "How did you feel when you were doing ____?" and "Why do you think we included that step?" The students especially enjoy this reflecting, and find the latter question thought-provoking. Such reflection adds to students' sense of ownership of the curriculum because they are asked to evaluate it. It also strengthens their learning by making them aware of the processes that lead to success in school (pp. 134–137).

- How does Yolanda Simmons get to know her students?
- How does she try to integrate the curriculum across subject areas?
- How are students given responsibility for their learning?
- What might be the difficulties with this method when getting to know students?
- What are some other ways that teachers can achieve an authentic curriculum that addresses real-life issues in students' lives?

Inquiring About Learning

There are numerous theories that try to explain how people learn. These theories have implications for how to teach students. For example, the implications of some theories are that teaching should involve a lot of direct instruction to students, including lectures to "fill" them with knowledge. Other theories imply that hands-on experiences result in greater student learning. Still other theories suggest that teaching should involve designing learning experiences that result in students' constructing their own knowledge about the topics being studied. Several learning theories will be discussed in greater detail in chapter 11. You also are likely to study learning theories in greater depth in other classes you will take in your teacher education program.

It is important to know various learning theories and to critically study their effects on students. For example, how well do students learn when you have used a lecture method of instruction? How well do they learn when you teach using hands-on instruction? Do some students learn better in one way than another? Are there some concepts that are better taught using one method rather than another?

In addition to the relationship between teaching practice and learning theory, there is also a relationship between teaching practice, culture, and learning. When students begin formal schooling at the age of 5 or 6, they have a knowledge of their local culture and the ways of learning acquired within that culture. These ways of learning may fit well with those required by school—or there may be a mismatch. Cultural issues of how students learn are inseparable from what they learn.

There are different ways that the relationship between learning and culture has been viewed. The *cultural deficit theory* suggests that cultural backgrounds (including language) may prevent some students from performing well in the classroom. *Expectation theory* focuses on the effect that teachers' and schools' expectations have on cultural minority and female students. Finally, the *cultural difference theory* asserts that learning is inhibited when there is not a fit between home language and cultural patterns, and school language and/or cultural patterns.

The following excerpt, which discusses how teachers and schools might work effectively with Hispanic students, illustrates the cultural deficit, cultural difference, and teacher/school expectation theories just mentioned.

> The staff needs to recognize that it is likely that the children of these newly arrived Hispanic families will be motivated, hard-working students. . . . Financial and time constraints may limit [parents'] availability for school conferences and parent meetings. School staffs need to learn about cultural differences that newly arrived children from Central or South American may exhibit. For example, such children might regard direct eye contact as a sign of disrespect, while teachers take the refusal to make eye contact as a sign that students are being rebellious or untruthful. . . . Schools should encourage Hispanic parents to work with their children in their native language. By reading to the child and engaging in rich verbal communication, the parent will build a strong foundation for second-language learning. (Holman, 1997, p. 648)

You can tell from the tone of this writing that the author is writing from a cultural difference rather than a cultural deficit perspective. That is, she expresses the value of Hispanic culture and does not imply that it is of lesser value than the dominant Anglo culture of most schools. The author also indirectly addresses the issue of teacher and administrator expectations, wanting teachers to hold high expectations for the children.

As teachers in democratic schools we should always ask ourselves: Whose interests are being served by the ways of teaching and the policies in this school? Are we serving the interests of only the white, middle-class students? How are we serving the interests of Hispanic students, African American students, Native American students, and students living in poverty? In the past it was simply assumed that all students were responsible for adapting to the dominant cultural way of speaking and interacting. Now, we recognize our moral responsibility as educators to inquire into and critically study how we deal with differences between the home and school lives of students who do not belong to the dominant cultural group.

The tale of Maribel, a 4-year-old Mexican American child, provides another example of how cultural differences can impact a student's learning in school.

> In school, Maribel's English-speaking teacher struggles to get her to speak more, to be more independent, and to participate in class. At home, Maribel still sleeps in a crib in her parents' room—her mother's youngest child who plays exclusively with dolls and hears no English. The Latino parenting that I observed in this home and others had a nurturing style. Children were not expected to be independent. . . . I had expected to find that parents had prepared their children with some readiness skills that teachers had overlooked. Instead, I had discovered an important social and emotional support system separate from school goals or objectives. For most Latino children, entrance into the school world brings a more abrupt and total change than it does for other kids. . . . [Children] are expected to obediently fulfill the teacher's directives [i.e., to be independent] and to respectfully, lovingly fulfill family responsibilities [i.e., to be dependent]. . . .

Parents can be included in classroom activities in more authentic ways than just bringing supplies for parties or running errands for teachers.

> In the case of young Maribel, the classroom teacher learned to gradually introduce new kinds of toys to her and to lend such toys, along with books, for home use. The teacher also learned not to view [Maribel's father's] rare communication with school in a negative light but to realize that Maribel's mother would warmly welcome school initiatives. (Carger, 1997, pp. 41–43)

We do not mean to overplay the "cultural differences" perspective. There are different ways of being raised and of learning and acting in school. To some extent we all adapt to differing circumstances. However, for some students the differences are so great that they negatively impact the student's ability to learn in school. We believe teachers should critically study how they might address student differences by listening, asking questions, and seeking information about other cultures.

Given the potentially powerful effects of culture on learning, we need to also think about how some students may choose to "not-learn" or to "unlearn" school knowledge (also known as "resistance"; see discussion in chapter 7). Herbert Kohl's (1994) story of Wilfredo represents one person's desire to not-learn.

IDEALS CHALLENGE: *Examining Equity*

(Excerpted from Kohl, 1994.)

Years ago, one of my fifth-grade students told me that his grandfather Wilfredo wouldn't learn to speak English. He said that no matter how hard you tried to teach him, Wilfredo ignored whatever words you tried to teach and forced you to speak to him in Spanish. When I got to know his grandfather, I asked, in Spanish, whether I could teach him English, and he told me unambiguously that he did not want to learn. He was frightened, he said, that his grandchildren would never learn Spanish if he gave in like the rest of the adults and spoke English with the children. Then, he said, they would not know who they were. At the end of our conversation he repeated adamantly that nothing could make him learn to speak English, that families and cultures could not survive if the children lost their parents' language, and finally that learning what others wanted you to learn can sometimes destroy you (p. 1).

- What are the implications of this passage for teachers and school?
- What are the implications of this passage for equity?
- What might be other reasons that people would choose to "not-learn"?
- Have you ever chosen to "not-learn"? If so, why did you make that decision?
- As a teacher, how would you deal with a student who was choosing to not-learn due to cultural reasons?

In line with previous discussions about the social and cultural aspects of learning, sometimes students *choose* not to learn for reasons that have nothing to do with their intelligence or abilities. Kohl notes that students may choose not to learn because there are "challenges to her or his personal and family loyalties, integrity, and identity. . . . To agree to learn from a stranger who does not respect your integrity causes a major loss of self" (p. 6). Students may choose to not-learn because they perceive the teacher to be unfair, the textbook to be biased, or the school curriculum to be at odds with what they believe. A conscious decision to not-learn may also result from students' fear of failure or a sense that what they are learning is of little value in their lives.

Kohl also raises the idea of "unlearning," which occurs when students decide to reject information or ways of thinking and speaking that were previously learned. He tells the story of a former student, Akmir, who was trying to unlearn the version of history he had grown up with and to replace it with a history that included African Americans. Kohl comments that as a result of Akmir's "unlearning" he, too, was able to unlearn: "I learned from Akmir's reading techniques how to unlearn habits of mine that let such racism in books pass unexamined" [i.e., he now critiques what he reads for examples of racism and challenges it when he identifies examples] (pp. 19–20). As educators and citizens we carry images and beliefs about how students learn, generally based on how we personally learn best. It is our responsibility to consider that we might have to unlearn some of these images and beliefs if we are to effectively educate all students.

Inquiring About Teaching

Teachers are besieged by classes, workshops, and written materials aimed at promoting some instructional practice or another. How does a teacher decide which practice is best? How does a teacher decide what is simply a fad versus what will result in improved student learning? Inquiring into various learning theories is one way of sorting out fads from practices that are more substantive. (Chapter 11 discusses several learning theories in detail.)

Screening practices against the IDEALS of democratic schooling is another way. Looking at the historical grounding of practices can also inform a teacher's inquiry. Educators have had different conceptions of what constitutes "best practice" over time. Sometimes best practices from the past have merit and are rediscovered at a later time. Often, however, classes, workshops, and written materials promote practices in a nonhistorical and noncritical manner. Left unaddressed are questions of how teachers in the past addressed particular types of teaching situations, the merits and demerits of those practices, and how they compare with current practices and ways of thinking. Without a historical basis for inquiry, we limit our options for ways of teaching to methods that are currently in vogue. In the Present to Past section that follows, we look at the historical basis for some common teaching practices as well as metaphors for teachers that have existed over time.

PRESENT TO PAST

Examining Historical Bases for Teaching Practices

THE 19TH CENTURY: MAINTAINING CONTROL

During the 19th century the growth of cities led to a tremendous increase in the number of urban schools. Urban schools were much larger than rural schools and urban classrooms often contained 40–48 desks per room, accommodating as many as 60 students. The growth of these schools and classroom populations combined with the effects of industrialization led to a push for greater efficiency and student control. Schools began using subtle but powerful means of control. For example, instead of working at communal tables or benches, students sat at desks bolted to the floor, in rows, facing forward. Schools became graded by age groups, and ability grouping within classes was expanded. Specific textbooks were mandated and curriculum guidelines became formalized. Blackboards replaced the individual slates of students in country schools, and individual report cards replaced student performances and exhibits as a means of showing learning or achievement.

IDEALS CHALLENGE: *Initiating Inquiry*

- Discuss each of the practices listed in the previous paragraph and discuss what you believe to be the advantage of the practice during the period in history when it first developed.
- Which of the practices still exist in schools today? Do the historical reasons for their development remain valid in schools today?
- Are these practices in the best interests of students? Why or why not?
- What alternatives are there to these practices?

During this period in both rural and urban schools, the teacher's authority was absolute. Obedience was assumed and inappropriate behavior, however defined, was punished severely. Some school reformers wanted to continue moral training but discontinue the physical coercion. There is evidence that corporal punishment diminished in the latter half of the century, though there may have been an increasing reliance on the fear of parental punishment.

There were three different styles of teaching during the 19th century (Finkelstein, 1989). Some teachers, particularly in rural one-room schools, acted as *overseers* who simply conducted the recitations and closely monitored students' actions to ensure obedience. Other teachers, particularly in urban schools, could be characterized as *drillmasters* because they focused on the reproduction of increasingly complex texts and drilled large numbers of students as a whole group. In these first two styles of teaching, the predominance of recitation and individual seatwork as teaching methods meant that learning was synonymous with rote imitation of skills and the parroting of information from standard texts. A small portion of teachers embraced a third style of teaching in which they acted as *interpreters of culture*, exposing children to a wider realm of literature or history and attempting to enable children to think more rationally about their world.

IDEALS CHALLENGE: *Initiating Inquiry*

Think about the teachers you had in elementary and secondary school.

- Which were overseers? Which were drillmasters? Which were interpreters of culture?
- What were the practices that caused you to classify them the way you did?
- What were advantages and disadvantages of each type of teacher?
- With what type of teacher did you have the most pleasant experience?
- With what type of teacher did you learn best?
- What can you learn from thinking about the teaching styles of your teachers that can help you as a prospective teacher?

During this period, however, most children, especially ethnic minorities and females, received little or no schooling. Only a small percentage of young people attended high school; most of them were apprenticing or laboring full time in the home from an early age. In fact, many children preferred working outside the home to attending schools, perhaps because of the "overseers" and "drillmasters" awaiting them at the schoolhouse door.

THE 20TH CENTURY: TUNING INTO STUDENTS

In the early 20th century, many educators continued to be concerned with efficiency and economy in schooling. These educators focused on how teachers could control the most students efficiently, and freely borrowed ideas and even language from business (a practice that continues to this day). Their instruction was primarily teacher-centered. This entailed whole-class interactions where teacher talk and student recitation predominated, individual seatwork in which students sat in rows of desks facing the teacher's desk and the chalkboard, and management systems intended to tightly control student movement and interaction.

CLICK ON IT

The Chicago Laboratory School started by John Dewey is still in existence today. To learn more about how the school's current philosophy and practices continue to reflect John Dewey's influence and to view the work of the school's students, visit the school's Web site at

www.ucls.uchicago.edu

Some *student-centered* practices, however, were also present during the 20th century. In some instances student-centered practices mirrored the practices of 19th century rural schools—students helped one another, often across age groups; movement around the room was allowed; there was individual attention from the teacher; students could progress at different rates through the curriculum; and on occasion the content was related to community life (Cuban, 1984, p. 38). In other instances, student-centered instruction grew out of the thinking and practices of educational theorists such as John Dewey at the Chicago Laboratory School and Marietta Johnson at the Organic School in Fairhope, Alabama. These new student-centered educators called for a curriculum that responded to children's interests, individual and small group learning, more freedom and creativity in the classroom, and a close connection with the community. They stood firmly in opposition to "fixed grades in the schools, fixed rules for the children, and fixed furniture in the classroom" (Cuban, 1984, p. 38). According to these theorists, the new ideal for student-centered teachers was to serve as *interpreters* and *guides*. Under this new ideal, teachers were to demonstrate and model, help students set directions, supervise group work, and lead students toward greater responsibility for their own learning while still providing structure and maintaining adult responsibility for curriculum and learning strategies.

IDEALS CHALLENGE: *Initiating Inquiry*

Recall a teacher you had in elementary or secondary school who served as a guide.

- How did she or he teach?
- What did she or he do to guide your learning?
- How do you assess your experience in her or his classroom?
- What can you learn from this teacher that can help you as a prospective teacher?

Educational experiments blossomed in the 1920s, 1930s, and early 1940s, which was the heyday of "progressive schools." As the number of experimental schools grew, educators wondered whether the curriculum in such schools would prepare students for college and later life. To answer that question, the Progressive Education Association sponsored the Eight-Year Study (1933–1941), the largest comparative evaluation of schools ever undertaken in this country. In the study the college performance of graduates from experimental secondary schools, both private and public, was compared with graduates from nonexperimental schools. The experimental schools tried innovative approaches such as a project-centered curriculum and broad student choice of course work. Results indicated that students from the experimental schools were comparable to graduates of nonexperimental schools in academic performance and superior in their attitudes about learning. The evaluation in some senses vindicated progressive philosophies of education that had been vilified by many people who believed such schools neglected the basics.

The publication of the findings of the Eight-Year Study in 1941, however, was overshadowed by the looming threat of World War II. School innovation took a backseat to war preparation. After the war there were other pressing concerns. Additionally, most of the progressive schools were small and many were private. As a result, the bulk of public schools never attempted to make large-scale innovations. Still, many of the ideas of progressive educators remain influential.

The 1950s and 1960s continued to witness competing instructional approaches. "Behavior management" represented an emphasis on rationality and science and was a technical approach derived from behavioral psychology and the social efficiency movement of the early 20th century. Behavior management was designed to "shape" students' behavior and learning. Using positive reinforcement, which often included "token systems" (i.e., rewards for correct answers and specific behaviors), behavioristic educators wished to make teaching systematic and "teacher proof." That is, they believed that if teachers had well-defined systems in which they always knew when and how to reward and punish students, all teachers could be good teachers, inappropriate student behaviors would be reduced, and academic achievement would be enhanced. This represented a systematic approach to controlling learning.

IDEALS CHALLENGE: *Initiating Inquiry*

Recall a teacher you had in elementary or secondary school who served as a behavioral manager.

- How did she or he manage your behavior?
- How do you assess your experience in her or his classroom?
- What can you learn from this teacher that can help you as a prospective teacher?

Many of the 1960s experimental or alternative schools offered a different approach to classroom learning. "Free" schools, which sometimes resembled the experimental schools of the Progressive era, often let students participate in determining what they would learn and how they would learn it. Quite informal classroom relationships were the norm, and teachers developed many methods to incorporate students' interests and give them choices. These experimental and alternative schools implied that the role of the teacher was to be a *negotiator*. Negotiating extends the idea of guiding, by allowing students a part in developing the curriculum and in determining how they will learn. The teacher tries to effectively negotiate with students what will happen, in whole group planning sessions and small group working sessions.

IDEALS CHALLENGE: *Initiating Inquiry*

Recall a teacher you had in elementary or secondary school who served as a negotiator.

- How did she or he teach?
- What types of things were negotiated in the classroom (try to recall specific examples)?
- How do you assess your experience in her or his classroom?
- What can you learn from this teacher that can help you as a prospective teacher?

What might these young men be learning from doing this project in this progressive school?

When considering these patterns of teaching over many decades, we see that teachers historically were seen as drillmasters, overseers, interpreters of culture, behavioral managers, guides, and negotiators. Inquiry into teaching involves being aware of these and other metaphors for teaching. It involves asking questions such as:

- What are the advantages and disadvantages of each approach to teaching?
- Which approach is best? In what situations is it the best? How do I know?
- What are the beliefs and values that support each style?
- Which are consistent with democratic IDEALS? Which are not? How are they consistent and inconsistent?
- What kinds of information and data do I have to support the effectiveness of my teaching approach? What kinds of information and data can I gather to study the effectiveness of my approach?

IDEALS CHALLENGE: *Learning Leadership*

We have discussed drillmaster, overseer, interpreter of culture, behavioral manager, guide, and negotiator as historical metaphors for teachers. Think of a metaphor that describes how you see yourself fulfilling your role as a teacher. Explain why you see yourself in this way and what the implications are for your practice as a teacher in your classroom. Does the metaphor you selected have implications for your practice as a teacher beyond your classroom walls? That is, does it have implications for your leadership as a member of a democratic school community? Is it sufficient for a teacher in a democratic school community to be concerned with only her or his classroom? Based on your responses, assess the adequacy of your metaphor and think of a new metaphor or an additional metaphor if appropriate. You may wish to revisit this IDEALS Challenge after you finish this book to see if your response to it has changed.

SUMMARY

Throughout this chapter we have emphasized the importance of inquiry and critical study. We made the point that excellent teachers engage in reflective inquiry about their teaching on a regular basis, and that they ask students to think about what they are learning. Many teachers keep a journal in order to document both what is happening in class and their thoughts about the events. Nearly all of the teachers quoted in this book have used a journal or some other consistent means of documenting and making sense of what happens in their teaching, classroom, and school.

Inquiry, however, involves more than listening to one's self. There is also a social dimension to inquiry. Teachers often reflect with other teachers, whether standing in the hall, sitting in the cafeteria, or working together on plans for a field trip. Teachers also talk with students, parents, and administrators as part of reflecting. Talking with others, listening to others, and reflecting on what they say are central social aspects of inquiry.

We think a note of caution is in order. One of our purposes in this chapter has been to encourage you to consider how you should teach. As authors we have our own beliefs about what schools should be like and how teachers should teach. Our beliefs are reflected in the democratic IDEALS and the framework for democratic schooling described in the first unit of this book. It is important, however, that you not simply accept our framework as yours. Rather, you should inquire into different theoretical, philosophical, and historical approaches to teaching and schooling and decide which best fit you and your context. Then you should proceed in continually learning from your practice by studying the effects of your practices on the students for whom you are responsible.

IDEALS CHALLENGE: *Supporting Service*

(Adapted from McLaughlin, Irby, & Langman, 1994, pp. 20–22.)

Buddy is European American, 19 years old, 6 feet, 5 inches tall, and 210 pounds, with a close-cut head of dark hair, save for one long lock at the nape of his neck. At first glance he is more likely to engender caution than respect. He is, however, one of the revered "seniors" at Cooper House, a Boys and Girls Club affiliate chartered at the turn of the century. In addition to sharing in the Senior Boys Club activities, he works at Cooper House regularly as a part-time receptionist and supervisor for the younger members.... At age 14, after a few scrapes with the police for car theft and street fighting, Buddy turned away from the streets to the Cooper House's red-bricked refuge.... Buddy credits his association with Cooper House with making fundamental changes in his attitudes toward others and toward himself. The opportunity to make friends with African Americans within the context of Cooper House values and traditions has been especially important to him....

At school Buddy received the message that "tough kids" and "poor white trash" would never amount to anything.... Buddy missed having rules at school at the same time as he suffered from strict but inconsistent rules at home.... He also missed compassion and caring. He feels that even his high school sports coaches had no interest in him as a person although he was a prized player. "They focus only on winning." At Cooper House, Buddy finds genuine caring and clear, consistent rules. Although Cooper House teams "want to win, too," Buddy experiences a key difference between the Cooper House and high school teams. Cooper House coaches know the youth as individuals. "Sometimes when ... I've had a bad day, Paul [the coach] realizes that. He doesn't ride me that hard. But if he sees me slackin', he'll get on my butt."...

The personal contact he gets at Cooper House has changed Buddy's goals. Once interested in a professional sports career, he now sees a future helping kids in his community in the way Cooper House has helped him.

- You have read in this chapter about different metaphors for teachers. Think of a metaphor that might characterize the practices of the educator's at Buddy's school? What metaphor might characterize the practices of the educator's at Cooper House?
- Apparently Cooper House has strict rules. Engage in inquiry about different ways of thinking about rules and student discipline (see also chapter 11). Are rules consistent with democratic IDEALS? How can rules be consistent with democratic IDEALS? Under what conditions are rules inconsistent with democratic IDEALS?
- Based on the description, how does Cooper House reflect and/or not reflect democratic IDEALS?
- Based on the description, how does Buddy's school seem to reflect and/or not reflect democratic IDEALS?

DOING DEMOCRACY

The previous sections posed many examples of the types of questions teachers and schools might ask as they inquire into their practice. Take one of these questions or another question in which you are particularly interested and collect and analyze data for a school in which you are working as part of your field experience. If you are currently not involved in field experience, identify a question on which you can collect data that does not require you to be working in a school. For example, you could interview teachers and other educators, or review documents such as those mentioned in the discussion of inquiry to help you address your question. Write a brief report on what additional insight and understanding you have gained by conducting your action research project.

REFERENCES

Anderson, G. L., Herr, K., & Nihlen, A. S. (1994). *Studying your own school: An educator's guide to qualitative practitioner research.* Thousand Oaks, CA: Corwin Press.

Bullough, R. V., Jr., & Gitlin, A. (1995). *Becoming a student of teaching: Methodologies for exploring self and school context.* New York: Garland.

Caivino, C. (1997). Teaching future members of the fourth estate. In T. S. Poetter, *Voices of inquiry in teacher education* (pp. 57–67). Mahwah, NJ: Lawrence Erlbaum.

Carger, C. L. (1997). Attending to new voices. *Educational Leadership, 54*(7), 39–43.

Cochran-Smith, M., & Lytle, S. L. (1993). *Inside/Outside: Teacher research and knowledge*. New York: Teachers College Press.

Cuban, L. (1984). *How teachers taught: Constancy and change in American classrooms, 1890–1980*. New York: Longman.

Delpit, L. (1995). *Other people's children: Cultural conflict in the classroom*. New York: The New Press.

Doyle, W. (1986). Classroom organization and management. In M. Wittrock (Ed.), *Handbook of research on teaching* (3rd ed., pp. 392–431). New York: Macmillan.

Finkelstein, B. (1989). *Governing the young: Teacher behavior in popular primary schools in Nineteenth-Century United States*. London: Falmer Press.

Good, T. L., & Brophy, J. E. (1994). *Looking in classrooms* (6th ed.). New York: HarperCollins.

Holman, L. J. (1997). Working effectively with Hispanic immigrant families. *Phi Delta Kappan, 78*(8), 647–649.

Hubbard, R. S., & Power, B. M. (1993). *The art of classroom inquiry: A handbook for teacher researchers.* Portsmouth, NH: Heinemann.

Jackson, P. (1968). *Life in classrooms*. New York: Holt.

Kohl, H. (1994). *"I won't learn from you" and other thoughts on creative maladjustment*. New York: The New Press.

McCaffrey, D. (1997). Moving the teacher's desk: Democracy in a fifth/sixth grade. In R. S. Charney (Ed.), *Habits of goodness: Case studies in the social curriculum* (pp. 121–136). Greenfield, MA: Northeast Foundation for Children.

McLaughlin, M. W., Irby, M. A., & Langman, J. (1994). *Urban sanctuaries: Neighborhood organizations in the lives and futures of inner-city youth*. San Francisco: Jossey- Bass.

Noffke, S. E., & Stevenson, R. B. (1995). *Educational action research: Becoming practically critical.* New York: Teachers College Press.

Richards, M. (1989). A teacher's action research study: The "bums" of 8H (A humanistic view of motivational strategies with low achievers). *Peabody Journal of Education, 64*(2), 65–79.

Simmons, Y., & Bearden, P. (1996). Getting to know you culturally. In S. Zemelman, H. Daniels, & A. Hyde (Eds.), *Best practice: New standards for teaching and learning in America's schools* (pp. 134–137). Portsmouth, NH: Heinemann.

What roles do conversation and storytelling play in Native American culture?

What role does conversation play in the culture of schools?

What benefits might result from it?

What factors often limit professional conversation in schools?

CHAPTER 6

Fostering Productive Discourse

IDEALS CHALLENGE: *Deepening Discourse*

(Adapted from Reitzug & O' Hair, 1998, p. 131. The voices are of teachers in schools.)

"I have heard teachers say that they would like to say something in a teachers' meeting but when five people are very vocal or angry other people shut down. They are afraid to speak out against a person who has slammed her fist down on the table and said, 'God damn it! We've done this 15 times and I'm sick and tired of this conversation.' Teachers who are really trying to solve that problem sort of shrink and they don't deal with it. . . ."

- What are the barriers to productive discourse illustrated in the example?
- What are other barriers to productive discourse in schools?
- How would you define or describe "productive discourse"?

INTRODUCTION

According to Deborah Meier (1995), former principal of the highly acclaimed Central Park East Secondary School, discourse in schools is essential. She writes,

> The kinds of changes required by today's agenda can only be the work of thoughtful teachers. . . . To find time for thoughtful discussion we need to create schools in which consensus is easy to arrive at while argument is encouraged (even fostered) and focused on those issues of teaching and learning close to teacher and student experiences, rather than on procedural rules and processes, buildingwide disciplinary codes, detention policies, filling out forms and checklists, scheduling, etc. . . . This continuing dialogue, face to face, over and over, is a powerful educative force. It is our primary form of staff development. (pp. 108–109)

If schools are to become democratic, teachers must have and take time to discuss, debate, and even disagree with each other about the truly important issues impacting student learning. Schools must create opportunities for creative knowledge building and social dialogue that enables democratic communication and participation.

Discourse is critical to successfully developing and extending democratic education. In democratic schools discourse serves four primary purposes.

1. It exposes us to new ways of doing things and different ways of thinking about issues.
2. It increases our understanding of viewpoints different than our own.
3. It permits exploration of the consistency between our personal and collective practices and the school's values and beliefs.
4. It results in the emergence of a sense of shared purpose among members of the school community.

In order for discourse to serve these purposes, it must be pervasive throughout the school community; inclusive of culturally diverse groups of teachers, students, parents, administrators, and community members; and extend over time.

In this chapter, we examine democratic discourse in schools and how it contributes to the education of children and adults, and to the development of community. After exploring in more detail what we mean by discourse, the chapter focuses on how we might engage in productive discourse.

WHAT IS DISCOURSE?

Discourse refers to conversations, discussions, and debates focused on professional issues. Discourse nurtures professional growth, builds relationships, results in more informed practice, and improves student achievement. In democratic schools, the objective of discourse is the development of a clear, shared purpose for schooling and for student learning and the exploration of how classroom and school practices fit with this shared purpose. Discourse involves asking ourselves and our colleagues difficult questions such as: Do we share our best practices? Do we engage in critical study of our best practices? How much do we trust each other? Is our

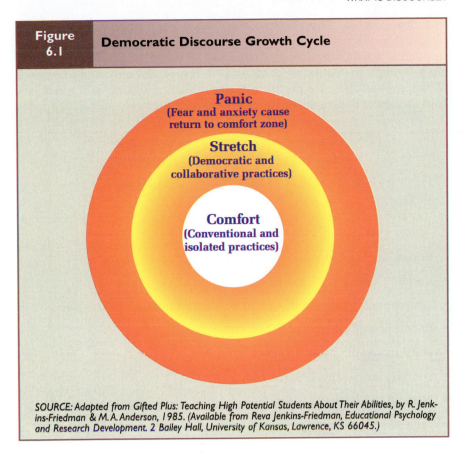

Figure 6.1 **Democratic Discourse Growth Cycle**

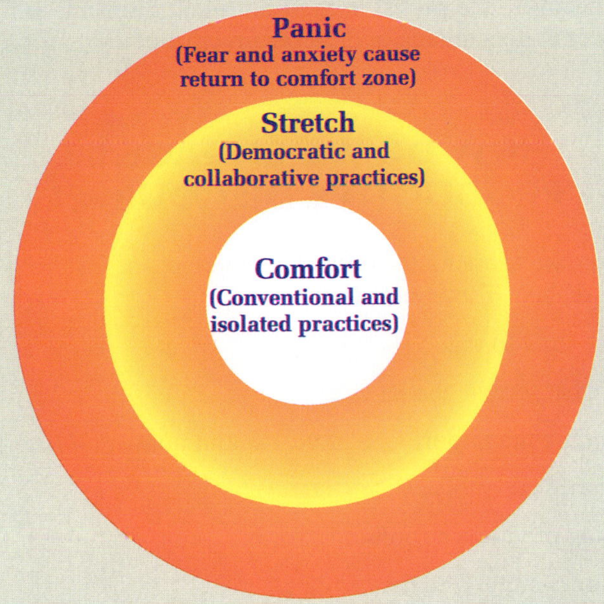

SOURCE: Adapted from Gifted Plus: Teaching High Potential Students About Their Abilities, by R. Jenkins-Friedman & M. A. Anderson, 1985. (Available from Reva Jenkins-Friedman, Educational Psychology and Research Development. 2 Bailey Hall, University of Kansas, Lawrence, KS 66045.)

teaching authentic? How do we know what students know? How do our practices match what we say we believe in?

The essence of democratic discourse in schools is more than just subject matter discussions. It is about reducing isolation and increasing within-school sharing, critique, and learning. Teachers engaged in democratic discourse grow and stretch as professionals. Discourse allows them to move beyond their comfort zone (i.e., conventional and isolated practice) to the stretch zone (democratic and collaborative). The stretch zone helps teachers challenge themselves and others to tackle obstacles, improve practice, and accomplish shared goals and objectives. In conventional school improvement efforts, change often occurs via programs and mandates that sometimes result in teachers being forced to stretch too quickly. Rather than stretching and growing, there is panic and teachers are filled with the fear and anxiety associated with dramatic change. As a result, teachers attempt to escape the panic zone by quickly returning to the comfort zone of conventional practice. The key to school and classroom transformation requires that teachers remain in the stretch zone. Democratic discourse helps provide the constant and steady growth accompanied by the support of others which helps us to stretch without causing extreme panic and fear. See Figure 6.1 for a visual description of the democratic discourse growth cycle.

Discourse in educational settings draws on the fundamental beliefs, skills, and concepts necessary to build strong relationships. While people bring different goals, backgrounds, styles, habits, and preferences to the discourse process, truly effective discourse is interactive, genuine, persistent, and nurturing. Each person taking part in discourse must listen and respond to others, be committed to providing accurate information, seek to work through conflict rather than avoid it, respect different and often conflicting perspectives, and persist in their faith that discourse will eventually lead to greater understanding and better practice.

HOW DO WE ENGAGE IN PRODUCTIVE DISCOURSE?

In this section, we examine the critical components of fostering productive discourse in schools. These include:

- finding the time to talk
- deciding what to talk about
- understanding the importance of verbal and nonverbal language
- providing critical feedback
- encouraging productive conflict
- building cross-cultural understanding
- facilitating productive meetings
- developing and participating on teams

Finding the Time

If schools are to be considered democratic, teachers must have time to engage in discourse. They must have regular opportunities to discuss, debate, and even disagree with each other about the truly important issues impacting student learning.

The number one complaint we have heard voiced by teachers with whom we work is the *lack of sufficient time* in their schools to discuss important teaching and learning issues. Our experience with schools, however, is that there is a distinction between the way teachers in conventional schools talk about time and the way in which teachers in schools striving to become democratic discuss time. Teachers in conventional schools complain that they have *no* time to talk collectively about classroom and school practice. Teachers in democratic school communities also bemoan the lack of sufficient time to talk about their practice, but individuals in these schools find or create times in which to meet, reflect, talk, and study their practice. In these schools faculty meeting time, staff development days, teacher professional days, banked time days, and other available time is used productively. For example, in one school, after a brief period of collective celebration of recent accomplishments, the remainder of faculty meeting time was devoted to work sessions of the school's five democratic practice committees.

By contrast, in conventional schools, faculty meeting time is typically consumed by announcements, instructions, and other insignificant matters. Other available time in conventional schools often inadvertently perpetuates the isolation in which teachers work. For example, schools often have an early student dismissal one day per month to give teachers an opportunity to meet and talk. Unfortunately, many schools do not use their time for this purpose. Instead, such time is often "given" to teachers to calculate grades, prepare lessons, or otherwise work individually in their classrooms. While the intent of this practice is to be "nice" to teachers by letting them get caught up, it comes at the expense of opportunities to further the collective democratic work of the schools and to develop democratic community.

GLOBAL CHALLENGE: *The Use of Time and Resources*

(Adapted from Darling-Hammond, 1997, pp. 193–194.)

Unlike U.S. teachers, teachers in other countries have broad professional roles that engage them in many aspects of school functioning. Administrative and support staff are reduced greatly in other countries. Teachers generally teach groups of students only about 15 to 20 hours out of a 40- to 45-hour work week. During the remaining time, they engage in preparation, joint planning, curriculum and assessment development, school governance, their own professional development (including study groups, observation of other teachers, research, and demonstration lessons), and one-on-one work with students, parents, and colleagues.

According to the Organization for Economic Cooperation and Development (1995), teachers constitute more than 75% of all public education employees in Belgium, Japan, and Italy and more than 60% in most other countries. These countries, rather than build up large external offices for inspecting, monitoring, and controlling teaching, invest more of their resources in supporting the efforts of better paid, better prepared teachers who are given the time and responsibility for managing most of the work in schools. It is because U.S. schools have invested in a relatively smaller number of lower paid, less well prepared teachers, directed and augmented by large numbers of administrators, supervisors, and specialists, that the United States far surpasses other countries in the share of nonteaching staff it employs in its schools.

Table 6.1 International Comparisons of Instructional and Other Staff

Country	Staff Who Are . . . . . . Teachers (Percent)	. . . Other Instructional (Including Principals & Supervisors) (Percent)		. . . Other Administrative & Support Staff (Percent)	Ratio of Teachers & Principals to Other Staff
Belgium	80.0	10.0		10.0	4.0 : 1
Japan	77.4	—		22.6	3.4 : 1
Italy	76.4	7.3		14.5	3.5 : 1
Australia	69.1	7.1		28.6	1.9 : 1
Finland	60.8	—>	39.2	<—	1.55 : 1
France	60.0	—>	40.0	<—	1.5 : 1
Denmark	57.9	28.1		15.8	1.3 : 1
United States	43.6	24.2		33.9	0.75 : 1

SOURCE: Education at a Glance: OECD Indicators, 1995. Published in Darling-Hammond (1997, p. 194).

For more data on international comparisons in education, visit the OECD Web site at

http://www.oecd.org/els/edu/eag98/list.htm

- How do teachers spend their professional time in other countries?
- How does this compare and contrast to the United States?
- What occurs when the ratio of teachers and principals to other staff are reduced greatly such as in the United States?
- What are the implications for democratic IDEALS and schooling?
- Under which staffing model would you prefer to teach? Why?

Democratic schools provide more time for discourse by allocating a greater portion of their funds for classroom teachers and by organizing teachers' schedules to give them more time with the same students and with each other. Through a combination of staffing choices (nearly everyone teaches, including administrators, counselors, and librarians), role designations (teachers take on a broader array of responsibilities), scheduling practices (block schedules with longer periods and fewer classes), and curriculum decisions (a core curriculum with no tracking), restructured schools provide faculty and staff more intense and intimate work time between and among students and teachers (Darling-Hammond, 1997). For example, in one democratic school in New York City, teachers meet once a week for a full morning with their disciplinary teams while students are engaged in community service placements. In addition they meet with other house teachers twice a month during an extended lunch and planning period and with the total staff twice a week. Altogether these teachers average seven and one-half hours a week for joint planning in addition to five hours weekly of personal planning time (Darling-Hammond, 1997). In most conventional secondary schools, teachers meet collectively on the average for one 45-minute staff meeting per week (Darling-Hammond, 1997).

Deciding What to Talk About

When we have time to talk, the question becomes, "What do we talk about?" Often, teachers find themselves engaged in professional conversations which have little impact on teaching and learning. For example, teachers in conventional schools often use their time to discuss nonteaching and learning related issues, such as parking spaces, bus duties, and lunchroom supervision. Carl Glickman (1993) has observed that many teachers and principals feel comfortable discussing students, parents, sports events, or community. He refers to these topics as zero impact topics and suggests that discussions likely to have a more comprehensive impact on teaching and learning include ones dealing with curriculum, staff development, peer coaching, instructional programs, student assessment, instructional and school budget, hiring of personnel, and deployment and evaluation of personnel (Glickman, 1993). Similarly, Deborah Meier (1995), in discussing her experiences at Central Park East Secondary School, observes,

> Nothing was or has ever been "undiscussable," although we have learned not to discuss everything—at least not all the time. This has actually meant more time for discussing those issues that concern us most: how children learn, how our classes really work, what changes we ought to be making, and on what basis. (p. 26)

Thus, the issue for schools may not be as much that there is no time to talk, as that the time that does exist be used wisely—that is, for collaborative discourse that is focused on the questions that are of greatest interest and importance.

Understanding the Importance of Verbal and Nonverbal Language

The importance of language is crucial in discourse and for students' and teachers' learning. It is through using and listening to language that we construct meaning and make sense out of our lives. Ernest Boyer (1993) notes that language is the most essential and awesomely important human function.

> It starts in the womb, as the unborn infant monitors the mother's womb, as the unborn infant monitors the mother's voice. . . . It is no accident that the three middle ear bones—the hammer, the anvil, and the stirrup—are the only bones that are fully formed at birth. We start by listening, and then we learn to talk, first through gurgles and coos and eventually through full sentences. As a requirement for life, for survival, we reach out to others from the earliest days of our lives through the miracle of language. (Boyer, 1997, p. 123)

Boyer (1993) also once asked, "Wouldn't it be great if every child heard good speech and received thoughtful answers to their questions instead of "be quiet" or "go to bed" (p. 6)? Thoughtful and respectful answers to questions are not limited to family communication. Teachers must also respond daily to student questions and to each other in thoughtful and respectful ways, no matter how trivial, uninformed, or uncomfortable another person's questions is for us. For example, students may ask, "Why do we have to learn this?" Unless we take the time to provide them with thoughtful responses which link learning to their lives beyond school, or

If this teacher answers "fine" to the question of how she is doing, her downcast nonverbal behavior will belie her verbal answer.

engage them in a discussion about why what we are trying to teach is important, we will waste "teachable moments."

It is not only what we say but also how we respond nonverbally to students, teachers, and others that makes a lasting impression. If we act disgusted or threatened by someone's questions, an opportunity for productive discourse has been lost. Similarly, if what we say or the way we say it is perceived negatively, or the other person feels professionally or otherwise threatened by our remarks, then current and future discourse is stifled. Thus, it is important that we carefully monitor and examine our verbal and nonverbal language in working with students, teachers, and other members of our school community.

Providing Critical Feedback

Discourse can serve to provide teachers with regular honest, but supportive feedback from their peers. When this occurs, not only does their own practice benefit, but student achievement goes up too (Cushman, 1998).

Across the country, many teachers are seeking ways of getting critical feedback from colleagues to help them improve their daily practices. Some teachers in democratic schools use a technique called *critical friends group* which was developed by the Coalition of Essential Schools. A critical friends group usually consists of six to eight teachers who meet regularly to study each other's practice and to assess student work. The group constantly works at articulating what constitutes good teaching and learning, calling on both outside sources and their own experience. Teachers visit each other's classes, give feedback on each other's teaching strategies or curricula, and gather evidence of what works best for student learning. For example, some teachers develop portfolios to demonstrate and reflect evidence of what is effective for them in their teaching; others meet with groups from different schools to share insights and dilemmas (*HORACE*, 1998). Steve Jubb, Director of the Bay Area Coalition of Essential Schools, describes the critical friends group philosophy in the following way.

> People who work within the school community understand their context better than anyone else. So as critical friends we do not offer advice; rather we ask questions that promote further inquiry on the part of those in the school community. Critical friends recognize what's positive in the work and help imagine its potential.

Recognizing that it is not easy to be both critical and friendly while working collaboratively to make schools better, the Bay Area Coalition of Essential Schools developed the following norms for critical feedback (*HORACE*, 1998).

- Describe only what you see.
- Resist the urge to work on "solutions" until you are comfortable with what the data says and does not say.
- Be aware of the perspectives and experiences you bring to the analysis. These are essentially your biases, as well as the knowledge you bring to bear on the situation.
- Seek to understand differences of perception before trying to resolve them. Early consensus can inhibit depth and breadth of analysis. Hear

from everybody and genuinely try to understand everyone's viewpoint before moving toward consensus or resolution.

- Ask questions when you don't understand. Find the answers to the questions together.
- Surface assumptions and use the data to challenge them. Look actively for both challenges to, and supports for, what you believe is true.

Team teaching is one way for teachers to give each other constructive feedback on their performances and to collaborate on better ways to facilitate learning.

Teachers often become frustrated when they do not receive constructive feedback or questions that cause them to think differently or more deeply about their practice. For example, one elementary teacher reports that communicating with her principal is frustrating due to a lack of feedback.

> He seems to hear me, but avoids taking any action. You never see a problem resolved. If he disagrees with you, he never tells you. I leave his office feeling that he understood and supported me, but I never see any follow-up or results. If he disagrees with me, why doesn't he tell me? I never know. (McIntyre & O'Hair, 1996, p. 57)

In this example, the principal is neither following up on things they have discussed, nor disagreeing with the teacher, nor even asking questions that challenge the teacher to think about the situation. The lack of legitimate feedback makes the teacher feel frustrated, wonder whether the principal understands what she is trying to say, whether he really agrees with her, and ultimately, whether he really cares about her work.

A positive example of constructive feedback involves Aaron Curtis, a first-year teacher, and the way he and his students provide critical feedback to each other about classroom practices.

> It is really hard to watch yourself on a videotape. I watched the tape twice before I could actually see past the way I looked and sounded! But I am so glad that I made myself do it. I saw myself from a completely different vantage point. I guess you could say it was from my students' perspective. I learned a lot about myself and how my actions affect my students. I even watched the tape with my students and asked them for their feedback. It was a very enlightening discussion. I think we all understand each other better now. Every teacher would benefit from routine classroom videotaping. You aren't always aware of how you are influencing your students. Videotaping will help you see what you are doing and how your students are responding to your influence. It also provides an opportunity to initiate student-teacher conversation about classroom influence. (McIntyre & O'Hair, 1996, p. 300)

Constructive feedback is one form of effective discourse. Feedback creates shared experiences and meanings among teachers, students, parents, administrators and others involved in schools and communities.

Encouraging Productive Conflict[1]

All of us have experienced what we deem to be conflict in our own lives. But what exactly is conflict? And, is conflict good or bad? It may depend on who you ask.

Webster defines conflict as the mental struggle resulting from incompatible or opposing needs, drives, wishes, or external or internal demands.

How you define conflict will make a difference in the way you approach it. For example, if you frame conflict as "negative," then you probably think of it as being destructive, as creating stress and anxiety and a host of damaging consequences both personally and professionally. If you see conflict from this frame, as a process of war where one side wins and another loses, you may find yourself acting aggressively and selfishly when a conflict situation manifests itself—a kind of "I'm out for blood" or "I'm protecting me and mine" perspective. If you adhere to this conflict perspective, it is understandable why you might see conflict as something to be avoided at all costs. On the other hand, you may frame conflict as potentially having positive benefits. You may see conflict as an opportunity to grow and improve.

Educators in democratic schools adhere to a positive perspective of conflict. In democratic schools conflict is valued. Educators believe that education for citizenship in a democracy cannot happen in an artificially conflict-free environment. To them, conflict is not something to be feared, ignored, or avoided at all costs. It is to be expected, welcomed openly when it arrives, and even fostered, because from conflict often spring new ideas and understandings about education that helps us do what is best for our students. As Gerzon (1997) describes,

> In a nation whose 21st-century population is projected to be increasingly diverse and contentious, dealing with conflicting values is a key component of citizenship. The core challenge of citizenship is learning to cope creatively with controversy and to make informed choices. (p. 9)

Democratic conflict can be defined as giving voice to *opposing* perspectives for purposes of securing greater understanding and in order to better serve the common good. Democratic conflict is fostered by diversity. That is, individuals from a diversity of experiential and cultural backgrounds are more likely to have different thoughts, opinions, suggestions, and knowledge about the process of education. Democratic schools must provide frequent opportunities for the full and free expression of each of these individual's true selves. When this occurs, conflict is inevitable. If there is no conflict in a school, or if conflict ceases to exist, it is a sign that opportunities to exchange perspectives are not occurring, that the educators in the school do not care enough to have developed perspectives of their own, or that they are too apathetic to challenge perspectives that disagree with their own. Noted change scholar Michael Fullan (1993) observes, "Successful schools did not have fewer problems than other schools—they just coped with them better. The absence of problems is usually a sign that not much is being attempted. . . . Avoidance of real problems is the enemy of productive change and democratic schooling" (p. 26).

Neil Clark Warren (1995), a noted psychologist, states that the amount of conflict in an organization determines the speed at which the organization is moving either toward greatness or toward destruction. That is, conflict can either be productive (move us to greatness) or unproductive (move us toward destruction). Whether conflict is productive or unproductive all depends upon how we think about it (our conflict perspective) and how we act in response to it (our conflict skills). For instance, if you let conflict rage by refusing to learn how to make it productive or choose to ignore it altogether, conflict can destroy you and your school. On the other hand, if you view conflict as an opportunity to explore conflicting ideas and learn the skills necessary to engage in discourse and inquiry that facilitates the exploration of a diversity of ideas, then conflict can lead you to positive growth and achievement.

IDEALS CHALLENGE: *Deepening Discourse*

(The discussion at a school staff meeting that follows is adapted from Nehring, 1992.)

As the meeting began Al, the principal, spoke: "At our last meeting we held a discussion about the small distractions that keep you as teachers from doing what you want to do and what you do best: teach. Here is the list we came up with: Walkmans in the hallways and in the classroom, tardiness to class, eating in the hallways, and disrespectful language. It was felt by the school management team that the sense of the faculty is that we have to start chipping away at all these small discourtesies which over the years have been allowed to multiply. It was agreed that if we came down hard all at once against all these problems, there would be a student backlash. So it was felt we should select, as a faculty, one of these problems and resolve to enforce with consistency across the board." . . .

Joe Grossi, a teacher, raised his hand. "Well now wait a minute. All of those things that you just listed we already have rules for. The problem has been that when we write a kid up for breaking any of those rules, we don't get backed up by the administration. I say let's enforce them all, as we should have been doing all along anyway, as long as we can get a pledge right here and now that we'll get the kind of backup we need."

Al answered. "I have no problem with enforcing all of the rules and I would be willing to make that pledge right here and now—"

"Then why don't you?" Joe interrupted.

"But I . . . I just don't think that—"

George Handelman, assistant principal, rose. "Let me elaborate on the answer Al just gave from my perspective as the school disciplinarian. As it were, I too have no problem enforcing all the rules as long as everyone in this room lends equal support. But you know, the business of getting backed up works both ways. Case in point: yesterday a student came into my office. She'd been written up for being late to class. I asked her how many times she was late. She said once, and then launched into a thing about how her friend Mary or whatever didn't get written up until she was late five times because she has a different teacher, and how her friend Sue tells her she's late all the time and never gets written up 'cause her teacher doesn't care.' Now I don't necessarily believe every sob story that a kid brings to my office, but I know, whether or not this one is actually true, that kind of thing goes on. I think if we're going to make any kind of pledging, and maybe that's not a bad idea, we all need to work together."

Hal Murray tried valiantly to suggest that it was administration's responsibility to reprimand those teachers who did not enforce school rules and that teachers should not have to police each other. But Al suggested that would not work since there are only two administrators and they can't see everything that goes on in a building. So the idea of policing each other seemed inevitable.

Shortly a vote was taken as to which of the "little distractions" everybody would resolve to work on, and Walkmans won out.

- Does the scenario reflect an example of productive conflict? Why or why not?
- What is an alternative way in which the conflict could have been addressed?
- What issues were not addressed or avoided?

We believe that conflict is a healthy, dynamic, and creative means to transform teaching and learning in schools so that it better meets the needs of children. In a democratic school, responding to conflict productively incorporates the democratic ideals of discourse along with other democratic ideals such as inquiry, a concern for equity, authenticity in relationships, shared leadership of discourse processes, and exploration via discourse of how schools can serve others. Productive responses to conflict can:

- increase involvement
- promote cohesiveness and relational growth
- improve group productivity
- develop commitment
- improve decision making
- promote positive change

Conflict is important and inevitable if growth and change is to occur. We believe that conflict facilitation, which is described in the next section is a complex but learnable skill. We encourage you to learn to participate in, and learn from, conflict situations.

IDEALS CHALLENGE: ***Deepening Discourse***

How do you view conflict? The way you view conflict will make a difference in the way you approach it. Answer the following questions:

- In the last conflict situation I experienced I responded by ________________.
- My response suggests that I defined and viewed conflict in this situation as ___________.
- In general, I think of conflict as ________________.
- The ways I think about and respond to conflict is compatible/incompatible with the democratic ideals in that ________________.

Turning Unproductive Conflict Around

Certain behaviors and situations create unproductive conflict and undermine democratic education. These behaviors and situations are outlined in Table 6.1. You should be aware of these factors and understand how detrimental they can be to democratic discourse. Most importantly, you must deal with these factors directly so as to preserve discourse that is grounded in democratic principles and values. The discussion that follows describes each of these factors and provides you with suggestions on how to diffuse them.

Issue-oriented versus person-oriented conflict. Perhaps you have heard statements in conflict situations that are personal attacks rather than issue-oriented objections. For example, you may have heard someone say something like, "You've never known what you're talking about before, and you don't know what you're talking about now." Or, "When you've been around this school as long as I have, come and talk to me." Or, "That is the

Table 6.2 Barriers and Facilitators of Productive Conflict

Barriers	Facilitators
focusing on people	focusing on issues
pushing personal interests & preferences	pushing collective interests & values
holding unrealistic expectations	growing from unfulfilled expectations
ineffective communication skills	listening
solving before listening	listening
negative attitudes	expressing appreciation & gratitude
unattended concerns	examining the others' point of view
focusing on solving problems	focusing on understanding problems
the "I told you so"/"Got you last" complex	initiating conciliatory gestures
lack of self-confidence	encouraging different perspectives
personal biases	examining your motives

stupidest idea I have ever heard." These are lines that reflect unproductive ways of dealing with conflicting perspectives. Strange as it may seem, teachers engaged in democratic discourse hear these types of lines occasionally. Notice that all of these statements are directed toward individuals, not toward topics. Productive conflict is issue-oriented rather than person-oriented. Sometimes we have difficulty separating an issue from the person who is arguing in favor of a position different than ours. At other times, there are simply personality differences between two members that can create problems when they work together. In either case, person-oriented comments are not productive for the decision-making process and do not assist schools in achieving their goals.

Some possibilities for redirecting person-oriented comments include:

- Focus the discussion on the topic, not the person. "Jim, that may or may not be true, but what we are talking about is the budget for next year."
- Stress the urgency of completing the task. "We only have 15 minutes to make this major decision. Let's not waste it by talking about who is better or worse than anyone else."
- Encourage the parties involved in the person-oriented conflict to meet at another time or place. "Jim, I think you and Phil really need to talk about your differences. We can't do this here. We have too much to do."
- Make light of the conflict. "I'm glad we're working on the really important issues!" (spoken ironically).

The central challenge in working with person-oriented conflict is to get people refocused on the task at hand. While the only way to resolve any type of conflict is by working through it, faculty meetings, committee meetings, and other school-based group meetings are appropriate arenas for dealing with issue-oriented conflicts, but not person-oriented conflicts. More productive, beneficial, and long-lasting results can be obtained by encouraging the resolution of personal differences as soon as possible outside of professional meetings.

IDEALS CHALLENGE: *Examining Equity*

(Adapted from Meier & Schwarz, 1995, p. 27.)

CENTRAL PARK EAST SECONDARY SCHOOL, EAST HARLEM, NEW YORK CITY

It was Friday, May 2, 1992. Our students had spent the week talking, organizing, and dealing with powerful feelings in the wake of the Rodney King verdict and the riots in Los Angeles. As luck would have it, an all-white choir from a small Michigan town was scheduled to sing for us that day. While L.A. was burning, and probably scared to death, the choir faced an audience of mostly African American and Latino teenagers, many still brimming with eagerness to protest. There was tension in the air as one of our seniors stepped up to ask if he could say a few words that he thought might help.

"I took it on myself to come up here and talk to all you students about what we've been going through. I know from the Senior Institute that a lot of students have been talking about what's been going on in L.A., and it bothers them a lot.

"I just wanted to tell you that no one here is our enemy . . . and that we have to stick together.

". . . and that there's lots of people from . . . Michigan, right?" The students laugh. "Michigan, not California, right?" There is more laughter from students.

"What they are doing here, they are doing for us. They are not here to make us feel better. They are here because they like to sing, and they're here to show us what they've got.

"They are not our enemies either. There is no one in this room that is our enemy. If we can stick together and stay with each other, we can show these people that we are not falling apart like some other people are." Cheers and whoops fill the room. "You got to do what you got to do, but showing your anger at these people here isn't going to do anything for any of us."

- Describe the conflict facing the school.
- What are the person-oriented and issue-oriented aspects of this conflict?
- What happened in the conflict that could be considered productive?
- Have you encountered situations like this? What did you learn from it? If faced with a similar situation today, how would you handle it?

Pushing personal interests and preferences. The challenge of democracy in schools and other environments is striking a balance between the needs of the masses and the wants of a few. While the democratic way of life values individual freedom and the personal preferences that result from it, it does not promote personal preferences to the extent that they infringe on the rights and opportunities of others (i.e., the common good).

Trying to impose your preferences on others or having others impose their preferences on you creates unproductive conflict. For example, let's suppose you prefer a very structured and organized classroom environment. Your classroom is neat and uncluttered—everything has a place and is in its place. It is in this same manner that you approach your lesson preparation and presentation—you outline your instructional plan and it

Classroom set-up often reflects a teacher's personal style; a messy classroom doesn't necessarily mean a teacher is unorganized, but perhaps is very creative, just as a neat classroom might reflect a teacher who finds that being organized helps him teach better.

serves as a guide throughout your lesson presentation. However, your colleague, who has a classroom next door to you, is just the opposite. She sees organization as being restrictive to her and her students' abilities to think creatively. Her classroom looks cluttered and disorganized to you. You can't imagine how she finds anything. She does not outline her lesson presentations as you do. She prefers a more spontaneous approach to teaching. What would happen if you tried to impose your classroom and teaching style on your colleague? What would happen if she tried to impose her style on you?

Thus, you can see that your personal preference is simply one option for how to do something. It is not necessarily the "best" way of proceeding for everyone. For instance, in the example above, both you and your colleague agree wholeheartedly on the goals of democratic education, you just have different views of how to get there. There will be many times when your preferences differ from others, whether they are colleagues, students, parents, or principals. Unproductive conflict occurs when individuals assume that their way of doing things is the only way. To prevent this type of conflict, you must be open and accepting of different approaches and styles. Be open-minded enough to listen and look at alternative ways of accomplishing tasks. Allow others the freedom to be different from you. If someone tries to impose their preferences upon you, listen carefully and respond slowly. They just might have a suggestion that would work for you. If not, discuss with that colleague or parent why you do what you do and how you see it fitting in with the bigger picture. Explain to them that while your preferences may differ, your basic educational beliefs and values are the same—that of doing what is best for students.

Unrealistic expectations. Unrealistic expectations also can create unproductive conflict. They are one-sided and are imposed by one individual upon others, rather than the product of discourse between all those affected. Discourse can serve to mutually identify what can realistically be accomplished.

Unrealistic expectations create tension and pressure both personally and interpersonally and often lead to frustration and failure. When you hold unrealistic expectations for another person, you create tension or pressure in that person and they may respond in anger—not always at the situation, but at you. For instance, what if you had a child in your kindergarten class who was experiencing tremendous pressures in his home life and who frequently lost control and began crying and screaming at the top of his lungs in your class. What if the next time he cried and screamed you told him, "The very next time you cry or scream in this class you will not be allowed to share in recess with the rest of the class!" Are your expectations realistic? Maybe not when you consider that change takes time. This child needs to learn new, more appropriate ways of controlling his emotions and frustrations, a time-consuming process in which you and his parents must work together to help provide him with new strategies and skills. Without a doubt, this child will cry and scream again. When he does, under your rules he will be punished with a loss of recess. This will frustrate him even more and cause him to see you as the enemy, creating unproductive interpersonal conflict between you and him that affects every area of classroom life. Thus, your unrealistic expectations have created negative results for both you and the child.

To prevent unrealistic expectations, discourse between the involved parties is essential (even if one of them is a kindergarten student—even young children have insight into their behavior and what they can accomplish). One rule of thumb in mutually developing realistic expectations is to consider whether the expectations are likely to result in success or failure. It hardly seems surprising that people who anticipate that they will fail or actually experience failure get into far more unproductive conflicts than anyone else (Harvey & Drolet, 1994).

Ineffective communication skills. How effective are your communication skills? Are you a good listener? Does your nonverbal behavior communicate the same message to others as your words? Are you able to verbally express yourself clearly and succinctly? A negative response to any of these questions by you or your colleagues creates an atmosphere for unproductive conflict and will certainly impede efforts at productive discourse in your school.

How does ineffective listening cause conflict? By missing important messages you may miss deadlines, parent or student conferences, assignments, or messages that could negatively affect students, colleagues, or yourself. In addition, poor listeners are essentially in a conversation by themselves. They say what they want to say, regardless of what others have said before them. When a roomful of poor listeners attempts to have a conversation or engage in discourse, the result is a series of monologues—lots of talking, but little responsiveness, thoughtfulness, or interaction. This, of course, results in poor interpersonal relationships between school members.

In democratic schools, we must be prepared to establish strong interpersonal relationships within our school community. We cannot do this without effective communication skills. One skill that gets overlooked is nonverbal communication. When we realize that 75% of the feedback we receive in a conversation is nonverbal, we can begin to see the impact and importance of our nonverbal communication.

IDEALS CHALLENGE: *Initiating Inquiry*

As an experiment, answer the following question: What is a good teacher? Take your time and write out all of the characteristics of a good teacher. Now refer back to your list. How many of these characteristics have a strong nonverbal component?

Conflicts often occur when verbal and nonverbal messages contradict. For example, if you tell your students, "You had better not chew gum in my class," while smiling at them, they may interpret your message as "It's really OK; she doesn't mean what she is saying." If you then punish your students for chewing gum, you have created a conflict situation based on contradictory verbal and nonverbal communication. To prevent this type of conflict, be sensitive to the nonverbal messages you are communicating. When used appropriately, nonverbal communication should enable us to reinforce our verbal message and thus prevent miscommunication that could result in interpersonal conflict.

What about creating unproductive conflict through verbal means? It is easy to see how an "unleashed tongue" can create conflict. To keep your tongue in check, utilize the following suggestions.

- Make sure you concentrate your comments on a person's behavior or perspective and not on the person.
- Think before you speak—engage in wait time.
- Be aware of your own biases and how they affect what you see and think.
- Don't impose your feedback on another; instead, offer your input.
- Monitor the verbal and nonverbal responses of the other person before providing feedback. Be sensitive to the receiver's emotional state. In the same manner, be aware of your own emotional state and how it may affect your communication.

- Don't overload others with information. Be selective with your comments, selecting key points and presenting them in a manageable and concise verbal package.
- Be selective as to when and where you engage in discourse so that it is not likely to produce conflict. Ask yourself, "Is this a good time and place to discuss this?"

Negative attitudes. Have you ever had a day surrounded by negative people? Did you find yourself leaving that environment with very little patience toward anyone or anything? Negative people can drain a school of both energy and excitement. Negative environments breed unproductive conflict.

There is a difference between democratic conflict and negativism. Negativism is disagreement without hope. It is finding fault for its own sake, with no hope or desire to seek out better ways of doing things. By contrast, democratic conflict is disagreement with hope. It is disagreement with the hope of finding better ways of doing things via gaining the understanding that comes from exploring differing perspectives. Negativism is about speaking and tearing down; democratic conflict is about challenging, listening, and building up.

People who experience negative environments are less likely than others to practice effective communication and more likely to pick a fight with the first unfortunate person they encounter. The opposite is also true. Environments full of people who think in positive and challenging ways are more productive. A positive and challenging environment breeds risk taking, sharing, and tolerance for diverse perspectives. Positive and challenging environments are characterized by responding to undesirable situations with inquiry and discourse until the best possible way of responding is identified and agreed upon.

Unattended concerns. Small concerns or problems can easily become large ones if left unattended. In democratic schools, individuals are encouraged to express their concerns in discourse or through other channels. It is important to listen to others, even when their concerns seem insignificant to you. In the same vein, make sure you express your concerns early and find suitable answers before the situation mushrooms into unproductive conflict.

A focus on* solving *others' problems. Don't fall into the trap of always having to come up with a solution to a problem. Many problems are so complex that they have no solution—there are simply better ways of addressing them. Effective discourse in democratic settings focuses on exploring a variety of alternatives. When you try to solve unsolvable problems, you do several perilous things. First, you close down discourse about the problem. If you have the "answer," there is no need to take time to discuss other possible responses to the situation. Second, you rob yourself and others of the opportunity to grow by discussing, reflecting, and generating a variety of ways to address the situation. Third, you are most likely imposing a simplistic and ineffective solution on a complex dilemma. Does this mean that we should avoid problems? No, it simply means that instead of addressing problems individually with the first acceptable response that pops into our head, we should respond to them collaboratively, via discourse, reflection, and inquiry.

Solving before listening. Productive discourse involves good listening. Yet, many of us take listening for granted. We fail to recognize that listening is hard work. It is a skill that needs to be practiced and perfected. When you fail to listen you fail to learn, and you create a mass of additional problems. For example, if you fail to listen to the whole situation, you may try to solve a problem without having all the facts. Your solution is doomed to fail because it was not based on all the facts surrounding the problem. Often, your solution will be based on the problem's symptoms rather than on the root cause. When presented with a situation, make sure you listen purposefully in order to get all the relevant information. To be sure, ask questions to clarify the situation, ask for the thoughts and insights of others, and allow everyone involved time for reflection and discussion before collaboratively deciding what to do.

The "I told you so" or "got you last" complex. Typically no one likes, welcomes, or wants to collaborate with a person who glories in the "I told you so" complex. The last thing we need when we are facing an unpleasant or uncertain situation is someone who feels compelled to remind us of how we could have avoided a situation if we would have "done it their way." In moments such as these, what is welcome is a sympathetic ear and a supportive attitude.

In democratic schools, there is a spirit of exploration and experimentation. With this freedom, some miscalculations naturally will occur. All experiences (even miscalculated ones) can help us grow and learn. After all, we learn just as much if not more from our mistakes than from our successes. The person who glories in saying, "I told you so," casts a negative light on the positive aspects of good tries that didn't work out but that are part of the growth of democratic schools. Such comments tend to poison discourse and create a defeatist attitude among participants.

The "got you last" complex originated as a children's playground game. Unfortunately, this same game is played in subtle ways by some adults. The "got you last" complex contaminates democratic principles and values. It creates divisions between groups and individuals as well as distracting everyone from the important work of schools. Refuse to participate in such games. While you can't control what others are doing, you can control how you respond to them.

Lack of self-confidence and courage. Democratic schools value the full and free expression of their members. Each member is viewed as an important participant in the process of schooling. To withhold your participation is, in a sense, to limit or undermine the process.

There are many reasons why some members participate less than others. Perhaps you can remember attending meetings when you contributed very little. You are not alone. Teachers have offered a number of reasons for not participating in groups: "I felt intimidated," "I couldn't get a word in," "I didn't know anything about the topic," "I'm too shy," "I was angry at the discussion facilitator," and "They never do what I want anyway, so why bother?" We sometimes feel that our ideas or concerns are not worthy of consideration, or that we have inadequate ability, training, or experience to participate. Other times we are intimidated by what others might think of us—that we might say something that seems stupid or obvious to others or that our input will be met with ridicule or will be rejected.

While others' opinions are important, we must respect ourselves and believe in our own abilities. This type of self-confidence is essential to democratic schooling. There is only one you, and without your participation, your school cannot be complete. You see things from your own individual perspective—a perspective that no one else has. Thus, your participation in democratic schooling is essential.

As educators, we must have the courage to speak out when we feel that our actions as a group, school, or community are incompatible with what is best for our students. It is often easier to go along with the crowd or to hang with the status quo. In doing so you can avoid conflict. In Doris Lessing's (1986) *Prisons We Choose to Live Inside,* this internal conflict is clearly portrayed:

> People who have experienced a lot of groups, who perhaps have observed their own behavior, may agree that the hardest thing in the world is to stand out against one's group, a group of one's peers. Many agree that among one's most shameful memories are of saying that black is white because other people are saying it. (p. 51)

This kind of conflict avoidance is contrary to democratic practice. Democratic schools believe in doing what is best for students. A lack of courage undermines this belief. Humanity's best moments have occurred when ordinary people have had the courage to stand up for what they believe in. Professional educators should have this same courage. Furthermore, by failing to stand up for what we believe, we must deal with internal conflict caused by the incompatibility of our beliefs with our actions.

It is vital that teachers not only have the courage to speak out, but that they do so in an appropriate manner. Stephen Covey (1990) states that a person should express his feelings and convictions with courage, but that it should be balanced with consideration for the feelings and convictions of others involved.

IDEALS CHALLENGE: *Learning Leadership*

Describe a difficult and challenging experience in which you disagreed with an opinion leader. Did you express your concerns or did you sit quietly? If you expressed your concerns, how successful were you? If you sat quietly, what actions might you take next time to participate even when it is difficult?

One of the requirements of democratic discourse is that no individual or group dominates another in terms of power (Dewey, 1916). Inequity in terms of real or perceived power inhibits the free and open exchange of ideas. Yet, in schools a variety of power imbalances regularly occur in decision-making discussions. In most schools there are one or two individuals who always participate in discussions, sometimes to the point of monopolizing and controlling the discussion and trying to force their perspective on the group. Often, other less aggressive individuals are intimidated or overwhelmed by these dominating members and remain quiet. Equity in discourse is essential and requires that the voices of all are heard—not simply those who are powerful, aggressive, or favored. Voices of others who are typically not asked or heard must be solicited—custodians, secretaries and other school support staff; parents, especially the less affluent and those who are members of minority groups; students; and community members.

Carl Glickman (1993) notes that one way of increasing the participation of less aggressive, powerful, or favored members is by providing them with opportunities to access specialized knowledge or information that others do not possess. He provides this example: A quiet teacher was given an opportunity to observe a practice in another school. When this practice was being discussed at her own school, she spoke up forcefully and informed a loud, dominating, and dissenting teacher, "No, it can work. I have seen how it works in other schools and know that it is workable and can be done in our school as well!" (p. 63).

"Gatekeeping" is another way that allows or encourages a nonparticipant to enter into the discussion. This technique is so called because the leader "opens a closed gate," or solicits input from the quiet nonparticipant in order that a member's contribution may be heard. Examples of gatekeeping comments are: "Maria, we haven't heard from you on this," or "Comments? Rick, let's begin with you. What do you think?"

If teachers are serious about engaging in democratic discourse that leads to better educational practices, they must concern themselves with improving self-confidence and inequity in discourse, and with utilizing strategies that encourage all members to participate and share their perspectives.

TECHNOLOGY CHALLENGE

Building Confidence Through Audiotaping

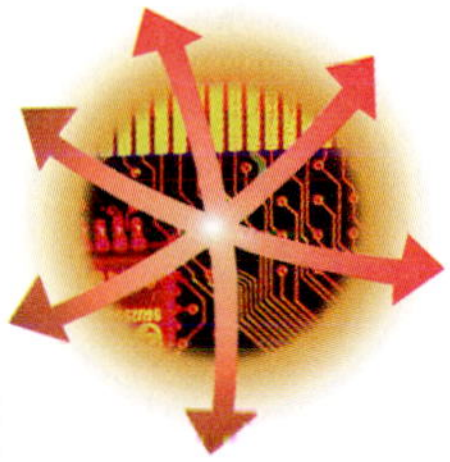

For many of us it is the unknown that scares us. For teachers it is the unknown in terms of participation in a democratic setting that is sometimes frightening. That is, it can be fear-provoking to not know just how we'll feel, act, or even sound when we speak in front of a faculty or at a meeting. Technology can help. Taping a discussion or group meeting provides us with information about our participation (or lack of it). It allows us to see how often and how much we participated, what effect our participation had, and if we were speaking clearly and at the right tempo. After listening and reflecting on our performance, we will begin to recognize our strengths. We also are likely to identify some weaknesses on which we may wish to work. This process can help build self-confidence.

- Ask the permission of other meeting participants to audiotape the discussion. (A university class is another possibility.) Analyze your participation. How much did you speak? What did you contribute to the discussion? What can you do the next time to improve your input?
- Analyze the participation of others. Was participation equitable? Or, did one or two individuals dominate the discussion? Did some individuals not participate at all? Did some appear ready to participate at various times, only to remain silent? Whose input appeared to influence the group the most? What could have been done to make participation more equitable?

Approaching Conflict Positively

Since democratic education involves the full and free expression of who we are and what we believe in, we know conflict is inevitable. As schools strive to become more democratic, conflict is desirable, because it can actually accelerate the change process by forcing us to confront the issues on which we differ. Viewing conflict as a positive, productive aspect of school life is not always easy. Behaving in ways that promote productive conflict is even harder but, as Emerson says: "That which we persist in doing becomes easier—not that the nature of the task has changed, but our ability to do has increased."

IDEALS CHALLENGE: *Achieving Authenticity*

(Adapted from McClure & Phillips, 1997. It is narrated by Lori McClure, a teacher.)

NORMAN, OKLAHOMA

"We are a group of friends who treat each other with respect." Said in unison, this chant begins the daily class meetings of our pre-first-grade transitional classroom. Each day I meet with my students to discuss curriculum ideas and to explore their interests, to encourage a climate of respect and appreciation for one another, and to collaboratively solve problems they have encountered since the previous meeting. The problems are recorded throughout the day in our "agenda book." The agenda book is a place where children record their concerns and the differences that they are unable to work out independently. By writing or drawing in the agenda book, they realize that an unresolved issue has been put on the "agenda" for the next class meeting. At the class meeting we engage in discussion which will help generate suggestions and solutions. With young children, generally a handshake and an "I'm sorry," brings closure to a dilemma. Below are some excerpts from my journal.

SEPTEMBER 11

Many little incidents that are truly accidents are being reported in the agenda book. I'm trying to teach the children the difference in an offensive act and an accident. Through discussion and modeling, I have stressed the difference between throwing rocks and bumping into someone. I think the children are learning to differentiate between the degree and intent of occurrences. I noticed today that when several of the children's "brakes" weren't quite working and bumping into one another occurred, the offender would say, "Sorry." This seemed to be acceptable to the one who was bumped, and the action was not recorded in the agenda book. The children are already demonstrating much growth and understanding from our class meetings! They are developing lifelong skills for solving their own problems.

SEPTEMBER 17

Today on the way to lunch I asked Kevin to stop talking while he was in line. He said, "I can't right now. I'm working out a problem." The fact that Kevin was using the skills acquired through the class meetings was very exciting for me. But, more importantly, I think that the incident reflects Kevin's comfort level in his relationship with me. He knew that I respected him enough to listen to his explanation.

- How does Mrs. McClure approach conflict in her classroom?
- How does the class meeting time help children develop lifelong problem-solving skills?

- Why did Mrs. McClure want the children to distinguish between an accident and an offensive act?
- How are these children learning to respect and value each other?

Just as McClure's students are learning to approach conflict productively in her classroom, we encourage you to consider the following suggestions for promoting productive conflict in your own environment.

Examine your own motives. When facing a conflict situation, examine your own motives. What are you motivated by? Are your motives selfish and self-serving? Or, do you seek mutual benefit for all concerned? Do you have a commitment to democratic ideals?

Examine the situation from others' points of view. The old saying "put yourself in another's shoes" is still important today. When we can see an issue from another's point of view, we are better able to understand the issue. To help resolve conflicts, we must first understand why individuals holding a different viewpoint believe the way they do. Stephen Covey, in his book the *Seven Habits of Highly Effective People* (1990), encourages us to seek to understand before we seek to be understood. According to Covey, this requires emphatic listening, which means listening with the intent to understand. One principal described it as such:

> We walk in each others' shoes. We look at different perspectives. If we are on the staff, we look at it from the parental point of view. In the community we try to see things from the teachers' or staff's point of view. (O' Hair & Reitzug, 1997, p. 274)

Ideally, those whose perspectives we are trying to consider and understand should be involved in the discourse process. However, when this is

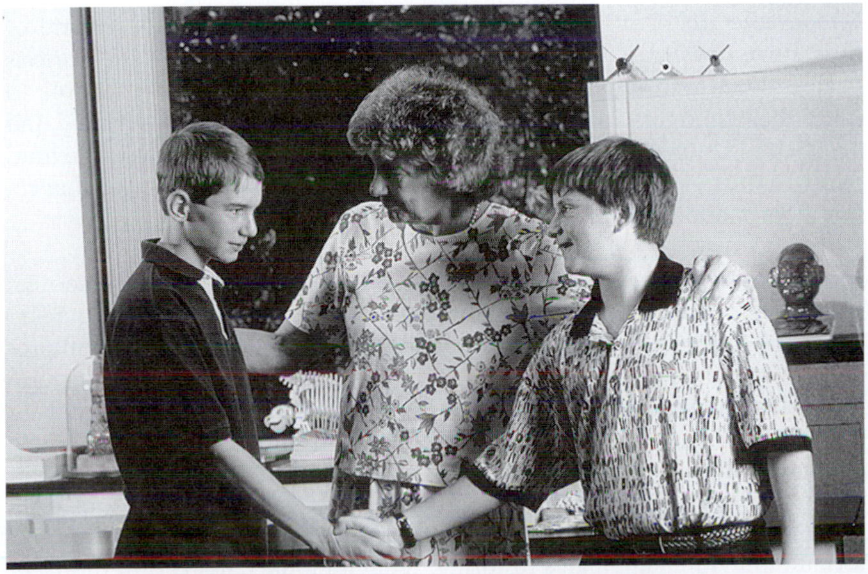

What are some of the positive benefits that can ensue from conflict?

not possible, efforts should be taken to explicitly ask questions such as, "How would students feel about this? How would parents feel about this? How would the community feel? What different viewpoints are likely to be represented within each of these groups?"

Express appreciation and gratitude to one another. To express your appreciation and gratitude to another is to show that you value the person and the perspectives they have to offer. Everyone wants and needs to feel valued. Expressing appreciation and gratitude keeps positive feelings and self-expression flowing, provides much needed personal encouragement, and prevents us from taking each other for granted.

IDEALS CHALLENGE: *Achieving Authenticity*

(Adapted from McClure & Phillips, 1997. The excerpts that follow are from Lori McClure's journal.)

JANUARY 10

Today I was told that a new student would be joining our class soon. When I told the students, they were very excited. As we discussed the arrival of our new student, I asked, "What's the first thing that we'll need to teach Josh?" Almost every child in the room said, "Respect!"

JANUARY 12

A new student has probably never felt better than Josh did today. We began our class meeting with everyone offering a compliment to him. Josh's smiles were heart warming! The intent was for him to feel connected to the group that is already well established and close-knit. He was readily accepted into our community.

- Why do you think the class chose respect as the first thing to teach?
- What other ways help new students feel welcome?

Encourage different perspectives. The secret of creating a climate of productive conflict is to demonstrate daily how much you value various perspectives, even when they differ from your own. Encourage people to share their thoughts and ideas with you and be open to both solicited and unsolicited feedback. Often, the easy part is listening to feedback, the hard part is letting go of old ways of doing things and initiating changes that result from the feedback.

Initiate conciliatory gestures. When you feel that unproductive conflict may be festering, don't wait for the other person to act. Instead, quickly make the first move yourself. Conciliatory gestures help to diffuse unproductive conflict. Most people believe that conciliatory gestures are only appropriate when an individual is at fault. We suggest that "who is at fault" is a secondary issue. The primary issue is clearing the air and reestablishing communication. Conciliatory gestures can assist us in doing just that. In addition, we have found that conciliatory gestures are even more powerful when we are not at fault. Conciliatory gestures take many forms from informal, individual apologies to formal team announcements of a desire to reduce tension.

IDEALS CHALLENGE: *Achieving Authenticity*

(Adapted from McClure & Phillips, 1997. The excerpt that follows is from Lori McClure's journal.)

JANUARY 15

Josh chose to kick Stephen today. Stephen was very confused about how to handle the situation. He wanted to write the incident in the agenda book, but was afraid of hurting "the new student's" feelings. I encouraged Stephen to write the problem down if he wasn't able to solve it. That afternoon in the class meeting Josh was mad and embarrassed because the episode was in the agenda book. However, he was relieved when the students explained to him that it was the action not the person who earned their disapproval. How mature!

- Why do you think Mrs. McClure encouraged Stephen to write the incident in the agenda book?
- How was the class's reaction consistent with effective conflict resolution?
- Give an example of when an action was separated from the person? How did the person feel? How was the conflict resolved?

Grow from unfulfilled expectations. Often we visualize exactly how certain events should happen. When they do not materialize as expected, we sometimes focus exclusively on our disappointment and fail to see new opportunity. Alexander Graham Bell states it best as, "When one door closes, another opens; but we often look so long and so regretfully upon the closed door that we do not see the one which has opened for us." What we decide to do in the school as a result of our discourse will undoubtedly sometimes result in "unfulfilled expectations." Further discourse is the perfect response for such situations. Participants serve as a natural, and potentially positive support group for each other. Simultaneously, the failed try can be the basis for further discourse, inquiry, and analysis that helps to collaboratively determine what steps should be taken next.

Building Cross-Cultural Understanding

In addition to the various factors we have already discussed that are important in fostering productive discourse, teachers must understand the traditions, language, and daily experiences of their students and the community to be able to communicate successfully in the classroom. Engaging in discourse with students and families, especially those from other cultures, can help develop understanding. This is essential if teachers are to know *all* their students well.

IDEALS CHALLENGE: *Examining Equity*

(The following is from a graduate course in educational leadership by Larry Hurst, an Oklahoma educator.)

My name is Chewng Nguyen, and my family and I recently immigrated from Vietnam. My father is a skilled tailor and is currently working for a clothing store doing alterations. My mother is working in a Vietnamese restaurant as a cook. We are living with relatives until we have saved enough money to get our own home.

I am currently a sophomore in high school. My first few weeks of attending an American high school were quite unusual and somewhat disturbing to me. Since I speak very little English, I had to enroll in the same classes that my cousin was taking so that he could act as an interpreter for me while I learn English.

My first day of school was depressing due to the obstacles I have to overcome to learn a new language and become aware of many new, and often conflicting, customs. For example, in my country, it is disrespectful to wave or use a hand signal for someone to approach another person. Using such a gesture in my country would represent what we use for calling a dog. In my Geometry class, the teacher wanted me to come to her desk. She called out my name and then waved her hand for me to come. Although this would have been a seriously humiliating event in my country, my cousin assured me that my teacher merely waved for me to prevent disturbing the rest of the class and that she meant no disrespect.

- What would have happened if Chewng's cousin had not been with him?
- Would the teacher have realized her mistake?
- What might teachers do to better understand and communicate with students from different cultures?

Discourse helps reduce cross-cultural discomfort. Understanding what others are saying often involves "reading between the lines." Reading between the lines is much more difficult if our culture is significantly different from the culture of the person we are trying to understand. Unless the backgrounds and experiences of both people are identical, problems may develop in accurately understanding another's intent. Let us provide two examples.

Example 1. A Hispanic mother poignantly expresses the discomfort she experiences when she interacts with Anglo teachers and parents. She says:

> [In] the Hispanic culture and the Anglo culture things are done different and you really don't know—am I doing the right thing? When they call me and say, 'You bring the plates' [for class parties], do they think I can't do the cookies, too? You really don't know. (Finders & Lewis, 1994, p. 52)

Example 2. A white, middle-class teacher in an urban school intending to call attention to the high degree of poverty that exists in the school's families says, "We have to consider the families the children in this school come from." An African American teacher interprets the white teacher's comment as meaning, "Since most of the kids in this school are black we can't expect much of them since their parents don't care about them."

Obviously, in each of these examples, cultural miscommunication has occurred. It is through discourse that cross-cultural understanding can be developed. Such discourse, if it is open and honest, develops trust between people. Once trust is established, people from different cultures feel freer to challenge each other's cultural assumptions and misconceptions without creating ill feelings and dysfunctional conflict. Understanding cultural differences is key to building meaningful relationships with students and families whose backgrounds differ from ours. Discourse is the best tool for developing cultural awareness and understanding and for monitoring the way our messages are received by students and families from other cultures.

Facilitating Productive Meetings

IDEALS CHALLENGE: *Learning Leadership*

(Excerpted from O'Hair & Reitzug, 1996, p. 14. The voice is that of a teacher with 18 years of teaching experience.)

We have in this district a lot of committees that people put tremendous amounts of energy into that go absolutely nowhere. And people will say afterwards, "What was that all about?" You know, we went through this process, we gave up evenings with our families and everything else to go to these meetings and "where does it go from here?" It just seems to fade and then another committee comes and then another committee comes. . . . It is like you are committeed to death. You go to work and you do your job and then you go to a committee meeting, and meeting, and meeting. . . .

- What are the sources of this teacher's frustration?
- How might the teacher's frustrations be addressed?

Most teachers, especially those working in democratic schools, spend a great amount of time in meetings. Meetings that are perceived by teachers and other participants to be a worthwhile expenditure of time are essential for fostering productive discourse.

In order to feel meetings are productive and worthwhile, teachers must see how their work in meetings relates to student learning and the values, beliefs, and shared purposes they hold as a school. Teachers must see how committees relate to each other and how they support each other's work. With today's technology, including conference-calling, computer networks, and video-conferencing, not all meetings are face-to-face interactions with members. However, face-to-face meetings remain the primary means by which decisions are reached, goals are established, and questions are answered, and one of the fundamental ways in which democratic schools conduct business. This section examines several factors that frequently serve to foster productive discourse at meetings.

Setting Agendas

To be efficient and effective and to stay on-task, meetings should have an agenda. An agenda is a map that guides the participants through the meeting process. The agenda contains topics or subjects that will be covered during the meeting. The agenda is not private information for only a few members. Most facilitators share the agenda with all participants in advance of the meeting so they may prepare and organize their thoughts or concerns. Often the agenda for a subsequent meeting can be developed by the participants at the previous meeting. This serves to make the meeting the group's meeting, not just the facilitator's meeting.

In some cases, the agenda contains time limits or targets for each of the topics for discussion. If one or more discussion topics become "bogged down," time limits help move the agenda forward. By announcing how much time should be devoted to a topic in advance, everyone may adjust their input accordingly. The agenda may also contain the names of the participants who are responsible for leading the discussion for certain subject areas.

One cautionary note: agendas should be used as guides only. Sticking too rigidly to an agenda may cause a group to miss opportunities for in-depth and enlightening, but unscheduled discussions. Having a focus is important, but don't let agendas become blinding and too rigidly enforced. Just as in a classroom, you do not want to miss that *teachable moment* by sticking too rigidly to the lesson plan or moving away from a topic prematurely.

Prioritizing Issues

In democratic schools, teaching and learning issues are the first priority on the agenda. How students construct knowledge; how the curriculum can be integrated; and how learning and instruction can be assessed; what is fair and just for individuals, groups, and the school community; and related issues are constant topics of discussion. In addition to student learning issues, teacher learning issues are also a high priority since you cannot improve student learning without improving teacher learning (Fullan, 1993). Zero-impact issues, as discussed in a previous section, become last on the agenda. Placing important issues first is essential because otherwise time may expire and the significant issues may not be discussed.

Staying on Course

One of the great challenges for teachers in meetings is to actually follow the agenda. There are many possibilities for how a meeting can "steer off course," and members become frustrated and feel they have accomplished little. Witness the following IDEALS Challenge.

IDEALS CHALLENGE: *Initiating Inquiry*

A school's Parent-Teacher Association appointed a task force to investigate how to retain members. At the beginning of the meeting, Jim, the chair of the task force, distributed an agenda. After the first several items on the agenda were addressed, the next agenda topic was a discussion of "Why do parents fail to renew their PTA membership?" After brief discussion, Jim repeated a remark that he had heard from one parent who was dissatisfied with last year's fund-raising activities and threatened to "never come back again." Bob followed Jim's comment with a personal attack on the parent, stating, "I know her and we're a lot better off if she doesn't come back." This spurned more comments and opinions about the woman from the other participants.

The meeting continued and the agenda moved to the item "Publicity efforts for membership retention." At this point Terry said, "Let's skip down to the topic on budget, because I'm not sure we have enough money to print another brochure." Everyone agreed that the financial matter was important, and the discussion moved to the agenda item "How much money do we have?" The meeting continued with time expiring prior to the committee's addressing the publicity agenda item.

- Was this meeting conducted in a successful manner? Why or why not?

Several techniques can be used to keep members focused during a meeting. First, the leader is responsible for directing discussion according to the agenda. The agenda is the "map" that ensures topics are discussed in a logical sequence. Second, to keep every participant on track, the leader *summarizes* the discussion at periodic points during the meeting. Before a group moves from one topic to another, the leader can give members a chance to correct what has been said or decided up to the time that the summary is given. For example, the facilitator might say, "Let me see if I understand what we have said so far . . . Is that correct?" The best time to give a summary statement is when the topic is about to change. If there are problems, or if the leader's interpretation is incorrect, corrections can be made at that time.

Developing and Participating on Teams

Working on a grade-level team or a cross-grade team typically fosters a great deal of productive discourse. Discourse in democratic schools springs from individuals working together as a team on issues or projects of mutual concern. Teaming helps to build trust, cohesiveness, and caring, all essential components in building democratic school communities. Teaming creates an opportunity to improve classroom and school practices by developing an atmosphere of "connectedness," inquiry, and discourse. As one teacher describes it:

> In my school we function as a team. It is a place where teachers are eager to work together. Don't get me wrong. We are all strong teachers individually, but together we make an awesome team. [Together], we listen, discuss, and come up with solutions to problems affecting our students. . . . We have this family concept in my school . . . I know that when I have a problem, it's no longer just mine, but it belongs to everybody. (notes from O'Hair, 1994)

Glickman (1993) believes that teaming should be characterized by purposeful, adult-level interactions focused on the teaching and learning of students. He believes that people do not necessarily have to socialize with one another, but that they should respect each other's differences of opinion about education. Mutual professional respect comes from the belief that everyone has the students' interest in mind.

Goodman (1992), in his examination of critical democracy, notes that if practices in classrooms and schools are to be truly democratic then,

> organization and practices must be deliberately established to cultivate a "connectionist" perspective among its administrators, teachers, and students—that is, a perspective that places one's *connection* to the lives of [others] . . . at the center of the educational process. (p. 28)

While autonomy is important and teachers must be effective teachers individually, if it is not in balance with a teaming or "connectionist" perspective that links individuals to others and to "causes beyond themselves" (Glickman, 1992), practice may over time be determined by self-interest and self-indulgence. For example, the focus of many teachers' unions on protecting the rights of individuals and one group (e.g., teachers) without connecting their position to the interests of other groups (e.g., students, families, community) illustrates the absence of a connectionist perspective. Self-interest that gives people license to pursue their own goals at the expense of others contradicts the very heart of democracy—concern for the common good (O'Hair & Reitzug, 1997).

Finally, teachers working collaboratively on teams significantly improves student learning. In their study of over 1,500 schools, Fred Newmann and his associates at the Center on Organization and Restructuring of Schools found high student achievement to be linked to the following teacher practices:

- participating in reflective dialogue to learn more about professional issues
- observing and reacting to one another's teaching, curriculum, and assessment practices
- engaging in collaborative planning and curriculum

Working on teams as well as teamwork among those not on formal teams are essential in democratic schools. Discourse is enriched by team structures that facilitate the sharing of similar and different perspectives. If a faculty does not intend to disagree, debate each other's ideas, or ask tough questions of one another, then why are they meeting in the first place?

Students and Teaming

IDEALS CHALLENGE: *Achieving Authenticity*

(Adapted from McIntyre & O'Hair, 1996; Good, Mulryan, & McCaslin, 1992.)

It is clear that self-concept can be modified, either positively or negatively, by experiences at school. Cooperative teamwork can improve a student's self-concept. It has been found that students working in cooperative teams have a better understanding of themselves than do students in traditional classes. . . . These students report that they both like and feel liked by the other members of the group more often than do students in traditional classroom settings. . . . It also appears that students are more successful in their schoolwork when they work in cooperative teams. This success leads to an increase in self-concept. Students who have a cooperative, supportive environment in school appear less likely to become withdrawn or antisocial.

- Can you think of other advantages of teamwork for students? As a student, do you enjoy working cooperatively in small groups? Why or why not? What are some disadvantages to working together?

As we have noted throughout this book, classrooms in which student work is driven by a purpose and where children's interests help shape the curriculum hold the most promise for our future as a democratic nation. This requires that teachers substitute lecture-dominated/passive teaching with projects that have a real audience for worksheets and quizzes, children's interests for textbook writers' agendas, and student-centered/active classrooms. The other classroom element that is essential for promoting life in a connected, democratic society is that students work cooperatively on learning tasks rather than in competitive, individualistic arrangements (Wood, 1993). Cooperative work has at its core students engaging in discourse with each other.

Students enjoy cooperative learning and pick up on cooperative routines quickly. George Wood (1993), in his book *Schools That Work,* provides descriptions of cooperative learning that he witnessed in several of the schools that were the basis of his book.

> When given virtually any task, they [students] pair up, figure out how to go about it, and share the work . . . It's not unusual to see a Hispanic girl teaching an African American girl new Spanish words to use during journal-writing time . . . Or to see Jeremy first searching Marcia Burchby's room for the spelling of a word he wants to use and then asking three of his classmates before he gets it right. Or Janelle teaching three other members of her group how to conduct a science experiment. . . . Or Joyce Hanenberg's students rewriting the story "Why Mosquitoes Buzz in People's Ears" in order to add enough characters so every group member has a part. (p. 164)

In addition to the fact that children learn best through cooperative rather than competitive strategies, one teacher provides yet another reason for teaching cooperatively:

> I am trying to teach the power of people working together. That even though one person may not have all the answers and may not be doing everything perfectly . . . all of us together can come up with something we can be proud of and that can be taken seriously by the class, the school, the community, whatever or whoever looks at it. . . .They have gained something by going through the cooperative process; the ability to work with people, to see things from a new perspective, to understand the power of working with a group. (Wood, 1993, p. 161).

Classrooms which are organized for collaboration rather than competition help students tackle problems and realize that they *can* make a difference by working *together*. Some might argue that competition is healthy and should be encouraged. However, if competition comes at the expense of the ability to work collaboratively toward a common goal, it is not only unhealthy but harmful. Most of what we accomplish in life is a result of collaborative efforts, "a fact that every school recognizes when children are encouraged to play together or help one another on the playground. But when students bring that same ethic inside the classroom and attempt to help one another on the real work of schools, then they are accused of cheating" (Wood, 1993, p. 160). Research supports that cooperative, as opposed to competitive, teaching strategies best enable children to learn, and to continue learning for a lifetime (Kohn, 1998; Slavin, 1996; Stevens & Slavin, 1995).

IDEALS CHALLENGE: *Supporting Service*

Think about how you might proceed in analyzing discourse in your university classroom or some other setting. Think about what concepts are significant in understanding discourse in the setting you choose, and how you might collect data on how these concepts are at play in the discourse process you are analyzing. After you have developed a plan for your analysis, proceed in conducting the analysis. Subsequent to your analysis, take appropriate actions to improve discourse in the setting you analyzed.

SUMMARY

In this chapter, we examined democratic discourse in schools and how it contributes to the education of children and adults. The chapter focused on how we might engage in productive discourse and the role of various factors such as conflict in enhancing or stifling productive discourse.

Productive discourse increases collaboration while reducing isolation in schools. Discourse between and among students and faculty is at the core of democratic schools and classrooms. It allows both children and adults to verbalize and sharpen their thinking as they learn from each other. For effective discourse to occur in schools we must develop the skills of meaningful communication—listening, speaking, facilitating and arguing. When these skills are exercised, they build strong relationships and help us tackle significant problems affecting schools. We end with the words of John Dewey (1916), as he aptly describes how communication, discourse, community, and education are related:

> There is more than a verbal tie between the words common, community, and communication. Men (sic) live in a community in virtue of the things which they have in common; and communication is the way in which they come to possess things in common . . . all communication . . . is educative. To be a recipient of a communication is to have an enlarged and changed experience. One shares in what another has thought and felt and in so far, meagerly or amply, has his own attitude modified. (pp. 4–5)

The next unit will discuss issues of equity.

DOING DEMOCRACY

Identify someone who disagrees with you on an issue or topic that is significant to you. Interview that person and develop an understanding of why they believe the way they do about the issue. Your objective is not to debate the issue with the individual or even to help the individual understand your viewpoint, but rather to gain a deeper understanding and appreciation of their viewpoint and how they came to hold it.

END NOTE

[1]An earlier draft of the conflict section was written by Angela McNabb Spaulding.

REFERENCES

Boyer, E. (1993, March). *In Search of Community.* Address delivered at the Association for Supervision and Curriculum Development Conference, Washington DC.

Boyer, E. (1997). *Ernest L. Boyer: Selected speeches 1979–1995.* New Jersey: The Carnegie Foundation for the Advancement of Teaching.

Covey, S. (1990). *The seven habits of highly effective people: Powerful lessons in personal change.* New York: Fireside.

Cushman, K. (Ed.). (1998, June). *HORACE.* Providence: The Coalition of Essential Schools.

Darling-Hammond, L. (1997). *The right to learn: A blueprint for creating schools that work.* San Francisco: Jossey-Bass.

Dewey, J. (1916). *Democracy and education.* Old Tappan, NJ: Macmillan.

Finders, M., & Lewis, C. (1994). Why some parents don't come to school. *Educational Leadership, 51*(8), 50–54.

Fullan, M. (1993). *Change forces: Probing the depths of educational reform.* Bristol, PA: The Falmer Press.

Gerzon, M. (1997). Teaching democracy by doing it! *Educational Leadership, 54*(5), 6–11.

Glickman, C. D. (1993). *Renewing America's schools.* San Francisco: Jossey-Bass.

Good, T., Mulryan, C., & McCaslin, M. (1992). Grouping for instruction in mathematics: A call for programmatic research on small-group processes. In D. Grouws (Ed.), *Handbook of research on mathematics teaching and learning.* New York: Macmillan.

Goodman, J. (1992). *Elementary schooling for critical democracy.* Albany, NY: State University of New York Press.

Harvey, T., & Drolet, B. (1994). *Building teams, building people.* Lancaster, PA: Technomic.

Kohn, A. (1998). Only for my kid: How privileged parents undermine school reform. *Phi Delta Kappan,* 569–577.

Lessing, D. (1986). *Prisons we choose to live inside.* Toronto: CBC Enterprises.

McClure, L., & Phillips, K. (1997). *Discourse and positive discipline.* Unpublished document.

McIntyre, D. J., & O'Hair, M. J. (1996). *The reflective roles of the classroom teacher.* Belmont, CA: Wadsworth.

Meier, D. (1995). *The power of their ideas: Lessons for America from a small school in Harlem.* Boston: Beacon Press.

Meier, D., & Schwarz, P. (1995). Central Park East Secondary School: The hard part is making it happen. In M. Apple & J. A. Beane (Eds.), *Democratic schools* (pp. 26–40). Alexandria, VA: Association for Supervision and Curriculum Development.

Nehring, J. (1992). *The schools we have, the schools we want.* San Francisco: Jossey Bass.

O'Hair, M. J. (1994). Data collected by M. J. O'Hair as part of the Melville (CT) School Restructuring Project.

O'Hair, M. J., & Reitzug, U. C. (1996, November). *Restructuring for Democracy: Co-reform in Schools and Universities.* Paper presented at the annual conference of the Coalition of Essential Schools, Albuquerque, NM.

O'Hair, M. J., & Reitzug, U. C. (1997). Restructuring schools for democracy: Principals' perspective. *Journal of School Leadership, 7,* 266–286.

Organization for Economic Cooperation and Development (OECD). (1995). *Education at a glance: OECD indicators.* Paris: Author.

Reitzug, U. C., & O'Hair, M. J. (1998). Struggling with democracy: Implications for career-long teacher education. In J. McIntyre and D. M. Byrd (Eds.), *Research on Career-Long Teacher Education: Teacher Education Yearbook VI.* Thousand Oaks, CA: Corwin.

Slavin, R. E. (1996). *Education for all.* Exton, PA: Swets & Zeitlinger.

Stevens, R. J., & Slavin, R. E. (1995). The cooperative elementary school: Effects on students' achievements, attitudes, and social relations. *American Educational Research Journal, 32*(2), 321–351.

Warren, N. C. (1995). *The triumphant marriage.* Dallas: Word.

Wood, G. H. (1993). *Schools that work.* New York: Plume.

UNIT 3

EQUITY

Just because all students now have a legal right to an equal education, does that mean that all students now receive an equitable education?

How does discrimination in schools today differ from discrimination that existed in schools during the 1960s when this photo was taken?

CHAPTER 7

INEQUALITIES OF OPPORTUNITY

IDEALS CHALLENGE: *Deepening Discourse*

(In this excerpt a group of high school–age young men from a low-income neighborhood are being interviewed. Excerpted from MacLeod, 1987, pp. 68–71.)

Interviewer: What sorts of jobs do you think the rest of the guys will have?

Stoney: Shitty jobs. Picking up trash. Cleaning the streets. They won't get no good jobs.

Slick: Most of the kids around here, they're not gonna be more than janitors or, y'know, goin' by every day tryin' to get a buck. That's it . . . I'd say the success rate of this place is, of these people . . . about 20 percent, maybe 15.

Steve: I dunno. Probably hanging around here. Shit jobs.

Jinks: I think most of them, when and if a war comes, they're all gone. In the service. Everyone's going. But for jobs—odds and end jobs. Here and there. No good high-class jobs. I think they'll all end up working for the city, roofers, shit like that.

Slick: Out here, there's not the opportunity to make money. That's how you get into stealin' and all that shit. That's why I went into the army—cuz there's no jobs out here right now for people that, y'know, live out here. You have to know somebody, right?
All right, to get a job, first of all, this is a handicap, out here. If you say you're from the projects or anywhere in this area, that can hurt you. Right off the bat: reputation.

Shorty: Is this dude gonna rip me off, is he . . .

Slick: Is he gonna stab me?

Shorty: Will he rip me off? Is he gonna set up the place to do a score or somethin'? I tried to get a couple of my buddies jobs at a place where I was working construction, but the guy says, "I don't want 'em if they're from there." . . .

- What is your reaction to the statements made by the young men?
- What do you believe about the following statement: "The United States is the land of equal educational and employment opportunity?"
- Do you believe the "achievement ideology" that we promote in this country; that is that anyone can be successful and be anything they want to be if only they work hard enough?
- What are the implications of your responses to the two previous questions for your work as a teacher?

INTRODUCTION

In the United States we believe in the concept of universal education. What this means is that we are strongly committed to providing a public education to all children. This differs from practices in some countries in which formal education was (or continues to be) something that is the right of only the rich and powerful. In providing an education for all students it is important to recognize that not all students will come to school equally ready to learn the things that we as teachers intend to teach them. Although we, as a society, believe that all people are created equal and are entitled to certain inalienable rights, various social and cultural factors affect who we are, how we respond to others—both those who are similar to us and different from us—and how others respond to us. This is true as well for children as they enter schools and progress through their formal schooling experience.

As teachers in democratic schools we have a responsibility to educate all students—rich, poor, black, white, male, female, disabled or not. In order to equitably educate all students we must continually develop our understanding of students who are growing up in circumstances that are different than those in which we grew up. All too often we view our personal cultural values and norms as the values and norms that are best. We believe that our way of doing things is the way that everyone should do things. It is important that we understand and appreciate norms, values, and beliefs emanating from various cultures and that we view our way of doing things as only one of many ways of doing something. Democratic schools view the diversity of cultures and experiences that children bring to the classroom as enriching for all students.

Our difficulty or inability to view life through cultural or social perspectives different than those we have experienced can result in inequality of educational opportunity for students. As a result, some students have a better opportunity to receive a quality education while other students have a lesser opportunity. In this chapter we discuss the relationship between various social and cultural factors and educational opportunity. We begin by discussing several concepts related to educational opportunity.

FOUNDATIONAL CONCEPTS RELATED TO EDUCATIONAL OPPORTUNITY

IDEALS CHALLENGE: *Deepening Discourse*

"Schools have been accused of being places in which Western family values, moral fundamentalism, and a Eurocentric "Great Book" ethic reassert a nostalgic and mythical view of what it means to be a citizen. The result is that the key values for schools become domestic production, moral regulation, and cultural uniformity."

- What do you think the above statement means?
- Do you agree with it? Why or why not?
- What do you think are the characteristics of the "nostalgic and mythical view" of citizenship that is referred to above? What do you think it means to be a citizen in a democratic society? What are the implications for schools and for your teaching?

Schools frequently serve as a scapegoat for a variety of problems this country faces. For example, in recent years schools have been blamed for the lackadaisical performance of the American economy internationally. As a result, the rhetoric of competition rather than cooperation has been instilled in our young people. Beating Japan and other countries on international assessments of math and science achievement are national educational goals. The language of individualism and competition is often emphasized instead of democratic concerns for the common good and social attentiveness to the problems of poverty, homelessness, discrimination, abuse, violence, greed, and oppression. As was stated in the above IDEALS Challenge, schools have been accused of being places in which Western family values, moral fundamentalism, and a Eurocentric "Great Book" ethic reassert a nostalgic and mythical view of what it means to be a citizen. The result is that the key values for schools become domestic production, moral regulation, and cultural uniformity (see, e.g., the work of Michael Apple, Henry Giroux, and other critical theorists).

The emphasis on the supremacy of "our way of doing things" and on maximizing educational opportunities for "the best and the brightest" students detract from earlier emphases on providing quality education for *all* students. The result is a promotion of elitist, racist, and sexist attitudes. These attitudes inhibit educational opportunity for all students except those belonging to the favored social class, race, or gender. Elitist, racist, and sexist attitudes are grounded in concepts such as ethnocentrism, assimilation, stereotyping, and prejudice and discrimination. Let's look closer at each of these concepts.

Ethnocentrism and Cultural Myopia

When members of one group believe their culture is superior to all other cultures, they are acting in an ethnocentric manner. Ethnocentrism is the belief that one's particular culture is the "best" culture, that its norms and values are appropriate in all situations, and that it should be embraced by

How do teachers and students from diverse cultural and racial backgrounds add richness to learning in democratic schools?

all others. One's own culture is perceived to be the only "real" one, and anything that does not fit comfortably within this perception is considered wrong, bad, or unworkable. This perception is often held by members of the majority culture toward the minority culture or cultures (e.g., when white members of our society view their way of doing things as superior to the cultural norms of African Americans, Asians, or Hispanics).

Ethnocentric individuals who are unable to view other individuals or events through any but their own cultural perspective have cultural myopia. While a high level of cultural myopia leads people to evaluate other cultures based on their own cultural frame of reference, openness about the legitimacy of various cultural perspectives facilitates effective cross-cultural communication, something toward which all of us should strive. When we limit meaningful communication to only those who look or act like us, we severely limit our school and ourselves. For example, a school hiring team that refuses to hire a male Native American teacher because of long, flowing hair that is in keeping with his cultural tradition is losing a potential opportunity to expose students to an outstanding teacher. Similarly, a hiring team that refuses to hire a teacher who uses a wheelchair because of concerns about his or her ability to supervise students or attend to playground duty may lose a great teacher who could readily assume those duties with some minor accommodations.

Ethnocentrism or cultural myopia in members of the dominant cultural group (in the United States, middle-class whites) leads them to be insensitive toward and unaware of the needs and values of other cultures. Furthermore, the dominant group is unlikely to perceive how their cultural norms and beliefs affect members of other cultures. For example, Christmas parties in schools may conflict with the cultural or religious beliefs of students who are from cultures or religions that do not recognize this holiday. A more subtle example may be the culturally grounded belief that the *best* family structure consists of a mother and a father living in the same house raising their children. Such a cultural belief conflicts with other cultural notions of family that have had good results in raising children, including single-parent family structures, gay family structures, or extended family structures.

Valuing homogeneity rather than diversity is one of the factors that leads to communication difficulties at school and in the community. The more we interact with people different from ourselves, the more likely it is that our information about other people will be correct, thus boosting effective communication. Conversely, the more we avoid individuals different from ourselves, the less likely it is that accurate perceptions will be formed, thus harming effective communication all the more.

Assimilation

One form of ethnocentrism is assimilation. Currently, many schools expect students to reject their own cultural characteristics and adopt (assimilate) the dominant culture's ways of experiencing and learning. The belief of those promoting assimilation is that for students, assimilation equals success in school. That is, that the more completely a student can adopt the values, practices, and worldview of the dominant culture, the more successful a student coming from a nondominant culture will be.

Becoming assimilated into the dominant culture, however, can teach students that their characteristics are deficient. Assimilation demeans students' images of themselves as learners and ignores aspects of students that are at their core as a people. Schools that promote assimilationist views send negative messages to students from cultural minority groups that their culture is not as good as the dominant culture and, thus, that they are not as good and as valued as students. This can lead to the development of a negative self-concept that makes school success less likely. For example, many people with disabilities do not see their disabilities as deficiencies; they see them as characteristics. Individuals who are deaf and use sign language may not be able to hear, but they can be very effective learners, even though their ways of receiving and expressing language are different from those of the majority culture. Learning the dominant culture's modes of communication is neither reasonable nor necessary. Individuals who are deaf need the dominant culture to accept their characteristics as valuable and to make changes that create opportunities for them to flourish. Nieto (1996) argues that research and her work with students indicate that it is important for students to maintain their dominant culture. She observes that the more students are able to do this, the more successful they will be in school.

Nieto (1996) and others, however, recognize that nonmajority students cannot reject the dominant culture either. As Lisa Delpit (1995) has pointed out, proficiency in using the dominant culture's language and knowing its way of being is a "code of power" (p. 40) for nonmajority students. Nonmajority students need to know and be able to operate by these codes of power in order to have access to opportunities. Thus, nonmajority students need to both maintain their pride in their culture and language while learning the codes of power of the dominant culture. Nieto (1996) notes that the implications of this for school policies and practices is that they must "stress cultural pride, build on students' native language ability and use, and emphasize the history and experiences of the students' communities" (p. 293).

One significant arena in which beliefs about assimilation have been played out are in the area of bilingual or second-language education. Specifically at issue is how students who are not proficient in English are to be educated. Beliefs range from a sink-or-swim attitude, in which non-English speaking students are expected to learn English on their own, to two-way bilingual education where English-speaking and non-English speaking students are integrated with each other with the goal that *all* students will become bilingual, achieve academically, and be cross-cultural in their attitudes. Individuals holding the sink-or-swim perspective might argue, "This is our country. If someone wants to live here and go to school here, it's their responsibility to learn our language and way of doing things." This position reflects an extreme assimilationist stance. The passage in California of Proposition 227, which essentially prohibits non-English language instruction, is an example of this belief. The IDEALS Challenge that follows provides more detail of the various perspectives on this issue.

IDEALS CHALLENGE: *Examining Equity*

(Excerpted and adapted from Schnaiberg, 1998.)

California's educators and its 1.4 million limited-English proficient students are in limbo.

Voters last week overwhelmingly approved a ballot initiative that calls for the virtual elimination of bilingual education from the state's public schools. Now officials in districts are waiting to find out what happens next.

Gloria Matta Tuchman, the Orange County teacher who cosponsored Proposition 227, said that by perpetuating what she calls a failed bilingual education system, advocates, policymakers, and some educators themselves compelled voters to take matters into their own hands.

The measure calls for limited-English proficient (LEP) students to be taught in a special English-immersion program, in most cases for no more than a year, before moving into mainstream English classrooms.

Opponents of the measure say spending one year in an English-immersion program could mean students' access to grade-level instruction is delayed by a year—a charge Tuchman vehemently rejects.

And many administrators and teachers predict that all children—not just LEP students—will be affected as mainstream teachers grapple with students who may not be prepared to deal with grade-level work in English after one year in immersion.

Civil rights groups say 227 would violate students' rights to equal educational opportunity.

- Do you believe that Proposition 227 is an example of an assimilationist perspective? Why or why not?
- Do you believe that Proposition 227 limits "students' rights to equal educational opportunity"? Why or why not?
- Conduct some research on the various options for bilingual programs and the advantages and disadvantages of each.
- Conduct research on the status and impact of Proposition 227 since its passage in June 1998.

CLICK ON IT

For more information on bilingual education, visit the Web site of the National Council of Bilingual Education at

http://www.ncbe.gwu.edu

Stereotyping

Stereotyping is the process of organizing information about groups of people into categories that make generalizations about their attitudes, behaviors, skills, morals, and habits. In some ways stereotyping is a natural process that makes our thinking, perception, and communication processes more efficient. Categorizing and grouping information helps individuals to manage a complex array of information. However, stereotypes have a powerful influence on our perceptions and judgments of other people. If you have a difficult experience with a member of another culture, stereotyping could cause you to generalize this instance onto all members of that cultural group.

Stereotypes are often very resilient and remain in place in spite of contrary evidence. That is, stereotypes often compete successfully with reality and serve as explanations for racist and/or sexist thought and behavior. Even stereotypes that seem to be positive still work as stereotypes— they restrict identity and offer narrow representations of groups of people. Saying that women are sensitive, African Americans have rhythm, Asians are smart, Mexican Americans are romantic, or that persons with disabilities are heroic is merely the flip side to: women are irrational, African Americans are violent, Asians are cowardly, Mexican Americans are lazy, or persons with disabilities are slow. All stereotypes establish prejudicial and reductive views of others. It is through their simplicity, one-directionality, and claims to commonsense knowledge that stereotypes can be so powerful and difficult to dislodge. Indeed, sometimes the victims of stereotypes begin to believe in the validity of the stereotype. By regularly attributing certain characteristics to a group (i.e., stereotyping them), members of that group over time may come to believe in the truth of the attributes. This may serve to limit their confidence and their opportunity (Capper, 1993; Reitzug, 1994). For example, girls may begin to believe the stereotype that females are poor at math and end up lacking confidence in their mathematical ability or avoiding higher level math courses.

Children who are educated in classrooms and schools which are culturally diverse can learn that all students are very much alike as people, even though their physical and cultural characteristics are different. Students in diverse classrooms also can discover how to learn from one another. For example, a technique that helps a student with learning disabilities focus his attention in reading may be quite helpful for other students who struggle to maintain their interest in social studies.

Reducing stereotypes requires learning to perceive others in more complex and different ways. To perceive others from multiple perspectives means, most importantly, learning how people themselves wish to be understood. Among the necessary conditions to achieving this are engaging in ongoing conversation and cultural contact. In turn, meaningful dialogue with members of different cultures requires more than mere physical proximity. That proximity alone will not produce better relations between different groups is most clearly demonstrated by the long history of coeducation in the United States, which has not ended gender discrimination. Moreover, schools sometimes use physical proximity in ways that undermine positive cross-group relations. A traditional means of classroom control with younger students is to seat males and females next to each other precisely because they commonly have sex-segregated friendships and social lives. In this situation, the lack of communication between the sexes at this age is exploited and physical proximity becomes a disciplinary technique that reinforces existing gender roles and relations.

One element in the effort to educate all students together in heterogeneous classrooms is overcoming stereotyping.

Prejudice and Discrimination

Prejudice is a deep-seated feeling of resentment and or hostility toward a particular group based on faulty and erroneous stereotypes. Negative stereotypes categorize thoughts and feelings about cultural groups leading to prejudicial attitudes. These prejudicial attitudes, in turn, inhibit effective relationship development. Just as stereotypes facilitate your thinking and perceptual processes, prejudices make it easy to protect your attitudes and behaviors by criticizing other people. Prejudices prey on the insecurities and fears we have about the legitimacy or value of our own existence.

Prejudicial attitudes range from intolerance about race and gender to attitudes about appearance and social background. When schools allow prejudices to influence decisions, prejudice becomes discrimination. *Discrimination* is the mistreatment or denial of opportunity to members of a particular cultural group. There are laws and policies that protect students from being discriminated against in schools. Laws and policies are necessary but insufficient to combat prejudice and discrimination. Students learn not to be prejudiced by having positive experiences with other students who do not look, act, or learn like they do and by learning that their stereotypes limit their understandings of others. We all know of examples of students who have been oppressed by racial or ethnic stereotypes. But there are more subtle stereotypes that are similarly oppressive. For example, how often have we chosen students to take leadership positions on the basis of their good looks or their parents' social position in the community? Simply because some students do not match society's stereotypes about beauty does not mean that they cannot be good class presidents or inspirational cheerleaders.

Ethnocentrism, assimilation, cultural myopia, stereotyping, prejudice, and discrimination all serve to limit the opportunities of those who are victimized by them. These concepts, however, are not solely the domain of *society*. They also exist in schools—often in subtle and unknown ways—in the attitudes and practices of students, teachers, administrators, support staff, and other members of the school community. The following sections explore specific ways in which factors related to race, ethnicity, social class, gender, disability, and sexual identity serve to limit educational opportunity.

FACTORS RESULTING IN INEQUALITY OF EDUCATIONAL OPPORTUNITY

Racial and Ethnic Diversity

The United States is becoming increasingly racially and culturally diverse. Currently, half of the United States' population growth is accounted for by individuals of color, with about one-fourth of the U.S. population qualify-

Figure 7.1 **Current and Projected U.S. Minority Group Population Percentages**

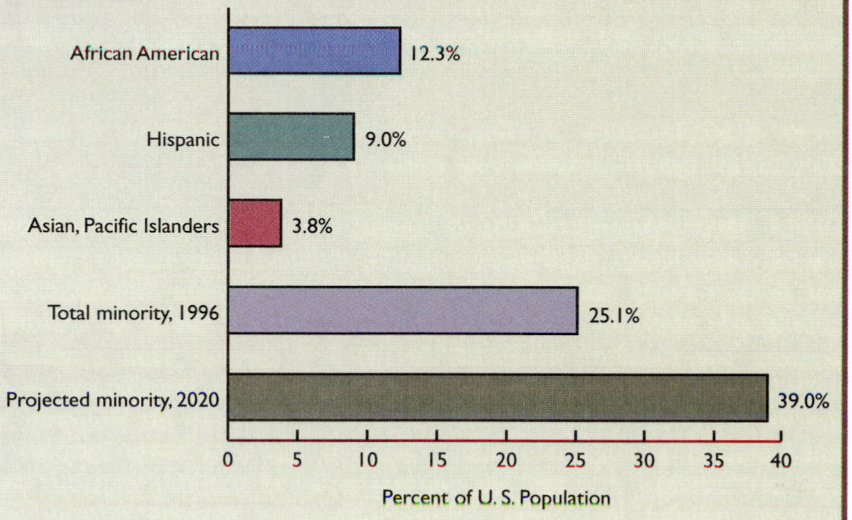

SOURCE: U.S. Bureau of Census, 1996.

ing as being minority (Ward, 1994). African Americans make up 12.3% of the total U.S. population; Hispanics, 9.0%; and Asians, Pacific Islanders, and other races, 3.8%. It is projected that in the next 25 years, the nonwhite segment of the U.S. population will increase to 39% (U.S. Bureau of the Census, 1996; see Figure 7.1).

Public school populations, particularly in urban areas, also are becoming increasingly nonwhite. Minority group members make up approximately 33% of public school enrollment, with some large urban districts having over 90% minority enrollments (U.S. Department of Education, 1996a). Between 1980 and 1994, the number of Hispanic students in public schools increased by 46% and the number of African American students by 25%, while the number of Caucasian students increased by only 10% (U.S. Bureau of the Census, 1996).

Although the differential birth rates of various races and ethnic groups have a great impact on population growth, immigration also has contributed to the growth of minority group populations. The United States now admits more immigrants annually than ever before. Whereas most immigrants came from Europe in decades past, most now come from Asian and Hispanic countries (America's Changing Face, 1990). The combination of high birth rates, low median age, and high immigration rate makes the continued growth of the nonwhite segment of our population likely.

Students belonging to many racial and cultural minority groups have traditionally had low achievement in schools. The reasons for low achievement are complex. After reviewing a great deal of research on minority group achievement, Nieto (1996) concludes that "school achievement can be understood and explained only as a multiplicity of sometimes competing and always changing factors" (p. 245). Some of these factors are briefly discussed below.

Language difficulty. For students from some minority groups, such as recent Hispanic immigrants, not being proficient in the English language can affect school achievement. This is particularly true if these students do not have access to high-quality bilingual education programs or if judgments about their achievement are based on tests that are written in English.

Overt discrimination. In some instances, educators continue to overtly discriminate against students from minority groups.

Covert discrimination—Cultural mismatch. Many times educators and schools unknowingly discriminate against students from minority groups due to the cultural mismatch between middle-class, white conceptions of appropriate education and the norms, values, and needs of minority students. For example, a cultural mismatch is present when a school's curriculum is Eurocentric, excluding knowledge and perspectives from non-European cultural groups, and the school's students are primarily of non-European heritage. A cultural mismatch may also occur between a teacher's teaching style and the learning styles of minority students. For example, scholars have cited cultural differences between African and European cultures that have an effect on the learning styles of African American and Caucasian students and have implications for how a teacher's behavior will effect students (e.g., Hale-Benson, 1982; Irvine, 1991). Jacqueline Jordan-Irvine (1991) highlights the following cultural differences between African and European cultures:

- an orientation in African culture to expressive movement as opposed to the European orientation to impulse control
- an orientation in African culture to affect as opposed to the European orientation to reason
- an orientation in Africa to an orally based culture as opposed to the European orientation to a print-based culture

Each of these cultural orientations have significant implications on how a student is likely to learn best and how she or he is likely to respond to different teaching practices.

IDEALS CHALLENGE: *Examining Equity*

(Excerpted from Carger, 1996, pp. 98–99. Alejandro Juarez is an eighth-grade student at a school in Chicago. His family immigrated to this country five years ago. On his most recent standardized achievement test, Alejandro scored in the 15th percentile in reading and in the 1st percentile in spelling, grammar, vocabulary, and math (meaning that 99% of the students across the country who took the exam scored better than he). In the following excerpt the author discusses Alejandro's academic ability, his performance on another test, and how his teachers perceive him.)

Interestingly, Alejandro recently was assessed as English dominant based on a standardized language dominance test given during the summer ESL (English as a Second Language) program. His English proficiency was rated as slightly higher than his Spanish proficiency. But in this test, as is the case for many current language dominance instruments, only conversational skills are assessed rather than the more complex language needed for academic work. Nestled in the security of his home, Spanish was his language of choice even if some words escaped him. . . . No language dominance test I knew could measure the effect of context. In addition to language . . . I remained convinced that a memory problem and visual perception weakness hindered Alejandro's performance.

His diagnostician was a well-balanced LD (Learning Disabled) specialist, which is a luxury many second-language children are not afforded in the assessment process. . . . [On the individual assessment he administered] Alejandro scored strongly within the average range, at the 47th and 92nd percentiles, on nonverbal mental ability tests. Luz, his diagnostician, who had tested him in the fifth grade as well, and I were delighted to see those scores. It gave some credence to our suspicion that mainstream language depressed other scores significantly.

The interviews I conducted showed that his teachers, with the exception of remedial reading, chose to explain his academic performance as lack of sufficient effort. Even Mr. James, although aware of memory problems affecting math, pointed to peers and low self-expectations as underlying problems in math achievement. None, not even the remedial reading teacher, voiced major concerns about his lack of English proficiency.

- What are the factors that appear to be affecting Alejandro's school achievement?
- How can the differing results between the standardized test and the individual assessment be explained?
- What does the author mean by "the effect of context" in the first quoted paragraph? How might one's home and community context affect their performance on intelligence and achievement tests?
- Mr. James claimed that Alejandro's learning difficulties were due to lack of effort. As a teacher, how could you inquire in order to determine when a student is not trying versus when other learning difficulties are hindering their performance on schoolwork?

Resistance. In some instances, the low achievement of students from racial and cultural minority groups is due to political resistance. That is, sometimes students consciously or subconsciously resist what educators and schools are trying to teach them. In some instances students may resist simply because they dislike school policies or structures, or they do not want to be subjected to authority. In other instances resistance may be the result of "moral and political indignation" (Giroux, 1983, p. 288). That is, students may consciously or subconsciously resist learning or the wishes of educators because they believe that they are being mistreated and that this is the only way in which they can be heard. Frequently, perceived mistreatment is grounded in issues of race, ethnicity, or class. For example, students from racial or ethnic minority groups may resist because they do not see people who look like them in their textbooks, they do not see education as leading to economic opportunity for them (see the IDEALS Challenge that opened this chapter), or they see schools as trying to assimilate them or make them "act white" (see the IDEALS Challenge that follows).

CLICK ON IT

For more information regarding African Americans, including discussion of current issues, visit the Web site of the NAACP at

http://www.naacp.org

IDEALS CHALLENGE: *Examining Equity*

(*Excerpted and adapted from* Blacked Out: Dilemmas of Race, Identity, and Success at Capital High *by Signithia Fordham, 1996, p. 236–237, 283.*)

High-achieving African American adolescents at Capital High are resisting the dominant society's minimal academic expectations for black students. High-achieving students seek to validate African Americans' ability to perform academically in ways that parallel and even surpass those of their white American counterparts. Hence they often eagerly seek to become indistinguishable from their dominant group counterparts in behavior, worldview, language usage, and so forth. This leads to the emergence of a raceless "self" through denying connectedness to other black Americans, their African ancestry, and all things black. Students who seek academic success risk being accused of acting white.

Among *underachieving* African American students, resistance to being academically successful is used to reclaim African American humanness. The dominant ideology postulates that academic achievement is the primary route to success; but to Capital students academic success is the primary route to becoming the "other" [that is, to "acting white"].

- In what ways do *high-achieving* students show resistance to society's expectations of them? What are they resisting?
- In what ways do *underachieving* students show resistance to society's expectations of them? What are they resisting?
- What factors are identified in the excerpt and in this chapter that help you understand the underachievement of black and other minority group students in school?
- In what ways can democratic schools respond to underachievement by minority group students?

A Response: Multicultural Education

Even though most educators harbor good intentions toward *all* students, achieving school environments that honor multiple cultures and provide equality of educational opportunity for all students is not easy. It is not simply a matter of seeking out and terminating the employment of racist educators. Educators who belong to the dominant cultural group (i.e., the white middle class), or have been acculturated to accept the norms, values, and beliefs of the dominant cultural group as their own, often view schooling through a narrow cultural lens. Thus, they may be unknowing or insensitive to cultural differences in learning styles, to the Eurocentric content of the textbooks they use, or to the incongruency of some school policies and practices with the norms and values of nondominant cultural groups. Unfortunately our own frequently culturally narrow experiences constrain us from being culturally sensitive enough to always realize when the focus of the education we provide delegitimizes the cultures of children with other cultural backgrounds and thus ensures *in*equality of educational opportunity for most of these children. As teachers in democratic schools it is important that we engage in inquiry and discourse in furthering our understanding of cultures other than our own. Without understanding various cultural perspectives we are likely to inadvertently engage in inequitable practices in our classrooms. Additionally, without multicultural understanding, it will make it more difficult for us to work toward equity in our school.

In addition to learning about the clothing, heroes, holidays and foods of other cultures, what else is necessary for true cultural understanding?

IDEALS CHALLENGE: *Achieving Authenticity*

(Excerpted from Fordham, 1996. The excerpt is a letter a teacher wrote to her colleagues in reaction to the school's celebration of St. Patrick's Day. The setting is a large, urban high school in Washington, DC, that is attended by predominantly African American students.)

Recognizing the rights of the leprechauns to sponsor today's activities in celebration of St. Patrick's Day, I wonder why there was no such effort to sponsor a party, fun, or merriment to celebrate Black History Month! That was month, not day. Oh yes, there was the assembly that almost did not take place, to which only selected teachers were invited to take their classes. A few individuals did make bulletin boards. But there was no cake, no schoolwide merriment, no leadership to celebrate the accomplishments of black heroes. The birthday of Martin Luther King Jr. was properly ignored by all but a few. As you take a bite into that piece of green cake today, I want you to feel GUILTY, especially if you are black. During February you were not black and proud, you were black and hiding, or black and ashamed. Today you are pretending to be Irish! It's not the leprechaun that will get you the real pot of gold, it's more black pride and the dedication that accompanies that pride.

Y.B.C.
Your Black Conscience

- What is your reaction to the teacher's letter?
- How do you think the school should have celebrated Black History Month?
- How do you feel about dedicating a month to black history? What are the advantages of this type of approach? What are the disadvantages?

- Is celebrating Black History Month, or recognizing black heroes, an authentic approach to multicultural education? Why or why not? How can schools help members of other minorities, such as Hispanics, Native Americans, and Asians, celebrate their cultures?
- What is multicultural education and why is it important? Why is it especially significant for democratic schools?

Practice in democratic school communities requires that we rethink and reconstruct schooling in a way that recognizes and honors multiple cultures and ways of being. Noted scholar James Banks (1994) describes four levels of multicultural school reform. He calls the first level the *contributions approach.* This approach has also been called the "heroes, holidays, and foods" approach to multiculturalism because it focuses solely on these aspects of other cultures. A school using this approach might discuss Martin Luther King, celebrate Cinco de Mayo or Black History Month, or have a "Soul Food Evening."

The second level of multicultural curriculum is the *additive approach.* In this approach, content, concepts, themes, or perspectives are added to the curriculum, but the focus of the overall curriculum remains Eurocentric. Adding a Multicultural Issues class or a unit on Diversity are examples of this approach. When teachers or schools become stuck at the first two levels of multicultural reform, they fall short of democratic school practice. The contributions and additive approaches may be better than not addressing multicultural issues at all and may be a necessary first step for many teachers and schools before engaging in more systemic reform. However, by themselves and without additional growth and reform in this area, they may simply serve as token responses that allow the more systemic and cultural incongruencies of overall school practices to be ignored.

Banks (1994) terms the third level of multicultural school reform as the *transformational approach.* This level requires a more systemic restructuring of the curriculum and school practices, so that all curricular concepts, issues, and themes, as well as all school events, are viewed from the perspectives of multiple cultural groups.

The fourth and final level of multicultural curriculum reform is called the *social action approach* and requires students to develop stances on important social issues and to take action to address these issues. The third and fourth levels are congruent with democratic IDEALS, particularly inquiry, discourse, equity, and service.

Replacing the dominant cultural perspective with a minority cultural perspective, however, is also antithetical to democratic schooling. Democratic schooling requires that we continually attempt to understand how education might best proceed when it integrates a variety of cultural perspectives. Exposure to multiple cultural perspectives stimulates inquiry, enriches discourse, enhances equity, facilitates authentic learning, provides leadership opportunities for all students and teachers, and promotes service on social issues.

CLICK ON IT

For more information about multicultural resources for teachers, visit

http://curry.edschool.virginia.edu/go/multicultural

For an online magazine devoted to multicultural education, visit

http://www.inmotionmagazine.com

PRESENT TO PAST

The Cultural Homogeneity of Teachers

In 1993, although about 30% of public school children were from minority ethnic groups, only about 12% of teachers were from minority groups (U.S. Department of Education, 1996b). How did we come to this disparity between those who teach and those who are taught? Let's examine historical trends in the teaching force, particularly with respect to African American teachers.

Historically, most African American educators taught in the South, where, until the 1960s and 1970s, black teachers taught black students in segregated school systems. The teachers were mainly female. In 1890 there had been roughly equal numbers of men and women in the African American teaching force, but by 1910 women held more than two-thirds of the teaching positions (Schwager, 1987). Teaching was a respected job in the community, although African American teachers earned less money and worked with far fewer resources than did European American teachers.

In the North, African American teachers have a long history of teaching, and in Chicago, Buffalo, and other cities they sometimes taught in schools with no minority students. In Buffalo, New York, for example, there have been black teachers in the public schools for more than 150 years (though until 1972 they taught in the segregated African School). African American teachers were required to demonstrate the highest possible character and, if they did so, were seen as fine "representatives of their race," a pressure that many minority teachers since then have also felt.

Ironically, the expansion of civil rights in the late 20th century commonly resulted in a decrease of minority teacher representation and community involvement in schools. School desegregation often led to the elimination of jobs for minority teachers, especially in the South where parallel school systems had been mandated. In hundreds of towns and cities, the African American schools were torn down or turned to other purposes and students attended formerly all-white schools. These schools consequently had low percentages of African American teachers and administrators, although in some cases efforts were made to maintain ethnic balance.

As opportunities for black professionals have grown recently in other fields, the number of African American teachers has decreased. In addition, because society evaluates one's worth and status according to income, low salaries have contributed to the decline in teacher status within the black community as it "assimilates the values of the larger society" (Perkins, 1989, p. 363). This comment applies to other ethnic minorities as well. In 1993, Asian/Pacific Islanders were far more likely than European Americans to major in biological and life sciences, computer and information sciences, or engineering; African Americans were more likely to major in business management; and Hispanics were more likely to major in the social sciences or history—but all were less likely than European Americans to major in education (U.S. Department of Education, 1996b).

Social Class

The socioeconomic class from which students come also affects their access to educational opportunity and their achievement while in school. Children are poorer than any other age group in America. One out of every five children lives in poverty (Children's Defense Fund, 1997). Almost half of all children born in the United States today will spend a part of their lives in poverty. In fact, the United States has one of the highest child poverty rates of any industrialized nation.

Poverty is closely correlated with race, ethnicity, and gender. For example, 42% of African American children, 21% of Hispanic children, and 18% of Caucasian children live in poverty (U.S. Department of Education, 1996b). Additionally, 33% of single women with children live in poverty (U.S. Bureau of the Census, 1998; see Figure 7.2). Although we frequently associate poverty with urban areas, it is actually more prevalent in rural parts of our nation. The poverty rate for rural children is 50% higher than that for urban children (Cohen, 1992). The federal government has made some recent overtures toward improved health and human services, but many eligible children still do not receive free or reduced lunches nor reap the benefits of food stamps.

Figure 7.2 **Percentages of Children Living in Poverty by Group**

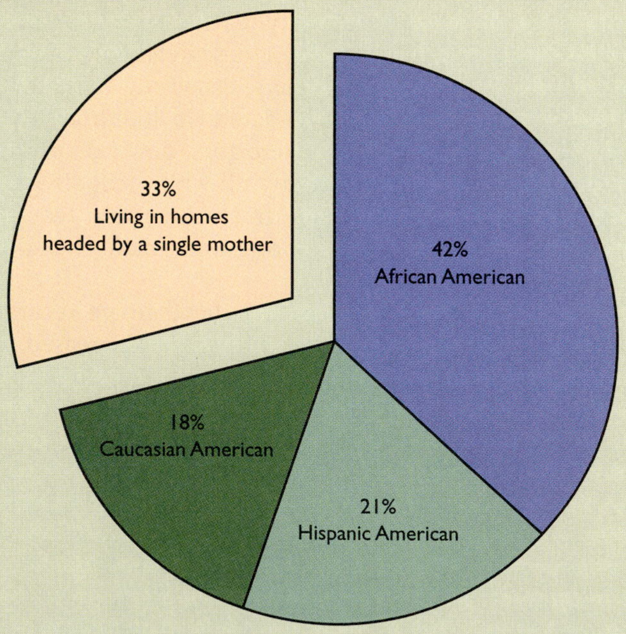

SOURCE: U.S. Department of Education, 1996b; U.S. Bureau of Census, 1998.

What might be some of the effects on children of growing up in poverty?

IDEALS CHALLENGE: *Examining Equity*

(*Excerpted from* There Are No Children Here: The Story of Two Boys Growing Up in the Other America *by Alex Kotlowitz, 1991.*)

The apartment bulged with people that winter. Weasel's girlfriend moved in, as did LaJoe's mother, Lelia Mae, who had been depressed from a stroke that paralyzed one side. She had been shifted from one child's or grandchild's house to another. . . . The apartment seemed to collapse under the weight of all these people. The oven stopped working, and for most of eight months LaJoe couldn't bake. The wooden door to Lafayette and Pharoah's room could be opened and shut only with great care, otherwise the top came unhinged and the door leaned precariously into the room as if it had been battered down. A cheap, unadorned light fixture, which the housing authority had only partly installed, hung loosely down from the wall, unfinished. A friend of Lafayette's stuck a screwdriver in its opening—and recoiled from the electric shock.

And the pipes leading to the kitchen sink sprang a leak. LaJoe tied rags around them to keep them from dripping onto the floor, and for two weeks, while she waited for them to be repaired, she washed the dishes in the bathtub, which still ran day and night . . . (pp. 166–167).

As it did every winter, the temperature in the apartment approached a dry, crackling 85 degrees. Stripping down to their underwear was of no relief to Lafayette and Pharoah; it was like being inside an oven. Their only remedy was to open a window, even in the dead of winter, but then they had to put up with a frigid draft. Pharoah had developed a blistering cough; his throat was parched and sore. The scorching heat tired the boys and put everyone on edge . . . (p. 171).

At night, Pharoah frequently read until his eyes hurt. Because he had no lamp or working overhead light in his bedroom, he would lie on his belly on the brown floor with his head poking out the door to take advantage of the hallway light. The naked, 60-watt light bulb did little to brighten the narrow hallway, so Pharoah's eyes quickly grew weary (p. 62).

- To what is the author referring when he uses the term "the other America" in the subtitle of the book from which this excerpt is taken?
- Based on this excerpt, what are some of the factors that influence Pharoah's ability to learn and fully access his education?
- Identify, compare, and discuss how out-of-school factors affect Pharoah's access to education and how they affected your education.

The impact of poverty on children and young adults is significant. As might be expected, living in poverty significantly affects the childhood experience and impacts the ability of children to learn. The greatest single predictor of academic achievement is not race, ethnicity, or gender, but social class. Young adults growing up in poverty have lower academic achievement and lower job and career expectations and opportunities (as illustrated by the IDEALS Challenge that opened this chapter). Children from economically disadvantaged families experience greater rates of generally poor physical health, serious illness, developmental disability, teenage pregnancy, and dropping out of school. Additionally, children from families living in poverty have lower academic achievement and lower self-reports of happiness. They spend twice as many days in hospitals as do other children but are unlikely to be covered by health insurance. Thus, poor children generally do not receive preventative health care such as physical examinations and dental check-ups. Conditions for the near poor (those with incomes slightly above the poverty line) are little better. Frequently they are ineligible for services at public expense and thus do totally without health care and other services.

The past decade has also seen a tremendous increase in the number of homeless individuals in our society. Most homeless families consist of single women with two or three children under age 5. Additionally, almost half of the homeless are families with children (Cohen, 1994) with almost 1 million school-age children being homeless (Nunez & Collignon, 1997). Single mothers typically pay over 50% of their income toward housing costs even though mortgage approval ratios suggest that this figure should be no more than 28%. As a result, one significant unexpected expenditure can quickly throw single mothers and their children into the ranks of the homeless (Hodgkinson, 1991). Although the temptation sometimes is to blame the parents of poor and homeless children for shirking their economic responsibility to their children, in 87% of poverty families and 24% of homeless families, at least one member of the household is employed (U.S. Conference of Mayors, 1989).

CLICK ON IT

For more information on how poverty and other social conditions affect children, visit the Web site of the Children's Defense Fund at

http://www.childrensdefense.org

Homeless children experience health problems, psychological problems, and school-related problems to an even greater extent than poor children who live in homes with their families. Problems include depression, aggressiveness, lower school attendance, and difficulty establishing peer friendships (Pawlas, 1994), all illustrated by Michael in the IDEALS Challenge.

IDEALS CHALLENGE: *Examining Equity*

(Excerpted from Polakaw, 1998, p. 8.)

Michael is a bright articulate 8-year-old who has experienced four episodes of homelessness in his young life. . . . During his latest episode of homelessness, when the family fled from drug and gang violence at a public housing site, Michael was so traumatized that as we drove to a shelter, he lay on the floor of the car, screaming and clutching his pillow as he cried: "I hate this life—why can't I live in a place like other kids—it's not fair—I won't have friends no more at school—it's the worst thing in the world when you don't got no home. I never want to go in that shelter." . . . Michael lay crying on the floor, curled up in a fetal position, and refused to leave the car to set foot in the shelter. An hour later, after being coaxed inside, he sat on the stairway, angrily shouting about his mother, "Why does she do this to us—why can't we have a regular home like other kids—I can't go to school no more 'cos my friends will find out I'm in a shelter—I hate her, I hate her—I'm gonna run away from here." . . . During the three months Michael spent alternating between the shelter and a "welfare motel" he experienced terrible nightmares, became very fearful, and lashed out aggressively at classmates in school. He ran away from school twice in the middle of the day and was punished by suspension. . . . One afternoon the school janitor found him trying to crawl into the furnace, saying he wanted to die. Soon after he was hospitalized for 14 days at a children's psychiatric unit. When I visited him in the hospital he told me, "I don't got no reason to live."

- What special needs of homeless children are evident in Michael's story? How might teachers and schools address these needs?
- What do you think of the school's response to Michael's behavior?
- How do teachers and schools balance the need to maintain standards (for example, school attendance) and protect the safety of other students (that is, against Michael's lashing out aggressively at other students) with empathy and understanding of Michael's situation?

The plethora of physical and psychological problems that accompany poverty and homelessness have a significant effect on the opportunity children facing these conditions have to obtain a quality education. Socioeconomic class has been found to have a stronger correlation with achievement on standardized tests than race, ethnicity, gender, or any single other factor. That is, children from affluent families consistently score higher on standardized tests than children from families living in poverty—regardless of whether the students are white, black, male, or female.

Ways Schools Can Respond

Following the need for shelter, the most significant needs of homeless students (Rafferty, 1998) are:

- individual academic assistance, school materials, and clothing
- support services (for example, counselors)
- transportation
- extended day and summer school programs (providing for such needs as food, shelter, and recreation)

- educational program continuity
- sensitivity, awareness, and caring by teachers, school staff, and other students

There are a number specific practices that teachers and schools have implemented to address these needs (Pawlas, 1994; Rafferty, 1998). These include:

- developing a buddy system where all new students are provided a buddy to show them around and introduce them to others when they first begin attending a school (there is a high degree of transiency among poor and homeless students)
- being an advocate for poor and homeless children (for example, ensuring that they receive appropriate educational and support services, helping them make friends, assisting them in learning how to deal with classmates questions about poverty or being homeless)
- reaching out to involve poor and homeless families in the education of their children (for example, visiting parents at home or at a homeless shelter)
- developing a collaborative relationship with homeless shelters that serve the school's students
- sharing copies of all school-to-home correspondence with homeless shelters
- enlisting the help of school or community organizations to provide school supplies and clothing for poor and homeless students
- providing family support services

In general, schools that are *communities* of learning for poor and homeless children follow three general strategies. First, they must provide specialized education for these children as needed. Second, they must provide parent education that is responsive to individual parents. Finally, they must link students and families to needed services (Nunez & Collignon, 1997).

IDEALS CHALLENGE: ***Supporting Service***

Visit a homeless shelter in your community and volunteer to assist them in their work. During your service as a volunteer be especially sensitive to the needs of any children who might be at the shelter with their caretaker(s). Inquire into the relationship, if any, the shelter has with nearby schools. Keep a journal of your thoughts, feelings, and what you are learning from your work.

Examples of Schools Addressing the Needs of Poor and Homeless Children

A number of schools have made extensive efforts to address the needs of poor and homeless students.

The Brownstone School in New York City provides one-on-one tutoring, homework help, and educational activities organized around themes. Recognizing that new students will be arriving daily at the shelter, educational activities are offered in brief cycles to provide continuity. There is also an adult education program with a literacy component in which parents read, write, and discuss a variety of topics such as parenting, health and nutrition, stress management, budgeting, housing, and apartment maintenance. The adult education program also includes an alternative high school component through which parents can earn a high school equivalency degree and an employment component that provides workshops on employment referral and placement services. On-site day care is provided so that parents can more easily participate in these programs (Nunez & Collignon, 1997).

The Recovering the Gifted Child Academy in Chicago recognizes that children and adults are better able to make learning a priority if their needs for basic essentials are addressed. The academy provides a "survival kit" including underwear, socks, deodorant, toothpaste, and a toothbrush for any student who needs them. The academy also offers three meals a day for its students (Nunez & Collignon, 1997).

The Benjamin Franklin Day School in Seattle acts as a liaison between landlords and families to ensure that buildings in undesirable neighborhoods do not fall into disrepair, but remain occupied and maintained by families (Nunez & Collignon, 1997). The principal of this school remarked,

> I want teachers who are willing to go the 22 yards when it comes to letting children know we will never give up on them. If that translates into hugging and holding a psychologically beaten child, if it means walking down the street and buying him a hamburger, or washing that child's face and combing his hair—whatever—I expect it. (Quint, 1994, p. 33)

The Salem Keizer Public Schools in Oregon have developed a Homeless Children and Families Program that is involved in the activities of five local family shelters. The program serves as a bridge between individual schools and the shelters, works with children while they are in school, and provides after-school and preschool enrichment programs. Additionally, the program provides life-skills classes for the parents of homeless children and helps in case management (Nunez & Collignon, 1997).

Gender Issues

For many years, gender was largely an invisible issue in American schools. It was assumed that the quality of education that male and female students received was very similar. It was not until recently that we became aware that the school experiences of male and female students differed greatly. One recent report noted, "It is clear that sex and gender make a difference in the nation's public elementary and secondary schools. The educational system is not meeting girls' needs" (American Association of University Women, 1992, p. 1). The report argues that even though boys and girls enter schools with roughly similar measured abilities, 12 years later when they exit high school, female students are significantly behind male students in a number of areas such as mathematics and science. Additionally, in terms of self-esteem, as girls move from childhood to adolescence their loss of self-confidence is twice that of boys.

How do the experiences of female students in school differ from those of male students? A report commissioned by the American Association of University Women entitled "How Schools Shortchange Girls" reviewed research on the experiences of female and male students in schools to attempt to understand why girls fell behind in certain key areas during their schooling experience. The report identified many ways in which girls were treated differently than boys during their schooling experience. Specifically, the report found the following.

- Girls receive significantly less attention from teachers than do boys.
- Teachers have a tendency to select activities that appeal to boys' interests more than to girls' interests.
- Teachers continue to use teaching methods that foster competition even though research has demonstrated that all students, but particularly female students, learn better using cooperative rather than competitive methods.
- The contributions of females continue, to a large extent, to either be ignored or marginalized in textbooks.
- African American girls have fewer interactions with teachers than do European American girls, even though the black girls attempt to initiate more interactions than the white girls.
- When African American girls did as well or better than European American boys, teachers attributed their success to hard work (rather than ability) and assumed that the white boys were not trying as hard as they could.
- Issues dealing with the relationship between gender and power are largely ignored in schools even though our society and popular culture both exploit and idealize female sexuality while clearly assigning women less valued roles than men (American Association of University Women, 1992).

GLOBAL CHALLENGE

Educating Teachers in Developing Nations

(Excerpted from Iredale, 1993, pp. 19–24.)

Gender differences are the best documented of inequalities in most developing countries. Literacy rates among females over the age of 15, compared with those of men, provide one of the clearest indicators of the considerable gap between men's and women's educational opportunities. In 1990 male literacy in sub-Saharan Africa stood at 59% to 36% for women; the difference between countries in southern Asia was even more dramatic at 59% to 32%. . . . On balance, the most disadvantaged position that any group of human beings can occupy is to be born female to poor and illiterate parents in the rural part of a developing country. . . .

As a first step in teacher training it is necessary to ensure that teachers are made aware of the inevitable tendency for materials to portray women as less important, as stereotyped in trivial roles, and as less involved in the key areas of science, mathematics, and the use of international languages such as English, French, or Portuguese. . . .

Teacher preparation, however, is not the only issue. The very absence of female teachers from classrooms in many countries or parts of countries reduces the opportunities for girls to find suitable role models. UNICEF figures show that only 20–45% of teachers are female even at the primary level in Asia, Africa, and the Middle East. . . .

Increasing female access to education has to be a multipronged effort. It should include:

1. nonformal education opportunities for girls outside the formal school curriculum (e.g., attending classes that take place in the home of a local community member, often after regular school hours)
2. entry to teacher training that discriminates in favor of female recruits by allowing them to enter college with lower qualifications, supplemented by additional tuition
3. teacher training that helps male and female trainees to perceive gender bias in both books and their own teaching styles
4. female literacy classes

The challenges of using a highly diversified approach to the provision of education for the underprivileged rural societies, both male and female, will require a major rethink of how teachers are trained, supported and deployed.

- How do the issues associated with females in schools and in teacher education programs in developing nations compare with the situation in this country?
- What do you think of the author's suggestions for addressing these gender issues?
- Do you think a special effort should be made to recruit female teachers in developing nations—or minority teachers in the U.S.? Why or why not? If so, then what should we do to effect these changes?

CLICK ON IT

For more information on gender discrimination in schools, visit the Web site of the American Association of University Women at

http://www.aauw.org

TECHNOLOGY CHALLENGE

The Gender Gap in Technology

(*From* The Parents' Guide to the Information Superhighway, *2nd ed., 1998, Washington, DC: The Children's Partnership; FIND/SVP,* American Internet User Survey, *May 1997.*)

Research reports conclude:

1. In elementary school, there is little difference between boys' and girls' computer use and ability.
2. Many girls lose interest in computers because the computer world is more oriented toward males. For example, video games and other software for home computers are overwhelmingly developed for and marketed to boys.
3. By the mid-teen years, when computer courses in schools are typically elective, the gender gap grows and continues to widen through college and graduate school. Two and a half times as many men as women now earn computer science degrees.

4. Girls use home computers for schoolwork more than boys and use computer games far less.

5. In 1997, there were three men using the Internet for every two women who were online.

6. Future employment opportunities will depend in a large part on an applicant's skills involving computers and information technology. Girls will need these skills just as much as boys.

- How might teachers and parents address the inequity of boys' and girls' interest and use of computers?

Clearly the preferential treatment of male students is not consistent with the democratic ideal of equity. As teachers in democratic schools, it is important for us to be sensitive to the manner in which we treat female and male students. Although we may be well-intentioned and may intend to treat female and male students equally, we may be unintentionally falling short of reaching our goal. That is because our culture has ingrained in us images of males and females that ascribe particular roles and abilities to each. In order to become aware of differential ways in which we treat male and female students, we may need to engage in inquiry and critical study of our own practice. In some instances, critically studying practice in another classroom, as described in the IDEALS Challenge that follows, may also be helpful.

IDEALS CHALLENGE: *Initiating Inquiry*

(Adapted from Matthews, Binkley, Crisp, & Gregg, 1998.)

At a university seminar in elementary education, seniors disagreed about the importance of gender bias in elementary schools. Some argued that gender bias was not a problem for elementary children. Others contended that gender equity was a significant issue that could affect both the academic and personal success of elementary children. As part of a senior research project, we began a year-long study to test interventions designed to make elementary students and teachers more aware of gender equity issues and to give them tools to resolve these situations. We worked with fifth graders in a new school in Guilford County, North Carolina. We began our study in September by observing the classroom and taking notes. We conducted observations once a month for four months. Our initial observations were not surprising. We saw many instances of inequitable interactions. For example, during our first observation period, a guest speaker on drug prevention conducted a small group activity with students. Reporters came to the front of the room to share each group's findings. Of six small groups, one girl and five boys gave reports. On our second visit, the school guidance counselor worked with the class. Students again formed small groups. The counselor asked each group to create a machine. . . . When the small groups demonstrated their machines, they were asked to call on other students to name the machines. Boys were called on 31 times, and girls were called on 13 times.... Boys would shout out answers more frequently that girls.... Some teachers referred to all students as "guys."

We began our interventions with the class in February. Each month we introduced an activity, followed by written responses and then a discussion. We spent one session reviewing a CD-ROM on gender equity with them. Students also read and discussed case studies on gender equity issues. Each of us facilitated small-group discussions about the cases, and some of the most insightful comments about gender equity came from these conversations. Students were particularly struck by the statement in one of the cases, "boys will be boys." They had heard the phrase before and now they wanted to ... explore its hidden meanings.

We concluded our project by asking students to fill out the same questionnaire they answered in February. Some of the questions were:

1. Is your teacher fair? Give an example.

2. Are boys or girls the best students in your class in these subjects: English? Math? Science? Social Studies?

3. Are there certain jobs that only girls do in your class? Are there certain jobs only boys do?

4. What do you want to be when you grow up? Rate from 1 to 5: a doctor? a homemaker? a lawyer? a scientist? a teacher?

5. Do you like to answer questions in class?

One finding from the questionnaire was that boys preferred jobs as doctors and scientists while girls wanted jobs as teachers.

At the conclusion of the study, we began to see that just as members of our senior seminar had struggled to understand gender equity issues, so had the fifth graders who tried to decide for themselves what fairness meant. It is difficult for both college students and fifth graders to observe and understand gender inequity—because gender inequity is so common and familiar, it doesn't always grab your attention.

- Conduct a critical study similar to the one described in your class, another university class you are taking, or in a classroom in which you are engaged in a field experience. Make sure you obtain the teacher's or professor's permission prior to commencing the study and conduct the inquiry in a collaborative manner so that you, the students in the class, and the teacher/professor all learn from the experience.

Disability[1]

Students with disabilities cross all categories of race, ethnicity, class, gender, and sexual orientation. About 6 million students are identified as having disabilities. Typically, 10% to 12% of the students in a school district will be students with disabilities, although this number can widely vary. Students with disabilities have a variety of physical, emotional, and academic characteristics, and there are 14 categories of disability into which they are categorized (Office of Special Education Programs, 1998).

Students with disabilities are sometimes called handicapped, a term that has been used throughout this century to designate those people who have physical, mental, or emotional impairments that affect their ability to lead a normal life. That language, and the attitudes and actions it promoted, reflected a sense that people with disabilities are somehow defective or less than whole, that they cannot have a normal life, and that they should be objects of our charity because they are unable to help themselves. People with disabilities and we as a society, however, have come to understand that physical, emotional, and learning disabilities only limit people when society creates barriers and people have attitudes that discriminate against people with these conditions. People with disabilities recognize that their characteristics influence who they are as people, but that their characteristics do not necessarily have to limit what they can become. Although they may need some assistance, people with disabilities are able to become independent, fully participating members of our society.

People with disabilities look at their difficulties as characteristics to be accepted and overcome through adaptations to the way they lead their daily lives. So, people who are deaf use sign language in their work, play, and home lives; people with physical disabilities use wheelchairs, walkers, and canes; people who have learning disabilities use books on tape, instructional organizers, and note takers. The growth of technology and our desire for people with disabilities to participate fully in society have resulted in considerable creativity being used to think of ways to make social and work environments accessible.

The language that we use to talk and write about people with disabilities reflects important aspects of our attitudes and practice. The term *people with disabilities* has become the accepted language to use when discussing such individuals. People with disabilities are people first—people who happen to have physical, sensory, emotional, or intellectual disabilities. We should avoid using phrases like "the handicapped," "the disabled," "LD kids," and other wording that highlights the disability rather than the person. We should strive to use language that places the person first—"students with disabilities," "programs for students with emotional disabilities," "the student who is deaf." These changes emphasize that the disability is only one of an individual's characteristics. We should also remember that the assistive devices people with disabilities use give them the freedom to participate in schools and society. We often say people with physical disabilities are *confined* to wheelchairs, when in fact they are people who *use* wheelchairs to participate in schools and society. Assistive devices give people with disabilities the freedom to move about, communicate, and participate.

In addition to using language that puts people first, we must also strive to change the language we use to describe what happens to students with disabilities in school. We have become accustomed to using words and phrases that suggest that the problems of students with disabilities are the student's fault and that we can diagnose those problems precisely. Our habits of language come from a medical model that has dominated special education. We should strive to replace phrases like "differential diagnosis" with a phrase like "identifying problems at school"; "treating disabilities" with "teaching students what they need to know"; and "providing services" with "educating students so they can achieve valued outcomes."

Students with disabilities have a variety of needs and by law, programs that are provided to meet their needs must be individually tailored for each student. This personalization in educational programming is perhaps the most important innovation that has come about as a result of our

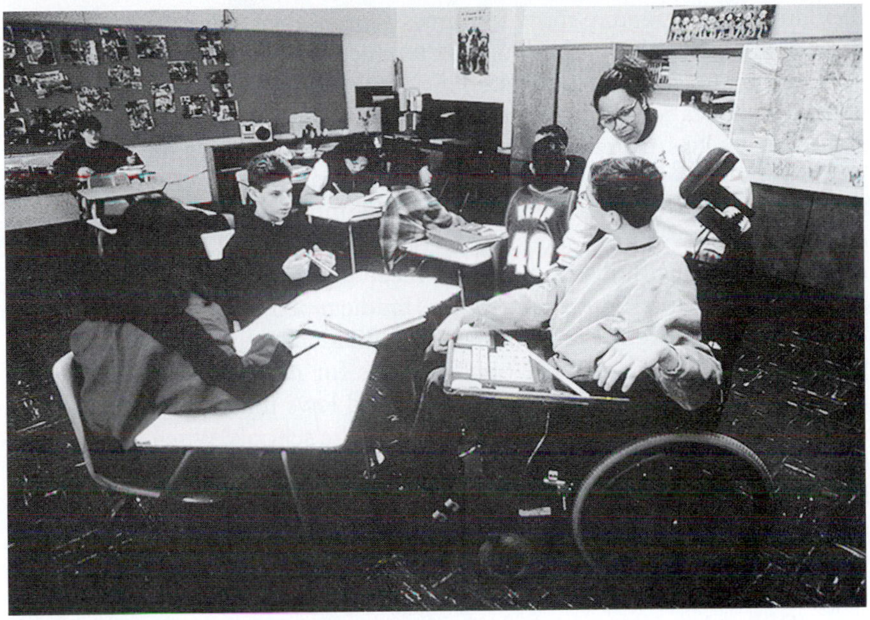

Democratic schools focus on inclusion and ability, rather than disability.

experience with students with disabilities in schools. Students with disabilities challenge educators and school systems to take seriously their responsibility for educating *every* student.

Planning an educational program for a student with a disability requires identifying the student's educational needs and designing a plan of individualized interventions that will enable the student to accomplish goals that are important to his or her future. For most students with a disability, their goals are the same goals that are expected for all students—an academic program that leads to a high school diploma. But such an academic program must be supplemented by students learning additional skills and dispositions that are necessary for them to be successful learners (e.g., skills like sign language, orientation and mobility, interpersonal skills, or dispositions such as the value of schooling). For a small number of students with significant disabilities, the goals to be accomplished are related to the goals we expect for all students, but their scope is not as broad. For example, such a student may need to learn to communicate his basic needs by using a language board or may need to learn to become economically productive by working in assisted employment with a job coach.

Because of their additional needs, students with disabilities need additional support in order to be ensured an equal educational opportunity as students without disabilities. Providing the same opportunities for students with disabilities that typical students have is not sufficient to assure that their needs will be met. Providing equal educational opportunity means that students with disabilities may require additional support and resources in the form of more teachers to provide a smaller class size; different instructional equipment like laptop computers, voice synthesizers, or FM communication systems; instructional aids to provide personal assistance; or different instructional materials that provide supplementary support as they learn reading or mathematics. If students with disabilities are to be successful students, they are likely to require more resources from the school. Fairness requires that these students have more support to reach standard outcomes.

Parents and advocates for students with disabilities are very zealous about the educational programs and rights of these students. Their fervor stems from a history that indicates that the public schools have not been particularly hospitable toward students with disabilities. In 1970, it was estimated that only 38% of students with disabilities were receiving the special educational services necessary to meet their unique needs and over 1 million students with disabilities were receiving no educational services of any kind (Bureau of Education for the Handicapped, 1970). Spurred on by the civil rights movement, advocates for individuals with disabilities began pointing out that educational opportunities for children and adults with disabilities were inadequate. Many states had laws that allowed the exclusion of students with disabilities from the public schools. When educational opportunities were available, special education services were provided only because of the good graces of the public schools, public health and mental health agencies, and private organizations, such as Associations for Retarded Citizens and the Easter Seals Society. In these instances, disruptive students were often placed in special education programs to remove them from the regular classroom, and disproportionate numbers of poor, black, Hispanic, and male students were placed without fair application of assessment procedures (Lashley, 1994).

Parents and advocates were understandably concerned that students with disabilities were being discriminated against by the educational system. Their concerns became lawsuits that stimulated state legislatures to pass laws requiring schools to educate children with disabilities. These actions in the courts and legislatures focused attention on students with disabilities and the importance of the democratic commitment to educate all children. A major victory for protecting the educational rights of students with disabilities was achieved when Congress enacted Public Law 94-142, the purpose of which was to ensure that all children with disabilities have available to them a free and appropriate public education (see further discussion of P.L. 94-142 in chapter 8).

As schools began to put programs for students with disabilities into place, they were first concerned with making sure that every child of school age was in a school program and that the programs were tailored to meet their individual needs. Schools relied on what has been called the "two box approach" in which there were "two kinds of classes (regular and special), two types of children (regular education children and special education children), and two sets of teachers (regular education and special education)" (Reynolds & Birch, 1982, p. 37). Special education was thought of as a special class, where special curriculum, special instructional methods, and specially trained teachers were available to educate students with disabilities. Sometimes, students with disabilities would be "mainstreamed" into regular classes for part of their school day.

A Response

The "two-box approach" to special education was very successful in putting programs into place and in bringing students with disabilities to the attention of teachers and administrators. However, the two-box approach also separated students with disabilities from their peers and tended to result in lower expectations for students with disabilities than for students without disabilities. During the 1980s, researchers and advocates began to recognize that programs for students with disabilities could be delivered in regular classrooms and that all students benefit when diverse students are educated together. This new approach, often called *inclusion,* is successful when accommodations are made to classroom routines, curriculum, instruction, and assessment. Inclusion provides students with disabilities with the opportunity to learn the regular curriculum, to develop relationships with their "typical" peers, and to participate in all that a school has to offer. You might ask why the regular classroom should be changed to accommodate the needs of students with disabilities. Those who advocate for inclusive classrooms argue that the changes they suggest represent good educational practice for all students— that is, inclusive practices help teachers create programs that meet the needs of all students and educate them to high standards. Some examples of inclusive practices are:

- using cooperative learning with heterogeneous groups
- implementing peer tutoring programs
- providing a variety of ways that students can learn and show that they have learned skills and content
- creating more opportunities for active learning
- creating approaches to instruction, assessment, and classroom management that take individual differences into account
- respecting individual differences and helping students learn from one another so they can understand and appreciate their differences
- teaching students that being treated equally and being treated fairly are different
- developing teacher-support systems that help teachers help each other solve instructional and behavioral problems by focusing on individual students
- providing opportunities for *all* parents to understand that treating students the same is not the same as treating students equitably

For students with disabilities, access to an equal educational opportunity may mean that they need more support, more assistance, or more attention—that more resources be available for them if they are to be successful. Equal treatment is not enough to assure that every student is successful. Achieving equity requires that some students be treated differently in order to reach the same goals that are expected for all students. Nonetheless, students with disabilities are more like typical students than they are different. They have goals, needs, aspirations, strengths, and limits. They want to participate in families, employment, recreation, and community life. Their parents want them to have a good education and to be successful adults. They look to the school to provide them with the knowledge, skills, and attitudes they will need to be successful—just like everyone else.

What are the responsibilities of democratic schools to students who are gay?

Sexual Identity

Other dimensions that result in inequalities of opportunity besides race, ethnicity, class, gender, and disability also exist in schools and should be considered as you develop your teaching practices. For example, some sources estimate that up to 10% of the U.S. population is gay (Sears, 1993). However, not only are the needs of homosexual students often overlooked in schools, these students also are regularly and overtly discriminated against by students, faculty, and school policies. Overt discrimination by some students against gay students includes name-calling and physical abuse, as illustrated by the incident described by a gay student.

> When I was changing classes, I had all the books in my hands. . . . I'd hear someone mutter "faggot" and have my books knocked down. People are walking over me as I'm trying to gather my books. I don't have time to turn around to see who said it. (Sears, 1993, p. 129)

Overt discrimination by schools includes forbidding gay students to attend school dances or the prom as a couple. Less overt discrimination, however, also exists. For example, turning the other way when gay students are harassed by other students, or pretending that homosexuality does not exist among students by not openly addressing it in the curriculum are inconsistent with the democratic ideal of equity because it denies gay students the type of school environment experienced by nongay students. Noted curriculum and gay studies scholar James Sears (1993) observes that in schools "Discussion of homosexuality is relegated to hallway gutter gossip, classroom sexual slurs, and locker room queer-baiting. The cruelty of the callous disregard of [such] malicious behavior among many educators is second only to the cruelty of the behavior itself" (p. 128).

Data indicate that many gay students are crying out for understanding. For example, there is a high degree of correlation between teenage suicide and homosexuality, which might well be attributed to the loneliness and harassment that gay adolescents frequently face both in and out of school (Sears, 1993).

Homosexual students, however, are not the only students who are harassed in school. Recent reports have indicated that sexual harassment of girls by boys is increasing (American Association of University Women's Report, 1992) and that *all forms* of peer harassment in schools are pervasive (Shakeshaft, Mandel, Johnson, Sawyer, Hergenrother, & Barber, 1997). Harassment is neither distributed nor responded to evenly. That is, some students are harassed more frequently than others and some students are more negatively impacted by even low levels of harassment. In both instances, harassment makes the school life of the student miserable and may lead to their not being able to respond maximally to the educational opportunities that are available to them.

The study by Shakeshaft and her colleagues found that harassment is initiated more by boys than by girls, although it is significant in both sexes. Boys harassed both boys and girls, while girls typically harassed only other girls. While almost everyone could be a target for harassment, the main targets included unattractive or unstylish girls, physically mature girls, and boys who did not fit the stereotypic macho male role. Harassment was often of a sexual nature. For example, Shakeshaft and her colleagues reported a boy sarcastically saying "I think I'm getting hard" when a girl walked by, and boys calling a girl a "slut" or a "ho" if other boys claimed that she was sexually active. Boys were called "pussy" or accused of being homosexual if they did not brag about being sexually active, if they were not athletes, or if they did not otherwise conform to a macho image (Shakeshaft et al., 1997, p. 23).

Students who were the targets of harassment reported feeling bad about themselves, beginning to believe in the substance of the harassment, and feeling powerless in responding to it. They said that harassment made them feel "sad and worthless," "powerless," and that it was "depressing" and "tiresome" (Shakeshaft et al., 1997, p. 24). Their responses included either ignoring the harassment, rationalizing it, trying to fight against it (by harassing their harassers), changing their behavior, or becoming part of a group to shield themselves from it. Teachers typically either ignored harassment or engaged in lame responses to it such as telling students they were "overreacting" and to simply ignore it, or by telling the harassers to stop the harassment but not following up with other actions if the students did not stop.

CLICK ON IT

For more data on sexual harassment, visit the following Web site

http://www.de.psu.edu/harass/intro.htm

A Response

Shakeshaft and her colleagues (1997) recommend three general strategies for teachers and schools as they deal with harassment of all forms. They recommend that teachers and other adults in the school community help students become aware of the ways in which they harass others and of their own feelings when they are the victims of harassment. Once awareness of harassment has been brought into the open and made a subject of public discussion, students and faculty need to discuss and define peer and sexual behavior that is respectful, caring, and appropriate. Finally, peer interaction needs to be monitored by making harassment the periodic topic of public and private conversation.

Addressing the climate of discrimination that exists in many schools against gay students requires additional steps. Sears (1993) makes a number of recommendations for schools. Specifically, he recommends that schools:

- develop an anti-slur and anti-harassment policy that includes sexual orientation
- review and assess policies, practices, and events (e.g., dances), for evidence of discrimination against gay students
- review textbooks for bias or misleading information about gay individuals
- review textbooks, instructional materials, and the school's curriculum to identify where material about sexual minorities can be included
- assess the adequacy of resource materials (e.g., library books) that deal with sexual identity
- provide and make students aware of a counseling service where students can discuss issues of sexual identity
- sponsor prejudice awareness workshops for students, teachers, and other school staff members

IDEALS CHALLENGE: *Learning Leadership*

(Examples of harassment adapted from Shakeshaft et al., 1997; it is narrated by a teacher.)

As you walk down the hallway to your classroom you hear the name-calling and insults flying back and forth across the hall from student to student. "Hey, Miss Piggy," "Cow," "She's a slut," "Ho," "fucking fag," "Man is she greasy," "popcorn face," "pussy," "I did her last night," "Gay boy." As you enter your classroom you hear one of the male students in your class tell a female student, "I know you do it with everyone. How would you like to do it with me right here?" From a different side of the room you hear one male student call another one "gay" in front of a group of students who are surrounding them and laughing. You turn away, only to see another male student snapping a female student's bra strap.

- If you were this teacher, how would you respond?
- What would you do in your classroom? (Consider role-playing your responses as a class.)
- How might the IDEALS of a democratic school inform your responses?
- What would you do if the harassment described did not seem as pervasive, but consisted of just one of the instances mentioned?
- What could you do that would impact the entire school?

SUMMARY

Sometimes students succeed despite racial and gender discrimination, poverty, and other negative influences in their lives. Frequently their success is facilitated by the presence of a loving parent or caregiver in their lives. Other times their success is facilitated by teachers and schools who care about them as individuals and who empower them through practicing the ideals of democratic schooling. As democratic educators we must ensure that the voices of the disenfranchised (e.g., racial and ethnic minorities; single parents; students with disabilities, students who are regularly harassed) and the invisible (e.g., the poor; the homeless; homosexual students) are heard and that their needs are addressed in the educational opportunities schools provide.

PRESENT TO PAST

Common Schooling—Assimilation or Equalization of Opportunity?

One of the major educational movements that shaped the modern American school was the 19th-century push to establish a nationwide system of "common" schools that were free and public. In the eyes of some, the common school movement was about providing equal educational and economic opportunity for everyone. In the eyes of others it was about ensuring that immigrants and others were assimilated into the American way of life. Some would argue that this latter perspective is an ethnocentric and inequitable perspective. As you read about the common school movement we ask you to consider how the past continues to be mirrored in present day practices and perspectives.

The Common School Ideal

Though the first public high school was opened in Boston in 1821, private academies remained the main form of secondary education in the U.S. through the first part of the 19th century. By the mid-1820s, the sentiment grew among some educators that it was time to press for free publicly sponsored education for all children, a revolutionary idea at that time.

Horace Mann's appointment as Superintendent of Education for Massachusetts turned out to be a centerpiece in the campaign for common schools. Mann fervently believed that America could—and should—create a more democratic educational system, serving more children, than the European nations.

Mann summed up his philosophy in the *Twelfth Annual Report* to the Massachusetts State Board of Education. In the report Mann expounded on numerous issues that still resonate in our times, including the question: "What should be *common* to all schools?" According to Mann, all children should have *common access* to public schools that are of similar quality (Mann was a strong abolitionist, so he included African Americans in the equation). To provide access, the schools must be free. Additionally, students should receive a *common moral education.* Mann and most common school reformers supported the teaching of nondenominational Christian values in the public schools. As we shall see, this idea did not prevent serious conflict between Catholics and Protestants over religion in the schools. Finally, Mann thought that education could help to equalize the economic conditions of society—to create *common conditions* of life that would abolish social class distinctions and conflict. This would only work if rich and poor attended the same publicly supported schools, so that they would learn a set of *common political beliefs.*

Notice what is *not* "common" here. Mann did not call for a common, nationalized curriculum. Nor did he and other reformers oppose the control of schools by local school boards; decentralization was a central tenet of American educational faith. In this way, and in their insistence on one school system for all, they departed from the direction of European educational systems.

Broad-Based Support and Perplexing Problems

The common school movement was not supported just by Mann and idealistic educational reformers. Working class people saw the chance for their children to attain an education similar to the middle and upper classes, not simply to advance economically but to have a voice in a democratic society. Working class publications stressed the equal sharing of power in society, which went beyond what Mann envisioned. Business owners and employers had different reasons to push for common schools. They wanted schools to educate future workers in order to increase productivity and provide for public order.

The point here is that more and more people came to support the idea of common schools, but they did so for different and sometimes conflicting reasons. Horace Mann and the thousands of common school reformers placed their faith in universal public education as the salvation of society. Schoolteachers would be the keepers of public order and a good education would enable people to be productive workers and increase the wealth of society. Not coincidentally, schools would also assimilate the growing numbers of immigrants into the American way of life, which meant primarily white, Anglo-Saxon, Protestant, and middle class.

Although the ideal of common schools gained many devoted adherents, the movement also faced substantial problems. One of the problems faced by school reformers and local educators was how to deal with the growing number of immigrants. The first wave of voluntary immigration to America had occurred quite steadily. In the 1840s a new wave of immigrants began and their presence had a powerful socioeconomic and religious effect.

The rise in immigration began because of the Irish Potato Famine that lasted from 1845 to 1854. The previously rural Irish tended to settle in Northeastern cities, and the magnitude of immigration in some places was startling. In 1847 alone, 37,000 Irish emigrated to Boston, at a time when the entire city population was 114,000 (Tyack, 1987). The Irish were predominantly Roman Catholic and working class, with traditionally low levels of formal education. They were saddled with stereotypes kept alive by their English conquerors and overseers. Nativists (those born in the United States) soon wanted to exclude the Irish or to assimilate them through churches, voluntary associations, and state-sponsored public education.

One reason for resistance to the new immigrants, especially the Irish and other Catholics, concerned religion. Many Catholic citizens were concerned about the religious sectarianism of the public schools. Catholics saw the schools as Protestant institutions, because textbooks contained overt anti-Catholic passages and religious instruction usually incorporated readings from the King James Bible, not the Catholic's version of the Bible. In 1840, Catholics in New York presented a petition to the Board of Aldermen requesting a share of the public school funding. The mayor agreed to their request, but tremendous controversy ensued. Subsequently, there was increasing anti-Catholic sentiment and opposition to public funding for parochial schools. It was not just a matter of religion; a basic point of the argument was how much local control of the curriculum was possible.

Because of continuing disagreements about funding and the curriculum, Catholics and other groups eventually chose to expand their private religious schools. In 1884 American Catholics were required by a church council to send their children to Catholic schools. This created a "full-fledged system of parish schools paralleling the public schools" (Welter, 1971, p. 117). Many other schools associated with the Lutheran, Baptist, Jewish, and other religions were also formed. Horace Mann's vision of *one unified system* of common schooling would not come to pass, even though the great majority of students across the country were enrolled in public schools.

REQUIRING SCHOOL ATTENDANCE

The common school movement resulted in states slowly passing compulsory attendance laws, requiring all students to attend school. By 1885, 16 out of 38 states had passed such laws, even though these laws frequently went unenforced.

The slow passage of compulsory attendance laws was due to several reasons. In some areas of the country people saw no need to coerce children into schools because parents already believed in public education. In Iowa, for example, there was no compulsory school law as late as 1897, yet Iowa was second nationally only to Kansas in the percentage of children enrolled in elementary schools. Other states did not pass compulsory attendance laws because of economic reasons; that is, it took time for the idea of financing schools through taxation to take hold in these states. Cultural beliefs also slowed the passage of compulsory attendance laws. Some school leaders did not want to mix working-class "street" children with the children of the middle class. Other educators saw lengthier schooling as a way to acculturate the masses of arriving immigrants and to compensate for what was perceived to be poor parenting by working-class and lower-class parents. In some cases, parents did not want compulsory attendance, because their children typically left school in their mid-teens to work in order to help support their families. The subsequent growth of a more economically stable middle class enabled children to attend school for longer periods, and resulted in greater parent support for compulsory schooling.

In spite of the various forms of resistance to compulsory schooling, the ideal of a public education for everyone proved to be powerful. By 1918, all 48 states had enacted compulsory attendance laws. In conjunction with the passage of laws prohibiting child labor below a certain age, this had a dual effect. More children were formally educated, thus increasing the literacy rate among the working class; and teenage workers were frozen out of the job market, thus further separating the lives of adults and children.

IDEALS CHALLENGE: *Examining Equity*

We titled the Present to Past section "Common Schooling—Assimilation or Equalization of Opportunity?" After reading the section, what do you think? Do you believe the historical efforts to promote common schooling resulted in equalization of opportunity? Or, do you believe public schools served more as agents of assimilation? Is it possible to do both? Or, maybe public schools do neither? Which purpose do you think present-day public schools serve—assimilation or equalizer of opportunity? What about Catholic and other religious schools—do they serve as agents of assimilation, of religious training, or both? How is religious training similar to and different from assimilation? Provide support for your answers.

DOING DEMOCRACY

Identify a community service project or organization that provides service to a group that is culturally different from yours. Spend some time as a volunteer in the project or organization. Make an effort to try to understand cultural differences and similarities between you and the individuals you are serving. Attempt to distinguish between personality differences and cultural differences. Keep a journal of your experiences and about what you learn from your volunteer work.

END NOTE

[1]The sections of this chapter on disability were written by Carl Lashley from the University of North Carolina at Greensboro. He also contributed the examples dealing with disability.

REFERENCES

American Association of University Women. (1992). *How schools shortchange girls.* Washington, DC: Author.

America's changing face. (1990, September 10). *Newsweek,* pp. 46–50.

Banks, J. A. (1994). *An introduction to multicultural education.* Boston: Allyn & Bacon.

Brumberg, J. J. (1983). The feminization of teaching: "Romantic sexism" and American protestant denominationalism. *History of Education Quarterly, 23*(3), 379–384.

Bureau of Education for the Handicapped. (1970). *Better education for the handicapped. Annual report FY 1969.* Washington, DC: Author.

Capper, C. A. (1993). *Educational administration in a pluralistic society.* Albany, NY: SUNY Press.

Carger, C. L. (1996). *Of borders and dreams: A Mexican-American experience of urban education.* New York: Teachers College Press.

Children's Defense Fund. (1997). *Twenty key facts about American children.* Washington DC: Author.

Cohen, D. L. (1992, January 8). Conditions "bleak" for rural children, C.D.F. finds. *Education Week,* p. 7.

Cohen, D. L. (1994, January 19). Children and families. *Education Week,* p. 8.

Delpit, L. (1995). *Other people's children: Cultural conflict in the classroom.* New York: The New Press.

Erickson, J. B. (1990). Poverty in Indiana. *F.Y.I., 2*(3), 1–2, 5.

Fordham, S. (1996). *Blacked out: Dilemmas of race, identity, and success at Capital High.* Chicago: University of Chicago Press.

Giroux, H. A. (1983). *Theory and resistance in education: A pedagogy for the opposition.* South Hadley, MA: Bergin & Garvey.

Hale-Benson, J. E. (1982). *Black children: Their roots, culture, and learning styles.* Baltimore: The Johns Hopkins University Press.

Hodgkinson, H. (1991). Reform versus reality. *Phi Delta Kappan, 73,* 8–16.

Iredale, R. (1993). Global apartheid: Disadvantage and inequality. In G. K. Verma (Ed.), *Inequality and teacher education: An international perspective,* pp. 15–27. London: Falmer Press.

Irvine, J. J. (1991). *Black students and school failure.* New York: Praeger.

Kotlowitz, A. (1991). *There are no children here.* New York: Doubleday.

Lashley, C. (1994). Criticizing special education as a social practice. *Special Education Leadership Review,* 2 (1), 40–58.

MacLeod, J. (1987). *Ain't no makin' it: Leveled aspirations in a low-income neighborhood.* Boulder, CO: Westview Press.

Matthews, C. E., Binkley, W., Crisp, A., & Gregg, K. (1998). Challenging gender bias in fifth grade. *Educational Leadership, 55*(4), 54–57.

Nieto, S. (1996). *Affirming diversity: The sociopolitical context of multicultural education.* White Plains, NY: Longman.

Nunez, R. C., & Collignon, K. (1997). Creating a community of learning for homeless children. *Educational Leadership, 55*(2), 56–60.

Office of Special Education Programs. (1998). *Twentieth annual report to Congress on the implementation of the Individuals with Disabilities Education Act.* Washington, DC: U.S. Department of Education.

Pawlas, G. E. (1994). Homeless students at the school door. *Educational Leadership, 51*(8), 79–82.

Perkins, L. M. (1989). The history of blacks in teaching: Growth and decline within the profession. In D. Warren (Ed.), *American teachers: Histories of a profession at work.* New York: Macmillan.

Polakaw, V. (1998). Homeless children and their families: The discards of the postmodern 1990s. In S. Books (Ed.), *Invisible children in the society and its schools* (pp. 3–22). Mahwah, NJ: Lawrence Erlbaum.

Quint, S. (1994). *Schooling homeless children: A working model for America's public schools.* New York: Teachers College Press.

Rafferty, Y. (1998). Meeting the educational needs of homeless children. *Educational Leadership, 55*(4), 48–52.

Reitzug, U. C. (1994). Diversity, power, and influence: Multiple perspectives on the ethics of school leadership. *Journal of School Leadership, 4,* 197–222.

Reynolds, M. C., & Birch, J. W. (1982). *Teaching exceptional children in all America's schools.* Reston, VA: Council for Exceptional Children.

Schnaiberg, L. (1998, June 10). Uncertainty follows vote on Prop. 227. *Education Week, 17*(39), 1, 21.

Schwager, S. (1987). Educating women in America. *Signs, 12*(2), 154–193.

Sears, J. T. (1993). Responding to the sexual diversity of faculty and students: Sexual praxis and the critically reflective administrator. In C. Capper (Ed.), *Educational administration in a pluralistic society.* Albany, NY: SUNY Press.

Shakeshaft, C., Mandel, L., Johnson, Y. M., Sawyer, J., Hergenrother, M. A., & Barber, E. (1997). Boys call me cow. *Educational Leadership, 55*(2), 22–25.

Strober, M. H., & Lanford, A. G. (1986). The feminization of public school teaching: Cross-sectional analysis, 1850–1880. *Signs, 11*(2), 212–235.

Tyack, D. B. (1987). *". . . schools and the means of education shall forever be encouraged": A history of education in the Old Northwest.* Athens, OH: Ohio University Libraries.

U.S. Bureau of the Census. (1996). *Statistical abstract of the United States: 1996 (116th ed.).* Washington, DC: U.S. Government Printing Office.

U.S. Bureau of the Census. (1998). *The official statistics.* Internet address: www.census.gov/hhes/www/povty96.html.

U.S. Conference of Mayors. (1989). *A status report on hunger and homelessness in America's cities, 1989.* (ERIC Document Reproduction Service No. ED 317 641.)

U.S. Department of Education. (1996a). *Mini-digest of education statistics 1996.* Washington, DC: Author.

U.S. Department of Education. (1996b). *The pocket condition of education 1996.* Washington, DC: Author.

Vinovskis, M. A., & Bernard, R. M. (1978). Beyond Catherine Beecher: Female education in the antebellum period. *Signs, 3*(4), 856–869.

Ward, J. G. (1994). Demographic politics and America's schools: Struggles for power and justice. In C. Marshall (Ed.), *The new politics of race and gender.* Washington, DC: The Falmer Press.

Welter, R. (1971). *American writings on popular education: The Nineteenth Century.* Indianapolis: Bobbs-Merrill.

Should children whose families have entered the United States illegally be entitled to a "free" public education?

What does the law say?

How do you feel about this?

Who should or should not have access to public education?

CHAPTER 8

The Legal Foundations of Equity: Protecting Access to Education

By Julie F. Mead
University of Wisconsin–Madison

IDEALS CHALLENGE: *Deepening Discourse*

Discuss the following statements:

- Access to education can be protected via legal means.
- Equity means that everyone must be treated the same.
- Integrated schools ensured equal educational opportunity for all students.
- Schools that include students with disabilities in regular classrooms are equitable for all students.
- Sex equity in athletics can be ensured by permitting male and female students to participate on the same teams.

As previous chapters have described, education in today's schools encompasses many dimensions, with the legal perspective being but one of them. Understanding legal principles serves each of the IDEALS of democratic schools, especially equity. A firm grounding in the legal aspects of education will give you one more avenue to initiate inquiry, deepen discourse, examine equity, achieve authenticity, learn leadership, and support service. Remember legal principles stem from legal documents (the United States Constitution, federal and state statutes, local ordinances) that define and protect democracy in our country. As such, understanding legal principles helps teachers and other school personnel understand the various interests that must be balanced and provides some direction in how that balancing can be accomplished. That balance is the essence of equity. In addition, the practical result of that knowledge is the prevention of legal problems. After all, the last thing a teacher wants is to play some role in a legal controversy!

In this chapter, we explore the following questions:

- What are the sources of legal authority that affect teachers' and students' lives?
- How do laws protect equitable access to education?

Subsequently, chapter 9 will focus on the legal foundations of equity as they pertain to protecting personal liberties.

One quick note before we tackle these questions. The type of school in which you teach dictates what legal principles apply to you. Public school teachers and students have considerably more rights and some additional responsibilities when compared with private or parochial school teachers. Therefore, this chapter and chapter 9 are written primarily with the public school context in mind. Nonetheless, if you work in a private or parochial school setting, many of these legal principles can still serve as guides for you.

WHAT ARE THE SOURCES OF LEGAL AUTHORITY?

Legal authority in our country comes from various sources and various levels of government that build on and complement each other (see Table 8.1).

The U.S. Constitution

The cornerstone of our system is, of course, the Constitution of the United States. Our system dictates that all laws, all rules, and all governmental practices must be consistent with the foundation established in the Constitution. The Constitution sets forth the powers of each branch of the federal government and balances the powers between branches. The Constitution also serves to protect our personal liberties. These liberties are delineated in the Bill of Rights (the first 10 amendments) and other amendments. As

Table 8.1 Sources of Legal Authority

	Federal	State	Local
	U.S. Constitution	State Constitution	(Derived from state constitution)
Legislative	Federal Statutes (U.S. Congress)	State Statutes (State legislature)	Board Policies (Local school board)
Executive	Federal Administrative Regulations and Rules (U.S. Department of Education)	State Administrative Regulations and Rules (State Educational Agencies [e.g., Dept. of Education, Dept. of Public Instruction])	Administrative Policies and Procedures (Superintendent and other administrators)
Judicial	Case Law (Federal District Courts, Federal Courts of Appeals, U.S. Supreme Court)	Case Law (All state courts)	Board Decisions From Hearings

SOURCE: Adapted from Underwood, J. K., & Mead, J. F. (1995). *The Legal Aspects of Special Education and Pupil Services.* Boston, MA: Allyn and Bacon, p. 1.

Case law is only one of the sources of legal authority that protects equity in schools.

will be explained in upcoming sections of this chapter, it is important to note that no right is absolute. Specifically, there are situations in which the liberties of the individual (the teacher) must be limited in order to balance the legitimate interests of the state—in this case, the local school district.

Other Federal Sources of Legal Authority

A second major source of federal legal authority affecting schools is federal statutes. Statutes are laws. Although statutes may create additional rights and protections, they may not contravene any Constitutional principle. You may be surprised to know that the U.S. Constitution does not directly mention education—anywhere. There is no federal right to an education and Congress has no enumerated power to legislate education directly. How, then, can Congress enact laws that affect public education? It does so indirectly through its power to "provide for the common defense and general welfare of the United States" found in Article I, Section 8 of our Constitution. Education is regarded as important both for the protection and the welfare of the United States.

Once Congress has enacted legislation, it falls upon the administrative branch of government to make certain that the law is properly implemented. The administration is charged with promulgating rules and regulations to implement the statute. These rules and regulations provide the detail needed to make a statute operational. For laws relating to education, the U.S. Department of Education assumes this responsibility.

The final source of federal legal authority is the federal judicial system. Courts may do three and only three things:

1. settle the controversy before them (answer the specific question they've been asked)

2. construe statutes (tell what a law means in a particular circumstance)
3. interpret the Constitution (tell how the Constitution applies to a particular circumstance).

Anytime a case is presented in court, a record is made of the facts surrounding the case and the resulting decision regarding the issue. These decisions or court opinions are referred to as "case law." Later, when a similar case is tried in court, this former case may be used as a legal precedent and applied to similar factual situations. Courts are bound by the precedents set by courts above them on the chain of appeals. In other words, federal district courts are bound by the Federal Circuit Court of Appeals that serves their location, and all courts (district level and appellate) are bound by the Supreme Court.

State Sources of Legal Authority

As mentioned earlier, education is not discussed anywhere in the federal Constitution. Therefore, it is a "reserved power" under the Tenth Amendment. That is, since the Constitution is silent on education, the power to address it is reserved to the states. The Tenth Amendment reads:

> The powers not delegated to the United States by the Constitution, nor prohibited by it to the states, are reserved to the States respectively, or to the people.

Thus, the issues and responsibilities of education belong to the individual states. Each of the 50 states has provided for education through its state constitution and delegates to the legislature the responsibility for creating some system of public education.

State legislatures then enact laws describing that system and creating requirements for the delivery of public education in that state. State statutes generally outline school board composition and election, teacher certification requirements, instructional obligations, the minimum number of days and/or hours of instruction required, curricular and graduation requirements, and many other items. The particulars of educational requirements vary considerably from state to state depending on the specific state laws enacted there. Remember, though, that all state laws must be careful not to violate any provisions of either the state constitution or the U.S. Constitution. Also, since ours is a system characterized by federalism, state laws may add to, but may not be inconsistent with federal statutes.

State statutes are also implemented by administrative rules and regulations. These regulations are developed by each state educational agency (SEA). An SEA is the agency within a state charged with the oversight of schools. An SEA is generally called a state "Department of Education" or state "Department of Public Instruction."

Each state also has a system of courts that sometimes examine educational controversies. These courts are limited to the same three tasks as federal courts. They also produce precedent, which is referred to as case law. Except for those rulings of the United States Supreme Court, state courts are independent from federal courts and are not bound by federal court rulings. State courts are bound by the precedents established within that state system.

Local Sources of Legal Authority

The final level of government directing the lives of teachers and students has the most direct impact—the local school district. The district's authority is derived from the state constitution and/or statutes. School boards then create district policies that are essentially "local law" for that district. Sometimes state or federal law requires those policies and sometimes they are an independent construction of the district. For example, each school district *must have* antidiscrimination policies to satisfy Title IX and Title VII. They may also have to have a student discipline policy describing prohibited student behaviors in order to satisfy state statutes. Then they *may have* policies regarding the evaluation of teachers that are created independent of any other level of government.

Once a board enacts policies, it falls on the administrators in the school to implement them. Like the other levels of government, the administration of a school may create policies and procedures. Finally, there are situations when the school board acts in a quasi-judicial role. For example, the board may serve as a hearing panel in student expulsion or teacher dismissal cases. Those decisions, although not termed as such, are the local equivalent of case law. All decisions at the local level must be consistent with the dictates of federal and state statutes, the state constitution, and the federal Constitution.

HOW DO LAWS PROTECT EQUITY?

The previous chapter examined how race, class, gender, and other factors sometimes result in inequality of educational opportunity for students. We now explore the legal foundation for equity. Equity is an issue of fairness and that principle has its home in the Fourteenth Amendment of the Constitution. Specifically, equity is defined in the Equal Protection Clause. It requires that states (or constructions of the state, such as school districts) provide individuals equal protection of the laws. Equal protection does not mean that all persons be treated identically, however. If that were so, states could not restrict driver's licenses to those age 16 or older. Rather, equal protection demands that the state have a legitimate justification for the classifications it makes. To use the driving example, it makes sense to restrict the operation of motor vehicles to those of an age most likely to be able to operate a vehicle safely. There is a rational connection between the state's goals (safe drivers) and the means (requiring a minimum age) it chose to achieve them. Therefore, it is not discrimination to require kids to be 16 before they are let loose on the interstate. Discrimination occurs when people are subjected to different treatment based on some characteristic and the state cannot justify the necessity of using that characteristic to achieve their goals. A law that allowed only women to obtain drivers licenses would be discriminatory because the state would be unable to show how a person's gender made the person qualified or unqualified to drive. There would be no connection between the state's goals and the means it chose to achieve them.

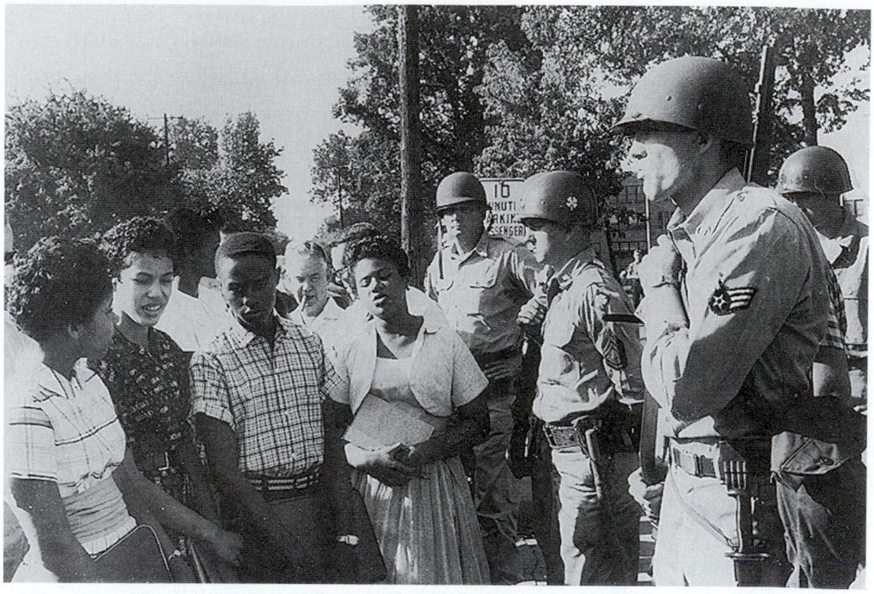

Prior to the *Brown* v. *Board of Education* case, black students were often educated separately from white students with segregation sometimes physically enforced as seen in this 1957 picture of black students trying to enter all-white Central High School in Little Rock, Arkansas.

Equal Protection for Students

The landmark case regarding equal protection for students is *Brown* v. *the Board of Education of Topeka* (1954). The case challenged the "separate but equal" doctrine that existed at the time. That is, it challenged the principle that states with racially segregated school systems satisfied the requirement for equal protection as long as the white and black schools were equal in quality. The "separate but equal" doctrine was established by the Court in 1896 in a case called *Plessy* v. *Ferguson* (1896). After reviewing the effects of segregated schooling on African American children, the *Brown* Court unanimously stated:

> We conclude that in the field of public education the doctrine of "separate but equal" has no place. Separate educational facilities are inherently unequal. Therefore, we hold that the plaintiffs . . . are, by reason of the segregation complained of, deprived of the equal protection of the laws guaranteed by the Fourteenth Amendment.

In other words, the Court held it was inappropriate to use race as the determinant of where children attended school.

The importance of *Brown* cannot be overstated. Of course, it marked the end of the reprehensible practice of state-sponsored or *de jure* segregation. However, the thinking articulated in the *Brown* opinion has influenced issues of equity and equal access for all student groups. The legal principles of equal educational opportunity for students regardless of gender, ethnic background, language ability, and disability can all be traced to this landmark opinion.

Twenty-eight years after *Brown*, the educational opportunities available to children of illegal aliens came under scrutiny. In the case of *Plyler* v. *Doe*

(1982), the Supreme Court ruled that funding for the education of illegal aliens could not be withheld from local school districts, nor could local school districts deny enrollment to children not legally admitted to the country. This decision struck down a Texas law denying free public education to these children. According to the court, education is of utmost importance in maintaining a democratic society. In denying a child an education, we deprive the child of the necessary tools for living a productive life and impose a lifetime of hardships on children who are not responsible for their illegal status. As Justice Brennan explained:

> If the State is to deny a discrete group of innocent children the free public education that it offers to other children residing within its borders, that denial must be justified by a showing that it furthers some substantial state interest. No such showing was made here.

However, the issue of educating the children of undocumented illegal aliens continues to create controversy. As recently as 1994, voters in California approved a referendum that forbids access to public services, such as education, for children whose parents are illegally residing in the state. This referendum, titled Proposition 187, was immediately challenged in court and, based on *Plyler*, the sections of the proposition affecting public education were immediately prohibited from implementation.

IDEALS CHALLENGE: *Examining Equity*

Discuss the following statement:

Legislation, such as Proposition 187, which restricts the educational services provided to the children of illegal aliens is justifiable. After all, educating the children of illegal aliens places a tremendous tax burden upon taxpayers as they try to make their tax dollars stretch to pay for the education of students whose parents are not contributing to the tax base.

The Supreme Court has also considered the educational opportunities of students whose first language is not English. The Court's decision in *Lau* v. *Nichols* (1974) illustrates the principle that mere physical access may be insufficient to provide equal educational opportunity. The children in *Lau* spoke Chinese and had been attending the San Francisco Unified School District. However, the school district provided no specialized assistance related to their language needs. In other words, although the students attended school, they had no way to meaningfully access the education provided there. In this case, the Court ordered the school district to address the students' needs in order to create meaningful access.

In similar manner, courts also examined the issue of meaningful access for children with disabilities. Two landmark decisions, *Pennsylvania Association for Retarded Citizens* v. *Pennsylvania* (1972) and *Mills* v. *Board of Education* (1972), established the concept of a Free Appropriate Public Education (FAPE) as the definition of equal educational opportunity for children with disabilities. At the time of these two cases, children with disabilities were often excluded entirely from public schools. Parents were simply told that no programs existed for their child. Those parents whose children were lucky enough to be allowed to attend school often had no say in the services their children received—which were frequently inappropriate for the children's needs. Like the children in *Lau*, the schools may have opened the doors to children with disabilities, but they made little or no attempt to make legitimate learning opportunities available to them once they were in school. Using the precedent set by the *Brown* case, the courts found these practices unconstitutional since they denied the children access to equal educational opportunity. The courts ordered the school districts to develop programs to meet the individual needs of children with disabilities and to involve parents in the process of designing those programs.

At this point it is necessary to point out some important issues that must be understood to fully comprehend equity. Usually we think of equity as sameness, and discrimination as difference in treatment. Using this way of thinking, we achieve equity by removing difference. Most of the time, such efforts achieve the desired result. This reasoning applied in both *Brown* and *Plyler*. It typically applies when the word discrimination is used (i.e., discrimination on the basis of race, gender, age, ethnicity, alienage, national origin).

Discrimination on the basis of disability requires a different way of thinking. Treating a person with a disability the same as those without disabilities may actually create discrimination. Consider this example: Two people approach a building with 10 stairs leading to the entrance. One can walk; the other uses a wheelchair. Although they are treated the same, they are not treated equitably because only one has true access to whatever is happening inside the building. In order to avoid discriminating against the person using the wheelchair, some difference must be applied (e.g., an alternate entrance or a ramp).

However, once inside the building the person may need no other differential treatment in order to "access" the events that are occurring there. Whether differential treatment is needed to achieve equity depends on the individual person, not any set way to treat the "class" of people with disabilities. Disabilities, even those that appear similar, manifest themselves differently in different people. For example, two people may have the same visual impairment but one needs large type in order to read, while the other uses Braille. Therefore, the only way to determine what differential treatment is necessary to achieve equity for someone with a disability is to examine the *individual* person. Then, only that differential treatment necessary to achieve equity should be applied, with the individual being treated the same as individuals without disabilities in all other respects.

Confusing? Let's return to the earlier example. One person in a wheelchair needs difference in order to achieve equity (a ramp or alternate entrance), but requires no other difference to achieve meaningful access. A second person in a wheelchair may need both a ramp and a sign language interpreter to accommodate her deafness. A third person may need only the interpreter and a fourth person with a disability may require no accommodations at all. The point is that equity in the case of disability demands an individualized determination of what constitutes meaningful access.

Finally, it is important to note that these differences in treatment are not "special treatment" that "favor" someone with a disability. Rather, they are accommodations that allow a person with a disability to have the same meaningful access to activities that those without a disability enjoy.

IDEALS CHALLENGE: *Initiating Inquiry*

As a teacher, you will be required to accommodate children with disabilities in a variety of ways. For example, a child with a learning disability may require extended time on a test.

- Why would this be necessary to achieve equal educational opportunity? Without that extended time, how might the child with a learning disability be treated unfairly?
- How do you explain to children without disabilities that you are not being "unfair" to them by accommodating their peers? Do such practices serve to lower academic standards?
- What if everyone had "extended time" on a test? Would that be "unfair" to anyone? Would it lower academic standards?
- Talk with one or more teachers who teach in inclusionary classrooms and ask them about the accommodations they make for the children with disabilities in their classroom. Ask them about the reaction of other students in their class to these accommodations and how they respond to the other students' reactions.

Not surprisingly, the exclusions described by the controversies in the cases of *Brown, Plyler, Lau, Pennsylvania,* and *Mills* eventually spurred Congress into action. Therefore, equal educational opportunity is now protected by various federal statutes in addition to the Fourteenth Amendment. Table 8.2 lists those statutes and describes their application. Although all are important, three statutes particularly impact the day-to-day life of teachers and students. They are described in more detail below.

Section 504 of the Rehabilitation Act of 1973

Section 504 of the Rehabilitation Act of 1973 is a civil rights act that prohibits discrimination on the basis of disability. As noted on Table 8.2, it has broad application to both students and adults in any setting that accepts federal monies. Since all public schools accept federal funds (perhaps even the college in which you're enrolled), Section 504 applies to all public school districts.

In a moment we'll discuss how Section 504 affects you as a teacher, but first let's focus on how it affects students. It means that students who have a "mental or physical impairment that affects one or more major life activities" must receive an education comparable to that of their peers without disabilities. Major life activities include walking, talking, hearing, seeing, breathing, and learning. The disability may be permanent (e.g., a visual impairment, cerebral palsy, or attention deficit disorder) or it may be temporary (e.g., a broken leg). It also applies to students with AIDS (acquired immune deficiency syndrome) and those who test positive for the HIV virus (human immunodeficiency virus).

Providing an education comparable to that of peers without disabilities means that you may be required to make reasonable accommodations in your classroom in order that the student's disability does not serve as a barrier to how the child can access information or demonstrate learning. Reasonable accommodations may be physical (e.g., Braille, preferential seating,

Table 8.2 Federal Statutes Affecting Equity

Statute	Year Passed	Purpose	Protected Classes	Affected School Members
Title VI of the Civil Rights Act (42 U.S.C. 2000d)	1964	"No person in the United States shall, on the ground of race, color, or national origin, be excluded from participation in, or be subjected to discrimination under any program or activity receiving Federal financial assistance."	race national origin	students staff members
Title VII of the Civil Rights Act (42 U.S.C. 2000e)	1964	"It shall be unlawful employment practice for any employer . . . to fail or refuse to hire or discharge any individual, or otherwise to discriminate against any individual with respect to his compensation, terms, conditions, or privileges of employment because of such individual's race, color, religion, sex or national origin . . ."	race religion gender national origin	school employees
Age Discrimination in Employment Act (29 U.S.C. 621 *et. seq.*)	1967	Prohibits discrimination on the basis of age in employment.	age (40–70)	employees
Title IX of the Education Amendments (20 U.S.C. 1681)	1972	"No person in the United States shall, on the basis of sex, be denied the benefits, of, or be subjected to discrimination under any education program or activity receiving Federal financial assistance . . ."	gender (including marital status and pregnancy)	students employees
Section 504 of the Rehabilitation Act (29 U.S.C. 794)	1973	". . . no otherwise qualified individual with a disability in the United States shall, solely by reason of her or his disability, be excluded from the participation in, or denied the benefits of, or be subjected to discrimination under any program receiving Federal financial assistance . . ."	persons with disabilities	students employees parents community members accessing school programs
Equal Educational Opportunities Act (20 U.S.C. 1703)	1974	"No state shall deny equal educational opportunities to an individual on account of his or her race, color, sex, or national origin . . ."	race gender national origin	students
Individuals With Disabilities Education Act (20 U.S.C. 1400 *et seq.*) (First passed under the title "Education for All Handicapped Children Act)	1975	Provides financial assistance to states in order to provide special education and related services to children with disabilities.	children with disabilities aged 3–21 whose disabilities adversely affect educational performance	students
Bilingual Education Act (20 U.S.C. 3281)	1978	Provides funds and ensures equal educational opportunity for students with limited English.	students with limited English	students
Pregnancy Discrimination Act (42 U.S.C. 2000 e) (amended Title VII)	1978	Prohibits employment discrimination against pregnant women.	pregnant women	employees
Stewart B. McKinney Homeless Assistance Act (42 U.S.C. 11301)	1987	Provides funds for the appropriate education of homeless children.	homeless children	students
Americans With Disabilities Act (42 U.S.C. 12101-122313)	1990	Prohibits discrimination against persons with disabilities who are qualified to perform the duties of a job with reasonable accommodations. Also reiterates prohibitions of Section 504.	persons with disabilities	students employees

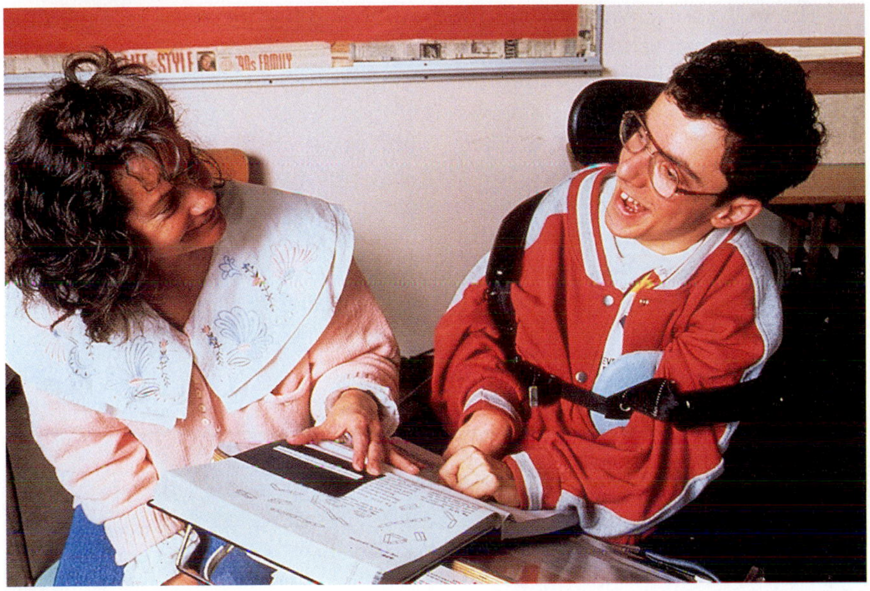

What does the Individuals With Disabilities Education Act require for students with severe disabilities? How might a democratic school meet the needs of this student?

a note taker, assistance with carrying supplies) or instructional (e.g., a sign language interpreter, extended time on a test, vocabulary assistance) and may include special education and related services. Accommodations are determined by staff members in consultation with the parents and are outlined in an accommodation plan. Although regulations do not require it, most schools generally use written accommodation plans. Remember, each accommodation plan must be based on the individual child and is essentially an equity plan for that child's educational experience.

Individuals With Disabilities Education Act

Two years after passing Section 504, Congress passed the Education for All Handicapped Children's Act, which was renamed the Individuals With Disabilities Education Act (IDEA) in 1990. This piece of child welfare legislation serves as a complement to Section 504. In recognition of the costs involved in providing equal educational opportunity to students with disabilities, Congress enacted IDEA to provide funds to states to assist them in serving those students with disabilities who are most adversely affected by their disabilities. You might say that Section 504 is the "stick" (it punishes those who violate it), while IDEA is the "carrot" (it provides financial incentives for the delivery of special education and related services).

Therefore, a student with disabilities will always be protected by Section 504, but may not be disabled enough to qualify for services under IDEA. For example, children with *temporary* impairments do not qualify under IDEA. In addition, a child could have an impairment that was not severe enough to qualify under IDEA (e.g., a hearing impairment, a learning disability). However, they may still have accommodation plans under Section 504. Thus, those served under IDEA are a subset of those protected under Section 504.

The Individuals With Disabilities Education Act is an extremely detailed law that requires school districts to document and justify the services provided to eligible children with disabilities. Figure 8.1 depicts the core components of IDEA.

IDEA creates a federal statutory right or an entitlement for each student with a disability. That entitlement is a Free Appropriate Public Education (FAPE) that consists of special education and related services designed to address the unique needs of the individual child. With parental participation, a team of school personnel knowledgeable about the child and his or her disability creates an Individualized Education Plan (IEP). In 1982, the Supreme Court explained that a Free Appropriate Public Education

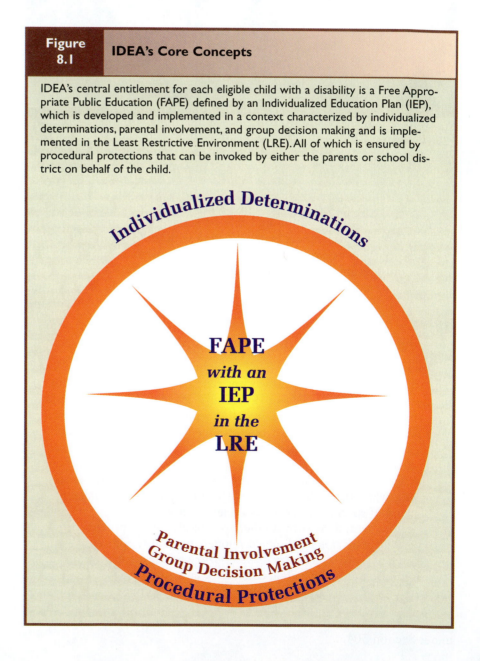

Figure 8.1 **IDEA's Core Concepts**

IDEA's central entitlement for each eligible child with a disability is a Free Appropriate Public Education (FAPE) defined by an Individualized Education Plan (IEP), which is developed and implemented in a context characterized by individualized determinations, parental involvement, and group decision making and is implemented in the Least Restrictive Environment (LRE). All of which is ensured by procedural protections that can be invoked by either the parents or school district on behalf of the child.

(FAPE) does not require that a child's potential be maximized, but rather that the IEP be "reasonably calculated to enable the child to receive educational benefits" (*Hendrick Hudson Central School District* v. *Rowley*). FAPE is a "floor opportunity," that is, a minimum level of service below which a district may not go.

Least Restrictive Environment (LRE) is another central principle of IDEA. It requires that children be educated with their peers without disabilities to the maximum extent appropriate. The 1997 amendments to the IDEA refocused the law on this principle and created a strong presumption in favor of educating children with disabilities in traditional classroom settings. If we decide to educate a child outside the regular education classroom, it is our responsibility as educators to show why a Free Appropriate Public Education cannot be achieved for that child in the regular class setting. In other words, the law requires that various other settings be made available (e.g., resource rooms, special classes, special schools) but that they be used only when equity demands such a difference.

What if you as a teacher think that a child with a disability is not achieving satisfactorily in the regular classroom? IDEA's principles suggest two possible reasons for such a problem: either (1) the child is inadequately supported in the traditional classroom; or (2) the child is inappropriately placed in that setting. The law requires that we carefully examine the first question before considering the second. Although the Supreme Court has never further defined the concept of Least Restrictive Environment, numerous other courts have. One of those cases, *Sacramento City Unified School District* v. *Rachel H.* (1994), established four factors to consider when determining the Least Restrictive Environment. Understanding these factors shows teachers what questions to ask and what information to gather if a teacher believes a child with disabilities "is not making it." Table 8.3 lists those factors and related questions for teachers.

LRE is related to, but not synonymous with "inclusion." Inclusion is an *educational philosophy* defined as "providing all students within the mainstream appropriate educational programs which are challenging and yet geared to their capabilities and needs as well as any support and assistance they and/or their teachers may need to be successful in the mainstream" (Stainback, 1990). Some even argue that all students with disabilities should be included at all times regardless of the nature and severity of their disabilities. This stance, often referred to as "full inclusion," is inconsistent with IDEA. IDEA does not require that students with disabilities be included as much as *possible*. It requires that students with disabilities be included as much as *appropriate*. IDEA is predicated on the principle that sometimes appropriateness (read equity) requires something other than what is traditional to meet the unique needs of an individual child. However, it is certainly true that for the vast majority of students with disabilities, an individualized examination of the needs of the child and the appropriate settings to address those needs will result in an "included" placement for all or part of the school day.

Refer once again to Figure 8.1. The final core component of IDEA is procedural protections. In order to protect the child's entitlement to Free Appropriate Public Education (FAPE) with an Individualized Education Plan (IEP) in the Least Restrictive Environment (LRE) and to ensure that all decision making occurs in the proper context (IDEA mandates detailed

Table 8.3 Least Restrictive Environment Considerations and Related Questions

Factor 1:	"The educational benefits available to [the child] in a regular classroom, supplemented with appropriate aids and services as compared with the educational benefits of a special education classroom." • What academic progress (as measured by the IEP) is the child showing? What problems are apparent? • What instructional strategies have I tried? To what effect? • What curricular adaptations have been tried? To what effect? • What supplemental and supportive services does the child receive now? Why isn't this enough? What's working and what's not? • What other supplemental and supportive services are needed to help this child? What additional support and/or training do I need? • How could we, as a team of educators, make this a successful environment for this child?
Factor 2:	"The nonacademic benefits of interaction with children who are not disabled." • What socialization benefit does the child receive? • Does the child appear to model his or her behavior on that of classmates? What evidence do you have? • Does the child interact with classmates? In what ways? • Are there differences in the way the child interacts with people in this setting compared with the ways she or he interacts in other settings you've observed (e.g., lunch room, recess)?
Factor 3:	"The effect of [the child's] presence on the teacher and the other children in the classroom." • How much class time do you use to work specifically with this child on academic skills? • Is the child disruptive? In what ways? How much class time is expended getting the child's behavior under control? • How do classmates respond to this child? Has anyone complained? • Have you received any feedback from parents?
Factor 4:	"The cost of mainstreaming [the child] in the regular classroom." • This factor is a consideration for the administrative team of your school. Although cost alone cannot rule out a setting or a service, the court's use of this factor suggests there is a limit (although undefined) to the measures required by a district to make a regular classroom placement available to the child.

SOURCE: *Sacramento City Unified School District* v. *Rachel H.*, 14 F.3d 1398 (9th Cir.), *cert. denied*, 129 L.Ed.2d 813 (1994).

procedural requirements and safeguards). If parents believe that the school is not providing at least an appropriate education for their child, they can challenge the district through a "due process" hearing. Likewise, if the district believes that parents are obstructing the school's ability to meet its obligation of FAPE for the child, the district can request a due process hearing to settle the dispute.

One last word about your responsibilities under IDEA. Teachers, including both "regular and "special" education teachers, have four main responsibilities under IDEA:

1. referral for testing and assessment of a child suspected of having a disability

Does excluding female students from participating on the football team violate Title IX?

2. participation in the evaluation of the child to determine eligibility and/or educational needs
3. participation in the development of the IEP goals and objectives
4. participation in the implementation of the IEP

How you will be involved in each of these steps depends on the position you hold in the school. However, no one is exempt from responsibility under IDEA. Children with disabilities are not "those kids." All students are "our kids" and each educator brings his or her talents to bear on the education of every member of the community. Each IEP team (the group of people that develops a child's IEP) must include at least one "regular class teacher" unless the child will not spend any part of his or her day in the regular classroom. Therefore, you will be directly and intimately involved in the implementation of IDEA. Ultimately, the question for democratic schools is, "How can all students (including students with disabilities) be equitably treated and have access to experiences that promote inquiry, discourse, authenticity, leadership, and service?"

Title IX of the Education Amendments of 1972

Title IX of the Education Amendments of 1972 prohibits discrimination on the basis of sex in educational settings. This includes prohibiting schools from sex discrimination in admissions, counseling, financial aid and scholarships, and extracurricular activities. For many schools, girls had no interscholastic sports opportunities until the passage of Title IX. Girls also endured exclusions from stereotypically "male" courses such as car mechanics or even advanced math and science, while boys were similarly

CLICK ON IT

For more information about how schools can better serve students with disabilities, visit the Web site of the Office of Special Education at

http://www.ed.gov/offices/OSERS/

excluded from stereotypically "female" courses. Title IX changed all that. In general, if a school notices that a course is either over- or underrepresented by one gender, it must investigate to ensure that sex bias has not created the situation. Still, some segregation on the basis of sex may occur in some contact sports and in courses where gender may influence the activity (e.g., playing contact sports in physical education classes, separating choral groups by vocal range).

Title IX has also had an increasing impact on a school's response to aggressive behavior on the basis of sex. In the last chapter, we discussed the issue of sexual harassment. There are two types of sexual harassment. The first is *quid pro quo* harassment, which means conditioning benefits or rewards on the granting of sexual favors. For example, if a teacher told a student he could receive an "A" if he engaged in sexual intercourse, that would constitute *quid pro quo* harassment. The second type of sexual harassment is *hostile environment* harassment. A hostile environment exists when behavior of a sexual nature makes it difficult or impossible for the student to learn. For example, a hostile environment might exist if a student was subjected to unwelcome comments of a sexual nature with such frequency and of such a degree that he or she began to skip that class. While even one incident of *quid pro quo* harassment may be sufficient to found a claim, hostile environment harassment necessitates the showing of a pattern of behavior over time.

In addition to being antithetical to the concepts of democracy and equity, sexual harassment is legally defined as one form of discrimination. Therefore, under Title IX, schools must have policies in place to investigate complaints of sexual harassment and make appropriate responses to stop any harassment that is verified. That response may mean reprimanding the harasser or may include harsher penalties such as expulsion for students or dismissal for teachers. In addition, many schools have sexual harassment policies that require teachers to report any observations of harassing behavior. Be sure to check your teacher's handbook so that you know what your responsibilities are and to whom you should report any concerns.

IDEALS CHALLENGE: *Learning Leadership*

Consider the following scenario:

Tina Harris is an eighth-grader at Washington Middle School and is in your fourth-period class. She has been a model student—attentive in class, considerate of her classmates, and willing to work hard to complete the work assigned to her. During second quarter, you notice that her work is markedly falling. She also seems very distracted while in class and appears to become more and more anxious as the hour progresses. You ask Tina if anything is wrong, but she gives no explanation for the change. One day, you notice Tina speaking with Mr. Grafton, her fifth-hour English teacher. Tina has her back to the lockers and Mr. Grafton is standing with his hand on the wall near her shoulder and is leaning toward her. As you approach, Tina sees you and immediately begins to blush. Mr. Grafton removes his arm and backs away. You exchange greetings. Although you can think of several innocent reasons for the encounter you witnessed, you can't seem to shake the nagging sour feeling in the pit of your stomach.

- What would you do?
- Should you say something to Tina? To Mr. Grafton? To anyone else?
- What if you do make a report and it turns out that your concerns were unfounded?
- Do you have a legal responsibility to do anything? What about an ethical or moral responsibility?

Equal Protection for Teachers

Teachers are also protected from discrimination. In the case of teachers, however, the focus moves from equal educational opportunity to equal employment opportunity. Again, the Fourteenth Amendment's equal protection and due process clauses provide the foundation for our protection from discrimination. As explained at the beginning of this section, discrimination does not mean that school districts cannot treat people differently. It means that differential treatment based on some status characteristic such as race, gender, or disability, must be justified as necessary to the achievement of the district's legitimate goals.

In addition to the constitutional protection you enjoy, several federal statutes safeguard your rights. Table 8.2 lists those statutes and their application. Some of these acts are particularly relevant for teachers and are discussed below.

Title VII of the Civil Rights Act of 1964

Title VII of the Civil Rights Act prohibits any practice in which an employer refuses to hire an individual, or chooses to dismiss an individual, based on that individual's race, color, religion, sex, or national origin. This statute also prohibits an employer from segregating or classifying employees based on race, color, religion, sex, or national origin when such practices deprive employees of opportunities or adversely affects their job status. In addition, the provisions of the statute and an explanation of how and where to file an employment discrimination complaint must be posted in an area accessible to all employees. If a court finds an employer guilty of employment discrimination, the court can order appropriate action such as the reinstatement of a dismissed employee or the hiring of an individual for employment.

It is legal to hire employees based on color, religion, sex, or national origin if those characteristics are essential qualifications necessary for the normal operation of the particular business doing the hiring. For example, it is legal for a school, university, or other educational institution to hire employees of a particular religion if the school is substantially supported or controlled by that religion.

IDEALS CHALLENGE: *Examining Equity*

In the spring of 1997, Steve Jubb circulated a job announcement via an Internet listserv that specifically requested that teachers of color apply for the position. He received the following response from one reader.

E-MAIL MESSAGE FROM STEVE LANGFORD TO STEVE JUBB, DATED 6/19/97, 8:03:22 PM

I find: "Title VII of the 1964 Civil Rights Act, as amended, and other Federal Laws and regulations forbid discrimination by employers, labor organizations, employment agencies, State and local government and public agencies . . ."

Are there exemptions to existing laws that now permit racial discrimination by employers?

—*Steve Langford*

REPLY FROM STEVE JUBB, EXECUTIVE DIRECTOR, BAY AREA COALITION OF ESSENTIAL SCHOOLS

Thank you for sharing the text of the antidiscrimination law. The e-mail I passed along should have read something like, "Teachers of color are encouraged to apply." Your implied feedback is accepted vis à vis being more careful about the wording of a job description and the importance of using the correct code words . . .

The spirit of the request, however, is to bring more role models into a school that will ultimately serve mostly poor students and/or students of color. At this time in our development as a nation we seem to lack the shared language (and shared experience) to discuss issues of race and poverty honestly and with sufficient directness to truly understand what is being said. So while you and I might agree with the law as written, in practice we may differ on whether it is appropriate to be direct in encouraging teachers of color to apply for a particular job. Personally, I'm willing to take the risk that people will be offended because the cost of not addressing racism directly is too high otherwise.

In California 80% of the teaching force is white while nearly 50% of the students are not. In areas like San Francisco and Oakland (where I live), the student population is overwhelmingly of color. So if it means taking risks on behalf of creating a multicultural faculty so be it. The positive effects of providing students with role models and teachers whom they perceive as being successful and like them are well documented (see Delpit, Cummins, Banks, Asante, Howard, & Hilliard to name a few) and it's something I have seen with my own eyes. We could argue all day about whether or not you believe that systemic racism exists in our education system. I happen to think it does.

You asked: Are there exemptions to existing laws that now permit racial discrimination by employers? I would ask you a question in return: Are there any laws that have resulted in really preventing racial discrimination in schools? If so, how would you explain the horrific achievement gaps for poor, Latino, and African American children?

—*Steve Jubb, Executive Director, Bay Area Coalition of Essential Schools*

- Discuss Title VII of the 1964 Civil Rights Act with your classmates. Does having an anti-discrimination law prevent discrimination? What implications for schools and hiring practices are raised by Steve Jubb's reply?

Title VII of the Civil Rights Act is designed to protect you from unfair practices with respect to employment. Employment discrimination can be difficult to prove. In most cases, courts look for a pattern of discrimination

Can telling a joke constitute sexual harassment? If so, what criteria would you use to determine whether it was sexual harassment?

and not a one-time event. Sustaining a charge of discrimination requires surviving three separate inquiries. First, the complainant must show a "*prima facie*" case of discrimination. In other words, without any further explanation, the situation appears to be discriminatory. If the complainant cannot do so, the process is over and the school district prevails. Second, if the individual succeeds, then the school district will have an opportunity to advance evidence of a nondiscriminatory reason for the actions they took (i.e., the district hired the other person, not because of his race, but because of better qualifications). If the district cannot do so, they have violated Title VII. If the district shows a nondiscriminatory rationale for their actions, then the burden of proof shifts back to the complainant. Third, the person filing the complaint must provide evidence that the district's rationale was merely a pretext to hide discriminatory behavior. Only if all three inquiries can be substantiated will the complaint be sustained. Clearly this is a difficult process and requires not just a suspicion of discrimination, but actual evidence of wrongdoing in order to prevail.

As explained in the discussion about Title IX, sexual harassment is one form of discrimination. Thus, Title VII also prohibits sexual harassment in the workplace. Both *quid pro quo* and *hostile environment* claims may be brought under Title VII. Districts must have policies in place to prohibit such discrimination against employees and a procedure to investigate and process complaints.

In 1998, the Supreme Court decided three separate cases regarding sexual harassment and Title VII. The first, *Oncale* v. *Sundowner Offshore Services, Inc.* (1998), established that same-sex harassment is prohibited under Title VII. In other words, if woman harasses a woman or a man harasses a man because of sex, Title VII provides an avenue for relief. The second two cases both considered the employer's liability if a supervisor harasses a supervisee and refuses requests by the supervisee to stop. The Court concluded that the employer was liable in such a situation and that the employee could collect monetary damages under Title VII for such improper conduct. However, if the employer has appropriate policies in place, that are well articulated and publicized, that liability may be relieved. If policies to investigate and respond to complaints were available and the person did not use the complaint process, then the employer is not liable for damages (*Faragher* v. *City of Boca Raton*, 1998; *Burlington Industries, Inc.* v. *Ellerth*, 1998).

For our purposes these decisions mean that any teacher subjected to sexual harassment should (1) tell the harasser to stop; and (2) make an appropriate complaint with the designated person responsible under the district's policy. Then, if the district fails to respond adequately, further remedies and/or damages can be sought in court.

Age Discrimination in Employment Act of 1967

Teachers are protected from age discrimination under the Age Discrimination in Employment Act of 1967. The purpose of this act is to see that individuals are employed based on their merits or abilities rather than their age. For example, this act protects older, experienced teachers who have higher salaries from being replaced by younger, inexperienced teachers who typically receive much lower salaries. Under this act, an employer cannot refuse to hire an individual, dismiss an individual, or reduce the salary of an individual based on the age of the individual. To be eligible for protection under this statute, individuals must be at least 40 years old, but less than 70 years of age.

Section 504 and the Americans With Disabilities Act

Teachers with disabilities are also protected from discrimination by both Section 504 and the Americans With Disabilities Act. These acts mean that any person with a disability who can perform the essential functions of a job with reasonable accommodations is eligible for that job. In addition, persons already employed who become disabled must be given reasonable accommodations to allow them to continue working. Some examples of reasonable accommodations are "making necessary facilities accessible and usable, restructuring work schedules, acquiring or modifying equipment, and providing readers or interpreters" (McCarthy, Cambron-McCabe, & Thomas, 1998, p. 352). Accommodations become unreasonable if they cause the employer undue administrative or financial burden. Accordingly, a school would not have to hire or promote unqualified persons, redesign the essential functions of the position, or require another worker to change jobs in the name of "accommodation." Whether an accommodation is too costly depends on the size of the organization and the impact on that organization both in the short and long term. However, schools do need to be built to ADA specifications, or appropriate changes should be made when remodeling.

IDEALS CHALLENGE: *Achieving Authenticity*

You are being interviewed for a teaching position. The principal interviewing you seems very friendly and begins by engaging in what you assume is just some chitchat to try to get to know you better and make you feel at ease. However, she begins to ask questions that make you feel uneasy. "Are you married? Would you like to have children? Were you born in this country? What religion do you practice? What political party do you belong to?" You wonder if these questions are even legal.

- What should you do? Can you refuse to answer?
- What do these questions tell you about the principal? Would you want to work for her?
- If you wanted to complain, whom would you contact?
- Now assume that your principal has asked you to serve on an interviewing team to hire a new teacher for your school. With one or two of your classmates, conduct a mock interview of another classmate. As a group, debrief after the interview. Were the questions you asked legally defensible? Did they help give you a sense of your classmates qualifications and abilities for the position?

SUMMARY

This chapter has discussed the sources of legal authority that affect teachers' and students' lives as well as how laws attempt to protect the access of all individuals and groups to education. Remember though that the law can serve only as a minimum in terms of providing access to educational opportunity for students and opportunities in education for teachers. In a sense, the law serves only to let individuals and groups get their foot (or feet) in the door. What happens to them once they have crossed the threshold and are actually inside the room (or school) is equally important. As was discussed in chapter 7, the nature of policies, practices, actions, and behaviors within schools also play a major role in creating equity or inequity. This is where you as an individual and a member of a school community can make a significant difference as you continuously strive to implement the IDEALS of democracy. You will learn more about protecting personal liberties in chapter 9.

PRESENT TO PAST

Minority Access to Education Prior to *Brown* v. *Board of Education*[1]

Earlier in this chapter we discussed the 1954 *Brown* v. *Board of Education* case, which ruled that separate educational facilities for blacks and whites were inherently unequal and thus, unconstitutional. As noted, the *Brown* ruling influenced equity and access to educational opportunity not only for African Americans, but for students from various racial and ethnic backgrounds from that day forward. This Present to Past section explores the access four racial and ethnic groups had to public education prior to the *Brown* ruling. Specifically, we will discuss four major groups of *involuntary* ethnic minorities. These groups did not choose to leave their previous life behind. Rather, they were forced to do so. They include:

- Africans who had been captured, enslaved, brought to America, and later freed
- Native Americans, primarily in the Midwest and West who were conquered and whose land and way of life was taken from them
- Mexicans whose lands became part of the United States after Mexico lost the Mexican American War in 1848
- Hawai'ians whose islands were claimed by the United States

ACCESS FOR AFRICAN AMERICANS

For African Americans, one of the repercussions of the Civil War was that at last they had the opportunity to attend public schools. Charlotte Forten (1837–1914) was an African American woman from a well-to-do Philadelphia family that was active in the abolitionist movement. From 1862–1864 Forten taught in a school for recently freed children, with the express purpose of proving that African Americans were educable and would be good soldiers for the Union cause. Here is an excerpt from her journal:

> I never before saw children so eager to learn, although I had had several years' experience in New-England schools. . . . The older ones, during the summer, work in the fields from early morning until eleven or twelve o'clock, and then come into school, after their hard toil in the hot sun, as bright and as anxious to learn as ever. . . . Many of the grown people are desirous of learning to read. It is wonderful how a people who have been so long crushed to the earth, so imbruted as these have been,—and they are said to be among the most degraded negroes (sic) of the South,—can have so great a desire for knowledge, and such a capability of attaining it. One cannot believe that the haughty Anglo-Saxon race, after centuries of such an experience as these people have had, would be very much superior to them. (Forten, 1997, pp. 128–129)

Some Northern educators supported the idea of "redeeming" the South and raising up freed slaves and poor whites by educating all citizens. For the first time, legal actions were taken and direct federal aid was given to support elementary education. Remedies to halt inequality came in the form of the Thirteenth Amendment of 1865, the Reconstruction Acts of 1867, the Fourteenth Amendment of 1868, and the 1875 Civil Rights Act.

Senator Charles Sumner of Massachusetts had tried since the 1840s to eliminate legal and social discrimination in education. He led a congressional group dubbed the "Radical Redeemers," who passed legislation to establish the Freedmen's Bureau in 1867. The Freedmen's Bureau was intended to help the newly freed slaves better their lives and to control the expected transformation of the South. The powers of the bureau included hiring teachers (mainly European American females from the North) and leasing buildings for schools. The schools were funded by the bureau, benevolent associations, and freedmen themselves. By 1870, when the Freedmen's Bureau ended its work, there were 4,239 schools in the South under its supervision, but only 10% of the 1.7 million African Americans of school age were actually in school—although many of them in separate schools from white students (Du Bois, 1992). Although there were successes during Reconstruction, African Americans still faced discrimination, unequal access, and unequal schools.

An 1896 court decision, *Plessy* v. *Ferguson*, had implications for African American schools. Homer Plessy, whose ancestry was seven-eighths European and one-eighth African, was told that he could not ride on a "whites only" train car in Louisiana. Plessy sued and lost his case before the United States Supreme Court. The court rejected the argument that "the enforced separation of the two races stamps the colored race with a badge of inferiority" (Noll & Kelly, 1970, p. 270). The court further asserted that social prejudices and inequalities could not be overcome by legislation, and that the "two races" already had equal civil and political rights. This ruling was used as a justification to maintain the segregated educational system that had existed since the end of Reconstruction. The ruling held that separate schools for African American students were acceptable, as long as they were equal to the schools white students attended. This ruling would be bitterly opposed by many African Americans over the next 58 years who argued that black schools were separate but unequal in terms of resources when compared with white schools.

In the first half of the 20th century segregation and inequality had been largely maintained, in spite of heroic struggles by many citizens. The 1940 federal census showed that 17 states and the District of Columbia mandated segregation of blacks and whites by law—75 years after the end of the Civil War. The inequities were glaring (Cremin, 1988):

- 2.8% of whites and 11.7% of blacks had never attended school
- 11.6% of whites and 37.0% of blacks were illiterate
- 13.2% of whites and 2.9% of blacks had completed four years of high school

IDEALS CHALLENGE: *Deepening Discourse*

(Adapted from Washington & Du Bois, 1907.)

At the turn of the 20th century two powerful, but conflicting, educational and social visions were proposed for African Americans, one by Booker T. Washington (1856–1915) and the other by W. E. B. Du Bois (1868–1963). In 1907 Du Bois and Washington engaged in a debate about these matters, which was published under the title *The Negro in the South*. Excerpts follow. See if you can identify the nature of each man's argument and how their visions for African Americans differ.

BOOKER T. WASHINGTON

I have learned that the man of my race who has some regular occupation, who owns his farm, is a taxpayer and perhaps has a little money in the bank, is the most reliable and helpful man in the Sunday-school, in the church, and in all religious endeavor. The man who has gotten upon his feet in these directions is almost never charged with crime, but is the one who has the respect and the confidence of both races in his community. . . . " (pp. 72)

- What does Washington see as the purposes of education for African Americans?
- What are his major arguments?
- How might you argue against Washington?

W. E. B. DU BOIS

It is becoming distinctly obvious to Negroes that today, in modern economic organization, the one thing that is giving the workman a chance is intelligence and political power, and that it is utterly impossible for a moment to suppose that the Negro in the South is going to hold his own in the new competition with immigrants if, on the one hand, the immigrant has access to the best schools of the community and has equal political power with other men to defend his rights and to assert his wishes, while, on the other hand, his black competitor is not only weighed down by past degradation, but has few or no schools and is disfranchised [unable to vote]." (pp. 119–120)

- What does Du Bois see as the purposes of education for African Americans?
- What are his major arguments?
- How might you argue against Du Bois?

ACCESS FOR NATIVE AMERICANS

Following the Trail of Tears in the 1830s, Native Americans in the South had been given a huge swath of territory in the Western plains. For a time, the tribes in Oklahoma were once again isolated on land that belonged to them and could develop their own educational systems. For example, in conjunction with missionaries the Choctaws had established nine boarding schools and a system of day schools by 1848 (Spring, 1997). The Cherokees used bilingual teachers and texts written in the new Cherokee alphabet (created in 1821 by Sequoyah), and attained nearly 100% literacy at a time when European Americans in neighboring states were far less literate (Spring, 1997).

After 1850, however, this policy of simply moving people west was replaced by a policy of setting aside limited reservations for the forced resettlement of all Native American groups. In order to "civilize" those who lived on the reservations, two types of schools were created: manual labor schools and boarding schools.

Manual labor schools on the reservations served to teach Native Americans the European work ethic and prepare them to be farmers, while making them literate. The curriculum of these schools resembled other one-room rural schools of the time, with the important exception that it intended to replace Native American culture with the European-based American culture.

In order to fully assimilate Native American children, the Office of Indian Affairs also established off-reservation boarding schools. The first such school was Carlisle Indian School in Carlisle, Pennsylvania, which opened in 1879. By 1905 there were 25 off-reservation boarding schools across the country. The purpose of these schools was made apparent by the U.S. Commissioner of Education, William T. Harris, in the introduction to an 1889 bulletin. Harris praised the effort to "obtain control of the Indian at an early age, and to seclude him as much as possible from the tribal influences. We cannot save him and his patriarchal or tribal institution both together. To save him we must take him up into our civilization" (Spring, 1997).

Assimilation for Native Americans remained the goal of the Bureau of Indian Affairs until the 1930s. The reservation status of most Native Americans ensured that they would be segregated from other ethnic groups, except for those Native American students who were sent to boarding schools. Some government officials in the Bureau of Indian Affairs, however, were influenced by progressive ideas. The *Meriam Report,* a study of Native American education that was published in 1928, stated that the previous policy of removing children from their homes to attend boarding schools and prohibiting tribal language and customs was wrong. Bureau schools on reservations were also criticized for being too rote and rigid. There was direct support for day schools that encouraged children to keep their own culture while learning how to live in a non-Indian world. After 1928, the idea of "biculturalism" became the new watchword (Spring, 1997, pp. 34–35).

ACCESS FOR NATIVE HAWAI'IANS

In the 1890s, United States government leaders put aside their previous isolationism and began pursuing the acquisition of colonies for the United States. They did this by winning the Spanish-American War in 1898 and claiming Puerto Rico, the Philippines, and Guam from Spain, and by acquiescing in the overthrow of a sovereign nation—Hawai'i. The story of Hawai'i and the education of Pacific Islanders is an important tale about a communitarian society being made to fit into a modern liberal nation.

Although traditionally children in Hawai'i were educated within the family and through apprenticeships with non-family adults, two kinds of schools developed in Hawai'i in the 1830s. The first type of schools were common schools taught by a missionary-trained Hawai'ian teacher and attended by the common people. The second type of schools were "select" schools for the Hawai'ian elite and church-related private schools for the American or British elite. The church-related schools were taught by missionaries and, because of their strong Christian and Western European cultural values, dancing the hula and dressing in traditional Hawai'ian clothing were strictly prohibited in public (although classes were taught in Hawai'ian until the 1870s).

Political changes led to greater problems for the Native Hawai'ian culture. In January 1893 a group of American businessmen led by plantation owner Sanford Dole took control of the 'Iolani Palace where Lili'uokalani lived, and the nation of Hawai'i ceased to exist. Though President McKinley opposed this insurrection, by 1898 Hawai'i was annexed as a territory of the United States.

After annexation, the de facto segregation of education into public schools for commoners and elite church schools (especially Catholic and Anglican) continued. Asian immigrants were often educated in plantation schools, while the public schools in Honolulu and the few other cities in the islands had inadequate facilities and lackluster leadership. European American parents whose children attended the public schools complained about the poor education, the use of "pidgin English" by local children, and the separatist Japanese language schools (which only operated before or after public school hours). In response, a new institution was created in the 1920s: the "English Standard School." This school emphasized a strong training in speaking standard English and learning the social customs of middle-class European Americans, and for decades few Asian or Pacific Islanders attended the schools.

After World War II the English Standard School idea was dropped and the Japanese Language Schools were drastically curtailed. Not until the 1960s would Native Hawai'ians begin to change the curriculum in the public schools so that Hawai'ian culture and language could be included. There is now a required Hawai'ian Studies curriculum at different grade levels. Groups of parents and educators also created "Hawai'ian Language Immersion Schools" on several islands in the 1990s. In these schools, some classes are taught in the Hawai'ian language and the aim is for children to become bilingual and meld traditional Hawai'ian culture with modern Western cultures.

In spite of the successful push for a multicultural curriculum, the split between commoners attending public schools and the elite attending private schools has persisted. Hawai'i has the highest rate of private school attendance of any state in the nation, and Native Hawai'ian children (except those in elite private schools) have relatively low rates of school success. Native Hawai'ians have not experienced the same level of legal segregation as other groups described in this section, but like Native Americans they have had to struggle to save their language and customs, and like African Americans they have faced overt, deep-seated prejudice.

ACCESS FOR MEXICAN AMERICANS

There are many Spanish-speaking groups in the United States, but the largest group with the longest history as part of this nation is Mexican Americans. After the United States won the war with Mexico in 1848, Mexico was forced to sell a huge expanse of land in the Southwest, and millions of Spanish-speaking peoples suddenly became a part of this country. Throughout much of the 1800s, Catholic schools dotted the Southwestern landscape, but most Mexican Americans worked to eke out a living and their children attended few years of school. A pattern of segregation from the "Anglo" (European American) population developed, because the public schools taught classes only in English and disregarded the history and culture of Mexican Americans. Parents who had some resources started private "Mexican schools."

In the first decades of the 20th century there was a large influx of Mexican immigrants to the United States. The response of Anglos to the changing demographics was contradictory (Spring, 1997). On the one hand, the immigrants were coming to work on the large farms in Texas and southern California, and their children were needed as planters and pickers in the fields. Schooling would not only take them away from the fields for the short term, but they might not return to farmwork if they became more educated and had more economic opportunities. The simplest method to deal with the situation was not to enforce compulsory school laws. As a result, non-enforcement was widespread. Recent immigrant families needed the money earned by their children, and the parents had generally not attended school themselves.

On the other hand, the immigrants needed to be "Americanized" by learning English and fitting into the cultural ways of the dominant Anglo society. This required public education—but schools were to remain segregated according to ethnicity. As late as the mid-1930s, 85% of the schools districts in the Southwest were segregated into Anglos and Mexicans (Gonzalez, 1990). Perceptions of Spanish-speaking children were routinely stereotypical. Here is what some Anglo educators of the era said about Mexican American girls:

> Mexican girls have inherited this remarkable aptness with the needle. We should strive to foster it in them. . . . Many of the [Mexican] girls will very likely find employment as house servants. They should be taught something about cleaning, table-setting, and serving. . . . The fact that the Mexican girl marries young and becomes the mother in the home at the age the American girl is in high school means that the junior high school is trusted with her education for homemaker. For this reason, it seems to me that all or most of her junior high school training should be directed toward making her a better wife, mother and homemaker. (Gonzalez, 1990, pp. 49, 168)

The quote exemplifies how educators thought the school curriculum should reflect the probable occupations of students, and they remind us of the limiting nature of a strictly vocational track in schools. Given these educational conditions, it is not surprising that there were astronomical dropout and retention rates for Mexican Americans, a problem that has affected their communities to this day.

Some Mexican Americans were dissatisfied with their "separate and unequal" status and their children's low levels of formal education, and they fought to improve the schools. The *de jure* segregation of Mexican American students was forever altered by the *Mendez* v. *Westminster* court decision of 1946. The court ruled that there was no educational justification for school segregation (partly because of the need for Mexican Americans to learn English). This landmark case was the first one to employ the Fourteenth Amendment to overturn school segregation for ethnic minorities. The attorney for the plaintiffs gave copies of all the briefs and notes from the case to Thurgood Marshall, an African American attorney who was instrumental in the *Brown* v. *Board of Education* ruling almost a decade later.

IDEALS CHALLENGE: *Deepening Discourse*

Revisit the following statements that you discussed at the beginning of this chapter. Are your responses still the same?

- Access to education can be protected via legal means.
- Equity means that everyone must be treated the same.
- Integrated schools ensured equal educational opportunity for all students.
- Schools that include students with disabilities in regular classrooms are equitable for all students.
- Sex equity in athletics can be ensured by permitting male and female students to participate on the same teams.

DOING DEMOCRACY

The schools you attended and maybe even some of your classes probably had students with disabilities. Others of you may have a family member with a disability. Still others of you may have a disability yourself.

- Based on your past experiences, how were students with disabilities treated?
- What did you gain from interactions you have had with students or adults with disabilities?
- How do your experiences help you understand and conceptualize the potential of inclusion?
- How can you use your experiences to help other teachers conceptualize and understand the potential of inclusion?
- How will your experiences impact your ability to equitably treat students with disabilities?
- Volunteer to work in a classroom or other setting where you will be able to work with students with disabilities. Keep a journal of your thoughts, actions, reactions, and what you are learning form the experience.

END NOTE

[1]This section was written by the text's main authors.

REFERENCES

Cremin, L. A. (1988). *American education: The metropolitan experience, 1876–1986*. New York: Harper & Row.

Du Bois, W. E. B. (1992). *Black reconstruction in America, 1860–1880*. New York: Atheneum. (Originally published in 1935 as *Black Reconstruction*.)

Forten, C. (1997). Life on the Sea Islands. In R. M. Cohen & S. Scheer (Eds.), *The work of America: A social history through stories* (pp. 125–131). Mahwah, NJ: Lawrence Erlbaum.

Gonzalez, G. G. (1990). *Chicano education in the era of segregation*. Cranbury, NJ: Associated University Presses.

McCarthy, M., Cambron-McCabe, N., & Thomas, S. (1998). *Public school law: Teachers' and students' rights* (4th ed.). Boston, MA: Allyn and Bacon.

Noll, J. W., & Kelly, S. P. (1970). *Foundations of education in America: An anthology of major thoughts and significant actions.* New York: Harper & Row.

Spring, J. (1997). *Deculturalization and the struggle for equality* (2nd ed.). New York: McGraw-Hill.

Stainback, S. (1990). Inclusive Schooling. In W. Stainback (Ed.), *Support networks for inclusive schools: Interdependent integrated education.* Baltimore, MD: Paul H. Brookes.

Underwood, J. K., & Mead, J. F. (1995). *The legal aspects of special education and pupil services.* Boston, MA: Allyn and Bacon.

Washington, B. T., & Du Bois, W. E. B. (1907). *The Negro in the South.* Philadelphia: George W. Jacobs.

CASES CITED

Brown v. *the Board of Education of Topeka*, 347 U.S. 483, 74 S.Ct. 686 (1954).

Burlington Industries, Inc. v. *Ellerth,* — U.S. —, No. 97-569 (June 26, 1998).

Faragher v. *City of Boca Raton,* — U.S. —, No. 97-282 (June 16, 1998).

Hendrick Hudson Central School District v. *Rowley,* 458 U.S. 176, 102 S.Ct. 3034 (1982).

Lau v. *Nichols,* 414 U.S. 563, 94 S.Ct. 786 (1974).

Mills v. *Board of Education,* 348 F. Supp. 279 (D.D.C. 1972).

Oncale v. *Sundowner Offshore Services, Inc.* — U.S. —, No. 96-568 (March 4, 1998).

Pennsylvania Association for Retarded Citizens v. *Pennsylvania,* 334 F. Supp. 1257 (E.D. Pa. 1971), 343 F. Supp. 279 (E.D. Pa. 1972).

Plessy v. *Ferguson,* 163 U.S. 537, 16 S.Ct. 1138 (1896).

Plyler v. *Doe,* 457 U.S. 202, 102 S.Ct. 2383 (1982).

Sacramento City Unified School District v. *Rachel H.,* 14 F.3d 1398 (9th Cir.), *cert. denied,* 129 L.Ed.2d 813 (1994).

Do students have a right to come to school dressed in whatever they choose?

In general, what rights do students have to express themselves?

CHAPTER 9

The Legal Foundations of Equity: Protecting Personal Liberty[1]

By Julie F. Mead
University of Wisconsin–Madison

IDEALS CHALLENGE: *Deepening Discourse*

(Narrative is by Amber Brook, a middle school student, and is based on events that occurred in a suburban Wisconsin school district.)

Sometimes adults are so narrow. I mean especially teachers and principals. Some of them are OK, but some of them get so freaked for the wrong reasons. Like, take my principal. He doesn't like me at all. Actually, he doesn't even know me—the real me. All he knows about me is how I dress. He gets so freaked by the way I dress. Maybe I do dress a little differently than he does and than most of the other kids. But then, I'm not about to wear blue suits and boring ties to school, or preppy sweaters, or even super baggy pants. I should be allowed to dress the way I want to dress as long as it doesn't hurt anyone. And the way I dress doesn't hurt anyone. How does wearing black lipstick hurt anyone anymore than wearing red lipstick? How does wearing white face make-up and black fishnet stockings hurt anyone? My principal claims it's "disruptive of the educational environment." It's not the way I dress that disrupts things, it's the narrow-minded students who can't tolerate anyone being different. I mean out here in the suburbs almost everyone is rich, white, and thinks and acts exactly the same. If you're black or Hispanic or not as rich as they are, or if you think or act at all differently, you're looked down upon. I mean I just come to school, go to my classes, and do my work like any good student. Because I dress differently than the other students, I get called names and get harassed in other ways by some of the students. I don't like it, but I basically ignore it. That's not the way some of my friends feel. They talk back and the other day a fight started between some of my friends and the kids that harass us. Since then it's been harder to ignore the harassment, because it's gotten worse. I can't even walk the halls anymore without some snide remark being made about how I look or the way I act. I've even been pushed while I'm riding the bus to and from school. Now, the principal and superintendent have adopted a policy that says students can't wear black lipstick, white face make-up, or black fishnet stockings. Instead of using this incident as an opportunity to teach us a little bit about tolerance for people who look, act, and think differently than we do, they punish the innocent and ignore the students who have really done something wrong. I think they're violating my rights to freedom of expression. I mean, if I were a Muslim girl and were wearing a black scarf because of religious reasons, would they have done the same thing? Just because the way I dress is the way my favorite rock group dresses, they don't like it. Just because they say the group is against Christianity, against women, and are devil worshipers, I can't dress like them. What gives them the right to tell me what I can and can't believe? What makes their beliefs right and mine wrong? I'm glad my parents are pretty cool. They've hired an attorney and we're thinking of filing a suit against the school district for violating my free speech rights.

- What are Amber's rights as a student?
- Is Amber within her rights in dressing the way she does?
- Is the school's concern about disruption legitimate?
- How do you balance her rights against those of the district?

(Based on events in Erb v. *Iowa State Board of Public Instruction, 216 N.W.2d 339, Iowa, 1974.)*

Richard Erb taught in the Nishna Valley Community School in Iowa. He was married, with two sons. In addition to his teaching duties, for which he had a spotless record, Erb coached wrestling and football, and was a senior class sponsor. Margaret Johnson taught home economics at Nishna Valley. Erb and Johnson were caught engaged in sexual intercourse by Johnson's husband, who was hidden in the trunk of the car that Erb and Johnson chose as a rendezvous point. Johnson's husband, furious as he was, proceeded with divorce proceedings and brought the issue to the school board of Nishna Valley School. He wanted Erb fired for immoral behavior.

In the meantime, Erb and Johnson terminated their relationship. Erb apologized and was successful in making amends with his family, friends, and coworkers. Based on his spotless teaching record and the testimony of various community members, the school board did not seek to terminate Erb. The case, however, moved on to the State Board of Educational Examiners, pushed by Johnson's husband. The state board voted 5 to 4 to revoke Erb's teaching certificate. A trial court held that Erb's adulterous conduct was sufficient reason for revoking his teaching certificate on the grounds of immorality. Erb appealed the case to the Supreme Court of Iowa.

- Should Richard Erb have been dismissed from his teaching position?
- Did his conduct warrant revocation of his teaching certificate?
- As a teacher, what are his rights to lead his personal life the way he chooses?

INTRODUCTION

How common are stories like Amber's and Erb's? What do you as a teacher need to know about your legal rights and responsibilities? What about the legal rights of students? These questions are significant for any teacher, but especially a beginning teacher. This chapter is designed to address these questions:

1. What personal liberties do students and teachers enjoy in schools?
2. What are the rights of students and teachers and should their actions become subject to discipline?

3. What responsibilities do teachers have to protect their students from harm?

WHAT PERSONAL LIBERTIES DO STUDENTS AND TEACHERS HAVE?

One characteristic of our system of laws that distinguishes us from many other countries is our protection of personal liberties and the restrictions placed on the rights of the government. We enjoy freedom of speech, religion, association, and privacy, for example. These freedoms are contained in the Bill of Rights—the first 10 amendments of the U.S. Constitution—and exist to protect individuals and the minority from the tyranny of the majority. That said, it is important to note that sometimes the rights of the state outweigh the rights of the individual. No right is absolute.

While examining these rights as they apply first to students and then to teachers, consider whether you believe the courts have struck the right balance between personal freedom and legitimate state control in the school setting. In addition, consider whether, even if schools have the legitimate authority to restrict some liberties, they ought to in all circumstances. Are there ever legitimate educational reasons why you, as a teacher, or the school as a whole may not wish to assert the authority you have at your discretion?

Student Freedoms

For many years, conventional wisdom said that schools and teachers had nearly absolute authority, similar to that of parents, over students. This doctrine is known as *in loco parentis*, which means "in place of the parents." Just as your parents had broad authority to direct your upbringing (including telling you when to be quiet, where to sit, and perhaps even looking through your drawers or school backpack), school personnel were assumed to command similar latitude with the students who attended their school. Although that doctrine has been curtailed to some degree by a landmark court case, discussed below, *in loco parentis* "is viable and operates to help define the relationship between school and student in the public schools today. Its justification is found in the necessity for an orderly and well-behaved student in keeping with an agreeable learning environment" (Alexander & Alexander, 1998, p. 309). As we examine each issue of student freedom, note how the Supreme Court balances the rights of the students with the rights of the school.

Freedom of Expression: Students

Freedom of speech is an explicit right guaranteed by the First Amendment. It includes any form of expressive activity and so is frequently called "freedom of expression." In 1969, the U.S. Supreme Court first recognized that students do not "shed their constitutional rights to freedom of speech or expression at the schoolhouse gate" in the landmark case of *Tinker* v. *Des Moines Independent Community School District* (1969). The case involved a group of students who planned to wear black armbands in silent protest of the U.S. involvement in the Vietnam War. Upon learning of the students'

Do students' rights to freedom of expression mean they can say whatever they want when they address other students?

plans, the school enacted a policy prohibiting the wearing of armbands. Mary Beth and John Tinker and Christopher Eckhardt ignored the ban and subsequently were suspended from school until they returned without the armbands. The Court ruled that students have the right to express their views by speech or other forms of expression as long as the conduct does not "materially and substantially disrupt the work and discipline of the school." As Justice Fortas explained in the Court's written opinion, "any action to prohibit such freedom of speech must show that the action was caused by more than a mere desire to avoid the unpleasantness that always accompanies an unpopular viewpoint." In this case, the students' protest caused no disruption and therefore the school violated the students' First Amendment rights.

CLICK ON IT

To look up more information about legal cases or other information about education law, visit the following Web site

http://www.law.emory.edu/LAW/refdesk/subject/ed.html

or the Internet Law Library at

http://uscode.house.gov

Many thought *Tinker* tolled the demise of *in loco parentis*. Fear was rampant among schools that *Tinker* had provided students with the freedom to act as they pleased. The Court's ruling in *Bethel School District No 403* v. *Fraser* (1986) laid those fears to rest. Although Matthew Fraser, a student at Bethel High School in Bethel, Washington, had been advised by two teachers that the speech he planned to deliver at an all-school assembly was inappropriate and would result in severe consequences, he delivered it anyway. The short speech, nominating a fellow student for an office in student government, was as follows:

> I know a man who is firm—he's firm in his pants, he's firm in his shirt, his character is firm—but most . . . of all, his belief in you, the students of Bethel, is firm. Jeff Kuhlman is a man who takes his point and pounds it in. If necessary, he'll take an issue and nail it to the wall. He doesn't attack things in spurts—he drives hard, pushing and pushing until finally—he succeeds. Jeff is a man who will go to the very end—even the climax, for each and every one of you. So vote for Jeff for A.S.B. vice-president—he'll never come between you and the best our high school can be.

Responses to Matthew's speech were mixed among the 600 high school students. Some students seemed shocked, others embarrassed, and others cheered and nonverbally simulated the sexual activities that Matthew was describing. As a result of the speech, Matthew was suspended for three days. Matthew sued.

The Supreme Court had no sympathy for Matthew. Applying the "material and substantial disruption" test established in *Tinker*, the Court held that the school officials acted within their authority by first warning Matthew not to deliver the speech and then suspending him as a consequence of presenting it. The Court noted that Matthew's appeal was not based on any political viewpoint, that his speech was lewd and vulgar, and that it disrupted the schooling process. The Court also noted the educational purpose of teaching appropriate civil discourse.

> The undoubted freedom to advocate unpopular and controversial views in schools and classrooms must be balanced against the society's countervailing interest in teaching students the boundaries of socially appropriate behavior. Even the most heated political discourse in a democratic society requires consideration for the personal sensibilities of the other participants and audiences.

IDEALS CHALLENGE: *Achieving Authenticity*

Some educators believe that Matthew's speech in *Bethel* v. *Fraser* is a good teaching tool for a democratic school at the high school level to discuss free speech rights, the responsibilities of free speech, and whose values a school uses to decide what constitutes appropriate speech. Discuss the use of Matthew's speech as a teaching tool with your university classmates. If you decide the speech is appropriate to use at the high school level as a learning tool, how would you structure the learning environment to ensure that discussion was serious? In your university classroom, role-play the discussion of Matthew's speech that might occur in a high school classroom. What did you learn? What do you think your high school students might

The Supreme Court also has provided guidance with regard to freedom of expression in student publications. In *Hazelwood School District* v. *Kuhlmeier* (1988), students challenged the principal's decision to withhold two articles from publication in the student newspaper. One article dealt with actual pregnancies that had occurred at Hazelwood East High School and the consequences surrounding these pregnancies. While the author had changed the names of the students to maintain confidentiality, the principal stated that the anonymity of these pregnant students was not adequately protected. The second article dealt with students' experiences with their parents' divorce and included one student's harsh comments about her father. The principal was concerned that the comments amounted to personal attacks without providing an opportunity for response.

The Supreme Court centered its conclusion on one telling fact: the student newspaper was produced as part of the curriculum of a journalism class. Therefore, the publication could not be considered a public forum, but rather was a supervised, school-sponsored curricular activity. Since the school district unquestionably had the authority to set its curriculum, it likewise had the authority to restrict the expression printed in the school newspaper as long as it behaved reasonably. In other words, just as any teacher can set and control proper topics for an assignment, the school can exercise similar control over a student newspaper. In this case, the Court noted that the principal had a reasonable rationale for his decision and, as such, sustained his actions.

IDEALS CHALLENGE: *Deepening Discourse*

The *Hazelwood* decision reaffirms the school's authority in the case of student publications. The Court opined that the principal could justify his actions on the reasoning "that the students who had written and edited these articles had not sufficiently mastered those portions of the Journalism II curriculum that pertained to the treatment of controversial issues and personal attacks," that the school needed to protect the privacy of individuals whose most intimate concerns were potentially revealed in the newspaper, and that the school had a responsibility to impose "legal, moral, and ethical restrictions . . . upon journalists within [a] school community that includes adolescent subjects and readers."

- Do you agree with the decision? Do you agree that these rationales justify the principal's actions?
- Even though he could legitimately pull the two articles, do you think the principal should have? What would you have done in the principal's place?
- If you had been the Journalism II instructor, what would your response to the articles have been? To the principal's decision?
- Are there other actions that could have addressed the principal's concerns without removing the articles from publication?

Dress codes also have been frequently challenged as violations of students' freedom of expression. However, courts have generally not accepted such arguments. First, unlike the expression in *Tinker*, students have difficulty showing what message, other than personal preference, they are trying to convey by their manner of dress. Therefore, schools have a relatively easy task to articulate various legitimate rationales for the existence of dress codes. Various courts have accepted justifications such as training students for the work world, creating an orderly learning environment, and quelling gang-related activity. Courts generally have upheld school dress codes that prohibit clothing that is immodest or suggestive, that is unsanitary or unhealthy, or that creates a disturbance and disrupts the educational process.

IDEALS CHALLENGE: *Learning Leadership*

Remember Amber's story at the beginning of this chapter? Applying the precedents set in *Tinker* and *Bethel,* the school's actions would likely be upheld if challenged in court. The style of dress chosen by Amber and her friends had already caused a disruption as evidenced by the verbal and physical fights that had occurred. But what about Amber's point that the school was targeting the wrong disrupters? Reread Amber's story and discuss the school's response and any alternate responses available to the school. Would you be an advocate for Amber's choice? Why or why not? If you were a teacher in the school Amber attends, what, if anything, would you do?

Freedom of Religion: Students

Religion in public schools continues to be a controversial issue. Freedom of religion stems from the first two clauses of the First Amendment. The Establishment Clause, which says that "Congress shall make no law respecting an establishment of religion," prohibits the government, in this case a public school district, from privileging a particular religion or privileging religion over nonreligion, or vice versa. The Free Exercise Clause, which says that Congress shall make no law prohibiting the free exercise of religion, makes a citizen's spiritual life a matter of personal choice. Together these clauses create a "separation of church and state."

While religion cannot be promoted in public schools, schools are not necessarily religion-free zones. In this section, there are several guidelines that will help you interpret the separation of church and state and help you understand students' religious rights under our current understanding of these principles.

The general rule of thumb regarding religion in the classroom is that you may teach about religion, but you may not teach religion. Religious texts and music may be studied for their literary, historic, or artistic merit, but not for the spiritual message they convey. You may not do anything that suggests to students that their religious beliefs are wrong, nor can you use your classroom to proselytize. In general, religious belief or nonbelief should have no bearing on your treatment of students or their access to the learning you provide. You must be conscious of the fact that you represent the state (a public school district), and therefore you must not do anything that violates either the Establishment of Religion or Free Exercise of Religion clauses of the First Amendment.

Students may carry Bibles or other religious materials with them at school. Students are free to read these materials, silently, during free time or when personal activity time is allowed. Students also may pray and discuss their religious views with each other in informal school settings, such as in hallways or the cafeteria. They may even speak to and attempt to persuade their peers about religious topics, just as they attempt to persuade their peers about other topics. However, they have no right to a captive audience, no right to compel other students to participate or to listen, and no right to create a disruption or badger others in their attempts to express their religious views. In addition, these informal discussions and prayers are subject to the same rules and regulations that apply to other school activities and to other forms of student speech.

On the other hand, audible prayer during formal class time or at school-sponsored events raises concerns. Audible prayer is often viewed as having the potential of coercing disinterested individuals to endure a religious act that they may not accept or choose to practice. For example, in the case of *Lee* v. *Weisman* (1992), the Supreme Court held that prayers at a public school graduation ceremony were unconstitutional because they used the "machinery of the state" (a school-sponsored event and the input of the school principal) to coerce graduates and attendees to pray. The school had arranged for a rabbi to deliver a "nonsectarian, non-proselytizing prayer" at the ceremony. As the Court explained, "[t]he potential for divisiveness is of particular relevance here though, because it centers around an overt religious exercise in a secondary school environment where . . . subtle

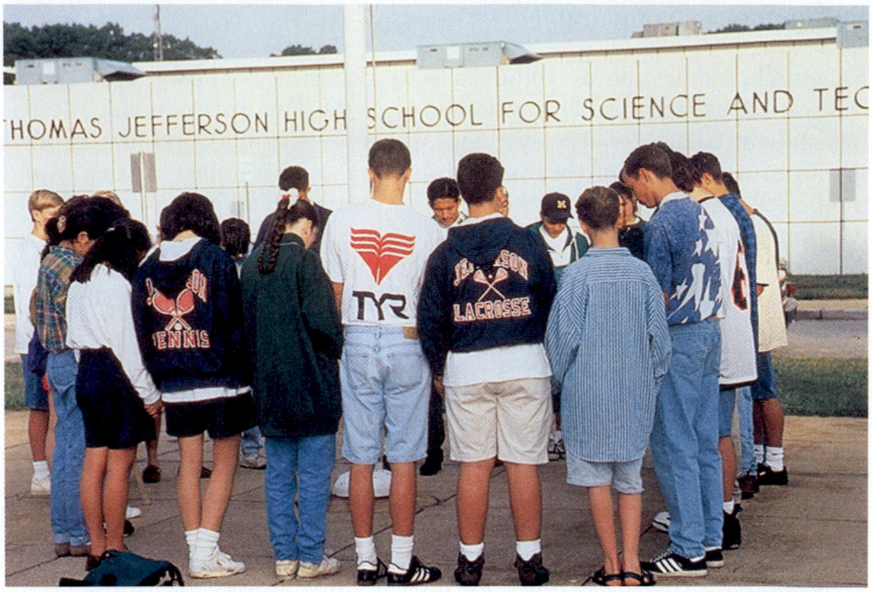

Is the prayer service in which these students are involved constitutional? What would you need to know in order to be able to decide? Is making school prayer unconstitutional consistent or inconsistent with democratic education?

coercive pressures exist and where the student had no real alternative which would have allowed her to avoid the fact or appearance of participation." School-sponsored prayer during class time is even more offensive to the Constitution, since compulsory school attendance laws effectively create a captive audience.

The Equal Access Act of 1984 states that student-led religious groups, such as the Fellowship of Christian Athletes, have the same rights of access to high school facilities as other noncurricular student groups. This means that student religious groups can meet on the school site during noninstructional time if other noncurriculum related groups are allowed to meet. Noninstructional time usually means before or after school or during lunchtime. These groups also may utilize school media (e.g., bulletin boards, school newspapers, and public address systems) to announce their club events, according to the same policies that govern such access for other student groups. However, it is important that the group be truly student-initiated and student-led. School personnel cannot suggest or encourage the creation of such groups. In addition, any teacher or other staff member who serves as an adviser may act only in a custodial capacity. This means if you are an adviser to a student-led religious group, you may advise them about school policies and supervise their use of equipment and facilities, but may not engage in religious discussions or exercises. In other words, you are there to make sure they don't start a fire in the middle of the room or walk off with the computers, but you are not there to engage in any devotional activity or to disrupt their religious activities.

Finally, schools need to make reasonable accommodations for students' religious beliefs. That includes excusing absences for religious observances as long as those absences do not become excessive (e.g., being absent every Friday). Likewise, students may be exempt from certain school activities because of their religious beliefs. For example, over 50 years ago the Supreme Court determined in *West Virginia School Board of Education* v. *Barnette* (1943) that students cannot be compelled to salute the U.S. flag or say the Pledge of Allegiance if it compromises their religious principles. Students who do not wish to say the pledge may sit or stand (you *cannot* compel the latter) and maintain a respectful silence while others complete the exercise. You also may have to provide reasonable alternative activities to some class activities for students. However, this does not mean that individual students can dictate the curriculum or curricular materials in the name of religious exemptions (see, for example, *Mozert* v. *Hawkins County Board of Education,* 1987).

IDEALS CHALLENGE: *Examining Equity*

You have just learned that one of your elementary students is a Jehovah's Witness. You want to be sensitive to his religious practices, but you do not want to single him out or separate him from his classmates during class activities. How could you use his parents as a resource? What questions would you ask them? What other resources might you have? Give an example of an art activity you could do around Halloween that would honor his religious liberties, while still allowing other students to examine the themes of the holiday.

Freedom From Unreasonable Searches and Seizures: Students

Searches of students are governed by the Fourth Amendment to the Constitution, which protects us from unreasonable searches and seizures. Government authorities have no general authority to search except when "probable cause" exists that the items being searched for will be found in the possession of those being searched.

The Supreme Court considered the application of the Fourth Amendment in schools in the landmark case *New Jersey* v. *T.L.O.* (1985). The Court had to balance students' rights to be free from unreasonable searches with the school's responsibility to provide a safe learning environment. The Court determined that the probable cause standard that applies to law enforcement officers was too stringent for application in a school setting where administrators must enforce reasonable school rules and protect the safety of students. Therefore, the Court held that school officials may search a student when they have *reasonable suspicion* that the child has violated a school rule. The search must be reasonable at its inception and reasonable in scope given the suspected violation. In other words, you must be reasonably confident that the information is correct and you must tailor the search according to what you are searching for. You would not look for a shotgun in someone's pocket, for example. However, the greater the potential harm, the more extensive the search may be. Accordingly, you could search more extensively for a weapon than you could for a package of cigarettes. You also must be certain that the search is not excessively intrusive in light of the age and sex of the child, and the nature of the infraction. Finally, while consent of the student for searching is always sought, it is not necessary to validate the search.

In general, the closer the search comes to the person, the more intrusive it is and the more evidence is needed to warrant the intrusion and validate the search as reasonable. When searching a student's person, as opposed to possessions such as a backpack or purse, extreme caution should rule. Once a student is identified as having an item of contraband, school personnel are advised to have students remove the items from their clothing instead of removing it themselves. Although courts have generally ruled in favor of students with regard to strip searches, even these highly intrusive searches have been upheld when the target was drugs and the search was sufficiently grounded by reasonable suspicion (Alexander & Alexander, 1998). Still, most schools avoid this type of search at all costs. In addition, some state statutes prohibit the use of strip searches by school personnel for any reason.

Generally searches must be based on an individualized suspicion of wrongdoing. Courts have recently carved three exceptions to that rule. One such exception is locker searches. The Wisconsin Supreme Court held that students have no expectation of privacy in the contents of their lockers, and therefore school officials could randomly search lockers whenever they chose (*In re Isiah B.,* 1993). In this case, school officials had randomly searched lockers after there were several reports of weapons on campus, an incident over the weekend where shots were fired on school grounds at a school-sponsored event, and reports that some retaliatory action was planned. In upholding this random, suspicion-less search, the court pointed to the fact that the school had a well-publicized locker policy that informed students that the school retained ownership and control of the lockers, that the lockers were provided to students for their convenience, and that lockers were subject to search at any time.

A similar exception to the requirement for individualized suspicion involves what are sometimes termed "administrative searches" (Rossow & Stefkovich, 1995). An example of an administrative search is the use of metal detectors at a school. The use of such devices has been upheld if the school can show that its actions were motivated by previous incidents of weapons possession at school. Courts found that the intrusion created by the metal detectors is outweighed by the compelling need for the school to maintain a safe and secure learning environment (see, for example, *People* v. *Pruit,* 1996).

Finally, the most recent Supreme Court ruling addressing student searches upheld a policy requiring random urinalysis as a prerequisite for participation in extracurricular sports. The Vernonia School District in Vernonia, Oregon, had created the policy in response to concerns about student drug use, particularly by student athletes. James Acton, a seventh grader, objected to the policy and challenged it in court. Justice Scalia, writing for the six-member majority, noted several elements of the policy that weighed in its favor (*Vernonia School District 47J* v. *Acton,* 1995):

1. Extracurricular sports are a privilege, not a right.
2. Student athletes have a lowered expectation of privacy in that they dress and bathe in communal locker rooms.
3. The district had evidence of a drug problem in the school and evidence that some athletes had used drugs.
4. Student safety while competing was advanced by the policy.
5. Student athletes serve as role models for other students.

6. The test was conducted unobtrusively and the results were not used for disciplinary purposes, but rather to assist students with alcohol or drug-related problems.

IDEALS CHALLENGE: *Deepening Discourse*

The three-person dissent in the *Vernonia* case argued that the goals of the policy could adequately be met by using individualized suspicion. In other words, instead of having students tested randomly, only those students whom school officials reasonably suspected were using drugs or alcohol would be tested.

- What do you think?

Recently, the Seventh Circuit Court of Appeals extended the reasoning in *Vernonia* by upholding as constitutional a policy that required any student who wished to participate in any extracurricular activity (e.g., athletics, student clubs) to consent to random urinalysis (*Todd* v. *Rush County Schools,* 1998). The student challenging the policy has petitioned the Supreme Court for review, although at this writing the Court has not yet determined whether it will hear the case.

- Applying the factors listed above, do you agree that schools should have this authority?
- Do you see any characteristics of extracurricular activities that make the *Vernonia* reasoning inapplicable?
- Should different reasoning apply to student clubs than to sports?
- Even if, for the sake of argument, such policies are constitutional, do you believe they are necessary? Desirable?

One final note about student searches. Because of the constitutional nature of the act and the potential harm to the student and legal liability of the district if used inappropriately, school districts may have additional policies directing how searches will be conducted and who is authorized to perform them. Do not assume that you as a teacher have this authority without first checking with your principal about your district's policies.

Right to Privacy: Student Records

There is no explicit constitutional right to privacy. However, the Supreme Court has found that a fundamental right to privacy is implicit in the Constitution (*Griswold* v. *Connecticut*, 1965). Schools keep lots of personal information about students. These records may be sensitive and are certainly confidential. So who has the right to view these records? Student records are protected by the Family Educational Rights and Privacy Act (FERPA). This act guarantees parental access to student records and restricts the school's use and dissemination of them. Students over age 18 also have the right to view their own records. In essence, access to student records is restricted to persons within the school system and the state and federal governments who have "legitimate educational interests" in the information contained within a student's file. As a teacher, you fit that bill. Express parental permission is required before the records may be made available to anyone else unless a court orders the release of the records. If a school district refuses or fails to comply with the Family Educational Rights and Privacy Act, it risks the loss of all federal funds.

FERPA further requires that parents and adult students be allowed to challenge material in the student record file that they believe is inaccurate or misleading. In such cases, parents or adult students can ask that the offending document be removed from the file. The district must consider the request, but does not have to honor it if the district believes the information is accurate and there is a purpose in retaining it. The person making the complaint has the opportunity to attach his or her version of events or comments about the situation to the document.

Parents retain rights under FERPA even if they do not have physical custody of the child, such as in the case of separation or divorce. Unless a court terminates parental rights, and the district has documentation of that order, a parent maintains all rights under FERPA.

Many teachers are not aware that all written comments or notes they submit as part of a student's record are subject to parental viewing. However, parents do not have the right to view your personal notes if these notes are in your sole possession and not openly shared with others.

As a beginning teacher, you should also keep in mind other privacy issues frequently overlooked by educators. For example, having students call out their grades in class is a violation of their privacy under FERPA, not to mention the negative effects this practice can have on a struggling student's self-esteem. Similarly, posting a chart that lists all students' scores violates FERPA. Leaving student files or papers in plain view of others and "telling tales" about students in the teacher's lounge also are questionable activities. As a caring professional, you have a responsibility to protect your students' rights to privacy.

Finally, districts frequently have additional policies in place to assist in complying with FERPA, and teachers should know those policies as well. These local policies may include rules about where files may be kept and where you may look at them.

Teacher Freedoms

Teachers do not shed the constitutional and statutory protection of their personal liberties while at school. However, the rights enjoyed as a public employee do not precisely match the rights enjoyed while in your living room. Sometimes the rights and obligations of the school district will outbalance those of the individual teacher. In this section we will explore teachers' freedom of expression, academic freedom, freedom of religion, and freedom from unreasonable searches and seizures.

Freedom of Expression: Teachers

As a teacher, are you free to say or write anything you want? Good common sense tells you that you are not. But, what are your rights? The historic Supreme Court decision in *Pickering* v. *Board of Education of Township High School District 205* (1968) provides the answer.

A teacher, Marvin Pickering, was fired from his teaching position for sending a letter to a local newspaper criticizing the school board over the way tax proposals were being presented to the public. Pickering was concerned with the inequity of funds being targeted for athletic programs versus those allotted to educational programs. He further stated that the school board had failed to tell taxpayers that athletic funding motivated the new request for additional tax funds. In a hearing before the school board, Pickering was accused of making false statements and impugning the honesty, integrity, and motives of the school board and school administration.

The Supreme Court agreed with the school board that Pickering had made many false statements in his letter. However, they found no proof that his statements had damaged the professional reputation of the school board or school administration. The Court overturned Pickering's dismissal. In so doing, the Court fashioned what has become known as the Pickering Balance Test. The test has two parts to it:

1. Was the speech about a "matter of public concern" or simply an employer-employee dispute?

2. Does the district have a "compelling state interest" that outweighs the employee's right to speak?

In this case the Court found that Pickering had spoken about matters of public concern, just as any taxpayer might, and that there was not a compelling enough state interest to outweigh his right to speak. The Court ruled that without proof of false statements being knowingly or recklessly made by Pickering, he had a right to speak on issues of public importance.

Thus, as a teacher, you have the right to speak out on issues of public concern. However, you may not do so to such an extent that you disrupt the educational environment of the school. For example, you cannot disrupt faculty meetings, knowingly or recklessly denigrate the administration or school board, or use your classroom as a platform to express your views while neglecting your responsibility to teach the required curriculum. In essence, you may disagree with the official position of the school district, but you may not be overly disagreeable in the process. Nine years after Pickering, the Court added some additional considerations in *Mt. Healthy City School District Board of Education* v. *Doyle* (1977). At its core, *Mt. Healthy* stands for the idea that public employees cannot use free speech rights as a shield to protect them from adverse employment action (e.g., dismissal, demotion, or suspension) that is properly motivated by other factors. In other words, if you believe you are about to be dismissed for poor classroom management and insubordinate behavior, you cannot dash off a letter to the editor of your local newspaper in order to preempt that dismissal. Therefore, when considering a teacher's freedom of expression, most courts now apply a hybrid test, the Pickering–Mt. Healthy Test. It asks:

1. Was the speech protected by the First Amendment as a matter of public concern?

2. Was the speech a substantial and motivating factor in the adverse action taken by the school district?

3. Would the district have taken the same action, justified by other factors, even in the absence of the protected speech? Or, do the district's legitimate concerns as an employer outweigh the protected speech rights of the employee?

Do teachers have a right to publicly protest when they disagree with administrative or school board policy?

IDEALS CHALLENGE: *Achieving Authenticity*

Earlier we asked you to consider the use of Matthew Fraser's speech as a teaching tool when examining civil discourse. How could you use the Pickering–Mt. Healthy Test to accomplish the same goal? Imagine that you as a teacher feel strongly that the administration is too quick to punish student speech it finds "disruptive." Would that be a matter of public concern? How could you and your students advocate for a review of the school's practices without violating the principles articulated in both *Bethel* and *Pickering*? Discuss your strategies and role-play the challenges you and your students might experience due to your advocacy.

The First Amendment also has been employed to challenge dress codes for teachers. The personal appearance of teachers has always been an important issue and has received a great deal of attention from students, parents, school administrators, and the courts. There are two sides to this issue. On one side of the issue are those who believe that attention to proper grooming and dress establishes a professional image that is important for gaining the respect of students, parents, and society. On the other side of the issue are those who feel that dress codes limit their rights of expression and do not have any correlation with the ability to teach. Nonetheless, many schools have established various dress or appearance codes for teachers. In the past, dress code conflicts have involved immodest attire; clothing with questionable graphics or slogans; the wearing of long hair, beards, mustaches, and neckties for men; and the length of dresses worn by women.

It is interesting to note that in the 1960s and the 1970s, courts tended to rule in favor of teachers' rights to dictate their own appearance choices. Then in 1976, the Supreme Court considered the issue of dress codes for public employees in a case concerning police officers (*Kelley* v. *Johnson*, 1976). The court found that choice of dress only raised concerns about a general "liberty" interest under the Fourteenth Amendment, not a more carefully scrutinized First Amendment expression claim. Therefore, as long as the regulations were not "so irrational that [they could] be branded 'arbitrary'" the dress requirements could withstand constitutional scrutiny. In the 1980s and 1990s, courts have applied this thinking to teachers. Thus, a public school board may impose reasonable regulations governing the appearance of the teachers it employs. You should research the school dress code prior to accepting a contract with the school if you have doubts about your ability to conform to it.

IDEALS CHALLENGE: *Achieving Authenticity*

(The voice is that of the author of this chapter.)

As a fourth-year teacher, teaching my first year in a new school, I noticed that one of the first-grade teachers always dressed up. One day I asked her why. She told me she once received an unexpected hug from a little boy in her class. She thanked the boy and asked why he hugged her. His response was, "Because you look so pretty. You dress fancy almost every day. You must think we are really important." The teacher said that until the boy's comment, she had never really thought about the way she dressed or the clothes she wore. However, after that day, she made sure she dressed up every day for the "really important" kids she served.

- What is your response to this story?
- Whatever your choice of dress, how will you be sure it communicates what you intend and not something else?
- What other symbolic expression might you engage in as a teacher without really thinking about it?

Academic Freedom

Academic freedom also falls under the protection of the First Amendment. However, unlike the speech in *Pickering*, academic freedom relates to "curricular speech." Teaching, by its nature, is an expressive activity. The ways in which teachers deliver the curriculum, from choosing materials to employing various methods, forms the heart of academic freedom. As Justice Brennan wrote:

> Our nation is deeply committed to safeguarding academic freedom, which is of transcendent value to all of us and not merely to teachers concerned. That freedom is, therefore, a specific concern of the First Amendment, which does not tolerate laws that cast a pall of orthodoxy over the classroom. (*Keyishan* v. *Board of Regents of the University of the State of New York*, 1967)

Like many other freedoms, however, this one must also be balanced against the legitimate concerns of the school district (see Figure 9.1). The school board holds the authority to set curriculum and reasonable rules and regulations regarding its delivery. The curriculum and related regulations may prescribe the content you teach or it may proscribe topics. Likewise, specific books may be required while others are declared off limits. As such, school board authority serves as a boundary to academic freedom.

An additional boundary to academic freedom is the concept of teacher reasonableness. In other words, even if your teaching choices are within the mandates of district policies and the curriculum, your decisions still must be reasonable. What constitutes reasonable academic choices? They are choices that:

- have a legitimate pedagogical purpose (i.e., a defensible connection to the adopted curriculum)
- utilize accepted professional standards (e.g., you don't try to teach gravity by jumping off of a roof)
- consider the students' age and maturity level
- do not violate a students' constitutional or statutory rights (e.g., you do not teach creationism)
- avoid disruption of the educational process

As you might surmise, conflict over academic freedom generally occurs when teachers discuss controversial issues such as religion, politics, abortion, morals, or sex. If these issues are a part of the adopted curriculum and the issues are brought before the board, the issue will be dealt with as a curricular concern, not a concern with an individual teacher. However, if an individual teacher adds such controversial topics to the curriculum, he or she must make sure that the additions are relevant to the curriculum and meet all the other considerations of reasonableness.

Figure 9.1 **The Bounds of Academic Freedom**

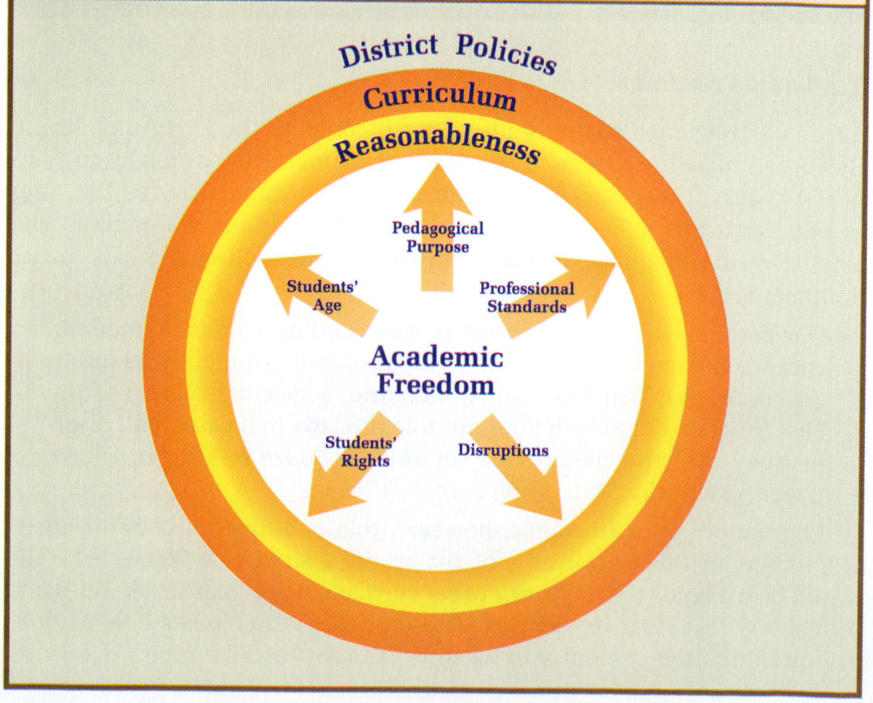

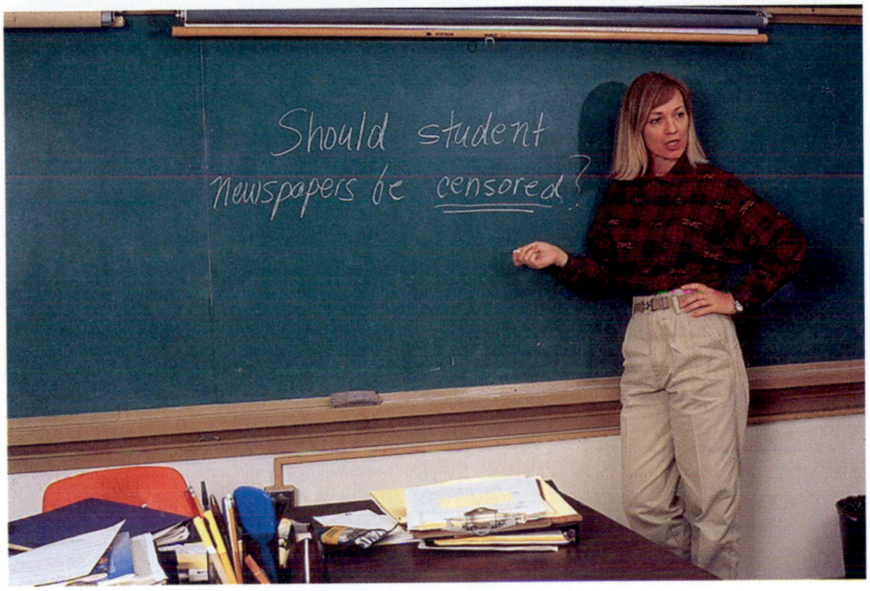
Should student
newspapers be censored?

What is the legal answer to the question on the board? How would you respond as an individual? Would you grant more rights than the law requires?

IDEALS CHALLENGE: *Achieving Authenticity*

Several "academic freedom" cases have concerned the use of R-rated movies in classrooms. As the discussion above indicates, teachers who have been able to show that they had a legitimate pedagogical purpose for using the movie, previewed the movie, and considered the age and maturity of their students have prevailed. Those that have used it to fill time have not fared as well. Many districts have procedures that must be followed before any R-rated (or sometimes even PG or PG-13) movies can be shown. One common requirement is to have teachers send parents notices that describe the movie, explain its connection to the curriculum, the rationale for using it, and identify issues that may be objectionable (violence, sexual content, language). Parents are then requested to return a permission slip before the child may participate in that class. Children whose parents deny permission are given alternative assignments.

- Think of an R-rated movie you believe has educational merit for high school students. Draft a permission slip like the one described above. Pay particular attention to your rationale for its use. Now role-play with a classmate a conversation with a parent who is reluctant to grant the permission you seek. What concerns will the parent be likely to have? Explain how you believe the movie's educational merit justifies its use, despite its rating.

Freedom of Religion: Teachers

Public school teachers do not have to disavow their religious lives as a condition of their contracts. In addition to First Amendment protections, recall from our section on equal protection that Title VII prohibits discrimination on the basis of religion. Therefore, school districts must reasonably accommodate a teacher's religious beliefs and practices. For example, a teacher may be given leave to observe religious holidays. That leave does not have to be paid, however. It would be unreasonable, though, to redefine the job in order to accommodate a teacher's religious practices. It also would be unreasonable for the teacher to refuse to teach large portions of the required curriculum because of religious objections. After all, delivery of the curriculum is what we are hired to do.

Again, you must search your own conscience. If these restrictions place too heavy a burden on the manner in which you believe you must practice your faith, you need to think twice about accepting a public school position. You may be better suited to teaching in a private sectarian school where none of these concerns would be present.

You should also be cognizant of the fact that when you become a teacher in a public school, you now wear a new hat; that of "state actor." Since you work for a public agency and are charged with educating impressionable children, you should not do anything that could be seen as using your position to promote or hinder religious activity or thought. Nor may you do anything that would create a symbolic link between the school and religion.

Freedom From Unreasonable Searches and Seizures: Teachers

Workplace searches of teachers have much less case law to guide us than do searches of students. However, by now you might be able to guess the issues that must be weighed in the balance between the school's authority and the teacher's expectation of privacy.

First, let's examine teachers' expectation of privacy. The Supreme Court held in 1987 that certain areas and items in the workplace have a limited expectation of privacy because they are within the employer's control. The Court specifically identified "hallways, cafeteria, offices, desks, and file cabinets" as subject to workplace searches (*O'Connor* v. *Ortega,* 1987). Personal items, such as purses, backpacks, and brief cases, would generally not be subject to search without a warrant. For most searches, though, the reasonable suspicion standard from *New Jersey* v. *T.L.O.* applies and any search must be reasonable at its inception and reasonable in scope given the target of the search and its potential harm to the school community.

Random drug testing of teachers and other school employees generally has not been found constitutional, unless the job created a high safety risk (e.g., bus driver). However, drug testing or physical examinations as a precondition of employment have been upheld, provided the results are strictly confidential and the employer pays for them. In essence, these tests are seen as just another way of getting to know you and ensuring your fitness to teach.

WHAT ARE THE RIGHTS OF STUDENTS AND TEACHERS? SHOULD THEIR ACTIONS BECOME SUBJECT TO DISCIPLINE?

As a teacher, you have a responsibility to establish reasonable rules and guidelines that maintain an educational climate necessary for effective learning. However, you must be careful to balance the rights of students with your own responsibilities. You must make sure not to violate students' constitutional rights or deny them rights provided by federal or state statutes.

Schools must adopt policies that are legally and educationally sound and must communicate these policies clearly to teachers, students, and parents. It is your responsibility to know, understand, and abide by these policies.

This section will explore students' and teachers' rights when these policies have allegedly been violated. These rights reside in the Fourteenth Amendment's due process clause. The Fourteenth Amendment guarantees that government institutions cannot "deprive any person of life, liberty, or property without due process of law." Due process has two components: substantive due process and procedural due process. "Substantive due process encompasses the basic concept of fairness; the state may deny a person of life, liberty, or property only for reasons that are considered fair or legitimate" (Underwood & Mead, 1995, p. 189). The proportionality of the misbehavior and the consequence is also a matter of substantive due process. You wouldn't expel a student or dismiss a teacher for chewing bubble gum, for example.

Procedural due process exists to protect the substance. In other words, in order to ensure that we have been fair and just, we employ certain procedures as checkpoints. Procedural due process includes three primary aspects: *notice, hearing*, and a *decision based on the facts*. The procedures also must be proportional to the potential deprivation. The more at stake, the more elaborate each component of due process must be. If the potential deprivation is slight, the process may be immediate and verbal.

Student Discipline

Student discipline raises constitutional concerns over potential liberty and property deprivations under the Fourteenth Amendment. As such, discipline of students should be handled fairly and consistently. We will examine the legal aspects of three of the most severe sanctions, suspension, expulsion, and corporal punishment.

IDEALS CHALLENGE: *Supporting Service*

(Adapted from F. M. Lappé & P. M. Du Bois, 1994, pp. 218–219.)

For 18 years, at Schaefer Elementary School in Tappan, New York, children have taken responsibility for their school by serving on the Due Process Board. They don't make decisions, but they do issue opinions about the fairness of the treatment a child receives. The Due Process Board also can hear cases brought by one student against another. In these cases it can even determine consequences.

Here's just one example of the kinds of challenges these elementary students have resolved effectively. A few years ago a youngster was caught drawing swastikas on the books of Jewish students. Students brought him before the Due Process Board. The offender, Raymond, "seemed unable to tell them why he had been doing this," explained Principal JoAnn Shaheen. So the board finally decided the only reason someone would do this is that they didn't understand Nazi mentality and its consequences. When Raymond admitted he didn't understand, a Jewish child who had lost his grandparents in the Holocaust volunteered to help Raymond research and write a paper on Hitler and Nazism. "Months later," Shaheen told us, "when a little first grader was drawing swastikas, it was Raymond who came to my office to ask if he might teach him about Nazism."

"The mistake we make in this country," Shaheen concludes, "is that we keep thinking kids need to be older to take on big ideas—justice, fairness, equality—the landmark ideas of our country . . . You can teach fairness to 7 and 8 year olds like you can never do later."

- How is this an example of the democratic IDEAL of service?
- How is this an example of authentic instruction?
- What are the benefits of this practice?
- Are there any potential pitfalls, legal or otherwise?

Suspension and Expulsion

Students can be suspended or expelled for failure to conform to reasonable rules of student conduct. However, because school attendance is a right and responsibility of students, all disciplinary action involving expulsion or suspension requires due process. Due process is designed to protect individuals from arbitrary, capricious, or unreasonable policies, practices, or actions and involves providing students with a series of steps and procedures that allow them to present their side of a case.

Suspension can be defined as student exclusion from expected educational services for a short period of time. Expulsion is student exclusion from educational services for a period exceeding 10 days, usually the remainder of a semester, term, school year, or even permanently. Expulsion usually occurs after chronic or repeated misbehaviors. However, a single incident of sufficient proportions (e.g., bringing a gun to school) may justify expulsion.

In 1975, a U.S. Supreme Court case, *Goss* v. *Lopez* (1975), established procedures for suspensions. In this case, nine students were suspended for 10 days each without a hearing. The students and their representatives said that this action deprived them of a property right, their right to an education, and thus violated the due process clause of the Fourteenth Amendment. The Court agreed and held that suspension and expulsion implicated students' liberty and property interests. Students have a liberty interest in their reputations and good names. They have a property interest in the educational services themselves, as earning power is directly tied to educational achievement. Therefore, the students were denied substantive due process rights without the requisite procedures to ensure fairness.

The decision of the Court in *Goss* provided minimum guidelines for suspension and began by distinguishing between short- and long-term suspensions. For suspensions of 10 days or less, the Court instructed that the student must be given "oral or written notice of the charges against him, and, if he denies them, an explanation of the evidence the authorities have and an opportunity to present his side of the story." However, there need be no delay between the "notice" and the "hearing."

Consider the following example that satisfies the *Goss* requirements for procedural due process. A principal enters the girls' bathroom and sees a student smoking a cigarette, a clear violation of school policy. The administrator waits for the girl to emerge and then says, "Susie, I saw you smoking in the bathroom [*notice*]. What do you have to say for yourself?" Susie responds, "I didn't do it" [*hearing*]. To which the principal replies, "Susie, I saw you with my own eyes. Let's go call your parents; you've just earned a day's suspension" [*decision based on the facts*]. Notice that the entire exchange might take only 30 seconds, but all aspects of due process are present.

Since the deprivation is much greater for exclusions exceeding 10 days, the *Goss* Court cautioned that more formal procedures would be required. Those procedures for expulsion generally are spelled out in state statutes and are far more elaborate. Notice must be in writing and sufficiently specific for the student and the parents to prepare a "defense," if they choose to do so. The hearing before an impartial hearing officer or panel (often the school board itself) would include a right to be represented by counsel, an opportunity to present evidence including witnesses, and cross-examining the district's witnesses. The decision, too, would be in writing and a transcript or recording of the proceedings would be made available so that the student could appeal the decision, if desired.

Suspension and expulsion of special education students raise additional considerations to ensure equity. In essence, officials must be careful that the disciplinary consequences do not unwittingly have the effect of disciplining a child because he or she has a disability. In addition, the Supreme Court held in *Honig* v. *Doe* (1988) that exclusions of 10 days or more constituted a change in educational placement that cannot be made without convening the Individualized Education Plan (IEP) team to effect that change. Therefore, a special education student may not be suspended for more than 10 days unless a change in his or her IEP is made. In addition, the team must consider whether the misbehavior is a manifestation of the child's disability.

The 1997 Amendments to the IDEA added a new section detailing the additional procedures required to ensure the equitable application of discipline policies to children with disabilities. Different procedures must be used if the consequence exceeds 10 days, but general disciplinary policies apply if the deprivation is less than 10 days. Although equity demands these additional inquiries, it must be stressed that IDEA does *not* say that children with disabilities should escape the consequences of their actions. Rather, it requires in some circumstances that the IEP, rather than general disciplinary policies, be used as the vehicle for meting out those consequences. In other words, the endpoint may be the same, but the path to get there is different.

Corporal Punishment

We consider corporal punishment an inappropriate disciplinary tool and strongly urge its elimination because it is contrary to the IDEALS of democratic education. In fact, as of 1994, approximately one half of states already specifically prohibited its use (Huefner, 1994). Yet, the sad fact is that corporal punishment is still legally practiced in a number of states. Keep in mind that corporal punishment is not limited to spanking. It includes any form of physical discipline. Although the Supreme Court rejected the assertion that corporal punishment violated the Eighth Amendment's prohibition against cruel and unusual punishment (*Ingraham* v. *Wright*, 1977), it has been found to implicate the liberty interest of "bodily integrity" (see, for example, *Garcia by Garcia* v. *Miera*, 1987). Corporal punishment that is "grossly excessive" and/or "shocking to the conscience" may create a constitutional violation for which the school district and personnel involved could be held liable in civil court. In addition, the personnel involved potentially can face criminal penalties for unreasonable or unauthorized corporal punishment (e.g., assault, child abuse).

Teacher Discipline

Teachers, too, have protected interests in their reputations (liberty) and their employment (property). But before we can discuss your legal rights as a teacher, you must first qualify to be a teacher. Therefore, this section begins with a review of teacher certification requirements and issues involved in the revocation of certificates. Then we will explore employment contract issues related to adverse employment consequences.

Teacher Certification

States have requirements for certifying competent people to teach in their schools. You must meet these minimum standards in order to qualify for the appointment as a teacher. Each state sets its own requirements, and although they may be similar, each state has its own set of expectations. Your university has a certification officer who can help you understand the requirements and process of applying for state certification. Certification requirements usually include all of the following: specific educational courses from an accredited institution, evidence of citizenship, good moral character, good physical health, and a minimum age. Many states also require that you pass a teaching area exam or competency test. They also may require that you take an oath of loyalty pledging faithful professional performance in teaching and support for the state and U.S. constitutions. As long as the requirements have a connection to the goal of a competent, qualified teaching force, and do not violate constitutional rights, courts have upheld them against challenge. The certificate is the state's to give and therefore each state can set the bar or hurdle where it sees fit. This fact means that if you move from one state to another, you probably will have to meet additional requirements in order to be certified in your new state.

Revocation of a teaching certificate is a different matter and raises important due process concerns. In this case, the deprivation is great. In essence, the question being considered is whether the individual is fit to teach, not just in that one locale, but anywhere in the state. In addition, since many states withhold certificates from applicants who have had certificates revoked in other states, the question essentially becomes, "Is this person fit to teach anywhere?" Obviously an answer of "no" carries severe consequences for the individual. Therefore, the amount of evidence necessary to justify such a sanction must be great and the process used to examine the issues must be detailed and formal (the specifics of which are described in each state's statutes or administrative rules and regulations). The most frequently named grounds for revocation are immorality, incompetency, contract violation, and neglect of duty (McCarthy, Cambron-McCabe, & Thomas, 1998).

Remember the case of Richard Erb that appeared at the beginning of the chapter? He faced possible revocation on the charge of immorality. You can see from this case that the definition of immorality is not simple. For

What legal rights do school districts have to hold expectations for teachers' personal lifestyles?

your information, in Richard Erb's case, the Supreme Court reversed the lower court's ruling, stating that no evidence had been submitted to show that Erb's teaching effectiveness had been affected by the actions in his personal life. Accordingly, Erb's teaching certificate was reinstated. In general, though, commission of a serious crime that violates the public's trust always constitutes immorality and will render the individual permanently unfit to teach. Revocation decisions are administrative but can be appealed in a court of law. Also, some states allow individuals to petition for reinstatement after a set period of time.

Employment Contracts

A teaching contract is a written, legal agreement between you and the school district that employs you. A contract usually includes statements about your rights and responsibilities as well as the rights and responsibilities of the school district. The contract describes other such matters as salary, contract length, and teaching assignment. Many beginning teachers are so glad to finally be finished with their university preparation programs, and so relieved to find a teaching position, that they neglect to read the contract carefully. "Just tell me where to sign" seems to be their mentality. We encourage you to take your time and consider the responsibilities that come with your signature. Ask yourself, "Will I be happy with this contract?" If you have doubts, you may want to discuss the contract with a representative of a teacher organization or another informed professional.

There are three types of contracts: term, continuing, and tenure. The type of contract you have is important because it defines the type of property interest you have under the Fourteenth Amendment and therefore what process you are due should the district wish to end its relationship with you. A *term contract* has a fixed beginning and end point. After the contract expires, you have no continuing expectation of employment and therefore have no property interest. New teachers are generally given this type of contract. What it means is that as long as the school district upholds its end of the bargain (it pays you), they have no further obligation to you once the contract expires. Therefore, as long as they notify you by the date established by state statute or in the contract, you are not entitled to any explanation or hearing. You may simply be told that your services are no longer needed. In fact, some attorneys advise districts not to publicly disclose a reason because that could implicate a liberty interest, thereby requiring a full hearing. However, if the district wants to terminate your contract during its term, you would be entitled to an explanation and a full due process hearing.

You may have also heard of *tenure contracts*. Tenure is a statutory construct. Some states have it and some do not. A tenure contract has a fixed beginning point but no end point. Therefore, once you have tenure, you always have a continuing expectation of employment and the district cannot dismiss you without showing just cause and a full hearing. In addition, the longer your tenure, the greater the property interest and therefore the greater the justification the district must have to demonstrate that its "punishment fit the crime." Not surprisingly, teachers generally have to serve a probationary period under term contracts (usually three years) before being awarded tenure.

The third type of contract is a hybrid of the other two. Called the *continuing contract*, it, too, is awarded after a probationary term. Under a continuing contract, a date is set. Unless notified by that date of nonrenewal, the contract will be renewed for another year. If the district moves for nonrenewal, it must specify just cause and you have a right to a hearing to challenge their evidence and conclusions.

A "just cause" for nonrenewal of your contract is defined by state statute, the district's collective bargaining agreement, or both. Immorality, incompetency, contract violation (e.g., insubordination), and neglect of duty are the most frequent causes. Although these terms may vary in their precise definitions, they all relate to the expectation that teachers will serve as role models for their students.

As a teacher, you should be aware of the values that are important in the community where you will be teaching. The parents of that community are likely to expect you to pass on the community's values through your teaching and your example. As a teacher in a democratic school you will need to determine the extent to which the community's values coincide with democratic IDEALS. When they do not coincide you will need to decide whether you want to perpetuate the status quo and pass on the existing community values, or whether you wish to work toward transforming undemocratic values. You should be forewarned that the latter choice may well lead to controversy and potentially even dismissal.

IDEALS CHALLENGE: *Initiating Inquiry*

Discuss the following statement:

As a teacher it is your responsibility to support the values of the community in which you teach.

- Do you agree with this statement?
- If you disagree, which values should you and will you teach?
- How will you know that the values you decide to teach are better than the community's values?
- What are the values of the community in which your university is located? How can you use inquiry processes to find out?

Issues concerning the personal lifestyles of teachers raise the specter of "immorality" and therefore continue to be played out in our courts. These lifestyle issues range from alcohol and drug activity to homosexuality, and further include such things as teacher physical appearance, criminal behavior, and group affiliations. The courts have typically ruled that in order for a teacher's actions to be held as morally unfit, it must be proven that the conduct in question adversely affects the teacher-student relationship. In other words, it must be proven that the teacher's actions disrupt the educational process or erode the credibility and professionalism of the teacher in the eyes of the students, community, or colleagues. If proven that a teacher's actions disrupt education or result in a loss of credibility, the teacher may be dismissed.

WHAT RESPONSIBILITIES DO TEACHERS HAVE TO PROTECT THEIR STUDENTS FROM HARM?

Recall the doctrine of *in loco parentis*. In addition to affecting student rights, it places responsibilities on teachers to care for the children in their charge. Teachers have a responsibility to protect students from known dangers and to report any concerns about a child's well-being. This section focuses on two such issues, negligence and reporting child abuse. Because teachers have responsibilities to children, they also face liability if they fail to discharge that duty faithfully.

Negligence

You, as a teacher, can be held liable for an injured student if you are proven to be negligent. Negligence is a failure to exercise appropriate care and foresight for your students when such failure results in an injury to a student. To be negligent, it must be proven that a student's injury could have been prevented if you had anticipated the potential for danger and taken the appropriate actions. To determine if negligence has occurred, the question is often asked: Was a reasonable and prudent degree of care shown? In other words, would a reasonable and prudent person have acted in a similar way, in a similar situation, and under similar circumstances?

There are four components of negligence. In order for a claim of negligence to be successful, all four questions must be answered "yes."

What are a teacher's responsibilities to protect students' safety?

1. *Did the person being charged with negligence owe a* ***duty*** *to the injured person?* In a school setting, you may have one or a combination of the following duties: to supervise, to warn of known hazards, to maintain a hazard-free environment, to inspect equipment for hazards, to teach safe handling or use of materials and equipment, to teach safe methods of performing physical tasks.

2. *Did the person* ***breach that duty*** *(i.e., fail to exercise an appropriate* ***standard of care****)?* This standard of care is not specifically stated, but varies according to the age and grade of students, the mental capacity and maturity of students, and the context in which the injury occurs. The standard of care is different during kindergarten story time than it is in a high school chemistry lab, for example. The appropriate standard of care is determined by the negligence question stated previously: What behaviors or actions would a reasonable and prudent teacher with similar teaching responsibilities exercise in similar circumstances? This is where the issue of foreseeability comes into play. Could you have reasonably foreseen the possibility of an injury? Have other similar accidents occurred that should have put you or the school on notice that there was a problem? Could you have done anything to prevent the injury or would this injury likely have happened regardless of your actions? For example, even if a teacher is standing right next to a play structure, he or she may not be able to do anything to stop a child from stumbling and falling off.

3. *Was the breach of duty the* ***proximate cause*** *of the injury?* It must be proven that a responsible party's actions or lack of action had a substantial causal connection to the resulting injury in order for negligence to be proven. Other possible intervening causes will be taken into consideration (e.g., student misconduct, the intervening act of a third person). In other words, even if you breached a duty, if that breach did not directly lead to the injury, you cannot be found negligent.

4. *Did someone suffer an actual* ***injury?*** To be held negligent, it must be proven that actual loss or injury has occurred as a result of the breach of duty.

The best advice for you as a beginning teacher is to always think ahead or anticipate the potential for danger that might be involved in any situation involving your students. Once you have reflected on possible dangers, take the appropriate actions to prevent them. As a teacher, you must remember it is your responsibility to exercise forethought in terms of potential hazards to which you may be exposing your students. Your student's physical well-being could easily depend on your ability and efforts to do so. That said, it may be comforting to remember that you will not be held to a standard of perfection, just reasonableness.

IDEALS CHALLENGE: *Supporting Service*

Imagine you are on your school's site-based decision-making council. At the last meeting, the subject of a playground safety audit came up. You asked for and received permission from the group for your sixth-grade class to conduct the audit and then report back to the council.

- Using the legal negligence framework outlined above, what information should your students gather?
- How could they go about collecting it?
- What questions should they ask? Of whom?

Reporting Child Abuse

National reports tell us that nearly 2 million children are abused physically or mentally each year and that over 2,000 of these children die each year from this abuse. These statistics are a sad reality and teachers may be witnesses to this reality. Teachers are required by law in all 50 states to report suspected child abuse or neglect. To report child abuse, you do not need absolute proof that the child has been abused. Your job is to file a report with the appropriate state social services agency (e.g., Division of Health and Social Services) whenever you have reasonable cause to believe that abuse or neglect may be occurring. Someone from that agency will be charged with investigating your report. As a teacher, you should educate yourself about how to recognize abused students. Table 9.1 provides you with some possible symptoms that a child who is abused or neglected might display. In addition, addresses and numbers of three child abuse organizations that will gladly provide you with additional information are provided.

The United States Department of Justice reports that a child is abused every two minutes in the United States. With such an overwhelming rate of occurrence, it is very likely that you will encounter abused students who need your help. You, as someone who has frequent contact with children, are required by law to report any suspicions you have. That responsibility is an individual one. *You* must make the report. Failure to provide help by reporting the abuse may result in your being found criminally liable, with

Table 9.1 Possible Signs of Child Abuse

Signs an Abused Child May Exhibit:
Fears or a reluctance to leave school and go home.
Sudden changes in physical, academic, or social behaviors.
Lack of medical provision by parents for identified problems.
Overcompliance or trying to please everyone.
Skittishness or being extremely watchful and distrustful of adults.
Flinching when touched or pulling away from appropriate shows of affection.
Statements or behavior demonstrating a lack of adult supervision at home.
Complaints of pain in genitals.
Physical evidence such as cuts, burns, or bruises.
Excessive excuses by parents concerning physical evidence of harm.
For More Information, Contact:
1. American Humane Association, 9725 East Hampden, Denver, CO, 80231; (303) 695-0811.
2. CALM, Child Abuse Listening Mediation, Inc., P.O. Box 718, Santa Barbara, CA, 93102 (805) 682-1366 or (805) 963-1115 (hot line).
3. Clearinghouse on Child Abuse and Neglect Information, P.O. Box 1182, Washington, DC, 20013, (202) 245-2856.

possible fines and imprisonment. You also may face civil liability for negligence or disciplinary sanction from your school district for failure to abide by district policies. Be sure to familiarize yourself with your district's policies and procedures for fulfilling your responsibility under the law. You may be asked to file any reports in the presence of an administrator, social worker, or other colleague and/or complete a written report for the district. However, be aware that even if no one else believes a report should be made and *you* do, the law *requires* you to make the report.

Also, you should know that child abuse reporting statutes grant you immunity from liability in the event your suspicions prove to be unfounded. As long as you made the report in good faith and did not maliciously report something you knew to be false, the parents of the child will not be able to collect any damages if you were in error. Because child abuse and neglect are so pernicious, these statutes are designed to overreport incidents of abuse and neglect in the hope that our vigilance will protect children before it is too late.

SUMMARY

You are now aware of many legal issues surrounding life in schools. However, it would be foolhardy to believe that this chapter and chapter 8 covered all the legal aspects of education. Rather, they serve as an introduction to the topic.

As you continue to develop a greater understanding of the legal aspects of being a teacher, keep these final thoughts in mind. Knowing the legal principles that undergird your role as a teacher and advocate for children will assist you in working toward the challenge of democratic education. But remember, the protection provided by the law ensures only a minimum standard. As some of the IDEALS Challenges discussed, sometimes there are valid reasons for granting more rights than the law requires. Other times it may be better to resist asserting your authority. As a democratic educator you must ensure that practices in your classroom and your school extend well beyond the minimum. Meeting the letter of the law is a start, but our goal should be the intent of our Constitution and laws—the promise of a more just and equitable society.

TECHNOLOGY CHALLENGE

Using Software Legally

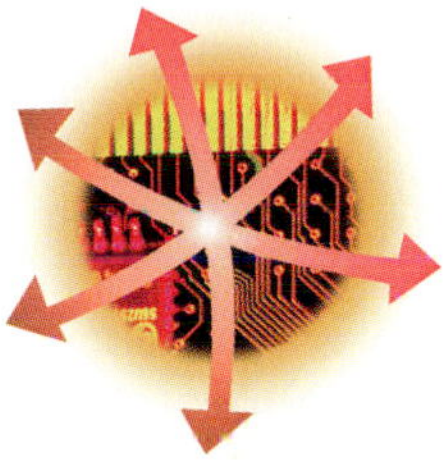

(Adapted from Blair, 1998.)

An internal audit of one school in the Los Angeles Unified School District has uncovered hundreds of pirated computer-software programs, and that could end up costing the district millions of dollars. Under a tentative agreement, the district would be required to pay $300,000 to the Washington-based Business Software Alliance for infringement. The accord also would require the 681,500-student district to come into compliance with federal copyright law in three years, an effort officials say could cost the Los Angeles schools $4.5 million. Industry specialists say the problems in Los Angeles can be found in educational institutions across the country. In Los Angeles, the illegal copies were most likely made by well-intentioned teachers or administrators who did not realize they were doing anything wrong, said Rich Mason, the general counsel for the district. "Employees are simply not knowing they're not supposed to do this."

- This chapter did not discuss copyright laws with respect to printed materials and computer software. Conduct research on copyright law that governs printed material and computer software, including the Fair Use Act of 1976.
- What are the moral and ethical dimensions of illegally using copyrighted material for the benefit of students?
- Is ignorance of the law, which the attorney for the school district claimed was the reason for copyright violations in the district, an acceptable excuse for breaking the law?

DOING DEMOCRACY

We have reviewed the legal aspects of three disciplinary sanctions: suspension, expulsion, and corporal punishment. Visit a local school or school district and ask for a copy of the student handbook, the student discipline policy, or the district's policy handbook. What other sanctions does the school or school district use to further discipline? What behaviors are students "put on notice" will not be tolerated? What procedural due process rights are spelled out in the policy? What do you think about the school or district's discipline policies from a legal perspective? From a democratic schools perspective? You may also wish to look at some of the school's or district's other policies from a legal and democratic schools perspective.

END NOTE

[1]The original draft of this chapter was written by Angela McNabb Spaulding.

REFERENCES

Alexander, K., & Alexander, M. D. (1998). *American public school law* (4th ed.). Belmont, CA: West/Wadsworth.

Blair, J. (1998, August 5). Pirated software could prove costly to L.A. district. *Education Week, 17*(43), 3.

Huefner, D. S. (1994). Federal and State Legislation. In *The yearbook of education Law 1994.* Topeka, KS: National Organization on Legal Problems in Education.

Lappé, F. M., & Du Bois, P. M. (1994). *The quickening of America: Rebuilding our nation, remaking our lives.* San Francisco: Jossey-Bass.

McCarthy, M., Cambron-McCabe, N., & Thomas, S. (1998). *Public school law: Teachers' and students' rights* (4th ed.). Boston, MA: Allyn and Bacon.

Rossow, L., & Stefkovich, J. (1995). *Search and seizure in the public schools,* (2nd ed.). Dayton, OH: National Organization of Legal Problems in Education.

Underwood, J. K., & Mead, J. F. (1995). *The legal aspects of special education and pupil services.* Boston, MA: Allyn and Bacon.

CASES CITED

Bethel School District No. 403 v. *Fraser,* 478 U.S. 675, 106 S.Ct. 3159 (1986).

Erb v. *Iowa State Board of Public Instruction,* 216 N.W.2d 339 (Iowa, 1974).

Garcia by Garcia v. *Miera,* 817 F.2d 650 (10th Cir. 1987).

Goss v. *Lopez,* 419 U.S. 565, 95 S.Ct. 729 (1975).

Griswold v. *Connecticut,* 381 U.S. 479, 85 S.Ct. 1678 (1965).

Hazelwood School District v. *Kuhlmeier,* 484 U.S. 260, 108 S.Ct. 562 (1988).

Hendrick Hudson Central School District v. *Rowley,* 458 U.S. 176, 102 S.Ct. 3034 (1982).

Honig v. *Doe,* 484 U.S. 305, 108 S.Ct. 592 (1988).

Ingraham v. *Wright,* 430 U.S. 651, 97 S.Ct. 1401 (1977).

In re Isiah B., 176 Wis. 2d 639, 500 N.W.2d 637 (Wis. 1993).

Kelley v. *Johnson,* 425 U.S. 238 (1976).

Keyishan v. *Board of Regents of the University of the State of New York,* 385 U.S. 589, 87 S.Ct. 675 (1967). *Lee* v. *Weisman,* 505 U.S. 577, 112 S.Ct. 2649 (1992).

Mozert v. *Hawkins County Board of Education,* 827 F.2d 1058 (6th Cir. 1987).

Mt. Healthy City School District Board of Education v. *Doyle,* 429 U.S. 274, 97 S.Ct. 568 (1977).

New Jersey v. *T.L.O.,* 469 U.S. 325, 105 S.Ct. 733 (1985).

O'Connor v. *Ortega,* 480 U.S. 709, 107 S.Ct. 1492 (1987).

People v. *Pruit,* 663 N.E.2d 540 (Ill. App. 1 Dist. 1996).

Pickering v. *Board of Education of Township High School District 205,* 391 U.S. 563, 88 S.Ct. 1781 (1968).

Tinker v. *Des Moines Independent Community School District,* 393 U.S. 503, 89 S.Ct. 733 (1969).

Todd v. *Rush County Schools,* 133 F. 3d 984 (7th Cir. 1998).

Vernonia School District 47J v. *Acton,* 115 S.Ct. 2386 (1995).

West Virginia School Board of Education v. *Barnette,* 319 U.S. 624, 63 S.Ct. 1178 (1943).

What are the needs of plants in order to be able to grow?

What are the needs of schools in order to be able to grow?

What role does adequate financial support and having a voice in school governance play in school growth?

Who should have a voice in schools?

CHAPTER 10

Governing and Supporting Schools Equitably

IDEALS CHALLENGE: *Deepening Discourse*

Decide whether you believe the following statement is true or false. Then discuss the reasons for your belief with your classmates.

The rules, policies, legislation, and other regulations that guide and direct the work of schools are always developed with the best interests of students in mind.

INTRODUCTION

As a teacher you will have great freedom to make many decisions within your classroom. It has been said that once teachers' classroom doors are closed, they are free to do essentially whatever they want in terms of what to teach and how to teach it. Although there is some truth to this statement, restrictions on your practice as a teacher will exist. There are rules and regulations that teachers and schools are required to follow and there always seems to be a shortage of funding that restricts your ability to do what you ideally would like to do. In fact, while some argue that teachers have extensive autonomy within their classrooms, others argue that this autonomy exists within a context of limited funding and excessive regulation that interferes with the ability of schools to respond to local conditions and to improve their practice. Many of the guidelines and restrictions on teacher and school practice come from governing bodies (e.g., the state legislature) and from those in positions of authority (e.g., the school board, the superintendent of schools), exercising the leadership opportunities that their authority provides them. In this chapter we will explore the governance and financing of schools as it exists in many schools and districts. We will also focus on how governance and finance can enhance or detract from equity in schooling. We begin by examining federal, state, and local roles in the governance of schools.

WHO GOVERNS THE SCHOOLS?

When we talk about the governance of schools we are talking about the people, agencies, institutions, and factors involved in making decisions and developing policies that direct, guide, and sometimes control the work of schools. Essentially, governance refers to who makes and develops decisions and policies, which decisions and policies they make and develop, and what processes they use. How many days must schools be in session each year? How many instructional hours need to be part of the school day? What should students learn at each grade level? How should the financial resources of a school district be distributed? How should financial resources allocated to a school be spent? These are just a few of the many decisions that are made by various individuals and agencies involved in the governance of schools.

The governance of schools comes from different levels. One common way of thinking about the different levels of school governance is to divide them into governance that originates from the federal level, the state level, and the local level. Subsequent sections of this chapter will examine school governance that comes from each of these levels, including the major agencies and individuals influential at each level.

IDEALS CHALLENGE: *Achieving Authenticity*

(Conversation between teachers at Axeton Elementary School in Oklahoma.)

Teacher #1: Sadly, in this school a child's merit is based on his or her standardized test score.

Teacher #2: Yes, we have booklets of objectives to meet. In science alone, we have 72 objectives we have to meet for our kids to do well on the science test. We're told, "Just do it. Make your test scores go higher."

Teacher #3: You don't think you can free up your room for two hours to work on a hands-on project because you know you have to be to a certain point by May 24th when they're going to tell you whether you taught well for the year. We know what is right, the right way to teach, the way children internalize a concept. But then, we also know what we *have* to do to keep test scores up.

Teacher #4: I feel like I'm doing a disservice to kids when I'm not teaching authentically.

Teacher #5: We are doing some things that are more hands-on. The children seem to be really enjoying those and are really enthused about learning when we do hands-on things.

Teacher #6: The structured teaching may lead to higher test scores, but they are not retaining or really understanding.

Teacher #1: Just because students score high on the standardized test doesn't mean they learned a lot. I'm pretty sure standardized tests don't really reflect what kids have learned.

Teacher #2: Should we be evaluating all kids by the same stick [i.e., standardized tests] or should we be assessing their growth by using portfolios and other forms of authentic assessment? How do we reconcile the struggle between "what is reality and what is required"?

Teacher #3: Yes, the laws and regulations we must follow as teachers have become so restrictive as to make teaching more difficult all the time—teaching, testing, discipline, assistants in the classroom—the laws are putting a lot of strings on what we do in the classroom.

Teacher #4: In addition to laws and regulations, our superintendent, our principal, and the state really decide what we need to teach. The state does so through the PASS document, which reflects our state objectives. We also use the test company's list of objectives that are covered on the test.

Teacher #5: When we get a copy of all objectives being tested, integrate them with state requirements and manage to get it all taught, our test scores are around 98%.

Teacher #6: Yes, but it's such a struggle. We're all on blood pressure and ulcer medicine. It was so rushed and so pushed. Yes, they knew it for the test, but whether they actually learned it—I don't know. They may be able to repeat it on a test, but they don't really get it.

Teacher #1: We're giving them a lot, we're giving it to them fast, but whether they're really able to break it down in their minds and understand it, I don't know.

- What are the considerations that are influencing the practice of these teachers?
- What is the source of these considerations? Which are coming from beliefs and knowledge the teachers' hold? Which are coming from external levels of governance?
- How might the teachers reconcile their beliefs about hands-on, authentic teaching with the external pressures to "teach to the test"?

Governance From the Federal Level

Although the federal government affects what occurs in schools in this country, they have little direct control over education. As was discussed in chapter 8, the U.S. Constitution does not specifically delegate responsibility for education to the federal government, and thus the state has primary responsibility for public education in this country. State responsibility for education is somewhat at odds with the principle of local control—a principle that has long guided the governance of public schools in this country. The principle of local control holds that what occurs in schools should be in the hands of the local public, rather than in the hands of individuals and agencies at the state or national level. This is a very democratic principle that is implemented to some extent through publicly elected local school boards. School boards will be discussed more extensively later in this chapter.

Educational governance at the federal level thus occurs primarily through actions that influence education in a manner consistent with the federal government's perception of what is needed to protect the public's general well-being. Typically the federal government influences education in four ways:

1. through federal legislation (e.g., Title IX, special education legislation)
2. via federal funding for special programs (e.g., Title I programs)
3. as a result of federal court rulings that deal directly with education or have implications for education
4. through "the bully pulpit"

Examples of landmark federal *legislation* that have impacted education in recent decades include Public Law 94-142, often referred to as the Education for All Handicapped Children Act, and Title IX (see chapter 8). An example of a *program* from the federal level that promotes the federal agenda via providing significant funding for schools is the Title I program. The intent of Title I is to improve the educational opportunities for children from low-income families. Title I has gone through various name, structural, and directional changes during its 30-year history. While at one point in its history, schools were required to use Title I funds for direct services for students from low-income families who were underachieving, these funds now may be used for resources and services that impact all students in a qualifying, low-income school, even though many students may be neither from low-income families nor underachieving.

A third way in which the federal level influences education is via *federal court decisions.* Supreme Court decisions sometimes have tremendous implications for school policy and practice. For example, the 1954 case *Brown* v. *Board of Education of Topeka* has had long-term implications for the desegregation of schools (see chapter 8).

A fourth way the federal government influences school direction is via what has been termed the *bully pulpit.* Like preachers who influence their flock from the pulpit, the government influences the practices of U.S. schools through federal officials and agencies advocating certain educational policies and practices. They do this when giving speeches, issuing reports, and communicating with the public about education. For example, the Secretary of Education, as well as some U.S. presidents, frequently address particular educational viewpoints in their speeches. The bully pulpit also was in use during the 1980s when a number of educational reports criticized education. Perhaps the most notable of these was the federal government sponsored *A Nation at Risk,* which strongly advocated school purposes that result in economic growth (as opposed to other purposes, such as preparing students for life in a democratic society).

In addition to the Supreme Court, the Secretary of Education, and Congress, the Department of Education also influences education nationally through its duty to implement and administrate educational programs passed by Congress. This includes the development of rules and regulations to guide states, school districts, and schools in developing and implementing programs at the local level.

Governance From the State Level

Whereas the governance role of the federal government is frequently indirect, governance at the state level is more direct. At the state level, governance occurs primarily through the governor, the state department of education, the state board of education, the chief state school officer (called the state Superintendent of Instruction in many states), and state courts.

Governors primarily influence through their power to appoint individuals to important educational positions in the state; their fiscal authority in preparing the state budget, including the portion to be allocated to education; their influence with legislators particularly in terms of promoting specific initiatives, such as merit pay plans and competency testing; and their use of the bully pulpit.

The state education agency's responsibilities include administering, monitoring, and ensuring adherence to both federal and state regulations and legal mandates; providing technical assistance to schools and districts as needed; and developing new proposals for state legislatures.

The role of the state board of education is a bit of an anomaly and varies from state to state. In many states the state board of education has limited influence, being usurped by the state legislature, the state education agency, the governor, and the chief state school officer. Typically the state board of education takes a broader and longer range perspective than the other agencies or offices. Frequently it also must write the rules and regulations for education policies emanating from the state legislature.

The influence of the chief state school officer also varies from state to state. This official, in a sense, serves as the principal or superintendent of the state education agency, overseeing and providing leadership for the agency's work. The chief state school officer also is a link between the various individuals and agencies that are influential in educational governance at the state level, as well as a link between the state level and educators throughout a state.

The state courts serve a similar role as federal courts, except that the decisions of a state court are applicable within that state (although they may set a precedent for another state). Frequently, state courts are involved in legal interpretations of school funding formulas, collective bargaining agreements, and a variety of other education-related issues in which legal aspects are involved.

In terms of the relative influence of these individuals and agencies, one study ranks the state legislature as most influential, followed by the chief state school officer and senior members of the state department of education. Next in influence is the governor and the governor's executive staff, and, finally, the state board of education (Marshall, Mitchell, & Wirt, 1986).

A number of special interest groups also are indirectly influential in state education governance. Marshall and colleagues (1986) found that education associations were the most influential. Education associations include the state-level umbrella organization for teacher and administrator associations/unions, state school boards associations, and similar groups. Next in influence among special interest groups are noneducator groups, such as business leaders and taxpayers' groups. These are followed in influence by lay groups, such as Parent-Teacher Associations, school advisory groups, educational research associations, and producers of educational materials (e.g., textbook or multimedia publishers).

The 1980s and 1990s saw an expanding state role in the governance of education. This expansion was partially a reaction to the plethora of reports issued during the 1980s that criticized school performance. The public demanded better schools than the ones described in the national reports, although in most instances they were satisfied with the schools their own children attended (see e.g., Rose & Gallup, 1998). Business and industry, facing difficulties of their own, found a convenient scapegoat in education,

CLICK ON IT

To visit the Web site of your state education agency go to

http://www.ed.gov/Programs/bastmp/SEA.htm#N

Then follow the on-screen directions to access your state's education agency Web site.

CLICK ON IT

To visit the Web site of the Council of Chief State School Officers go to

http://www.ccsso.org

blaming their woes on the poor preparation their workers had received in public schools. (Note again the assumption that the purpose of schools is to prepare students for the economic sector rather than for democratic citizenship.) In short, education became enough of an interest to the general public to merit the status of a hot political issue.

In response to the increased interest in education, governors and legislatures mandated a variety of reforms, such as standardized testing for students and competency testing for teachers and administrators, longer school days and school years, more stringent graduation requirements, merit pay, and numerous other reforms focused primarily on establishing more stringent standards in general. Other players in educational governance at the state level such as professional teacher, administrator, and school board associations were not as active in generating reform proposals of their own and frequently openly opposed state-mandated reforms. The increasing role of the state level in school governance is in sharp contrast to past practices. Previously, state level governance was primarily concerned with setting minimum standards for curriculum, school building construction, graduation, and educator certification.

One important factor to remember when reflecting on the decisions and initiatives emanating from various levels of educational governance and decision making is that decisions are not always made with the best interests of students in mind. Whether we are considering the actions of the president, governors, state legislators, or other departments or offices, the educational agenda frequently is dependent on individual vested interests, such as trying to please the public and garner votes. Unfortunately, vested interests often are a key factor in decision making at the school level, where teachers, principals, and parents may make decisions based on their own interests rather than on the interests of all students (see, for example, the following IDEALS Challenge).

IDEALS CHALLENGE: *Deepening Discourse*

(Narrated by Phyllis Blanford, Orlando, Florida, elementary school teacher.)

I am so irritated at my principal! I can't believe he did what he did. I've been teaching first grade for four years and all of a sudden he tells me that I am teaching fourth grade next year. I don't want to teach fourth grade. To make matters worse, he's moving me so that some teacher who has never even taught before can get her wish and teach first grade. Why does she get her wish and I don't get mine? I mean I have been a good teacher and have always tried to do what's best for students. The principal told me that he needed me in fourth grade because he knew I was a strong teacher and could do well in fourth grade too. So, what is this—am I being punished for being a good teacher? He said that the new teacher was the best applicant they interviewed, but that her certification is in early childhood education. That's when he came up with the brilliant idea of having me fill the fourth-grade opening so that she could then fill the first-grade opening left by my moving to fourth grade. He said that way our students would have strong teachers in both grades. I can't believe he doesn't care about what I want. I told him I was thinking of filing a grievance with the teacher's union. We'll see who teaches first grade!

- What does Blanford *claim* is the basis for her decisions in the classroom? What is really the basis for her decision in this situation?
- Whose and what interests are guiding this decision?
- What is the relationship of the democratic IDEALS to this situation?

Governance From the Local Level

Although the U.S. Constitution relegates responsibility for education to the states, the formal authority of the states is at odds with the principle of local control that has existed throughout the history of American public education. State governance is concerned with a wide array of issues that touch many aspects of a state's educational system. Influence from the state level typically occurs through legislative mandates or state board of education policies. These policies and mandates limit local control over education because the local school district must adhere to and implement these policies and mandates. The local role also includes developing policies and mandates of its own that address remaining aspects of daily school operations. The primary players in the local governance of schools include the district board of education (or school board), the superintendent, teacher associations/unions, and administrators and teachers within schools. Playing an indirect role in local governance are the community and special interest groups.

The Board of Education

The Board of Education is the legal governing body of a local school district. The board is given authority by law to establish policies for the district as long as those policies fall within the laws and statutes established at the state and federal levels. School boards are elected by the public, and either represent a particular geographic portion of the school district or are elected as at-large members, representing all constituents within the district. Terms of office for school board members are typically three years, with members' terms staggered so that some terms expire each year. This helps to ensure continuity in board operations. Boards vary in size, but most boards consist of five, seven, or nine members.

Ideally Boards of Education should represent the diversity of perspectives present in the community. Ideally they should engage in inquiry about an issue or policy and eventually come to consensus based on the best interests of all students in the district. A school board operating in this manner is very consistent with the ideals and principles of democratic education. Unfortunately, this is not always the case. School board members nationally do not reflect gender, race, and class demographics of our society (Tarazi, Curcio, & Fortune, 1997). Specifically,

- males are much more likely to be school board members (54% of members) than females (40%)
- African Americans and Hispanic Americans constitute only 4% of school board membership nationally, although they make up over 12% of the U.S. population

The governance of schools is influenced by various federal, state, and local forces, including school boards.

- 87% of school board members have incomes of over $40,000 annually and 66% earn over $60,000 annually

Thus, from a representation perspective, it is likely that school boards represent the dominant cultural perspective in our society—that of white, middle-class males—and underrepresent the perspectives of racial and ethnic minorities, the economically poor, the working class, and females.

Also interfering with democratic representation in school board governance is that candidates frequently run for office because of an interest in a single issue (e.g., school prayer, outcomes-based education, sex education). These single-issue board members are less likely to be open-minded and listen to perspectives or information that conflicts with their perspective on their pet issue. They also are less likely to be interested in the big picture of teaching and learning in the school district because of their obsession with one issue. Thus, the Board of Education structure has the potential to be consistent with democratic schooling but, in reality, frequently falls short of democratic ideals and principles.

CLICK ON IT

To learn more about school boards, visit the Web site of the National School Boards Association at

http://www.sba.org/

The School District Superintendent

A school district superintendent is the educator in the school district with the most authority. Superintendents are selected by a district's Board of Education and may be dismissed by the board.

Superintendents are involved in some fashion in all of the district's operations. Officially, their role is to ensure that school board policies get implemented in the district in the manner intended by the board. Additionally, the superintendent must see to it that the school district complies with state and federal laws, mandates, and regulations. The superintendent's role, however, extends well beyond implementation and compliance. Typically, superintendents do not merely ensure implementation of policy but also initiate the development of policy based on what they and their staffs perceive as district needs. Frequently, however, their time is so consumed by what one veteran superintendent termed the three B's of the superintendency—budgets, busses, and buildings (Baldwin, 1987)—that little time remains for them to be involved with the district's instructional program.

Teacher Associations/Unions

In order to protect their rights, teachers began to form unions. Unions were initially formed in the early 1900s with rapid growth in teacher unionism occurring in the 1960s. As a teacher you likely will have the opportunity to join the local teacher association (or union) and be collectively represented by it in contractual and other personnel matters. Teacher unions are involved not only in negotiating with school boards the salaries teachers in the school district receive, but also in negotiating various other working conditions. These typically include the length of the school day; the number of contractual days in each school year (i.e., the number of days for which teachers are to be paid, including planning and professional days when students are not in attendance); the amount of planning time each teacher must have daily; tenure, seniority, and transfer rights; and a variety of other working conditions. The scope of working conditions that are negotiable varies by district: some districts negotiate only a limited number of conditions while others negotiate virtually all conditions of employment.

Teacher unions initially were formed to protect teacher rights that were being regularly abused. However, in some districts the power of the teacher union and the stipulations of the collective bargaining agreement have evolved to where they interfere with the school district's capacity to address student needs. Indeed, sometimes the leadership of a teacher association promotes an agenda with which many of the teachers they represent disagree. For example, one executive director of a teacher association in a large urban school district, who was a former teacher himself, noted in a speech to a university class that the union had little interest in doing what is best for students. Instead, he argued, the role of the union is to do what is best for teachers regardless of whether that is good for students. Thus, he continued, the union will pull out all stops to defend a teacher who the district is trying to terminate even if the teacher is clearly a poor teacher. In subsequent discussion, many of the teachers in the class (who were members of the union) voiced strong disagreement with his conclusion.

IDEALS CHALLENGE: *Deepening Discourse*

- Do you agree or disagree with the statements made by the executive director of the teacher union?
- What should be the role of a teacher union?
- Is it possible for a teacher union to serve the interests of both teachers and students? Can you think of examples where the interests of teachers and students might conflict? How should a union proceed in these instances?
- What is your role as a teacher who believes in democracy when the philosophy of the teacher union conflicts with your personal beliefs?

In some school districts, teacher unions view any reform and restructuring efforts in the district as items subject to contract negotiation. That is, they adopt a blanket policy that any change resulting from reform efforts must yield in concessions in other working conditions for teachers, even if the reform initiative does not negatively affect those conditions. In still other districts, the union promotes the vested interests of teachers even if doing so conflicts philosophically with what collaborative efforts are trying to accomplish. For example, in one district that was moving to a decentralized decision-making structure, where teachers, parents, and community members were to be equitable partners in school-level decisions, union representatives insisted that 51% of school decision-making councils be composed of teachers, even though this would result in inequitable representation of parents.

These positive and negative examples of teacher unions are not intended to lambaste them. Many unions are engaged in collaborative partnerships with the school district administration and school board and keep the needs of students' forefront. The significance of these examples, however, is their implication for your work as a teacher striving to carry out your role in accordance with democratic ideals and principles.

Now we turn to local control at the school building level and explore the implications for teachers.

IDEALS CHALLENGE: *Supporting Service*

Using newspaper reports, other documents, interviews, conversations, and observation, study a current educational issue in your school, district, community, or state. Determine the levels of governance and the individuals or groups involved at each level. Identify the public stance of each individual and group.

- Why do you think each believes the way it does? Speculate on what vested interests or "hidden agendas" each might have.
- Analyze the issue in terms of how various perspectives do or do not reflect democratic IDEALS.
- Become involved in the local debate about the issue in whatever way seems most appropriate.

CLICK ON IT

To learn more about teacher unions/associations, visit the Web sites of the American Federation of Teachers and the National Education Association at

http://www.aft.org//index.htm

and at

http://www.nea.org

Democratic Governance at the School Building Level

In all likelihood, the level of governance that will most affect your life as a teacher is the governance that occurs at the school building level. Assessing governance in your school involves asking questions such as:

- How are decisions that affect my practice as a teacher made in this school?
- How are policies developed that affect my students and me?
- Who is involved in decision making and policy development?
- What power and authority do those involved hold?
- What issues and topics do they have authority over?

Democratic governance and decision making includes teachers, parents, administrators, and often students.

In recent years many schools have attempted to move toward more democratic forms of governance that involve teachers, parents, and other members of the school community in decision making. These democratic forms of shared governance are often called school-based management, site-based management, site-based decision making, and a variety of similar terms.

School-based management (SBM) is the decentralization of decision-making authority from the district level to individual schools. That is, rather than the school board and school district administration making curriculum, personnel, and budget decisions for all the schools in a district, teachers, the principal, parents, and students at each school make decisions for their own school. School-based management intends to facilitate change in educational practice by providing schools with greater autonomy from the influence, authority, mandates, and regulations that come from other levels of educational governance. Autonomy permits a school to make decisions that better fit the specific needs of the school, rather than decisions made at other levels of educational governance to generically fit many schools.

Even though schools and districts may use the term *school-based management* to describe their governance structure, the way shared governance is practiced varies greatly between districts and even within different schools in the same district.[1] The range of practices in shared governance can best be understood by thinking in terms of three components: authority, involvement, and influence.

Authority refers to the power given to a school's decision-making body; *influence* refers to the issues and questions over which a school has authority; and *involvement* refers to who is involved in making school decisions. Each of these components can range from practices that are very restrictive to practices that are very inclusive. The more inclusive the practices, the more shared governance is truly democratic. The following sections examine the range of shared governance practices, and the IDEALS Challenge looks at practices that sometimes keep shared governance from being truly democratic.

Practices Related to Authority

As noted, authority refers to the power given to a school's decision-making body to make decisions. A school's authority is narrow when decisions made by the school's formal decision-making committee (commonly called the school council) are merely advisory. At the other end of the spectrum, a school's authority is broad when the school council's decisions are binding. Mid-range authority is when the principal, the district administration (including the superintendent), or the school board can veto a decision made by a school council (see Figure 10.1).

Practices Related to Involvement

Involvement refers to who is involved in making school decisions. Involving a broad range of individuals is based on the following assumptions:

- Teachers, principals, and other members of the school community are closer to the work of the school and know its needs better than district level personnel or school board members and thus are able to make better decisions about issues affecting the school.
- Hearing a broad range of perspectives on an issue results in more holistic understanding of all the perspectives that exist on an issue and thus better decision making.
- Equity requires giving voice to the perspectives of all parties, including those who are typically not heard (e.g., members of racial and cultural minority groups, individuals living in poverty).

In the least inclusive form of involvement in shared governance, the principal and a few teachers make school decisions with little input from others. In the mid-range of involvement, most or all teachers and staff

Figure 10.1 **Practices Related to Authority in Shared Governance**

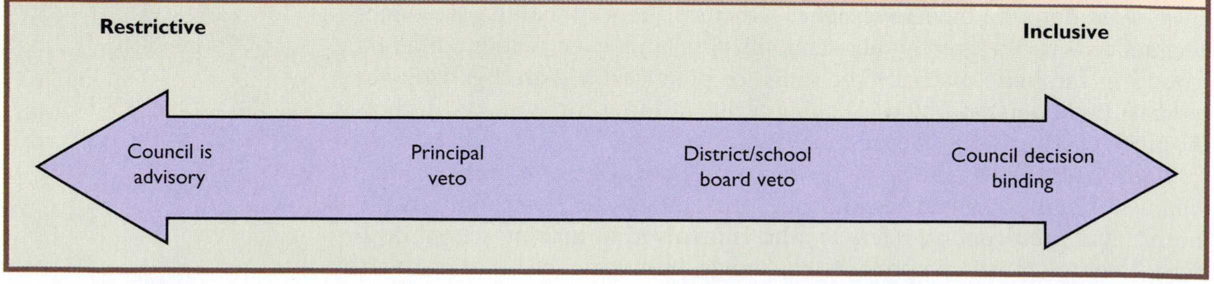

participate in making school level decisions, typically via membership on the school council or a subcommittee (e.g., curriculum committee, personnel committee, budget committee). At the most inclusive level of involvement, teachers, administrators, staff, and other patrons (i.e., parents, students, and/or community members) are represented in shared governance and all groups have an equal voice in the decision-making process (see Figure 10.2).

IDEALS CHALLENGE: *Examining Equity*

(Narrated by Linda Smith, a teacher at Hillside Elementary School, Milwaukee, Wisconsin.)

Since we became self-governed, my life as a teacher has changed tremendously. . . . There is hardly a day that goes by that there isn't a meeting. . . . At the beginning there were some days when I would have two meetings a day. One in the morning, one after school. . . . Also summer, we spent a lot of *gratis* time here during the summer. . . . It's not all bad, it just gets hectic. . . . in addition I'm still teaching. It isn't like I can give up my teaching job and do all this other work. And it's not just the meetings, it's the prep for the meetings. You know, I have to have agendas and handouts and what we're going to talk about—all those things are in addition to what I was already doing as a teacher. . . . [In addition to] preparing for teaching, now I have to spend time at a meeting or in prep for a meeting or whatever. So yes . . . that's hard. But it can't be done any other way. If you want input into decision making, you have to be part of it. And the only way you're going to do that is if you join a committee and commit to it and go to meetings. . . .

Before we began the move toward authentic assessment we surveyed the staff. . . . The staff actually chose what we decided to do. . . . When you start looking at change, and you start saying, "Well the majority of us want to go there. If you don't want to go there then you have to think of your options. We're getting to a point where we can't let you do whatever you want. You've had input all along, so it's time to commit or it's time for you to make other choices." I don't think that I would be willing [to accept it] a year from now if someone says, "Forget it, I don't want to do that." Well, they should have given their input all along and tried to work with us to

Figure 10.2 Practices Related to Involvement in Shared Governance

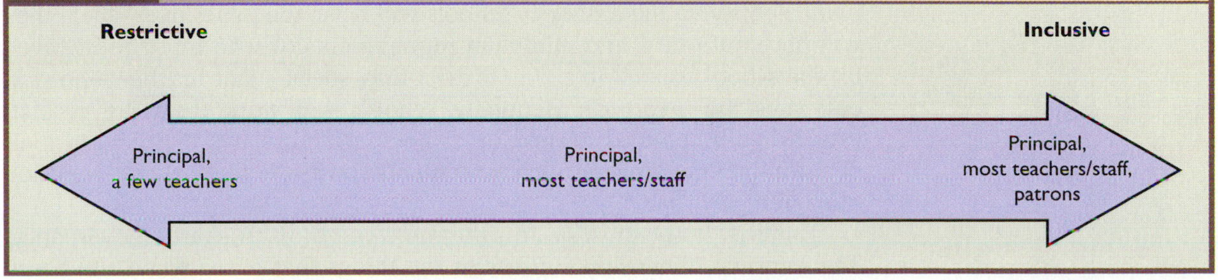

change that focus if that's what they want, or voice their opinion long before it becomes a mandatory thing. I guess I don't have any patience with that after a certain point. I will help you and work with you after we've put it into place. . . . if you want to learn anything here, we've got some bright people who'll be more than happy to help you get started. And I guess after a certain point, you have to do it and go for it.

Reflect on and discuss the following statements. Consider what you believe Smith's opinion is on each statement, but develop and support your own opinion.

- In schools that are democratically governed, it is fair and equitable for some teachers to not participate in self-governance processes if they have other commitments.
- Teachers should be paid extra for the time they spend in democratic governance activities.
- If a teacher in a democratically governed school disagrees with a decision the majority of teachers have made, it is acceptable for that teacher to not adhere to the decision.
- Increased school autonomy sometimes results in decreased classroom autonomy.

Practices Related to Influence

Influence in shared governance refers to the issues and decisions over which schools have authority. School influence can be thought of in terms of the *areas* over which they have authority and the *range* of decisions within each area. The three areas in which most school decisions fall are budgeting, personnel, and curriculum and instruction. In some instances, the decisions over which schools have authority may be only peripherally related to these areas (e.g., what the color of the new couch for the faculty lounge should be). In most instances, schools have authority over some budget, personnel, and curricular and instructional decisions, but the range of decisions within each area is limited. For example, the budgeting decisions a school is able to make may be restricted to how to allocate funds not devoted to personnel and building maintenance costs—a marginal portion of the school budget. In a few cases, schools have a lot of latitude and are able to make a broad range of budgeting decisions, such as whether to hire several instructional aides in lieu of an additional teacher. Figure 10.3 graphically shows the range of decisions over which schools may have authority.

Practices That Facilitate or Constrain Democratic Governance

Typically school districts establish agreements for school-based management, specifying the authority schools will have, the issues over which they will have authority, and minimum requirements of who must be involved on the school council (e.g., the district may specify that teachers and parents must be involved). Generally, schools will work from the district-established minimums to develop more specific by-laws that govern their decision-making process. Such agreements constitute the *formal* dimension of shared governance.

There is, however, also an *informal dimension* to shared governance. The informal dimension consists of the things that occur when site-based

Figure 10.3 Practices Related to Influence in Shared Governance

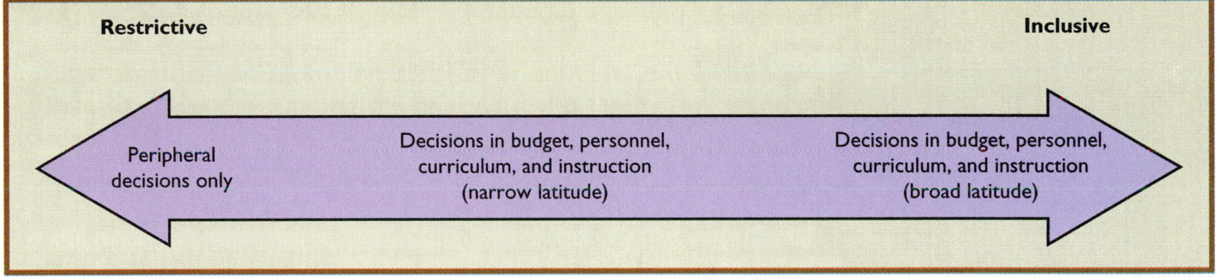

Figure 10.4 Formal and Informal Dimensions of Authority, Influence, and Involvement

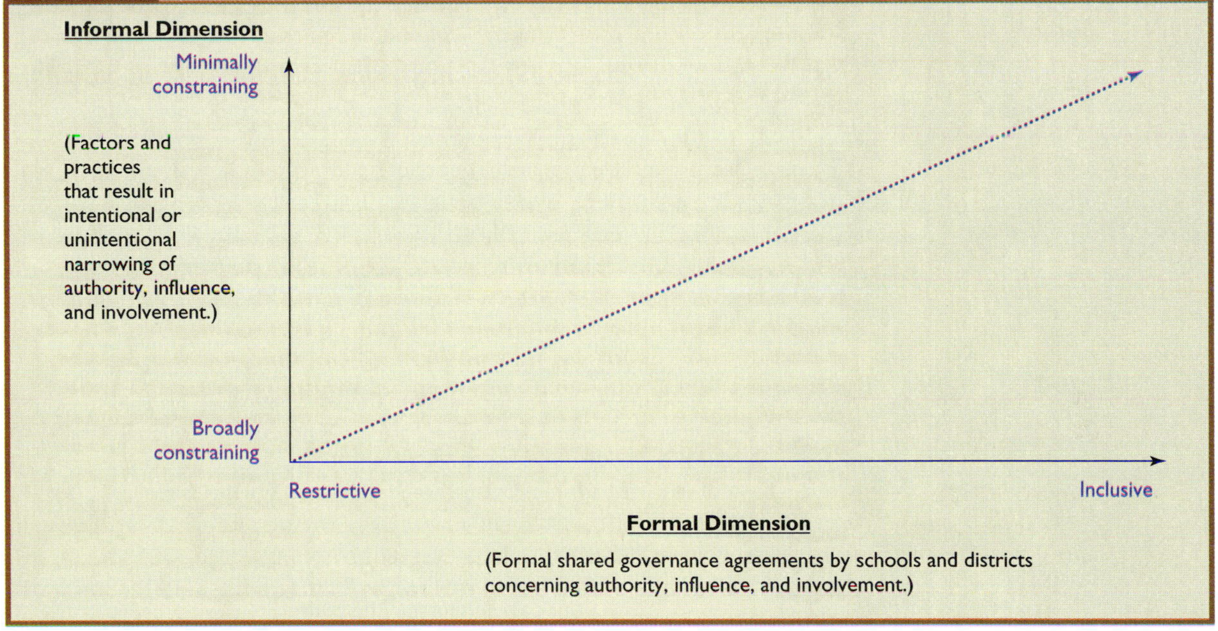

management is put into practice and that cause authority, influence, and involvement to be narrowed. As illustrated by the case study in the IDEALS Challenge below, various factors and practices may restrict the formal dimensions of authority, influence, and involvement established by a school district. Each of the restricting factors keeps school-based management from being as democratic as it might otherwise be. The maximum potential for democratic governance occurs when practices are inclusive (formal dimension) and minimally constraining (informal dimension). This is depicted by the diagonal line and arrow in Figure 10.4.

IDEALS CHALLENGE: *Examining Equity*

Lake City is a medium-size city in a state where the legislature is increasingly influencing education through legislation mandating practices previously left up to local districts.

At the end of last year, the Lake City School Board decreed that all schools in the district would participate in school-based management. However, prior to acquiring formal authority, the schools must file an application with the school district office that describes specific programs or innovations the school wishes to implement through the use of school-based management.

Simultaneous with the push toward school-based management the district also is implementing several other initiatives. These include:

- the implementation of a new curriculum
- a more stringent student testing program
- a more detailed school evaluation program
- a uniform, districtwide staff development program

Additionally, the district is in the first year of a three-year contract with teachers that has a reputation as being one of the state's most prescriptive contracts in terms of working conditions.

You are a teacher in the Lake City schools and were recently appointed by the principal to be a member of the school council, your school's decision-making committee. The council is meeting this morning and you are on your way to what will be your first meeting. As you enter the principal's conference room for the before-school meeting, the principal hands you a copy of the meeting agenda, which he developed. Looking around the room, you see almost entirely white, well-dressed men and women—which somewhat surprises you given the significant minority population of your school. As the meeting begins the principal stands at the head of the conference table and presents information on the agenda topics. One item that provokes discussion concerns the school budget. After some discussion, in which two individuals are the primary participants, the topic is tabled because information regarding enrollment projections, fringe benefit costs, and carryover funds is not available. As the principal continues to work his way to the bottom of his agenda, a teacher raises an issue that is not on the agenda. However, the bell signaling the beginning of the schoolday rings, and the meeting is adjourned. The principal announces that the November and December meetings have been canceled due to the holiday season, but that the council will meet again in late January. As you leave the conference room the principal is discussing the budget item with the assistant principal and you overhear him reassuringly tell the assistant principal, "That's OK, I communicated the information I needed to get out there on the other topics—the budget is my responsibility anyway." In walking down the hallway to your classroom, you discuss the meeting and the schools "shared" decision making with several teachers who are also on the school council. One teacher says, "We seem to spend a lot of time listening to the principal talk. When we get a chance to discuss, it's always what the principal or district office want us to talk about. We never talk about what we believe should be happening with kids or what we can do to make it happen." Another teacher adds, "I get kind of frustrated sometimes. The time I put into school-based management is a major increase in my workload but yet we deal mostly with clerical and general organizational work. We mostly talk about trivial issues." A third teacher notes, "The few times we do talk about a significant issue, we seem to make the decision in a vacuum. We solve a budget problem that creates a curriculum problem. We solve the curriculum problem but now we're going against what we've agreed is best for kids." The fourth teacher that is part of your group observes, "Plus, we can never put the few things we've made decisions about into practice because we don't have any money. It's all taken up by salaries, building maintenance, and other fixed costs from the district. We aren't even allowed to decide whether we want to spend our budget on less teachers and more aides or more aides and less teachers, what support staff we need—it's all prescribed by contract or district policy."

You enter your classroom somewhat ambivalent about your new responsibility. Maybe you should just concentrate on your classroom and forget about the rest of the school.

- What are the practices that constitute the informal dimension of shared governance in the case study (i.e., the practices that restrict authority, influence, and involvement)?
- How do the events described reflect or not reflect democratic IDEALS?
- What equity issues are raised by the case study?
- How could the equity issues you identified be addressed?
- What would you do if you were a teacher in this situation?

In addition to being aware of the practices that you identified as limiting in the IDEALS Challenge case study, we believe there are several other aspects that are important in democratic governance. These include:

- addressing issues in relationship to how they impact other issues and to the school's values and beliefs
- incorporating democratic IDEALS of equity and inquiry as part of shared governance

Addressing issues in isolation. School districts involved in democratic governance processes sometimes address issues without considering:

- their impact on other issues
- their significance in terms of the values they project about what is important in the school

Any decision that is made impacts other aspects of the school and sends messages about the values of the school. For example, scheduling decisions may impact the opportunity you have to interact with other teachers and to collaboratively engage in critical study of your practice; setting parent-teacher conference times may affect which parents will be able to attend their child's conference; and, budgeting decisions are ultimately an expression of your school's instructional mission. Even a discussion of parking space allocation may be significant in that it symbolically expresses the school's beliefs about equity (i.e., are some individuals or groups given preferential treatment with parking spaces close to the school, sending the message that they are more valued than others?). Democratic schools should strive to address issues not as singular decisions about budget, personnel, or curriculum, but rather as related to and impacting other areas and signifying the values and ideals that are important in the school.

Many factors can limit a diversity of voices being heard in building-level decision making. What seems to be a limiting factor in this picture?

GLOBAL CHALLENGE

Centralization Versus Decentralization

(The following description discusses democratic governance in Israel and raises some issues of equity. The excerpt is taken from A. Vollansky & D. Bar-Elli, 1996, p. 60.)

The ethos of equality has been a driving force of Israel's education system since Israel became an independent state in 1948. . . . To help support this goal of equality, the education system that emerged featured a high degree of central control. By centralizing decisions and policies on administrative and pedagogical matters, the Israeli government sought to avoid inequities among schools.

For example, through a policy of "positive discrimination," the Ministry of Education tried to reduce gaps between various parts of the population by increasing allocations to schools serving disadvantaged students and providing funds for instruction.

In recent years, however, educators have raised questions about the ill effects of this centralization in Israeli education. Many believe that more power and autonomy should be delegated to individual schools, so that local educators can tailor educational programs to the needs of their students and their vision of the school. In the last decade, Israel has begun to move in this direction—but will continue to monitor carefully the effects of decentralization on the equality deeply cherished here.

- How can centralization contribute to equality? To inequality?
- How can decentralization contribute to equality? To inequality?
- Which educational issues do you believe should be centralized to promote equality?
- Which issues should be decentralized to promote equality?

Incorporation of the democratic ideal of equity. In order for shared governance to be truly democratic, it must incorporate democratic IDEALS. But frequently overlooked is explicit discussion of the implications for equity of decisions. For example, how do budget, personnel, and program decisions affect various student groups? Does a decision benefit white students more than students from minority groups? Does it benefit male students more than female students? Whose interests are served by specific school policies and practices? Instructional improvement is a laudable objective for democratic governance. However, democratic governance is not truly democratic if it does not consider instructional improvement in terms of whether it equally benefits male and female students, rich and poor students, and students from all races and ethnicities.

Incorporation of the democratic ideal of inquiry. Inquiry (or critical study) is also frequently not as pervasive in shared governance as it could be. Without critical study, shared decision making may become more democratic, but will not necessarily result in better decisions. Inquiry:

- uses data, information, and knowledge to study the effectiveness of decisions
- relates decisions to democratic ideals and principles
- explores the congruence between decisions and the school's vision, values, beliefs, and goals

As previously noted (see chapter 5), inquiry involves asking questions such as:

- What evidence or support do we have to justify our decision? What information, data, and knowledge can we gather and study to assist us in making our decision?
- What perspectives are represented as we discuss this issue? What perspectives are missing?
- How does what we are deciding to do serve the needs of our broader community as well as the diverse individuals and groups who make up our community?
- What individuals or groups benefit from our decision? What individuals or groups might be negatively impacted by our decision?
- How does what we are deciding to do fit with the values and beliefs of our school community?

You may wish to refer to chapter 5 for more extensive discussion of inquiry.

WHO FINANCES THE SCHOOLS?

Closely related to the governance of education is the financing of education. There is a popular saying that goes something like, "Where the money is, the power is." In the remainder of the chapter we examine financial

IDEALS CHALLENGE: *Initiating Inquiry*

(A Madison Elementary School teacher discusses her school's decision to become a member of the Oklahoma Networks for Excellence in Education [ONE].)

When Dr. O'Hair first came to talk to us about the network, we had lots of questions. What's a network? What does it do? What do you mean by democratic schools? What other schools have been in networks? What have they gotten out of it? What's in it for us? What's the Coalition? What does it stand for? The questions went on and on. We felt kind of sorry for Dr. O'Hair because it probably seemed to her like we were attacking her. We weren't really. We just wanted to know what we were getting into. After that first meeting with her we got to work. Some of us went to the library and looked up articles. Others of us got on the Internet. We researched networks, democratic schools, the coalition, and anything else that we thought had to do with our participating in this school renewal network. We brought information back to the other teachers and the principal and discussed, argued, and disagreed with each other. We wrote little suggestions all over the ONE document in the margins. It helped us see all the different ways others saw the proposal. I'd find myself thinking, "Oh, I never thought about that" or, "Why are they saying that?" Going through what we did helped us develop an open communication process with each other and to learn about networks and democratic schools. This wasn't whining like some previous times. It was a working through. It helped us realize that you don't just need to accept, but that you can question and voice your opinion.

- How does the example illustrate the use of inquiry/critical study in decision making?
- What other democratic IDEALS are represented in the example?

support for schools at the local, state, and federal levels. Our focus will be on exploring how funding inequities lead to conditions such as those described in the IDEALS Challenge that follows.[2]

IDEALS CHALLENGE: *Examining Equity*

(These descriptions of urban schools are excerpted from Jonathon Kozol's book, Savage Inequalities, *1991).*

SCHOOL #1

There are scores of window frames without glass, like sockets without eyes. Hallways in many schools are dark, with light bulbs missing or burnt out. One walks into the school...and you can smell the urinals a hundred feet away. . . . Each year . . . there's one more toilet that doesn't flush, one more drinking fountain that doesn't work, one more classroom without texts . . . certain classrooms are so cold in winter that the students have to wear their coats to class, while children in other classrooms swelter in suffocating heat that cannot be turned down (pp. 36–37).

SCHOOL #2

In the street in front of the school there is an elevated public transit line. Heavy traffic fills the street. The existence of the school is virtually concealed within this crowded city block.... Beyond the inner doors a guard is seated. The lobby is long and narrow. The ceiling is low. There are no windows.... The principal ... tells me that the school's "capacity" is 900 but that there are 1,300 children here.... Two first grade classes share a single room without a window, divided only by a blackboard. Four kindergartens and a sixth-grade class of Spanish-speaking children have been packed into a single room in which, again, there is no window. A second-grade bilingual class of 37 children has its own room but again there is no window.... By 11 o'clock, the lunchroom is already packed with appetite and life. The kids line up to get their meals, then eat them in ten minutes. After that, with no place they can go to play, they sit and wait until it's time to line up and go back to class. On the second floor I visit four classes taking place within another undivided space. The room has a low ceiling. File cabinets and moveable blackboards give a small degree of isolation to each class. Again, there are no windows. The library is a tiny, windowless and claustrophobic room. I count approximately 700 books. Seeing no reference books, I ask a teacher if encyclopedias and other reference books are kept in the classrooms. "We don't have reference books in classrooms," she replies. "That is for the suburbs." ... There is one small gym and children get one period, and sometimes two, each week. Recess, however, is not possible because there is no playground. "Head Start," the principal says, "scarcely exists in District 10. We have no space." The school, I am told, is 90% black and Hispanic; the other 10 percent are Asian, white, or Middle Eastern.... There seems to be no ventilation system, or, if one exists, it isn't working.... On the top floor of the school, a sixth grade class of 30 children shares a room with 29 bilingual second graders.... There are, at least, some outside windows in this room—it is the only room with windows in the school—and the room has a high ceiling. It is a relief to see some daylight. I return to see the kindergarten classes on the ground floor and feel stifled once again by the lack of air and the low ceiling.... The kindergarten children are sitting on the worn rug, which is patched with tape (pp. 85–88).

- Would we as a society tolerate the deplorable conditions under which some black, Hispanic, and other minority group children experience schooling if those children were white?
- Are funding inequities best explained by our inability to develop better models for funding schools, or are they better explained by a societal lack of will in providing equal access and educational opportunity for "other people's children" (Kozol, 1991; Delpit, 1995)?

In the United States the three levels of government (federal, state, and local) have developed clearly defined roles not only in the governance of education but also in its funding. In most nations, the federal government is the primary source of funding for public education. In the United States, however, the federal government takes a limited role in the financing of education. State governments have a much larger and ever expanding role and bear primary *responsibility* for funding education. However, local communities continue to typically provide as much revenue for public education as does the state. Although this can be viewed positively from the perspective of giving jurisdiction over school decisions and operations to the individuals closest to them, it has also resulted in substantial inequities in the funding of schools—what Jonathon Kozol (1991) calls "savage inequalities"—between urban schools and suburban schools.

It is important to keep in mind, however, not only technical explanations for inequities but also sociocultural reasons. As one urban principal

Due to inequities in funding, inner city schools are often not maintained at the same high level as schools in affluent suburban school districts.

whose school resembled the schools described in the IDEALS Challenge observed, "This would not happen to white children" (Kozol, 1991, p. 90). Or, as a teacher in another run-down school answered when asked if the students saw the deplorable condition of their school facility as a racial message, "All these children see TV. They know what suburban schools are like. Then they look around them at their school. This was a roller rink, you know. . . . They don't comment on it but you see it in their eyes. They understand" (Kozol, 1991, pp. 88).

We must consider these issues as we read about our current ways of funding schools and the inequities created by them.

The Local Role in Funding Education

In most states and school districts, about half of the funding for education is raised locally. Locally controlled and funded schools developed during the 19th century, with the trend of local support continuing during the first part of the 20th century. During this time, school enrollments grew enormously, as education became available to a larger part of the population and the number of years students spent in school increased. In the face of this quantitative educational expansion came increasing expenditures for public education for which local school districts bore the majority of the costs. This emphasis on local support resulted in extremely wide disparities from community to community in terms of education funding. For example, one district might spend $6,000 per student every year, while another might only spend $3,000. Differences in the amount of funding were primarily due to two factors:

- a local community's wealth—that is, its financial *ability* to provide funding for education

- a local community's desire—that is, its *willingness* to provide funding for education

Although ample funding for schools does not guarantee high quality education, to some extent, "you get what you pay for." That is, more funding for schools makes it possible to provide enhanced educational services and programs and decrease teacher-student ratios so that greater individual attention can be given to each student.

The major source of *local* revenue for education typically comes from property taxes. Property taxes are made up of three components:

- the tax base
- the tax rate
- the revenue generated by applying the tax rate to the tax base

The tax base in a community is typically the total assessed value of all the taxable property in the community. For example, your home may be assessed at $100,000 and the land and buildings of the business several blocks away at $500,000. When the assessed value of all the taxable homes, businesses, and other taxable properties in a community are added together, the total is the tax base. The tax base of a community is important for schools, because the greater the tax base the more money can be generated for schools without excessively high taxes. The tax rate is the percentage of taxes one pays on something. For example, a sales tax rate of 5% indicates that for every dollar spent an additional 5% must be paid in sales tax. Instead of percentages, property tax rates are usually given in mills per $1,000 of assessed valuation. We use mills in the following example to illustrate how the varying tax bases of different communities can lead to inequitable financing of schools (see Table 10.1).

District A is an urban school district with many older homes, a few businesses, but a number of vacant buildings caused by the "white flight" of families, businesses, and industries to the suburbs. District A has a tax base of $300,000 per student and the tax rate that taxpayers in the community pay for schools is 10 mills per $1,000 of assessed valuation. This results in $3,000 of revenue per student to fund the education of District A students. District B is a suburban district with many expensive homes, several industrial and business parks, a large mall,

Table 10.1 Comparison of Revenue and Effects on Educational Services of High and Low Local Tax Bases

District	Tax Base per Student	Tax Rate	Revenue per Student	Effects
A	$300,000	10 mills/$1000	$3000	Crumbling buildings Inadequate books/supplies Large class sizes
B	$600,000	10 mills/$1000	$6000	Modern buildings Ample books/supplies Small class sizes

and many other stores and businesses. District B has a tax base of $600,000 per student. The tax rate that taxpayers in the community pay for schools is the same as in District A: 10 mills per $1,000 of assessed valuation. Even though the tax rate in District B is the same as in District A, the higher tax base results in $6,000 of revenue per student for District B students. Thus, seemingly District B students are able to receive twice the educational services that students in District A receive. Students in District A would likely attend school in crumbling buildings like the ones described by Kozol, with inadequate books and supplies, large class sizes, and few enrichment opportunities. By contrast, District B would be able to afford to provide its students well-kept, high-tech buildings, the latest books and ample supplies, small class sizes, and many enrichment opportunities.

Variations in educational funding per student of the magnitude described in the example exist widely throughout the United States. Kozol (1991) notes that in New Jersey some districts spend as little as $3,500 per student while others spend over $7,700 per student. Similarly, in the Chicago metropolitan area the Chicago Public Schools are able to spend only $5,200 per student while the nearby Niles Township Schools spend over $9,300.

As a result of local inequities in the funding of schools, states stepped into the school funding picture. The next section discusses the state's role in funding education.

The State Role in Funding Education

To mitigate inequities in educational funding, state governments developed a variety of models or formulas for distributing funds to local school districts. The intent of these formulas is to increase financial equity among the school districts in a state by supplementing local funds at differential levels with state funds. Although in many cases financial equity across a state's school districts has been improved, substantial inequities between local school districts continue to exist. As a result, there are a frequent lawsuits that challenge the constitutionality of the state's way of funding schools. The courts have regularly declared a state's manner of funding schools unconstitutional and required the state to modify its funding formula to achieve greater equity. Nonetheless, substantial funding inequities remain in many states.

Currently in the United States nearly as much revenue for funding schools is derived from the state level as from the local level. The state versus local funding proportions vary considerably, although state contributions typically are 45% to 50% of total education funding, the local share usually constitutes another 45% to 50%, and the federal share makes up the remaining percentage (typically 3% to 9%). See Figure 10.5.

The Federal Role in Funding Education

The federal role in financing education traditionally has been limited and thus typically does not significantly enhance or detract from financial equity. The federal government has become involved in education funding in four areas. These are:

Figure 10.5 **Sources of School Revenue**

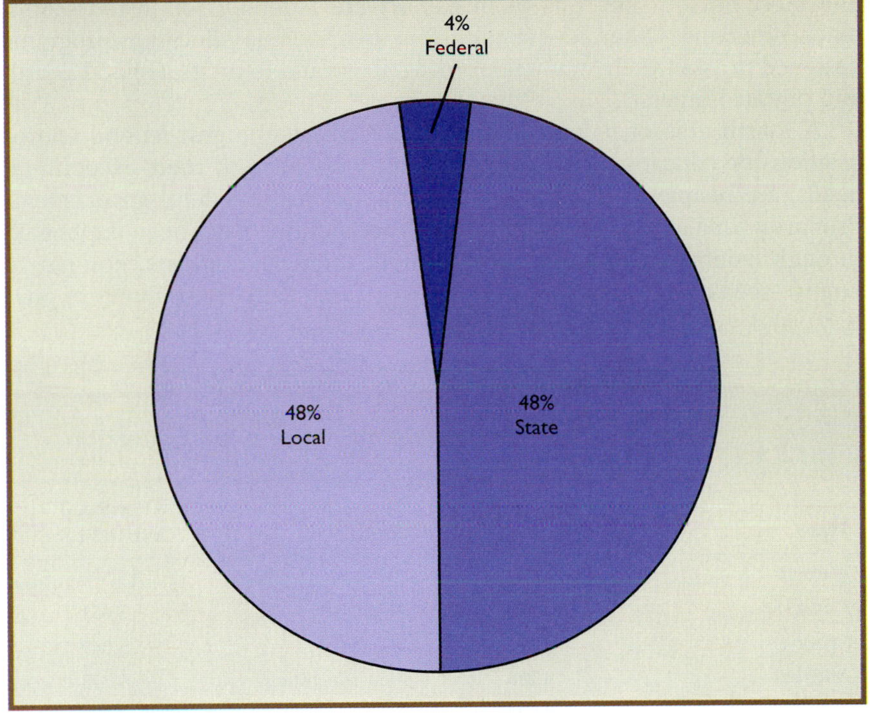

1. maintaining national defense and international relations
2. enhancing national productivity
3. promoting health and nutrition
4. providing aid to special populations of students

The federal government bears ultimate responsibility for national defense and relations with other nations. As part of this responsibility many federal education funding initiatives have been developed in an effort to help maintain national security and increase American economic competitiveness. For example, in the aftermath of the 1957 Russian launching of Sputnik, the first manned spacecraft, and the proliferation of the cold war in the 1960s, the federal government developed funding initiatives to support education. Fearing the United States had lost its technological advantage, the funding initiatives focused on mathematics, sciences, and foreign languages.

Education is significant to the further development of the nation's economy; hence, the federal government has an interest in funding education to enhance national productivity. For example, during the 1980s the United States' position as the world economic leader had eroded. Thus, there was a renewed interest at the federal level in maintaining our economic competitiveness internationally. As a result the federal government provided funding to assist initiatives it believed would educate students to compete in the global economy.

A third area of federal involvement is improving health and nutrition. The most obvious portions of this effort are federally supported school lunch programs. Other programs in this area include education programs designed to assist in the war against drug abuse and to promote good health and physical fitness.

A fourth area of federal funding represents the largest federal appropriation for education. Special populations, because of their exceptional needs, are recipients of additional funding from the federal government. Primarily four groups of special school populations have been supported through federal funding, including Native American students, non-native English-speaking students, at-risk students (especially those living in poverty), and students with disabilities.

Table 10.2 Average State per Pupil Expenditure for Education

State	Per Pupil Expenditure	State	Per Pupil Expenditure
Alabama	$4,037	Montana	$5,598
Alaska	8,882	Nebraska	5,651
Arizona	4,611	Nevada	5,049
Arkansas	4,280	New Hampshire	5,723
California	4,921	New Jersey	9,677
Colorado	5,097	New Mexico	4,261
Connecticut	8,473	New York	9,175
Delaware	6,621	North Carolina	4,894
District of Columbia	10,180	North Dakota	4,674
Florida	5,516	Ohio	5,971
Georgia	4,915	Oklahoma	4,697
Hawaii	5,879	Oregon	6,263
Idaho	3,844	Pennsylvania	6,983
Illinois	5,893	Rhode Island	7,333
Indiana	5,630	South Carolina	4,761
Iowa	5,288	South Dakota	4,586
Kansas	5,659	Tennessee	4,149
Kentucky	5,107	Texas	4,898
Louisiana	4,519	Utah	3,439
Maine	6,069	Vermont	6,600
Maryland	6,958	Virginia	5,109
Massachusetts	6,959	Washington	5,751
Michigan	6,658	West Virginia	5,713
Minnesota	5,720	Wisconsin	6,717
Mississippi	3,660	Wyoming	5,899
Missouri	5,114		

Note: *Figures are from 1993–94 and taken from U.S. Department of Education (1996).*

Additional Financial Inequities

Other than financial inequities that occur between *districts* in a state, resource inequities also occur at a number of other levels.

1. Resource inequities exist between *states* in the United States. For example, some states spend over $9,000 per year to educate a student while others spend less than $4,000 per year (see Table 10.2).
2. Resource inequities exist between *schools* within a district. For example, in some school districts, high schools are allocated a much larger amount of funding per student than elementary schools. Additionally, sometimes some schools receive more funds than other schools due to a variety of factors including location, influential parents, or a politically aggressive principal (see IDEALS Challenge that follows).
3. Resource inequities exist between *classrooms* in one school with classrooms of a favored, aggressive, or "squeaky wheel" teacher receiving more resources than other teachers' classrooms.
4. Resource inequities exist between *students* due to differential access to materials and equipment during nonschool hours. For example, in some homes children have access to hundreds of books; in other homes to virtually no books. In some homes children have access to multiple, cutting-edge computers and the Internet; in other homes there is no computer access.

IDEALS CHALLENGE: *Examining Equity*

(Philip Gasteau is the principal of an urban elementary school striving to be a democratic community school in which teachers, parents, community members, and the principal collaboratively make decisions for the school. In many respects the school is viewed as highly successful by the public. Yet others criticize the school, arguing that it receives more than its share of financial resources from the district. The excerpt below is the principal's voice reflecting his perspective on resource distribution and acquisition.)

It was never truer that nice guys finish last than in the politics of the central office. There is a very thinly veiled shoving match for resources. Sometimes it gets to be very nearly a physical shoving match. You spend a lot of time in that environment getting your piece for your school. It's a little bit like when the lions bring down the prey . . . the game is to do like I did at the meeting. . . . The big players were dividing up 6 million dollars. . . . And the people at the table were the lions. They just went around and had their choice of, "I'll take a leg, I'll take a rib." When you're running a little school like Hilltop, you have to understand that you have to put in your hours on those commitments. . . . If I weren't at that meeting our school would not have gotten any additional money. But I was there when they were eating it. As a result we will have more money per student than some of the other elementary schools. I don't feel badly about that. Look at the kind of results my colleagues have achieved with their money. They've wasted it. Thrown it away. It's a lot better here being used to provide services for kids and families than in their schools being used for something that makes absolutely no sense at all.

- Do you agree or disagree with Philip Gasteau's perspective?
- Do you believe Gasteau is acting in an equitable manner?
- What do you think Gasteau's response would be to a suggestion that all administrators in the district should engage in discourse and inquiry in determining how money should be distributed? Why do you believe he would respond this way?
- Moving the example from the school level to the classroom level, do you believe it is equitable and appropriate for you as a teacher to lobby for a greater share of the school's resources for your classroom than what other classrooms in the school are receiving? Why or why not?
- Are "equal" and "equitable" synonymous concepts?

IDEALS CHALLENGE: *Learning Leadership*

(Paraphrased from George Woods, principal of Federal Hocking High School in rural southern Ohio.)

Our school district is a rural school district and we are the only high school in the district. Our students come from a very wide geographic region; in fact, our district covers the second largest geographical region of any district in Ohio. We are also a very poor district overall. Some of our students have computers in their homes and can access the Internet. Others have computers but cannot access the Internet. Many do not have computers. This presents a dilemma for us as a democratic school concerned with equity. How do we ensure that all of our students have access to computers, the Internet, and other resources that they need to further their education? In more densely populated areas, students can visit the local library during nonschool hours to use computers, access books, etc. In our case, the local library is very small and is too far from most of our students' homes to be readily accessible during nonschool hours. In order to deal with this dilemma, we have an hour-long, open lunch period every day. We call it an open lunch period not because students can leave the building during that time—they can't—but because all the facilities in our building are open to students during that time. They are not required to stay in the cafeteria or in some other "holding" area, but may go to the school library, the computer lab, to see teachers for individual tutoring, to the gym to play basketball. All facilities are open. Our objective in this is two-fold. First, we wanted to send a message to our students that we trust them to be independent, to make good decisions, and to use the facilities responsibly. Secondly, we want to create more equitable access among students by giving those students who do not have access to computers, the Internet, or other materials and equipment at home, some "down" time during the school day during which they can access these things according to their needs and desires.

- What other issues of equity exist for students in classrooms and schools?
- What is your responsibility as a teacher for addressing issues of equity in your classroom?
- What is your responsibility as a teacher for exerting leadership toward addressing issues of equity that exist in your school?
- How would you proceed as a teacher in exerting leadership toward addressing the type of school-level equity issue described above?

George Woods, principal of Federal Hocking High School in Ohio, meeting with students who are involved in school governance.

TECHNOLOGY CHALLENGE

Exploring Equitable Access

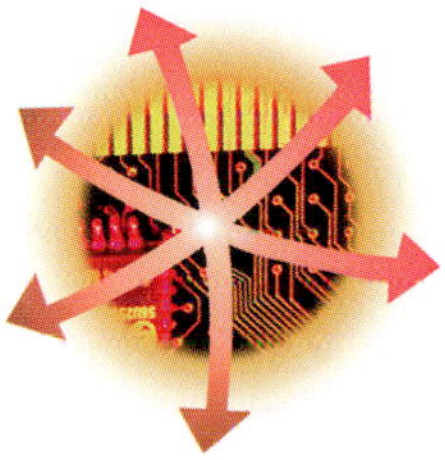

Gather data from students in one or more schools to determine the access they have to various types of material and equipment (e.g., computers, color printers, scanners, the Internet, books, etc.). Data could be gathered via conversations, a survey, or interviews. Do students have equitable out-of-school access to these items? If equitable access does not exist, talk with teachers and administrators to determine whether the school is using any strategies to equalize access. Discuss with your fellow university students other ways schools could address issues of inequitable out-of-school access to materials, equipment, and experiences. (If you do not have access to nonuniversity students for your data gathering, gather data from your university class in terms of their current or past access to materials and equipment.)

RECENT INITIATIVES AND EQUITY

Several recent controversial initiatives have implications for equity in financing and governance. Specifically, we will discuss school choice, charter schools, and vouchers.

School Choice and Vouchers

In most public school districts, students are assigned a school which they must attend. Typically this is the public school that is the closest to their place of residence. In some instances students may be bussed out of their neighborhood for purposes of achieving racial desegregation of schools in the district. In other cases, several districtwide magnet schools may exist that any student living in the school district may attend. Magnet schools usually specialize in an area (e.g., technology) and usually are located in central city areas with high minority populations. The intent of magnet schools is to promote voluntary desegregation by developing within the magnet schools sufficiently desirable programs to make attending the school attractive to European American students not living in the area. In some respects magnet schools are a form of school choice.

School choice refers to parents having a choice about which school their children will attend. The intent of choice plans is to improve schools by increasing competition between schools and to provide access to good schools to all students—not just to middle-class students whose families can afford to pay private school tuition or to be selective about where they choose to live (i.e., they can choose to live in an area where a high-quality school exists).

There are several major variations to school choice. One variation is a within-district choice. In this variation, students may choose to attend any public school within the district, no matter where they live in that district. A second variation is intra-district choice, where a student can choose to go to a school that is located in another school district. This form of school choice is intended to promote desegregation across school districts between highly minority urban districts and primarily European American suburban districts. Intra-district choice arrangements are usually voluntary agreements between the participating school districts. The most radical variation is where students may choose to attend any school—public, private, or parochial. If students attend a nonpublic school, they receive a *tuition voucher* from the public school district to help pay their costs at the private school. Radical choice plans include public and private schools, but *usually* exclude religiously affiliated parochial schools since there are unresolved legal issues regarding the separation of church and state when religiously affiliated schools are involved.

Critics of school choice are most opposed to public-private school choice plans. They argue that such plans are unfair since private schools do not have to adhere to all the regulations to which public schools must adhere. Additionally, they argue that private schools can be selective about which students may attend the school and therefore can refuse to admit students who have had various difficulties. A third argument of those critical of public-private choice plans is that they reduce funding for public schools by diverting money to private schools. Finally, critics argue that public-private choice does not result in increased access for students from economically poor families to a variety of schooling options. Rather, they argue, it simply makes it easier for middle-class families to afford private schools and may well destroy public education in this country.

Charter Schools

Charter schools could be considered radical schools of choice. Essentially charter schools are schools that are typically under the jurisdiction of the local public school district, but have been granted freedom from many of the state and local regulations that govern schools. The intent of charter schools is to increase schooling options for students and to improve schools by allowing creativity to flourish via lifting regulations that may restrict creativity. Charter school proponent Joe Nathan argues that charter schools give people "a chance to create distinctive public schools," that they "empower people who have ideas, passion, and vision," and that "thousands of teachers . . . have stepped forward to create the kinds of schools they think make sense" (Willis, 1997, p.1). Charter school laws vary widely by state with the majority of states now having charter school laws.

Charter schools can be "sponsored" by a variety of different groups or organizations. For example, a group of Native American parents may be dissatisfied with their local school(s) and decide to develop a charter school that better meets the needs of their students. In many states, after developing the plan for their school they would submit the plan to the local school board for approval. If approved, the parents would then put their plan in operation. They would receive funding from the local school district for the school and would remain under the loose jurisdiction of the public school district.

Critics of charter schools argue that charter schools divert our energies from improving all public schools. Further, they argue, if freedom from most regulations permits charter schools to be better schools, then all schools should be freed from regulation so that they can be better schools. Finally, charter school critics argue that money spent on charter schools diminishes the amount of money available to be spent on other public schools. Charter school critic Alex Molnar, in speaking about his daughter who is an inner-city public school teacher, argues, "What she needs is more resources behind her, not somebody starting up a charter school in the projects, four blocks away from her school" (Willis, 1997, p. 5).

CLICK ON IT

For more information on charter schools, school choice, and vouchers, visit the Web site of The Center for Education Reform at

http://www.edreform.com/

School choice, tuition vouchers, and charter schools are three initiatives that are unlikely to go away. As democratic educators we must become knowledgeable about these issues so that we can promote the debate and implementation of these initiatives in a manner that is consistent with the IDEALS of democratic schooling.

SUMMARY

This chapter has explored the governance and financial support of education. It is important to remember that decisions made at local, state, and federal levels of governance are not always made in democratic ways, nor with the best interests of students in mind. Unfortunately, decisions are often made to satisfy the personal or political interests of individuals or groups. However, placing blame on others for things that displease you is an unproductive practice. Rather than blaming individuals or influences from other levels of governance, a more productive practice is to challenge decisions that you believe do not best serve student interests or that are inconsistent with democratic ideals. One way of accomplishing this is through participation in shared governance.

This chapter has also discussed the manner in which schools are financially supported and noted the financial inequities that exist between rich and poor districts. As a democratic educator it is important that you proactively be concerned with issues of equity. In your classroom this means ensuring that all students have equitable access to educational materials, equipment, and experiences. This may mean using the classroom as a place where inequities created by differential access to equipment (e.g., computers) or experiences in the home can be equalized. At the state level this may mean lobbying legislators for more equitable ways of distributing funds to districts throughout the state. The next unit will discuss achieving authenticity in teaching and learning.

PRESENT TO PAST

Teacher Unions and Professional Organizations

One of the ways in which teachers can participate in the governance of schools and school districts is through participation in their union and in other professional organizations. Professional organizations provide opportunities for inquiry and discourse by sponsoring meetings and conferences, and publishing professional journals. Teacher unions also can facilitate teacher leadership, although they are frequently misunderstood and sometimes engage in practices that are not good for students (the same, of course, can also be said about some schools). There are many misconceptions about the history and the changing nature of unions. The discussion that follows reviews the history of the teacher unions in the United States, with a focus on the two major unions, the National Education Association (NEA) and the American Federation of Teachers (AFT).

TEACHER UNIONS/ASSOCIATIONS

At the turn of the 20th century, newly forming unions sought to gain the *right to organize* laborers by entering the workplace or by making literature describing their beliefs available to workers. They fought, often literally, to gain the right to *collectively bargain* for increases in wages and improvements in working conditions and to enter into collective bargaining agreements with school districts. Collective bargaining agreements specify the wages and working conditions that unions and school districts have agreed upon. When an agreement is reached, both parties are then required to abide by the terms of the signed agreement. If an agreement cannot be reached, then the union has a number of options to put pressure on the employer to settle, including various forms of work stoppages and *strikes*.

THE NATIONAL EDUCATION ASSOCIATION

The National Education Association (NEA) began operation in 1857, well before the rise of the unions in the late 19th century. Because of its inclusion of administrators and its historical development outside of the union movement, NEA leaders until quite recently tried hard to distinguish their "association" from unions. NEA documents did not use the common language or actions of unions such as *labor organizing, collective bargaining*, and *strikes*. The NEA did no collective bargaining with school districts until 1962 and did not engage in what could be termed strikes until the 1970s. NEA literature still does not use the word "strike" to describe its actions.

With 2.2 million members, the National Education Association is larger than any union in the nation except the Teamsters and has a budget approaching $150 million. About two-thirds of teachers in the United States belong to the NEA.

The American Federation of Teachers

The American Federation of Teachers arose from the turmoil of the early union movement. Activist teachers, almost entirely female and teaching in elementary schools, created the Chicago Teachers Federation in 1897. They were associated with the Chicago Federation of Labor (CFL), a union whose leaders wanted the children of workers to receive a broad liberal education while employers' organizations wanted them to get the "3 R's" and manual training for factory work (Wrigley, 1982, p. 48). From its inception, the CFL engaged in labor organizing and collective bargaining. In 1916, the CFL affiliated with the AFL-CIO, the largest industrial union in the country. John Dewey, the eminent educational philosopher, became the first card-carrying member of the new American Federation of Teachers.

The AFT remained relatively small, certainly compared with the less militant and longer-lived NEA, until the 1960s. In a now-legendary confrontation, Albert Shanker, the brash young president of the AFT, went head to head with the NEA to convince teachers in the New York City school system to join the AFT. When the smoke had cleared, Shanker's aggressive organizing tactics had triumphed. The 50,000 New York City teachers had voted to affiliate with the AFT. Union militancy about salaries and conditions resulted in great increases in the AFT's membership, especially in urban areas. Urban teachers were familiar with unions and they saw the need for a powerful organization to represent their interests against a large bureaucracy. Consequently, the AFT is to this day predominantly urban, while the NEA dominates in suburban and rural school districts, which historically have been more antagonistic to unions. Union leadership became more aggressive after the 1960s. In 1966 there were only 30 teacher strikes in the United States; in 1975 and 1980, there were more than 200 strikes across the country. Those high-water marks have since receded. In the period from 1981–1991, there were less than 100 strikes per year.

Today, after the upheaval of the 1960s and 1970s, the AFT has about 907,000 members. After 1976, the union became open to nonteachers and now includes other professionals, such as nurses, social workers, and media specialists—but still no administrators. The organization publishes *American Teacher,* a monthly newspaper; and *Changing Education,* a monthly magazine.

New Directions for the Unions

Both the NEA and the AFT have moved in some new directions recently. AFT leadership has tried to move beyond a singular focus on the "bread-and-butter" issues of salaries, benefits, and working conditions. Albert Shanker and many other union leaders, in their efforts to promote teacher professionalism, became involved in discussions about how to improve schools and ensure teacher quality. Shanker, who died in February 1997, promoted the idea of minimum-competency testing for teachers and national teacher certification, stances which were certainly controversial within his own organization. Both the NEA and the AFT oppose *privatization* of school operations and *vouchers* for children to attend private schools, and both support (with some reservations) the notion of *charter schools* within the public school system. The NEA has initiated a National Center for Innovation to encourage teacher reforms. The AFT's "Lessons for Life" program encourages high standards of conduct and academic achievement by doing away with automatic ("social") promotion of students and not allowing administrators to change teachers' grades. Both organizations are gingerly exploring the possibilities of other reforms: renewable teacher contracts to replace tenure, pay-for-performance plans for teachers and schools, and rewards and sanctions for school improvement. Such initiatives are not entirely popular, of course, and often the local chapters have strong disagreements with directions taken by the national organization. Adam Urbanski, president of the Rochester, New York, Teachers Association (an AFT affiliate) described the current issues faced by unions in his eulogy to Albert Shanker:

> He refuted the phony choice between compensation and dedication (no reason why teachers shouldn't do well while doing good); equity and excellence (the most insidious form of racism is to lower standards for someone because of race, ethnicity, or socioeconomic status); and unionism and professionalism (the stronger our union, the more able we are to build a genuine profession). (Urbanski, 1997, p. 43)

Finally, there has been talk for more than a decade about the merger of these two unions in order to deepen their impact on national education policies. A merger would create the largest public employees' union in the United States. In the first votes of their kind, more than 60% of the representatives to the NEA's annual meeting in July 1998 voted against a proposal to merge with the AFT, while two weeks later AFT representatives voted overwhelmingly for the merger. The NEA and AFT are still making their way through the shoals of public opinion, congressional pressure, and their members' varying views about where to head in the future. In the IDEALS Challenge that follows, you have a chance to express your views on some fundamental issues facing teachers' unions.

IDEALS CHALLENGE: *Deepening Discourse*

- Do you believe that teachers, who are public employees, should have the right to bargain collectively with school boards over issues related to their salary and working conditions? Why or why not?
- Should teachers be awarded tenure if they perform well in their first two or three years on the job? Determine the key points you would make if you were to argue for tenure as well as the key points you would make if you were arguing against tenure.
- What should be the limits on teachers' academic freedom? Imagine a situation in which academic freedom would become controversial. For example, should a teacher be able to espouse her or his beliefs in favor of socialism as part of a unit on different political systems?

IDEALS CHALLENGE: *Deepening Discourse*

At the beginning of this chapter you completed the following exercise. Now that you have read about the governance and financing of schools complete the exercise again. How did your responses after reading and discussing the issues raised in the chapter compare with your responses prior to reading the chapter?

- The rules, policies, legislation, and other regulations that guide and direct the work of schools are usually developed with the best interests of students in mind.

DOING DEMOCRACY

From your state department of education or another source, gather data on the amount of revenue spent per student by each district in your state.

- Is there equitable school funding across districts in your state?
- If inequities exist in your state, write to your legislators or lobby them in some other way, requesting that they give attention to developing a more equitable manner of distributing funds to schools.

END NOTES

[1]Portions of the section "Democratic Governance at the School Building Level" are adapted from Reitzug and Capper (1996).

[2]Portions of the "Who Finances the Schools?" section are adapted from material written by Jeffrey Maiden of the University of Oklahoma for this book.

REFERENCES

Baldwin, H. (1987). Personal communication.

Delpit, L. (1995). *Other people's children: Cultural conflict in the classroom.* New York: The New Press.

Kozol, J. (1991). *Savage inequalities: Children in America's schools.* New York: Harper Collins.

Marshall, C., Mitchell, D., & Wirt, F. (1986, April). *The context of state level policy formation.* Paper presented at the American Educational Research Association Conference; San Francisco.

Reitzug, U. C., & Capper, C. A. (1996). Deconstructing site-based management: Possibilities for emancipation and alternative means of control. *International Journal of Education Reform, 5,* 56–69.

Rose, L. C., & Gallup, A. M. (1998). The 30th annual Phi Delta Kappa/Gallup poll of the public's attitudes toward the public schools. *Phi Delta Kappan, 80,* 41–56.

Tarazi, G. J., Curcio, J. L., & Fortune, J. C. (1997). Where you stand: Do school board members' religious and political beliefs affect their board decisions? *American School Board Journal, 184*(1), 26–29.

U.S. Department of Education. (1996). *Digest of Education Statistics 1996.* Washington, DC: U.S. Department of Education, Office of Educational Research and Improvement.

Vollansky, A., & Bar-Elli, D. (1996). Moving toward equitable site-based management. *Educational Leadership, 53*(4), 60–62.

Willis, S. (1997). Debating charter schools: Will they revitalize or undermine public education? *Education Update, 39*(5), 1, 4, 5, & 8.

Wrigley, J. (1982). *Class politics and public schools: Chicago 1900–1950.* New Brunswick, NJ: Rutgers University Press.

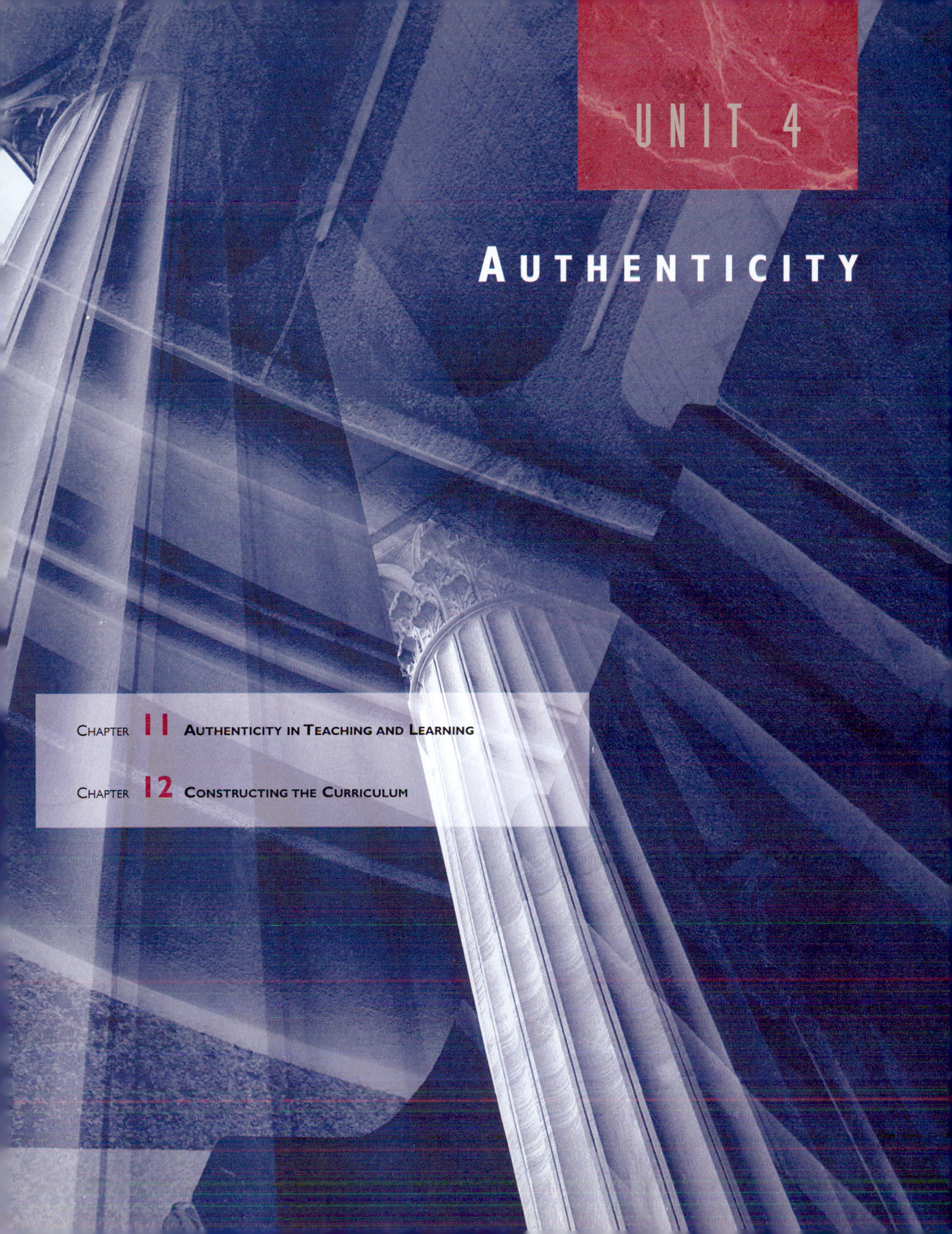

UNIT 4

AUTHENTICITY

How do you think these students learned to distinguish authentic gold from "fools gold" and ordinary rocks?

Why will these students be more excited when they find authentic gold than when they find ordinary rocks?

What are the students likely to do with the ordinary rocks they find?

How is panning for gold like learning?

What makes students more excited when they learn "authentic" things than when they learn other things?

What makes learning authentic?

What is likely to happen to the inauthentic things students are taught?

CHAPTER 11

AUTHENTICITY IN TEACHING AND LEARNING

IDEALS CHALLENGE: *Deepening Discourse*

My most meaningful learning experience was ______________________.
I learn best when the teacher or instructor ______________________.

This chapter is about teaching, learning, and democratic classroom practice. In chapter 2 we noted that authentic teaching is a way of teaching that is consistent with democratic schooling. In this chapter we will explore authentic pedagogy in greater detail. We will discuss authentic pedagogy's connection to constructivist learning theory and compare authentic pedagogy with conventional pedagogy. We will also explore the skills of teaching, the characteristics of democratic classrooms, and how the skills of teaching are practiced in democratic classrooms. We will conclude the chapter by taking you from the present to the past, exploring the foundations of constructivist learning and authentic teaching in the progressive education movement of the late 19th and early 20th century and in the work of several learning theorists.

THE CONSTRUCTION OF KNOWLEDGE

Learning is a process in which we *construct* knowledge. One way of thinking about this idea was articulated by the late Paulo Freire (1970), a Brazilian educator. Freire worked as an adult educator with poor people in Brazil, and he rejected what he called the "banking metaphor" of education. The banking metaphor represented traditional views of teaching, in which we "deposit" knowledge in students just as we would deposit money in a bank. The student is simply a recipient, essentially powerless and voiceless in the process. Freire developed a way of teaching that encouraged

CLICK ON IT

To learn more about Paulo Freire visit the Web site

http://www.infed.org/thinkers/et-freir.htm

students to raise questions about the social conditions in which they lived, and then to learn basic literacy skills while considering how those conditions might be changed.

Approaches such as Freire's are related to the ideas of *constructivism*, a recent term created to encompass a philosophy of learning. The idea of constructivism is quite complex and there is a voluminous amount of writing about it. To put the ideas in practical terms, educators such as Walker and Lambert (1995) have outlined the principles of constructivist learning and other educators such as Brooks and Brooks (1993) have discussed the implications of constructivist learning principles for teaching.

Walker and Lambert (1995) list the following principles as distinguishing *constructivist learning* theory from other theories of learning.

"Knowledge and beliefs are formed within the learner" (p. 17). Rather than being viewed as "empty vessels," learners are recognized as bringing important knowledge and experience to the learning process. They integrate new information with what they already know, by reframing what they know.

"Learners personally imbue new experiences with meaning" (p. 17). In constructivist theory, rather than a teacher telling students what something means (e.g., the interpretation of a painting, a passage, a story), students draw their own interpretations, which may vary from student to student.

"Learning activities should cause learners to gain access to their experiences, knowledge, and beliefs" (pp. 17–18). The manner in which things are taught in constructivist learning approaches should prompt students to call forth what they know in order that they can connect new information and experiences to their existing schemas, resulting in the construction of new iterations of what they know.

"Learning is a social activity that is enhanced by shared inquiry" (p. 18). One of the types of new experiences that is key in the construction of new understandings is access to the perspectives of others. Access to other perspectives helps the learner to see that multiple ways of viewing situations exist and that some views are very different from their own. This creates disequilibrium, which is reconciled as the student makes sense and integrates the new perspectives with the old perspectives.

"Learners play a critical role in assessing their own learning" (p. 18). In addition to teacher-developed evaluations that measure how well students have met goals and learning criteria established by the teacher, constructivist evaluation focuses on student self-assessment. Students play an active role in assessing what and how much they have learned as well as attempting to identify and understand the processes they have used to learn. Student self-assessment also serves to provide insight for the teacher about how students view what and how they have learned.

"The outcomes of the learning process are varied and often unpredictable" (p. 18). Unlike linear models of teaching, in constructivist-oriented teaching, teachers need to embrace a greater degree of flexibility. Students may bring different perspectives to classroom learning experiences than the teacher had anticipated or, they may respond in other unanticipated ways. Thus, the teacher "gives up a degree of control over both the process and the outcomes" (Walker & Lambert, 1995, p. 18) and engages in decision making during teaching that modifies the decisions made during planning.

Brooks and Brooks (1993) observe that the principles of constructivist learning have the following implications for *constructivist teaching*:

- The curriculum is presented whole to part with emphasis on big concepts.
- The pursuit of student questions is highly valued.
- Curricular activities rely heavily on primary sources of data and manipulative materials.
- Students are viewed as thinkers with emerging theories about the world.
- Teachers generally behave in an interactive manner, mediating the environment for students.
- Teachers seek students' points of view to base future lessons on student conceptions.
- The assessment of student learning is interwoven with teaching and occurs through teacher observations of students at work and through student exhibitions and portfolios.
- Students work primarily in groups. (p. 32)

We want to make several concluding points about the constructivist perspective on learning.

1. *What* knowledge is being "constructed" is of great importance to politically oriented educators such as Freire. Like all other ways of thinking about learning, constructivism is not value free.
2. Proponents of a constructivist stance speak of teachers as "guides" and "facilitators." It is often unclear when and why direct instruction should take place.
3. We should not overstate the extent to which children—or adults—actually construct their own world or even their own understandings. Our lives are invisibly shaped by the language and ideas we are socialized into using in a certain way. We will discuss in greater detail in chapter 12 how the cultural understandings with which we grow up affect how we learn.

For a listing of Web sites dealing with constructivism, visit

http://members.it.tripod.de/Knowing/Constructivism-links.htm

Authentic Pedagogy

Growing out of our knowledge of constructivist learning is authentic pedagogy. Authentic pedagogy refers to *teaching* students and *assessing* student progress in ways that are connected to the real world—that is, that are authentic. In chapter 2 we briefly discussed the nature of authentic pedagogy. We noted that rather than teaching in a didactic manner that focuses on the memorization of factual information, teachers using authentic pedagogy design and facilitate learning experiences for students that have positive outcomes (Newmann & Wehlage, 1995). They:

- engage them in the personal construction of new knowledge
- result in their conducting disciplined inquiry about the topic at hand
- have some value beyond the school

We also noted that authentic pedagogy is democratic because it treats students as individuals rather than assuming they are all the same. That is,

Authentic teaching helps students construct knowledge and engage in disciplined inquiry, while participating in tasks that have a value beyond school.

authentic pedagogy recognizes that students bring different experiences to the classroom and that they construct knowledge in different ways. In contrast, conventional teaching is grounded in assumptions that all students can be taught in the same way and that those students who do not respond to this manner of teaching have a deficiency that needs to be "fixed."

The development of authentic learning experiences begins with what children know and what they are interested in. Before teachers can help students learn, they need to know their students. When Stanley Zehm and Jeffrey Kottler (1993) asked a 10-year-old boy what he most wanted to learn, the student replied:

> I don't like learning about periods and question marks and multiplication problems and stuff like that. I like learning about things that are more interesting. For example, when I am playing computer games and I press the button to make a figure on the screen jump, how does that work? All the information goes through a little wire from the controller to the power box. However, what happens after the information goes there?
>
> Drugs are something else I wouldn't mind knowing about. Where do they come from? How are they made? If they are supposed to be so bad for you, how come some people say they feel so good? I've got a whole long list of other things I wish we could learn about in school instead of the boring stuff we have to study. How can I dribble the basketball better with my other hand? How can I get my mom to let me stay up later at night? How can I have more friends sleep over? How can I get my older sister to stop bothering me? How can I make some money so my parents don't have to work so hard and then they could come home early? How do I prove myself to other people? I would love to know the answers to these questions. (p. 25)

In contrast to conventional pedagogy, in authentic pedagogy, lessons, skill learning, and problems are presented within a surrounding context that

Table 11.1 Comparing Conventional and Authentic Pedagogy

Conventional Pedagogy	Authentic Pedagogy
Reproduction of Knowledge	***Construction of Knowledge***
• memorizing information	• organizing, synthesizing, interpreting, explaining, and evaluating information
	• considering alternatives
Transmission of Knowledge	***Disciplined Inquiry***
• repeating information	• collecting information via methods of inquiry
• superficial understanding	• in-depth understanding via exploring issues, relationships, complexities
• brief communication (1–2 word responses)	• elaborated communication
Value for School	***Value beyond School***
• problem connected to book, tests, etc.	• problem connected to world beyond classroom
• audience is teacher	• audience beyond classroom
Implicit View of Students	***Implicit View of Students***
• students as a generic mass	• student as an individual
• assumes sameness	• assumes difference
• difference is a deficit	• difference is natural
• difference is undesirable and to be rectified	• difference desirable & results in enhanced learning
• attempts to silence student difference	• gives voice to student difference

connects them to the real world. Lessons are conducted not simply for the sake of learning, but rather for purposes that extend beyond the classroom.

Authentic practices require activities in which students study disciplinary content, organize information, consider alternatives, gather new information, and link the information and alternatives to what they already know. This result is the construction of new knowledge. Teachers who use authentic practices frequently ask students to communicate newly constructed knowledge via such means as elaborated written or oral communication. Additionally, teachers are concerned that the learning experiences they design and facilitate for students have a value beyond school. Learning experiences should address problems connected to the world beyond the classroom, and students need to have an audience beyond the school with which they can "communicate their knowledge, present a product or performance, or take some action" (Newmann & Wehlage, 1995, p. 14). Table 11.1 provides an overview comparison between authentic and conventional pedagogy.

IDEALS CHALLENGE: *Initiating Inquiry*

(Excerpted from Cherkasky-Davis, 1993. As you read the description, note the examples that reflect authentic pedagogy.)

The children enter the classroom for family-style breakfast at 8:45. They "sign in" outside the door, thereby taking their own attendance. The first day of school the children may draw their "portrait" as signature, or may choose a color and shape to use as theirs until they are able to sign their names or parts thereof. From the first day, children use writing for authentic purposes, never for isolated tasks. . . .

Following breakfast the children blend into the rest of the classroom for family reading. Children may read alone, in pairs, or in small groups. Volunteer parents, a part-time teacher aide, and I read with the kids. We listen to them picture read, approximate read, or actually read—whatever stage they're at. . . .

The rest of our day is spent in a literate, "hands on," problem-solving environment. The children circulate to various learning centers—some of their own choosing, some as a result of teacher and child evaluation. . . .

Let's tour the classroom to view some of these activities as they're organized in thematic centers. We have a home and family center where children role-play, write shopping lists (while consulting peers and other class resources for color sequencing and correct spellings) and family stories.

Continuing our tour, we find the science center . . . the transportation center . . . the fine arts center . . . These are but a few of the learning centers the children can work at. What ties all these centers together are books, books, books, and writing, writing, writing! Out in the hallway you will find the kids' mailboxes. Children write to each other, to me, parents, principal, volunteers, upper graders, and anyone else. . . . On the walls around the room, the writing that the children do fills so much space that we're continually in trouble with the fire marshal. . . . Each kid has a folder with his or her name and picture, and a list of the books selected. . . .

My eyes scanned the room. Donald was in the math center making three-part patterns and recording them. He was using Unifix cubes, chips, and colored toothpicks. Another student was checking him. Donald put his findings in his math journal and went on to seek out books in our class library that will reinforce his patterning. . . . Donald has integrated math and reading. I noted this behavior in my anecdotal records. That, with his recordings, will go into his evaluation portfolio. . . .

At 2:15 we completed our daily diary. Children got coats, and signed out. Patrice quickly went to the "out" mailbox, carefully opened the envelope to her pen pal, and did something to it. The bell rang and she didn't have time to re-glue or tape her envelope. I told her I'd do it. Patrice gave me a hug, filled out her exit slip, and ran to meet her auntie.

The children are home. For the first time since 8:30, it is quiet. I read the student exit slips (I too am a learner!) and review and alter my plans for the rest of the week. . . . Creating a literate, problem-solving, risk-free, higher-level critical thinking, encouraging environment for all 25 Patrices, taking into account their individual needs, desires, and learning styles—this is the embodiment of Best Practice in any developmentally appropriate classroom, not just kindergarten but preschool through grade 12 (pp. 39–43).

- What are the examples of authentic pedagogy in this description?
- How might the description differ if a classroom grounded in conventional pedagogy were being described? Identify as many examples as possible.
- Identify examples from the description of ways in which students in this classroom were involved in:

1. the construction of knowledge (In deciding how to construct their signature "portrait" and what to include in it about themselves, they are constructing knowledge about how they see themselves.)
2. disciplined inquiry ("Consulting peers and other classroom resources" is an example of disciplined inquiry at this age level.)
3. value beyond school (Writing a shopping list has value beyond school if there will be an actual shopping expedition.)

Authentic teaching is not simply a concept that has achieved prominence in the United States. As illustrated in the Global Challenge that follows, teachers around the world are facilitating learning experiences for students that engage them in authentic ways.

GLOBAL CHALLENGE

Authentic Teaching

(Adapted from Posch & Mair, 1997, p. 264.)

In a secondary school in Austria, a biology teacher started an "energy network" with a group of 14-year-old students. In a pilot phase, they began to study the energy situation in their school building and in their own homes. A year later they tackled a major task: to analyze the use of energy in four small villages (the home communities of most of the pupils). The first step was the elaboration of a questionnaire with 50 questions and—supported by an energy expert—an intensive learning phase to understand the issues and to master the theoretical and social demands of collecting the necessary data. Through role plays, possible reactions of inhabitants were anticipated and discussed, then groups of two to three students went from house to house with their questionnaire, informed people about their intentions, and offered assistance in filling it in. Nearly 70% of the households completed the questionnaire.

The students processed the data at school and produced a comparative analysis of the use of energy for each house and for each village, and of the possibilities to use renewable energies (such as biogas, wood, and solar energy). The teachers involved, and their students, kept research diaries to facilitate reflection on the progress of their work. The results were presented by the students at a public event, where they enacted sketches to illustrate experiences and conflicts during data collection. The main part was the presentation and discussion of findings and proposals.

Two months after the event, a few pupils with their parents started to build sun collectors for their own house. This stimulated the foundation of an association for renewable energy and within two years, 700 installations for solar water-heating were built in the whole region. A number of other investments followed. In one village, for example, the school building was insulated to reduce energy consumption.

- Could the learning experience described above have taken place in a classroom in the United States? Why or why not?
- How does the learning experience reflect the dimensions of authentic teaching (i.e., the construction of knowledge, disciplined inquiry, and value beyond school)?
- What do you think is the most important aspect of this learning experience?
- What problems might the teacher and students have encountered in trying to do the project?
- Can you think of an analogous situation in our country, or even in your home town, in which students and teachers could conduct a study and take action on an important social problem?

THE SKILLS OF TEACHING

Planning and Organization

In chapter 12 you will read about how the formal curriculum is developed, who develops it, and the rationale for different sorts of curricular approaches. For now, we want to focus on the classroom level: How do teachers develop learning experiences and decide what and how to teach? To answer this question, we will explore how teachers plan and organize.

Teachers in most public schools are held accountable for teaching a set of objectives developed at the state and district levels. As you will read about in chapter 12, teachers meet these objectives by organizing a *scope and sequence* for the curriculum. To do this, they create an *annual outline* of the topics and activities they intend to address during the school year; *unit plans* that are devoted to a certain topic or theme and that represent the curriculum plan for a period of several weeks, and *lesson plans* that detail what is planned for a particular day. Even though researchers have claimed that teachers should first determine objectives and then build classroom activities around them, teachers often do not do that. Rather, in practice, teachers usually begin by thinking about vital content and worthwhile activities for students rather than with what they are trying to accomplish.

It is important that teachers establish a balance in planning. Routines are important for teachers, in part to reduce the complexity of classroom interactions and to be more efficient in managing materials and tasks. Routines, however, can also limit us by overly prescribing and routinizing what we do. We risk missing opportunities and "teachable moments" because we are so committed to our plan that we miss the spontaneous learning opportunities that occur around us. An unexpected student response, a question we did not anticipate, a sudden violent storm outside, a bird flying in the window, two students fighting, a light bulb burning out—all present potential teaching and learning opportunities for which we cannot plan. Sometimes we forget that teaching and learning are much more about life, and much less about books.

Few teachers, however, can be effective without planning. Outstanding teachers seem to strike a balance between planned activity and spontaneity. Their teaching reflects a combination of planned lessons, of responding to the environment and context of the moment, and of developing and facilitating activities that simulate other environments and contexts. Outstanding teachers also strike a balance between short-term and long-term learning needs. You have already read about a number of teachers who incorporated student interests, considered community issues, and created integrated curriculum. Though these teachers feel pressure to address the district objectives and prepare students to perform adequately on standardized tests, they also realize that they have a responsibility to address the long-term learning needs of students—which have more to do with democratic citizenship and less to do with test scores.

Grouping students is another central part of planning and organizing. *Tracking* is a form of grouping students across classes, which separates students according to achievement test scores, teacher recommendations from previous years, and behavioral patterns. Tracking has been found to be inequitable, restricting the educational opportunities of students in the lower-ability tracks. Nonetheless, teachers frequently group students for various purposes. In doing so they should remember that long-term, inflexible grouping arrangements, particularly those based on academic ability, are inequitable. Additionally, they should ask three basic sorts of questions in making determinations about how to group students within their class. These include:

1. Who will choose the groups? The teacher may decide on the grouping (see possible criteria in the next question), students may choose who to work with, or the groups may be chosen at random.

2. According to what criteria will the students be grouped? The teacher may group according to students' prior achievement on a certain topic or task, either to make the groups heterogeneous (students of varying ability levels working together) or more homogeneous (students with similar ability levels). Teachers may also want to disperse students according to ethnicity and gender, or group according to students' interests or their choice of a certain project. You will recognize that these decisions relate to democratic beliefs about equal opportunity, group solidarity, and freedom of choice. Grouping students for different reasons at different times in the year means that different features of democratic teaching are being fulfilled.

3. What are the guidelines for group work? There has been a great deal written about cooperative learning and other forms of group work, and five issues surface in this writing. Teachers need to think about how they will give specific, clearly understood directions; what size the groups will be; how long the different parts of a group exercise will last; what roles students may play in the group and how leadership will be established; and how to hold students responsible for the quality of their work, as individuals and as a group.

If much of this sounds quite prescriptive and top-down, and you're wondering where students fit into the picture, then you're thinking on the right path. You'll recall in chapter 4 we discussed the debates over "subject-centered" and "child-centered" teaching. This is a false dichotomy. The planning challenge is for teachers to develop goals and objectives for subject matter learning in a way that is student-centered and respects the student's needs and desires. Indeed, the challenge is to engage students in setting goals for their own learning. That process begins with communication.

Communicating

Communication begins with *listening to students* and thinking about them individually. One way to do this is to confer regularly with students. This might entail a one-on-one conference where you ask four basic questions (Zemelman, Daniels, & Hyde, 1993, p. 152). They are:

1. "What are you working on?
2. How is it going?
3. What do you plan to do next?
4. What are you learning?"

It takes good planning and classroom organization to arrange student conferences, but it can make a significant difference in your relationship with students and in how much you know about their learning.

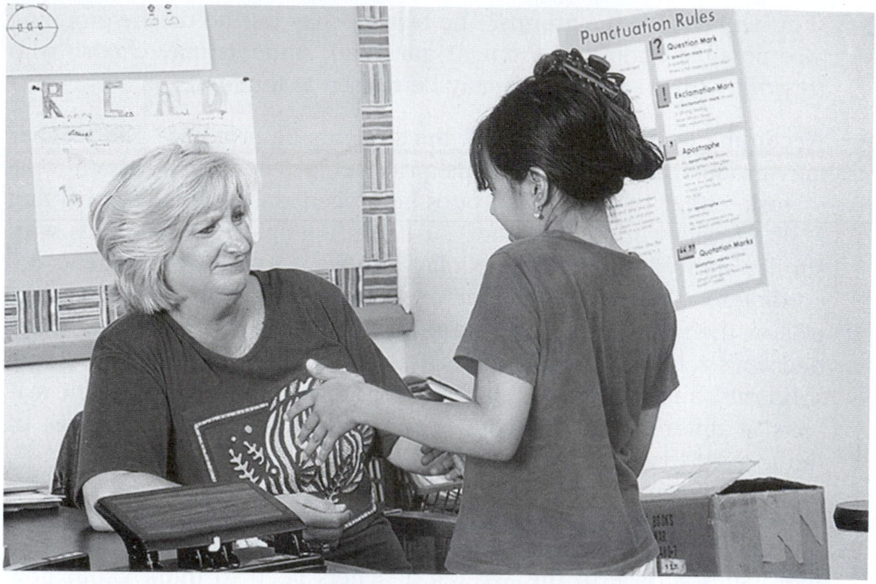

One of the skills of teaching involves listening to students.

IDEALS CHALLENGE: *Achieving Authenticity*

(Communication entails both questioning students and allowing them to ask "real questions." Bob Strachota, 1996, teaches second grade and has these observations.)

I've come to define a real question as one which engages the teacher and the learner in exploring the mysteries of the universe, rather than one which engages the learner in exploring the mysteries of what the teacher wants her to say or know or do . . . (p. 8).

Since I believe that peer interactions are just as important for promoting academic and social growth as teacher/student interactions are, I have tried to find a way that my students can offer each other the same sort of invitation to share, discuss, and debate their thinking. After several tries in math, I have hit on a very productive way for them to do this. . . .

Since . . . the focus has to be on the thinking rather than the answer, I always ask, "*How* are you thinking about this" instead of "*What* did you come up with?" This question is very nonthreatening and when the children use it with each other, their work together becomes very productive. If the problem that they are working on is an intriguing one, they naturally want to unravel it; this question—*How did you get that?*—focuses them on understanding both their partners' and their own thinking so that they are better able to think through the problem.

I have come to believe that this question lies at the heart of how we can talk with each other in any situation.

- Why does Strachota think that questioning should begin with the "how" rather than the "what"?
- What are some other questions that teachers should ask students, whether in mathematics or some other subject, in order to gauge students' thinking?
- There *are* answers to academic questions that students should know. Can you think of a situation where you might initially ask students "what" instead of "how"?

One more aspect of communication is *listening to yourself*. You can listen to yourself by considering how you explain information, how you respond to students, or how you monitor yourself while teaching. This is difficult to do, as Strachota (1996) points out:

> It helps me get out of ruts with children to be able to figure out which personalities rub me the wrong way. . . . [D]ishonesty especially rankles me, so I've had to work on my knee-jerk reactions to it. In fact I have quite a few pet peeves. I am easily put off by children who brag or whine and those who are controlling or act entitled. If I don't notice that these things are operating for me, I usually wind up in a power struggle with these children. . . .
>
> I have found that one of the best ways to avoid these power struggles is to ask myself in what ways I have the trait that is bothering me. In what situations do I talk out during meetings? When do I shirk work? How do I put people down? Don't I sometimes exaggerate my accomplishments? Why? What makes me grouchy? I've found that if I hunt a little, I can almost always find a situation when I do the same things that are bothering me. . . .

What a great idea: to see yourself in your students' actions! Questioning students and one's self is central to teaching. So, too, is the ability to negotiate what happens in classrooms.

Negotiating

Negotiation, which is a basic aspect of democratic teaching, takes place in two arenas. Teachers can negotiate the curriculum and instructional activities with students, and students negotiate with each other whenever they engage in group work. Let us consider both situations by listening to teachers.

IDEALS CHALLENGE: *Examining Equity*

(You have already read about teachers who involve students in developing curriculum, which we see as a negotiated process. This excerpt is the voice of Sue Hazzard, a second-grade teacher, as she develops class rules with her students; from Nicholls & Hazzard, 1993.)

"Now there's another thing about the second grade. We are going to become a family. You will be able to count on everyone to be your friend. Look at all the different faces. Every one of you is special. And every one of you can be friends to each other. Look at this poster. What does it say?"

"If you want a friend, be a friend."

"What does it mean?"

"Be nice to people and they'll like you and be your friend."

"What happens when someone doesn't want to be your friend?"

"You can find another one." "Find something to do by yourself."

"If someone doesn't want to be your friend, should you cry?"

"No!"

[There is a brief conversation about yelling at each other.]

"And what would you do if your teacher yelled at you and it wasn't your fault? What would you do?"

"I could say it wasn't me."

"Good. So, if I make a mistake you tell me." There is no doubt who is in front of the class. There is only one teacher here. But the messages keep coming. Respect and consideration is the order of the day. The teacher can be corrected. Things can be negotiated. The rules are not arbitrary.

"There shouldn't be any yelling anyhow. I won't yell at you. I don't like that, and I know that with you sitting and listening and thinking like you are, there won't be any yelling. I think we will be a real family and help each other learn" (pp. 14–15).

- What is being negotiated here?
- Why does Hazzard believe that some matters should be negotiated with her students?
- What are some limits on negotiation—what should not be negotiable in a classroom?
- Think of an instance in your educational experience when you or your classmates have negotiated with a teacher. What happened? How might you do things differently than what happened?

An example of students negotiating with each other occurs if they are able to determine who they might work with on a project. Here is a scene where Candace Jordan (Thorkildsen & Jordan, 1995), a teacher of fourth and fifth graders, talked with her students about how they chose their own collaborators to do a project:

> At a class meeting the day the projects were handed in, Jordan asked, "I'm really curious, and so is Terri, about why this project was so much better than the last one. Last time I had to get on your case every day to get to work and remind you of the deadlines. This time you worked together so well, and you all got your projects done on time. What was the difference? How did you choose your groups? How did you decide whether to work in groups or work alone?"
>
> "I didn't join a group because when you're by yourself, you can decide how much you want to do and when," interrupts Debbie.
>
> "I choose my friends that work good together," begins Jim, eagerly. "I like that. I like it when we choose our own groups because you get put with people that work good, friends that work good, and not with others. I like working with friends, not because they are friends, but because they *work good* together."
>
> "Why do you choose the people you do?" Jordan asks.
>
> "It feels more *comfortable*," responds Dionne, who, during the experiment, maintained harmony with DeAndre by giving up her position as leader. She regularly helps classmates find collaborators and resolve conflicts, yet never asserts a formula for making such decisions." (p. 157)

Notice how this conversation raises issues we have already discussed: Jordan tries to listen to students, she asks questions about how they're doing, and she wonders how they negotiated with each other about the composition and working style of the groups. Engaging in such actions enables her to learn about students, and forms the basis for equitable assessment of their learning.

Assessing

Assessment entails making a judgment about students' learning. Let's examine why we assess student work, what we can assess, and how we can assess.

Why Do We Assess Student Work?

When students begin a school year or even a new unit of study, some teachers give a "pretest" over the ideas and information that seem most important in the upcoming weeks. Teachers and other school staff may also administer tests to determine a student's capabilities in reading or some other skill area. These assessments are *diagnostic*. They are an attempt to diagnose what a child knows and is able to do so that the teacher can think about how to help the student.

Teachers also assess students' learning day-by-day and almost minute-by-minute as they observe and think informally about how the students are doing, who is struggling, and what they should do next. This kind of ongoing assessment, which is often unwritten and may be reported to students informally, is called *formative*.

Assessment can also be *summative*. Summative assessment does what it says—it sums up a child's level of achievement at a certain point. Any time we grade or score, or try to summarize in some manner what a student has learned, we are conducting a summative assessment. Teachers are contractually obligated to do this, because report cards are issued every six or nine weeks in schools and most teachers have to assign grades or even numerical scores to every student.

What Should We Assess?

We know that teachers assess students' knowledge of information, their understanding of ideas, and their development of certain skills (such as writing). Teachers also evaluate students' conduct and sometimes non-quantifiable skills such as "leadership." Teachers who assess only students' recall of factual information have frequently been criticized. Without question, it is important to have a firm grasp of information in many topics, if students are to think deeply and intelligently about the issues involved. We think, however, that the ability to assess students' skill development and students' social development is also crucial to good teaching.

How Should We Assess?

The method teachers choose to assess student learning should reflect *what* they want to assess and their purposes for assessment. Tests, products made by students, samples of student writing, conferences with students—all represent different ways to assess learning. Some key questions teachers should ask themselves as they think about assessment include:

- Should I consider requiring students to keep a portfolio of their work?
- How will I assign and structure homework assignments?
- In what ways should portfolios or homework assignments be authentic—that is, related to real-life tasks?
- What sort of standards for good work will I establish?
- What sort of grading or rating system will I use?
- What part will students and parents play in developing and implementing the assessment procedures?

- What sort of self-assessment can students do?

Authentic assessment is one form of assessment. When teachers assess authentically, they embrace the same principles as they do in authentic teaching. That is, in authentic assessment students are asked to:

- develop products that show construction of knowledge (i.e., doing tasks that ask them to organize or reorganize information and consider alternatives)
- engage in disciplined inquiry (i.e., doing tasks in which they use ideas, theories, or perspectives; gather and organize new information; and communicate information in elaborated written or oral communication)
- complete tasks which link learning to a value beyond school (i.e., showing that what they have learned connects to public problems or personal experiences)

You will learn more about authentic assessment and other forms of assessment as part of your teacher education program. The IDEALS Challenge that follows provides an example of how one school, Central Park East Secondary School (CPESS), has integrated a form of authentic assessment into their graduation requirements.

IDEALS CHALLENGE: *Achieving Authenticity*

(Excerpted from Meier & Schwarz, 1995, pp. 30, 33–34. The voice is that of the codirectors of Central Park East Secondary School in New York City.)

Our operational definition of a thoughtful person . . . was one who could demonstrate to us, in a variety of ways and in numerous disciplines, that he or she was in the habit of tackling the following five questions:

1. How do you know what you know? (Evidence)
2. From whose viewpoint is this being presented? (Perspective)
3. How is this event or work connected to others? (Connections)
4. What if things were different? (Supposition)
5. Why is this important? (Relevance)

The biggest step we took was deciding that a student would graduate CPESS almost entirely on the basis of evidence of such thoughtfulness, over and over again in 14 designated fields of work. We called this Graduation by Portfolio. . . . We [also] invented graduation committees. . . . Each committee includes at least two faculty members, an adult of the student's choice, and another student member. Their job is to read, review, observe, listen to the evidence, and make appropriate recommendations for revision or approval.

A MEETING OF THE GRADUATION COMMITTEE

It is a warm Friday afternoon in September and Monique is so nervous she can't sit still. "I've got to go to the bathroom," she says, and makes her third trip in 15 minutes.

Finally we all settle around a table in my office and Monique begins her presentation. She has chosen to present a paper on AIDS discrimination in health care. She refers to her paper, but only occasionally. At the start, she is somewhat ashen-faced.

Monique finishes her presentation and asks if there are any questions. She knows there will be. This is the part of the meeting where committee members probe to see if she has acquired our five habits of mind, the hallmark of a CPESS graduate. We begin gently asking her for the sources of her information. She handles these questions easily.

But the questions quickly become less predictable. "Monique," I ask, "you spoke of doctors who screened patients for the HIV virus without their knowledge or permission. You see this as a bad thing, an invasion of privacy. . . . In Cuba they test everyone. They don't ask permission. When they find an HIV-positive person they quarantine them. . . . One result is that they have greatly lessened the spread of the disease. What if they were to do that here?"

Monique is on her own here. She certainly did not anticipate this question. . . . But something happens to her at that moment; a physical change takes place, one that I've often seen at a graduation committee meeting. Monique doesn't hesitate. She straightens up, leans forward, looks me right in the eye, and says, "My father died of AIDS and that's why I decided to present this portfolio first. It is real important to me."

She continues, "I would be in favor of anything that prevents AIDS or even slows it down a little bit, but I don't know about not telling people that you are testing them. I can see both sides of the question and I don't want to decide. I think we should take a vote."

"Who should vote?" I ask.

"Everyone," she answers immediately. "Even little kids. This is so important that everyone should be able to vote."

- What do you see as the benefits and drawbacks of "graduation by portfolio"?
- What are some other ways of getting students involved in assessing their own learning?
- Is there anything you would add to CPESS's five habits of mind?

This student is presenting and explaining a portfolio of her work to her teacher and parents.

Teachers and other educators have written extensively about assessment. One honest account of a teacher's struggle to be flexible and equitable in grading and to involve students in the process was authored by Lee Colsant (1995), a high school French teacher in a low-income, inner-city school. Colsant determined that to reach his students, many of whom showed no interest in French, he had to listen to them and involve them in some aspects of decision making.

IDEALS CHALLENGE: *Examining Equity*

(Excerpted from Colsant, 1995, p. 52.)

With midterm exams over, grades must be given. I decide to try something I've never done. They will give themselves their semester grade. They already know their exam grade. They know what effort they've made and the results of past tests. So, it seems to me they know where they stand in terms of an overall grade.

"Would you all take out a sheet of paper?" I ask. "Put your names on them." There is a nervous scurry.

"What's up?" I hear in various renditions.

"I'd like you to put your heads on your desks, close your eyes, and go deep into yourselves." There are some fearful resisters. Most heads go down. Eventually all.

"Imagine you are finishing your studies abroad; you are alone in the French Alps. There is just you and the surrounding beauty of the mountains. What you see is nature's truth. The beauty you are surrounded with is all true. You have just finished your short stint in learning French. You know how much effort you have given to this adventure. Now, alone on this mountain top, all alone, search your interior and give yourself a grade. Stay within yourself, give yourself a grade and justify it." My hope is to bring them more into collaboration, to face the process of evaluation, and avoid dividing them from me by assigning grades. They are left to confront the truth or the lie.

Quietness reigns. It's still-life. Then heads begin to perk up. Pens and pencils move. Papers are passed in. Of the 24 who submitted a grade with its justification, I disagreed with only two students, who I thought inflated their grades and whose justifications also seemed inflated. Others were too harsh, and I pushed them up. I held private conferences with the two. We discussed what I thought were inconsistencies, and a new grade was agreed on.

- Why does Colsant want the students to grade themselves? How does his story relate to the idea of equity and to being democratic?
- What sort of classroom climate would need to be created in order for Colsant's approach to work well?
- What could be some difficulties or problems of this approach to grading?
- Have you ever been asked to assess yourself? How did you feel about it?

CLICK ON IT

For a listing of Web sites dealing with authentic assessment, visit

http://people.delphi.com/TJ3/authass.html

TEACHING IN DEMOCRATIC CLASSROOMS

The skills of planning and organizing, communicating, negotiating, and assessing are generic skills that are important for all teachers. However, these skills have specific implications for teachers who wish their classrooms to function as democratic communities. In this section we will discuss the characteristics of democratic classrooms. Embedded in the characteristics

IDEALS CHALLENGE: *Achieving Authenticity*

(Adapted from Kohn, 1993, pp. 9–10.)

Educators are painfully well acquainted with the phenomenon known as "burnout." But what if, hypothetically speaking, this syndrome also affected students? How would *they* talk and act? Teachers . . . to whom I have put this question immediately suggest such symptoms as disengagement and apathy—or, conversely, thoughtlessness and aggression. Of course, no sooner is the sketch of the hypothetical student begun than we recognize it as a depiction of real life. The fact is that students act this way everyday.

But now let us ask what we know from research and experience in the workplace about the cause of burnout. The best predictor, it turns out, is not too much work, too little time, or too little compensation. Rather, it is powerlessness—a lack of control over what one is doing. Combine that fact with the premise that there is no minimum age for burnout, and the conclusion that emerges is this: much of what is disturbing about students' attitudes and behavior may be a function of the fact that they have little to say about what happens to them all day. They are compelled to follow someone else's rules, study someone else's curriculum, and submit continually to someone else's evaluation. The mystery, really, is not that so many students are indifferent about what they have to do in school but that any of them are not.

- Think about your school experience. Did you like or dislike school? What factors contributed to your impression of school?
- What are the implications of Kohn's commentary for the way in which the skills of teaching are practiced?
- What are the implications for authentic teaching, classroom governance, and decision making?

you will witness specific ways of communicating, planning, negotiating, and assessing that are grounded in democratic IDEALS.

As the IDEALS Challenge graphically illustrated, the primary role of students in conventional classrooms is to be passive participants in their own education and to be receptive to the teaching and directives of the teacher and the school. In contrast with conventional classrooms, in democratic classrooms students play a much more active role in their education. What does this mean in terms of specific classroom practices? What follows are what we believe to be specific characteristics of democratic classrooms.[1]

Characteristics of Democratic Classrooms

Characteristic 1: Frequent Opportunities for Student Choice and Inquiry

At the heart of democratic schools and classrooms is the notion of *student choice*. Students in democratic schools and classrooms have many choices. They have frequent opportunities for input and decision making about school and classroom life. Students share ownership and responsibility for classroom and school property, space, and environment (Cunat, 1996). For example, students develop and evaluate classroom rules, procedures, routines, and activities and are involved in addressing social problems that occur during the schoolday. Essentially the focus in democratic classrooms shifts from teacher responsibility for student learning and behavior to student self-responsibility for learning and behavior.

At the heart of student choice are the skills of communication, collaborative planning, and negotiation. Teachers in democratic classrooms provide structured opportunities such as classroom meetings and classroom committees in which students and teacher communicate, plan, and negotiate in making decisions and taking action. Such opportunities indicate to students that they are respected by making it clear to them that their opinions matter and that they have a sense of agency—that is, that they can impact their environment and living conditions. They help build a sense of belonging and community and help students see issues through others' perspectives. Finally, opportunities for input, decision-making, and action help students develop skills important for democratic life—skills such as perspective taking, conflict resolution, and rational analysis (Kohn, 1993).

Democratic classroom practice does not mean, however, that there are no structures or limits and that students are allowed to run free and do as they please. The fear that democratic practice means a lack of adult guidance and results in chaos is a misguided notion. It is not a question of whether limits and rules are needed, but rather a question of who develops the limits and rules: the adults alone or the adults and students together (Gordon, 1989).

Guidelines for student choice. Alfie Kohn (1993, 1996) and other observers of democratic classroom practice have noted that adult guidance in democratic classrooms is essential. Students frequently do not come to school ready to think critically, to reflect, to make decisions, and to solve problems cooperatively. Children have been socialized in a culture of individualism. To expect them to naturally operate from the perspective of the good of the community is unreasonable. As Jesse Goodman (1992) has noted, giving students choices and opportunities to exercise power does not necessarily result in democratic living. Power can be used for self-serving purposes or socially responsible purposes.

Teachers in democratic classrooms strive to help students understand the relationship between freedom, the exercise of power, and social responsibility (Goodman, 1992). They help students develop community and social consciousness by providing opportunities that assist them in seeing beyond their personal self-interest to what is in the best interest of the classroom community or for the common good. In conventional classrooms, students are sometimes empowered toward economic purposes with teachers helping students develop skills to be more competitive in the economic marketplace. In contrast, democratic classrooms empower students in a manner that develops their sense of social responsibility and caring and teaches them how to exercise power toward these purposes. In democratic classrooms, teachers ensure that students are provided with "occasions to directly confront the tension between their freedom to act in accordance with their own desires and their social and moral responsibility to others who share their world" (Goodman, 1992, p. 120).

In democratic classrooms, adult guidance is also provided to help students discover and nurture their voices. Sometimes students believe they have nothing to offer because they have never been asked for their opinion. Teachers need to work with these students to help them discover that they have valuable thoughts to offer, to help them gain confidence in their ideas and opinions, and then to voice them publicly in the classroom, school, and community (Poduska, 1996).

Finally, in democratic classrooms, adult guidance is provided to help students develop the ability to make informed and value-driven choices (Sorenson, 1996). Specifically, teachers should strive to incorporate the democratic IDEAL of *inquiry*. Voicing ideas and opinions is important, but equally important is identifying, collecting, and sharing data and information that provide support for (or refute) ideas and opinions. Inquiry should inform student choice by helping students identify the basis of support for various choices and decisions and project the impact of decisions (see chapter 5 for more detail about inquiry). Democratic ideals and principles should be an explicit part of the inquiry process. For example, do various choices safeguard individual rights as well as enhance the welfare of others? Or, will pursuing one course of action benefit some individuals or groups and harm others? Do various courses of action have implications for equity? Do they promote collaboration or isolationism?

In addition to adult guidance, there are other essential factors in establishing reasonable limits for student choice. A second guideline for reasonable student choice is that the choices students make may not violate the rights of others. Choices and decisions should take into account the impact on others in the classroom. The tension between meeting the needs and interests of individuals versus meeting the needs and interests of the community is at the heart of democratic practice. As Kohn (1993) notes, "It is the integration of these two values, community and choice, that defines democracy . . . one person's freedom to choose is always compromised by a set of obligations to others" (p. 15). Ideally, students will develop a sense of "connectionism" (Goodman, 1992) which results in their automatically considering their individual needs and interests in the context of classroom, school, and community interests.

A third factor in establishing reasonable limits for student choice is a consideration of student age. Some choices that are appropriate for a 14 year old may not be appropriate for a 6 year old. Kohn (1993) notes, however, that we often use age as an excuse in overly limiting student choice. He notes that students and even young children can make far more decisions than we frequently let them and that it is only through entrusting students with responsibility to make *some* decisions that they become capable of making *other* decisions.

A fourth factor in establishing reasonable limits for student choice is time. Involving students in making decisions takes far more time than making those decisions for students. Often teachers will say, "I'd like to involve students in making decisions, but we don't have the time for that. I have to cover the curriculum for this grade." There is a degree of truth to this statement. Time does not exist to involve students in all decisions. Decision-making discussion, however, should not be viewed as a barrier to getting to the "real" lesson. As we previously noted, with teacher guidance, involvement in decision making helps students see issues from others' perspectives, resolve conflict, make a rational analysis, and develop a concern for others. In many ways, student involvement in decision making is the real lesson. As Alfie Kohn points out, "at least to some extent, *the process is the point*" (Kohn, 1993, p. 14).

TECHNOLOGY CHALLENGE

Good Citizenship and Cyberspace

(From: Online crime: Dealing with kids who send threats on the Internet, by K. J. Amundson, January 1998, Electronic School, pp. 32–33.)

In her article, author Kristen Amundson describes online crime and effective ways that teachers and schools may prevent and respond.

1. A student in a Fairfax County, Virginia, high school was angry at his physics teacher over a low grade that he feared might keep him out of a good college. So he decided to let the teacher know exactly what he thought of him—by sending death threats to the teacher's home e-mail address. The student didn't worry about being caught. After all, he had logged on to someone else's account and had used a false screen name.

2. After playing a computer game at home, two students at another high school logged onto their school's home page. What would happen, they wondered, if they sent a bomb threat over the Internet to the school—anonymously, of course? No one could catch them, right?

3. Two Massachusetts students used their school's computers to e-mail the White House, "Kill Bill, signed Mr. Deftos [the school principal]." The students thought their message would be seen as a joke. It wasn't. Following a grilling by the Secret Service, the students were suspended. Agent Richard Oliver observed, "In most cases, the kids don't fully appreciate or respect the capabilities of the technology they're using."

- How might a democratic school respond to the types of situations described above? How might a conventional school respond?
- How might a democratic school proceed in terms of developing a policy regarding Internet usage? What might the substance of the policy be? How might a conventional school proceed and what might be the substance of its policies?
- The previous section discussed the importance of allowing students to make choices in democratic classrooms. Does establishing a policy regarding Internet usage restrict student choice? Is such a policy incompatible with democratic classrooms? What are the responsibilities of a democratic school to its students and to its various communities regarding Internet usage?

The following excerpts and examples are from the Acceptable Use Policy (AUP) designed by the Fairfax County Public Schools to help students learn to use the Internet appropriately.

1. Respect for others. Users should respect the rights of others using the network. (For example, log off after finishing your work and leave the equipment and room in good condition.)

2. Ethical conduct for users. Accounts on the network, both school based and central, are considered private, although absolute security of any data cannot be guaranteed. (For example, use only your own account or password, and do not read, modify, or remove files owned by other users.)

3. Respect for property. The only software, other than students' projects, to be used on school computers or the school network are those products that the school may legally use. Copying copyrighted software without full compliance with terms of

a preauthorized licensing agreement is a serious federal offense and will not be tolerated. Modifying any copyrighted software or borrowing software is not permitted.

4. Appropriate use. Do not use offensive, obscene, or harassing language when using the network system. Students are not to reveal personal information (last name, home address, phone number) in correspondence with unknown parties. All Web pages should reflect the mission and character of the school.

• Do you agree with the above policy statements? Are critical elements missing?

Democratic classrooms engage students in discourse and provide them with choices about issues that affect them.

Characteristic 2: Student Engagement in Discourse

In addition to frequent opportunities for student choice, a second characteristic of democratic classrooms is that they provide students on-going opportunities for *discourse*. At the heart of discourse is the teaching skill of communication. Discourse involves listening, discussing, debating, critical thinking, reflection, and encouraging students to come to their own conclusions on issues. Discourse should develop "habits of mind" in students that focus on evidence, perspective, connections, supposition, and relevance (see IDEALS box on page 336).

Discourse results in students actively pursuing and constructing knowledge as a result of dialogue, interaction, and discussion (Sorenson, 1996). Refer back to chapter 6 for a more detailed discussion of discourse.

Characteristic 3: Equitable Student Access to Resources

A third characteristic of democratic classrooms is that all students have equitable access to resources (the democratic IDEAL of equity). Students should have equitable access to tangible resources such as supplies, materials, and equipment, but also to less tangible resources such as knowledge, information, decision making, and instruction. Access to these resources impacts the intellectual and emotional outlook of students and thus affects the quality of the decisions they are able to make about their own lives and the lives of others.

One growing area of inequitable access for students is technology. Some students have state-of-the-art computers in their homes and thus have access to word processing, spreadsheets, the Internet, and a variety of other information and productivity programs. These students literally have a world of information at their fingertips. Meanwhile other students do not have computers in their homes and may live a long distance from libraries or other locations where they can access a computer or the Internet.

In order to ensure equitable access to resources for all students, teachers and other educators use the teaching skills of planning and organization. An example of how one school planned and organized their school to promote equitable access to resources for all students is the case of Federal Hocking High School in rural southern Ohio (described in more detail in the IDEALS Challenge: Learning Leadership in chapter 10). In order to address the issue of inequitable access, the school developed a "flex" time period, which is essentially an extended lunch period of one hour where students can access computer labs, the library, the gymnasium, and other school resources. Principal George Wood (1997) notes that the flex time period has served not only to "equalize access to resources for those who don't have them at home," but that the different context for student-teacher interaction has resulted in meaningful conversations between students and those teachers who serve as resource persons in the areas students frequent during flex time.

Inequitable access to information and knowledge also can occur as a result of the Euro-centric nature of a school's curriculum or the instructional practices of its teachers. These issues are discussed in detail in chapters 7 and 12.

Characteristic 4: Authenticity in Relationships and Pedagogy

A fourth characteristic of democratic classrooms is authenticity. Authenticity in democratic classrooms has two dimensions. One dimension is authenticity in relationships. Developing authenticity in relationships involves the teaching skills of communicating and negotiating and intangible qualities such as knowing, respecting, and caring about each other as human beings. The other dimension of authenticity refers to authenticity in pedagogy and involves connecting curriculum and instruction to things that are meaningful to students (see the section "Authentic Pedagogy" at the beginning of this chapter).

In order to achieve authenticity in relationships, everyone should know each other *as a human being* (that is, not just as a teacher or student). Authentic relationships are facilitated by structuring classroom activities so that they require peer input and collaboration in the learning process, thus helping class members get to know each other. Structures that facilitate this include cooperative group work, small and large group discussions, cooperative learning, peer tutoring, peer editing, cooperative researching, and sharing creative writing (Sorenson, 1996).

Educators should help students take an active part not only in decisions that are directly related to academics, but also to those that are only indirectly related to academics. School is about more than academics. It is about learning to become a responsible, caring person—about education of the spirit as well as of the intellect (Kohn, 1996). Deborah Meier (1995), former director of Central Park East Secondary School, observes that caring for and respecting each other is essential in democratic schools because you cannot care about the world if you do not care about each other.

One way in which caring and responsibility for others are developed is by establishing classroom rules together. Kohn (1996) notes that students should be engaged in thinking about the general basis for rules (e.g., Why do we have rules? What rules do we really need? What happens if we don't have those rules? Which rules don't we need?). Students also should be engaged in discussing the basis for specific rules (e.g., How much noise is too much? Is it necessary to raise one's hand before talking or to line up before walking through the school?). Rules protect the right of all to learn. Developing rules together creates a statement that guides the classroom environment via a democratic process.

In terms of authenticity in pedagogy, in democratic classrooms what is being taught and how it is taught must be meaningful and significant to students. What students are learning and the products that result from their learning should have "value beyond school" (Newmann & Associates, 1996). Krista Sorenson (1996) writes that in her classroom students learn about "vital problems in the real world" (p. 91) and then engage in follow-up actions that result in changes that benefit their community.

Students should also be involved in discourse about why they are learning certain things. Teachers should be able to respond to the question, "Why do we gotta do this stuff?" (Kohn, 1993, p. 13). Indeed, teachers should regularly engage students in discussion about the curriculum. Teacher responses such as, "Because I'm the teacher and I said so" are inadequate in democratic schools. Democratic classrooms value and respect student knowledge, input, and curiosity. Knowledge is seen not as something that resides in the teacher and is delivered to students, but rather as something that is constructed out of the interaction of the ideas and experiences of the students and the teacher. Sorenson (1996) notes that "sharing ownership of knowing is key to the possibilities for student empowerment" (p. 88).

IDEALS CHALLENGE: *Achieving Authenticity*

(Angelo Patri was a high school teacher and administrator in New York City in the early 20th century. In the following excerpt, he reflects on his classroom experiences; from Patri, 1917, pp. 206–212.)

I knew little of subject matter, pedagogy, or psychology, except a number of words that had never become a part of me. I had one notion that was strong—discipline. . . . Discipline—my favorite word—why, discipline was failing, failing terribly. If I kept the children after hours they would not come to school the next day until they had made up the time that I had taken from them. If I went to their parents, the parents simply said they could not help it; they knew that these were bad children. . . .

What was I to do? I began to tell over again the stories I faintly remembered having heard in the days when father sat and talked and we listened, not daring to move lest we lose a syllable of what he said. I told them about my own childhood in the mountains of Italy, about midnight expeditions when we loaded the mules with provisions and carried food to our friends. . . . I told them about a wolf that attacked the sheep at night until my father seized and killed it barehanded. When I related these stories they listened. They hardly breathed. Each day I would end so that more could be expected. Then I began to bargain with them, trading what they liked for what the schools said they should have. I bribed them with promises of more stories to come if they would be "good" and do the work assigned. . . .

Then a new trouble arose. I had been teaching a year when "Methods" became the school watchword, and everybody set about learning how to teach arithmetic, spelling, history, and geography. Each teacher had his own methods, and supervisors going from one room to another were puzzled by the variety. The principal restored order out of chaos. A method book was written. Every subject was treated and the steps of procedure in each were carefully marked out. A program of the day's work was prescribed and we were expected to follow the stated order. . . . When I failed to follow directions, I was severely criticized. I began asking the reason for it all.

Why should I teach history in the prescribed way?

"Class, open books to page 37. Study the first paragraph."

Two minutes later.

"Close books. Tell me what you learned."

In such instruction there was no stopping, no questioning, no valuation: nothing but deadly, mechanical grind. Every teacher and every class had to do these things in just this way. . . .

(Patri then took a course that focused on John Dewey's thinking. He discusses some of the most important ideas for his teaching.)

The greatest fallacy of the child education was the "training-for-the-future" idea. Training for the future meant dying for the present. . . . I realized then that the child must move and not sit still; that he (sic) must make mistakes and not merely repeat perfect forms; that he must be himself and not a miniature reproduction of the teacher. The sacredness of the child's individuality must be the moving passion of the teacher. . . .

I tried to put into practice the results of what I had learned. . . . My supervisors objected to the variations I was trying to introduce into the teaching of history, spelling, and the rest.

"You'll find those things may be all right in theory but they will not do in practice," they said. But I refused to compromise, to yield to beliefs merely because I was told to do so or because others about me yielded to beliefs and policies. . . .

(Eventually, Patri works with a principal who is a great educational leader.)

To each of us he seemed to say . . . "You must not think too much of arithmetic, and rules and dates and examinations, for these are not teaching; the children don't grow because of them. They grow because of their contact with you . . . look into the hearts of children . . . work with the earnestness of a discoverer patiently awaiting revelations."

- How do Patri's efforts relate to authenticity in relationships and pedagogy?
- How do his efforts reflect inquiry?

Students in democratic classrooms are involved in presenting *and* assessing their work.

Characteristic 5: Student Involvement in the Assessment of Their Work

In democratic classrooms, teachers practice the skill of assessment by involving students in the process. Specifically, students help determine the criteria by which their work will be judged and then assess their work by these criteria. This is a learning experience in itself. Kohn (1993) notes, "students can derive enormous intellectual benefits from thinking about what makes a story interesting, a mathematical proof elegant, or an argument convincing" (p. 13).

One way in which students can be involved in assessing their work is through the development of reflective portfolios. The portfolio should tell the story of what students have learned and know, but should go beyond that. It should include a reflective component in which students individually as well as with groups of other students and with the entire classroom community evaluate their goals and decisions and how they as individuals have contributed to the group or community (Cunat, 1996). Further, the reflective component should assess what they have done as part of their learning to improve conditions in any of the multiple communities in which they reside (e.g., classroom, school, home, neighborhood, global) as well as what else they can do.

Characteristic 6: Assuming Responsibility for Leadership and Service

The final characteristic of democratic classrooms requires that students assume responsibility for leadership and service. Leadership and service are an essential follow-up to student choice and inquiry, discourse and input into school and classroom decision making, a concern for equitable access (within and beyond the school and classroom), and authenticity of relationships and pedagogy. In a sense, student leadership is involved in many of the activities that promote these characteristics in classrooms and schools. Providing opportunities for student leadership also involves all the teaching skills we have discussed—planning, organizing, communicating, negotiating, and assessing.

IDEALS CHALLENGE: *Supporting Service*

(Narrated by Dennis Littky, principal of Thayer Junior/Senior High School in Winchester, New Hampshire; adapted from Wood, 1992, pp. 213–214.)

It was a Friday afternoon and two kids come into my office and are really excited. They say, "Hey Doc, you gotta see this." And they go around pulling down the shades in my office, and closing the door, and then they play the videotape. And it's a tape they made of the area in Winchester where the state wanted to put a toxic waste dump. And what they had on tape was all the natural beauty of the area as well as the fact that there were several springs in the area and several varieties of protected plants.

Of course, the students' work had not gone on by accident. In Dan Bisaccio's science classes students had first been alerted to the potential of the dump. Dan, when offered such a great opportunity to teach science, couldn't turn it down. . . . Outsiders saw Winchester as a poor town with apathetic people who would jump at the opportunity of having one or two more jobs and an increase in tax revenues. How wrong those outsiders were.

"The kids were really excited about the issue," relates Dan. "At first I don't think that they really believed they could make a difference. But they were willing to try." Several of Dan's classes moved into action almost immediately, and Dan describes their work:

> One group quickly became involved with looking at some of the plants and animals in the area, and they found some endangered species which right away began to cast doubt on whether or not this was an area that was suitable. . . . Another group actually took a perk test and found the soil was glacial sand and that even with the liners [in the dump] there would be a contamination problem. . . . And then another group took a selectman and actually rented a video camera and filmed a spring on the site of the area's aquifer. . . . The fourth group organized a hearing on the dump here at school. They invited proponents and opponents and key people who were leading both campaigns. . . . The kids had been doing a lot of homework and reading about what was going on and they asked some really good questions.

Those questions were asked in front of a packed gymnasium, much to the surprise of state officials who attended. Those questions caught the attention of community members who began to ask hard questions of their own. Those questions ultimately ensured that no dump was to be dumped on the residents of Winchester.

- Which democratic ideals does the narrative illustrate?
- How does the example illustrate service?
- How does the example illustrate students learning about "vital problems in the real world" (Sorenson, 1996, p. 91) and engaging in follow-up actions that result in changes that benefit their community?

Making choices, engaging in discourse, and being concerned with equitable access to resources, while prerequisites for student leadership, are insufficient. Students should also take responsibility for engaging in appropriate follow-up action. The discourse and action aspects of leadership have been called the dual responsibilities of critique and "possibility" (Giroux, 1992). That is, democratic practice requires not only that we critique existing conditions, but also that we see the possibility of acting on our critique and take advantage of that possibility by acting to improve conditions. Democratic classrooms cannot be islands unto themselves. Rather, students should interact with others in the school and in society, discussing social issues both within the school and beyond it, and engaging in service that makes conditions more equitable and empowering for everyone. Chapter 14 will discuss student service in greater detail.

IDEALS CHALLENGE: *Learning Leadership*

(Adapted from A. Fowler & T. Jones, 1997. The authors were students at Federal Hocking High School in rural southern Ohio at the time the events described occurred.)

On Friday, March 20, about 260 Federal Hocking High School students walked out of the school building's front door in protest of the board of education's decision [to fire our principal]. Students felt violated by not having an active voice in the matter of who their principal should be. Our high school is unique in the way teachers, staff, and students interact in the curriculum, the hiring of teachers, and what rights the students have. The feeling was that by walking out of the school we could and would be heard by not just one but many of the members of the community. The walk-out was totally voluntary, which the students understood. Some supporters, as well as nonsupporters, stayed inside.

Outside, students gathered and waited for the superintendent, Mr. Bill White, to arrive so the students could present him with a letter requesting the presence of Mr. Koehler, board president. . . . After giving the letter to Superintendent White, a member of the Student Concerns Committee, Jeremy Ford, thanked students for coming out to support our principal, Dr. Wood, and asked that everyone return to class. All the students went back inside with no argument and continued on with the rest of the school day. . . .

The students waited on Koehler to reply. He declined to meet with the students. . . .

The next Monday a sit-in occurred at the school in which about 50 students participated. It was decided that an after-school action would be best so as not to disrupt the school day. . . . A phone call was made to inform Koehler that the students had a list of questions and were waiting for him to come to the school and meet with them. . . .

On Monday, April 9, another letter was mailed to all board members, along with a copy of the questions that were prepared during the sit-in.

In this country our schools are supposed to teach us how to live in a democracy. Many times in schools, however, we as students are told to sit and listen in order to learn. At Federal Hocking High School we have been taught to take responsibility, take a stand for what we believe in, and voice our opinions loud and clear. If there was a chance that we could be punished for what we saw as right, then that was a chance we thought we needed to take. . . .

We feel that many parents look at us as kids with a future, but with no influence on the present. Many seem to think that just because we are students, we should have no part in how the school we attend is run. We—not the parents or board members—have to live with the decisions made about our school. It is our attitudes as students which make an environment in which we can learn. [As students we will] continue to exercise our democratic right to seek answers.

(Postscript: Subsequent to the initial publication of the article from which this IDEALS Challenge was adapted, the Federal Hocking Board of Education rescinded the nonrenewal of Dr. Wood's contract.)

- What do you think of the students' actions in the IDEALS Challenge?
- What is the connection between the IDEALS of democratic schools and classrooms and the students' actions?
- How else might they have responded?
- Was the students' leadership responsible or irresponsible?

After reading chapter 13, revisit this IDEALS Challenge and identify aspects of the students' leadership that could be considered "conventional leadership." Identify aspects that could be considered "constructivist" leadership.

The Stability of Conventional Practice

In spite of the attention that has been given to authentic and democratic teaching and assessment practices in the past few years, and in spite of the research supporting their effectiveness, most teachers continue to follow traditional patterns of teaching. Tyack and Cuban (1995) refer to this stability of instruction as the "grammar of schooling." They note,

> Little has changed in the ways that schools divide time and space, classify students and allocate them to classrooms, splinter knowledge into "subjects," and award grades and "credits" as evidence of learning. . . . Indeed, much of the grammar of schooling has become taken for granted as just the way schools are. . . . Once established, the grammar of schooling persisted in part because it enabled teachers to discharge their duties in a predictable fashion and to cope with the everyday tasks that school boards, principals, and parents expected them to perform: controlling student behavior, instructing heterogeneous pupils, and sorting people for future roles in school and later life. . . . Established institutional forms come to be understood by educators, students, and the public as necessary features of "real school." (pp. 85–86)

Not only has the grammar of schooling become taken for granted by many teachers, it has been internalized by many students, as illustrated by the following IDEALS Challenge.

IDEALS CHALLENGE: *Deepening Discourse*

(Excerpted from Pate, Homestead, & McGinniss, 1997, pp. 138–139.)

Not everyone embraced the idea of a democratic classroom. Some students, especially those who had learned to do well within the traditional structures of schooling, were uncomfortable with some aspects of our curriculum. These students were more comfortable with teachers directing every lesson, rather than accepting responsibility for their own learning. Some students were also unhappy with the fact that democratic education takes more time. It requires listening, debating, withholding judgment until all opinions are voiced, making decisions, accepting responsibility, and tolerating ambiguity. Because we all had varying ideas about what democracy and living democratically is or ought to be, the next time we would discuss these ideas more often. We (students and teachers) might pose questions such as the following: What does democracy mean? What does living democratically at home and at school mean? What is my role as an individual or as part of a group in relationship to democratic living? What responsibilities go along with democratic living?

Sometimes we found ourselves talking too much and not letting our students voice their opinions enough. It was also easy to fall into our old teacher role and provide answers. . . . Time was also problematic. Although our students understood that it would take time to work collaboratively, they were impatient. It took time to come to consensus, develop action plans, codevelop units, and so on.

- What dilemmas of democratic practice are evident in the excerpt above?
- How might you address these dilemmas as a democratic teacher?
- How would you respond to the questions posed at the end of the first paragraph? Discuss your responses with your classmates.

The grammar of school structures and instructional practices is quite powerful, though there have been changes. Especially in elementary schools, there may be more informality, greater flexibility in seating and room arrangements, more student movement and exploration of the environment, more varied groupings, more frequent use of group work, and more independent activities such as learning centers than in past eras. However, whole group instruction, the predominance of textbooks and prepackaged curriculum resources, and teacher talk still prevail (Tyack & Cuban, 1985). It is not that direct instruction—the well-articulated lecture, the enlightening demonstration—is bad. The point is that these forms of instruction are often used to such an extent that students have few authentic learning experiences and little voice in what happens to them in their classroom and school. They have few experiences that recognize and give voice to their individuality and the unique and differing ways in which they construct knowledge.

SUMMARY

Democratic teaching requires that we help students develop the tools they need to make informed choices. Students need to work within society, but need not accept that which they find unjust and can influence in a positive direction. Democratic citizenship means having an awareness of the realities and expectations of the "system" but not accepting the status quo as unchangeable. Democratic citizenship requires questioning and challenging authority and the status quo when things appear unfair and engaging in discourse and inquiry to determine whether appearances reflect reality.

The implications of this for you as a teacher are that students may occasionally challenge you as a teacher. Democratic teachers do not view student challenges of their decisions and practices as signs of disrespect, but rather as students engaging in the practice of democracy. Student questions and suggestions should be viewed as opportunities for exploration and inquiry rather than as disrespectful, or as struggles for power. Democratic teachers should help students learn how and when to challenge the way things are, to hone their sense of what is just and unjust, to see how else things might be done, and to nurture a personal and collective sense of efficacy in terms of impacting the course of events (Cunat, 1996).

Rather than being expected to passively conform to what adults know is best for them, as is the case in many conventional classrooms, in democratic classrooms students play an active and collaborative role with adult educators in initiating ideas and suggestions, exploring them, and constructing practices that fit with democratic principles and ideals.

DOING DEMOCRACY

Spend some time volunteering at an adult literacy center. Study the ways in which the adult students you are tutoring seem to learn best. Compare this with what you have learned about teaching and learning in this chapter. If possible and appropriate, learn about your adult students' educational histories and try to understand how their educational history contributed to their current situation.

PRESENT TO PAST
The Foundations of Authentic Pedagogy

THE PROGRESSIVE EDUCATION MOVEMENT

One of the foundations of authentic pedagogy is the progressive education movement. Progressive education began as a reaction by social critics against the purposes and practices of traditional education. It was grounded in the larger social reform movement of the late 19th and early 20th centuries that attempted to change many aspects of society during the Industrial Revolution.

Harold Rugg's progressive critique of traditional schooling summed up much of the thought of progressives. Rugg argued that:

1. education should take place in the community
2. life and work in schools ought to be seen not merely as preparation for the future but as a present opportunity to grow
3. the arts and experiential learning ought to augment or even supplant standard textbooks
4. "applied," "modern" subjects needed to enter the curriculum

Many of Rugg's ideals came from the writings of John Dewey (1859–1952), the most famous American educational philosopher of the 20th century.

Dewey constructed his philosophy of education around the idea of *experience*. He believed that much of traditional school experience was actually miseducative. For an experience to be educative, there needed to be at least three conditions met (adapted from Noddings, 1995):

1. There should be "continuity" between the students' past knowledge and experiences, their present experiences, and the possibility of future experiences. The present is not simply an abstract preparation for the future. Dewey wrote,

   > What avail is it to win prescribed amounts of information about geography and history, to win ability to read and write, if in the process the individual loses his own soul: loses his appreciation of things worth while, of the values to which these things are relative; if he loses desire to apply what he has learned and, above all, loses the ability to extract meaning from his future experiences as they occur? (Dewey, 1938, p. 49)

2. Education should be centered around providing experiences for children who take into account "the powers and purposes of those taught" (Dewey, 1938, p. 45). By this Dewey meant that students should have more freedom in classrooms, but their freedom should be coupled with thinking intelligently about their purposes—that is, what it is they want to learn and why they want to learn it.

3. Although students' powers and purposes should be a part of the educational process, students should not simply be left on their own to learn as they can. Dewey believed there needed to be an "interaction" between what he called the "internal conditions" and the "external conditions" at play in the learning process. That is, the "internal conditions" of learning, which include the needs, capacities, and interests of the individual student, and the "external conditions," which include the environment, the social setting, and the teachers' actions, had to interact in a congruent manner in order for learning to occur (Dewey, 1938). Over the years, Dewey became concerned about erroneous interpretations of progressive education, which implied that progressive education meant "anything goes." Such interpretations fell short of key objectives of progressive education in that they failed to develop students' sense of self-control and their participation in a form of social control built on collective activity rather than on authoritarian dictates.

One of Dewey's legacies was the Chicago Laboratory School, an experimental school sponsored by the University of Chicago that he created and led from 1896–1904. Dewey and the teachers who started the school envisioned it as a small community. The teacher's task was to act as a facilitator of children's self-directed learning and as an organizer of educative experiences. The IDEALS Challenge that follows provides a brief description of the school, as seen through the eyes of a visiting parent of a prospective student.

CLICK ON IT

For more information about progressive education visit the Web site

http://newmaine.com/progressive-educator/ped.htm

IDEALS CHALLENGE: *Achieving Authenticity*

(The narrator is describing his observations in a school where he is a visitor. From Runyon, 1900, p. 591, as cited in Katch, 1991, pp. 64–65.)

Everywhere the children were busy, but the morning was half gone and I had heard nothing that reminded me of a school except a class talking Latin as I passed. I had heard a class discussing whether John Smith or George Washington was the greater man, and another group, with a relief map, trying to decide where it would be best to erect forts to protect the English colonies from the French aggressions from the north and west. But I always know at home when the children get on those subjects that they are *not* studying their lessons. I wondered why the teacher did not tell them, if she thought it worthwhile, and then have them bound states and name the capitals and principal cities. In all the classes the children talked—sometimes two at once; but with a freedom of expression and an ability to stick to the point which surprised me. . . .

I found my way to the kitchen, which I had previously mistaken for the laboratory, with its rows of gas fixtures and asbestos mats. I learned that earlier in the morning the group had had a cooking lesson in which they experimented with the food given them. Each child had cooked one third of a cup of flaked wheat in two thirds of a cup of water. Each had calculated how much water he would need if he cooked half a cup, and then one child was told to find out how much he would need for the whole group and to cook it, while other tasks were assigned to the rest. . . . I thought how Fred [her son] worried over his fractions, and here were children two years younger [probably about 8 years old] working out the number of cupfuls of water and cereal that would be needed for a family of three, five, or eight, on the basis of the number for which one third of a cupful would be sufficient. . . .

From time to time during the morning, a line from Dr. Dewey's book had come into my mind: "Education is a process of living, not a preparation for future living."

- What are some examples of how Dewey's ideas are being implemented in this school?
- How are the democratic IDEALS evident in the school?
- How does the description of the school reflect authentic pedagogy?

ENDNOTE

[1] This section relies heavily on the work of Sorenson (1996) and Kohn (1993; 1996).

REFERENCES

Amundson, K. J. (1998, January). Online crime: Dealing with kids who send threats on the Internet, *Electronic School,* 32–33.

Brooks, J. G., & Brooks, M. G. (1993). *In search of understanding: The case for constructivist classrooms.* Alexandria, VA: Association for Supervision and Curriculum Development.

Cherkasky-Davis, L. (1993). A day in the life of a developmentally appropriate whole language kindergarten. In S. Zemelman, H. Daniels, & A. Hyde, *Best practice: New standards for teaching and learning in America's schools* (pp. 38–44). Portsmouth, NH: Heinemann.

Colsant, L. (1995). "Hey man, why do we gotta take this . . . ?" Learning to listen to students. In J. G. Nicholls & T. A. Thorkildsen (Eds.), *Education as adventure: Lessons from the second grade* (pp. 62–89). New York: Teachers College Press.

Cunat, M. (1996). Vision, vitality, and values: Advocating the democratic classroom. In L. E. Beyer (Ed.), *Creating democratic classrooms: The struggle to integrate theory and practice* (pp. 127–149). New York: Teachers College Press.

Dewey, J. (1938). *Experience and education.* New York: Macmillan.

Fowler, A., & Jones, T. (1997). FHHS students want Dr. Wood and democracy. *Democracy & Education, 11*(3), 47–48.

Freire, P. (1970). *Pedagogy of the oppressed.* New York: Herder & Herder.

Giroux, H. A. (1992). Educational leadership and the crisis of democratic government. *Educational Researcher, 21*(4), 4–11.

Goodman, J. (1992). *Elementary schooling for critical democracy.* Albany, NY: State University of New York Press.

Gordon, T. (1989). *Teaching children self-discipline.* New York: Times Books.

Katch, J. (1991). John Dewey's school. In K. Jervis & C. Montag (Eds.), *Progressive education for the 1990s* (pp. 61–70). New York: Teachers College Press.

Kohn, A. (1993). Choices for children: Why and how I let students decide. *Phi Delta Kappan, 75,* 8–20.

Kohn, A. (1996). *Beyond discipline: From compliance to community.* Alexandria, VA: Association for Supervision and Curriculum Development.

Meier, D. (1995). *The power of their ideas: Lessons for America from a small school in Harlem.* Boston: Beacon Press.

Meier, D., & Schwarz, P. (1995). Central Park East Secondary School: The hard part is making it happen. In M. W. Apple & J. A. Beane (Eds.), *Democratic schools* (pp. 26–40). Alexandria, VA: Association for Supervision and Curriculum Development.

Newmann, F. M., & Associates. (1996). *Authentic achievement: Restructuring schools for intellectual quality.* San Francisco: Jossey-Bass.

Newmann, F. M., & Wehlage, G. G. (1995). *Successful school restructuring.* Alexandria, VA: Association for Supervision and Curriculum Development.

Nicholls, J. G., & Hazzard, S. P. (1993). *"Reasons for learning": Expanding the conversation on student-teacher collaboration.* New York: Teachers College Press.

Noddings, N. (1995). *Philosophy of education.* Boulder, CO: Westview Press.

Pate, E. P., Homestead, E. R., & McGinnis, K. L. (1997). *Making integrated curriculum work: Teachers, students, and the quest for coherent curriculum.* New York: Teachers College Press.

Patri, A. (1917). "A schoolmaster of the great city." In R. M. Cohen & S. Scheer (Eds.), *The work of teachers in America: A social history through stories* (pp. 205–214). Mahwah, NJ: Lawrence Erlbaum.

Poduska, K. (1996). To give my students wings. In L. E. Beyer (Ed.), *Creating democratic classrooms: The struggle to integrate theory and practice* (pp. 106–126). New York: Teachers College Press.

Posch, P., & Mair, M. G. (1997). Dynamic networking and community collaboration: The cultural scope of educational action research. In S. Hollingsworth (Ed.), *International action research: A casebook for educational reform* (pp. 261–274). London: Falmer Press.

Sorenson, K. (1996). Creating a democratic classroom: Empowering students within and outside school walls. In L. E. Beyer (Ed.), *Creating democratic classrooms: The struggle to integrate theory and practice* (pp. 87–105). New York: Teachers College Press.

Strachota, B. (1996). *On their side: Helping children take charge of their learning.* Greenfield, MA: Northeast Foundation for Children.

Thorkildsen, T. A., & Jordan, C. (1995). Is there a right way to collaborate? When the experts speak, can the customers be right? In J. G. Nicholls & T. A. Thorkildsen (Eds.), *Education as adventure: Lessons from the second grade* (pp. 137–161). New York: Teachers College Press.

Tyack, D. B., & Cuban, L. (1995). *Tinkering toward utopia.* Palo Alto, CA: Stanford University Press.

Walker, D., & Lambert, L. (1995). Learning and leading theory: A century in the making. In L. Lambert, D. Walker, D. P. Zimmerman, J. E. Cooper, M. D. Lambert, M. E. Gardner, & P. J. Ford Slack (Eds.), *The constructivist leader* (pp. 1–27). New York: Teachers College Press.

Wood, G. (1992). *Schools that work: America's most innovative public education programs.* New York: Penguin Books.

Wood, G. (1997, June). *Democratic schools: The case for community.* Presentation at the Oklahoma Networks for Excellence in Education Summer Institute, Norman, Oklahoma.

Zehm, S. J., & Kottler, J. A. (1993). *On being a teacher: The human dimension.* Thousand Oaks, CA: Corwin Press.

Zemelman, S., Daniels, H., & Hyde, A. (1998). *Best practice: New standards for teaching and learning in America's schools.* Portsmouth, NH: Heinemann.

Given the immensity of all there is to know, how do we decide what is most worth knowing?

Who makes these decisions?

Who should make these decisions?

CHAPTER 12

Constructing the Curriculum

IDEALS CHALLENGE: *Deepening Discourse*

(Excerpted and adapted from the "Conversations" section of High Strides *magazine, 1997, pp. 8–9.)*

For the past 10 years, Gail Peddle has taught math and science to middle-level students at the Overbrook Educational Center, a K–8 public school in Philadelphia that includes a large number of visually impaired children. She also has been a leader in the movement to establish rigorous academic standards in the Philadelphia Public Schools. What follows is an interview we conducted with her.

High Strides: What do you believe the curriculum should be for middle school math and science?

Gail Peddle: Right now we're doing algebra in eighth grade. I would like to see algebra concepts integrated K–8, and geometry also. I would like to see by sixth grade everyone being competent in basic mathematics, the level that's usually reached by ninth grade. I'd like to see that type of review course in sixth grade, that they would have achieved all the basic level of competency in sixth grade in math and science. . . . In science I think we need to look at integration of science and look at it in terms of a lifelong learning experience. Science is all around us. Kids hear about new medications, different things that impact the environment, every day. I'd like to see more emphasis placed on making a difference in the community with the uses of science. I don't want so much science taught in isolation. The reason I teach math and science is that I think we need more integration.

High Strides: Is it possible for all students to reach high standards in math and science?

Gail Peddle: I think so. I think we have to look at what we mean by high standards. Whose definition do we use? Is the child intellectually satisfied? Not everybody is going to be a mathematician or a scientist, but if they can learn to love math and see its necessity and not be afraid of it, that's a lot. . . .

High Strides: What does it mean to have high standards as a teacher?

Gail Peddle: First, we have to know that all children can learn. You have to believe it, but you also have to know that. . . . Once you believe that all children can learn, you raise your standards. Then the kids will raise their standards. . . . I always get slightly shaken because I feel that I'm constantly asked to lower my standards for certain people.

> People say, "That's too much homework," or "That's too difficult." I know when they hang in there, kids can move to a new level of learning. . . .

- What role should teachers play in determining the curriculum in democratic schools?
- What role should teachers play in determining the standards for learning that represent the curriculum?
- Should standards for learning be applied to all children in the same way?

Chapter 12 concerns how we think about curriculum. You will consider the varied meanings of curriculum and learn about the history of curricular reform. We also want you to understand how the curriculum gets constructed, who the stakeholders in the construction process are, and how the curriculum might need to be reconstructed.

The term curriculum is layered with different meanings. The original Latin term *currere* means "to complete the course." For a long while, curriculum was essentially seen as the content of what educators intended to teach, or what educators thought they were teaching. Since this definition depends solely on the interpretation of educators, some have broadened the definition to include all the experiences students have while at school. We find it helpful to define curriculum as the "what" of education: what others think students are supposed to learn, what we hope they will learn, and what they actually get a chance to learn.

Curriculum is a complex concept when we try to describe how it is developed and enacted. This is because:

- the educational curriculum assumes multiple forms (including academic and social forms)
- the scope and sequence of the curriculum alters over time
- responsibility for curriculum development is widely shared
- curriculum is a cultural artifact

Each of these characteristics will be dealt with in this chapter.

CURRICULUM TAKES ON MULTIPLE FORMS

A school's curriculum can be seen as having five forms. First, curriculum is what others think students should learn; this is called the ideal curriculum.

In a second form, it is what educators intend for students to learn by setting objectives and creating curricular materials; this is called the formal curriculum. In a third form, curriculum is what really happens in the classroom and school; this is called the enacted curriculum. In a fourth form, curriculum is what students implicitly learn in schools without being directly taught in schools; this is called the hidden curriculum. Finally, a fifth form of curriculum is what students do *not* get a chance to learn; this is called the null curriculum. As we describe these multiple forms of curriculum, we want you to relate the ideas to your education and the various curricula that you have been required to learn.

The Ideal Curriculum

What is worth teaching and learning? Why is it worthwhile? Questions such as these reflect our *ideal curriculum*. They stem from philosophical and practical concerns about what it means to be an educated person in a democracy, and why one should become "educated." We derive our ideals from many sources. On one level, the ideal curriculum comes from philosophical writings. In our society there are many publications that express the author's philosophical beliefs about the curriculum. These may take the form of speeches such as Ernest Boyer's "What Is an Educated Person? Eight Core Commonalities" (1993), essays such as Philip Jackson's "Untaught Lessons" (1992), compilations of different approaches to the curriculum such as Landon Beyer's *Creating Democratic Classrooms* (1996), books about teaching that are coauthored by university and school faculty, such as *Education as Adventure* by John Nicholls and Susan Hazzard (1993), and autobiographical accounts by teachers such as Sylvia Ashton-Warner's *Teacher* (1963). These writings are always influenced by the societal conditions and prevailing beliefs of the time, but they can provide us with a coherent set of beliefs to weigh against our own.

There also are many professional books about curriculum that you may want to read. Some of the authors present different curricular topics and ask the reader to learn about them, while other authors take a position and present their own approach. If you become a teacher, you will find that in-service workshops, conference presentations, and packaged curricular programs also express what ought to be taught in school. In any case, all texts, speakers, and resources related to curriculum present their ideal explicitly or implicitly.

Finally, ideal curriculum is developed through *personal* experience. Every teacher has an interpretation of what they have read and discussed and thought about, an interpretation that can be expressed as a set of ideals. If you were to ask several teachers why they teach and why students should learn what they are teaching, the teachers would tell you in some way about their curricular ideals, just as a teacher named Mr. Guy will do later in this chapter in an IDEALS Challenge.

Teachers' views of what constitutes the essential or ideal curriculum are similar to the views of noneducators in many respects, although they are different in a few areas. A recent poll (Wadsworth, 1997, p. 45) asked respondents "What subjects are absolutely essential to teach?" Teachers and respondents from the general public agreed on four of their top five choices: (1) "basic reading, writing, and math skills"; (2) "good work habits such as being responsible, on time, and disciplined"; (3) "the value of hard

How might the curriculum in a democratic school differ from the curriculum in a conventional school?

work"; and (4) "values such as honesty and tolerance of others." Teachers felt more strongly than the public about teaching "American history and geography" (72% to 63%), "habits of good citizenship such as voting and caring about the nation" (77% to 66%), and especially "curiosity and love of learning" (76% to 57%). Public respondents placed "computer skills and media technology" third on their list (80%), while this ranked only seventh with teachers (72%). What ranked lowest with both groups? "Classic works from such writers as Shakespeare and Plato," "modern American writers such as Steinbeck and Hemingway," and "sports and athletics" were rated as essential by less than 25% of both teachers and the public. If this poll is representative of common opinions, what people define as "basic" skills, values, and habits are the most important aspects of the curriculum. Two essential parts of the Western classical curriculum—literature and physical education—are no longer highly valued. Not surprisingly, public respondents are more utilitarian and less interested in children's curiosity, creativity, and learning about the world than are teachers.

The Formal Curriculum

The *formal curriculum* is comprised of the written intentions, guidelines, plans, resources, and activities intended to further the growth of individual students and the community life of the classroom and the school. As with the ideal curriculum, there are many sources for this form of the curriculum. For example, state legislatures and school district personnel usually determine the outlines of a formal curriculum that is mandated for school districts and publish it in a curriculum guide, which should be readily available to all teachers. We will delve more deeply into the formal curriculum in a subsequent section that deals with the "stakeholders" in the curriculum.

The Enacted Curriculum

The *enacted curriculum* consists of what actually occurs in classrooms and other school sites, regardless of the formal or ideal curriculum. What gets enacted may not parallel what was intended by the teacher, in part because students embody the community's culture as well as school culture. In any school, students have diverse ways of responding to adults and communicating with peers. If there is a mismatch between the cultural background of the teacher and some of the students, the discrepancy between a teacher's intentions and what actually occurs in the classroom may loom large. Cultural diversity can be seen as a boon to social learning or as a barrier to communication, as we will discuss in a section on multicultural issues.

Students' and teachers' actions also are influenced by the customs and contexts of schools. Each classroom has its own culture that differs in subtle or overt ways from other classrooms. Ideals or formal processes are constantly being reshaped by the teacher (and perhaps challenged or reinforced by the students) in the flux of classroom life. In the following IDEALS Challenge, a teacher and a student discuss the curriculum in their class. Look at how they talk about the ideal, formal, and enacted curriculum.

IDEALS CHALLENGE: *Deepening Discourse*

This challenge presents excerpts from an end-of-year conversation between an eighth-grade student, Meghan, and her science teacher, Mr. Guy. They have been teaching and learning together in a middle school of 650 students, located in an ethnically mixed area of a small urban community. The conversation concerns their views of curriculum.

Why Should Students Learn Science?

Mr. Guy: It's the world we live in. Technology and science have played an essential part in the way we are. . . . It's also a way of thinking about why, how, when, how much—finding answers to questions we have. . . . We think of science as people in white coats, but it's everywhere around us.

Meghan: It's observing your surroundings. I think science gives you a chance to get a closer look at everyday life and then analyze it. When we looked at atoms, we tried to figure out what makes them up—and the different types of weather, what it affects. . . .

What Was the Curriculum About This Year?

Meghan: I learned about animals, like arthropods, in life science—habits and habitats—energy, like electromagnetism, kinetic and potential—rocks and geology, you know, the continental drift and plate tectonics—oh, and we did a project where we had to take one element and do a visual of what the components would look like. . . . But the most important part was not just in the regular curriculum. Throughout the year, it was the way we did things and the way we talked—we had a lot of discussions, guest speakers, and three different student teachers. So you had different opinions from people. Plus, a lot of hands-on things because you lose interest with just talking. Mr. Guy would stand up and talk with us about what we wanted to do, to get our viewpoints. Then, we would do an experiment and talk about it, or write.

Mr. Guy: This year was a new integrated science curriculum, which was video-driven, with much of the content in videos. The teachers thought we needed content in a format adolescents would enjoy, and activities tied in that reinforce the videos. I liked some videos and didn't like others, and we spent a bit too much time watching them. Next year, the videos will be no more than two days, a total of 30 minutes during the week. Because I always stop the video to talk with students. This year, we wanted to validate this curriculum and learn how to work with it. . . . I put my own video together every year and show it to the students at the end. Socialization is an important part of teaching; content at this age is not as important as turning them on to science—that it's real and it's fun. There is plenty of time for them to learn more content. In fact, I'm going to place even more emphasis next year on process skills. . . . We have only four units in the curriculum: waves, energy, stages, and environment. Some of them are difficult to grasp—for example, the difference between sound waves and light waves. I *do* think there are big ideas in this curriculum, so next year I'll do fewer topics in more depth. How the facts fit with the ideas, and not in isolation.

- How do Mr. Guy and Meghan describe the purpose of science?
- What do *you* think should be the purpose?
- In as much detail as possible, describe the different aspects of the ideal, formal, and enacted curriculum, as presented by Mr. Guy and Meghan.
- What do you think about Mr. Guy's discussion of content, process skills, and "big ideas"?
- How do Mr. Guy's and Meghan's descriptions of the curriculum relate to the IDEAL of authenticity?

The Hidden Curriculum

The *hidden curriculum* is what is implicitly taught in schools. We might think of the hidden curriculum as the "messages" interpreted by students—what they learn without being directly taught. For example, what do students learn when classes are canceled for a pep rally but not for an academic competition or exhibit? What do students learn when those who blindly follow teacher requests are rewarded and favored, while others who sometimes ask "Why do we have to do this?" are told "Because I said so, and I'm the teacher!" Students also may learn things from the way the physical environment of the school and classroom is arranged. For example, the arrangement of student desks in rows makes it easier for the teacher to separate students and survey the room, but quite difficult for students to talk with each other. Students might learn that isolation is more important than collaboration in this classroom. When students' names are placed on the board for disciplinary action, students might learn that control is more important than learning. When some students get called on frequently and others do not, students might learn about favoritism and privilege. All of these aspects of classroom life are part of the hidden curriculum.

What we value is transmitted through our interpretations of subject matter and teaching methods. One teacher may focus more on how accurately students recall the content of a text, while another might focus on the relevance of the content to students' lives. Teachers may give more praise for being quiet than for asking an insightful question. Such differences will likely result in different responses by students.

Values expressed implicitly are not always consistent. Directly teaching about these values as a set of curriculum topics, moreover, may differ from the messages students derive by observing how teachers act. The point has often been made, for example, that we talk about democracy but students seldom have a chance to practice *acting* democratically in schools and classrooms.

The hidden curriculum also is structural and economic. What is important in schools is reflected in the time allotments for certain subjects, as well as the amount of resources that support the subject. If we relegate art to a trailer site, require that the art specialist travel by rolling cart to each classroom, or make art an elective so that only a few students take it, we send the message that art is not one of the important "real" subjects like science.

One interesting example of a hidden curriculum is documented in Philip Jackson's (1992) description of veteran teacher Elaine Martin's first-grade classroom. In this excerpt, Jackson describes her means of handling student disagreements that arise on the playground.

> After recess on days when the teacher has no supervisory duty and thus has remained indoors, the children who have been outside return to the room in various states of readiness to resume their schoolwork. Some are excited, others are tired, a few quite matter-of-factly take their seats, and, almost invariably, one or two have stories to tell the teacher, sometimes tearfully, about what happened on the playground. Many of the stories are about injustice and cruelty. They often include accusations. Martha yanked Sarah's ball away. Freddy pushed Billy and then kicked him when he was down. . . .
>
> Mrs. Martin always takes these incidents seriously, but seldom deals with them privately. Even when she bends down to comfort a crying child, she rarely speaks in subdued tones. Instead, she discusses what happened in a voice that conveys sympathy and concern, and also usually can be heard several feet away, often across the room. . . .
>
> In addition to expressing the teacher's concern, something else seems to me to be conveyed to the class as a whole by the way these brief exchanges are conducted. Their semipublic nature announces to one and all that there are few secrets in this room, few subjects that cannot be talked about openly and loudly enough for everyone to hear. No need to go whispering behind people's backs, accusing them of this or that. Have a complaint? Then speak up and have it dealt with out in the open, the way one might discuss a difficulty one was having in arithmetic or reading. The voice of solace and the voice of instruction are practically indistinguishable. (pp. 51–52)

Jackson believes that the hidden curriculum in Mrs. Martin's room has to do with settling disputes in public and with making her ideals for social interaction an integral, apparent part of her instruction. By considering how other teachers act out a hidden curriculum, perhaps we can consciously consider aspects of teaching that may foster—or hinder—students' growth.

The Null Curriculum

We can think of the *null curriculum* as what students do *not* get a chance to do and to learn. Elliott Eisner sees the null curriculum as "the options students are not afforded, the perspectives they may never know about, much less be able to use, the concepts and skills that are not a part of their intellectual repertoire" (Eisner, 1985, p. 107). Part of the null curriculum is academic. For example, in a 10th-grade class on American history, students may not learn about the bloody conflict during the early years of the U.S. labor movement; in eighth-grade mathematics, they may not be allowed to take algebra; in fifth-grade language arts, they may not learn about root words and the etymology of our language; and in third grade, they may not engage in dramatic play.

Resources play a role in the null curriculum. Depending on how teachers use them, students may have access to some knowledge and experiences and be deprived of others. For example, the textbooks and learning materials teachers use impact the enacted and the null curriculum. Textbooks have mainly conveyed a picture of middle-class society and have neglected the disparities of poverty and great wealth found in our country. If teachers do not use supplementary learning materials to expand the narrow perspective presented by textbooks, they will develop an image of society that provides "a shallow social consciousness and narrow sense of history and culture . . . alienating from school lower-class children and children of color" (Sleeter & Grant, 1991, p. 101).

The null curriculum also relates to students' interactions. When we do not allow students to interact in small groups within a classroom, we are not teaching them how to work cooperatively. When students take no part in keeping the school environment clean or when they are not involved in helping to resolve disputes among students, we are not teaching them how to be environmentally or socially responsible.

In summary, the curriculum assumes different forms at any given point in time. Let's say that a teacher is solving math problems on an overhead projector. The problems deal with skills and concepts that are part of the *formal curriculum*. During this whole-class activity, a student calls out a question without being recognized by the teacher. The formal curriculum in this class includes a rule that "call-outs" are not allowed. The teacher then reminds the student of the rule about call-outs and continues to write on the transparency. The teacher's *ideal curriculum* in situations like this may be that students will take responsibility for their own actions and consider how to change. The student, however, feels frustrated and chagrined. She knows that the teacher often moves through mathematical problems too quickly. The only recourse that results in slowing down the delivery is to interject questions during explanations. A *hidden curriculum* in this classroom may be the implicit message that mathematics is a subject with fixed answers, that the best way to learn is by the teacher being active and the students listening passively. The entire episode constitutes the *enacted curriculum* at that point.

IDEALS CHALLENGE: *Deepening Discourse*

Choose a grade level and a subject area about which to think about the following questions. You might write in response to the questions and then talk with other students about your responses.

- What is your *ideal curriculum*? What should students learn and why should they learn this?

- Come up with four ideals you hold about the school curriculum. Share your ideals with another student, and see where you converge or diverge in your views.
- What was the *formal curriculum* of a teacher or a team of teachers in one of your former schools?
- What was the *enacted curriculum* in a school in which you have taught or have been a student? In a particularly memorable situation, what occurred that was *not* part of the apparent ideal or formal curriculum?
- What was the *hidden curriculum* in your school? What was an implicit message that you or other students picked up? How was this hidden curriculum conveyed?
- What was the *null curriculum* in your school? What was *not* taught or expected of students?

TECHNOLOGY CHALLENGE

Danger on the Internet?

(Excerpted and adapted from Sherman, 1998.)

Education and political leaders regularly call for all schools to be "connected." For most, what constitutes "connected" probably is best expressed in the president's goal of every 12-year-old being able to log on to the Internet. . . .

Until recently, almost no one asked if connecting our classrooms would produce genuine benefits. . . . That our 12-year-olds will be advantaged by getting on the Internet is rarely debated. . . . It is clear that every technology that brings benefits also carries a monetary and social price. . . .

The Internet is a medium with the potential to be more powerful and influential than any to precede it; the great promise to educate may be matched by possible negative consequences. . . . Children clearly should be protected from offensive material that can be accessed easily. But there are more fundamental reasons to be concerned about Internet access for children that are intrinsic to the technology itself rather than to the content delivered over it. It may well be that the Internet is a developmentally inappropriate experience for young children and perhaps for adolescents as well. . . .

To what extent is the Internet consistent with the intellectual capabilities of young children? . . . The following is an analysis of four features that characterize the Internet as a medium and define its promise as a communication technology.

First, the Internet provides virtual rather than actual experiences. . . . [This] may be at odds with the developmental needs of children. Generally, early childhood development emphasizes physical manipulations coordinated with observation and social interaction about the effects of manipulation. . . . It is unclear if virtual manipulation will generate the same intellectual skills and sense of personal agency. . . .

Second, the Web provides quick and easy access to an enormous amount of information. However, it has long been the practice in early childhood development to limit children's access to information. . . . In this way young children are not overwhelmed with information . . . that is inconsistent with their information-processing abilities. . . .

Third, the information on the Web is essentially anarchic. Anyone can post literally anything. . . . The consequence may be that children are less able to discriminate between what is real and is not real, with no means to reality-test any concepts in the virtual world.

Finally, . . . multimedia presentations can be powerful ways to communicate. . . . Children on the Web may be more vulnerable both to overt messages and to subtle or thematic innuendoes . . . [this] may result in distorted interpretations of the complete range of human emotions and broad misunderstanding of nature.

- What do you think about the author's arguments? Do you agree or disagree? Do you believe he is overreacting, or that his concerns are legitimate? What evidence can you provide to support your opinions?
- What are the implications of the author's arguments for the various forms of curriculum?
- What is your leadership responsibility as a teacher in a democratic school to ensure that your school addresses the issues raised by the author?
- How would you proceed in raising awareness and addressing issues raised by the author and/or other issues of Internet access and use?

THE SCOPE AND SEQUENCE OF FORMAL CURRICULUM CHANGES OVER TIME

How can we characterize the contemporary curriculum in American schools? One way to think about curriculum is to consider the *scope* and *sequence*. The scope consists of the information and ideas that make up the curriculum, what teachers metaphorically call the "material" they teach. When we talk about scope we must think about *breadth* and *depth*. Breadth refers to the range of content to be addressed in a curricular approach. The concept of depth expresses how detailed the information and how complex the ideas will be. Teachers are constantly deciding on the scope in terms of breadth and depth, because there are unlimited topics that might be raised but only a limited amount of class time in which to raise them. Should a

What are the things students learn as part of the hidden curriculum of schools?

mathematics teacher spend three weeks on multiplying fractions? Is it better to spend less time on studying cells in October, and more time in April studying environmental effects on animal populations? Often, such questions are phrased in terms of what to "cover" in the curriculum.

IDEALS CHALLENGE: *Achieving Authenticity*

Think back on your most meaningful learning experience as a student in school.

1. Describe for a colleague your most meaningful learning experience. Listen carefully to colleagues describe their experiences.
2. What did your experiences have in common?
3. Do your experiences represent authentic learning? Why or why not? Were any of the following represented in your experiences:

   active learning in real-world contexts that called for higher-order thinking

   consideration of alternatives

   use of core ideas and modes of inquiry in a discipline

   extended writing or speaking

   an audience beyond the school for your work

- Do meaningful learning experiences require more time than superficial topic overviews?
- Would meaningful learning experiences occur if the teacher were only allowed a certain amount of time to cover a topic? Would the learning experience that you described have been as meaningful for you if the time devoted to it had been abbreviated? How much time is enough?
- What does all this have to do with the scope of the curriculum? Who should decide the scope of the curriculum?

Democratic educators believe that "less is more" (e.g., Sizer, 1992). Gardner, Torff, and Hatch (1996) note,

> If we wish to teach for understanding, we have to accept a painful truth: it is simply not possible to cover everything. Indeed, the greatest enemy of understanding is "coverage." Only to the extent that we are willing to choose certain topics as worthy of exploration, and then to devote the time that is needed to explore these topics in depth and from multiple perspectives, is there any possibility that genuine understandings will be widely achieved. (p. 49)

- Do you agree with Gardner, Torff, and Hatch?
- Does the "less is more" philosophy relate to your description of meaningful learning experiences?

Sequence refers to how the curricular subject, concepts, or topics are arranged. Publishers of textbooks and educational resources frequently provide a scope and sequence chart to help the teacher set objectives, and state standards are usually built on a structured scope and sequence agenda. A chart or matrix is not the only way to represent a scope and sequence, however. Teachers (and textbook publishers) also may develop concept webs or maps.

The scope and sequence of curriculum are not necessarily logical or linear. The formal curriculum has been forged from countless historical struggles over issues large and small, national and local. We could write many different histories about how the scope and sequence of the school curriculum has been constructed and reconstructed. There are histories of bodies of information (e.g., the divisions into subject areas), of curricular ideas (e.g., vocational education), and of philosophical beliefs about curriculum (e.g., a "classical" education). In chapter 4 you read about broad philosophical and historical patterns from the past; in the next section you will learn in more detail about the scope and sequence of American curriculum in the last two centuries.

PRESENT TO PAST

Curricular Reforms Through the Years

Curriculum reform may have many different catalysts. In some cases, grassroots efforts by educators have led to the adoption of a new program or to the spread of an idea. Other changes have been spurred by major reports issued by leading groups of educators and by legislative and judicial decisions related to education. Now, we want to introduce you to some of the most influential calls for curricular reform in the last two centuries.

THE CLASSICAL 19TH CENTURY CURRICULUM

Some background information about 19th century curriculum is necessary to understand the implications of curriculum initiatives in the last 100 years. The two most influential curricular announcements in the 19th century portrayed the power of a Western classical approach to curriculum. The Yale Report of 1827 was fashioned by university academicians who wanted to preserve the classical curriculum. They emphasized classical languages, mathematics, and the natural sciences because these subjects disciplined the mind—not because studying Latin or Greek would result in a better job or a more practical understanding of the world. This idea of "mental discipline" was connected with the theory of "faculty psychology," which entailed a belief that reason, will, imagination, moral judgment, and especially memory were faculties that could be strengthened simply by exercising the mind through the study of certain disciplines. Have you ever been told, as we have, that algebra (or some other subject) is "good for you"? This is similar to the idea of faculty psychology.

The Yale Report was written for an elite audience of university professors and high school educators in a time when very few students went to school for any appreciable length of time. During the 19th century, most teachers taught what they wanted, always subject to the pressures of community standards, and the teachers' beliefs about teaching and learning derived from their prior schooling. This localized, personalized curriculum, which was especially evident in one-room schools, came under increasing challenge. Beginning in the mid-1800s, urban school leaders in the United States tried to develop formal curriculum guidelines that were age-graded, sequential, and often tied to early forms of standardized examinations. By the century's end, such approaches to curriculum had a firm foothold in American schools.

Whether or not the curriculum was tightly structured, the actual content in secondary schools remained focused on college preparation. In 1893, the National Education Association issued its *Report of the Committee on Secondary School Studies.* Members of this "Committee of Ten," as it was known, included five university presidents, the present and former U.S. Commissioner of Education, a professor, and two principals. Given the committee's makeup and the powerful beliefs of its leader, Charles W. Eliot, the president of Harvard University, it seemed a foregone conclusion that the committee would focus on academic curriculum suitable for college. Though the committee proposed that high schools offer four tracks for students, there was an obvious preference for classical and modern languages, mathematics, and the traditional approach to natural sciences. There was no mention of art, music, drama, physical education, or vocational education (then called manual training).

Critics such as G. Stanley Hall challenged the committee's assertions that subjects should be taught in the same way to all students and that subjects were primarily of value as a means of "exercising" the mind, along with the committee's unwillingness to incorporate practical studies into the curriculum. As Herbst (1996) notes:

> What the committee deliberately disregarded and excluded from its consideration was that for most Americans the battle over the high school was not one of the classics versus the modern sciences but one of academic culture versus practical training—the well-known confrontation between those who wanted to prepare for college and those who wanted to prepare for life. (p. 115)

This confrontation (or confusion), perhaps in a more muted form, still characterizes debates over curriculum today in vocational education, and initiatives such as Tech Prep and School-to-Work.

IDEALS CHALLENGE: *Initiating Inquiry*

Using the Internet, ERIC (an educational resources data base available at all university libraries and usually online through the university's Internet home page), your local school district, your state department of public instruction, and other sources, learn more about school-to-work. What is it? What do proponents argue are its good points? What arguments and cautions do opponents cite? What other advantages or disadvantages can you identify? How do you believe it relates to democratic IDEALS?

Seven months after the appointment of the Committee of Ten, the Committee of Fifteen on Elementary Education began its deliberations. William T. Harris, a renowned superintendent of schools from St. Louis and the first U.S. Commissioner of Education, chaired the committee. From 1893 to 1895, its members struggled to develop an appropriate curriculum for elementary school students. In the end, they settled for a curriculum that focused on grammar, literature and art, mathematics, geography, and history—just the sort of subjects to prepare students for high school. The committee also introduced Latin and other languages, as well as algebra, into the elementary curriculum. Such a vision did not deal with the reality that a very small percentage of students even attended high school, much less college, but that they would still be citizens and workers in the society. It would take another 20 years for the next major commission to propose a more "present-oriented" curriculum.

LIBERAL CURRICULUM IN THE 20TH CENTURY

American educational leaders—those who promoted their vision of an ideal curriculum—had traditionally refused to consider manual training or vocational education as part of formal education. In the first two decades of the 20th century, however, many school-level educators pushed for vocational education to be a part of the school curriculum. Not more than half of students who entered school in the late 1800s completed eight grades. While children, especially the children of new immigrants, left school in order to augment their family's income, the majority of students left school because they disliked being there. The Committee of Ten's plans for a college-oriented curriculum did not address the interests of the students who perceived school as having little value and who had no intention of attending college.

The most influential curriculum report was issued by the Commission for the Reorganization of Secondary Education, which held meetings from 1913 to 1922 to review the state of American education and offer a vision for the future. Unlike the previous committees' decidedly professorial look, the commission's 26 members represented diverse positions in education (although there was only one woman and no ethnic minorities).

In 1918 the committee published a curriculum report, *Cardinal Principles of Secondary Education,* which opposed major tenets of the classical curriculum and proposed an alternative. The committee chair, Clarence Kingsley, a Massachusetts high school supervisor, emphasized the importance of democracy and efficiency for education. Kingsley and other committee members adhered to the idea of "scientific curriculum building," meaning that curriculum would be "constructed from small, concrete objectives that corresponded to specific activities that particular adults performed in their lives. . . . Efficiency in education meant to find the most perfect fit between instruction and what were considered the needs of students and society" (Herbst, 1997, pp. 144–145). The committee's definition of students' "needs" are evident in the seven cardinal principles: (1) health, (2) the "three R's," (3) "worthy home-membership," (4) vocation, (5) citizenship, (6) "the worthy use of leisure," and (7) "conduct founded upon right principles." Notice how the school was being asked to venture beyond its well-traveled territory. Students' everyday lives—including family life and how students used their "free time"—were now to be accounted for in the school curriculum. Coupled with the political progressives' push for more social services in schools, the overall effect was to strengthen the image of schools as the primary social agency of the society. We still live with this image of schools as the salvation of the society and with the enlargement of teachers' responsibilities for students' lives.

As a result of the *Cardinal Principles of Secondary Education,* there arose the notion of high schools as "comprehensive" institutions that would combine academic and vocational concerns. The subsequent expansion of vocational programs resulted in a quandary: How could homogeneous grouping, separate classes for students who had been tested and labeled as "slow," and specialized vocational programs coexist with the ideal of a democratic institution where students from all backgrounds stood on common ground? In comprehensive high schools the "college-prep" programs would assume a privileged status and vocational tracks would be seen as inferior.

The committee also proposed that there be three levels of schooling: elementary school and two levels of secondary school (which were called junior high school and high school). An "academic" curriculum should be introduced in earlier grades, and all children should be required to attend six years of elementary school. The junior high school should introduce departmental instruction, electives, and prevocational courses in order to serve as a bridge between the elementary school and the high school.

As you can see, the *Cardinal Principles* provided the outline for much of our current approach to curriculum. Many school districts across the country accepted the recommendations and instituted a broader curriculum, junior high schools, and the comprehensive high school. There remained, however, controversies about curriculum. Kliebard (1995) gives a good description of varying reform groups, which he calls "social efficiency," "developmentalism," and "social reconstructionism":

> Three seemingly irreconcilable reform thrusts were represented. One derived its impetus from the standards of adult living . . . and sought to reorient the curriculum in the direction of preparing children and youth for a distinct adult role. A second took the immediate life of the child as the starting point, and essentially discarded the subject matter whether traditional or directly utilitarian, and conceived of the curriculum as the forum where the child can realize his or her own purposes. . . . [A third movement] derived its central thrust from the undercurrent of discontent about the American economic and social system. That last movement, establishing itself under the banner of social reconstructionism by the 1930s, saw the curriculum as the vehicle by which social injustice would be redressed and the evils of capitalism corrected. (p. 158)

People promoting social efficiency pushed for better vocational programs and the more efficient organization of school curriculum. The other two groups are associated with innovative schools in the early part of the century.

THE LAST 50 YEARS

In the last 50 years there have been various curriculum reform efforts that in one way or another mirror what happened in the early 20th century. The Council on Basic Education, formed in 1956 to push for a "return" to basic skills, was a classical reaction to earlier ideas. Arthur Bestor, a historian, argued that the curriculum should be organized around the structure of subject matter disciplines and called the schools' focus on socialization and vocational preparation "anti-intellectual." A more utilitarian and economically based approach arose after the Soviet Union launched Sputnik I, the first space satellite, in October 1957. Congress passed the National Defense Education Act (NDEA), which promoted mathematics and science education in an effort to match the technological advances of the USSR. In addition, President Eisenhower pushed for federal funds to enhance and expand the teaching of foreign languages and research in education, and vastly increased the federal role in funding research projects and educational programs.

What are the advantages and disadvantages of a "back to the basics" curriculum?

The political turmoil of the 1960s led to further curriculum reforms. Teachers and schools, already burdened with mandates to expand the curriculum, were told they had to meet the special needs of poor children in order to help fight President Johnson's "War on Poverty." At the same time, other educational critics attacked the rigidity and narrowness of the curriculum. One such critique was Charles Silberman's scathing study of American schools, *Crisis in the Classroom,* published in 1970. While the "basic educators" had seen a school curriculum that was unfocused or not attuned to the country's economic needs, Silberman saw in the same sorts of schools a deadening and limited curriculum that did not foster children's creativity or address fundamental social issues. Silberman called for "open classrooms" and alternative schools, which in many ways resembled the experimental schools of the progressive era. A third approach to contemporary reform can be read in *A Nation at Risk*, published in 1983. This book laid the problems of society at the feet of schools (who were accused of putting the nation "at risk"). The report indicted the American educational system for failing to educate students in the basics and in the new technologies needed to be a worker in the booming information economy. The call for more testing and stronger mathematics and science education echoed Eisenhower's words from 25 years earlier.

One point to be made here is that the groundwork for all such reforms was done between the 1890s and the 1940s. Schools across America have many more similarities than differences. Today, we have a five-part organization of schooling: preschool, elementary school, middle or junior high school, high school, and higher education (only preschool is a recent addition to the structure, and it is not universal). School leaders still predominantly divide the curriculum into four "core" subjects (language arts, mathematics, science, and social studies), along with "elective" or "exploratory" subjects (e.g., the arts, physical education, vocational education, industrial arts, home economics, computer/media education, and foreign languages). This division accords status to the core subjects, which are required of all students nearly every year until they graduate from high school. Such an organization also de-emphasizes apprenticeships with adults and neglects certain components of the Western classical curriculum, such as drama, art, and foreign languages.

You can see that the school curriculum in the United States has changed over time, while the tensions between competing perspectives and aims have continued. Other countries have developed a "modern" curriculum, but their curricular decisions may differ from ours. Mexican curriculum is a good example of a different approach.

GLOBAL CHALLENGE

A Nationalized Curriculum

(Excerpted from Martin, 1994, pp. 49–51.)

The most remarkably consistent feature of classroom teaching in Mexico must be the following of the subject matter as set down in the national textbook in all schools throughout the country. This is remarkable not only for the degree of uniformity that this implies ... but also because so many other aspects of the Mexican educational system do not display the same degree of uniformity.... [E]very child receives a free series of textbooks. This is the keystone of Mexican curriculum implementation.

The most recent set of textbooks appeared in 1992.... These texts are based on an integrated or "global" approach to learning in the sense that subject divisions are down-played in an overall attempt to connect different skills to different areas of knowledge through an emphasis on themes.

At all levels and in all phases of the school curriculum, what stands out ... is the extent to which the teacher is made to conform to specified learning modules to a greater extent than before. This is effected in the first place by a meticulous periodization of learning matter into units.... The result is a set of graded units grouped around themes in which key skills predominate.

Public criticism has questioned the value of the changes in the primary school curriculum over the last 15 years or so, of which the 1992 textbooks are but the most recent example. An earlier change ... was the introduction of the so-called "new maths," which until recently was the preferred system of the current textbooks.... [T]he frequent changes to the curriculum cause greater losses than gains when one considers the disruption created for teachers, pupils, and parents, whose previous knowledge is continually and perhaps unnecessarily being rendered obsolete by such changes.

- What would be the benefits and the drawbacks of having a national curriculum, in which all children at a certain grade level receive the same free textbooks?
- To what extent do you think that individual teachers or teacher teams should be required to conform to curriculum guidelines set down by a centralized agency such as a state or federal government?
- What do you think the author means when he says that "previous knowledge is ... being rendered obsolete by such changes"? Can you think of an example in our country where that might be happening?

Changes in Subject Areas

There have also been changes over time *within* subject areas, and again those changes were initiated in the early part of this century (Popkewitz, 1987). To make the point, let's take a look at what has happened in the subject of social studies.

In the traditional 19th-century approach to curriculum, history, geography, and possibly government were taught as separate subjects. Noah Webster's readers, with titles such as *The Little Reader's Assistant*, were one of the primary curriculum resources for elementary schools, and there were hundreds of different textbooks that vied for adoption in the country's far-flung school districts.

In the first few decades of this century, sociology, economics, psychology, and political science began to emerge as separate studies in colleges and universities. Strong arguments were made that there ought to be a new school subject that would integrate geography and history with the rising disciplines. At the same time, there were debates about whether history should remain simply an academic study of the past. James Harvey

Robinson, a dissident historian, spoke for a group who believed that learning history should contribute to one's understanding of modern social conditions and of ways to improve the present (Smith, Palmer, & Correia, 1995, p. 396).

Some educators finally tried to face the swirling arguments about the social sciences curriculum. In 1913 the Commission for the Reorganization of Secondary Education (which created the *Cardinal Principles*) appointed a Committee on Social Science, later renamed the Committee on Social Studies. In a 1916 report the committee proclaimed that good citizenship should be the purpose of a new subject called "social studies," and that a "problems of democracy" course for seniors in high school should be the capstone experience to enable students to examine modern social problems. The committee had come down firmly on the side of James Harvey Robinson and the proponents of a unified social science curriculum.

The term "social studies" has continued to be used, although not without controversy, and several ideas within the subject have proven to be provocative. Jerome Bruner (1960) and various social scientists in the late 1950s promoted the notion that the "structure of the disciplines" (the major concepts, theories, and especially methods of investigating the world) should provide the structure for social studies. The "new social studies" emphasized the use of original source documents, methods of student inquiry, and higher-level conceptual thinking (Greenawald, 1995, p. 420). This led to discussions, which still continue, about the extent to which social studies should center on citizenship education or the disciplinary structures, and on the balance between transmitting given social values and inquiring in ways that might challenge those values.

Furthermore, other educators argued that the sequence of social studies should be based on an "expanding horizons" approach, in which young children would initially study family and community life, then gradually expand their horizons by learning about American culture and history in the intermediate grades, and finally by sixth grade enter into a study of life in other countries. This idea has been criticized for its developmental assumptions about when children are able to gain a historical perspective or imagine life in other environments.

IDEALS CHALLENGE: *Initiating Inquiry*

(Excerpted from Leonard, 1998, e-mail.)

In 1996, the American Political Science Association organized a task force, consisting of top political scientists from around the country, to examine the issue of mounting political apathy in the United States and to study the responsibilities of teachers and professors who have chosen to teach politics as their profession in addressing the problem. Preliminary findings of the Task Force include:

1. Teaching "about government" will not in itself provide the political education we need.
2. "Value neutrality" must be adjusted in the civics education classroom to reflect the need to promote and enhance basic democratic values.

3. Reliance on "critical thinking," without a moral framework within which to think critically, may be part of the problem. [This lack of a framework] feeds unhealthy cynicism and political disengagement rather than healthy skepticism.

4. If we are to teach politics as the practice of competent and effective problem solving in human groups, then we must also teach tolerance, collaboration, analysis, and our traditions.

5. Factual political knowledge can only become meaningful in political practice when presented within a valuation framework; therefore, we must teach the specific virtues on which effective political practice depends.

The Task Force concludes with the following: "We believe we must unequivocally teach the value of democratic aspirations to human liberation and human dignity. Without this framework, our descriptions of political facts and political virtues will not inspire and motivate people to the level of civic engagement that a healthy democratic polity requires."

- Discuss each of the statements above. Do you agree with the Task Force's preliminary findings?
- If the Task Force's findings are implemented, how might a social studies or political science curriculum differ from the status quo? What might a "valuation framework" look like?
- In what ways might a "valuation framework" make the curriculum meaningful to students?
- What effect might it have on developing democratic school communities?

All subject areas have a history. The continual controversies about the content of subject areas—their scope and sequence—are vital for us to consider. They remind us that decisions about what gets taught are not merely handed down from some higher authority. At the end of all the talking and reporting by curricular committees, individual teachers in classrooms across the country decide what materials to use and what content to stress. The more you understand about what curriculum our educational ancestors have proposed and argued about, the more choices you'll know you have in constructing a worthwhile curriculum.

Connecting the Curriculum

In addition to scope and sequence, there are three other important curricular concepts that relate to how the curriculum is connected. *Articulation* has to do with how closely the curriculum will be connected within a certain subject area and across years. This issue becomes especially important when students move from one level of schooling to another. For example, it is difficult enough for elementary school teachers to communicate with one another about the progression of the science curriculum from kindergarten through fifth grade. It becomes quite a task for teachers to talk about the changes and continuities in curriculum between fifth grade in elementary school and sixth grade in a separate middle school.

Another key curricular concept is *balance*, which refers to the relative standing and emphasis given to different subjects in the curriculum. In elementary schools, many hours are devoted to teaching students how to read and do mathematics, some regular time is devoted to physical education and the arts, and science and social studies are often taught in a haphazard fashion. In junior high schools and middle schools, science and social studies are legitimated by making them part of the core curriculum (along with language arts and mathematics), while the arts and other subjects are demoted to mere electives that can even be omitted when school boards face tight economic times.

To determine a balance in the curriculum (thus assigning priority to certain subjects and not to others), high schools across the country use the concept of "Carnegie Unit." Each Carnegie Unit, which is defined as a minimum of 120 instructional hours, constitutes one high school credit. High schools commonly demand 20–23 units of credit for students in the "college prep" track. The usual balance in this curriculum is to require 3–4 units of language arts (called "English" in many schools), mathematics, science, and social studies. There are frequently 2 units of foreign language and 1 unit of physical education, while the remainder of the required units may be electives. Students not in the college prep track will take some other courses and they may have a different balance among the subject areas. You might note how the null curriculum is represented in the idea of balance in course work. Where is science in third grade? Where is foreign language in seventh grade? Where is drama in 10th grade? Where is a vocational curriculum at any level of schooling? People might argue that the curriculum is "out of balance" if these curriculum areas are not offered or not required.

A third concept, *integration*, connotes how different aspects of the entire school curriculum are brought together or "integrated." On one level, integration may involve teachers ensuring that their students, for example, write in all the subject areas, so that they recognize the value of writing skills and the need to write in various contexts. On a deeper level, integration may represent a challenge to the traditional patterns of separate subject areas and practices of top-down curricular guidelines. For example, there are teachers who develop, sometimes in negotiation with their students, a thematic curriculum that incorporates content from many subjects. The themes or problems chosen may be derived from students' concerns and interests. In this light, curriculum integration may be seen as a way to connect the curriculum with students' nonschool experiences or with community life.

The idea of curriculum integration has been around for a long time (using phrases such as "correlation of curriculum" and "core curriculum"), and especially in the past 10 years there has been a great deal of writing about integrating the curriculum. The IDEALS Challenge that follows is an example of one teacher, Steven Levy (1996), writing about how he integrates curriculum.

IDEALS CHALLENGE: *Learning Leadership*

(Steven Levy is a teacher in Lexington, Massachusetts. During the 1992–93 school year he embarked upon a grand curriculum journey. He and his teaching partner decided to confront the incoming fourth-grade students with a completely empty classroom and develop a curriculum around creating an environment! Here is part of the proposal to colleagues at the school, which includes Levy's rationale for doing this, his ideas for how the curriculum might be integrated, and some former students' comments.)

The curriculum we are required to teach is vast and fragmented. Each different department (math, science, language arts, social studies, reading, and, more recently, life skills) has independently developed a curriculum for each grade level. Thus, what is taught in one discipline is not related to what is taught in another. Units often come packaged in textbook kits. Not only do they lack integration with each other, they often lack relevance to the child's real world. . . . (p. 182)

Our first subject of study would be the classroom environment. We would begin the year with no furniture or supplies. The children would come together and the first order of business would be to anticipate equipment and supplies we would need for the year and design an environment for learning. We would purchase our own supplies and would build the furniture needed for work space and storage with the help of retired carpenters in the community.

For funding we would turn to the Pilgrims for guidance. We study their voyage in the fourth grade social studies curriculum, and how they settled in the new world. How did they fund their journey? They got individuals and businesses to invest. We would re-create their ingenuity and perseverance. We would begin by selling shares in the fourth grade class to local businesses and citizens. . . . The price of the original shares would be paid back to the owners at the end of the year after a culminating gala event, at which we serve dinner, entertain, and liquidate all our assets in a raffle.

Here are just a few of the curriculum ideas that could arise from such a project:

MATH

Estimating materials needed for the year: how many pencils?

Accounting and business: planning events, keeping records, setting up a class bank account, allocating funds to different projects, determining profit margins.

Measurement in furniture design and manufacturing.

SCIENCE

Where do the materials we need to use in the class come from? How are they produced? Where? By whom? What effect does that have on our environment?

Simple machines in tools we use to construct equipment.

How people and animals create spaces for themselves.

Inventions.

SOCIAL STUDIES

We would experience firsthand what the Pilgrims faced in starting from scratch in a new land.

Tremendous opportunity to practice cooperation, compromise, democracy, listening to each other, working together, social skills in a real-life context.

The environment: what we use and how we use it . . . (pp. 180–181).

I once had a reunion with a class two years after they had graduated from fourth grade. I wanted to hear what they remembered. . . . Here's what I found out:

They were able to articulate my interdisciplinary approach: "We liked the way you mooshed all the subjects together."

They caught the authentic nature of the curriculum: "We got to apply the stuff you taught us to real life. I mean, like, it wasn't just in a, like, book."

They appreciated the way we involved the community: "We worked harder and more carefully because we thought that people out there cared about what we did" (p. 160).

- The children—along with parents and community members—did literally construct the desks, chairs, and other things needed for the classroom. What do you think about this idea?
- In what different ways is the curriculum in Mr. Levy's class "integrated"?
- What other ways could you think of to integrate the curriculum?
- What problems do you see in Mr. Levy's approach to the curriculum?

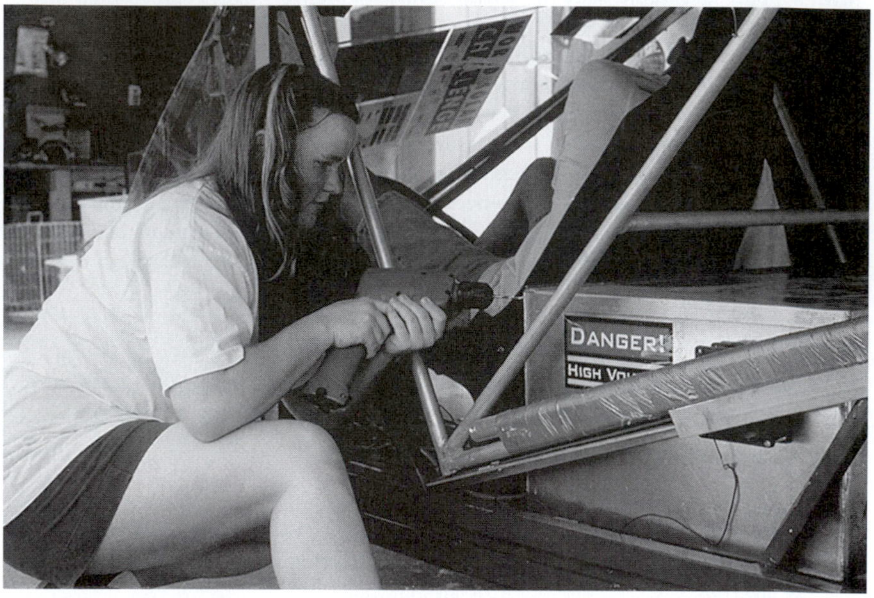

How might the teacher of this student integrate curriculum around the activity in which the student is involved?

THE RESPONSIBILITY FOR DEVELOPING FORMAL CURRICULUM IS SHARED

As the previous writing on the history of social studies showed, many people have been involved in developing and shaping curriculum to its current state. We should not assume that there has been constant progress or an easy consensus. Indeed, there has been historical conflict and struggle over what sort of knowledge is seen as most worthy of being "school knowledge," and who gets to determine what constitutes "legitimate" knowledge in schools. The following section deals with influences on the curriculum, the nature of curriculum standards, and decision making.

Stakeholders in the Curriculum

The societal context, as we have detailed throughout this book, affects the development of curriculum. Many citizens and school participants today define themselves as "stakeholders" in the curriculum process. The stakeholders are people "attempting to influence the allocation of resources or intended direction of the school system" (Mauriel, 1989). Stakeholders may be individuals, groups, businesses, institutions, and government officials.

On a national level, institutional influences on the curriculum include *private foundations, nonprofit lobbying groups,* and *professional organizations.* The Southern Poverty Law Center, National Parent-Teacher Association, Citizens for Excellence in Education, People for the American Way, National Education Association, and American Federation of Teachers, all with widely differing political stances and philosophies of education, vie for influence. Likewise, professional organizations related to subject areas (such as science), grade levels in schools (such as elementary school organizations), and curriculum topics (such as multicultural education) develop curriculum standards and attempt to shape the formal curriculum.

There are also *national, regional,* and *local businesses* that feel they have a stake in the school curriculum. Nationally, the three major business groups that influence the curriculum are textbook publishers, makers of standardized tests, and media companies. Publishers market books, workbooks, computer software, audiovisual materials, and many more educational items. Each textbook series promotes its own scope and sequence, which often parallels the current curriculum guidelines of its largest purchasers. Texts outline in detail how to introduce, practice, and assess student skills. Texts are modified to be more appealing to populous, growing states such as California, Texas, and Florida that have statewide adoption of textbooks. These giant markets may have an inhibiting effect on the content of textbooks and other resources (Haynes & Chalker, 1997, p. 24). Publishers are understandably reluctant to risk losing sales by including topics that might be controversial or dissatisfactory to their best customers.

Producers of standardized tests are also curriculum stakeholders. Educational Testing Service, the largest such company in the country, publishes the Scholastic Aptitude Test (SAT). This test was developed in the 1940s, and since the 1960s has been used widely by universities to make judgments about which students are admitted. There is much debate about the extent to which teachers "teach to the [standardized] test," by mimicking the test's objectives and gearing class instruction directly to improving students' test scores.

Media companies like Whittle Communications (the producers of Channel One), or television programs like Sesame Street, may also affect the curriculum. Media are a direct part of the curriculum whenever students and teachers tune into Channel One or teachers assign students to watch a particular television program. Students' ideas and information derived from television indirectly affect how they respond to the school curriculum. There is a continuing concern that more students now have a "television" mentality, and only feel compelled to learn when they are being entertained by someone.

State governments are powerful participants in the curriculum process. Formal curriculum guides are prepared by state department of education staff in conjunction with advisory groups of curriculum consultants, professors, and selected teachers and community members. Most guides contain curriculum goals and provide an outline or a map to describe the scope and sequence for different subjects at specific grade levels.

In addition, state funding decisions made by legislators have a direct effect on what curriculum gets offered to students. Some states, such as North Carolina, have sponsored a school for the arts, while in other states there have been severe cutbacks in funding for the arts. The Kentucky Education Reform Act is an example of a statewide initiative to reform curriculum that is having an effect on what and how students are learning.

Local school districts also have a stake in the curriculum. District educational officials, who may include subject area specialists, determine how state guidelines will be implemented. Many times in larger urban and suburban communities, the district will develop its own version of curriculum objectives. Districts typically appoint parents and other community members to serve with teachers and administrators on committees that make decisions about films to be used in schools and about potentially controversial topics such as sex education. These committees not only establish procedures (e.g., for teachers to order films that have been approved by the committee), they may also shape what can and cannot be taught (e.g., information about contraceptives).

Local civic and religious groups also are involved in the curriculum process. Such groups have been largely reactive, ready to protest if certain curricular resources offend their sense of what is best. Textbook adoptions, for example, have been influenced by the concerns of parents who want to see more multicultural representation, as well as those who are concerned that creationism have a status equal to that of evolutionary theory.

Teachers, support staff, and administrators in schools understandably influence curriculum. Teams of teachers sit on committees to choose texts for their school (even when there is statewide adoption of textbooks, local districts have a choice of which approved text to use). Schoolwide committees, grade-level groups, and interdisciplinary teams of teachers discuss the scope and sequence in different subject areas, how to articulate the curriculum from year to year, and sometimes how to integrate the curriculum across subject areas.

Parents and students certainly affect curriculum. In addition to being part of an organized civic group, individual parents may express a concern about some curricular topic, offer materials for the teacher to use, volunteer to speak in class, or take other steps toward being part of the formal and enacted curriculum.

Last but certainly not least, teachers on a daily basis construct and reconstruct the curriculum by the on-the-spot decisions they make about what to emphasize and what to de-emphasize as they interact with their students. Thus, at the most fundamental level, students' questions and comments direct the enacted curriculum via teacher decision making during the act of teaching.

Curriculum Standards

Local, State, and National Curriculum Standards

The stakeholders just discussed have all tried, in some form or another, to determine what students should know and be able to do. Guided by a set of National Education Goals developed in President Bush's term in office, his successor, President Clinton, also supported national standards. In

1994, the goals were formalized by Congress in the "Goals 2000: Educate America Act." During a speech to the Maryland legislature, President Clinton (1997) highlighted his reasons for setting federal standards:

> Let me say the most important thing we can do in education is to hold our students to high standards. . . . When 40% of our third graders are not reading as well as they should . . . we have a lot to do. When students in Germany or Singapore learn 15 to 20 math subjects in depth each year, while our students typically race through 30 to 35 without learning any in depth in a given year, we aren't doing what we should be doing to prepare them for a knowledge economy that demands that they be able to think and reason and analyze. . . . To compete and win in the 21st century, we must have a high standard of excellence that all states agree on. That is why I called, in my State of the Union address, for national standards of excellence in the basics—not federal government standards, but national standards representing what all our students must know to succeed in a new century.

You can detect a number of themes in the president's speech. The focus on economic purposes, the demand for depth of knowledge, the emphasis on thinking skills—all represent fundamental ideas about curriculum in the 20th century.

Standards From Professional Organizations

Professional organizations also set curriculum standards. Some organizations focus on subject area standards (e.g., the National Council for Teachers of English), while others support learning for a certain age range (e.g., the National Association for the Education of Young Children). In addition to their work on standards, professional organizations may influence curriculum by publishing journals, making research available to the public, developing Internet Web sites to dispense information, offering grants for teachers and schools, conducting state and national conferences or workshops, helping to support affiliate organizations for university students, initiating task forces that target certain concerns, and lobbying for passage of pertinent legislation. These groups have a large influence on what comes to be seen as the "best" curriculum in a particular subject area, and they are vital resources for anyone interested in curriculum and in educational issues.

Curricular Decision Making

On What Basis Are Decisions Made About Curriculum?

Decisions about the makeup of the formal curriculum are quite complex. Although there is some agreement from state-to-state and district-to-district about curriculum, there are also some differences in interpretations about what the curriculum should be and why it should emphasize certain information or skills. Let's listen to another part of the conversation between Mr. Guy and Meghan, in this case about how curriculum is constructed and the role of teachers.

CLICK ON IT

Visit the Web sites of the following organizations that have published highly publicized curriculum standards in recent years and find information about the curriculum standards proposed by each.

National Council of Teachers of Mathematics

http://www.nctm.org

National Council of Teachers of English

http://www.ncte.org

National Council for the Social Studies

http://www.ncss.org

National Center for History in the Schools

http://www.ssnet.ucla.edu/nchs/>

IDEALS CHALLENGE: *Learning Leadership*

WHO CREATES THE CURRICULUM IN YOUR SCHOOL?

Mr. Guy: The school board approves it in this district. Well, the state does that, with the QCC [a set of state guidelines], and the school board adds to it. We buy the materials from somebody whose objectives correlate with what we're supposed to teach. Teacher representatives from the schools made a recommendation to the superintendent about textbooks, then the school board okayed it. What we teach, in a basic sense, is not up to the teacher because other people make decisions. But we decide how to do it.

Meghan: And the teachers talk about it on the teams, so they can be on the same wavelength. The teacher decides the extent, and they decide on creative ways to teach.

Mr. Guy: That's a nice point. Our curriculum used to be a mile wide and an inch deep; now it's going to be a foot wide and a mile deep.

WHAT PART DO STUDENTS PLAY IN THE CURRICULUM?

Mr. Guy: The pace. You either go back, if they don't get it, or move on. Also, the depth; if there's interest, you take the time. So it's monitoring students' interest and motivation—

Meghan: —And performance.

Mr. Guy: Yes—and then making internal decisions. "Tomorrow, we'll stay on this." I do that a lot. I plan on the weekends. But the plans are a starting point, not an ending point. The more experience you have as a teacher, the more accurate judgments you can make.

Meghan: It's also how he tests us to determine how well we've done. Maybe it's a multiple choice test with discussion questions. Or a project. How he monitors our progress is affected by this. And we always ask questions!

- How do Mr. Guy and Meghan differ in how they talk about the curriculum?
- Do you agree with them about the part that students do play—and should play—in the curriculum?
- In this school, teams of 2–4 teachers meet frequently to discuss what they are doing and to determine how they wish to collaborate across the different subject areas. How might the leadership of such teacher teams affect curriculum development?

Mr. Guy described the top-down nature of curriculum development in his district and state, which is certainly not unlike many other areas of the country. In the past 25 years state departments of education have become more assertive about requiring school districts to adhere to state curriculum standards. However, in many districts, particularly in large districts, local officials have produced their own renditions of state standards. Schoolwide committees and subject area groups of teachers then hone the curricular objectives. Individual teachers and teacher teams further develop the formal classroom curriculum in the form of written plans.

How Do Teachers Make Curriculum Decisions?

In the end, after numerous stakeholders have had some impact on what becomes the formal curriculum guidelines, teachers have to interpret what information, skills, and attitudes are important for their students to learn. Think of all the possible ways that teachers might approach the curriculum. They could make judgments according to certain criteria and ask the following questions:

What are the standards of the community? This is a question that might be asked out of worry ("If I show this film, will I get nine phone calls tonight?") or, out of a desire to connect with people in the community ("What do parents want their children to learn, and what are they learning outside of school?").

What is the structure and what are the most important ideas of my discipline or subject? This question focuses on subject area knowledge. When teachers make long-range plans, no matter how open-ended the plans may be, they think about scope and sequence questions like this one.

What are society's economic needs and what are my students' vocational possibilities? This question concerns the practical outcomes of schooling. Elementary school teachers may be less likely than high school teachers to ask this question, because at the secondary level teachers are faced directly with students dropping out and making crucial career decisions. Still, most teachers consider at some point the future vocations of their students.

According to their developmental level, when will the students be ready for this curriculum content? This question leads us to consider issues such as when to formally teach reading, when to teach algebra, and whether we should use a more structured, academic curriculum with kindergartners. Individual teachers frequently ask themselves this question about certain information or ideas.

What are the talents and interests of students? One response to this question is to offer "exploratories" and "electives" so that students can identify and broaden their interests. Many teachers have built entire curricula around this question.

What factors do teachers consider when they interpret curriculum guidelines?

What are the societal problems that need to be addressed? This broader question may lead to involving students in social learning and perhaps social action of some sort.

Whatever questions teachers ask themselves—whatever their curricular approach—teachers have to consider the local context when they develop their plans and enact the curriculum. How much will they depart from the curriculum outlines developed at the state and district levels? Are they willing to take a risk by bringing in guest speakers and offering supplementary curriculum materials? Will they talk about evolution, race, and other controversial topics in our society?

We think the answers to these challenging questions depend on certain social and pedagogical beliefs, and on the conditions of teaching. Teachers face novel challenges posed by our increasingly complex society. They have been asked to teach more topics in each subject area than ever before, while administrators and parents monitor and sometimes challenge what gets included in the curriculum. The following IDEALS Challenge portrays how a teacher addresses these issues.

IDEALS CHALLENGE: *Learning Leadership*

(Excerpted from Cunat, 1996, pp. 136–137. The writer, Mary Cunat, teaches in a private religious school in Chicago. She describes how the faculty at her school tried to develop curriculum in a new way.)

For me, one of the biggest impediments to democratic teaching is a safe, known, "commonsense" form of security. . . . I know myself to be a teacher invested, theoretically and practically, in reflective and democratic activities. But I often take the more convenient route: using prepackaged materials and scripted teacher manuals, following stated "guidelines." The complexities, demands, and frustrations of being a classroom teacher are frequently overwhelming. Planning to do the next page in the text is so much less work and takes so much less energy, and there is little risk to me professionally. There is also little risk in coercing students to behave "appropriately"; it's always safe to dress "professionally"; it's wonderful to work diligently at improving standardized test scores. But do not take chances in allowing students to question authority. Don't go against the trends. Don't make waves. Democracy in the classroom could be dangerous. . . .

Unfortunately, at the local level it always seems to boil down to what is easiest, most convenient, and looks best on paper. Textbooks are chosen, and the written objectives are established by the scope and sequence provided by the textbook series.

Until recently. Somehow, the message finally got through that we as a faculty could determine what and how we want to teach in the area of religious education. . . . I led an in-service session primarily for reflection and brainstorming about what the individuals on our faculty wanted under the general topics. Further steps were taken to get input from parents. Administratively the idea was to refrain from giving parents "too much" space for input because that could complicate things. Asking for student input was not even a consideration. Nevertheless, the progress in giving teachers the responsibility to set their own objectives, inviting parents to express their ideas and concerns, and then choosing a text that would be closest to what was desired was a big step in a more democratic direction.

A complaint I hear frequently about teaching is that there is more and more to teach and less time to teach it in. That is why the choice of what and how to teach is so vital. I've tried so many times as a classroom teacher to "fit" it all in, to the detriment of my own sanity and the real education of my students. . . . Classroom life is becoming even more intense as schools bravely deal with the issues facing children and society today. These issues include violence, poverty, homelessness, child abuse, drug abuse . . . racism, crime, pollution, injustice, unemployment, and so on. . . . I believe that my school is struggling and grappling with these issues. . . . As a democratic educator I am glad to be part of this process. But the very breadth of the demands placed on me often forces me to choose the convenient route, going for what seems the quickest and most "effective strategies," leaving me little time and energy to reflect.

- What is the usual process of curriculum development in Mary Cunat's school? How does she think curriculum should be developed?
- In what ways was the development of religious curriculum a democratic process? How was it not truly democratic?
- What makes it difficult for teachers to be leaders in developing curriculum? How can they combat those difficulties?

You can see from the previous story that making decisions about curriculum involves our basic philosophical beliefs about schools, knowledge, and society. To what extent should teachers "follow the textbook" or "teach to the test" or adhere to the curricular guidelines set by district and state officials? How should teachers' interests and understandings about what is important knowledge be a part of curriculum development? And where do parents and students fit into the equation? How should educators deal with conflict over the curriculum? These are all essential questions that will continue to face us in the coming years.

CURRICULUM IS CULTURAL

Curriculum is also a cultural artifact, a representation of the beliefs, knowledge, and ways of thinking that have been assigned legitimacy by educators. As you read in the historical section of this chapter, parts of the curriculum have changed over time. In the United States in 1901, most students were expected to know Latin; in 2001, most students will be expected to learn how to use computers. There also may be disagreement about the nature of knowledge. In some groups and societies, knowledge is a "thing," perhaps the right answer on a multiple-choice test. Other societies may see knowledge as shifting, contextual "understandings," or believe that knowledge is shown by what young people can *do* in society. People may also disagree about exactly what knowledge should be taught in the official formal curriculum. Will the beliefs and customs of local culture be represented in the curriculum?

These are not matters decided by debates in a rational public forum. People from different cultural groups have long struggled to have their knowledge and interests represented in the curriculum, and have challenged local and national policies affecting them. We want you to think about three main ideas concerning culture and curriculum: *assimilation*, *integration*, and *separation*. To what extent should we assimilate students into mainstream society by holding to a common core of knowledge in the school curriculum? How can we integrate diverse cultural knowledge into the school curriculum? Should there be a separate curriculum that represents a "single studies" or ethnocentric approach to culture and curriculum?

Stirring the Melting Pot: Cultural Assimilation and the Curriculum

Assimilation is a process of socializing people so they fit into the dominant social norms and patterns of behavior. The objective of assimilation is make members of minority cultural groups "similar" to those who belong to the dominant cultural group in society.

Schools in every society transmit cultural knowledge, assumptions, and preferences in order to assimilate students from varying backgrounds. In societies consisting of multiple ethnic groups, there is usually a group whose culture dominates the school curriculum. For 150 years, public schools in American have transmitted cultural knowledge derived from Western Europe and from ancient Greece and Rome, but reshaped into a peculiarly American culture. When there was a tremendous influx of immigrants earlier in this century, some educators called for an even more overt process of "Americanization," so that the newcomers would be assimilated into a national culture.

School knowledge today is really an amalgam of classical and modern curriculum. In the same classroom, children may learn scientific classification and study about AIDS. They also learn ways of speaking and writing, along with information and ideas that portray what certain adults in the society value. E. D. Hirsch (1987) and William Bennett (1992) are two major proponents of "cultural literacy," a traditional curricular approach based on the premise that all students in the nation need to know a common core of information and values. They speak forcefully for the intellectual benefits of a classical liberal arts education, and they express a fear held by many people that American society will splinter even more into ethnic enclaves. There must be a common culture that we share in order for the society to hold together, and our common beliefs are represented in the Constitution and a large body of cultural knowledge derived mainly from Europe. Calling for a core does not necessarily omit non-European cultures from the curriculum. Bennett, in particular, has pushed to include information about diverse cultures in the curriculum, often in the form of literature. Banks and Banks (1997) refer to this as a "contributions" or "additive" approach, because the cultural information does not alter the core curriculum.

Sometimes the school curriculum suppresses certain cultural ways by denying the worth of different cultures and by substituting dominant cultural elements. The result is the overt suppression of nondominant cultures, what Joel Spring refers to as "deculturalization" (Spring, 1997). For example, throughout the 1800s and much of the 1900s, the languages of Native Hawai'ians and Native Americans were suppressed in the schools. Children were punished for speaking their native language, and many Native

American children were sent to boarding schools with the express intention of supplanting traditional cultural understandings. Mexican Americans also had their language suppressed, but they were able to attend Catholic schools and develop private schools in which Spanish and English both were spoken.

Spring argues that overt deculturalization is often unsuccessful: the groups just mentioned have tried to maintain their languages, religious beliefs, and certain forms of cultural knowledge (pp. 48–50). However, the devaluing of local language and culture can have devastating effects on cultural life, as witnessed by the continuing disappearance of native languages and traditional crafts.

The predominant metaphor used to describe how cultural groups were assimilated is the "melting pot," a phrase from the early 20th century. Immigrants and minority cultures within the United States may begin with diverse cultural understandings and knowledge, but a major purpose of schools has been to assimilate them so they are "melted" into one unified culture.

Tossing the Salad: Cultural Integration and the Curriculum

A metaphor commonly used to describe the *culturally integrative* approach to curriculum is the "salad bowl." The "salad bowl" metaphor comes from the notion that as Americans we are a multicultural nation. We come from various ethnic, racial, and cultural backgrounds, and we may look different and maintain some different ways of speaking, thinking, and acting, but yet we are all in the same "salad bowl" together.

Multicultural education is an essential ingredient in cultural integration. Multicultural education is a set of ideas about equal educational opportunity and is concerned with three types of practices. First, multicultural education is related to *institutional practices* such as the tracking of students. Second, it centers on *instructional practices* like calling on all students in class and recognizing how different students learn in different ways. Third, it addresses *curricular practices* like the inclusion of knowledge from multiple cultural perspectives in the regular curriculum. Schools integrate multicultural knowledge by incorporating other languages, providing information about diverse cultures, and including local culture in the curriculum.

Rather than focus only on ethnicity, proponents of multicultural education are concerned with the many human characteristics that constitute one's culture. Ethnicity, language, religion, gender, socioeconomic status, and physical or mental exceptionalities are usually included in these discussions. The goals for students relate to:

- knowledge (to reduce the amount of ignorance about other people and to consider important ideas that impact our society)
- attitudes (to reduce prejudice and engender respect for people who are different from you)
- skills (to enhance skills such as critical thinking skills, writing skills, and collaborative skills)

These are worthy goals, but when translated into actual practices, some of the everyday curricular issues can be quite controversial. For example, what should we teach about religion in social studies? Should we try to reduce prejudice against homosexuals? How should we deal with bilingualism and the call for an official "national language"? What if critical thinking skills result in students challenging the opinions of adults?

Such difficult questions have led some writers on multicultural education to broaden the scope and conceive of it as a reform movement. James and Cherry Banks (1997), who have written extensively about multicultural education, call for fundamental changes in the school environment, while Christine Sleeter and Carl Grant (1994) have argued for "multicultural and social reconstructionist" education. Sleeter and Grant call for social action that challenges societal inequities and social stratification. They believe students should have the chance to consider serious social issues from the viewpoint of different cultural groups in society.

Should there be special schools for certain cultural groups who are failing in the public schools? These are cultural and, of course, political issues and must be knowledgeably addressed by educators.

Another less common and more localized way of thinking about cultural integration of the curriculum is to consider community knowledge. Often, multicultural curriculum, especially related to ethnicity, can seem quite abstract. When students at a Crow reservation school in Montana read about African Americans, or students in an all-white Kentucky Appalachian town talk about Hispanics, it can seem as foreign as learning about aboriginals in Australia. What about local knowledge and culture? For example, Luis Moll (1992) has written about the "household funds of knowledge" in the Hispanic communities of Tucson, Arizona. He and his fellow researchers have found that families in poor areas often have a wide range of knowledge about topics that educators and more affluent members of society know little about. For example, "household funds of knowledge" may include such areas as agriculture and mining, economics, construction and repair, medicine (both contemporary and folk medicine), and religion. Moll works with groups of public school teachers who engage in discourse with families, spend time in the local community, and try to determine how the cultural knowledge of parents, children, and other community members can be a central part of the curriculum. The goal is not simply to address cultural issues that are national and international in scope, but to truly connect local culture with the schools.

Staying in Separate Rooms: Cultural Ethnocentricity and the Curriculum

In recent years, a more radical approach to cultural issues has emerged. Rather than focus on curricular integration as an outgrowth of the movements toward social and political integration, some educators have called for the establishment of schools that present an ethnocentric curriculum—for cultural minorities. Instead of being part of a melting pot or a tossed salad, we could say that this approach calls for people to stay in "separate rooms."

The goals of ethnocentric curriculum are to strengthen traditional languages and customs, help students see the relevance of the curriculum, increase students' understanding of social and political issues, and raise students' self-esteem and self-confidence. Educators who work in schools with an ethnocentric curriculum believe that students will drop out less frequently, learn how to read and write capably, and give back to their community when they graduate because they know about and are proud of their native culture.

Ethnocentric curriculum has been played out in different ways. In Hawai'i, educators and community activists have created "immersion schools" on several islands. The term "immersion schools" comes from the schools' practice of "immersing" students in the values, beliefs, and cultural norms of a particular culture. The immersion schools, which go through eighth grade, have a Hawai'ian Studies Program and language classes for all students in Hawai'ian and English (which are the official languages of Hawai'i). Students also speak Hawai'ian in one or two other classes, and the entire curriculum is suffused with the values of traditional Hawai'ian society, which is more collectively and ancestrally oriented than mainstream American society. The goal is to have children be bilingual and multicultural, a perfect fit for state demographics (there is no ethnic group in Hawai'i that makes up more than 26% of the population).

Cultural minorities on the mainland have also organized immersion schools with an ethnocentric curriculum. For example, educators on the mainland have developed Afro-centric schools in Milwaukee, New York City, Detroit, and elsewhere. These schools emanate from the belief that African American students, perhaps males in particular, are being failed by traditional school systems. Others have argued in favor of sex-segregation for female students due to gender discrimination (see chapter 7), citing research that indicates that female students perform better in all-girl schools. The IDEALS Challenge that follows provides the perspective of Alvin Poussaint, a noted psychiatrist and media consultant, on separate schools for African American *males*.

IDEALS CHALLENGE: *Examining Equity*

(Excerpted from Poussaint, 1996, p. 14.)

[The] assumptions are that regular schools support the educational needs of nonblack children and black girls better than those of black boys and that separate schools for black boys could address their needs more appropriately—in style, in structure and in curriculum. . . . Black boys may have a lot of issues around what it is to be a male. Many of them come from homes where adult males are absent and females run everything. The school system is largely female at the elementary level. The all-boys schools try to provide more male teachers. Remember that same-sex schools have been very successful for boys and girls for a long time. The rush toward coeducation didn't have to do with educational academic needs; it had to do with social needs. . . . Today, maybe we have a different set of social needs.

- What do you believe about Poussaint's perspective?
- Is sex-segregation in schools acceptable when the reasons for it seem legitimate?
- Do you believe ethnocentric schools are appropriate for cultural minorities?
- Do you believe ethnocentric schools are appropriate for cultural majorities?
- If your answer to the previous two questions differed, justify the reasons for your differential response.

Poussaint's concerns are stated even more forcefully by Afro-centric thinkers like Molefi Asante (1990). Asante believes that Afro-centric schools provide a view of history and culture from an African perspective. Afro-centric schools often incorporate the study of African languages such as Swahili. This approach to curriculum is controversial, even within ethnic groups. Some people who fought for civil rights and integration are disturbed by what they see as an emphasis on resegregation, while others have claimed that some content in the Afro-centric curriculum is narrow and inaccurate. Spring (1997) points out that ethnocentric approaches tend to be more concerned with ethnicity than with gender, exceptionalities, and other differences addressed in multicultural education. These criticisms may be legitimate, but so is the criticism that current educational practices and attitudes are unhelpful to many ethnic minority children, especially those living in urban poverty. The complexity of the issue is illustrated by the IDEALS Challenge that follows.

IDEALS CHALLENGE: *Examining Equity*

(Excerpted from Paley, 1995, pp. 81–82. Vivian Gussin Paley is a kindergarten teacher at the University of Chicago Lab School who has written a number of books about teaching and learning. A recent book, Kwanzaa and Me, details her confusions about issues related to race and her conversations with people from diverse cultural backgrounds about the idea of integration and separation. Here are excerpts from two conversations with African American teachers, "Louise" and "Mr. Arnold.")

Louise [an African American teacher] looks around the table at all of us as if she is deciding whether or not to make a statement. "Look, it didn't matter if you were black or white, your education left out more than it put in. The thing I'm trying to do now is find out more about blacks and their contributions to the world. If I were white I'd want to be doing the same thing even if I didn't have a single black child in my class. It's not Afro-centric, it's history. And," she stops for emphasis, "*and* it has to be in the regular curriculum. We are one people, one nation, made of many different people. We must learn this together from the earliest age. . . . I haven't met anyone who thinks we should go back to the way we were. If you're in an all-white or all-black school, there might be nothing you can do about it, but it shouldn't be the goal. At least you can integrate the curriculum."

"We're still pretty ambivalent," he [Mr. Arnold] says . . . "My wife especially. She'd like Jeremy to remain in an African American public school until he's older. But I know the public schools better than she does. I teach in one. Jeremy would get into trouble because he's curious, argumentative, questioning everything, like me. They don't like that in the public schools. They want obedience. He'd be labeled bad immediately. This has already happened in preschool."

While I [Paley] am flying home it occurs to me that several old premises of mine need to be reexamined. Homogeneity, I have stated, is fine in a bottle of milk but not in a classroom. What is this quality I call homogeneity? Does it exist in any classroom or is it found in the perception of the beholder? . . . This notion of homogeneity may well lie in the attitude of the teacher. Perhaps if we called ourselves *integrators* we would be better at identifying the "minorities" built into any group, those who act, feel, look, think, or learn differently. Then each child's special attributes could be included in the common culture.

- Why does Louise want a culturally integrated curriculum in socially integrated schools?
- Why do you think Mrs. Arnold might want her son to stay in a predominantly African American school?
- What does Paley mean by the statement that the "notion of homogeneity may well lie in the attitude of the teacher"? What do you think she means by "minorities" in the last paragraph?
- What are some of the things a teacher would do if he or she is an "integrator"?
- Do you think Paley's definition of "common culture" resembles the idea of a core curriculum described in an earlier section? How might it be similar? Different? How would you define a "common culture"?
- How would educators embracing the IDEALS of democratic schools respond to the notions of core curriculum and homogeneity?

SUMMARY

In the end, we are left to grapple with a number of dichotomies and dilemmas that will continue to trouble us because they have no resolution. "Dichotomies" are dualisms which are often posed as either-or choices we must make. For example, will our curriculum be "child-centered" *or* "subject-centered"? Will we focus on "basic skills" *or* what are considered to be nonbasic skills like those in the arts? Democratic educators reject such forced choices because they restrict thinking and make it appear as if there is no negotiated middle ground, no synthesis of child and content or of science and the arts.

"Dilemmas" are difficult problems we face as educators, which are related to scope and sequence, balance, and integration of the curriculum. What electives should students be able to take and when should they be given such choices? What should be the balance between an academic and a vocational curriculum? Between the extracurricular and the regular curriculum? In several senses, to what extent should we have a separated curriculum and an integrated curriculum? These dilemmas can be seen as insolvable, too difficult to reach a consensus on, or even too far removed from daily life. We disagree. As educators, our job is to constantly rethink what we are doing and why we are doing it. In small, local ways, we can try to reach consensus with our colleagues about what is important in the curriculum and determine how to include students and parents in the process. We are the people who must reconstruct the curriculum to ensure that it represents our democratic beliefs.

DOING DEMOCRACY

(Excerpted and adapted from Brodhagen, 1995, pp. 88–89.)

In Barbara Brodhagen's seventh-grade classroom in Madison, Wisconsin, students plan curriculum with the teacher. She encourages students to express their questions and concerns about their lives and the world. Here is an example of what students want to understand about themselves:

How did my skin color come about?

What will happen to me after I die?

Why was I born who I am and into my family?

How do my bodily organs keep going and going?

Why is school so hard for me?

Here are sample students' questions about the world, followed by Brodhagen's explanation of the process of curriculum construction:

Why do some people/groups think they are better?

How did religions evolve?

Will there ever be enough for all to survive?

How was the universe created?

How can birds fly?

Will other planets be livable?

Why can't teenagers vote?

How do roller coasters work?"

Students first develop their questions individually and then work in small groups to try to find common or shared questions. Once the whole class has identified these questions, students are asked to find connections between the self and world questions. These connections form themes around which the curriculum is organized. Students have developed such themes as Isms; Outer Space; Time: Past and Present; Mind Bogglers; Environment; Death, War, and Violence; and Conflict. As students consider each theme, they identify activities that respond to the self and world questions included in the theme. . . . Students know that they have to develop a variety of skills, however. When asked what should happen if the only suggested activity was "to read," students were quick to respond that there has to be a balance; everyone needs to do the basics, "like reading, writing, and math, and all that other stuff we learn in school."

The teacher's role in this process is not the traditional one of always directing the action from the front of the classroom, but rather one of facilitating activities and collaborating with students. . . . Early group planning creates a climate of openness for the rest of the year, a large part of which is a curriculum with far fewer "hidden" aspects than a traditional curriculum.

- What are the possible benefits of the children directly constructing the class curriculum?

- What do you foresee as potential problems with this approach?
- How can students' questions be in the curriculum? How are students "stakeholders"?
- How does Brodhagen's approach relate to the IDEALS and practices of democracy and education discussed in chapters 1, 2, and 3?
- Brodhagen is "doing democracy" in her classroom. What is your judgment of what she is trying to do? How might you teach in similar or different ways than she?

REFERENCES

Asante, M. K. (1990). *Kemet, Afrocentricity, and knowledge.* Trenton, NJ: Africa World Press.

Ashton-Warner, S. (1963). *Teacher.* New York: Simon & Schuster.

Banks, J. A., & McGee Banks, C. A. (1997). *Multicultural education* (3rd ed.). Needham Heights, MA: Allyn & Bacon.

Bennett, W. L. (1992). *The devaluing of America: The fight for our culture and our children.* New York: Summit Books.

Boyer, E. (1993). *What is an educated person? Eight core commonalities.* Presentation at the annual meeting of the Association for Supervision and Curriculum Development, Washington DC.

Brodhagen, B. L. (1995). The situation made us special. In M. W. Apple & J. A. Beane (Eds.), *Democratic schools* (pp. 83–100). Alexandria, VA: Association for Supervision and Curriculum Development.

Bruner, J. (1960). *The process of education.* Cambridge, MA: Harvard University Press.

Conversations. (1997). *High Strides, 9*(3), 8–9.

Cunat, M. (1996). Vision, vitality, and values: Advocating the democratic classroom. In L. Beyer (Ed.), *Creating democratic classrooms: The struggle to integrate theory and practice* (pp. 136–137). New York: Teachers College Press.

Eisner, E. (1985). *The educational imagination.* Stanford, CA: Stanford University Press.

Ford, P. L. (Ed.). (1899). *The New England primer.* New York: Dodd, Mead.

Gardner, H., Torff, B., & Hatch, T. (1996). The age of innocence reconsidered: Preserving the best of the progressive tradition in psychology and education. In D. R. Olson and N. Torrance (Eds.), *Handbook of education and human development: New models of learning, teaching, and schooling* (pp. 28–55). Cambridge, MA: Blackwell.

Greenawald, D. (1995). Maturation and change, 1947–1968. *Social Education, 59*(7), 416–428.

Haynes, R. M., & Chalker, D. M. (1997). World class schools. *The American School Board Journal, 184*(5), 20–26.

Herbst, J. (1996). *The once and future school: Three hundred and fifty years of American secondary education.* New York: Routledge.

Hirsch, E. D., Jr. (1987). *Cultural literacy: What every American needs to know.* Boston: Houghton-Mifflin.

Jackson, P. W. (1992). *Untaught lessons.* New York: Teachers College Press.

Jones, J. (1980). *Soldiers of light and love: Northern teachers and Georgia blacks, 1865–1873.* Athens, GA: University of Georgia Press.

Kliebard, H. M. (1995). *The struggle for the American curriculum, 1893–1958* (2nd ed.). London: Routledge.

Levy, S. (1996). *Starting from scratch: One classroom builds its own curriculum.* Portsmouth, NH: Heinemann.

Martin, C. (1994). *Schooling in Mexico.* London: Avebury.

Mauriel, J. (1989). *Strategic leadership for schools: Creating and sustaining productive change.* San Francisco: Jossey-Bass.

Moll, L. (1992). Bilingual classroom studies and community analysis. *Educational Researcher, 21*(2), 20–24.

National Commission on Excellence in Education. (1983). *A nation at risk: The imperatives for educational reform.* Washington, DC: U.S. Department of Education.

Nicholls, J. G., & Hazzard, S. P. (1993). *Education as adventure: Lessons from the second grade.* New York: Teachers College Press.

Paley, V. G. (1995). *Kwanzaa and me.* Cambridge, MA: Harvard University Press.

Popkewitz, T. S. (Ed.). (1987). *The formation of the school subjects.* New York: Falmer.

Poussaint, A. (1996, Spring). Reaching all children. *Teaching Tolerance,* pp. 11–15.

Sherman, T. M. (1998). *Another danger for 21st-century children?* Education Week, 17(38), 30, 32.

Silberman, C. E. (1970). *Crisis in the classroom.* New York: Vintage Books.

Sizer, T. (1992). *Hoarace's School.* Boston: Houghton Mifflin.

Sleeter, C. E., & Grant, C. A. (1991). Race, class, gender, and disability in current textbooks. In M. W. Apple & L. K. Christian-Smith (Eds.), *The politics of the textbook* (pp. 78–110). New York: Routledge.

Sleeter, C. E., & Grant, C. A. (1994). *Making choices for multicultural education: Five approaches to race, class, and gender* (2nd ed.). Englewood Cliffs, NJ: Macmillan.

Smith, B. A., Palmer, J. J., & Correia, S. T. (1995). Social studies and the birth of NCSS, 1783–1921. *Social Education, 59*(7), 393–398.

Spring, J. (1994). *The American school, 1642–1993.* New York: McGraw-Hill.

Spring, J. (1997). *Deculturalization and the struggle for equality* (2nd ed.). New York: McGraw-Hill.

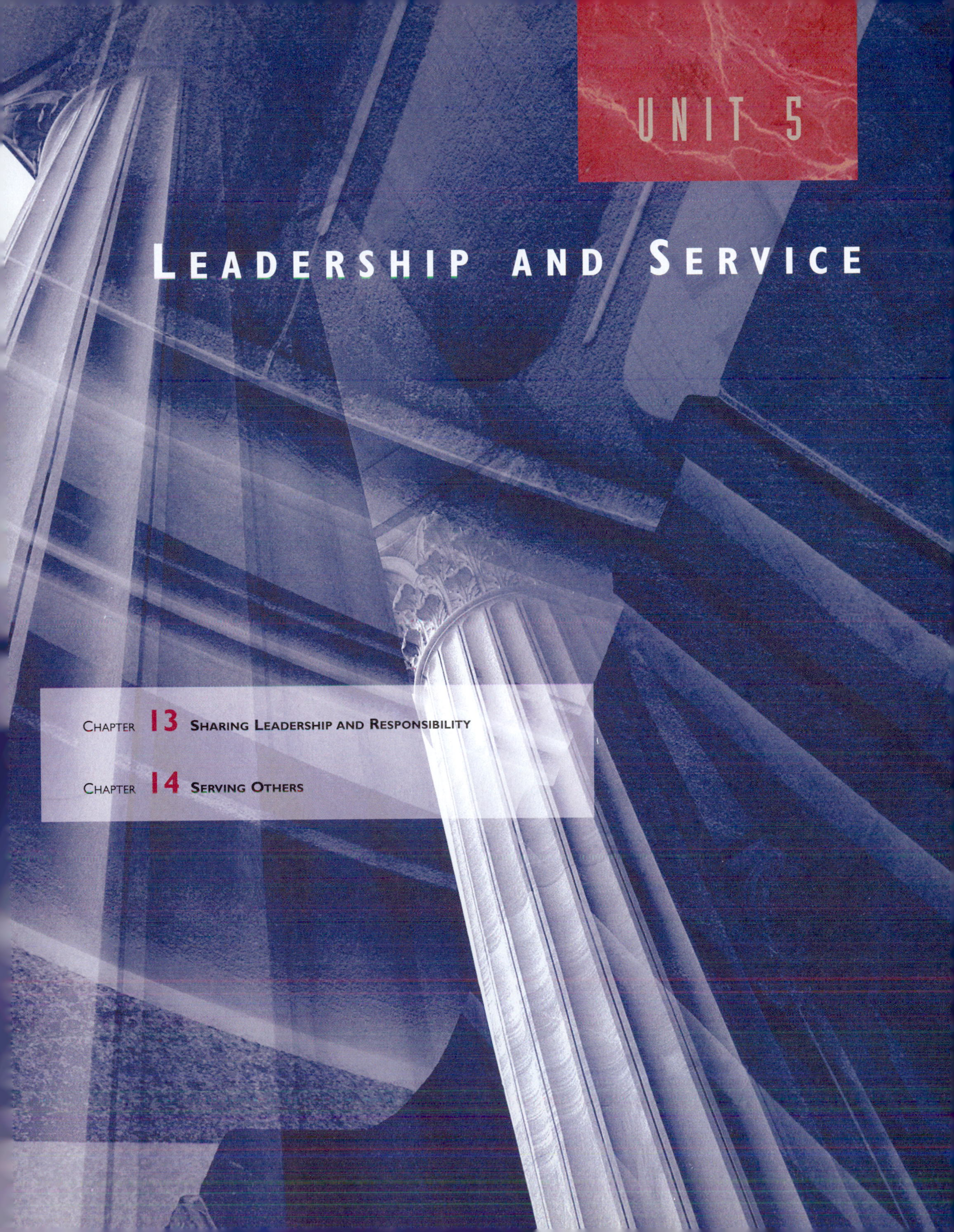

UNIT 5

LEADERSHIP AND SERVICE

What can we learn about leadership from this flock of geese?

Who is the leader of the geese in this picture?

Has this goose always been the leader?

Will this goose continue to be the leader?

Why are the geese flying in a V-formation rather than in a straight line?

What are the implications of geese flying patterns for school and teacher leadership?

CHAPTER 13

SHARING LEADERSHIP AND RESPONSIBILITY

IDEALS CHALLENGE: *Deepening Discourse*

Complete the following statement. Then discuss your response with your classmates.

- The role of teachers in democratic schools is to ______________.

INTRODUCTION

What is leadership? Who is a leader? What does it mean to lead? Toward what purposes should we lead? From whom should leadership come in a democratic school? Are teachers leaders? Should they be? Toward what purposes should leadership be exercised? Why do we need shared leadership? In what ways is it superior to hierarchical leadership?

We believe there are several purposes that shared leadership should strive to accomplish.

- Shared leadership should work toward the integration of the democratic IDEALS of inquiry, discourse, equity, authenticity, leadership, and service in all aspects of the school's practice.
- Shared leadership should work toward the development of common understandings that lead to a unified direction for the school and which improve the educational experience for all members of the school community.
- Shared leadership should result in, and work toward, the empowerment of all members of the school community.

By "empowerment" we mean more than simply giving individuals more power to make decisions. Rather, by empowerment we mean an intentional, ongoing process through which people lacking an equitable share of valued resources gain greater access to and control over those resources (Cochran & Dean, 1991). Resources include commonly thought of items such as money, materials, and supplies, but also less commonly thought of resources such as knowledge, respect, opportunities to have a say in one's daily destiny, and access to decision making. Empowerment includes three characteristics:

- the power to inquire into and make the decisions that affect one's life
- the ability to be able to address decisions in a manner that serves the interests of various communities while satisfactorily addressing one's personal interests
- the ability to pursue courses of action that put the decisions one has made into practice

As you read the descriptions that follow of the roles and responsibilities of various members of conventional schools, we ask you to reflect on the ways in which the roles and responsibilities fall short of empowering people and constrain them from sharing in leadership.

CLICK ON IT

Here are Web site addresses of several school reform networks that promote shared leadership as central in working toward more democratic schooling. Visit the sites and identify the networks' conception of democratic schooling and who the networks cite or imply are partners in school leadership:

Coalition of Essential Schools

www.essentialschools.org

League of Professional Schools

www.coe.uga.edu/lps/

Oklahoma Networks for Excellence in Education

www.ou.edu/org/one/network.html

ROLES AND RESPONSIBILITIES IN CONVENTIONAL SCHOOLS

Teacher Roles and Responsibilities in Conventional Schools

In conventional schools teachers are responsible for the teaching and learning that occurs in their classroom and for the smooth daily operation of their classroom. They are responsible for students while the students are in their classroom. Other students belong to other teachers and thus are not their responsibility. Additionally, events that occur outside the walls of the classroom are the responsibility of the principal and administration or other appropriate support staff. Typically, teachers in conventional schools work in isolation from other teachers, with little collaboration or professional interaction across classes or grades occurring. The curriculum is prescribed by the district's formal curriculum document and by textbooks, with teachers occasionally interjecting a unit on a favorite topic. School-wide decisions are of little concern to teachers in conventional schools unless the decisions have significant implications for their classroom practice. Teachers in conventional schools view the principal as being responsible for schoolwide leadership, for managing the smooth operation of the school, for maintaining discipline in the school's common areas, and for supporting them in severe classroom discipline cases. Typically, however, they see the principal as having little direct effect on what occurs in their classroom. Occasionally, teachers in conventional schools assume a leadership role, such as chairing an ad hoc committee, or being "put in charge" of a schoolwide project or upcoming event.

Student Roles and Responsibilities in Conventional Schools

The expectation for students in conventional schools is that they are passively receptive to the teaching and directives of the school. Students are provided few opportunities to be responsible for their own learning. Rather, they are told what to do and provided with knowledge, which they are expected to absorb as a result of listening and schoolwork. Schoolwork and homework is determined by the teacher and assigned to students. Students are provided with few leadership opportunities. They are seldom given a legitimate role in classroom or school governance. The teacher determines classroom activities and standards for classroom behavior; the principal determines school activities and standards for school behavior. Students are expected to passively conform to what adults know is best for them in order to develop similar levels of knowledge and wisdom that they can call on in their adult years.

Principal Roles and Responsibilities in Conventional Schools

In conventional schools the principal is expected to both manage and lead the school. In terms of management, the principal is responsible for ensuring the smooth daily operation of the school—that buses run on time, supplies are available, and classes and hallways are orderly. In conventional schools, if something does not operate smoothly, it is at least indirectly the responsibility of the principal. In terms of leadership, principals are responsible for making sure that the school continues to improve and progress. The principal in the conventional school is the individual who makes the various decisions that impact school operations and then informs others of the decision. Although the formal curriculum (i.e., what is to be taught at each grade level) is typically determined by the school board and central district administration, principals may mandate or forbid certain instructional approaches. Principals also typically make budgetary decisions about how a school's money should be spent. Personnel decisions, such as which grade or classes a teacher should teach and who should be hired for new positions, are also made by the principal. Finally, responsibility for evaluating teachers in terms of their overall performance as well as identifying areas for teacher growth are the purview of the principal. Principals are responsible for developing the rules, regulations, and procedures that guide the operation of the school and objectively enforcing them.

Parent Roles and Responsibilities in Conventional Schools

In conventional schools, parents are often encouraged to become involved in the school. Parent involvement, however, is usually thought of by teachers and principals as parents assisting the school with various tasks such as conducting bake sales, running book fairs, helping supervise field trips, helping with classroom holiday parties, and other similar tasks. Essentially, parents are viewed as an extra helping hand, rather than as a source of leadership. Additionally, an underlying assumption of this traditional perspective on parent involvement is that children will indirectly benefit by their mother's or father's involvement in the school. The assumption is that this will happen because of improved student behavior resulting from the presence of the parent in the school, the parent's stronger relationship with the teacher, or because of the symbolic message about the importance of school that the parent's involvement sends to the child.

The Community in Conventional Schools

In conventional schools the community is viewed as largely disconnected and irrelevant to the work of the school. Once students enter school, the experiences they bring with them from their communities are considered unimportant. The conventional school perspective on community holds that students are in school to learn what the school has decided they need to know, not what students may want to know based on their experiences in the community. Conventional schools are concerned with what occurs within the walls of the school building. They believe they do not have sufficient financial or human resources to be concerned with the community. The school believes its focus should be on academic matters and that their efforts should not be diluted by investing time or energy on providing community service or by bringing other social services for students and their families into the school. Additionally, the perspective of conventional schools is that the formal education and professional experiences of the school's teachers, principal, and professional support staff have resulted in expertise being collected within the school. The belief is that community members and business people have little expertise or leadership to offer to the professionally trained staff of the school.

Summary: Leadership in Conventional Schools

As you may have concluded from the description of roles and responsibilities in conventional schools, most individuals have limited opportunities to share in leadership. Leadership in these schools is thought of in traditional ways, and position responsibilities are structured in a manner that is consistent with these conceptions of leadership. Consequently, only very few positions have opportunities and expectations for exercising leadership.

Leadership is traditionally thought of as *influencing* the thoughts and actions of people *toward* the achievement of particular goals, directions, or courses of action (e.g., Argyris, 1976; Bass, 1985; Bennis & Nanus, 1985; Zalesznik, 1977). Leadership that is conceptualized in this way embraces the following set of assumptions about the nature of reality and life in schools and other organizations.

Traditionally school leadership has been a responsibility given to principals with teachers, students, and parents expected to passively follow the principal's leadership.

- Only one best course of action exists in any situation.
- There is only one best way of achieving that direction.
- The course and the way of achieving it can be identified by an individual with superior abilities.
- The "leader" of an organization (e.g., a school) achieved her or his position due to superior abilities. Thus, the leader is the person that is most qualified to identify the goals the organization should attempt to accomplish and the best way of accomplishing these goals.
- The members of an organization can be influenced, directed, persuaded, or otherwise controlled to accept and implement the leader's goals for the organization.

This form of leadership is grounded in bureaucratic thought, particularly in the principle of hierarchy. We will call this type of leadership, *conventional leadership*, since it is the form of leadership most typically practiced in conventional, bureaucratically driven schools.

The implications of these assumptions are that leadership is associated with a position and specifically with positions that have authority attached to them. For example, in conventional schools and school districts we usually think of leadership as the principal's or superintendent's responsibility rather than the responsibility of teachers, support staff, students, parents, community members, and universities. Thus, leadership directly or indirectly imposes one person's will upon others. That is, it imposes one person's conception of what goals should be pursued and how these goals should be accomplished upon others. This raises several important questions for democratic schools:

- How does the leader know that his or her conception of what should be done is somehow better than the conceptions of others in the school community (Angus, 1989; Reitzug, 1994)?
- What happens to the wisdom and knowledge of teachers and others who are not involved in decision making and direction setting?

LEADERSHIP IN DEMOCRATIC SCHOOLS

Democratic conceptions of leadership are grounded in a different set of assumptions about the nature of reality and life in schools and other organizations. The assumptions of a democratic conception of leadership include the following.

- Individuals at all levels of the organization have knowledge and insight to contribute that can enhance the work of the organization.
- Individuals will construct different interpretations of what they perceive to be appropriate ends for the organization and appropriate means for achieving those ends.
- Multiple appropriate courses of action exist in any situation.
- Due to practical reasons as well as the moral right to have a voice in determining one's destiny, all members of the organization should be involved in reflecting on and discussing appropriate means and ends for the organization.

These assumptions, of course, have implications for the practice of leadership in democratic school communities. Rather than being embodied in a

Leadership in democratic schools comes from students, teachers, parents, and the principal.

Table 13.1 Comparison of Conventional and Democratic School Leadership

	Conventional Leadership	Democratic Leadership
Definition	influencing others to pursue the principals' goals for the school	facilitating processes that engage members of the school community in inquiring into and discussing issues, dilemmas, goals, directions
Embodiment	in *positions* with authority/power (e.g., principal or superintendent)	in *acts* from anyone
Processes	directing, influencing, persuading, controlling	asking, challenging, forming discussion/study groups, creating community spaces, initiating collaborative events
Result	imposes one person's or group's will upon others	enhanced understanding, construction of new knowledge, development of shared understanding, identification of new and better ways of doing things

position, leadership in democratic schools is viewed as being embodied in *acts* that may come from anyone in an organization. Thus, rather than leadership being the principal's or superintendent's responsibility, responsibility for leadership in a democratic school belongs to everyone and should come from many different individuals—teachers, support staff, students, parents, community members, principals, superintendents, and perhaps even university faculty. Rather than leadership being thought of as the process of influencing or directing others to pursue the goals and direction identified by *the* leader, leadership in democratic schools is thought of as the facilitation by anyone in the school community of processes that engage people in examining, studying, and challenging beliefs and ways of doing things. In a sense it causes examination of "the way we do things around here" and helps authentic democratic communities increase their capacity for learning how to be more democratic.

Linda Lambert (1995) has termed this form of leadership "constructivist leadership." Constructivist leadership is based on the belief that adults learn just like children do—through reflection and the construction of knowledge. The function of constructivist leadership is to engage people in processes that cause them to wrestle with issues and dilemmas which result in their constructing new knowledge about the issue or dilemma. Table 13.1 compares conventional school leadership with democratic leadership.

IDEALS CHALLENGE: *Learning Leadership*

Maria, Blaine, and Cheryl are teachers at Riverside High School in Milwaukee, Wisconsin, and are part of a teacher leadership team from their school. All three believe that block scheduling will improve the school's instructional program and lead to more genuine relationships between teachers and students. However, not all their colleagues agree with them. Some are open in their disagreement. Others know little about block scheduling, but would like to know more. Still others know little about block scheduling and don't care to know more. Maria, Blaine, and Cheryl, in discussing how they should proceed, decide that they should not try to influence, persuade, or direct others to believe as they do. They decide that they need to give other teachers the opportunity to learn more about block scheduling and to engage in discussion about whether block scheduling is appropriate for their school. With the limited amount of funding to which they have access, they plan a luncheon that will span the school's multiple lunch periods. During the luncheon, submarine sandwiches from a nearby sub shop will be available free of charge to all teachers. The only requirement is that teachers must eat in the room in which the luncheon is being held—they may not take the sandwiches back to their classroom and eat alone. Additionally, while they are eating their lunch they must discuss block scheduling with others in the room.

- What is the relationship between Maria, Blaine, and Cheryl's actions and leadership?
- What type of leadership are they practicing?
- What are other examples of how teachers can practice this type of leadership?

Although constructivist leadership contains some democratic elements (e.g., it honors individual voice), it may still fall short of being democratic. For *leadership* to be *democratic*, in addition to a concern for giving voice to all, there must be:

- inquiry into the nature of equity *in the school*
- inquiry into the nature of equity *in society*
- *acting* on the results of inquiry in working toward achieving more equitable conditions in the school and in society

It is the concern for *inquiring into* and *acting on* issues of equity that transforms leadership from being merely constructivist to also being democratic.

What are the implications of democratic conceptions of leadership for teachers and other members of democratic school communities? We turn first to a discussion of teacher leadership. Specifically, we will discuss the settings in which teacher leadership occurs, its nature, and the ways in which teacher leadership is practiced.

Teacher Leadership in Democratic Schools[1]

The Settings of Teacher Leadership

Although as a teacher in a democratic school your primary responsibility remains the teaching and learning that occurs in your classroom, your responsibilities move well beyond that. Teacher leadership should occur in the classroom, the school, and the community.

1. Teachers serve as leaders in the *classroom* via their interaction with their students. Some teachers also lead their colleagues through the example they set by the way in which they fulfill their classroom responsibilities.

2. Teachers serve as leaders at the *school* level through their participation on committees, in governance, and via engaging in collaborative critical study and discussion of school practices and policies.

3. Teachers serve as leaders in the *community* by the way in which they link what happens in their classroom to the world beyond their classroom. In some instances this may simply be by modeling democratic citizenship. In other instances it may be by more explicitly connecting their community service with their teaching. They may accomplish this via constructing classroom experiences around the issues and dilemmas in which they are engaged in the community, or by involving their students or the school community in service learning projects.

The Nature of Teacher Leadership

Often discussions of teacher leadership imply that teacher leadership occurs by teachers filling a particular leadership role. The conception of teacher leadership as occurring via the fulfillment of responsibilities that are part of formal or informal roles, however, is more consistent with conventional than democratic notions of leadership. Specifically, such a conception of teacher leadership implies that teacher leadership comes from "expert" teachers who have assumed or been assigned a particular role (e.g., master teacher, lead teacher, mentor, committee chair, department chair, teacher-on-assignment) and whose responsibility is to set a direction and influence others to pursue that direction via typical administrative processes, such as coordinating, commanding, controlling, and directing. By contrast, as previously noted, democratic conceptions of leadership suggest that the essence of teacher leadership is found in daily leadership *acts* rather than occasional leadership roles. The next section discusses the "process" of leadership acts.

The Process of Teacher Leadership

The process of teacher leadership refers to the way in which teacher leadership is practiced. While, in some instances, there is nothing intrinsically wrong with the conventional leadership notion of influencing the course of school events in personally desirable directions (e.g., when such directions are grounded in what is good for students and the community), using influence processes in teacher leadership can be problematic in several respects. For example, sometimes influence is exercised in pursuit of results that lead to personal gain for the individual teacher leader but are not necessarily in the best interests of students, other teachers, or the community (e.g., a new program, policy, or curriculum that results in an easier teaching load for the teacher leader). In other instances influence is exercised toward an end the teacher leader believes is good for students and the community, but where others do not agree that such an end is desirable. Essentially, focusing on *individually predetermined* notions of best practice closes down the *collaborative* conversation among members of the school community, which can result in a *shared understanding* about what constitutes best and democratic practice for the school.

Rather than attempting to influence others to predetermined ends via holding leadership roles and using administrative processes, such as

Teacher leadership involves initiating inquiry and discourse, drawing attention to equity and authenticity, or providing service.

coordinating, commanding, and directing, we believe that teacher leadership involves processes that utilize the democratic IDEALS of inquiry, discourse, equity, authenticity, and service that we have discussed throughout this book.

Inquiry and discourse. Democratic leadership is not about trying to influence colleagues and others to "buy into" your way of doing things. Rather, democratic teacher leadership involves developing and facilitating processes that engage others in inquiry, discourse, and the construction of knowledge.

The events in your classroom do not occur in a vacuum. Your students will move to other classrooms or grades. Events within your classroom are impacted by curricular, budgetary, and personnel decisions made at the school level. Adopting a school-to-work focus, allocating money for an instructional aide instead of for curricular materials, deciding which applicant should replace the third-grade teacher who is going on parenting leave—all these school-level decisions will directly or indirectly affect events in your classroom. Additionally, what students are taught and how they are taught in your classroom is related to the curriculum and instructional methodology that occurs in other classrooms in which your students will spend time. Schoolwide discipline, attendance, and other policies will also impact practices in your classroom. These practices and policies are grounded in particular values, beliefs, and assumptions about students and the purpose of schooling. These values, beliefs, and assumptions should be identified and critically studied to determine how congruent they are with your individual beliefs, the school's shared beliefs, and with democratic ideals. As a teacher in a democratic school, you have a responsibility not only to study your own teaching, but also to work toward ensuring that the values, beliefs, and assumptions communicated by school-level policies and practices are examined.

Inquiry results in decisions that are based on careful study rather than on educational trends or fads. Teacher leadership involves promoting inquiry by finding various ways to stimulate the school and individuals to constantly ask, "How can we improve our practices? Is this the best decision for our students? On what data or information are we basing this decision?"

TECHNOLOGY CHALLENGE — *Using Web Resources*

A rich source of information that can fuel inquiry, discourse, and teacher leadership toward school change are the Web sites of various subject area organizations. Below are the names of selected professional subject matter organizations. Search the Internet for their Web sites.

- What can you learn from the Web site that might fuel inquiry, discourse, or teacher leadership toward curricular change in a school? What can you learn from the Web site that might fuel inquiry or discourse in your university classroom?
- Obtain the e-mail address of at least one listserv that provides a forum for teachers in a certain subject area to communicate. Join the listserv and monitor what educators are talking about.

ARTS AND PHYSICAL EDUCATION

American Alliance for Theater and Education
Music Teachers National Association
National Art Education Association

VOCATIONAL AND TECHNOLOGICAL

American Home Economics Association
American Industrial Arts Association
American Vocational Association
International Technology Education Association
Future Farmers of America
National Association of Classroom Educators in Business Education

SOCIAL SCIENCES

National Council on Economic Education
National Council of Geographic Education
Center for Civic Education
National Council for the Social Studies
National Center for History in the Schools

LANGUAGE

American Association of Teachers of French
American Association of Teachers of German
American Association of Teachers of Spanish and Portuguese
American Council on the Teaching of Foreign Languages
International Reading Association
Modern Language Association
National Association for Bilingual Education
National Council of Teachers of English

SCIENCES AND MATHEMATICS

American Association of Physics Teachers
National Association of Biology Teachers
National Science Teachers Association
National Council of Teachers of Mathematics

Constructivist teacher leadership entails getting colleagues engaged in discourse and inquiry about the issues, dilemmas, and decisions the school faces for purposes of discovering and determining what ends and means are most appropriate. Linda Lambert (1995) notes that constructivist leadership occurs through simple everyday acts such as "the next essential question is asked, ideas and traditions are challenged, people volunteer to lead, groups form, curiosity is aroused, verbal and nonverbal interactions change" (p. 50). More formally constructivist leadership may involve (Lambert, 1995):

- the formation of groups that discuss and inquire in some fashion (e.g., leadership teams, reading or study groups, or action research teams)
- the creation of spaces and places where collaborative inquiry, discourse, and discovery can occur (e.g., a professional library, a faculty research and development center, a user-friendly faculty room)
- the initiation of events where joint conversation, work, and action that enhances individual and shared understanding of the school's work can occur (e.g., workshops, dialogue sessions, parent breakfasts, afternoon teas)

One way of facilitating critical study is by being actively involved in school governance and decision making. As a teacher in a democratic school you should view your classroom responsibilities in the context of the entire school. Similarly, you should view school decisions in the context of the community and global society. Failure to do so marginalizes your concern for all students by implying that you are concerned only with the students in your classroom and for them only while they are physically present in your classroom. Such a disconnected perspective is incongruent with a democratic focus on collaboration, individual and social responsibility, and social justice. In a democratic school there is a sense of collective responsibility for all students at all times.

IDEALS CHALLENGE: *Learning Leadership*

(From Lambert, 1995, p. 91.)

The staff at Bryant School in San Francisco regularly use their faculty meetings for protocol discussions. Barbara Karvelis, former principal, describes a shift in the dynamics of professional inquiry, at first initiated and directed by the principal.

"It was agreed that all teacher information that was normally disseminated (verbally) at a staff meeting be placed in a binder where staff could read it at their leisure. In place of one of the monthly staff meetings, a protocol session took place in which a teacher team prepared a burning question and shared information centered around the examination of student work. After several protocol sessions, two teachers came to the meeting somewhat confused about the task. At this point the staff took over the session and helped the teachers rethink their question and place it in the proper context. A shift in thinking occurred whereby the process was no longer driven by the principal, but owned by the staff. From that point on the staff took charge of the protocol process."

- How did the principal participate in sharing leadership in this example?
- How did the teachers participate in sharing leadership?
- How does the example reflect the inquiry and discourse aspects of shared leadership?

Equity. In addition to engaging colleagues in determining what ends and means are most appropriate, discourse and inquiry in democratic teacher leadership must include a focus on equity and action. Equity refers to seeking fair and just practices both within the school and outside the school. There are many dimensions to equity. Equity in discourse and in having a voice in school decision-making processes for teachers, students, and the community is one dimension. A second dimension of equity is access to schools, school programs, and educational opportunities (e.g., how do school attendance area and choice policies, instructional practices, discipline policies, and other practices intentionally or unintentionally favor white, middle- and upper-class students and discriminate against students from economically poor families or students from racial or ethnic minority groups?). A third dimension of equity is achieving a balance between the rights of the individual and the welfare of others (i.e., the common good).

IDEALS CHALLENGE: *Learning Leadership*

(From Lambert, 1995, pp. 90–91. This discussion took place at a high school leadership team meeting.)

George: As you recall, we agreed to look at the available school data and disaggregate those data for race, ethnicity, and gender. Here is what we have: attendance (daily and period), suspensions, expulsions, district test scores, grade analysis sheets.

Joan: We separated the data into columns so that we can look at the patterns that arise in all categories. We've enlarged each sheet and posted it, and you each have your individual copies. Let's take some time to look at it.

Lillie: A number of patterns are beginning to form. Look at the consistent patterns for Latino and African American males; more suspensions and expulsions, but not necessarily poorer attendance! Latina girls have the best attendance, yet . . .

Gary: What?

Lillie: Their test scores are slightly above average, but their grades reveal that they are getting D's and F's in more than half their classes. I wonder why?

[The discussion continued to discover patterns and possible interpretations.]

Joan: How will we present this to the faculty?

George: They need to go through exactly the same process that we did. The most powerful aspect of inquiry is discovering the patterns yourself.

Joan: Agreed?

- How does the scenario reflect inquiry and discourse in shared leadership?
- How does it reflect equity in shared leadership?
- How does the scenario contrast with conventional conceptions of teacher leadership?

Authenticity. Teacher leadership should also be focused toward promoting authenticity in instruction and relationships. Authenticity in instruction actively engages students in disciplined inquiry and in constructing new knowledge that they see as having some value beyond their classroom (see chapter 11).

As previously noted, the Internet is a rich source of information that can fuel inquiry, discourse, and teacher leadership toward school change. Listed here are several Web sites that include a wealth of information on a variety of topics and, in some cases, links to other information-rich sites:

Education Week

www.edweek.com

U.S. Department of Education

www.ed.gov/

Education World

www.education-world.com

Consortium for Policy Research in Education

www.upenn.edu/gse/cpre

The following Web site provides links to all the federally funded regional education labs and their research and literature. Regional labs include the Appalachia Education Lab; WestEd; Mid-Continent, North Central, and Northwest Regional Education Labs; Pacific Resources for Education and Leadership; Laboratory at Brown University Education Alliance; the Lab for Student Success; Southeast Region Vision for Education; and the Southwest Development Lab.

www.upenn.edu/gse/cpre/frames/links.html

An initial focus for teacher leadership in promoting authentic instruction and relationships might be to inquire into and discuss school-level factors that impede movement toward greater authenticity. For example, conventional school curriculum typically emphasizes the concept that "more is better," with students receiving superficial exposure to hundreds of pieces of isolated information. By contrast, Ted Sizer (1992) and others argue that "less is more" because exposure to less information can lead to more in-depth exploration, deeper understanding, and more meaningful learning. In addition to a fragmented, superficial curriculum, other factors that might be examined as barriers to authenticity in instruction and relationships are teaching loads, school schedules, and planning time. All these factors can be structured to promote isolation or collaboration, personal relationships or impersonalization.

Service. Simply engaging in inquiry and discourse and being concerned with equity, authenticity, and sharing leadership is insufficient for democratic teacher leadership. Indeed, a fourth dimension of equity (see discussion earlier in this chapter) is working toward more just conditions *in society* through service learning and other connections and relationships with the community (see also chapter 14). Democratic teacher leadership requires connecting processes such as inquiry, discourse, and examination of equity, to actions within and outside the school. As a result of these processes, the *perspectives and practices* of members of the school community should be modified or changed. This involves moving beyond inquiry and study to action and service. It is imperative that teacher leadership focuses not only on *changes in thinking* and deepened understanding but also on *changes in school practice* and the relationship of schools with their community.

Sharing Leadership With Students, Principals, Families, and Communities

We noted earlier in this chapter that the purposes of shared leadership in democratic schools include:

- the integration of the democratic IDEALS in all aspects of the school's practice
- the improvement of the educational experience for all members of the school community
- the empowerment of all members of the school community

We have discussed how these purposes apply to the practices of teachers. We have not discussed how they apply to the lives and practices of students, parents, and the community. The descriptions that follow reflect the attitudes, environments, and relationships that need to exist or be developed to facilitate shared leadership from throughout the school community.

Student Leadership

In democratic schools and classrooms, students play a much more active role in their education than they do in conventional classrooms. In order for student leadership to flourish, classrooms and schools must be environments where students have many choices and much responsibility. In contrast to conventional classrooms where the implication is that only adults have worthwhile knowledge, in democratic classrooms both adults and students are viewed as knowledgeable and experienced—they simply have different experiences and knowledge to offer. Students bring the knowledge and experiences of childhood and adolescence—knowledge and experiences adults have frequently forgotten. Silencing the voices and input of students results in a lack of understanding between students and teachers. Because communication is from adults *to* students and seldom from students *to* adults or *between* adults and students, dysfunctional conflict occurs. As a result, adult desires do not mesh with student needs and student desires remain invisible to adults or are dismissed as unrealistic or insignificant.

In democratic classrooms, student ideas, needs, and desires have intrinsic worth. That is, if students view something as important it is deemed important. This does not mean that all student ideas and desires are viewed as acceptable and to be implemented. Student ideas and desires have intrinsic worth because students in democratic classrooms have intrinsic worth and thus their ideas and desires are important. The task of students and educators is to jointly explore whether specific student (and adult) ideas, needs, and desires are acceptable and should be honored. We refer you back to the second half of chapter 11, which discussed the characteristics of an empowering classroom environment for student leadership in greater detail.

Principal Leadership

In the conventional school, the principal is the primary decision maker, is directly or indirectly responsible for everything that happens in the school, ensures that decisions are clearly communicated to organizational members, and holds individuals accountable for complying with decisions. This places an unrealistic burden on principals to be all-knowing and all-seeing. By contrast, principals in democratic schools widely share decision-making responsibility with other members of the school community, including teachers, support staff, students, parents, and community members. Similarly, in a democratic school the principal is not held solely accountable for what happens in the school. Rather, accountability is shared, with the principal *and* the school community being responsible for implementing decisions, studying the products of the decisions, and making adjustments as necessary. Additionally, the entire school community shares responsibility for the orderliness of the school and all other aspects of daily school operations.

Principals of democratic schools help ensure that there is an environment in which critical study of school practice and democratic discourse about practice can occur. One study (Reitzug, 1994) found that principals in democratic schools:

- create an environment that supports and facilitates the critical study of practice
- engage in practices that stimulate instances of critical study
- acquire resources and develop structures that make it possible for individuals to implement the products of critical study

In terms of management, the principal in democratic schools remains the primary individual responsible for ensuring the smooth daily operation of the school, although this responsibility is dispersed more throughout the school than it is in conventional schools. Additionally, in democratic schools, management practices are not viewed in isolation from instruction. Rather, the impact of management practices on instruction is explicitly considered and discussed.

In summary, leadership in a democratic school does not come solely from the principal. The principal's role is to help create the type of context in which all members of the school community can take responsibility for making sure that the school continues to improve and progress.

The Community and Shared Leadership

In democratic schools the community is viewed as central to the work of the school. Rather than treating students acontextually—that is, as if their backgrounds and communities did not impact how they experienced school—democratic schools recognize the pervasive influence of community and sociocultural experiences on students.

Democratic schools recognize that in order to effectively teach and raise students, they must understand those students. Understanding students involves understanding the cultural and geographic communities from which they come. The values, beliefs, and knowledge of students are significantly influenced and shaped by the social and cultural factors to which they are exposed. Democratic schools build upon students' community and cultural experiences by developing curriculum and school practices in a manner that places these experiences as central. For example, rather than viewing cultural and community speech patterns as inappropriate (e.g., as some do with ebonics or "black English"), democratic schools view such speech patterns as an alternative but legitimate way of communicating. Nonetheless, democratic schools also teach students the importance of standard English because this is the "power code" that will facilitate their success in a society where the rules and standards are established by the majority culture (Delpit, 1995).

IDEALS CHALLENGE: *Examining Equity*

In 1997 the Richmond School District in Oakland, California, considered a policy that raised significant national controversy. The policy had to do with "ebonics" and would have resulted in it being considered a separate language from English, enabling the school district to receive bilingual education funds for all students who spoke ebonics.

Conduct research on ebonics and discuss the following questions.

- What is ebonics?
- Why do you think many people were upset when the Richmond School District wanted to consider ebonics a separate language?
- What does ebonics have to do with the empowerment of students in democratic classrooms?

- What are the implications of ebonics for you as a teacher in a democratic classroom and school?
- Should ebonics be taught in democratic classrooms and schools?
- From a democratic education perspective, what do you think should be the key issues in terms of ebonics?

Democratic schools also view the community as a teaching and learning laboratory. That is, learning is not restricted to within the walls of the school building. Learning can occur anywhere. Furthermore, in keeping with democratic ideals and principles, it is imperative that schooling extend beyond school walls. Specifically, democratic ideals and principles of inquiry, discourse, equity, authenticity, leadership, and service, demand interaction between students, educators, and the community. Rather than merely discussing democratic ideals and principles, democratic schools must also practice them within the walls of the school and in the community. Many schools are making this effort by facilitating student and school involvement in service projects that focus on improving conditions in the immediate school community and extended communities.

IDEALS CHALLENGE: *Supporting Service*

(Excerpted from Boyer, 1993.)

Margaret Mead said on one occasion that the health of any culture is sustained when three generations are vitally interacting with each other . . . developing a "vertical culture." And yet, in America today, we are creating what might be called a "horizontal culture." Each generation living all alone . . . disconnected from the other . . . Infants are in nurseries, toddlers are in day-care centers, older children are in schools and we layer them by age, college students are isolated on campuses living in a climate of low-grade decadence (at best), adults are in the workplace, and older citizens are in retirement villages . . . living and dying all alone.

For several years my own parents lived in a retirement village where the average age was 80. I called my father one day and he said, "No big deal being 80 around this place. You have to be 90 just to get a cake!" But the nice feature was that they had a day-care center there. Every morning 50 little 3- and 4-year-olds would come truckin' in and every little day-care child had an adopted grandparent. They met with them every day and had a sense of bonding. And when I called my father he wouldn't talk about his aches and pains, he'd talk about his little friend who he was sure was going to be governor or perhaps president someday. And when I would visit him he would have the paintings and the drawings taped on the wall. There was something powerful about the authenticity across the generations—the connectedness of things. An older person being inspired by the energy and innocence of youth and a little boy being inspired and learning lessons about the courage and agony of aging.

- How does Ernest Boyer's story reflect democratic IDEALS?
- What are the implications of Boyer's story for schools?
- What is the relationship between the story and an attitude that "the community is essential"?

In many democratic schools formal or informal relationships with community agencies that provide social services for families have been established. In these schools there is a proactive effort to identify services from the community that can serve to strengthen school programs, family practices, and student learning and development. The objective of such collaborative relationships is to provide a more integrated and efficient system of support services for families or for students and the school. School-community-family relationships recognize that a democratic school's responsibility is to the whole student, and not just the student's mind. Additionally, such relationships recognize that academic success is closely linked to a child's family environment and physical and emotional well-being. Thus, to promote holistic student and family health, democratic schools develop relationships with community agencies that make agency services more accessible to all students and families.

Finally, democratic schools recognize the value of multiple and diverse perspectives. They recognize that community members and business people, although not professionally prepared as educators, have perspectives to offer that can be helpful in improving schooling for all children. Many schools have developed partnerships with businesses. In the past this generally meant that the business provided additional funding to the school for meeting special school needs. Recently, the partnerships have become more encompassing with business partners actually spending time in the school as instructors or tutors. Students also often spend time in businesses, learning about careers and the type of skills and work habits desired by employers.

IDEALS CHALLENGE: *Achieving Authenticity*

(Excerpted from Ladson-Billings, 1994, p. 7.)

As a member of the baby boom generation, I went to urban schools that were bursting at the seams; every classroom had at least 30 students. Further, almost all of the children and most of the teachers were black. But the important thing was that the teachers were not strangers in the community. We students knew them and they knew us. We saw them at church, in the beauty parlor, in the grocery store. One of the sixth-grade teachers had served in the Army with my father. Most importantly, the teachers knew our families and had a sense of their dreams and aspirations for us.

- What does it mean to be part of a community? Does being part of the community refer only to living in the community?
- How important is it to be part of the community in which you teach? How can being part of a community enhance authenticity in relationships? How could it detract from authenticity in relationships?
- Is it important for children from racial or ethnic minority groups to be taught by someone from the same cultural background? What are the advantages? Disadvantages? Does your response differ when you think of cultural majority students rather than cultural minority students?
- How will you proceed in getting to know the families of your students and having "a sense of their dreams and aspirations" for their children?

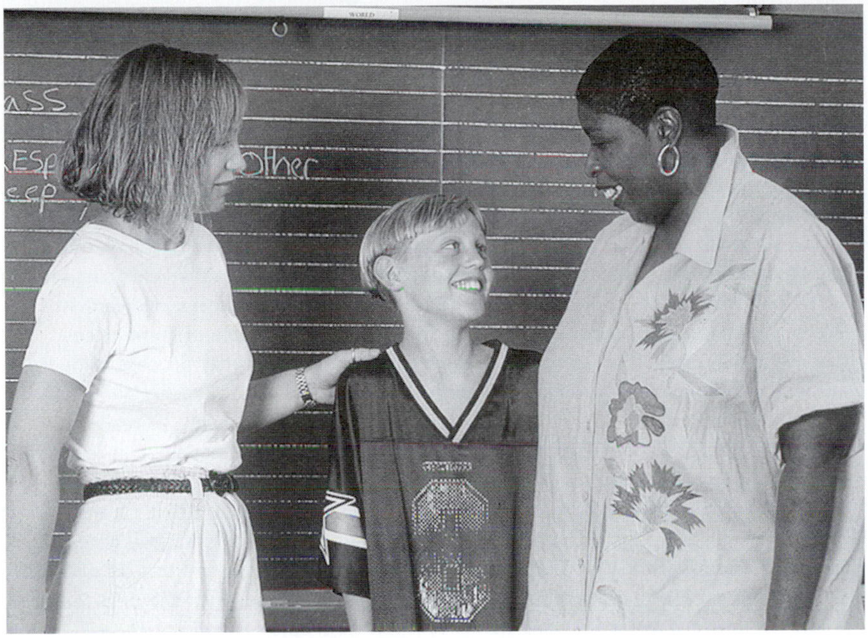

In democratic schools, families and the school are involved with each other for the good of students.

Parents, Families, and Shared Leadership

Democratic schools strive to develop a relationship with families that is not concerned as much with how *parents* can be *involved with the school* as with how *parents, families, and schools* can be *involved with each other* in meaningful and legitimate ways that positively impact the lives of students and children. (We will refer to "families" as well as to "parents" since, in many instances, the primary caretakers of students are not their parents but rather extended families or individuals or groups without a biological connection to the student.) Joyce Epstein (1995) reports that we know three things from research on parent/family-school relationships.

1. Almost all parents care about their children and want them to succeed.
2. Almost all teachers and administrators want parents and families to be involved with schools, but frequently do not know how to go about doing so.
3. Almost all students want their parents or caregivers to know more about their school and their schooling.

Given this positive foundation, it should be readily possible to develop shared leadership between families and schools that result in positive benefits for students.

IDEALS CHALLENGE: *Initiating Inquiry*

(Narration is by Eileen Andrews, parent, former PTO president, Hillside Elementary School, Milwaukee, Wisconsin.)

I really wanted parents to feel a part of the school. We are all intricately related to what's going on with our children's education. What I was struck with my first several years here is that parents were always being asked to do things and I never saw the flip side of what the school was offering parents. I felt that in order to be effective and to have parents feel that they had a part in the education of their children and weren't there just to bake cookies or when you were going on a field trip, that we really needed to focus on what we were offering families in terms of an environment and in terms of special services. Once we have met some of the family's needs, I think more parents will be willing to come in and help with some of the things that are going on.

I would like to see us do more than just give lip service to parent involvement. We can't say that just because we have some parents on a couple of committees that we are a community school. If we don't look at the day-to-day process of being a *community* school, a few events here and there don't make that happen.

Most important I think is communication . . . I question how much we really engage each other in conversations. We've never been invited to sit together in terms of talking about what are the specific questions or concerns we have. I think even offering social times . . . inviting parents to breakfast . . . It's real important that parents have a place to express their concerns and their issues. We need to solidify parents' voices, so that it's not just a handful of parents who are speaking. And that it's not just the angry parents who are voicing their opinions. I think it's sad when the only parent voices we hear are the angry ones versus all the ones that are simply concerned about the education of their children and want a place to share what they believe.

- How is Andrews's perspective on parent involvement in schools similar and different from your own?
- Conduct interviews with parents regarding (1) how they believe parents should be involved with schools; (2) how they are involved in the education of their children; and, (3) how they believe schools encourage and discourage parents from being involved with schools.
- What do you think Andrews meant when she said, "We can't say that just because we have some parents on a couple of committees that we are a community school. If we don't look at the day-to-day process of being a community school, a few events here and there don't make that happen"?
- What do you think makes a school a "community school"?
- How can schools involve the family and community in "the day-to-day process of being a community school"?

As Andrews observes, in conventional schools parent involvement is usually thought of as parents assisting the school with various tasks. Teachers and other school personnel typically perceive the parent's presence in the school as resulting in better effort and behavior from the parent's child, thus making the work of school personnel easier. This essentially constitutes a one-way relationship of parents serving schools. In some instances, schools believe they give back to parents by providing workshops to assist them in their child-rearing efforts. While such workshops may be a valuable service, by themselves they imply a deficit view of parents. That is, the workshops suggest that parents are deficient in their child-rearing and that a workshop can fix their deficiency. As Rioux and Berla (1994) note, schools should avoid "putting the parents in a box" by assuming that they and their families "have things wrong with them that have to be fixed" (p. 31).

How do we facilitate the development of a relationship where *families and schools* are *involved with each other* in meaningful and legitimate ways for the benefit of students/children? Meaningful and legitimate involvement extends beyond viewing parents and caretakers as "extra bodies" in the school building that provide clerical assistance or as revenue generators via their work in PTO fund raising activities. Parents and caretakers must be given opportunities to share their hopes and dreams for their children with education professionals and to inquire with us as we mutually identify ways in which hopes and dreams might be realized. We must recognize and acknowledge that families are full educational partners with the school and that families have perspectives, insight, and knowledge that can contribute to the key questions and tasks with which we, as educators, wrestle. Families can have a voice in the practices of the school via participation in Parent-Teacher Organizations, school decision-making councils, advisory groups, ad hoc committees, and standing committees. They may also have a voice in informal ways such as through informal parent networks and conversations with teachers, principals, and other school personnel.

There is, however, a potentially negative aspect to parent/family involvement in decision making. Ursula Casanova (1996) observes that some parents try to control what happens in schools so that it serves their interests and the interests of their child, but not necessarily the interests of all children. For example, some parents may argue for special programs for gifted students or against the inclusion of students with disabilities in the regular classroom, because they are concerned with the best interests of their child without considering the effect on all children. This is why in a democratic school we must ensure that all perspectives are heard, studied, and discussed, and that concerns for equity are strongly considered (i.e., the democratic IDEALS of inquiry, discourse, and equity). This helps prevent the pursuit of some individuals' interests at the expense of others' interests or the interests of the community.

Schools should be cognizant of the need to include families who have traditionally been disenfranchised from schools. Parents and caretakers, especially the disenfranchised, may not come to school even if schools invite them. This may be because they harbor unpleasant memories of school from their own student days. Visiting the imposing physical structures that were the site of unhappy days may be unappealing. Thus, schools must both develop relationships with families that break down preexisting barriers as well as make efforts to meet them on their turf—in community centers, churches, or even in their homes. Additionally, sometimes barriers that are negligible for middle class parents (e.g., child care and transportation to meetings) may restrict the participation of the less economically fortunate (Capper & Hammiller, 1993). These barriers can be overcome by providing baby-sitters for younger siblings and perhaps even bus service to the school for parents.

Democratic schools and teachers should attempt to create more *familylike* schools (Epstein, 1995). Familylike schools view *students as children*. They see the family and community as partners and as having shared interests and responsibilities in the education and development of children. This contrasts with schools where children are viewed only as students and where families and schools are viewed as being separate from each

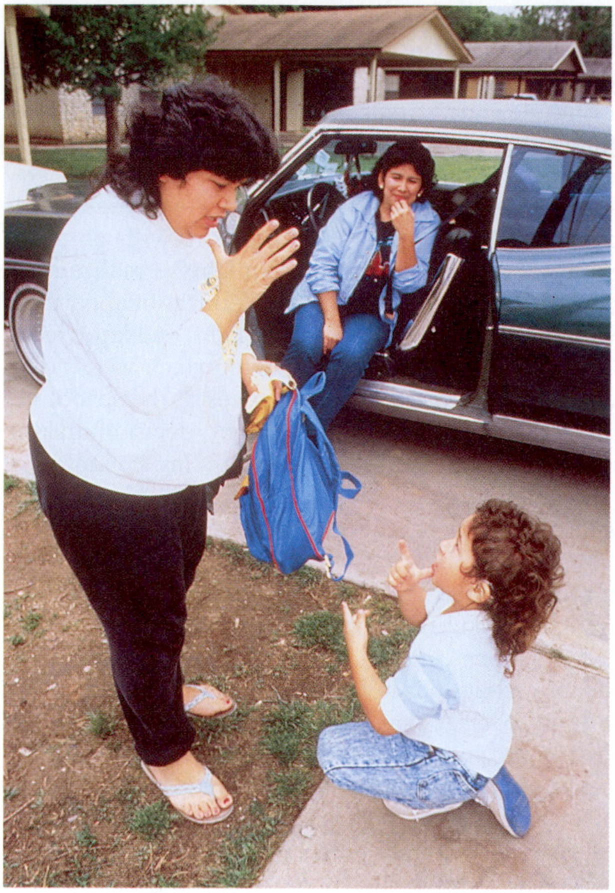

What can teachers do for parents and students who are deaf and/or don't speak English?

other—each with their own nonintersecting responsibilities. Family-like schools are characterized by a recognition and honoring of each child's individuality, by efforts to make each child feel special, and by *always* making *all* families feel welcome in the school, not just those who are affluent, powerful, or frequently involved in school functions and events.

Just as school personnel should attempt to create more familylike schools, parents and other caregivers should attempt to create more *school-like* families by incorporating school-like elements into their families (Epstein, 1995). School-like families recognize that each *child is also a student.* They reinforce the value of school, homework, and help their child build skills and feelings of success, including feelings of academic success.

Obligations of schools and families to each other. In order for schools and families to be in a mutually empowering relationship that permits them to share leadership for a child's/student's development, each has basic obligations to the other.

The most essential *obligation of families* and most important way in which they can be in relationship with schools is via carrying out the basic functions of caring for their children. The manner in which these functions are carried out impacts more significantly than any other factor on the child's ability to attend to her or his work as a student. Basic obligations of families require providing for the child's health and safety and ensuring that the child feels loved and cared for. Additionally, parenting and child rearing approaches that are consistent with the characteristics of empowering schools and classrooms discussed earlier in this chapter are important.

The establishment of a home environment that supports a child as a student is a second essential and significant way that parents and families can be involved in the education of students. Being physically present in school may be helpful in communicating the parent's support for education to the child, but it is not essential to the child receiving a good education. On the other hand, family support of their children through concerned parenting and through active interest and involvement in their children's learning at home is almost always essential to getting a good education. When we think of parent involvement in schools, our first thought should not be of how frequently the parent is physically present in the school building. Rather, our first thought should be of how frequently and pervasively the parent is emotionally and intellectually present in their child's schooling via involvement with the child in his or her education. Emotional and intellectual presence includes not only time spent with the student at home on learning activities, but also providing a home environment that is conducive to working on school-related tasks. Supportive practices will vary by student and family but might include such things as ensuring that there is a quiet area in the house where school tasks can be completed (although some children may not need to have quiet, but may work equally well with television, stereo, and other sounds competing for their attention), having a daily "study/homework" time, having books available in the house, modeling reading and writing, and having materials and supplies needed for schoolwork readily available.

Practices for schools which empower the family in their parenting work include parent education programs; programs that support families with health, nutrition and other information and services; home visits where schools and families mutually discuss their goals for students/children; and neighborhood meetings where information is exchanged and discussion occurs that is focused on helping families understand schools and schools understand families (Epstein, 1995).

Schools should be cautious, however, when working with families on two fronts. First, they should ensure that they do not position themselves as superior to families, viewing families as deficient. Second, they should be careful not to impose dominant cultural perspectives of families and parenting on those who come from diverse backgrounds and/or hold different perspectives of parenting and family life. If schools offer parenting classes, it is important that they be offered in an interactive fashion that gives all participants an opportunity to explore different ways of parenting, rather than presenting one model of parenting as the best model.

The most essential *obligation of schools and teachers* to families is communication. What communication channels exist between school and home? How does the school communicate information to families? How can families communicate information to the school? What is the nature of information that flows from school to home and from home to school? Is information communicated primarily about the individual student or about the school as a whole? When information is communicated about the individual student, is it only negative information, or does positive information

The Web sites of the following organizations contain more information about parent involvement in the education of their children:

The National Parent Information Network

http://npin.org

Project Appleseed

http://members.aol.com/pledgenow/appleseed/

also get communicated? How does communication with non-English speaking families occur? These are some of the many issues involved in schools communicating with families.

Practices which enhance school-home communication include common practices such as newsletters, parent-teacher conferences, handbooks, and other forms of written communication that contain clear written information on school programs, policies, and choices. Less common practices which facilitate parent empowerment as they work with schools include providing written communication in multiple languages in multilingual school communities; providing language translators as needed; establishing other communication structures that facilitate communication with non-English speaking families, nonliterate families, and families without telephones; a voice mail system that makes it possible to establish efficient oral communication with all families having telephones; establishing multiple channels of communication (e.g., written bulletins, voice mail, phone calls, newsletters, postings on bulletin boards, telephone trees); sending home folders or portfolios of student work, especially when combined with an interactive communication structure; and developing two-way and "multiple-way" channels of communication that pass information interactively between schools, families, and communities (Epstein, 1995).

The communication obligation of schools and teachers to families, however, goes beyond the need to pass on information about events, programs, and policies. It extends to developing channels through which parents, families, and schools can share with each other their dreams and aspirations for children, students, schools, and families and collaboratively develop ways in which their visions can be pursued.

Section summary. Democratic school communities move beyond conceptions that suggest that educating students is the work of the school, while raising children is the work of parents and families. Instead, in democratic schools, parents and schools discuss and grow to understand how schools can assist families in raising and educating children who are also students and how families can assist schools in educating and raising students who are also children. Rather than labeling parents who do not spend time volunteering in the school as uncaring, democratic schools (1) respect cultural differences (e.g., some cultures hold teachers in very high regard and believe in deferring to teachers and the school in educational matters); (2) recognize the reality of family life in our society (e.g., the scarcity of time, especially in homes where the single parent or both parents work during school hours); and (3) recognize that the most important and powerful way in which parents can be involved in schools does not require being physically present in the school.

Democratic schools recognize that the most important and powerful way in which parents and families can be involved in schools is by being interested and supportive of their children's educational efforts at home. In democratic schools the key question for educators is not, "How do we get parents involved in the school?" but rather, "How do we get schools and families involved with each other?" Ultimately, the most important issue is how schools and families can work together to benefit children.

GLOBAL CHALLENGE

South Africa's Curriculum Reform

(Adapted from "South Africa Tackles Ambitious Curriculum Reform Effort," by G. Carter, 1998, Education Update, 40(4), p. 2.)

The exhilaration and excitement of South Africa permeate every sense and sensibility. It is a breathtakingly beautiful country filled with startling contrasts. It is an extraordinary country of immense charm and magnificent adventure. But as we approach the 21st century, South Africa is also a country with many inequities striving to build a new nation.

South Africa's education system is crippled by a legacy of apartheid as it struggles to deal with issues of inequity and quality. These issues stem from the previous regime's purposeful allocation of ample resources to white schools but woefully inadequate resources to black schools. Consequently, the brew of raised expectations among the ever-growing numbers of the poor and the government's inability to respond portends trying times ahead.

The new government is trying to respond to this situation through an enterprise called the National Qualifications Framework (NQF), an innovative education and training paradigm that uses outcomes-based education [OBE] to prepare students to be lifelong learners. . . .

Sangaliso Mkhatshwa, deputy minister of education, asserts that "this system offers much in South Africa's move away from the rote learning and content-driven curricula of the past." He further contends that it represents a "head, hands, and heart approach, as learners are required to indicate what they have learned in terms of knowledge, skills, and attitudes."

In response, outspoken critics like Professor Jonathon Jansen, University of Durban-Westville, contend that, "OBE will fail, not because politicians and bureaucrats are malintended, but because the policy is being implemented [in a top-down way and] in isolation and ignorance of almost 50 years of accumulated experience with curriculum change."

- Engage in additional inquiry about South Africa, its educational system, and current efforts underway to democratize the country and its education system.
- Search the Internet for information about the efforts described in this Global Challenge. Find out more about the National Qualifications Framework. Do you believe it is "innovative"? Why or why not? How is it congruent or incongruent with democratic IDEALS?
- What is meant by outcomes-based education?
- Discuss the ways in which outcomes-based education might be congruent and incongruent with democratic IDEALS.
- What is the relationship of "rote learning" and "content-driven curricula" to democratic IDEALS?
- What is the relationship between the way education policy in South Africa is purportedly being implemented and democratic IDEALS?
- What are the parallels between the South African situation as described here and policies and practices in American schools? What are the differences?

SUMMARY

In democratic school communities your role and responsibilities as a teacher are different than they are in conventional, more bureaucratic and hierarchical schools. In democratic school communities simply "doing your job" is insufficient. Merely doing your job implies completing individual, isolated duties that fulfill minimums specified in job descriptions rather than the more encompassing, interconnected responsibilities that are part of membership and shared leadership in a community. Your role and responsibilities as a member and leader in a democratic school community should be guided by a sense of collective responsibility for each member of the local school community and the broader global community. As a teacher you are no longer simply responsible for students while those students are in your classroom nor for only the events that occur in your classroom. Rather, you have a collective responsibility with the other members of your school community for all students and for everything that occurs in your school community.

The ways and means of shared leadership described in this chapter are concerned with empowerment, relationships, democratic IDEALS, and collective responsibility. Ultimately they have to do with the intersecting concerns and needs of students, families, schools, and communities. This is in contrast to conventional schools. As Goodman (1992) has noted, "The language . . . in traditional schools is dominated by notions of management, control, and discipline, that is, concepts common to groups of strangers rather than to people who are working together as a community" (p. 95). It is only through viewing teachers, students, families, schools, and communities as a collectivity, rather than each trying to control or manage the other, that we will be able to work together in an effective, caring, and democratic manner. In the end, it is only when we are effective in facilitating the empowerment of others that we too become empowered. As members and leaders in a democratic school community, we not only have the potential to serve as agents of empowerment, but we too are empowered when we work with students, families, and communities in the ways described in this chapter.

DOING DEMOCRACY

- Conduct interviews with teachers, principals, and other school staff members regarding how they would like families to be involved with the school, with the education of their children, and ways that they believe the school encourages and discourages family involvement.
- Conduct interviews with students regarding how they think their parents and families are involved with their school and with their education and how they would like to see them involved.

- Offer to discuss your data with the school community or communities in which you collected your data. Collaboratively analyze the data and its implications.
- If the school or school communities in which you collected your data are unable or unwilling to collaborate with you, analyze your data by yourself. In either case you should determine what you have learned: how students, parents, and educators differ in their responses; how their responses are similar; what the implications of what you have learned are for your practice as a teacher in a democratic school.

IDEALS CHALLENGE: *Deepening Discourse*

At the beginning of this chapter you completed the following exercise. Now that you have read about sharing leadership and responsibility in schools complete the exercise again. How did your response after reading and discussing the issues raised in the chapter compare with your response prior to reading the chapter?

Complete the following statement.

- The role of teachers in democratic schools is to ______________.

PRESENT TO PAST

The Feminization of Teaching

Teachers today are overwhelmingly middle class, European American females. At the start of the 19th century, it is estimated that females comprised only 10% of the American teaching force (Brumberg, 1983, p. 379). By 1870, a 30-state sample revealed that 56% of teachers were women (Strober & Lanford, 1986, p. 223), and by 1900, 80% of teachers nationally were women. Today about 70% of public school teachers are female. This includes more than four out of five elementary teachers and somewhat more than half of high school teachers.

How did the teaching force get to be primarily female? The reasons have to do with the cultural and social beliefs of the time. These, in turn, affected the economics of supply and demand.

In the early 19th century, due to the enormous influence of Locke and Rousseau on educational thinkers such as Johan Pestalozzi, the cultural image of children as miniature adults began to change. Pestalozzi felt that children needed nurturing in a supportive learning environment and that school should resemble a family or home. Using this image, females would therefore be the best teachers because of their nurturing dispositions. Other advocates of a primarily female teaching force included Catherine Beecher, Mary Lyon, Horace Mann, and Henry Barnard, who all intoned about the "female virtues" of patience, nurturance, and understanding of children. Barnard, a famous common school advocate, expressed the idea succinctly when he stated in 1850 that women should be trained to be "daughters, sisters, wives, mothers, companions, and teachers" (Vinovskis & Bernard, 1978, p. 862). Note that teaching was the only occupation mentioned.

Additionally, cultural stereotypes of women's character promoted the notion that women were happiest when engaged in "self-effacing service" because they were "natural Christians" (Brumberg, 1983, p. 383). Females were seen as having moral character, which was the most important ingredient in the makeup of a good teacher, and thus "morally suitable" for teaching.

With the onset of industrialization and urbanization, increasing numbers of young women were being educated. Women variously saw teaching either as a job, a calling, or a way-station to marriage and motherhood. Some women chose to teach because they wanted to earn extra income but had few occupational choices and teaching was the best job available. Other women became teachers based on religious commitments. They could not preach in the local church, but they could teach in the local school.

During this period there was also a call for females to be educated for political responsibility and civic virtue in the new republic. It became the political responsibility of females to become self-reliant, rational, literate mothers and pass on the values of democracy to one's children. The work of teaching was compatible with a female's future roles as wife and mother. Educating other people's children was in essence training for the job of motherhood, and was thus a respectable occupation at a time when most occupations were off limits to females. Women's political responsibility could also be argued to relate to the need to teach the two million immigrants who entered the U.S. in the 1850s of American values and the American way of life. Women were essential if the common schools were to help assimilate the masses.

As schools became bureaucratized and professionalized, teaching became a less desirable occupation for males because they had traditionally viewed teaching as supplementary work. Farmers who wanted a little extra cash or students home on break from the academy often filled in as teachers. Wages were kept low, due to the seasonal nature of the work and the fact that schools depended on the financial support of reluctant taxpayers. With the advent of more demanding teacher certification requirements, longer school terms, compulsory summer institutes, and greater curriculum standardization, being a teacher became more than a part time job and teaching became less desirable for men. Women, with fewer career options, were more willing to accept the lower wages. As women assumed a larger proportion of the teaching force, teaching came to be seen even more as a female job and some men who might otherwise have considered teaching opted for occupations which were "male" and not "female."

The feminization of teaching has had a number of effects:

- Teaching provided a new occupational and intellectual role for women. It enhanced their chances to be self-supporting, and was certainly a key part of the 19th century women's social movement. The work of women outside the home helped to foster change, and was a link to the suffrage movement.
- During the 19th century the common schools which customarily went through eighth grade, were the only teaching opportunity for the great majority of female students. In essence, females were "tracked" into *elementary* teaching, in part by the schools that trained teachers. This was

due at least in part to the traditional perception that men were better disciplinarians with older students.

- As school enrollments expanded schools became more bureaucratic. "Head teachers" gave way to "principals" and the position of superintendent was created to administer urban systems. These new leadership perches were assumed by men, so that women stood at the bottom of the hierarchy.
- When women accepted low wages (and men rejected them), teaching was institutionalized as a low-wage occupation. Because women were viewed as inferior, or at least subordinate, to men, their profession could not equal male professions such as law and medicine—or perhaps even be considered a profession at all.

IDEALS CHALLENGE: *Deepening Discourse*

- What effect might the feminization of teaching have on the way in which schools have been (and continue to be) led?
- What effect might the feminization of teaching have on the education students receive?
- What are the implications for equity of the feminization of teaching?

END NOTE

[1]Parts of this section are adapted from O'Hair and Reitzug (1997).

REFERENCES

Angus, L. (1989). "New" leadership and the possibility of educational reform. In J. Smyth (Ed.), *Critical perspectives on educational leadership* (pp. 63–92). Philadelphia: The Falmer Press.

Argyris, C. (1976). *Increasing leadership effectiveness.* New York: Wiley.

Bass, B. M. (1985). *Leadership and performance beyond expectations.* New York: Free Press.

Bennis, W., & Nanus, B. (1985). *Leaders: The strategies for taking charge.* New York: Harper & Row.

Boyer, E. (1993, March). *In Search of Community.* Address delivered at the Association for Supervision and Curriculum Development Conference, Washington DC.

Brumberg, J. J. (1983). The feminization of teaching: "Romantic sexism" and American protestant denominationalism. *History of Education Quarterly, 23*(3), 379–384.

Capper, C. A., & Hammiller, R. (1993). *The principal's role in neighborhood-based interagency collaboration: A peripheral and flexible link.* (ERIC Document Reproduction Service No. ED 378637).

Carter, G. (1998). South Africa tackles ambitious curriculum reform effort. *Education Update, 40*(4), 2.

Casanova, U. (1996). Parent involvement: A call for prudence. *Educational Researcher, 25*(8), 30–32, 46.

Cochran, M., & Dean, C. (1991). Home-school relations and the empowerment process. *The Elementary School Journal, 91*(3), 261–269.

Delpit, L. (1995). *Other people's children: Cultural conflict in the classroom.* New York: The New Press.

Epstein, J. L. (1995). School/Family/Community partnerships: Caring for the children we share. *Phi Delta Kappan, 76,* 701–712.

Goodman, J. (1992). *Elementary schooling for critical democracy.* Albany, NY: State University of New York Press.

Ladson-Billings, G. (1994). *The dreamkeepers: Successful teachers of African-American children.* San Francisco: Jossey-Bass.

Lambert, L. (1995). Toward a theory of constructivist leadership. In L. Lambert, D. Walker, D. P. Zimmerman, J. E. Cooper, M. D. Lambert, M. E. Gardner, & P. J. Slack (Eds.), *The constructivist leader* (pp. 28–51). New York: Teachers College Press.

O'Hair, M. J., & Reitzug, U. C. (1997). Teacher leadership: In what ways? For what purpose? *Action in Teacher Education, 19*(3), 65–76.

Reitzug, U. C. (1994). A case study of empowering principal behavior. *American Educational Research Journal, 31,* 283–307.

Rioux, J. W., & Berla, N. (1994). *Innovations in parent and family involvement.* (ERIC Document Reproduction Service No. ED367454).

Sherman, T. M. (1998, June 3). Another danger for 21st-Century children? *Education Week, 17*(38), 30, 32.

Sizer, T. R. (1992). *Horace's school: Redesigning the American high school.* New York: Houghton Mifflin.

Strober, M. H., & Lanford, A. G. (1986). The feminization of public school teaching: Cross-sectional analysis, 1850–1880. *Signs, 11*(2), 212–235.

Urbanski, A. (1997, April). Remembering Al Shanker. *Teacher Magazine,* 42–43.

Vinovskis, M. A., & Bernard, R. M. (1978). Beyond Catherine Beecher: Female education in the antebellum period. *Signs, 3*(4), 856–859.

Wrigley, J. (1982). *Class politics and public schools: Chicago 1900–1950.* New Brunswick, NJ: Rutgers University Press.

Zalesznik, A. (1977). Managers and leaders: Are they different? *Harvard Business Review, 55*, 67.

What are the roles of teachers, students, and others in democratic schools in serving others?

CHAPTER 14

SERVING OTHERS

IDEALS CHALLENGE: *Deepening Discourse*

(Adapted from Developmental Studies Center, 1994, p. 39.)

Dear Family Members and Friends,

This year we're making an extra effort to build a stronger sense of community, to create a place where children feel comfortable and cared for. As a start, we've been thinking about ways to help children get to know more of the other children at school.

Next week we're going to start a Buddies Program. Each classroom will be matched with another classroom in the school, and each child will be assigned a "buddy" from the other class. Children in grades K–2 will be matched with an older buddy, and children in grades 3–5 will be matched with a younger buddy. Our goal is to help older children experience being responsible, caring friends and to help younger children feel comfortable and cared for at school.

The School Staff

- How does this letter illustrate an example of serving others?
- What else might schools do to "build a stronger sense of community" and make school "a place where children feel comfortable and cared for"?

Serving others is the action component of democracy. In essence, in democratic schools inquiry, discourse, equity, authenticity, and shared leadership focus on connecting individuals with a concern for the good of other individuals and for the common good. Without an action component, however, the ideals of democracy can conceivably be "all talk and no action." Serving others connects our study, our talk, and our values and beliefs with our practice.

There are many dimensions to serving others. As illustrated in Table 14.1, these dimensions include:

- teachers serving others in *their school* via

  sharing their best practices with other teachers in the school

Table 14.1 Ways Teachers Serve Others in Democratic Schools

Serving the School	Serving the Community	Serving Students
• sharing best practices internally • serving on committees • collaborating about curriculum • participating in school governance and decision-making	• sharing best practices externally • participating in community service • working toward eliminating social inequities	• daily teaching • nonteaching work with students • facilitating service learning projects

serving on committees that help complete the work of the school

inquiring, engaging in discourse, and collaborating in various ways with others in terms of the curricular and instructional efforts of the school

participating in school governance and decision making (which may overlap with some of the previously mentioned dimensions)

- teachers serving *their communities* via

sharing their and their school's best practices with teachers from other schools

participating in providing service to others in the community

advocating and working toward rectifying local, national, or global social inequities

- teachers serving *their students* via

teaching

nonteaching work with students

creating and facilitating opportunities for students to serve their schools and community

We have dealt with many of these dimensions of service earlier in this book. In this chapter we will more closely examine the ways in which teachers can create and facilitate opportunities for their students to serve others.

RELATIONSHIP OF SERVING OTHERS TO DEMOCRATIC EDUCATION

Whereas we have previously described the "habits of mind" that characterize democratic schools, the involvement of students in providing service can be thought of as "habits of the heart." Service counteracts the rampant individualism that currently characterizes our society. Kinsley and McPherson (1995) note that "a fundamental and natural part of democracy is based on people helping and caring for one another" (p. 3). In democratic schools and society, there is a need for students to understand not only their rights as individuals, but also to understand their responsibilities toward each other (Neal, 1986).

Being involved in service activities helps students see the relationship between their private rights and interests and the common good. It helps them to see issues from a broader perspective. Through service, students can begin to understand how their community is governed and how they can have input. McPherson and Kinsley (1995) note that students serving others "Helps democratize our schools and communities by giving voice and influence to young people who are often the recipients of service, but are rarely asked to be 'of' service" (p. 115). When we create opportunities for students to serve others, we view young people as "resources who have the capacity . . . to contribute to the work of their schools and communities" (p. 115). Being involved in providing service allows students to become active participants in a democracy and helps them to see that they can make a difference. In essence, being involved in service helps students develop a sense of social responsibility.

IDEALS CHALLENGE: *Supporting Service*

(Often when teachers begin contemplating engaging their students in service activities, they wonder what they might do and where they might go to find service opportunities. Winifred Pardo, 1997, offers some suggestions in the following excerpt.

In asking "Where might we go? What might we do?" program developers learn to look with new eyes at the community and at school programs. For example, students in intermediate grades may tutor children, while they in turn are taught by high school students. . . . Work with handicapped children can provide a particularly productive service learning experience. . . . Many of the elderly are in special need of relationships with children and, in turn, have much to offer. . . . Many students visit centers [for the elderly] on a regular basis. . . . In Macomb, Illinois, adolescents can shop for and deliver food to the homebound elderly. And the Grandfriends Club in Commack, New York, pairs students with elderly "buddies." . . . Some schools forge links with animal shelters, recycling centers, marine refuges, wildlife preserves, and outdoor education sites. In Burns, Oregon, elementary children replant native flora in the Harney High Desert Interpretive Garden. Also in Oregon, ninth and tenth graders rehabilitate trails and other facilities in the Sunrise Youth Camp. . . .

Some service models are ideally suited to urban settings. Gardens sprout from formerly littered lots; walls are transformed by budding artists; city blocks are cleaned up. . . . Another New York City school [has created] a Kiddy Corner in a local welfare office, where the middle school students work with young children as

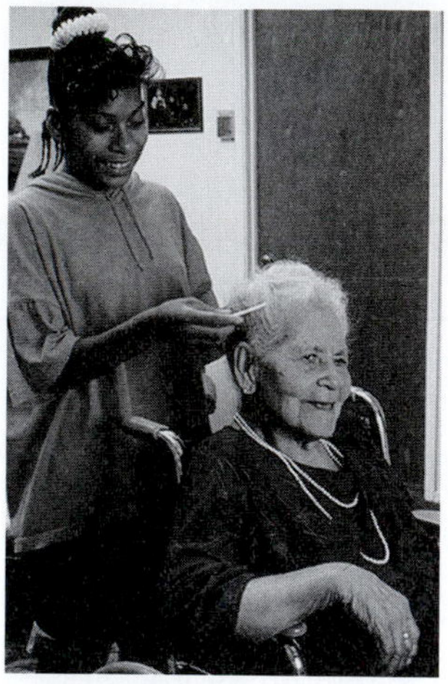

What benefits do you think this student is getting from providing service?

they wait, often for hours, with their parents. . . . Another important service grew in response to a riot. . . . The students, realizing that communication between the community and the police was unsatisfactory, helped the officers to learn Spanish, the language of many neighborhood residents.

- What additional ideas for service learning projects can you develop?
- What do you believe students might learn from each of the service projects mentioned in the excerpt?

MOVING FROM COMMUNITY SERVICE TO SERVICE LEARNING

Providing community service transforms students from passive recipients of schooling to active participants in their own education. It redefines the perception of youth in the community from a cause of problems to a source of solutions. There is, however, a difference between community service and service learning. Community service by itself can simply be students helping someone else, with no conscious efforts being made to ensure that students actually learn something from the service activity. Although community service can be a valuable experience in its own right, *service learning* takes community service a step further. In a sense, service can be altruistic without being academic. In *service learning*, however, teachers attempt to enhance and facilitate the student learning that occurs as a result of the service experience by developing "conscious and thoughtfully designed occasions for reflecting on the service experience" (Alliance for Service Learning in Educational Reform, 1995, p. 127). Reflection is the process of looking back at the actions taken, thinking about what has been accomplished, about what could have been done differently, and how the situation in which action was taken connects to the larger social context. For example, serving meals at a homeless shelter can be connected to the larger social context that explores and analyzes the reasons for widespread poverty.

When combined with formal education, service becomes a method of learning known as service learning. In service learning teachers teach in a way that is student-centered, interactive, and experiential. The curriculum is placed in the context of real-life situations. It reflects authentic pedagogy (see chapter 11). Students go through a continuing cycle of analyzing, evaluating, synthesizing, and acting as they provide service to others and learn from their service activities (Alliance for Service Learning in Educational Reform, 1995, p. 127).

There are a number of characteristics that distinguish service learning from community service (Alliance for Service Learning in Educational Reform, 1995, p. 126). Service learning activities and experiences:

- are thoughtfully organized
- meet actual community needs
- are coordinated in collaboration with the school and community
- are integrated into the student's academic curriculum

- include structured time for students to reflect, talk, and write about what they did and saw during the actual service activity
- provide young people with opportunities to use newly acquired academic skills and knowledge in real-life situations in their own communities
- enhance what is taught in the school by extending student learning beyond the classroom
- foster the development of a sense of caring for others

Essentially, service learning connects classroom study to the world beyond the classroom's and school's walls, as students learn math, science, social studies, and other subjects in the context of their service activities (Alliance for Service Learning in Educational Reform, 1995, p. 127). It reflects authentic pedagogy in that teaching and learning have a "value beyond school" (Newman & Wehlage, 1995, p. 16).

IDEALS CHALLENGE: *Achieving Authenticity*

(Adapted from Alliance for Service Learning in Educational Reform, 1995.)

Service at a community center that distributes food to the hungry and homeless by a group of secondary school students was connected to the curriculum in the following ways:

1. the study of crop rotation and rainfall in science and geography
2. computing individual and collective nutritional needs in math class
3. the economies of food distribution and efforts of government to address these issues in social studies class
4. the ways in which racism and classism affect the employment process
5. the impact of moving corporate production facilities to Third World countries on poverty in this country and in the Third World

- How do each of these links to the curriculum reflect authentic pedagogy (that is, how do they reflect construction of knowledge, disciplined inquiry, and value beyond school)?
- What else might be added to these curriculum linkages so that they reflect authentic pedagogy more thoroughly?
- In what other ways can linkages to the curriculum that reflect authentic pedagogy be created as a result of this service experience?

Principles of Service Learning

The Alliance for Service Learning has developed standards for high quality school-based service learning. The following discussion is based on the Alliance standards.

Effective service learning strengthens both service and academic learning. Rather than simply engaging in community service, service activities and experiences should be designed to facilitate student academic and civic learning. Teachers should use discussion, reading, and writing to enhance the reflection and learning that occurs as a result of participation in service activities and experiences. Researchers have found that when designed properly, service learning has many positive outcomes for students (Conrad & Hedin, 1991). These outcomes include:

fostering students' social, psychological, and emotional development

heightening their sense of personal and social responsibility

helping students develop more positive attitudes toward adults

ensuring more active exploration of careers

enhancing self-esteem

stimulating growth in moral and ego development

facilitating the development of more complex patterns of thought

helping students acquire a greater mastery of skills

Effective service learning provides opportunities for students to learn new skills, to think critically, and to test new roles. Many advocates of student service argue that service is not an end in itself, but that its ultimate objective is for students to further their academic learning and other skills. While we agree that this is true, we also partially disagree. We do not believe that the ultimate goal of service learning is the utilitarian goal of academic learning. It is rather to help students become more fully human, to learn what it means to be a citizen of a democratic society, to learn to be altruistic, but also to learn about the social and cultural forces that underlie the types of situations in which students provide service. (This is developed more fully below.) We agree that service learning helps students increase their academic skills, but we also believe that this is a secondary reason. The primary reason is to learn to become a democratic citizen. Nonetheless, as a result of service experiences students can develop abilities in public speaking, organizing meetings, analyzing problems, developing action plans, conducting evaluations, and a variety of other skills and roles (Boyte, 1991).

Preparation and reflection are essential elements in service learning. Community service should typically be preceded by preparatory study that helps students learn the most from the service experience. Preparatory study might include attention to history that is relevant to the service experience, and to underlying problems, policies, or social or cultural factors that have caused or are contributing to the situation in which service is being provided. In some instances, attention should be given to the development of skills and attitudes necessary to complete service. For example, if students are going to be working in a cultural context that is different from their own, they may need some preparatory study of that culture.

It is also important that teachers help students process, synthesize, and reflect on what they have gained from a service activity. Reflection should infuse all parts of the service learning process rather than merely following the field-based part of the service experience (Toole & Toole, 1995). As Peter Kleinbard notes, "experience by itself does not produce learning automatically and can be 'miseducative'" (1997, p. 7). Reflection should be concerned with the task itself; with the social, political, economic, vocational, and other aspects of the task; and with "related issues of the human spirit, such as questions of purpose, meaning, suffering, hope, friendship, justice, care, and responsibility" (Toole & Toole, 1995, p. 105).

Reflection should occur before, during, and after the actual field-based portion of the service experience. The Doing Democracy section at the end of the chapter highlights the type of questions that you might reflect on with your students during each phase of the service experience. Reflection can be stimulated via students writing in a journal, composing a song or poem, sketching a drawing or a cartoon, creating a slide show, authoring a short story, giving a speech, doing a dance, or "hosting" a "talk show" (Toole & Toole, 1995).

How might this service learning experience serve both altruistic and learning purposes?

Service experiences should be shared with peers and community. Sharing service experiences calls attention to the significance of what students are doing. While recognition should not be the objective of service activities, given all the negative publicity young people receive, it is important that we acknowledge the contributions they make. Publicly recognizing the service work of students helps them understand that individuals can make a difference in a democracy and that they can be contributing members of society as young people.

At one time children and adolescents were active participants in families, making contributions to the work of the household. They were valued for their work, realized they had things of value to contribute, and developed an intrinsic sense of self-worth. However, as our society became more industrialized and later more service- and information-driven, the workplace for many adults changed from the home where they might be engaged in running the farm or the family business to a distant office or factory. The relocation of adult work sites resulted in the disappearance of many of the opportunities young people had to contribute to the work of the household. Thus, there was a reduction in opportunities for young people to assume responsibility for themselves and others and to interact with adults. Schools typically offered youth few opportunities for taking responsibility, with schooling often being passive and merely requiring students to sit for many hours listening to adults (Kleinbard, 1997). Harold Howe, former U.S. Commissioner of Education, notes that we often implicitly communicate to students that we have no use for them in our economic system nor in our community affairs, essentially saying to them, "We suggest you sit quietly, behave yourselves, and study hard in the schools we provide as a holding pen until we are ready to accept you into the adult world" (Howe quoted in Kinsley & McPherson, 1995, p. 5). Service learning communicates a different message to students and can compensate for the disappearance of the naturally occurring opportunities for youth service that formerly existed in our society. It provides young people with opportunities to make real contributions to the school and the community (Kleinbard, 1997; Schine, 1997).

Effective service learning involves youth in the planning of service experiences. Involving youth in the planning of service learning activities and experiences helps them develop valuable skills and gains their support for the service activity. Students can be involved in the selection of service experiences, the making of contacts with individuals at the service site, making arrangements for site visits, and a variety of related tasks.

The service students perform should contribute in a meaningful way to the school or community. The work in which students engage as they provide service must be real. It must fill a recognized need rather than being artificially contrived. Additionally, the activity should be developmentally appropriate. Effective service learning is congruent with the learning and developmental needs of students as well as to the needs of the community. Determinations of developmental appropriateness include considerations of the type of service that will be performed, the duration of the service, the service role students will be filling, the desired outcomes, and the structure for reflection that will be used (Alliance for Service Learning in Educational Reform, 1995, p. 128).

GLOBAL CHALLENGE: Service Learning Around the World

(Adapted from Eberly, 1997, pp. 19–26.)

Throughout the world, increasing numbers of young men and women in other countries are utilizing their knowledge and skills to serve others and are learning from their service experiences. For example, Germany now has a de facto national service wherein young men can choose between spending 12 months in the military or 15 months in *Zivildienst* [Civil Service].

In Nigeria, to acquire a solid understanding of their diversity the national service law requires all university graduates to serve one year in a part of the country other than where they grew up. They work with villages on such projects as road construction and school building. At the end of the service year, Corps members gather at a number of sites around the country for a week of reflection and formulation of ideas to improve the program. . . .

Canada established a national service program in 1977. Twelve person teams of young people are deliberately made up to reflect the Canadian population: eight are English-speaking and four French-speaking; six are men and six are women; team members come from all parts of Canada. Each team carries on service projects in three locations—one in the east, one in the west, and one in the heartland—and at each of the three locations team members live separately for a two-week period with local residents. The total service period is nine months. Not only do these young people work together during the day, they also keep house together. While the Canadians refer to it as national service, service takes a back seat to the experience of living together and traveling around the country.

The United Kingdom is making significant strides toward the general adoption of service learning in schools. They have produced a pioneering set of guidebooks that will facilitate the incorporation of service learning in the curriculum. These guidebooks point out in detail how the individual teacher can integrate student community service with the curriculum.

- Several of the countries discussed have some form of mandatory service requirement. What are the advantages and disadvantages of a mandatory service requirement?
- Are you in favor of, or opposed to, a mandatory service requirement?

Service learning should include both formative and summative evaluation. Formative evaluation is focused on how the service learning experiences and program might continually be improved. What is the experience like for students? What is the experience like for service recipients? How can things be improved? What might be done differently? The idea of formative evaluation is to learn more about how things are going for purposes of on-going improvement. On the other hand, summative evaluation results in judgments and in documentation of outcomes, often to satisfy those who are providing funding for service learning that service learning is indeed making a difference. Summative evaluation addresses questions of how well service learning has met the needs of people it has tried to serve and how well it has met student academic, attitudinal, and citizenship objectives.

Service learning should connect the school and the community in new ways. Service learning has the potential to reduce barriers that typically separate the school and the community. Experiences that are on-going and result in the development of individual and group relationships are more likely to connect schools and communities in new ways than one-shot experiences such as serving a meal at a community shelter on Thanksgiving (not that there is anything wrong with this activity—it is simply unlikely to result in the formation of new relationships). Rather than viewing those with whom we are engaged as "clients" for our service, we are more likely to forge new connections if we view them as partners with whom we develop relationships and understanding. While we may serve some needs they have, they serve us by allowing us to learn from them. By taking education and service into the community, it helps communities become partners in the education of young people and to see young people as contributing members of society. Indeed, young people begin to see themselves in this same way and see that learning can occur in the community and not just in the school.

Service learning is seen and supported as an integral part of life in the school and its community. Service learning should not just be seen as an add-on. It should not be seen as something that occurs in only one or two classrooms, or on special occasions once or twice a year when time permits. It should be integrated as a key and continuing part of the curriculum. Service learning should also receive institutional support in terms of time and money. School schedules should be developed in a way that allocates time for planning and that provides the longer blocks of time needed for service activities. Financially, there should be support for the additional costs of service learning (for example, for transportation expenses to and from service learning sites).

Learning and service goals must be clearly understood by both educators and those in the community who are involved with students in service learning experiences. Sponsors at the service site should not simply view students as someone they are doing a favor to by letting them provide service. Students should be viewed as essential to the efforts in which they are involved. Thus, it is important that there be two-way communication about the goals and objectives of the service learning experience between teachers and service site partners. Parents also need to be educated about the value of service learning activities and involved in the actual implementation of service learning experiences to the extent that is appropriate.

Parents and the community should be brought into the planning process for service learning early rather than after planning has been completed.

Adult guidance and supervision are essential for effective service learning. The role of teachers in service learning is multidimensional.

- Teachers should help develop partnerships with the community that provide service learning opportunities for students. Teachers must become familiar with the communities in which they teach, including its agencies and organizations, so that they know the needs that exist, as well as the opportunities that are present (Carter, 1997).
- Teachers should replace rote learning with authentic learning, using activities that enable students to apply content information and skills to real-life situations which extend learning beyond classroom walls (Kinsley & McPherson, 1995).
- Teachers should make sure that the service experience is well-organized, that details are attended to, and that positive relationships are created and maintained with community participants. For example, teachers should ensure that definite dates and times for service work are established and that students arrive on time; that students and community participants have an orientation that establishes mutual expectations, and; that there is ongoing communication and collaboration between the school and community participants (Pardo, 1997).
- Teachers should be facilitators of learning who help students gather, examine, and synthesize information, and draw conclusions in service learning activities (Kinsley & McPherson, 1995).

In essence, teachers should provide *guidance* in every aspect of the service learning experience including the type of service that is to be provided, ensuring that there are connections between service and the curriculum, creating and facilitating reflective processes, attending to logistical considerations, providing for supervision at the service site, and assessing outcomes.

Teachers should engage in service learning activities of their own. In order to fully understand the nature and benefits of service learning and the things that can be learned from it, teachers should mirror service learning processes in their own work with the community. This will provide not only a valuable service in its own right, but will enhance their teaching around service learning experiences.

IDEALS CHALLENGE: *Learning Leadership*

There are many ways in which service learning can be integrated into the school curriculum. Listed below are a few examples.

1. Working at a senior center can be connected to learning about aging, the demographics of the community, and available social services.
2. Supervising young children at a day-care center can be connected to learning about child development, parenting, and social policy toward children.

CLICK ON IT

Visit "The Home of Service Learning on the Web" at

http://www.csf.colorado.edu/sl/index.html

Another excellent Web site about service learning is sponsored by the Corporation for National Service

http://www.cns.gov/learn/index.html

The U.S. Department of Education Web site also contains extensive information about service learning

http://www.ed.gov/

After locating the site, click on "Search" and enter the words "service learning."

3. Developing a school plan for recycling can be connected to learning about recycling, waste production, consumption, and deterioration.

4. Refurbishing a neighborhood park can be connected for younger students to learning about plants and growing flowers from seeds. For somewhat older students this experience can be connected to research about birds and building bird houses and feeding stations and maintaining them throughout the year. For older students the service experience can focus on the development of a recycling program for the park's waste, with students working with city agencies to institute such a program, decorating collection bins, and designing posters to increase awareness. For high school students the park project can include designing and building an exercise path, creating a mural for park buildings, surveying the community to determine who uses parks and what things they would like to see in a park, and reporting their findings to the public or to a community agency.

- Brainstorm other examples with your fellow students about how else service learning might be incorporated into the curriculum.
- Develop a unit around a service experience that incorporates both service and learning.

Moving Beyond Charity and Altruism

Providing service, developing skills, and learning academic concepts as a result of service learning experiences are valuable in their own right. However, service learning can move beyond objectives such as these, which essentially serve to maintain the societal status quo. Service learning can be structured in a way that works towards a more democratic and equitable society (Kahne & Westheimer, 1996). Thus, there are two approaches to service learning: service learning as reproducing existing (often inequitable) conditions in society, and service learning as promoting social transformation (see Table 14.2).

Service as Altruism

The first approach to service learning is to teach students the importance of charity and altruism. In a sense, this approach promotes service because it is good to help others and because it makes us feel good when we do. In this approach, the importance of civic duty, volunteerism, the need for responsive citizens, and compassion for the less fortunate are stressed. The belief of those using this approach is that helping others in need is sufficient and that

Table 14.2 Service Learning Approaches and Goals

	Moral Goals	Political Goals	Intellectual Goals
Altruistic approach	Giving	Civic Duty	Additive Experience
Transformational approach	Caring	Social Reconstruction	Transformative Experience

Adapted from Kahne & Westheimer, 1996.

analysis of the social and cultural factors that caused the situations to which students are responding is less essential. Students are neither asked to analyze, reflect on, nor articulate an understanding of the conditions and contexts that might have contributed to the social situations the individuals with whom they are interacting are experiencing. Thus, students do not investigate why poverty, racism, drug abuse, environmental exploitation, neglect of the elderly, or other social conditions came to exist and continue to be perpetuated. While the objectives of a "service as altruism" approach are valuable and noble in their own right, they fall short of what can ultimately be accomplished in using service learning to help students function as citizens in a democracy.

Service as Transformative

The second approach to service learning intends to accomplish more than developing students' sense of altruism. As Kahne and Westheimer (1996) note,

> Citizenship in a democratic community requires more than kindness and decency; it requires engagement in complex social and institutional endeavors. Acts of civic duty cannot replace . . . collective social action. Citizenship requires that individuals work to create, evaluate, criticize, and change public institutions and programs. (p. 597)

Essentially, service projects should not occur in isolation. They should be put into, studied, and analyzed in their broader social context. Related knowledge and perspectives should be brought into the service experience. Reflection is used to identify and explore the connections between the service experience and the myriad related social, cultural, political, and economic forces that have led to the situation (for example, the relationships between poverty, racism, economic exploitation by the corporate sector, and the deterioration of cities). In the service as transformative approach, learning is focused on promoting social change by incorporating a systematic and critical analysis of the causes of social and cultural factors that contribute to a social ill. It attempts to develop in students the ability to critically reflect about social policies and conditions,

IDEALS CHALLENGE: *Initiating Inquiry*

As noted previously, service learning should include a "critical analysis of the causes of social and cultural factors that contribute to a social ill" and that it should develop in students "the ability to critically reflect about social policies and conditions." Select one of the following potential service experiences and conduct your own inquiry into the social and cultural factors, policies, and conditions that have contributed to creating the situation.

- Working with individuals who are living in poverty or are homeless.
- Working for the alleviation of the environmental pollution of a lake, river, or stream.
- Working with students who have mental or physical disabilities and are being educated in settings where they are separated from students without disabilities.
- Working with senior citizens who live in nursing homes.

the acquisition of skills of political participation, and the formation of social bonds.

Service that works toward transformation should also explore the various ideological perspectives on an issue (for example, the varying ideological perspectives about welfare). Reflection without analysis can, in some instances, serve to reinforce simplistic or erroneous perspectives and conclusions or to reinforce irrational deep-seated prejudices by making them appear more rational. Structured, informed, and systematic analysis of the service experience won't prevent this, but it will make it less likely. For example, a service learning experience dealing with the less economically fortunate might include an analysis of the causes of poverty, strategies to prevent it, reasons for the growing economic disparity between the rich and poor, the impact of poverty on children, the balance between individual rights and collective responsibility, and the gathering of the life stories of individuals living in poverty. Neither a critical, but school-based assessment of homelessness, nor the service activity by itself alone could have this effect. They must be used in conjunction to have their full impact.

When students from different racial, ethnic, and economic backgrounds work together in service learning projects, stereotypes are often dispelled.

The value of the transformative approach to service learning extends far beyond the service students are providing (although that too is significant). Essentially, this is a socially *and intellectually* transformative approach that develops "analytic and academic skills . . . moral acuity . . . [and] social sensitivity" (Kahne & Westheimer, 1996, p. 595). The type of cognitive transformation that can occur as a result of service learning is exemplified by what occurred in a group of middle-class students who performed for and met with students from a poor community. Prior to meeting the poor students, the middle-class students harbored traditionally stereotypical attitudes about what students living in poverty would be like. As a result of the meeting and subsequent discussion, the middle-class students realized that the students living in poverty were not much different than them—they simply had less money. The transformation initiated by this activity could have been extended even further if the discussion had also encompassed the possible causes of stereotypes and their impact.

The transformative approach to service learning recognizes the explicitly political nature of service and community action. Service and political action are tied together.

IDEALS CHALLENGE: *Deepening Discourse*

Discuss the following statement from the previous paragraph:

"Service and political action are tied together. For example, working to limit deforestation efforts, to prevent institutionalization of Whittle Communications Channel One, to evaluate the representativeness of juries, to analyze the evening news, to assess and improve the availability of child care, are all efforts in which service and political action are inseparable" (Kahne & Westheimer, 1996).

- What is meant by "political action"?
- How is service provided in each of the cited examples?
- What forms might political action take in each example?
- How might each of the democratic IDEALS be served in each example?

IDEALS CHALLENGE: *Examining Equity*

Listed below are a variety of service learning experiences. (Examples are taken from Haynes & Comer, 1997; Kleinbard, 1997.)

working on the school newspaper
serving as a classroom monitor
serving as a crossing guard
raising and lowering the school flag
mentoring younger students
planting flowers around the school
contributing food and clothing to the needy
peer counseling programs
developing a car pooling plan for the school or community
documenting the pollution in a local river and publicizing this information
student internships in community work places and agencies
establishing a school career center and serving as career counselors for other students
producing artwork to be displayed in community settings or murals for buildings
developing a magazine for the immediate community surrounding the school
cleaning up a vacant lot in the community
creating videotapes to be aired on local access television channels that inform the public about community issues

Discuss the following questions with your classmates:

- Which activities are primarily service and which can become service learning experiences?
- How can the latter experiences be connected to the curriculum?
- Which experiences are primarily altruistic and which have possibilities for incorporating issues of equity, social justice, and social transformation?
- How might issues of equity, justice, and transformation be connected to the latter activities?
- Which experiences do you believe are worthwhile to pursue?
- How might you initiate these activities?

SUMMARY

Serving others is central to democratic schools and a democratic society. In serving others we are forging the connection that links our individual needs and interests to the needs of our own and other communities. In serving others we acknowledge that we live in relationship with others. Additionally, we acknowledge our responsibility for making that relationship one that serves not only us as individuals, but others as well.

Serving others is perhaps best exemplified in schools through students and teachers being engaged in service learning experiences. In their fullest implementation, service learning embraces all of the democratic IDEALS.

- *Inquiry* is essential in investigating and critically analyzing the cultural and social conditions and policies that have contributed to the context in which we are involved during our service experience.
- *Discourse* is necessary as we collaboratively reflect on and learn from our service experience.
- Concern for *equity* is central to our analysis of the cultural and social factors that have contributed to the service context we are experiencing.
- Because of their taking place in the world beyond the classroom, service learning experiences are grounded in *authenticity*.
- The collaborative processes between teachers, students, and community participants that are involved in planning and engaging in service learning experiences exemplify shared *leadership*.

IDEALS CHALLENGE: *Supporting Service*

Develop a unit of study around a service experience.

- Follow the service learning principles developed by the Alliance for Service Learning and discussed in this chapter.
- Develop curriculum connections with as many school subjects as you can.
- Write objectives for the experience both in terms of the altruistic and transformational aspects of the experience.

DOING DEMOCRACY

Become involved in a service learning project in your community. Keep a journal of your experiences and reflections about the experiences. Focus on the questions for reflection that are listed below. Questions are written as if you were using them with your students (adapted from Toole & Toole, 1995).

Reflection Before Service

- What do we wish were different in our community?
- What do we want to see happen?
- How do we feel about participating in this project?
- What are your current attitudes and beliefs about the individuals with whom you will be working?

- What is the source of your attitudes and beliefs?
- What evidence do you have to support them?
- What other attitudes and beliefs might exist about this context?
- What are the social policies and conditions that led to the context in which we will be serving?

Reflection During Service

- What are we experiencing?
- How does the social context in which we are working impact the lives of individuals in this social setting?
- What is troubling or problematic about our experience?
- What can we do to address any problems we are encountering?
- What can we learn from each other?
- What political skills can we acquire and use to work toward alleviating the social policies and contexts that contribute to inequitable or unjust settings in which we may be giving service?

Reflection After Service

- What difference have we made?
- What have I learned?
- Where else in my life might I apply the knowledge and skills I acquired?
- How has my conception of society changed and what does that mean for my life?
- What have I learned about myself, about those I served, and about academic skills and content?

PRESENT TO PAST

Progressive Education—Connecting School and Society

Most of the ideals and practices of democratic schooling that you have been reading about in this book are not new ideas. Many of them have historical roots in the progressive era of education that occurred in the early part of the 20th century. Some examples include:

- activities that are intended to help students examine social issues and community life, such as "service learning" and field trips;
- project-centered learning and authentic pedagogy;
- giving students a voice in classroom governance, and in what they read, write, and inquire about;
- integrated curriculum, in which the separate subjects are connected; and

Child labor laws passed early in the 20th century protected children from being forced into situations like the one depicted here.

- the idea of schools as community centers that include health services, counseling services, and vocational education.

As you read the historical description that follows see if you can identify the historical roots of many of the practices of democratic education that have been discussed in this book.

The Late 19th and Early 20th Centuries: Age of Smokestacks, Cities, and Working-Class Immigrants

In the 1890s, urban factories were expanding and the great cities of the Northeast and Midwest were teeming with new immigrants. The third wave of immigration from 1890–1929 brought in nearly 13 million eastern and southern Europeans (*Atlas of Our Country,* 1996). These new arrivals tended to have low levels of education and lived in ethnic ghettos in the cities. Adults and children worked long hours in factories, six or seven days a week, for low pay and no job security.

There was a great deal of talk about how to "Americanize" the immigrants. To some educators, that entailed radically changing immigrants' cultural beliefs and prohibiting them from speaking their native language in schools. Others, particularly community workers not located in schools, felt that immigrants' beliefs, customs, and language ought to be respected, even though the newcomers had to accept most of the prevailing social and political practices and also learn to speak English.

Simultaneously, a view of parenting developed which held that children should be raised as individuals who would find their own place in the world. Children began to attend the common schools for longer periods of time and the occupational apprenticeship systems decayed. The community had less and less to do with socializing young adolescents, and the peer group assumed greater importance. Educators assumed more responsibility for children's welfare, and began to talk more about children's individual capabilities and interests.

Industrialization also affected the purposes of education. Educators, especially in urban areas, felt compelled to prepare students to live in a fast-growing industrial society. The exponential increase in urban populations meant that school districts never had enough classrooms to accommodate incoming students, with the result that class size would extend up to 50 or more students per classroom. Given the difficult conditions there was a great deal of discussion about how to make schools more "modern" and "efficient"—in some sense, more like factories—and how to make teaching more "scientific."

The issues raised above—how to educate immigrants and those not in the economic or ethnic elites, how to take children's interests and needs into account, how to prepare students for life in a complex urban society, and how to be more efficient and scientific—were central to the efforts of progressive reformers beginning in the 1890s.

The Child Savers

The census of 1900 reported that 18.2% of the nation's 9.6 million children aged 10–15 years were employed—and this excluded all children who worked less than half time (Cremin, 1988). Jacob Riis, in 1892, wrote an exposé of life in the urban slums titled *The Children of the Poor*. This graphic account used hard-hitting photography to show the degrading conditions in which many children had to live and work. Books like this made an impact, and social reformers agitated for ways to help children. Orphanages, asylums, and the informal institutions of childhood apprenticeship were criticized as being in need of fundamental reform. The reformers were sometimes called, not necessarily kindly, "child savers," because they sought protective legislation that would save children from the ravages of industrial work conditions and adult exploitation. Ultimately, child advocates' efforts were successful. From 1890–1920, many state and federal laws were passed to ensure that children were not exploited in factories and sweatshops. In 1912 the United States Children's Bureau was created to promote the welfare of children and to educate parents about child care.

It is the hallmark of this era that educational opportunity continued to increase for many children, including the working class. It would take decades for child labor laws to pass and for women to obtain the vote, and more than a half century for ethnic minorities to achieve the legal right to an equal education. Still, the modern era of nearly universal, compulsory, long-term schooling was ready to rise.

Settlement Houses

One source of pedagogical innovation was the settlement houses. Settlement houses were places where social reformers lived and engaged in social inquiry and action designed to alleviate problems resulting from the poverty and social inequality of early industrial capitalism. By 1891 there were six settlement houses in U.S. cities, by 1900 there were more than 100, and in 1910 there were at least 400 (Cremin, 1988). Perhaps the most famous of these was Hull House, started by Jane Addams and Ellen Gates Starr in Chicago in 1889. Those living at Hull House engaged in a series of

Serving others and working for social transformation has historical roots in the settlement houses of the early 20th century, such as Hull House, pictured here.

experimental, often informal activities intended to better the lives of the community in which they lived. At Hull House there were:

> . . . college extension courses, a summer school, a student association, a reading room, picture exhibitions, and Sunday concerts; but there were also a Paderewski Club of young pianists, a Jane Club for young working women, a Phalanx Club for young typographers, various men's and women's clubs and a Nineteenth Ward Improvement Club, cooking and sewing classes, a free kindergarten and day nursery, public dispensary, and, possibly most interesting of all, a Labor Museum explicitly intended to convey to the immigrant young a respect for the arts and traditions their parents had brought with them from Europe. (Cremin, 1988, p. 79)

Imagine all this activity in one house! What made the settlement house movement so unusual in American educational history was its combination of openly political and educational aims. Intermittently since that time, educators have called for schools to become "community centers" and for schools and social agencies to become much more tightly linked. Although settlement houses have been criticized, particularly for their assimilationist approach to working with immigrants, we would do well to consider their strengths as we puzzle over how to help diverse families in contemporary schools.

Community Schools

Progressive education began as a reaction by social critics against the purposes and practices of traditional education. Although critics agreed on the need for government intervention to help children, educators and social activists sometimes staked out different positions about how to help children in this time of confusing societal change. Educators with widely varying views called themselves progressives.

The Present to Past section following chapter 11 discussed the beliefs of progressive educators like John Dewey about the relationship between students' experiences and their learning. Another important progressive idea that surfaced in the early 20th century was the concept of the *community school.* Some educational reformers of this era asserted that schools should serve as "social centers" that focus on the social and economic life of the local community, and involve community members in their day-to-day operation. One of the better documented experiments in community schooling was led by Elsie Ripley Clapp (1939), who initiated schools in Kentucky and Virginia from 1929 to 1938. Her first community school, Ballard Memorial School, opened near Louisville, Kentucky, in 1928. Clapp's students studied Kentucky life and history, they built a log cabin (in 1931–1932), they developed an annual "school country fair," they published a community magazine, and they organized a co-operative food market each Friday after school (the "woman's exchange"). Clapp created a health clinic in the school in order to conduct physical examinations and monitor the nutritional needs of students and parents. Parents came every day to help run this community school. Clapp moved on from there to begin another community school in Arthurdale, Virginia. There were many other schools like this one, which shared a common characteristic of trying to make the school a center of community life.

THE SECONDARY SCHOOL MOVEMENT AND JUNIOR HIGH SCHOOLS

The most significant organizational development of the early 20th century had to do with the expansion of secondary schooling. Many rural systems provided no secondary schooling. Traditionally, urban public school systems utilized an "8–4" structure, meaning that students spent 8 years in elementary school and 4 in secondary school. In 1870, only 2% of American 17-year-olds graduated from public or private high schools, in 1890 only 3.5%, and by 1900 still only 6.4%. Few employers required a high school diploma and entry positions were plentiful for those with little schooling. Secondary school enrollment exploded after 1900. Between 1900 and 1940, public high school enrollment grew tenfold (Cremin, 1988).

Along with longer years in schools, liberal reformers called for the expansion of the secondary curriculum and the creation of a "comprehensive" high school. From 1910–1930, the percentage of students studying French, English literature, and history stayed the same or rose. Study of the other subjects declined. The percentage of students studying general science, home economics, bookkeeping, typewriting, and industrial arts rose rapidly (Cremin, 1988). Extracurricular activities such as athletics, clubs of all kinds, and student government became an integral part of schools. Health care, counseling, meals cooked and served in a school cafeteria, and school libraries all came to be seen as "given" services provided by schools. New school buildings might include a gymnasium, a swimming pool, an auditorium, or other physical features of a more comprehensive school.

In the second decade of the 20th century a few university and public school educators began to talk about creating a level of schooling between the elementary schools and the high schools. This was a time when people were promoting a more "differentiated" curriculum, meaning that more vocational and applied subjects would be included, to account for students' interests (and for adult projections of children's probable future occupations). Growing enrollments had resulted in huge elementary schools, and students in the highest grades (sixth–eighth grades) seemed to be ill-served. Their academic needs were different and the child study movement had asserted that they had emotional needs that differed markedly from young children in the primary grades. The rise of the "junior high schools" in the 1920s led, most commonly, to a "6-3-3" or "6-2-4" school structure: 6 years of elementary education, 2–3 years in the junior high school, and 3–4 years in high school. The new level of schooling was intended to be a transition between the "child-centered," often interdisciplinary curriculum of many elementary schools, and the "subject-centered" curriculum of high schools. The junior high school soon became what the name implied: a junior version of the high school, a stepchild toeing the line of college and high school standards. Not until the middle school movement beginning in the 1970s would the purposes and practices of schooling at this level be reexamined.

Vocational Education

Since the late 1800s there have been two major patterns of formal vocational education. Although public school educators often do not know much about it, there is a long history of education conducted by business and industry. New workers in the 1890s, for example, might have been part of the John Wanamaker Commercial Institute, organized in 1897 for department store employees. Wanamaker himself claimed that the Institute, organized as part of his Philadelphia store, was nothing less than a school of practice in business methods, "giving daily opportunities to obtain a working education in the arts and sciences of commerce and trade." The curriculum of the school included reading, writing, arithmetic, English, spelling, stenography, commercial geography, commercial law, and business methods. The faculty consisted of 24 teachers, some drawn from the store, others from the Philadelphia schools. New employees spent two sessions a week at the school in the morning; more advanced employees spent two sessions a week in the evening, after having supper in the store's cafeteria (Cremin, 1988). Many larger businesses now have "workplace literacy" programs in place, the modern-day counterpart of Wanamaker's Institute.

For more than a hundred years there have also been what were called "manual training" classes in secondary schools, designed to teach work skills to students who might not attend college. Two major developments during the Progressive Era affected vocational education. First, we already noted that high schools were designated as "comprehensive," so that vocational education would be a track within high schools and not a separate school as it was in many European countries. Students and teachers in vocational schools, however, are fighting to this day to keep from being segregated and stereotyped. Federal legislation also made an impact on vocational education. The Smith-Hughes Act in 1917 provided aid to the states for vocational teachers' salaries and teacher education programs. There was strong support from business people and educators for vocational education, but pedagogical and administrative progressives disagreed about how narrow and utilitarian the education should be. John Dewey warned of the potential dangers of misguided vocational education early in the century:

> [We] should be united against every proposition, in whatever form advanced, to separate training of employees from training for citizenship, training of intelligence and character from training for narrow, industrial efficiency. (Rosenstock & Steinberg, 1996, p. 42)

The same issues are with us today, as shown by the story of the Rindge School of Technical Arts in Cambridge, Massachusetts. The school opened in 1888 and it was the second public vocational high school in the United States. Today, it is part of a comprehensive high school. The next excerpt describes the school's innovative CityWorks program.

IDEALS CHALLENGE: *Examining Equity*

(Adapted from Rosenstock & Steinberg, 1995, pp. 44–47.)

"Some people seem to have a problem with Rindge School of Technical Arts. They are always putting RSTA down and stereotyping us: . . . the students in RSTA are dumb; they will not go to college; they are going to drop out. Well, I will not take this anymore! . . . Being a freshman in RSTA, I am positive that I will go to college, and a lot of my confidence has come from my teachers. RSTA students have worked hard, demonstrated enthusiasm, and displayed some great exhibits. We are smart, not only in mind but also with our hands."

In March 1993, Paulina Mauras published this statement in our high school newspaper. . . . Paulina's notion of combining hands and mind, and the development of her skills in doing so, come directly from her experiences in CityWorks. . . .

Several features make this program unusual. . . . a project approach, apprentice-master relationships, and real clients. . . . students engage in problem solving, like deciding where on the map to locate a new teen center that would attract youth from all ethnic and racial communities of the city. . . . At a recent exhibition of students' work, several teams of students displayed drawings and scale models of a heritage museum they had designed for Cambridge. . . .

In choosing CityWorks, we rejected the purely consumerist notion of democracy so prevalent in American high schools today, which is that schools offering the most options in courses and shops are best—even if these offerings are shallow and force students into a track. Our goal was to move toward a more participatory model where teachers work together toward the collective interests of the students and the school; where students are engaged, active participants in their learning and in their community; and where parents and community members have real roles in the school's programs.

- What do you think of the form of vocational education described in this excerpt?
- Is this vocational education effort guilty of separating the "training of employees" and "training for narrow, industrial efficiency" from "training for citizenship" and "training of intelligence and character"?

EARLY CHILDHOOD EDUCATION

Proponents of early childhood education were also waging a long and difficult struggle during this period (a struggle which has not yet ended). The first kindergarten opened in St. Louis in 1873, and the innovation attracted wide attention within a short time. Eventually, teachers such as Maria Montessori (1870–1952), an Italian who developed a systematic experiential curriculum for young children, and parents who clamored for even longer years of formal education for their children, won the day. Still, it took more than 100 years to ensure nearly universal kindergarten education. From 1900–1940, kindergarten enrollment grew by 700%, and by 1980, 93.2% of all 5-year-olds were in school (Cremin, 1988).

SUMMARY: THE LEGACY OF PROGRESSIVE EDUCATION

Throughout the first half of the 20th century, progressive ideals were widely discussed but not commonly enacted. Most of the individual progressive schools in urban and rural areas opened with a promise, operated on a shoestring budget, and closed having had a small but insufficient impact on education. However, as you can see, the legacy of progressive practices continues in discussions about education and in the practices of democratic schools to this day.

REFERENCES

Alliance for Service Learning in Educational Reform. (1995). Standards of quality for school-based service learning. In C.W. Kinsley & K. McPherson (Eds.), *Enriching the curriculum through service learning* (pp. 126–134). Alexandria, VA: Association for Supervision and Curriculum Development.

Atlas of our country. (1996). Chicago: Nystrom.

Boyte, H. C. (1991). Community service and civic education. *Phi Delta Kappan, 72,* 766.

Carter, G. (1997). Service learning in curriculum reform. In J. Schine (Ed.), *Service learning: Ninety-sixth yearbook of the National Society for the Study of Education, part 1* (pp. 69–78). Chicago: The University of Chicago Press.

Conrad, D., & Hedin, D. (1991). School-based community service: What we know from research and theory. *Phi Delta Kappan, 72,* 743–751.

Cremin, L. A. (1988). *American education: The metropolitan experience, 1876–1986.* New York: Harper & Row.

Developmental Studies Center. (1994). *At home in our schools: A guide to schoolwide activities that build community.* Oakland, CA: Author.

Eberly, D. J. (1997). An international perspective on service learning. In J. Schine (Ed.), *Service learning: Ninety-sixth yearbook of the National Society for the Study of Education, part 1* (pp. 19–31). Chicago: The University of Chicago Press.

Goodman, J. (1992). *Elementary schooling for critical democracy.* Albany, NY: State University of New York Press.

Haynes, N. M., & Comer, J. P. (1997). Service learning in the Comer School Development Program. In J. Schine (Ed.), *Service learning: Ninety-sixth yearbook of the National Society for the Study of Education, part 1* (pp. 79–89). Chicago: The University of Chicago Press.

Howe, H. (1997). Foreword. In J. Schine (Ed.), *Service learning: Ninety-sixth yearbook of the National Society for the Study of Education, part 1* (pp. iv–vi). Chicago: The University of Chicago Press.

Kahne, J., & Westheimer, J. (1996). In the service of what?: The politics of service learning. *Phi Delta Kappan, 77*(9), 592–599.

Kinsley, C. W., & McPherson, K. (1995). Introduction: Changing perceptions to integrate service learning in education. In C. W. Kinsley & K. McPherson (Eds.), *Enriching the curriculum through service learning* (pp. 1–9). Alexandria, VA: Association for Supervision and Curriculum Development.

Kleinbard, P. (1997). Youth participation: Integrating youth into communities. In J. Schine (Ed.), *Service learning: Ninety-sixth yearbook of the National Society for the Study of Education, part 1* (pp. 1–18). Chicago: The University of Chicago Press.

McPherson, K., & Kinsley, C. W. (1995). Conclusion: Challenges for the future. In C. W. Kinsley & K. McPherson (Eds.), *Enriching the curriculum through service learning* (pp. 115–116). Alexandria, VA: Association for Supervision and Curriculum Development.

Neal, R. (1986). Speech presented at Youth Service Recognition Day, Springfield Public Schools, Springfield, Massachusetts.

Newmann, F. M., & Wehlage, G. G. (1995). *Successful school restructuring.* Madison, WI: Center on Organization and Restructuring of Schools.

Pardo, W. (1997). Service learning in the classroom: Practical issues. In J. Schine (Ed.), *Service learning: Ninety-sixth yearbook of the National Society for the Study of Education, part 1* (pp. 90–104). Chicago: The University of Chicago Press.

Rosenstock, L., & Steinberg, A. (1995). Beyond the shop: Reinventing vocational education. In M. W. Apple & J. A. Beane (Eds.), *Democratic schools* (pp. 41–57). Alexandria, VA: Association for Supervision and Curriculum Development.

Schine, J. (1997). Looking ahead: Issues and challenges. In J. Schine (Ed.), *Service learning: Ninety-sixth yearbook of the National Society for the Study of Education, part 1* (pp. 186–199). Chicago: The University of Chicago Press.

Toole, P., & Toole, J. (1995). Reflection as a tool for turning service experiences into learning experiences. In C. W. Kinsley & K. McPherson (Eds.), *Enriching the curriculum through service learning* (pp. 99–114). Alexandria, VA: Association for Supervision and Curriculum Development.

Tyack, D. B. (1974). *The one best system: A history of American urban education.* Cambridge, MA: Harvard University Press.

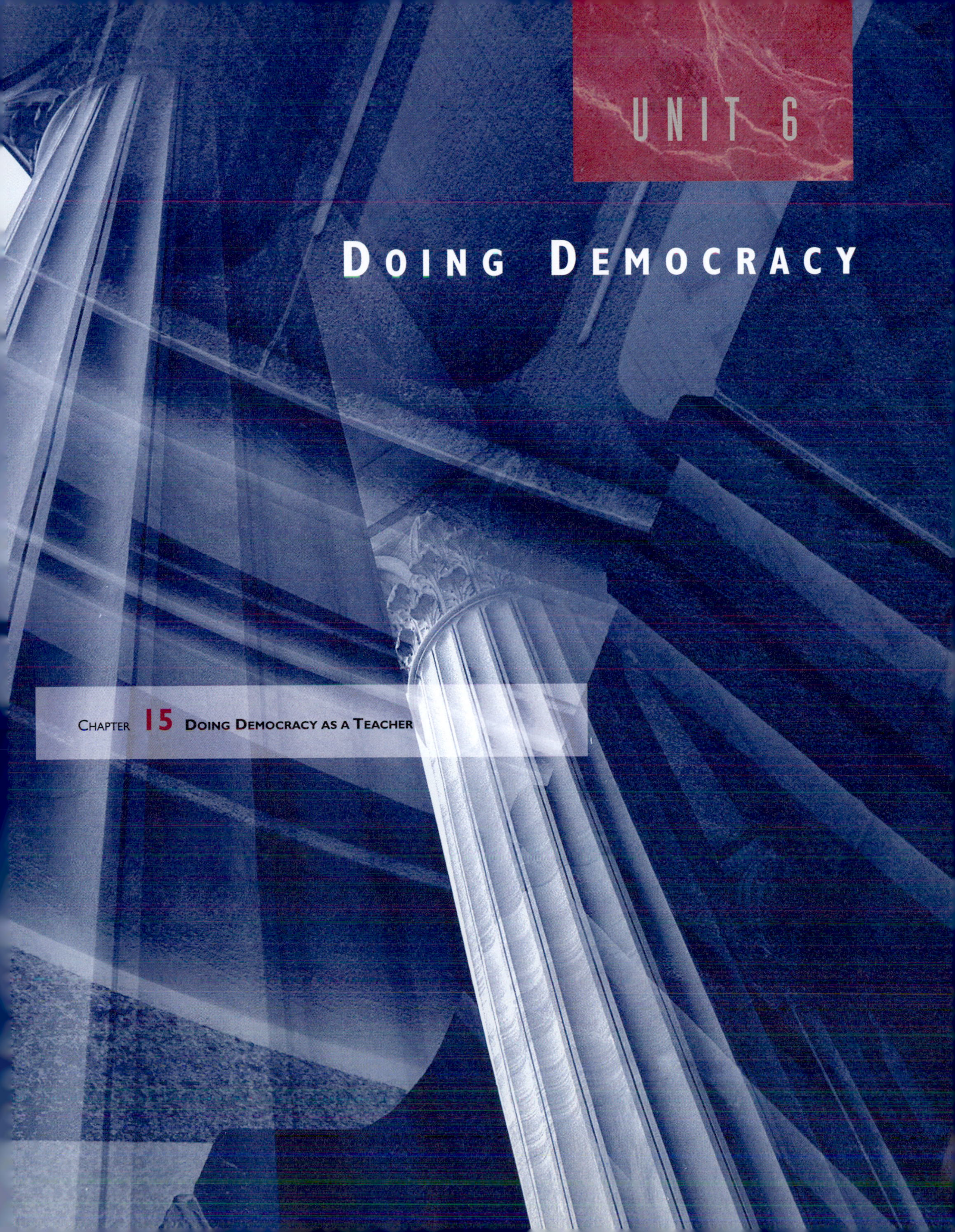

UNIT 6

DOING DEMOCRACY

CHAPTER 15 DOING DEMOCRACY AS A TEACHER

Do you think the individuals pictured in this school goal-setting meeting work mostly in isolation or as a school community?

What do you think they believe about schools, democracy, and teaching?

What do you believe about schools, democracy, and teaching?

CHAPTER 15

DOING DEMOCRACY AS A TEACHER

The central aim of this book was to help you see clearly the purposes, philosophies, and practices of public education that will serve as a foundation for you in your role as a teacher in a democratic society. Throughout this book we have encouraged you to explore ideals and practices and the journey of democratic education. Specifically, we examined the ideals of inquiry, discourse, equity, authenticity, leadership, and service and how these ideals help classrooms and schools move from bureaucratic, conventional schools to democratic learning communities.

Now it is time for you to reflect on, articulate, and act upon your own foundations of education. Remember, our purpose in writing this book was not to overload you with disconnected pieces of information about teaching and schools, but rather to assist you in examining and connecting new perspectives and information to your practice as a teacher and to help you examine your beliefs and values about teaching, learning, and schools. Rather than simply accepting our IDEALS as your foundation, we hope your reading, reflection, and inquiry associated with this book has helped you to make connections and begin to develop your own educational foundations. This foundation should help guide your actions throughout your teacher education program and in your future employment as a teacher.

We wish to conclude this book by giving you the opportunity to take the next step in the development of your educational foundation. In order to assist you, we provide you with a structure to help you articulate and explore your educational foundations. As authors we have shared with you our IDEALS and beliefs as well as those of a number of teachers, principals, students, and parents from around the United States and the world. Now it is your turn to articulate and explore your ideals, beliefs, and values.

Although as authors we firmly believe in, and have advocated for, democratic classrooms and schools, you may not necessarily agree with us. Alternatively, you may agree with us, but your conception or understanding of democratic classrooms and schools may be different than ours. Thus, as we walk you through the following exercise in exploring your current educational foundations, we will not use the term "democratic classrooms" or "democratic schools" but rather simply refer to "good" classrooms and schools since we want you to articulate your beliefs rather than attempting to mimic ours.

AN EXERCISE IN DOING DEMOCRACY

Description: Describing a Good Classroom and School

- If you walked into a good classroom, what would you see?
- If you walked into a good school, what would you see?
- In good *classrooms* what would you see each of the following doing?

  students

  teachers

  parents

  principals

- In good *schools* what would you see each of the following doing outside of the classroom?

  students

  teachers

  parents

  principals

Alternatives: Inquiry

- What perspectives or theories exist about good classrooms and schools that differ from what you described above (e.g., authentic pedagogy versus didactic instruction)?

Becoming a more democratic school is ultimately a joyful celebration of better meeting the needs of *all* children.

Alternatives: Comparison

- How is your description of good classrooms and schools similar to and different from the classrooms and schools you experienced as a student in elementary and secondary school, in your field experiences in your teacher education program, and/or as a volunteer in schools?

Discourse and Articulation

- Study and discuss your description of good classrooms and schools with someone else in your class and identify the 4–6 core ideals, beliefs, or values that run through your description.

Core Beliefs, Ideals, Values

1.
2.
3.
4.
5.
6.

Inquiry: Support

- Now take each of the beliefs/ideals/values you listed and provide support for it. Why do you think it is important? Support should come from

(1) research or other written material; (2) examples from your experiences as a student that led to positive outcomes; (3) examples from teaching or field experiences you may have had that led to positive outcomes, and; (4) other life experiences.

1. Belief/Ideal/Value #1:
2. Belief/Ideal/Value #2:
3. Belief/Ideal/Value #3:
4. Belief/Ideal/Value #4:
5. Belief/Ideal/Value #5:
6. Belief/Ideal/Value #6:

Taking Action

- Describe what you will do as a teacher to ensure that your classroom exemplifies the good classroom you described, and that your school moves toward being the good school you described. Address what you could do to stimulate school renewal in the school in which you teach, and to facilitate the examination of beliefs about good classrooms and schooling. In other words, what you will do in your school and practice during field experiences, internships, and your future employment as a teacher as a result of your beliefs about good classrooms and schools?

CONCLUSION

We leave you with one final challenge:

What will you do as a result of your work with this book that will extend beyond your university classroom? How will this book have "value beyond" your university course for you?

We invite you to share your examples of "value beyond" as well as your successes and struggles as a democratic educator with your professional colleagues.

Finally, we thank you for sticking with the journey throughout this book. However, you know as well as we do that the journey is just beginning. Teaching, and especially teaching democratically, is seldom easy. There will be struggles and frustrations—but also joys and successes. Through all of these, the good and the bad, we wish you patience, perseverance, progress, and fulfillment. You deserve it. For yours is the most noble of all professions—to be a teacher.

SUBJECT INDEX

NAME INDEX

LITERARY PERMISSIONS

CHAPTER 2

Excerpts from George Wood, principal of Federal Hocking High School, Ohio, keynote address reprinted by permission of George Wood.

CHAPTER 3

Excerpts from *Among Schoolchilren* by Tracy Kidder. Copyright ©1989 by John Tracy Kidder. Reprinted by permission of Houghton Mifflin Company. All rights reserved.

CHAPTER 5

From *Habits of Goodness: Case Studies in the Social Curriculum* by Ruth S. Charney. Copyright ©1997 by Northeast Foundation for Children, Greenfield, MA. Used with permission.

From C. Caivano (1997) in *Voices of Inquiry in Teacher Education* by T. S. Poetter, pp. 57–67. Reprinted by permission of Lawrence Erlbaum Associates, Inc.

Yoland Simmons and Patricia Beardon's "Exemplary Program" adapted by permission of Steven Zemelman, Harvey Daniels, and Arthur Hyde: *Best Practice: New Edition for Teaching and Learning in America's Schools,* Second Edition (Heinemann, a division of Reed Elsevier, Inc., Portsmouth, NH, 1998).

CHAPTER 6

Linda Darling-Hammond. *The Right to Learn,* pp. 193–194, text only. Copyright ©1997 Jossey-Bass, Inc., Publishers. Reprinted by permission.

Table 6.1 adapted from *Using What We Have to Get the Schools We Need,* reprinted by permission of OECD Washington Center, Washington, DC.

CHAPTER 8

From J. K. Underwood & J. F. Mead, *The Legal Aspects of Special Education and Pupil Services.* Copyright ©1995 by Allyn & Bacon. Reprinted/adapted by permission.

CHAPTER 10

From *Savage Inequalities* by Jonathan Kozol. Copyright ©1991 by Jonathan Kozol. Reprinted by permission of Crown Publishers, Inc.

CHAPTER 11

From A. Patri (1917) in R. M. Cohen & S. Scheer (Eds.) *The Work of Teachers in America: A Social History Through Stories,* pp. 205–214. Reprinted by permission of Lawrence Erlbaum Associates, Inc.

CHAPTER 12

Adapted by permission of Steven Levy: *Starting from Scratch: One Classroom Builds Its Own Curriculum.* (Heinemann, a division of Reed Elsevier, Inc., Portsmouth, NH, 1996.)

PHOTO PERMISSIONS

Page 2 © 1999 Frank Weiner
Page 8 © Robert D. Daemmrich / Tony Stone Images
Page 14 © Michael Newman / PhotoEdit
Page 16 © Bill Aron / Tony Stone Images
Page 17 © Robin Sachs
Page 21 © Robin Sachs
Page 28 © Michael Newman / PhotoEdit
Page 31 © David Young-Wolfe / PhotoEdit
Page 37 © Andy Sacks / Tony Stone Images
Page 39 © Paul Conklin / PhotoEdit
Page 41 © Mary Kate Denny / PhotoEdit
Page 48 © Robin Sachs
Page 54 © Tony Freeman / PhotoEdit
Page 59 © Robin Sachs
Page 62 © Robin Sachs
Page 63 © Mary K. Denny / PhotoEdit
Page 68 © Robin Sachs
Page 70 © Will Hart / PhotoEdit
Page 74 © Ariel Skelley / The Stock Market
Page 80 © Paul Kenward / Tony Stone Images
Page 86 The Granger Collection, New York
Page 89 The Granger Collection, New York
Page 100 The Image Works Archives
Page 106 The Granger Collection, New York
Page 116 © 1998 Mobil Corporation
Page 120 © Elizabeth Crews
Page 124 © Elizabeth Crews
Page 131 © 1999 Robin Sachs
Page 136 © Richard Hutchings / PhotoEdit
Page 142 © Mary Kate Denny / PhotoEdit
Page 146 © Jose Carrillo / PhotoEdit
Page 153 © Tony Freeman / PhotoEdit
Page 155 © Bill Aron / PhotoEdit
Page 161 top © Robin Sachs
Page 161 bottom © Robin Sachs
Page 169 © Robin Sachs
Page 182 © Spencer Grant / PhotoEdit
Page 186 © David Young-Wolfe / PhotoEdit
Page 195 © Elizabeth Crews
Page 199 © Alan Oddie / PhotoEdit
Page 209 © Paul Conklin / PhotoEdit
Page 212 © Spencer Grant / PhotoEdit
Page 222 © Mark Richards / PhotoEdit
Page 225 © Billy E. Barnes / Tony Stone Images
Page 228 AP / Wide World Photo
Page 233 © Michael Newman / PhotoEdit
Page 239 © Chandler H. McKaig / Tony Stone Images
Page 241 © Amy C. Etra / PhotoEdit
Page 252 © Michael Newman / PhotoEdit
Page 256 © Billy E. Barnes / PhotoEdit
Page 260 © Rob Crandall / Stock Boston
Page 266 UPI / Corbis - Bettmann
Page 269 © Robin Sachs
Page 275 © Tom Prettyman / PhotoEdit
Page 278 © Robert Brenner / PhotoEdit
Page 284 © David Young-Wolff / PhotoEdit
Page 292 © Michael Newman / PhotoEdit
Page 295 © Will Hart / PhotoEdit
Page 302 © Elizabeth Crews
Page 306 © Will Hart / PhotoEdit
Page 313 © Kellie L. Hayden
Page 322 © Tony Freeman / PhotoEdit
Page 326 © Tony Freeman / PhotoEdit
Page 332 © Robin Sachs
Page 337 © Bob Daemmrich / Stock Boston
Page 343 © Robert Daemmrich / Tony Stone Images
Page 347 © Michael Newman / PhotoEdit
Page 358 © Tony Freeman / PhotoEdit
Page 362 © Mark Richards / PhotoEdit
Page 368 © Mark Richards / PhotoEdit
Page 373 © Elizabeth Crews
Page 380 © Robin Sachs
Page 385 © David Young-Wolfe / PhotoEdit
Page 398 © Ronn Maratea / International Stock
Page 403 © Michael Newman / PhotoEdit
Page 404 © Elizabeth Crews
Page 408 © Elizabeth Crews
Page 417 © Robin Sachs
Page 420 © Robert Daemmrich / Tony Stone Images
Page 430 © Michael Newman / PhotoEdit
Page 434 © Michael Newman / PhotoEdit
Page 437 © Mark Richards / PhotoEdit
Page 443 © Mark Richards / PhotoEdit
Page 447 Lewis W. Hine, Child Labor in Cotton Mills, 1909-1913. George Eastman House
Page 449 Courtesy Chicago Historical Society
Page 456 © Lawrence Migdale / Stock Boston
Page 459 © Spencer Grant / PhotoEdit